Fodor's

NORTHERN CALIFORNIA

Welcome to Northern California

It's easy to tap into the good life in Northern California. Between rounds of golf at Pebble Beach, winding drives along the breathtaking coast, or scenic treks through Yosemite National Park, you can indulge in a wealth of top-notch outdoor activities. In Napa and Sonoma, eating and drinking are cultivated as high arts. You can sip wine at picturesque vineyards and then dine at stellar locavore restaurants. Urban pleasures await in San Francisco, too, where cable cars zip through vibrant neighborhoods lined with chic boutiques and cutting-edge museums.

TOP REASONS TO GO

★ **San Francisco:** This diverse city beguiles with natural beauty and contagious energy.

★ **Wine Country:** Top-notch whites and reds in Napa, Sonoma, and beyond.

★ **Feasts:** Cutting-edge cuisine, food trucks, fusion flavors, farmers' markets.

★ **Stunning Scenery:** Picture-perfect backdrops from the Golden Gate Bridge to redwoods.

★ **Outdoor Adventures:** National park excursions, hiking, and golfing are all excellent.

★ **Road Trips:** The Pacific Coast Highway offers spectacular views and thrills aplenty.

Contents

Fodor's Features

MAPS

Chapter 1

EXPERIENCE NORTHERN CALIFORNIA

15 ULTIMATE EXPERIENCES

Northern California offers terrific experiences that should be on every traveler's list. Here are Fodor's top picks for a memorable trip.

1 Crane Your Neck at Redwood National and State Parks

Traveling north, you'll encounter one of the world's most stunning natural wonders. Redwood National and State Parks is home to the tallest trees on Earth (300–400 feet tall), and hugs 40 miles of coastline. *(Ch. 14)*

2 Enjoy the View from a Hot-Air Balloon

It's worth waking at dawn for a balloon ride over the vineyards. Depending on where you soar, you'll see how compact the Napa Valley or how vast Sonoma County is. *(Ch. 10)*

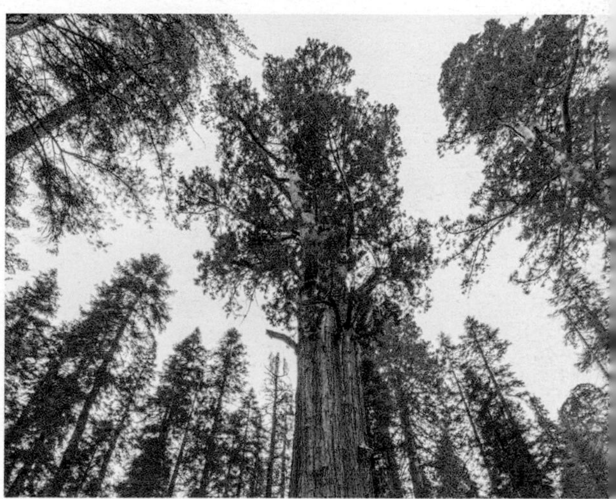

3 Ogle General Sherman

Sequoia National Park's General Sherman tree is the largest living tree in the world, at 275 feet tall and 36 feet in diameter at its roots. *(Ch. 4)*

4 Hike the Pacific Crest Trail in Kings Canyon National Park

The Pacific Crest Trail stretches 2,659 miles along the U.S. coast from Mexico to Canada. It peaks at Forester Pass in Kings Canyon National Park, at 13,153 feet. *(Ch. 4)*

5 Commune with Nature at Yosemite National Park

Nestled in the Sierra Nevada, Yosemite National Park is known for its giant sequoia trees, epic waterfalls, and abundant wildlife. Note that reservations are required to enter the park. *(Ch. 6)*

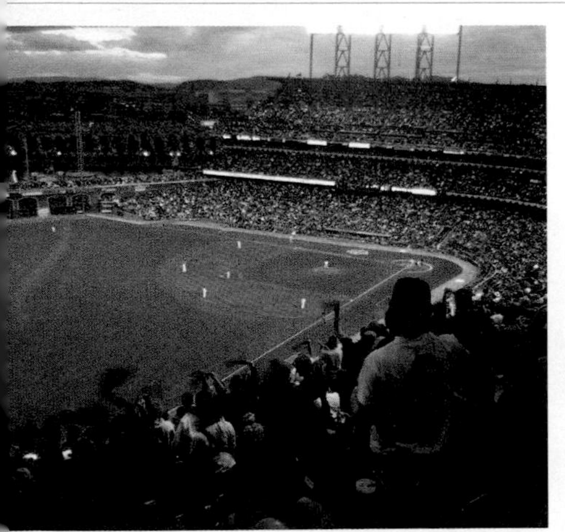

6 Witness Greatness in Sport

Sports fans have their pick of the litter in California, whether it's seeing the Giants, 49ers, or Golden State Warriors in San Franscisco, or the Kings in Sacramento.

7 Spot Whales in Monterey

Depending on the season, you can charter boats to view migrating gray, humpback, and blue whales. Monterey is also prime territory for killer whales, bottlenose dolphins, and more. *(Ch. 5)*

8 Get an Adrenaline Rush at Lake Tahoe

Straddling California and Nevada, Lake Tahoe is a wonderland for adventure enthusiasts year-round, with world-class skiing in winter and lake sports in summer. *(Ch. 13)*

9 Drink all the Wine

Don't tell the French, but the best wine is from Napa and Sonoma Counties. Only a few hours away from each other, both are flush with world-class wineries. *(Ch. 10)*

10 Dive into History in San Francisco's Chinatown

San Francisco's Chinatown is the largest outside of Asia and the oldest in the U.S. Don't miss the Dragon Gate, Golden Gate Fortune Cookie Factory, and the Old Telephone Exchange. *(Ch. 8)*

11 Take the Scenic 17-Mile Drive

This stretch of road in Pebble Beach takes you past enchanting sights, like Fanshell Beach, Point Joe, the Lone Cypress, and more. (Ch. 5)

12 Party at BottleRock

BottleRock Napa Valley, the Wine Country's hottest music fest takes place each Memorial Day Weekend, with headliners like Bruno Mars, Florence and the Machine, and others. *(Ch. 10)*

13 Play Arcade Games at Musée Mécanique

This quirky "museum" at Fisherman's Wharf in San Francisco has more than 200 antique arcade games, including coin-operated fortune tellers, moving dioramas, and stereoscopes. *(Ch. 8)*

14 Ski at Mammoth

Mammoth Mountain (a dormant volcano) is the largest ski resort in California; its 3,500 acres of skiable area hosts millions of skiers and snowboarders each year. *(Ch. 6)*

15 Cross the Golden Gate Bridge

Opened in 1937, the Golden Gate Bridge is one of the most iconic symbols of San Francisco. Visitors can cross the mile-long suspension bridge by foot, bicycle, or car. *(Ch. 8)*

WHAT'S WHERE

1 Monterey Bay Area. Postcard-perfect Monterey, Victorian-flavored Pacific Grove, and exclusive Carmel all share this stretch of California coast. To the north, Santa Cruz boasts a boardwalk, a UC campus, and plenty of surfers.

2 San Francisco. To see why so many have left their hearts here, visit the city's neighborhoods—posh Pacific Heights, the Hispanic Mission, and gay-friendly Castro.

3 The Bay Area. The area that rings San Francisco is home to some of the nation's great universities, fabulous bay views, Silicon Valley, and Alice Waters's Chez Panisse.

4 Napa and Sonoma. With award-winning vintages, luxe lodgings, and epicurean eats, Napa and Sonoma counties retain their title as *the* California Wine Country.

5 The North Coast. The star attractions here are natural ones, from the secluded beaches and wave-battered bluffs of Point Reyes National Seashore to the towering redwood forests.

6 Redwood National Park. More than 200

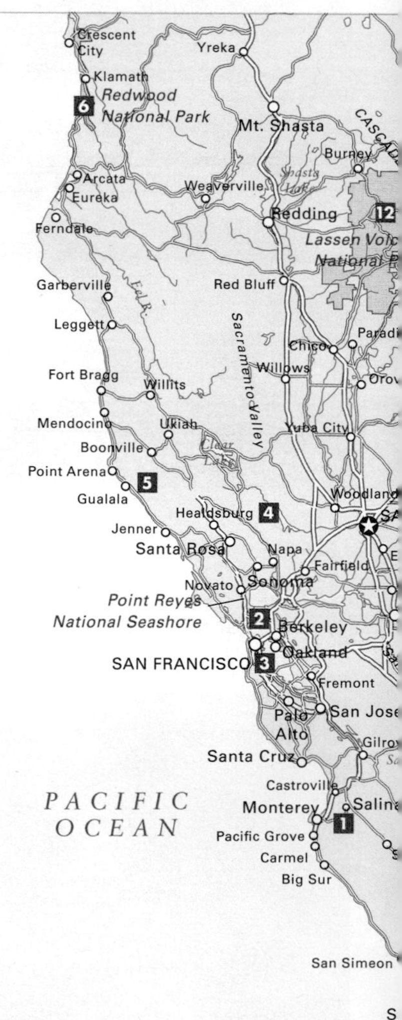

miles of trails allow visitors to see these spectacular trees in their primitive environments.

7 Eastern Sierra. In the Mammoth Lakes region, sawtooth mountains and deep snowdrifts create premier conditions for skiing and snowboarding.

8 Yosemite National Park. The views immortalized by photographer Ansel Adams—towering granite monoliths, verdant glacial valleys, and lofty waterfalls—are still camera-ready.

9 Sequoia and Kings Canyon National Parks. The sight of ancient redwoods towering above jagged mountains is breathtaking.

10 Sacramento and the Gold Country. The 1849 gold rush began here, and the former mining camps strung along 185 miles of Highway 49 replay their past to the hilt.

11 Lake Tahoe. With crystalline water reflecting the peaks of the High Sierra, Lake Tahoe is perfect for activities like hiking and golfing in summer and skiing and snowmobiling in winter.

12 The Far North. California's far northeast corner is home to Mt. Shasta and the pristine Trinity Wilderness.

What to Eat and Drink in Northern California

Oysters

SOURDOUGH BREAD

In California, sourdough history is tied to the Gold Rush, when French bakers set up shop in San Francisco to feed the miners. For the perfect loaf, head to Boudin Bakery in San Francisco where they've been perfecting their sourdough recipe since 1849.

WINE

You could throw a rock and hit a world-class wine up and down the coast of California. Napa, Sonoma, Los Robles, and Monterey all have some of the best vintages on the planet.

OYSTERS

One of the best places to eat oysters as big as your head is in Morro Bay, about half way between Los Angeles and San Francisco. It's the perfect stop on any west coast road trip, so pop into Tognazzini's Dockside where they serve fresh grilled behemoth bivalves, blast live music, and bask seaside with an outdoor deck.

IRISH COFFEE

Inspired by a drink in Ireland, the owner of the Buena Vista in San

Sourdough bread

Francisco set out to re-create the concoction and stumbled upon what we now know as an Irish Coffee. The mixture of coffee, whiskey, and floating cream can still be enjoyed out of a chalice at the same Buena Vista location since its humble beginnings.

BURGERS
If there's any debate about the home of the burger, just ask Fat Burger, Carl's Jr, McDonald's, In-N-Out, Umami Burger, The Habit Burger Grill, Hamburger Mary's, Johnny Rockets, The Counter, Original Tommy's, and Jack in the Box, which all started in the Golden State.

SUSHI
Outside of Japan, there is no better place to eat raw fish than in California. At Akiko in San Francisco, you can find the freshest, most savory cuts of fish that rivals any place in the world.

CHEESE
Wisconsin? Please. The best cheese is clearly from California. Have you heard of Humboldt Fog? That comes from Cypress Grove in Humboldt County. How about Red Hawk, that gooey triple-crème that melts in your mouth? Marin County. And cheddar? Sorry Wisconsin, but Fiscalini Bandaged Cheddar from Modesto has you beat any day of the week.

TACOS
They may have been invented in Mexico, but the Mexican influence on California has taken the taco to all new heights. If you're hankering for simple and classic, you can't miss at La Taqueria in San Francisco.

BEER
California is a hotbed of beer-making. From NoCal to SoCal, craft brewers are dominating the beer scene like never before. Check out 21st Amendment in San Francisco.

MAI TAIS
White rum, dark rum, Curaçao liqueur, orgeat syrup, and lime juice makes the perfect Mai Tai. The drink was invented (allegedly) by Victor Bergeron in 1944 of the famed restaurant Trader Vic's in Oakland, California, though Donn Beach (of Don the Beachcomber fame) claims he invented it in the 1930s in Hollywood.

What to Read and Watch

***WINE COUNTRY WOMEN OF NAPA VALLEY* BY MICHELLE MANDRO AND DONA KOPOL BONIK**
Winemakers, chefs, executives, and women holding other key positions share insights and recipes in this large-format volume filled with photography.

***THE MALTESE FALCON* BY DASHIELL HAMMETT**
There was a time when San Francisco's most notorious antiheroes weren't billionaires in T-shirts, but rather chain-smoking, hard-boiled detectives. In "The Maltese Falcon," detective Sam Spade criss-crosses an atmospheric 1930s San Francisco to locate a jeweled statue. Dashiell Hammett's novel is a legendary piece of noir fiction, but the film, which starred an in-his-prime Humphrey Bogart, is also a classic.

***THE GIRLS* BY EMMA CLINE**
In this nuanced coming-of-age story set in the Sonoma County town of Petaluma, the 14-year-old narrator yearns for excitement, attention, and beauty—and falls into the violent, psychological mind-trip of a Charles Manson–like cult. Beautiful and gripping, Cline's novel shares a gritty, late 1960s Sonoma County—one that couldn't be further from today's world of Cabernets and Pinots.

***GUN, WITH OCCASIONAL MUSIC* BY JONATHAN LETHEM**
Lethem started his career with a captivating but decidedly weird novel set in San Francisco and Oakland. In the sci-fi noir detective story, people rub elbows with talking, man-sized genetically engineered animals and everyone lives under a monetized "karma" system similar to what modern-day China has begun using to track and influence its residents. It's a compelling, not-quite-dystopian vision set in the near-yet-distant future and highlights what San Francisco might become with just a little (okay, a lot) of genetic experimentation.

***BURMA SUPERSTAR* BY DESMOND TAN AND KATE LEAHY**
Burmese food is increasingly popular in San Francisco, and Burma Superstar is a hit restaurant. Tan and Leahy's cookbook offers a look into the flavor-packed southeast Asian cuisine which is finally starting to get the recognition it deserves. If you're someone who wants to learn more about Burmese food, or are seeking to recreate the joy and bombastic flavors found at this San Francisco restaurant, this is a must-own.

***THE MAYOR OF CASTRO STREET* BY RANDY SHILTS**
Randy Shilts's biography of gay civil rights icon Harvey Milk is perhaps the most well-regarded and authoritative reckoning of his life to date. Milk was a bombastic, iconic figure whose advocacy and brutal murder permanently shaped the political landscape of not just San Francisco, but the entire country.

***MR. PENUMBRA'S 24-HOUR BOOKSTORE* BY ROBIN SLOAN**
This novel about a curiously quirky used-book store in San Francisco does double duty. Not only is it a story of mystery, love, code-breaking, secret societies, and adopted and inherited culture, it's also a narrative about the dangers of rapid technological advancement (and of rejecting technology), tribalism, and other issues currently affecting San Francisco.

***NOSE: A NOVEL* BY JAMES CONAWAY**
A fictitious Northern California wine-making region—couldn't be Napa or Sonoma, could it?—is the setting for a mystery.

THE BIRDS
Alfred Hitchcock's 1963 masterpiece centers around a small Northern Californian town under attack by swarming, possessed birds. Perhaps the focus on commonly found creatures is what makes this one of the director's most graphic thrillers. When you aren't distracted by the demonic winged creatures, there are breathtaking views of the Sonoma County's coastal drives and the charming 1960s small town of Bodega Bay, where almost all of the movie was filmed.

Northern California Today

THE PEOPLE

California is as much a state of mind as a state in the union, a perpetual promised land that has represented many things to many people. By most accounts, the ancestors of California's native peoples migrated from Asia, traversing a land bridge across the Bering Strait that formerly joined what's now Russia and Alaska. Some of these trailblazers continued south to California, flourishing for centuries off the land's bounty. Millennia later, Spanish explorers ventured north from Mexico in search of gold, with converts to Christianity the quest of 18th-century missionaries. Miners rushed here from the world over also seeking gold, followed in the 20th century by real estate speculators, would-be motion-picture actors and producers, Dust Bowl farmers and migrant workers, Haight-Ashbury hippies, sexual and gender pioneers, artists, dot-commers, and venture capitalists.

The result is a population that leans toward idealism without necessarily being as liberal as you might think. (This is Ronald Reagan's old stomping ground after all, and Richard Nixon was born here.) And despite the stereotype of the blue-eyed, blond surfer, California's population is not homogeneous either. Nearly 11 million people who live here —more than 27% of Californians—are foreign born. Almost half hail from Latin American countries; another 40% emigrated from Asia (now the single largest source of immigrants), following the waves of Chinese workers who arrived in the 1860s to build the railroads and subsequent streams of Indochinese refugees from the Vietnam War. Collectively California's 40 million residents speak more than 220 languages, making it by far the nation's most linguistically diverse state.

THE POLITICS

What's blue and red and green all over? Predominantly Democratic California, with an ambitious environmental agenda and policies that make this the nation's greenest state, supporting more green construction, wind farms, and solar panels. The last Republican governor, Arnold Schwarzenegger, left office in 2011, but the state is home to the Hoover Institution, a prominent conservative think tank based at Stanford University. In 23 counties in the North Coast, Far North, Gold Country, and elsewhere you're likely to come across signs proposing a breakaway, more conservative 51st State of Jefferson.

THE ECONOMY

As currently composed, California leads all other states in terms of the income generated by agriculture, tourism, entertainment, and industrial activity. With a gross state product of more than $2.8 trillion (median household income $71,805), by some estimates California would be the world's fifth-largest economy were it an independent nation. California took significant hits during two recessions in the 21st century's first decade, but the Golden State takes its boom and bust cycles—beginning with the mid-19th-century gold rush that started it all—in stride. A projected budget surplus of more than $21 billion for 2019 signaled a full recovery from previous economic woes, and optimists have their eyes focused on two potential booms: bioresearch and "green companies" focused on alternative energy, renewables, electric cars, and the like.

THE CULTURE

Cultural organizations flourish in Northern California. San Francisco—a city with less than 900,000 residents—has well-regarded ballet, opera, and theater companies, and is home to one of the continent's most noteworthy orchestras. Museums like San Francisco Museum of Modern Art (SFMOMA) and the de Young also represent the city's ongoing commitment to the arts.

THE PARKS AND PRESERVES

Cloud-spearing redwood groves, snow-tipped mountains, canyon-slashed deserts, primordial lava beds, and a seemingly endless coast: Northern California's natural diversity is staggering—and efforts to protect it started early. Yosemite, the first national park, was established here in 1890, and the National Park Service now oversees 33 sites in California (more than in any other state). When you factor in 280 state parks—which encompass underwater preserves, historic sites, wildlife reserves, dune systems, and other sensitive habitats—the number of acres involved is almost as impressive as the topography itself.

Due to encroaching development and pollution, keeping these natural treasures in pristine condition is an ongoing challenge. For instance, Sequoia and Kings Canyon, which is plagued by pesticides and other agricultural pollutants blown in from the San Joaquin Valley, ranks among the nation's smoggiest parks. During the summer the park's ozone levels often exceed those the Environmental Protection Agency considers safe for humans. Heavy ozone also damages plants by lowering their resistance to insects and disease.

There is no question that Californians love their 280 state parks. Nearly every park has its grassroots supporters, who volunteer as rangers and fundraisers and take on other tasks to keep the parks open.

THE CUISINE

California gave us McDonald's, Denny's, Carl's Jr., Taco Bell, and, of course, In-N-Out Burger. Fortunately for those of us with fast-clogging arteries, the state also kick-started the health-food movement. Back in the 1970s, California-based chefs put American cuisine on the culinary map by focusing on freshly prepared seasonal ingredients.

Today, this focus has spawned the "locavore" or sustainable food movement—followers try to consume only food produced within a 100-mile radius of where they live, since processing and refining food and transporting goods over long distances is bad for both the body and the environment. This isn't much of a restriction in California, where dozens of crops grow year-round. More than 700 certified farmers' markets operate in California, and their stalls are bursting with fresh produce and artisanal foods. By far America's top agricultural producer, California grows more fruits and vegetables than any other state. Dairies and ranches also thrive here, and fishing fleets harvest fish and shellfish from the rich waters offshore.

What's New in Northern California

FOODIE'S PARADISE

Great dining is a staple of the California lifestyle, and a new young generation of chefs is challenging old ideas about preparing and presenting great food. The food-truck frenzy continues to fuel movable feasts up and down the state. Esteemed chefs and urban foodies follow the trucks on Twitter as they move around cities 24/7 purveying delicious, cheap, fresh meals. You can find food-laden trucks at sports and entertainment venues, near parks and attractions, and on busy roads and boulevards—and the ensuing lines of hungry patrons.

Diners are also embracing the pop-up concept, where guest chefs offer innovative menus in unconventional settings for a limited time. These pop-up engagements are hosted anywhere from inside a warehouse to outside in a field. Often there is an air of secrecy and anticipation to them, with key details being revealed at the last moment. Visitors can look for local pop-ups listed on foodie websites such as Eater (🌐 *www.eater.com*).

California chefs continue to shop locally for produce and farmer-sourced meat, and many restaurants proudly display their vendors on the menu. Chefs and foodies alike engage in discourse on the ethics and politics of food and farming. Sustainably harvested seafood and "nose to tail" cooking, where as much of the animal as possible is used in an attempt to reduce food waste, are both hot topics these days.

FAMILY FUN

Both kids and adults will be fascinated by the creatures on display in "Tentacles: The Astounding Lives of Octopuses, Squid and Cuttlefishes," the newest exhibit at the Monterey Bay Aquarium.

The supersize and hands-on exhibits at San Francisco's Exploratorium continue to challenge and fascinate visitors of all ages. With trees as tall as they come, the Children's Redwood Forest in Humboldt Redwoods State Park is a great place for kids to romp through some awe-inspiring landscapes.

WINE DISCOVERIES

California offers oenophiles ample opportunities for new discoveries beyond the traditional California Wine Country. Across the state, vineyards are going up in unlikely places.

Venturing just beyond the traditional wine destinations of Napa and Sonoma counties will reward visitors with hidden gems. Areas such as the Petaluma Gap and the Sierra Foothills offer plenty of vineyards to explore. Visitors to Lake Tahoe can even take in some wine tasting at the Truckee River Winery, claiming to be the highest and coldest winery in the nation.

ALL ABOARD

Riding the rails can be a satisfying experience, particularly in California where the distances between destinations sometimes run into the hundreds of miles. You can save money on gas and parking, avoid freeway traffic, and see some of the best the state has to offer. California just broke ground on a high-speed rail project linking San Francisco to Los Angeles. In 2030, when the $68-billion project is complete, the train will make the run between the two cities in less than three hours.

Until then, the best trip is on the luxuriously appointed *Coast Starlight*, a long-distance train with sleeping cars that runs between Seattle and Los Angeles, passing some of California's most beautiful coastline as it hugs the beach. For the best surf-side viewing, get a seat or a room on the left side of the train and ride south to north.

HOMEGROWN HOSPITALITY

Agritourism in California isn't new, but it is on the rise, with farm tours and agricultural festivals sprouting up everywhere.

Wine Country is a particularly fertile area—spurred by the success of vineyards, the area's lavender growers and olive-oil producers have started welcoming visitors. Sonoma County Farm Trail maintains an excellent map and guide to visiting producers in the area.

STATE OF THE ARTS

California's beauty-obsessed citizens aren't the only ones opting for a fresh look these days: its esteemed art museums are also having a bit of work done.

The San Francisco Museum of Modern Art (SFMOMA) reopened in 2016 after a major expansion project vastly increased the museum's exhibition and support space.

Chapter 2

TRAVEL SMART NORTHERN CALIFORNIA

★ **CAPITAL:**
Sacramento

POPULATION:
40.1 million

LANGUAGE:
English

$ CURRENCY:
US dollar

COUNTRY CODE:
1

⚠ **EMERGENCIES:**
911

DRIVING:
On the right

ELECTRICITY:
120–240 v/60 cycles; plugs have two or three rectangular prongs

TIME:
Three hours behind New York

WEB RESOURCES:
www.visitcalifornia.com, www.parks.ca.gov, www.dot.ca.gov/cttravel, travel.state.gov

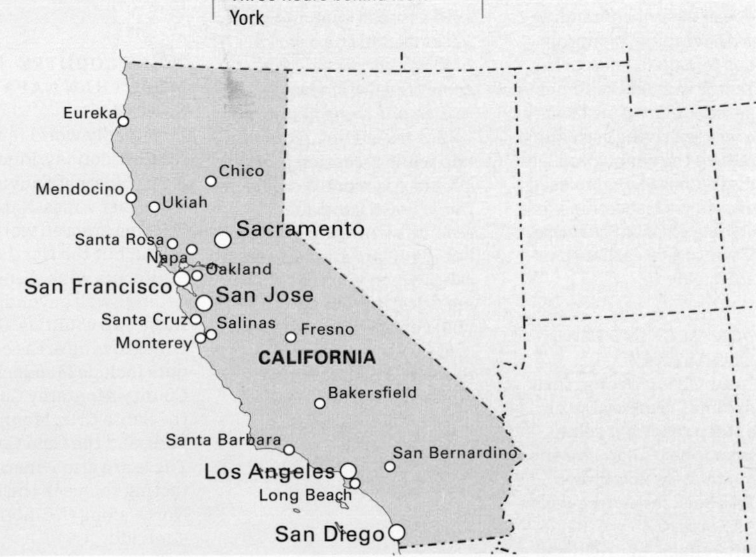

What to Know Before You Go

EXPECT SUMMER FOG ALONG THE COAST
The coast can be foggy in July and August because inland California's hot summer temperatures often cause cooler Pacific Ocean air to blanket areas nearest the shore. On a day when it's in 85 or 95 degrees inland, the temperature along the coast can be a crisp 55. Keep this in mind if you're planning a beach vacation in July. It might be sunny and warm, but then again not.

THAT ROAD TRIP TAKES TIME
Northern California is larger than many U.S. states. Traveling north–south from Lassen Volcanic National Park, say, down to Monterey Bay—or west–east from coastal San Francisco to Yosemite National Park or Lake Tahoe—takes several hours in the best of traffic (which frequently isn't the case). And that doesn't count contending with winding, mountainous terrain or coastal fog. Factor in an extra 20%–25% percent more time than the average driving estimate to reduce the chance you'll be disappointed over missed events or connections, and enjoy a pleasant surprise if you arrive earlier than anticipated.

DON'T LET GPS LEAD YOU ASTRAY
"Your GPS is Wrong: Turn Around," reads a sign on a steep road that some smartphone mapping apps mistake for downtown Truckee's main drag below. Although GPS is generally reliable in urban and suburban Northern California, this isn't always true in vast swaths of the rural North Coast, Far North, and Gold Country—not to mention Yosemite and Sequoia and Kings Canyon national parks and parts of Napa and Sonoma. If traveling to any of these places, in addition to referencing the maps in this book it's wise to back yourself up with old-school paper maps available at bookstores, auto associations, and some national and state parks. Also worth mentioning: some travelers may not realize one thing about how GPS works. If you plot out a trip while reception is good, should you move out of cell range you'll continue to receive turning directions, but if you are already out of range when you try to initiate a destination search, you won't be able to access route information. Be sure to seek GPS directions while you can.

"BEACH" DOESN'T NECESSARILY MEAN SANDY
The broad strands in Santa Cruz, Marin County's Stinson Beach, and way up north in Trinidad (Humboldt County) evoke the California beaches of countless media products, but much of the coastline is rocky. If you're looking for soft sandy beaches with bathtub-warm water, you're also in for a surprise. Even in July and August the water at most beaches north of San Francisco is cold. That said, some of the world's most majestic coastal terrain can be found here, and the sunsets are often nothing short of glorious. One other note about Northern California beaches: the surf at many of them can be treacherous. Take care when swimming and heed signs warning about riptides, forceful "rogue" waves that can appear suddenly and have caused even people onshore to drown.

"WINE COUNTRY" IS MORE THAN NAPA AND SONOMA
Deservedly world famous for Chardonnay, Pinot Noir, Cabernet Sauvignon, and other wines, Napa and Sonoma are well worth a visit, but the Northern California wine scene extends well beyond these two counties. Other winegrowing areas of note include Mendocino County, Monterey County, the Santa Cruz Mountains, Lodi, and the Gold Country. There are also wineries and tasting rooms in the Far North along the Interstate 5 corridor.

DRESS IN LAYERS

Among the conditions that make Northern California a nexus of wine production are the extreme shifts in temperature between night and day, especially in summer in coastal areas—Monterey, Santa Cruz, San Francisco, and Marin, Sonoma, Mendocino, and Humboldt counties—and in the Sierra Nevada range. Along the coast or at higher altitudes, it's best to dress in layers year-round.

NO NEED TO BREAK THE BANK

The San Francisco Bay Area ranks among the country's most expensive places to live, and travelers' costs in Napa and Sonoma rival those in major resorts (ditto for Lake Tahoe on summer weekends and during ski season), but away from these regions much of Northern California is affordable if not a flat-out bargain. Tasting fees in Mendocino County's Anderson Valley, for example, are generally half those of Sonoma County, and way less than the Napa Valley's on average. Likewise in the Gold Country and the Far North, except for the fanciest bed-and-breakfasts, room rates trend way lower than in San Francisco, Monterey, or Santa Cruz.

YOU CAN AVOID THE CROWDS

When you're stuck in rush-hour traffic heading from the Bay Area to the Wine Country or in weekend traffic to Yosemite National Park or Lake Tahoe, Northern California can seem mercilessly overcrowded. Since you're on vacation and have more flexibility than commuters, schedule your travel through densely populated areas to avoid peak driving times. Better yet, visit the attractions of the Far North and the North Coast's Humboldt County, many of which aren't usually awash with visitors even in summer.

DON'T MISS THE REDWOODS

Northern California is famous for sophisticated San Francisco, Napa and Sonoma's wines, the stunning coastline, and the rugged Sierra Nevada range. One experience not to miss while you're here, though, is walking among the region's magnificent redwood forests. If you're on a tight schedule, it's worth the time to zip a dozen miles north of San Francisco to Muir Woods. Even when this national monument is crowded—and it often is on weekends year-round and daily in summer—a stroll through the forest is still breathtaking. For more solitude, consider the off-the-beaten-path portions of Humboldt County's Avenue of the Giants or Redwood National Park or, south of Yosemite National Park, Sequoia and Kings Canyon National Parks.

POT IS LEGAL, BUT ...

In 2018 marijuana became legal in California for recreational purposes—medical use has been legal for more than two decades. A tug of war between local and state governments has led to inconsistencies from one county to the next that has inhibited marijuana tourism somewhat. Curious visitors do seek out weed, though, and as long as you are 21 and have proof, it's perfectly legal to acquire and use marijuana (albeit not always in public). Depending on the dispensary, cannabis might come in the form of flowers, edibles, concentrates, or something else. Keep in mind that dispensaries licensed solely for the sale of medical marijuana can't sell you pot without a prescription; without one you need to shop somewhere licensed for recreational use. As of mid-2019, such dispensaries are rare in Marin County and Napa, less so in Sonoma, and, because they're centers of cultivation, relatively easy in Mendocino and Humboldt counties. California's Bureau of Cannabis Control has a searchable database (🌐 *CApotcheck.com*) of licensed dispensaries.

Getting Here and Around

From San Francisco To:	By Air	By Car
San Jose	No flights	1 hr
Monterey	45 mins	2 hrs
Los Angeles	1 hr 30 mins	5 hrs 40 mins
Portland, OR	1 hr 50 mins	10 hrs
Mendocino	No flights	3 hrs
Yosemite NP/ Fresno	1 hr	4 hrs
Lake Tahoe/ Reno	1 hr	3 hrs 30 mins

From San Francisco to:	Route	Distance
San Jose	U.S. 101	50 miles
Monterey	U.S. 101 to Hwy. 156 to Hwy. 1	120 miles
Los Angeles	U.S. 101 to Hwy. 156 to I–5	382 miles
Portland, OR	I–80 to I–505 to I–5	635 miles
Mendocino	Hwy. 1	174 miles
Yosemite NP	I–80 to I–580 to I–205 to Hwy. 120 east	184 miles
Lake Tahoe/ Reno	I–80	220 miles

Air Travel

Flying time to California is about 6½ hours from New York and 4¾ hours from Chicago. Travel from London to either Los Angeles or San Francisco is 11 hours and from Sydney approximately 15. Flying between San Francisco and Los Angeles takes about 90 minutes.

Bus Travel

Greyhound is the major bus carrier in California. Regional bus service is available in metropolitan areas.

Car Travel

Two main north–south routes run through California: Interstate 5 through the middle of the state, and U.S. 101, a parallel route closer to the coast. Slower but more scenic is Highway 1, which winds along much of the coast.

From north to south, the state's main east–west routes are Interstate 80, Interstate 15, Interstate 10, and Interstate 8. Much of California is mountainous, and you may encounter winding roads and steep mountain grades.

GASOLINE

Gas stations are plentiful throughout the state. Many stay open late, except in rural areas, where Sunday hours are limited and where you may drive long stretches without a chance to refuel.

ROAD CONDITIONS

Rainy weather can make driving along the coast or in the mountains treacherous. Some smaller routes over mountain ranges and in the deserts are prone to flash flooding. When the weather is particularly bad, Highway 1 may be closed due to mud and rock slides.

Many smaller roads over the Sierra Nevada are closed in winter, and if it's snowing, tire chains may be required on routes that are open. ■**TIP→ It's less expensive to purchase chains before you get to the mountains.** Chains or cables generally cost $30–$75, depending on tire size; cables are easier to attach than chains, but chains are more durable. Most rental-car companies prohibit chain installation on their vehicles. If you choose to disregard this rule, your insurance likely will not cover any chains-related damage.

In Northern California uniformed chain installers on Interstate 80 and U.S. 50 will apply chains for about $30 and take them off for half that. Chain installers are independent businesspeople, not highway employees. They are not allowed to sell or rent chains. On smaller roads, you're on your own.

Always carry extra clothing, blankets, water, and food when driving to the mountains in the winter, and keep your gas tank full to prevent the fuel line from freezing.

ROADSIDE EMERGENCIES

Dial 911 to report accidents and to reach the police, the California Highway Patrol (CHP), or the fire department. On some rural highways and on most interstates, look for emergency phones on the side of the road.

RULES OF THE ROAD

All passengers must wear a seat belt at all times. A child must be secured in a federally approved child passenger restraint system and ride in the back seat until at least eight years of age or until the child is at least 4 feet 9 inches tall. Children who are eight but don't meet the height requirement must ride in a booster seat or a car seat. It is illegal to leave a child six years of age or younger unattended in a motor vehicle. Unless indicated, right turns are allowed at red lights after you've come to a full stop. Left turns between two one-way streets are allowed at red lights after you've come to a full stop. Drivers with a blood-alcohol level higher than 0.08 who are stopped by police are subject to arrest.

The speed limit on some interstate highways is 70 mph; unlimited-access roads are usually 55 mph. In cities, freeway speed limits are between 55 mph and 65 mph. Many city routes have commuter lanes during rush hour.

You must turn on your headlights whenever weather conditions require the use of windshield wipers. Texting on a wireless device is illegal for all drivers. If using a mobile phone while driving it must be hands-free and mounted (i.e., it's not legal having it loose on the seat or your lap). For more driving rules, refer to the Department of Motor Vehicles driver's handbook at 🌐 *www.dmv.ca.gov.*

CAR RENTAL

When you reserve a car, ask about cancellation penalties, taxes, drop-off charges (if you're planning to pick up the car in one city and leave it in another), and surcharges (for being under or over a certain age, for additional drivers, or for driving across state or country borders or beyond a specific distance from your point of rental). All these things can add substantially to your costs. Request car seats and extras such as GPS when you book.

Rates are sometimes—but not always—better if you book in advance or reserve through a rental agency's website. There are other reasons to book ahead, though: for popular destinations, during busy times of the year, or to ensure that you get certain types of cars (vans, SUVs, exotic sports cars).

■ TIP→ Make sure that a confirmed reservation guarantees you a car. Agencies sometimes overbook, particularly for busy weekends and holiday periods.

Getting Here and Around

A car is essential in most parts of California. In compact San Francisco it's better to use public transportation, taxis, or ride-sharing services to avoid parking headaches.

Rates statewide for the least expensive vehicle begin as low as $30 a day, usually on weekends, and less than $200 a week. This does not include additional fees or the tax on car rentals (8%–10%). Be sure to shop around—you can get a decent deal by shopping the major car-rental companies' websites. A few companies rent specialty cars such as convertibles or sport-utility vehicles.

In California you must have a valid driver's license and be 21 to rent a car; rates may be higher if you're under 25. Some agencies will not rent to those under 25; check when you book. Non-U.S. residents must have a license, valid for the entire rental period, with text in the Roman alphabet that clearly identifies it as a driver's license. In addition, most companies also require an international license; check in advance.

Train Travel

Amtrak provides rail service within California. On some trips—to Yosemite National Park, for example—passengers board motor coaches part of the way. The rail service's scenic *Coast Starlight* trip begins in Los Angeles and hugs the Pacific Coast to San Luis Obispo before it turns inland for the rest of its journey to Portland and Seattle.

Before You Go

Passport

All foreign nationals must possess a valid passport to enter the United States. This includes infants and small children. In most cases, the passport must be valid for at least six months beyond your scheduled return date. Keep in mind that having a valid passport and visa does not guarantee entry to the United States. The final decision about eligibility is made at your place of entry by a U.S. Customs and Border Protection agent.

Visa

Foreign citizens visiting the United States must have a visa—among the most common being the Nonimmigrant Visitor Visa—unless they belong to one of the three dozen or so nations participating in the Visa Waiver Program. To qualify for the waiver program, visitors need an e-passport with an embedded electronic identification chip and must have an updated Electronic System for Travel Authorization (ESTA). ESTA is the automated system used by the U.S. Department of Homeland Security to determine whether an individual qualifies for the waiver program. Note that even if your home country participates in the waiver program, you may not be eligible if you have recently visited a country on the U.S. terror-prevention list.

Immunizations

The United States has no traveler vaccination requirements. The U.S.-based Centers for Disease Control and Prevention (CDC) maintains a list of current infectious-disease outbreaks within the country. The CDC recommends that prospective U.S. travelers from abroad rely on resources within their home country for health recommendations.

U.S. Embassy/Consulate

Most U.S. embassies are located in host countries' capital cities, with consulates in additional cities. U.S. Foreign Service officers at embassies and consulates are available (usually by appointment) to interview foreign citizens wishing to visit the United States for business, tourism, or other eligible purposes, and paperwork can be filed with them.

When to Go

California is a year-round destination, so the best time to visit depends on your interests and where you're headed. The weather is pleasant nearly year-round, except for periods of high summer heat in the desert areas and low winter temperatures in the Sierra Nevada and other inland mountain ranges. The late spring and early fall are milder than in summer, and usually not rainy.

HIGH SEASON $$$–$$$$

High season extends from late May through early September. During this period expect the longest lines at the most popular attractions and the highest hotel occupancy rates and prices. In Northern California's wine country, high season lasts through October, until the grape harvest is nearly complete.

LOW SEASON $$

From December to March, tourist activity slows in much of the state, in part because temperatures are cooler but also because, drought years aside, this is the rainiest time of year. Except in the mountains, which may see snowfall (rare in coastal areas), winters here are mild. Lodging prices tend to be the lowest during this period.

VALUE SEASON $$–$$$

From April to late May and from late September to mid-November the weather is almost as pleasant as during high season, but hotel prices may seem more reasonable.

Essentials

 Accommodations

With just under 5,700 lodgings, California has inns, motels, hotels, and specialty accommodations to suit every traveler's fancy and finances. Retro motels recalling 1950s roadside culture but with 21st-century amenities are a recent popular trend, but you'll also see traditional motels and hotels, along with luxury resorts and boutique properties. Reservations are a good idea throughout the year but especially so in the summer. On weekends at smaller lodgings, minimum-stay requirements of two or three nights are common, though some places are flexible about this in winter. Some accommodations aren't suitable for children, so ask before you book.

The lodgings we review are the top choices in each price category. *For an expanded review of each property, please see www.fodors.com.* We don't specify whether the facilities cost extra; when pricing accommodations, ask what's included and what costs extra. *For price information, see the planner in each chapter.*

APARTMENT AND HOUSE RENTALS

You'll find listings for Airbnb and similar rentals throughout California.

BED-AND-BREAKFASTS

California has more than 1,000 bed-and-breakfasts. You'll find everything from simple homestays to lavish luxury lodgings, many in historic hotels and homes. The California Association of Boutique and Breakfast Inns has about 300 member properties that you can locate and book through its website.

RESERVATION SERVICES California Association of Boutique and Breakfast Inns *(CABBI). ☎ 800/373–9251 🌐 www.cabbi.com.*

Some properties allow you to cancel without any kind of penalty—even if you prepaid to secure a discounted rate—if you cancel at least 24 hours in advance. Others require you to cancel a week in advance or penalize you the cost of one night. Small inns and B&Bs are most likely to require you to cancel far in advance. Most hotels allow children under a certain age to stay in their parents' room at no extra charge, but others charge for them as extra adults; find out the cutoff age for discounts.

 Dining

California has led the pack in bringing natural and organic foods to the forefront of American dining. Though rooted in European cuisine, California cooking sometimes has strong Asian and Latin influences. Wherever you go, you're likely to find that dishes are made with fresh produce and other local ingredients.

The restaurants we list are the cream of the crop in each price category. *For price information, see the planner in each chapter.*

DISCOUNTS AND DEALS

The better grocery and specialty-food stores have grab-and-go sections, with prepared foods on a par with restaurant cooking, perfect for picnicking.

MEALS AND MEALTIMES

Lunch is typically served from 11 or 11:30 to 2:30 or 3, with dinner service starting at 5 or 5:30 and lasting until 9 or later. Restaurants that serve breakfast usually open by 7, sometimes earlier, with some serving breakfast through the lunch hour. Most weekend brunches start at 10 or 11 and go at least until 2.

PAYING

Most restaurants take cash or credit cards, though a few don't accept the latter. In most establishments tipping is the norm, but some include the service in the menu price or add it to the bill. *For guidelines on tipping see Tipping, below.*

RESERVATIONS AND DRESS

Regardless of where you are, it's a good idea to make a reservation if you can. For popular restaurants, book as far ahead as you can (often 30 days), and reconfirm as soon as you arrive in California. (Large parties should always call ahead to check the reservations policy.)

Online reservation services make it easy to book a table. OpenTable covers many California cities.

Money

Along the coast and at desert resorts, expect to pay top dollar for everything from gas and food to lodging and attractions. Prices in the Gold Country, the Far North, and the Death Valley/Mojave Desert region are somewhat lower than on the coast.

CREDIT CARDS

It's a good idea to inform your credit-card company before you travel. Otherwise, unusual activity might prompt the company to put a hold on your card. Record all your credit-card numbers—as well as the phone numbers to call if your cards are lost or stolen—so you're prepared should something go wrong.

Health

Smoking is illegal in all California bars and restaurants, including on outdoor dining patios in some cities. If you have an existing medical condition that may require emergency treatment, be aware that many rural and mountain communities have only daytime clinics, not hospitals with 24-hour emergency rooms.

Outdoor sports are a huge draw in California's moderate climate, but caution, especially in unfamiliar areas, is key. Drownings occur each year because beach lovers don't heed warnings about high surfs with their deadly rogue waves. Do not fly within 24 hours of scuba diving.

If you're spending time in the national parks or forests, be sure to follow posted instructions that outline how to avoid encounters with bears (e.g., store your food in bear lockers) and how to prevent exposure to hantavirus, carried in deer mouse droppings in remote areas.

Safety

California is a safe place to visit, as long as you take the usual precautions. In large cities ask the concierge or desk clerk to point out areas on your map that you should avoid. Lock valuables in a hotel safe when you're not using them. Keep an eye on your handbag when you're out in public. Security is high (but mostly invisible) at theme parks and resorts.

When hiking, stay on trails—rangers say that the majority of hikers needing to be rescued have gone off trail—and heed signs at trailheads about dangerous situations such as cliffs with loose rocks and how to react if you encounter predatory animals that live in the area. Bring plenty of water, hike with a companion if possible, and learn to identify and avoid contact with poison oak, a ubiquitous plant in California that causes a severe rash.

Taxes

Sales tax in the state of California is 7.25%, but local taxes vary and may be as much as an additional 2.5%. Sales tax applies to all purchases except for food bought in a grocery store; food consumed in a restaurant is taxed, but takeout food is not. Hotel taxes vary widely by region, from about 8% to 16.5%.

Packing

The California lifestyle emphasizes casual wear, and with the generally mild climate you needn't worry about packing cold-weather clothing unless you're going into mountainous areas between. Jeans, walking shorts, and T-shirts are fine in most situations. Few restaurants require men to wear a jacket or tie, though a collared shirt is the norm at upscale establishments.

Summer evenings can be cool, especially near the coast, where fog often rolls in. Always pack a sweater or light jacket. Comfortable walking shoes are a must. If you're headed to state or national parks, packing binoculars, clothes that layer, long pants and long-sleeve shirts, sunglasses, and a wide-brimmed hat is wise. You can pick up insect repellant, sunscreen, and a first-aid kit once in-state.

Visitor Information

The California Travel and Tourism Commission's website takes you to each region of California, with digital visitor guides in multiple languages, driving tours, maps, welcome center locations, information on local tours, links to bed-and-breakfasts, and a complete booking center. It also links you—via the Destinations menu—to the websites of city and *regional tourism offices and attractions. For the numbers and websites of regional and city visitor bureaus and chambers of commerce, see the Planning section in each chapter.*

Tipping Guidelines for California

Bartender	$1–$3 per drink, or 15%–20% per round
Bellhop	$2–$3 per bag, depending on the level of the hotel
Hotel Concierge	$5–$10 for advice and reservations, more for difficult tas*ks*
Hotel Doorman	$2–$3 for hailing a cab
Valet Parking Attendant	$3–*$5 when you* get your *car*
Hotel Maid	$3–$5 per day; more in high-end hotels
Waiter	18%–22% (20%–25% is standard in upscale restaurants); nothing additional if a service charge is added to the bill
Skycap at Airport	$1–$2 per bag
Hotel Room-Service Waiter	15%–20% *per delive*ry, even if a service charge was added since that fee goes to the hotel, not the waiter
Taxi Driver	15%–20%, but round up the fare to the next dollar amount
Tour Guide	15% of the cost of the tour, more depending on quality

Contacts

Air

AIRPORTS
NORTHERN CALIFORNIA Sacramento International Airport. 916/929–5411 *www.sacramento.aero/smf.* **San Francisco International Airport.** *650/821–8211, 800/435–9736 www.flysfo.com. San Jose International Airport. 408/392–3600 www.flysanjose.com.*

Bus

BUS TRAVEL Greyhound. *800/231–2222 www.greyhound.com.*

Train

TRAIN TRAVEL Amtrak. *800/872–7245 www.amtrak.com.*

Safety

SAFETY CALTRANS Current Highway Conditions. *800/427–7623 www.dot.ca.gov.*

Car

SPECIALTY CAR AGENCIES Beverly Hills Rent a Car. *310/448–2018 www.bhrentacar.com.* **Enterprise Exotic Car Rentals.** *866/458–9227 exoticcars.enterprise.com.* **Car (Midway Car Rental).** *866/717–6802 www.midwaycarrental.com.*

Weather

WEATHER National Weather Service. *707/443–6484 northernmost California, 831/656–1725 San Francisco Bay area and central California, 775/673–8100 Reno, Lake Tahoe, and northern Sierra, 805/988–6610 Los Angeles, 858/675–8700 San Diego, 916/979–3051 Sacramento.*

On the Calendar

January

Winter Wineland. In mid-January, wineries in the Alexander, Russian River, and Dry Creek valleys—including many not generally open to the public—offer tastings, seminars, and entertainment. 🌐 *www.wineroad.com.*

March

Flavor! Napa Valley Several days of dinners, cooking demonstrations, and wine-and-food tastings—many involving top chefs and winemakers—take place in late March. The event benefits the California campus of the Culinary Institute of America. 🌐 *www.flavornapavalley.com.*

Wine Road Barrel Tasting Weekends. In early March, more than 100 wineries open their cellars for two weekends of tastings straight from the barrel. More wineries participate on the first weekend than the second one. 🌐 *www.wineroad.com.*

May

BottleRock Napa Valley. An end-of-May three-day food, wine, and music festival, BottleRock gets summer rolling (and rocking) with acts headlined by the likes of Bruno Mars, the Red Hot Chili Peppers, and Halsey. Tickets sell out in early January when the lineup is announced. 🌐 *www.bottlerocknapavalley.com.*

June

Auction Napa Valley. Dozens of events culminate in the Napa Valley's glitziest night—with an opulent dinner and an auction of rare wines and other coveted items to benefit nonprofit health and other programs. It's held on the first full weekend in June. 🌐 *auctionnapavalley.org.*

July

Festival Napa Valley. This acclaimed mid-July event attracts international opera, theater, dance, and classical-music performers to Castello di Amorosa and other venues. 🌐 *www.festivalnapavalley.org.*

August

West of West Wine Festival. Wineries and grape growers along Sonoma County's coastline sponsor this early-August festival. You can sample Chardonnays, Pinot Noirs, Syrahs, and other wines of small producers with no tasting rooms of their own. 🌐 *www.westsonomacoast.com.*

September

Sonoma County Harvest Fair. This early fall festival at the county fairgrounds in Santa Rosa celebrates Sonoma agriculture with wine and olive-oil competitions, cooking demos, flower and livestock shows, carnival rides, and local entertainers. ✉ *Santa Rosa* 🌐 *www.harvestfair.org.*

Taste of Sonoma. Chefs, grape growers, and winemakers team up to celebrate Sonoma County food and wine on the first Saturday in September. Dozens of wineries pour current and library releases in the main, tented area and in outdoor VIP lounges, and there are seminars and presentations about wine-related topics. 🌐 *tasteofsonoma.com.*

October

Pinot on the River. Pinot Noir fans flock to the Russian River Valley in late October for a weekend of tastings, seminars, and lively discourse about what makes a great Pinot. 🌐 *www.pinotfestival.com.*

November

A Wine & Food Affair. For this November event, always a sellout, wineries prepare a favorite recipe and serve it with wine. Participants travel from winery to winery to sample the fare. 🌐 *www.wineroad.com.*

Chapter 3

NORTHERN CALIFORNIA'S BEST ROAD TRIPS

Updated by
Daniel Mangin

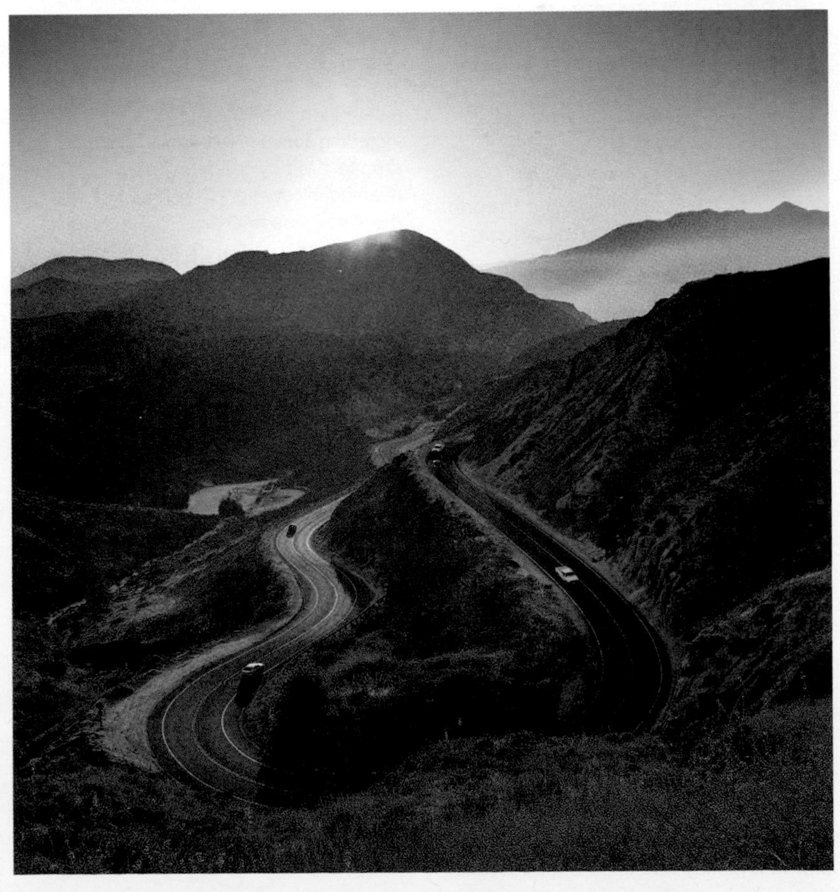

Great Itineraries

No trip to California would be complete without a drive through the state's spectacular scenery. However, adding a road trip to your itinerary is not just a romantic idea: it's often a practical one, too. A road trip is a great way to link together more than one urban area or to venture into some more remote areas of this massive state. Whether you have just a few days or longer to spare, these itineraries will help you hit the road.

The Best of the Northern Coast, 5 Days

Hit the highlights of Northern California in one itinerary: scenic coastal drives, quaint windswept towns, wine tasting, culinary delights, and majestic redwood forests. This route can be done as part of a longer trip north toward the Oregon border, or as part of a loop back down to San Francisco.

DAY 1: MARIN COUNTY AND POINT REYES NATIONAL SEASHORE

(Without stops, Point Reyes National Seashore is about 1½ hrs by car from San Francisco on Hwy 1. Point Reyes Lighthouse is 45 mins by car from the visitor center.)

As you head out of San Francisco on the Golden Gate Bridge, be sure to pull over at the **scenic lookout** on the north side and take in the spectacular views looking back at the city skyline. If you haven't yet checked out the picturesque harbor community of **Sausalito** just north of the bridge, now is your chance. It will be hard not to linger, but there is much to see today. Bidding San Francisco farewell, you will quickly find yourself in the natural beauty of Marin County. Exit the 101 onto Highway 1 at the chic suburb **Mill Valley,** and head toward **Muir Woods National Monument.** Walking among the coastal redwoods, it is hard to imagine San Francisco lies just a few miles away. However, the proximity to the city means that Muir Woods is often crowded, and parking can be difficult if you don't arrive early.

From Muir Woods, continue on Highway 1 past the laid-back beach towns of **Stinson Beach** and **Bolinas** before continuing on to **Point Reyes National Seashore.** Spend the remainder of the day at the park tide pooling, kayaking, hiking one of the many trails, or exploring the **Point Reyes Lighthouse.** In the winter, be on the lookout for migrating gray whales.

The tiny town of **Point Reyes Station** offers a selection of shops and dining options, including **Tomales Bay Foods,** a provisions stop favored by foodies. Spend a quiet evening in town and overnight at one of the small inns nearby.

DAY 2: HEALDSBURG

(Point Reyes Station to Healdsburg, via Jenner, is 2 hrs by car.)

Continue north on Highway 1 past **Bodega Bay,** made famous by the Alfred Hitchcock movie *The Birds.* At Jenner, known for its resident harbor seals, turn on Route 116 and follow the Russian River inland, taking time to stop at a winery or two along the way.

Ditch the car in **Healdsburg** and enjoy strolling through the appealing town square with its excellent selection of tasting rooms and boutiques. The town is home to many acclaimed restaurants and luxurious hotels and is an excellent place to stop for the night. The town's compact layout and quality offerings make Healdsburg a favorite among wine-country destinations.

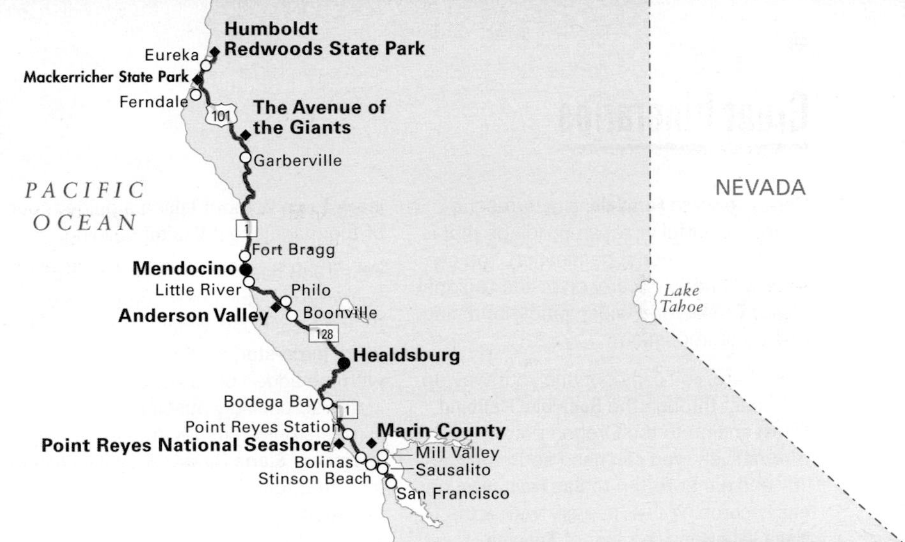

DAYS 3 AND 4: ANDERSON VALLEY AND MENDOCINO

(Mendocino is 2 hrs by car from Healdsburg. Budget plenty of time for stops in Anderson Valley to ensure the end of this scenic drive is done in the daylight.)

Driving north on the 101 from Healdsburg, pick up Highway 128 at Cloverdale and head into the **Anderson Valley.** This wine region is famous for its excellent Pinot Noir and Gewürztraminer, and the laid-back atmosphere of its tasting rooms can be a refreshing alternative to those in Napa Valley. **Navarro Vineyards, Roederer Estate,** and **Husch Vineyards** are all recommended. The small towns of **Boonville** and **Philo** have several high-quality dining options, and the latter is home to the **Philo Apple Farm's** beloved farm stand.

Continuing on to the coast, Highway 128 follows the Navarro River through several miles of dense and breathtaking redwood forest ending at the ocean. From here you meet up again with Highway 1 as it winds its way along a spectacularly scenic portion of the coast.

With their excellent dining and lodging options, the towns of **Mendocino** and **Little River,** just to the south, are great choices for your overnight stay. Spend the next day and a half exploring the area. Opportunities for stunning coastal walks abound, including **MacKerricher** and **Van Damme State Parks.** Hike through the unique Pygmy Forest in Van Damme and visit the **Glass Beach** in Fort Bragg. Be sure to save some time to explore the town of Mendocino itself with its quaint New England–style architecture and selection of art galleries and boutiques.

DAY 5: HUMBOLDT REDWOODS STATE PARK AND THE AVENUE OF THE GIANTS

(Mendocino to Eureka via the Avenue of the Giants is 3 hrs by car.)

Driving north on Highway 1, the road eventually curves inland and meets up with U.S. 101 near Leggett. Head north on the 101 to Garberville, a good place to take a break before heading on to the redwoods.

For all the hype, a drive through **The Avenue of the Giants** will still take your breath away. Pick up a copy of the self-guided tour as you enter the 32-mile stretch of road running alongside some of the tallest trees on the planet. The drive weaves through portions of the larger **Humboldt Redwoods State Park.** Take time to get out of the car and take a short hike through Founders Grove or Rockefeller Forest.

Great Itineraries

Continue on to **Ferndale,** a picturesque town of colorful Victorian buildings that is now largely a tourist destination. You can overnight here, or carry on to the regional city of **Eureka** for a wider variety of dining and accommodation.

From here, you can continue your way up the coast through the **Redwood National Forest** and on to the Oregon border. Alternatively, you can head south on the 101 and either return to **San Francisco,** or easily combine this itinerary with a trip to **Napa Valley** and the rest of **Sonoma.**

Roads Less Traveled: Discovering the Northern Interior, 5 days

Mountain peaks, alpine lakes, a lush waterfall, and a striking volcanic landscape are all included on this tour of California's far north. The drive packs a big scenic punch in a short amount of time, and without the crowds found elsewhere in California's national parks. The remote roads and high elevations make parts of this route subject to snow closures well into the spring. Check current road conditions before setting out.

DAY 1: SACRAMENTO TO CHICO

(1½ hrs by car.)

Start your trip with a tour of the highlights of California's capital city, **Sacramento.** Wander the cobblestone streets and historic storefronts of Old Sacramento to get a sense of the city during its gold-rush days. Enjoy a horse-drawn-carriage ride through the historic neighborhood or take a cruise along the riverfront. Train enthusiasts of all ages will enjoy the walk-through exhibits at the nearby **California State Railroad Museum.** Finally, don't leave town without taking a guided tour of the magnificent **Capitol** building.

When you have finished your tour of Sacramento, drive north on Highway 99 to **Chico.** Overnighting in Chico gets you a jump-start on the next day's drive, with the added bonus of spending time in this surprisingly bustling agricultural-meets-university town. Stop at the legendary **Sierra Nevada Brewing Company** for a free tour, or enjoy a meal at the brewpub.

DAYS 2 AND 3: LASSEN VOLCANIC NATIONAL PARK

(1½–2 hrs by car from Chico.)

Get an early start on your day, as spectacular scenery awaits you. From Chico, follow Highway 32 toward Chester and branch north at Highway 36 to reach the southern entrance of **Lassen Volcanic National Park.** Spend the next two days exploring the area's geothermal activity and dramatic landscape. Highlights include a hike alongside the bubbling mud pots and hot springs of **Bumpass Hell trail,** views of **Lassen Peak** from Manzanita Lake, or an ascent of the peak itself. The 185-mile **Lassen Scenic Byway** circles the volcanic park and neighboring Lassen National Forest. If you plan ahead, you might score a reservation at **Drakesbad Guest Ranch** or at one of the campgrounds within the park. Otherwise, you will need to bunk in Chester or another neighboring town. Note: in winter, the park is closed to vehicles. Check current road conditions before setting out. If the park is closed, the itinerary can easily be modified to skip it and continue straight to McArthur-Burney Falls from Chico via Highway 299.

DAY 4: MCARTHUR-BURNEY FALLS NATIONAL PARK AND MT. SHASTA

(McArthur-Burney Falls is about 45 mins by car from Manzanita Lake; the start of the Everitt Memorial Hwy. is approximately 1 hr and 10 mins from the falls.)

Follow Highway 89 north out of Lassen to **McArthur-Burney Falls Memorial State Park.** Arrive early on busy holidays and weekends, as the park entrance will close when filled to capacity. Inside the park, the 129-foot-high falls are a sight to behold as water cascades over the moss-covered rocks. The falls are located near the park visitor center, with a vista point and hiking trail leading down to the bottom.

When you've had your fill of the falls, continue north on Highway 89 to **Mt. Shasta.** Drive up the mountain on the paved Everitt Memorial Highway for incredible views. Time permitting, choose from one of the many day hikes along the route. Alternatively, in winter you can hit the slopes at the nearby **Mt. Shasta Board & Ski Park.** The charming town of Mount Shasta makes a great place to overnight. Train enthusiasts might prefer to venture 10 miles south to **Dunsmuir** and overnight at the **Railroad Park Resort,** a collection of antique cabooses transformed into a motel.

DAY 5: LAKE SHASTA AND REDDING

(The exit for Lake Shasta Caverns is approximately 50 mins by car from the town of Mount Shasta. It's another ½ hr by car to reach Redding.)

Drive south on Interstate 5 to Lakehead and take Exit 695 to the **Lake Shasta Caverns.** The two-hour tour of the glittering caverns also includes a boat ride. Tours are offered throughout the day, more frequently in summer.

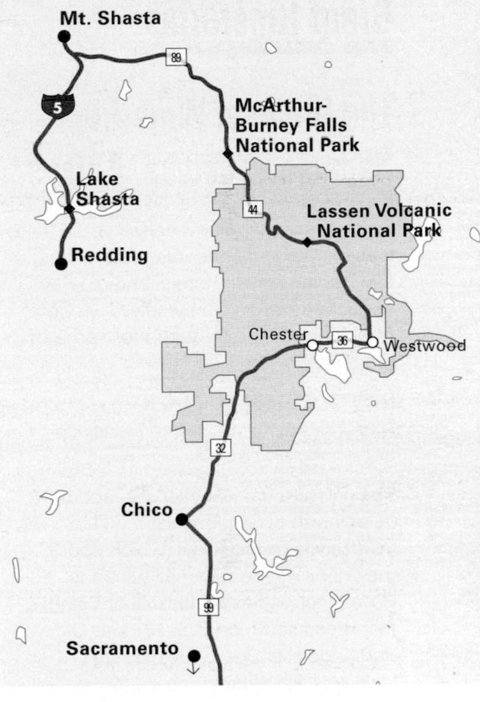

Back aboveground, anglers and boating enthusiasts should head to one of the marinas dotting the lakeshore to charter the craft of their choice. Houseboats are particularly popular on Lake Shasta, but many rentals come with a two-night minimum. For those more interested in engineering than angling, the hour-long tour of the **Shasta Dam** takes you inside the second-largest concrete dam in the United States. If you are not staying overnight on the lake, drive south and conclude your tour in the nearby city of **Redding** for the best selection of dining and accommodation. Note: this itinerary is designed for those wanting to loop back around to Sacramento and the Bay Area, or to continue on toward either Lake Tahoe or the North Coast. If you plan on driving north into Oregon, visit Shasta Lake prior to Mt. Shasta (take Highway 299 west from Burney) and then continue on Interstate 5 north across the state line.

Great Itineraries

The Ultimate Wine Trip: Napa and Sonoma, 4 Days

On this four-day extravaganza, you'll taste well-known and under-the-radar wines, bed down in plush hotels, and dine at restaurants operated by celebrity chefs. Appointments are required for some of the tastings.

DAY 1: SONOMA COUNTY

(1½–2 hrs by car from San Francisco, depending on traffic.)

Begin your tour in Geyserville, about 78 miles north of San Francisco on U.S. 101. Visit **Locals Tasting Room,** which pours the wines of special small wineries. Have lunch at nearby **Diavola** or **Catelli's,** then head south on U.S. 101 and Old Redwood Highway to **Healdsburg's J Vineyards and Winery,** known for sparkling wines, Pinot Grigio, and Pinot Noir. After a tasting, backtrack on Old Redwood to Healdsburg. **Hôtel Les Mars** and **h2hotel** are two well-located spots to spend the night. Have dinner at **Chalkboard, Bravas Bar de Tapas,** or **Campo Fina,** all close by.

DAY 2: SONOMA WINERIES

(1 hr by car from Healdsburg to Glen Ellen.)

Interesting wineries dot the countryside surrounding Healdsburg, among them **Dry Creek Vineyard, Jordan Vineyard & Winery,** and **Unti Vineyards.** Dry Creek produces Zinfandel, Jordan makes Cabernet Sauvignon and Chardonnay, and Unti specializes in Zinfandel, Sangiovese, and obscure Italian and Rhône varietals. In the afternoon, head south on U.S. 101 and east on scenic Highway 12 to **Glen Ellen.** Visit **Jack London State Historic Park,** the memorabilia-filled home of the famous writer. Dine at **Aventine Glen Ellen** or **Glen Ellen Star** and stay at the **Olea Hotel.**

DAY 3: NAPA VALLEY

(Glen Ellen to St. Helena is about 30 mins by car without traffic. St. Helena to Yountville is about 15 mins by car, without stops.)

On Day 3, head east from Glen Ellen on Trinity Road, which twists and turns over the Mayacamas Mountains, eventually becoming the Oakville Grade. Unless you're driving, bask in the stupendous **Napa Valley** views. At Highway 29, drive north to **St. Helena.** Focus on history and architecture at **Charles Krug Winery** or let the art and wines at **Hall St. Helena** transport you. Take lunch downtown at **Cindy's Backstreet Kitchen.** Check out St. Helena's shopping, then head south on Highway 29 to Yountville for more shopping. With its mix of gift stores and galleries, **V Marketplace** is a good place to start.

Stay overnight at **Bardessono** or the **North Block Hotel,** both within walking distance of Yountville's famous restaurants. A meal at **The French Laundry** is many visitors' holy grail, but dining at **Bouchon, Bistro Jeanty, Redd,** or Chiarello's **Bottega** will also leave you feeling well served.

DAY 4: OAKVILLE TO CARNEROS

(Just over 1 hr by car from Napa to San Francisco, without traffic.)

After breakfast, head north on Highway 29 to **Oakville,** where sipping wine at **Silver Oak Cellars, Nickel & Nickel,** or **B Cellars** will make clear why collectors covet Oakville Cabernet Sauvignons. Nickel & Nickel is on Highway 29; Silver Oak and B Cellars are east of it on Oakville Cross Road. Have a picnic at **Oakville Grocery,** in business on Highway 29 since 1881. Afterward, head south to Highway 121 and turn west to reach the Carneros District. Tour the **di Rosa** arts center (appointment required), then repair across the street to **Domaine Carneros,** which makes French-style sparkling wines. There's hardly a more elegant way to bid a Wine Country adieu than on the Domaine château's vineyard-view terrace before heading back to San Francisco. Give yourself plenty of time to get to your departure airport; traffic is generally heavy as you close in on the Bay Area.

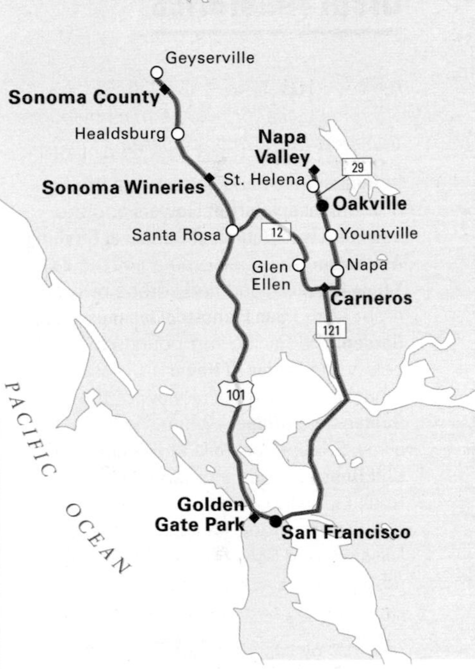

MODIFYING THE ROUTE FROM SAN FRANCISCO

The above itinerary is useful if traveling to Wine Country from points farther north. If you prefer to make a loop beginning and ending in San Francisco, the itinerary can be easily modified as follows: Day 1: Head north from San Francisco to the town of Sonoma (1 to 1½ hours by car, depending on traffic) and spend some time exploring the restaurants, shops, and tasting rooms lining the downtown plaza. Several excellent wineries operate nearby, including **Walt Wines** and **Patz & Hall.** From Sonoma, head north to Glen Ellen (20 minutes by car) and pick up the Glen Ellen itinerary described above. Day 2: Continue north to Healdsburg, following the above itinerary in reverse. Overnight in Healdsburg as described. Day 3: Head south on Highway 101 to River Road and then east on Mark Springs Road toward Calistoga (45 minutes by car), a town made famous by its hot springs and mud baths. If time permits, overnight at one of Calistoga's luxury retreats, such as the **Calistoga Ranch,** or enjoy a day of pampering at **Spa Solage.** Otherwise, head south to St. Helena (15 minutes by car) and complete the remainder of the road trip as outlined above.

Sierra Riches: Yosemite, Gold Country, and Tahoe, 10 Days

This tour will show you why Tony Bennett left his heart in San Francisco. It also includes some of the most beautiful places in a very scenic state, plus gold-rush-era history, and a chance to hike a trail or two.

DAY 1: SAN FRANCISCO

Straight from the airport, drop your bags at the lighthearted **Hotel Monaco** near **Union Square** and request a goldfish for your room. A Union Square stroll packs a wallop of people-watching, window-shopping, and architecture viewing. **Chinatown,** chock-full of dim sum shops, storefront temples, and open-air markets, promises authentic bites for lunch. Catch a Powell Street **cable car** to the end of the line and get off to see the bay views and the antique arcade games at **Musée Mécanique,** the hidden gem of otherwise mindless **Fisherman's Wharf.** No need to go any farther than cosmopolitan North Beach for cocktail hour, dinner, and live music.

Great Itineraries

DAY 2: GOLDEN GATE PARK

(15 mins by car or taxi, 45 mins by public transport from Union Square.)

In **Golden Gate Park,** linger amid the flora of the **Conservatory of Flowers** and the **San Francisco Botanical Garden at Strybing Arboretum,** soak up some art at the **de Young Museum,** and find serene refreshment at the **San Francisco Japanese Tea Garden.** The Pacific surf pounds the cliffs below the **Legion of Honor** art museum, which has an exquisite view of the **Golden Gate Bridge**—when the fog stays away. Sunset cocktails at the circa-1909 **Cliff House** include a prospect over Seal Rock (actually occupied by sea lions). Eat dinner elsewhere: Pacific Heights, the Mission, and SoMa teem with excellent restaurants.

DAY 3: INTO THE HIGH SIERRA

(4–5 hrs by car from San Francisco.)

First thing in the morning, pick up your rental car and head for the hills. Arriving in **Yosemite National Park, Bridalveil Fall,** and **El Capitan,** the 350-story granite monolith, greet you on your way to **Yosemite Village.** Ditch the car and pick up information and refreshment before hopping on the year-round shuttle to explore. Justly famous sights cram Yosemite Valley: massive **Half Dome** and **Sentinel Dome,** thundering **Yosemite Falls,** and wispy **Ribbon Fall** and **Nevada Fall.** Invigorating short hikes off the shuttle route lead to numerous vantage points. Celebrate your arrival in one of the world's most sublime spots with dinner in the dramatic **Majestic Hotel Dining Room** (formerly the Ahwahnee) and stay the night there (reserve well in advance).

DAY 4: YOSEMITE NATIONAL PARK

(Yosemite shuttles run every 10–30 mins.)

Ardent hikers consider **John Muir Trail to Half Dome** a must-do, tackling the rigorous 12-hour round-trip to the top of Half Dome in search of life-changing vistas. For a less technical route, hike downhill from Glacier Point on Four-Mile Trail or **Panorama Trail,** the latter an all-day trek past waterfalls. Less demanding still is a drive to Wawona for a stroll in the **Mariposa Grove of Big Trees** and lunch at the 19th-century **Big Trees Lodge Dining Room** (formerly the Wawona). In bad weather, take shelter in the **Ansel Adams Gallery** and **Yosemite Museum**; in fair conditions, drive up to **Glacier Point** for a breathtaking sunset view.

DAY 5: GOLD COUNTRY SOUTH

(2½–3 hrs by car from Yosemite.)

Highway 49 traces the mother lode that yielded many fortunes in gold in the 1850s and 1860s. Step into a living gold-rush town at **Columbia State Historic Park,** where you can ride a stagecoach and pan for riches. **Sutter Creek's** well-preserved downtown bursts with shopping opportunities, but the vintage goods displayed at **Monteverde Store Museum** are not for sale. A different sort of vintage powers the present-day bonanza of **Shenandoah Valley,** heart of the Sierra Foothills Wine Country. Taste your way through Rhône-style blended Zinfandels and Syrahs at boutique wineries such as **Shenandoah Vineyards** and **Sobon Estate.** Amador City's 1879 **Imperial Hotel** places you firmly in the past for the night.

DAY 6: GOLD COUNTRY NORTH

(2 hrs by car from Amador City to Nevada City.)

In **Placerville,** a mine shaft invites investigation at **Hangtown's Gold Bug Mine,** while **Marshall Gold Discovery State Historic Park** encompasses most of **Coloma** and preserves the spot where James Marshall's 1849 find set off the California gold rush. Old Town **Auburn,** with its museums and courthouse, makes a good lunch stop,

but if you hold out until you reach Grass Valley you can try authentic miners' pasties. A tour of **Empire Mine State Historic Park** takes you into a mine, and a few miles away horse-drawn carriages ply the narrow, shop-lined streets of downtown **Nevada City.** Both Nevada City and **Grass Valley** hold a collection of bed-and-breakfast inns that date back to gold-rush days. For more contemporary accommodations backtrack to Auburn or Placerville.

DAY 7: LAKE TAHOE

(1 hr by car from Nevada City, 2 hrs from Placerville.)

Jewel-like **Lake Tahoe** is a straight shot east of Placerville on Highway 50; stop for picnic provisions in commercial **South Lake Tahoe.** A stroll past the three magnificent estates in **Pope-Baldwin Recreation Area** hints at the sumptuous lakefront summers once enjoyed by the elite. High above a glittering cove, **Emerald Bay State Park** offers one of the best lake views as well as a steep hike down to (and back up from) **Vikingsholm,** a replica 9th-century Scandinavian castle. Another fine, old mansion—plus a nature preserve and many hiking trails—lies in **Sugar Pine Point State Park.** Tahoe City offers more history and ample dining and lodging choices.

DAY 8: EXPLORING LAKE TAHOE

(Sightseeing cruise lasts 2 hrs.)

The picture-perfect beaches and bays of **Lake Tahoe–Nevada State Park** line the Nevada shoreline, a great place to bask in the sun or go mountain biking. For a different perspective of the lake, get out on the azure water aboard the stern-wheeler MS *Dixie II* from **Zephyr Cove.** In South Lake Tahoe, another view unfurls as the **Heavenly Gondola** travels 2½ miles up a mountain. Keep your adrenaline pumping into the evening with some action at the massive casinos clustered in Stateline, Nevada.

DAY 9: RETURN TO SAN FRANCISCO

(About 4 hrs by car from Tahoe City.)

After a long morning of driving, return your rental car in San Francisco and soak up some more urban excitement. Good options include a late lunch at the **Ferry Building,** followed by a visit to the **San Francisco Museum of Modern Art,** or lunch in **Japantown** followed by shopping in **Pacific Heights.** There is excellent people-watching in the **Castro** and the **Haight.** Say good-bye to Northern California at one of the plush lounges or trendy bars in the downtown hotels.

Great Itineraries

DAY 10: DEPARTURE

(SFO is 30 mins from downtown both by BART public transport and by car, without traffic.)

Check the weather and your flight information before you start out for the airport: fog sometimes causes delays at SFO. On a clear day, your flight path might give you one last fabulous glimpse of the City by the Bay.

The Inland Route: San Francisco to Los Angeles via the Sierras, 5 days

This itinerary provides an alternate to the more frequented coastal route between San Francisco and Los Angeles and takes in the splendid scenery of the Sierras. This trip just touches the surface of all that Yosemite, Kings Canyon, and Sequoia national parks have to offer. Avid naturalists might want to extend their time in the parks. Either way, plan on spending a few days on either end of the road trip to explore California's two most popular cities.

DAY 1: SAN FRANCISCO TO YOSEMITE

(Yosemite is about 4 hrs from San Francisco by car, depending on traffic.)

Hit the road early for the day's long drive to **Yosemite National Park.** As you approach from Route 120, be sure to top up the tank as there are only a few gas stations within the park. Drive straight to the **Valley Visitor Center** to get an overview of the park. Stretch your legs on the easy loop trail to **Lower Yosemite Falls.** If daylight permits and you are looking for something a bit more strenuous, tackle the **Mist Trail** leading to **Bridalveil and Vernal Falls.** Reserve lodging early at the central valley lodges or campgrounds. Even if you aren't staying there, treat yourself to dinner at the renowned **Majestic Hotel Dining Room** (formerly the Ahwahnee).

DAY 2: EXPLORING YOSEMITE

Spend today tackling some of the sights in the northern and central areas of the park. Options include the 8½-mile **Panorama Trail** from **Glacier Point** back down to the valley or a drive along the impossibly scenic Tioga Road to **Tuolumne Meadows.** Alternatively, consider a horseback or photography tour. Hikers looking to tackle the strenuous ascent of **Half Dome** should plan on spending an additional day in the park. While some do attempt to complete the trail in one very long day, many consider camping overnight in Little Yosemite Valley to be preferable. If attempting Half Dome, don't forget to secure your wilderness permit in advance. Spend a second night in Yosemite Valley.

DAY 3: YOSEMITE TO KINGS CANYON

(The Wawona area of the park is about 1 hr by car from Yosemite Valley. From Wawona, Grants Grove Village in Kings Canyon is about 3 hrs by car.)

Make your way south to the **Wawona** section of Yosemite and don't miss the **Mariposa Grove of Big Trees** to see the famous Grizzly Giant before leaving the park. From here, drive south out of Yosemite and link up with Route 180 heading into **Kings Canyon National Park.** Again, remember to get gas along the route. Once inside Kings Canyon, continue along Route 180 for the 30-mile stretch known as the **Kings Canyon Scenic Byway** as it winds between Grant Grove Village and Zumwalt Meadow. There are several vista points or opportunities to stretch your legs en route. Toward the end, enjoy an easy 1½-mile hike along the **Zumwalt Meadows Trail.** Drive back (allow about an

hour without stops) and overnight in the Grant Grove area of the park.

DAYS 4 AND 5: KINGS CANYON TO SEQUOIA

(Allow ample time to drive Generals Hwy. as parts are steep and winding, and there are many stops to make on the way. Los Angeles is about 3½–4 hrs by car from the Foothills Visitor Center.

Spend the next two days exploring **Generals Highway,** the 43-mile scenic route connecting Kings Canyon and Sequoia national parks. Warm up with a hike into Redwood Canyon Grove, one of the largest sequoia groves in the world. You can choose between a shorter hike to an overlook point or longer 6- and 10-mile trails that lead deep into the grove. From there, continue the drive into **Sequoia National Park** and spend the rest of the day and the majority of the next exploring its highlights with an overnight at the **Wuksachi Lodge.**

Don't miss the 2-mile **Congress Trail,** an excellent opportunity to walk among the big trees, and the nearby **General Sherman Tree,** a massive specimen. If you want to tour the marble interior of **Crystal Cave,** be sure to reserve tour tickets in advance online or purchase them at the **Lodgepole visitor center.** Challenge your calves on the 350 stone steps of **Moro Rock** and reward your efforts with views over the Middle Fork Canyon. Don't leave the park without making the requisite photo stop at **Tunnel Log,** which, as its name suggests, is a drive-through tunnel carved out of the trunk of a fallen tree. It might take some discipline to pull away from the spectacular scenery, but a 3½-hour drive to Los Angeles awaits. With any luck, an evening arrival will mean you miss much of the city's notorious traffic. However, if you linger a bit longer than expected or simply don't feel up to the drive, Bakersfield is a closer alternative to stop for the night. Note: for the particularly intrepid traveler, this itinerary can be modified to take in **Yosemite and Death Valley national parks** via the **Tioga Pass** and **Mono Lake.** However, travelers should be aware that Tioga Pass is only open in the summer and early fall. By the time the pass opens (usually late May or June), temperatures in Death Valley are already searing hot and the extreme conditions should not be taken lightly. Always travel with an ample supply of drinking water and food, take precautions against the burning sun, limit physical activity, and time outings for early or late in the day.

Chapter 4

SEQUOIA AND KINGS CANYON NATIONAL PARKS

4

Updated by
Cheryl Crabtree

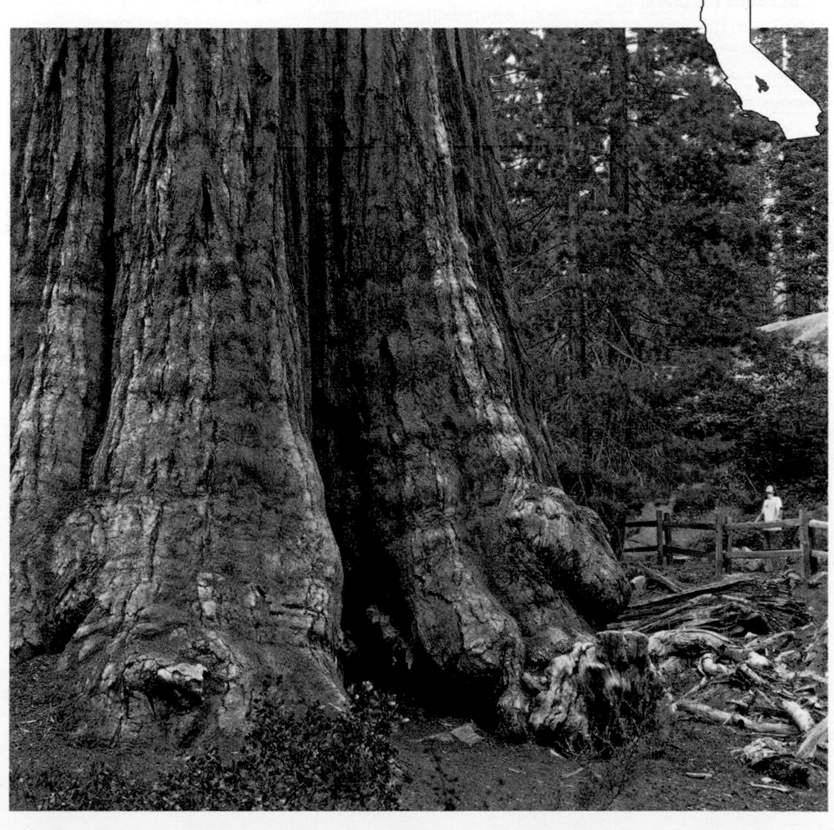

Sights ★★★★★ | Restaurants ★★★★☆ | Hotels ★★★★★ | Shopping ★☆☆☆☆ | Nightlife ★☆☆☆☆

WELCOME TO SEQUOIA AND KINGS CANYON NATIONAL PARKS

TOP REASONS TO GO

★ **Gentle giants:** You'll feel small—in a good way—walking among some of the world's largest living things in Sequoia's Giant Forest and Kings Canyon's Grant Grove.

★ **Because it's there:** You can't even glimpse it from the main part of Sequoia, but the sight of majestic Mt. Whitney is worth the trip to the eastern face of the High Sierra.

★ **Underground exploration:** Far older even than the giant sequoias, the gleaming limestone formations in Crystal Cave will draw you along dark, marble passages.

★ **A grander-than-Grand Canyon:** Drive the twisting Kings Canyon Scenic Byway down into the jagged, granite Kings River canyon, deeper in parts than the Grand Canyon.

★ **Regal solitude:** To spend a day or two hiking in a subalpine world of your own, pick one of the many trailheads at Mineral King.

The two parks comprise 865,964 acres (1,353 square miles), mostly on the western flank of the Sierra. A map of the adjacent parks looks vaguely like a mitten, with the palm of Sequoia National Park south of the north-pointing, skinny thumb and long fingers of Kings Canyon National Park. Between the western thumb and eastern fingers, north of Sequoia, lies part of Sequoia National Forest, which includes Giant Sequoia National Monument.

1 Giant Forest–Lodgepole Village. One of the most heavily visited areas of Sequoia contains major sights such as Giant Forest, General Sherman Tree, Crystal Cave, and Moro Rock.

2 Grant Grove Village–Redwood Canyon. The "thumb" of Kings Canyon National Park is its busiest section, where Grant Grove, General Grant Tree, Panoramic Point, and Big Stump are the main attractions.

3 Cedar Grove. The drive through the high-country portion of Kings Canyon National Park to Cedar Grove Village, on the canyon floor, reveals magnificent granite formations of varied hues. Rock meets river in breathtaking fashion at Zumwalt Meadow.

4 Mineral King. In the southeast section of Sequoia, the highest road-accessible part of the park is a good place to hike, camp, and soak up the unspoiled grandeur of the Sierra Nevada.

5 Mount Whitney. The highest peak in the Lower 48 stands on the eastern edge of Sequoia; to get there from Giant Forest you must either backpack eight days through the mountains or drive nearly 400 miles around the park to its other side.

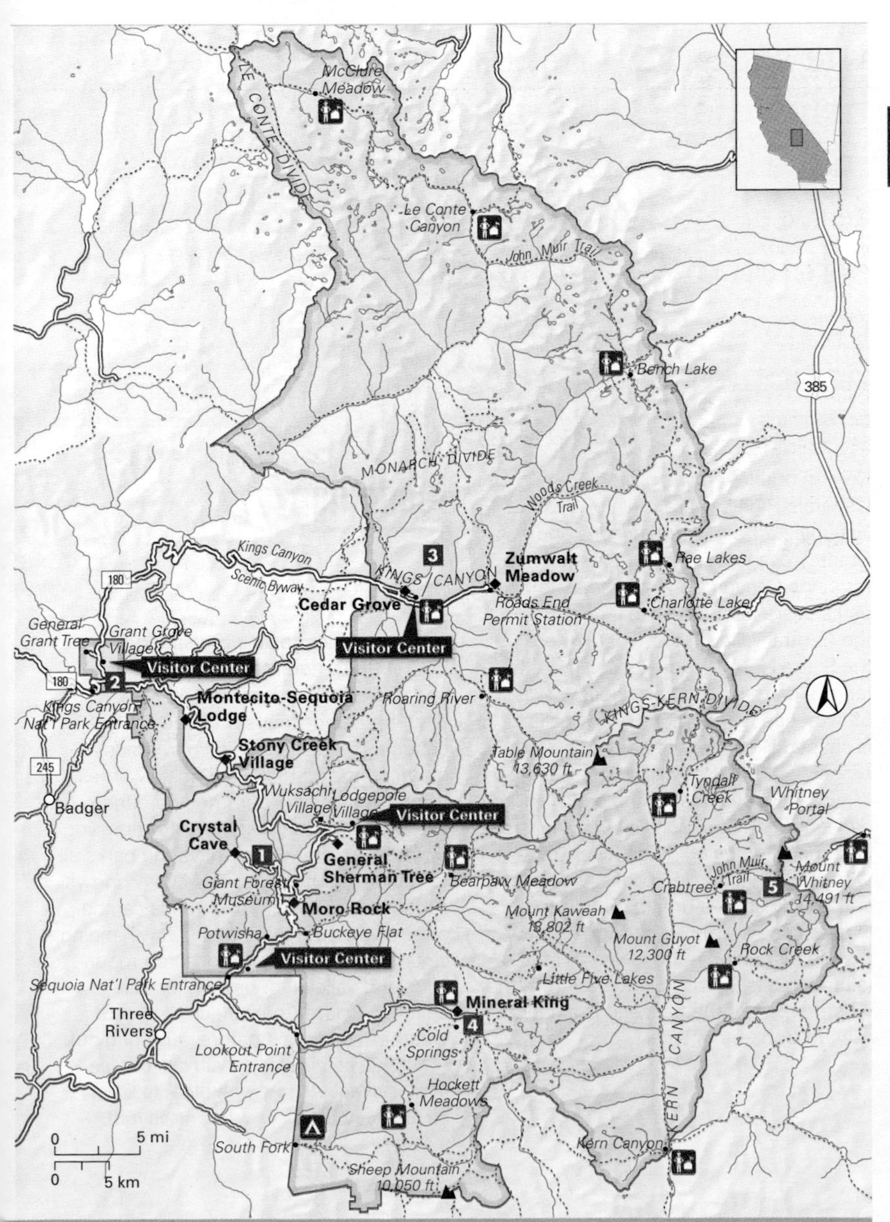
McClure Meadow
LE CONTE DIVIDE
Le Conte Canyon
John Muir Trail
Bench Lake
385
MONARCH DIVIDE
Woods Creek Trail
Kings Canyon Scenic Byway
KINGS CANYON
3
Zumwalt Meadow
Rae Lakes
180
Cedar Grove
Roads End Permit Station
Charlotte Lake
General Grant Tree
Grant Grove Village
Visitor Center
180
2
Visitor Center
Montecito-Sequoia Lodge
Roaring River
KINGS-KERN DIVIDE
Kings Canyon Nat'l Park Entrance
Stony Creek Village
Table Mountain 13,630 ft
245
Badger
Wuksachi Village
Lodgepole Village
Visitor Center
Tyndall Creek
Whitney Portal
Crystal Cave
1
General Sherman Tree
Bearpaw Meadow
John Muir Trail
Crabtree
5
Mount Whitney 14,491 ft
Giant Forest Museum
Moro Rock
Mount Kaweah 13,802 ft
Potwisha
Buckeye Flat
Mount Guyot 12,300 ft
Rock Creek
Visitor Center
Sequoia Nat'l Park Entrance
Little Five Lakes
Mineral King
4
Three Rivers
Cold Springs
KERN CANYON
Lookout Point Entrance
Hockett Meadows
0 5 mi
South Fork
Kern Canyon
0 5 km
Sheep Mountain 10,050 ft

The monstrously thick trunks and branches, remarkably shallow root systems, and neck-craning heights of the sequoias are almost impossible to believe, as is the fact they can live for more than 2,500 years. Many of these towering marvels are in the Giant Forest stretch of Generals Highway, which connects Sequoia and Kings Canyon national parks.

Next to or a few miles off the 46-mile Generals Highway are most of Sequoia National Park's main attractions and Grant Grove Village, the orientation hub for Kings Canyon National Park. The two parks share a boundary that runs from the Central Valley in the west, where the Sierra Nevada foothills begin, to the range's dramatic eastern ridges. Kings Canyon has two portions: the smaller is shaped like a bent finger and encompasses Grant Grove Village and Redwood Mountain Grove (two of the parks' largest concentration of sequoias), and the larger is home to stunning Kings River Canyon, whose vast, unspoiled peaks and valleys are a backpacker's dream. Sequoia is in one piece and includes Mt. Whitney, the highest point in the lower 48 states (although it is impossible to see from the western part of the park and is a chore to ascend from either side).

Planning

When to Go

The best times to visit are spring and fall, when temperatures are moderate and crowds thin. Summertime can draw hordes of tourists to see the giant sequoias, and the few, narrow roads mean congestion at peak holiday times. If you must visit in summer, go during the week. By contrast, in wintertime you may feel as though you have the parks all to yourself. But because of heavy snows, sections of the main park roads can be closed without warning, and low-hanging clouds can move in and obscure mountains and valleys for days. From early October to late April, check road and weather conditions before venturing out. **■ TIP→ Even in summer, you can escape hordes of people just walking ¼ to ½ mile off the beaten path on a less-used trail.**

Festivals and Events

Annual Trek to the Tree
FESTIVAL | On the second Sunday of December, thousands of carolers gather at the base of General Grant Tree, the nation's official Christmas tree. ☎ *559/565–3341.*

Big Fresno Fair
FESTIVAL | Over 12 days in October, agricultural, home-arts, and other competitions, plus horse racing and a carnival make for a lively county fair. ✉ *Fresno* ☎ *559/650–3247* 🌐 *www.fresnofair.com.*

Blossom Days Festival
FESTIVAL | On the first Saturday of March, communities along Fresno County's Blossom Trail celebrate the flowering of the area's orchards, citrus groves, and vineyards. ☎ *559/981–5500* 🌐 *www.goblossomtrail.com.*

Jazzaffair
FESTIVAL | On the second weekend of April, a festival of mostly traditional jazz takes place at several venues just south of the parks. 🌐 *sierratraditionaljazzclub.com.*

Woodlake Rodeo
FESTIVAL | The local Lions Club sponsors this rousing rodeo that draws large crowds to Woodlake on Mother's Day weekend. ☎ *559/564–8555* 🌐 *www.woodlakelionsclub.com.*

Planning Your Time

SEQUOIA NATIONAL PARK IN ONE DAY

After spending the night in Visalia or Three Rivers—and provided your vehicle's length does not exceed 22 feet—take off early on Route 198 to the **Sequoia National Park entrance.** Pull over at the **Hospital Rock** picnic area to gaze up at the imposing granite formation of Moro Rock, which you later will climb. Heed signs that advise "10 mph" around tight turns as you climb 3,500 feet on **Generals Highway** to the **Giant Forest Museum.** Spend a half hour here, then examine trees firsthand by circling the lovely **Round Meadow** on the **Big Trees Trail,** to which you must walk from the museum or from its parking lot across the road.

Get back in your car and continue a few miles north on Generals Highway to see the jaw-dropping **General Sherman Tree.** Then set off on the **Congress Trail** so that you can be further awed by the Senate and House big-tree clusters. Buy lunch at the **Lodgepole** complex, 2 miles to the north, and eat at the nearby **Pinewood** picnic area. Now you're ready for the day's big exercise, climbing **Moro Rock.**

You can drive there or, if it is summer, park at the museum lot and take the free shuttle. Count on spending at least an hour for the 350-step ascent and descent, with a pause on top to appreciate the 360-degree view. Get back in the car, or on the shuttle, and proceed past the **Tunnel Log** to **Crescent Meadow.** Spend a relaxing hour or two strolling on the trails that pass by, among other things, **Tharp's Log.** By now you've probably renewed your appetite; head to **Lodgepole Grill & Market** or the restaurant at **Wuksachi Lodge.**

KINGS CANYON NATIONAL PARK IN ONE DAY

Enter the park via the **Kings Canyon Scenic Byway** (Route 180), having spent the night in Fresno or Visalia. Better yet, wake up already in **Grant Grove Village,** perhaps in the **John Muir Lodge.** Stock up for a picnic with takeout food from the **Grant Grove Restaurant,** or purchase prepackaged food from the nearby market. Drive east a mile to see the **General Grant Tree** and compact **Grant Grove's** other sequoias. If it's no later than mid-morning, walk up the short trail at **Panoramic Point,** for a great view of Hume Lake and the High Sierra. Either way, return to Route 180 and continue east. Stop at Junction View to take in several

AVERAGE HIGH/LOW TEMPERATURES					
JAN.	**FEB.**	**MAR.**	**APR.**	**MAY**	**JUNE**
42/24	44/25	46/26	51/30	58/36	68/44
JULY	**AUG.**	**SEPT.**	**OCT.**	**NOV.**	**DEC.**
76/51	76/50	71/45	61/38	50/31	44/27

noteworthy peaks that tower over Kings Canyon. From here, visit **Boyden Cavern** or continue to **Cedar Grove Village,** pausing along the way for a gander at **Grizzly Falls.** Eat at a table by the **South Fork of the Kings River,** or on the deck off the Cedar Grove Snack Bar. Now you are ready for the day's highlight, strolling **Zumwalt Meadow,** which lies a few miles past the village.

After you have enjoyed that short trail and the views it offers of **Grand Sentinel** and **North Dome,** you might as well go the extra mile to **Roads End,** where backpackers embark for the High Sierra wilderness. Make the return trip—with a quick stop at **Roaring River Falls**—past Grant Grove and briefly onto southbound **Generals Highway.** Pull over at the **Redwood Mountain Overlook** and use binoculars to look down upon the world's largest sequoia grove, then drive another couple of miles to the **Kings Canyon Overlook,** where you can survey some of what you have done today. Make reservations for a late dinner at **Wuksachi Lodge.**

Getting Here and Around

AIR TRAVEL

The closest airport to Sequoia and Kings Canyon national parks is Fresno Yosemite International Airport (FAT).

AIRPORT CONTACTS Fresno Yosemite International Airport (*FAT*) ✉ *5175 E. Clinton Way, Fresno* ☎ *800/244–2359 automated info, 559/454–2052 terminal info desk* 🌐 *www.flyfresno.com.*

CAR TRAVEL

Sequoia is 36 miles east of Visalia on Route 198; Grant Grove Village in Kings Canyon is 56 miles east of Fresno on Route 180. There is no automobile entrance on the eastern side of the Sierra. Routes 180 and 198 are connected by Generals Highway, a paved two-lane road that sometimes sees delays at peak times due to ongoing improvements. The road is extremely narrow and steep from Route 198 to Giant Forest, so keep an eye on your engine temperature gauge, as the incline and congestion can cause vehicles to overheat; to avoid overheated brakes, use low gears on downgrades.

If you are traveling in an RV or with a trailer, study the restrictions on these vehicles. Do not travel beyond Potwisha Campground on Route 198 with an RV longer than 22 feet; take straighter, easier Route 180 instead. Maximum vehicle length on Generals Highway is 40 feet, or 50 feet combined length for vehicles with trailers.

Generals Highway between Lodgepole and Grant Grove is sometimes closed by snow. The Mineral King Road from Route 198 into southern Sequoia National Park is closed 2 miles below Atwell Mill either on November 1 or after the first heavy snow. The Buckeye Flat–Middle Fork Trailhead road is closed from mid-October to mid-April when the Buckeye Flat Campground closes. The lower Crystal Cave Road is closed when the cave closes (typically in November). Its upper 2 miles, as well as the Panoramic Point and Moro Rock–Crescent Meadow roads, close with the first heavy snow. Because of the danger of rockfall, the portion of Kings Canyon Scenic Byway east of Grant Grove closes in winter. For current road and weather conditions, call ☎ *559/565–3341* or visit the park website: 🌐 *www.nps.gov/seki*.

■ TIP→ Snowstorms are common from late October through April. Unless you have a four-wheel-drive vehicle with snow tires, you should carry chains and know how to install them.

Park Essentials

ACCESSIBILITY

All the visitor centers, the Giant Forest Museum, and Big Trees Trail are wheelchair accessible, as are some short ranger-led walks and talks. General Sherman Tree can be reached via a paved, level trail near a parking area. None of the caves is accessible, and wilderness areas must be reached by horseback or on foot. Some picnic tables are extended to accommodate wheelchairs. Many of the major sites are in the 6,000-foot range and thin air at high elevations can cause respiratory distress for people with breathing difficulties. Carry oxygen if necessary. Contact the park's main number for more information.

PARK FEES AND PERMITS

The admission fee is $35 per vehicle, $30 per motorcycle, and $20 per person for those who enter by bus, on foot, bicycle, horse, or any other mode of transportation; it is valid for seven days in both parks. U.S. residents over the age of 62 pay $80 for a lifetime pass, and permanently disabled U.S. residents are admitted free.

If you plan to camp in the backcountry, you need a permit, which costs $15 for hikers or $30 for stock users (e.g., horseback riders). One permit covers the group. Availability of permits depends upon trailhead quotas. Reservations are accepted by mail or email for a $15 processing fee, beginning March 1, and must be made at least 14 days in advance (☎ *559/565–3766*). Without a reservation, you may still get a permit on a first-come, first-served basis starting at 1 pm the day before you plan to hike. For more information on backcountry camping or travel with pack animals (horses, mules, burros, or llamas), contact the Wilderness Permit Office (☎ *530/565–3766*).

PARK HOURS

The parks are open 24/7 year-round. They are in the Pacific time zone.

CELL PHONE RECEPTION

Cell phone reception is poor to nonexistent in the higher elevations and spotty even on portions of Generals Highway, where you can (on rare clear days) see the Central Valley. Public telephones may be found at the visitor centers, ranger stations, some trailheads, and at all restaurants and lodging facilities in the park.

Educational Offerings

Educational programs at the parks include museum-style exhibits, ranger- and naturalist-led talks and walks, film and other programs, and sightseeing tours, most of them conducted by either the park service or the nonprofit Sequoia Parks Conservancy. Exhibits at the visitor centers and the Giant Forest Museum focus on different aspects of the park: its history, wildlife, geology, climate, and vegetation—most notably the giant sequoias. Weekly notices about programs are posted at the visitor centers and elsewhere.

Grant Grove Visitor Center at Kings Canyon National Park has maps of self-guided park tours. Ranger-led walks and programs take place throughout the year in Grant Grove. Cedar Grove and Forest Service campgrounds have activities from Memorial Day to Labor Day. Check bulletin boards or visitor centers for schedules.

EXHIBITS

Giant Forest Museum

MUSEUM | Well-imagined and interactive displays at this worthwhile stop provide the basics about sequoias, of which there are 2,161 with diameters exceeding 10 feet in the approximately 2,000-acre Giant Forest. ✉ *Sequoia National Park ✣ Generals Hwy., 4 miles south of Lodgepole Visitor Center ☎ 559/565–4436 🎫 Free ☞ Shuttle: Giant Forest or Moro Rock–Crescent Meadow.*

PROGRAMS AND SEMINARS

Evening Programs

TOUR—SIGHT | The Sequoia Parks Conservancy presents films, hikes, and evening lectures during the summer and winter. From May through October the popular Wonders of the Night Sky programs celebrate the often stunning views of the heavens experienced at both parks. ✉ *Sequoia National Park* ☎ *559/565–4251* 🌐 *www.sequoiaparksconservancy.org.*

Free Nature Programs

TOUR—SIGHT | Almost any summer day, ½-hour to 1½-hour ranger talks and walks explore subjects such as the life of the sequoia, the geology of the park, and the habits of bears. Giant Forest, Lodgepole Visitor Center, and Wuksachi Village are frequent starting points. Look for less frequent tours in the winter from Grant Grove. Check bulletin boards throughout the park for the week's offerings. 🌐 *www.sequoiaparksconservancy.org.*

Junior Ranger Program

TOUR—SIGHT | **FAMILY** | Children over age five can earn a patch upon completion of a fun set of age-appropriate tasks outlined in the Junior Ranger booklet. Pick one up at any visitor center. ☎ *559/565–3341.*

Seminars

TOUR—SIGHT | Expert naturalists lead seminars on a range of topics, including birds, wildflowers, geology, botany, photography, park history, backpacking, and pathfinding. Reservations are required. Information about times and prices is available at the visitor centers or through the Sequoia Parks Conservancy. ✉ *Sequoia National Park* ☎ *559/565–4251* 🌐 *www.sequoiaparksconservancy.org.*

TOURS

★ Sequoia Parks Conservancy Field Institute

TOUR—SIGHT | The Sequoia Parks Conservancy's highly regarded educational division conducts half-day, single-day, and multiday tours that include backpacking hikes, natural-history walks, cross-country skiing, kayaking excursions, and motor-coach tours. ✉ *47050 Generals Hwy., Unit 10, Three Rivers* ☎ *559/565–4251* 🌐 *www.sequoiaparksconservancy.org* 🎫 *From $40 for ½-day guided tour.*

Sequoia Sightseeing Tours

TOUR—SIGHT | This locally owned operator's friendly, knowledgeable guides conduct daily interpretive sightseeing tours in Sequoia and Kings Canyon. Reservations are essential. The company also offers private tours. ✉ *Three Rivers* ☎ *559/561–4189* 🌐 *www.sequoiatours.com* 🎫 *From $79 tour of Sequoia; from $139 tour of Kings Canyon.*

Restaurants

In Sequoia and Kings Canyon national parks, you can treat yourself (and the family) to a high-quality meal in a wonderful setting in the Peaks restaurant at Wuksachi Lodge, but otherwise you should keep your expectations modest. You can grab bread, spreads, drinks, and fresh produce at one of several small grocery stores for a picnic, or get take-out food from the Grant Grove Restaurant, the Cedar Grove snack bar, or one of the two small Lodgepole eateries. Between the parks and just off Generals Highway, the Montecito Sequoia Lodge has a year-round buffet. *Restaurant reviews have been shortened. For full information, visit Fodors.com.*

Hotels

Hotel accommodations in Sequoia and Kings Canyon are limited, and—although they are clean and comfortable—tend to lack much in-room character. Keep in mind, however, that the extra money you spend on lodging here is offset by the time you'll save by being inside the parks. You won't be faced with a 60- to 90-minute commute from the less-expensive motels in Three Rivers (by far the most charming option), Visalia, and Fresno. Reserve as far in advance as you can, especially for summertime stays. *Hotel reviews have been shortened. For full information, visit Fodors.com.*

What It Costs

	$	$$	$$$	$$$$
RESTAURANTS				
	under $12	$12–$20	$21–$30	over $30
HOTELS				
	under $100	$100–$150	$151–$200	over $200

Visitor Information

NATIONAL PARK SERVICE Sequoia and Kings Canyon National Parks ⊠ *47050 Generals Hwy. (Rte. 198), Three Rivers* ☎ *559/565–3341* 🌐 *nps.gov/seki.*

SEQUOIA VISITOR CENTERS

Foothills Visitor Center

INFO CENTER | Exhibits here focus on the foothills and resource issues facing the parks. You can pick up books, maps, and a list of ranger-led walks, and get wilderness permits. ⊠ *47050 Generals Hwy., Rte. 198, 1 mile north of Ash Mountain entrance, Sequoia National Park* ☎ *559/565–3341.*

Lodgepole Visitor Center

INFO CENTER | Along with exhibits on the area's history, geology, and wildlife, the center screens an outstanding 22-minute film about bears. You can buy books, maps, and tickets to cave tours here. ⊠ *Sequoia National Park* ✣ *Generals Hwy. (Rte. 198), 21 miles north of Ash Mountain entrance* ☎ *559/565–3341* ⏲ *Closed Oct.–Apr.* ☞ *Shuttle: Giant Forest or Wuksachi-Lodgepole-Dorst.*

KINGS CANYON VISITOR CENTERS

Cedar Grove Visitor Center

INFO CENTER | Off the main road and behind the Sentinel Campground, this small ranger station has books and maps, plus information about hikes and other activities. ⊠ *Kings Canyon National Park* ✣ *Kings Canyon Scenic Byway, 30 miles east of Rte. 180/198 junction* ☎ *559/565–3341* ⏲ *Closed mid-Sept.–mid-May.*

Kings Canyon Park Visitor Center

INFO CENTER | The center's 15-minute film and various exhibits provide an overview of the park's canyon, sequoias, and human history. Books, maps, and weather advice are dispensed here, as are (if available) free wilderness permits. ⊠ *Kings Canyon National Park* ✣ *Grant Grove Village, Generals Hwy. (Rte. 198), 3 miles northeast of Rte. 180, Big Stump entrance* ☎ *559/565–3341.*

Sequoia National Park

Sights

SCENIC DRIVES

★ Generals Highway

SCENIC DRIVE | One of California's most scenic drives, this 46-mile road is the main asphalt artery between Sequoia and Kings Canyon national parks. Some portions are also signed as Route 180, others as Route 198. Named after the landmark Grant and Sherman trees that leave so many visitors awestruck, Generals Highway runs from Sequoia's Foothills Visitor Center north to Kings Canyon's Grant Grove Village. Along the way, it passes the turnoff to Crystal Cave, the

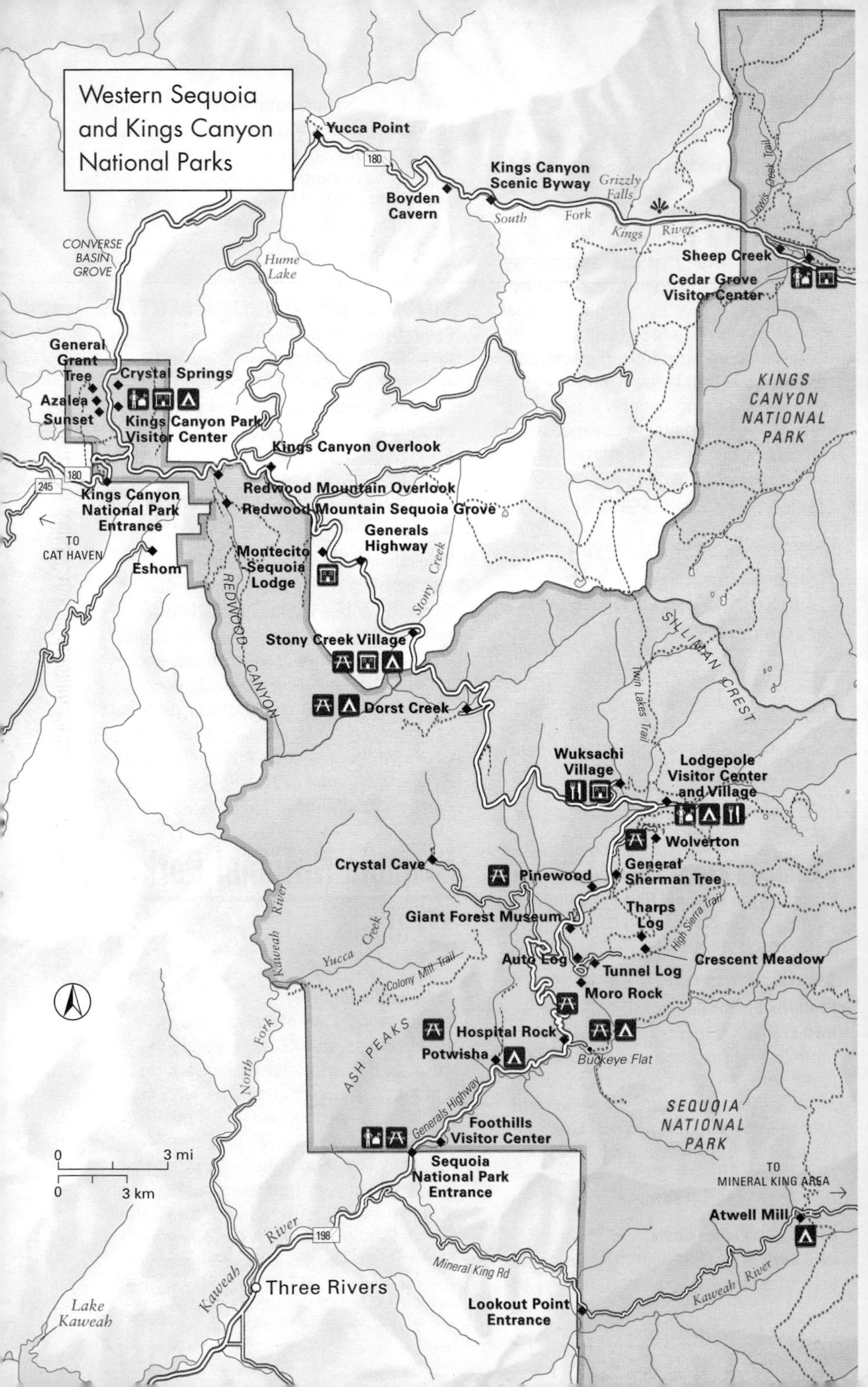

Western Sequoia and Kings Canyon National Parks
Yucca Point
180
Kings Canyon Scenic Byway
Boyden Cavern
Grizzly Falls
South Fork Kings River
Lewis Creek Trail
Sheep Creek
Cedar Grove Visitor Center
CONVERSE BASIN GROVE
Hume Lake
General Grant Tree
Crystal Springs
Azalea
Sunset
Kings Canyon Park Visitor Center
KINGS CANYON NATIONAL PARK
Kings Canyon Overlook
180
245
Kings Canyon National Park Entrance
Redwood Mountain Overlook
Redwood Mountain Sequoia Grove
TO CAT HAVEN
Eshom
Montecito Sequoia Lodge
Generals Highway
Stony Creek
REDWOOD CANYON
Stony Creek Village
SILLIMAN CREST
Twin Lakes Trail
Dorst Creek
Wuksachi Village
Lodgepole Visitor Center and Village
Wolverton
Crystal Cave
Pinewood
General Sherman Tree
Kaweah River
Giant Forest Museum
Tharps Log
High Sierra Trail
Yucca Creek
Colony Mill Trail
Auto Log
Tunnel Log
Crescent Meadow
Moro Rock
ASH PEAKS
Hospital Rock
Potwisha
Buckeye Flat
North Fork
SEQUOIA NATIONAL PARK
Generals Highway
Foothills Visitor Center
0 3 mi
0 3 km
Sequoia National Park Entrance
TO MINERAL KING AREA
Atwell Mill
River
198
Mineral King Rd
Kaweah River
Three Rivers
Lake Kaweah
Kaweah
Lookout Point Entrance

Giant Forest Museum, Lodgepole Village, and other popular attractions. The lower portion, from Hospital Rock to the Giant Forest, is especially steep and winding. If your vehicle is 22 feet or longer, avoid that stretch by entering the parks via Route 180 (from Fresno) rather than Route 198 (from Visalia or Three Rivers). Take your time on this road—there's a lot to see, and wildlife can scamper across at any time. ✉ *Sequoia National Park.*

Mineral King Road

SCENIC DRIVE | Vehicles longer than 22 feet are prohibited on this side road into southern Sequoia National Park, and for good reason: it contains 589 twists and turns. Anticipating an average speed of 20 mph is optimistic. The scenery is splendid as you climb nearly 6,000 feet from Three Rivers to the Mineral King Area. In addition to maneuvering the blind curves and narrow stretches, you might find yourself sharing the pavement with bears, rattlesnakes, and even softball-size spiders. Allow 90 minutes each way. ✉ *Sequoia National Forest* ✣ *East off Sierra Dr. (Rte. 198), 3.5 miles northeast of Three Rivers* ⏲ *Road typically closed Nov.–late May.*

SCENIC STOPS

Sequoia National Park is all about the trees, and to understand the scale of these giants you must walk among them. If you do nothing else, get out of the car for a short stroll through one of the groves. But there is much more to the park than the trees. Try to access one of the vista points that provide a panoramic view over the forested mountains. Generals Highway (on Routes 198 and 180) will be your route to most of the park's sights. A few short spur roads lead from the highway to some sights, and Mineral King Road branches off Route 198 to enter the park at Lookout Point, winding east from there to the park's southernmost section.

Auto Log

FOREST | Before its wood showed signs of severe rot, cars drove right on top of this giant fallen sequoia. Now it's a great place to pose for pictures or shoot a video. ✉ *Sequoia National Park* ✣ *Moro Rock–Crescent Meadow Rd., 1 mile south of Giant Forest.*

Crescent Meadow

TRAIL | A sea of ferns signals your arrival at what John Muir called the "gem of the Sierra." Walk around for an hour or two and you might decide that the Scotland-born naturalist was exaggerating a bit, but the verdant meadow is quite pleasant and you just might see a bear. Wildflowers bloom here throughout the summer. ✉ *Sequoia National Park* ✣ *End of Moro Rock–Crescent Meadow Rd., 2.6 miles east off Generals Hwy.* ☞ *Shuttle: Moro Rock–Crescent Meadow.*

★ Crystal Cave

CAVE | One of more than 200 caves in Sequoia and Kings Canyon, Crystal Cave is composed largely of marble, the result of limestone being hardened under heat and pressure. It contains several eye-popping formations. There used to be more, but some were damaged or obliterated by early-20th-century dynamite blasting. You can only see the cave on a tour. The Daily Tour ($16), a great overview, takes about 50 minutes. To immerse yourself in the cave experience—at times you'll be crawling on your belly—book the exhilarating Wild Cave Tour ($135). Availability is limited—reserve tickets at least 48 hours in advance at 🌐 *www.recreation.gov* or stop by either the Foothills or Lodgepole visitor center first thing in the morning to try to nab a same-day ticket; they're not sold at the cave itself. ✉ *Crystal Cave Rd., off Generals Hwy.* ☎ *877/444–6777* 🌐 *www.sequoiaparksconservancy.org/crystalcave.html* 🎟 *$16* ⏲ *Closed Oct.–late May.*

★ General Sherman Tree

LOCAL INTEREST | The 274.9-foot-tall General Sherman is one of the world's tallest and oldest sequoias, and it ranks No.

1 in volume, adding the equivalent of a 60-foot-tall tree every year to its approximately 52,500 cubic feet of mass. The tree doesn't grow taller, though—it's dead at the top. A short, wheelchair-accessible trail leads to the tree from Generals Highway, but the main trail (½ mile) winds down from a parking lot off Wolverton Road. The walk back up the main trail is steep, but benches along the way provide rest for the short of breath. ✉ *Sequoia National Park* ✣ *Main trail Wolverton Rd. off Generals Hwy. (Rte. 198)* ☞ *Shuttle: Giant Forest or Wolverton–Sherman Tree.*

Mineral King Area

NATURE PRESERVE | A subalpine valley of fir, pine, and sequoia trees, Mineral King sits at 7,500 feet at the end of a steep, winding road. This is the highest point to which you can drive in the park. It is open only from Memorial Day through late October. ✉ *Sequoia National Park* ✣ *Mineral King Rd., 25 miles east of Generals Hwy. (Rte. 198)* ⏲ *Closed late Oct.–May.*

★ Moro Rock

NATURE SITE | This sight offers panoramic views to those fit and determined enough to mount its 350 or so steps. In a case where the journey rivals the destination, Moro's stone stairway is so impressive in its twisty inventiveness that it's on the National Register of Historic Places. The rock's 6,725-foot summit overlooks the Middle Fork Canyon, sculpted by the Kaweah River and approaching the depth of Arizona's Grand Canyon, although smoggy, hazy air often compromises the view. ✉ *Sequoia National Park* ✣ *Moro Rock–Crescent Meadow Rd., 2 miles east off Generals Hwy. (Rte. 198) to parking area* ☞ *Shuttle: Moro Rock–Crescent Meadow.*

Tunnel Log

LOCAL INTEREST | This 275-foot tree fell in 1937, and soon a 17-foot-wide, 8-foot-high hole was cut through it for vehicular passage (not to mention the irresistible photograph) that continues today. Large vehicles take the nearby bypass. ✉ *Sequoia National Park* ✣ *Moro Rock–Crescent Meadow Rd., 2 miles east of Generals Hwy. (Rte. 198)* ☞ *Shuttle: Moro Rock–Crescent Meadow.*

Activities

The best way to see Sequoia is to take a hike. Unless you do so, you'll miss out on the up-close grandeur of mist wafting between deeply scored, red-orange tree trunks bigger than you've ever seen. If it's winter, put on some snowshoes or cross-country skis and plunge into the snow-swaddled woodland. There are not too many other outdoor options: no off-road driving is allowed in the parks, and no special provisions have been made for bicycles. Boating, rafting, and snowmobiling are also prohibited.

BICYCLING

Steep, winding roads and shoulders that are either narrow or nonexistent make bicycling here more of a danger than a pleasure. Outside of campgrounds, you are not allowed to pedal on unpaved roads.

BIRD-WATCHING

More than 200 species of birds inhabit Sequoia and Kings Canyon national parks. Not seen in most parts of the United States, the white-headed woodpecker and the pileated woodpecker are common in most mid-elevation areas here. There are also many hawks and owls, including the renowned spotted owl. Species are diverse in both parks due to the changes in elevation, and range from warblers, kingbirds, thrushes, and sparrows in the foothills to goshawk, blue grouse, red-breasted nuthatch, and brown creeper at the highest elevations. The Sequoia Parks Conservancy (☎ *559/565–4251* 🌐 *www.sequoiaparksconservancy.org*) has information about bird-watching in the southern Sierra.

CROSS-COUNTRY SKIING

For a one-of-a-kind experience, cut through the groves of mammoth sequoias in Giant Forest. Some of the Crescent

Meadow trails are suitable for skiing as well; none of the trails is groomed. You can park at Giant Forest. Note that roads can be precarious in bad weather. Some advanced trails begin at Wolverton.

Alta Market and Ski Shop

SKIING/SNOWBOARDING | Rent cross-country skis and snowshoes here. Depending on snowfall amounts, instruction may also be available. Reservations are recommended. Marked trails cut through Giant Forest, about 5 miles south of Wuksachi Lodge. ✉ *Sequoia National Park* ✣ *At Lodgepole, off Generals Hwy. (Rte. 198)* ☎ *559/565–3301* ☞ *Shuttle: Wuksachi-Lodgepole-Dorst.*

FISHING

There's limited trout fishing in the creeks and rivers from late April to mid-November. The Kaweah River is a popular spot; check at visitor centers for open and closed waters. Some of the park's secluded backcountry lakes have good fishing. A California fishing license, required for persons 16 and older, costs about $16 for one day, $24 for two days, and $48 for 10 days (discounts are available for state residents and others). For park regulations, closures, and restrictions, call the parks at ☎ *559/565–3341* or stop at a visitor center. Licenses and fishing tackle are usually available at Hume Lake.

California Department of Fish and Game

FISHING | The department supplies fishing licenses and provides a full listing of regulations. ☎ *916/928–5805* 🌐 *www.wildlife.ca.gov.*

HIKING

The best way to see the park is to hike it. The grandeur and majesty of the Sierra is best seen up close. Carry a hiking map and plenty of water. Visitor center gift shops sell maps and trail books and pamphlets. Check with rangers for current trail conditions, and be aware of rapidly changing weather. As a rule of thumb, plan on covering about a mile per hour.

★ Big Trees Trail

HIKING/WALKING | This hike is a must, as it does not take long and the setting is spectacular: beautiful Round Meadow surrounded by many mature sequoias, with well-thought-out interpretive signs along the path that explain the ecology on display. The 0.7-mile Big Trees Trail is wheelchair accessible. Parking at the trailhead lot off Generals Highway is for cars with handicap placards only. The round-trip loop from the Giant Forest Museum is about a mile long. *Easy.* ✉ *Sequoia National Park* ✣ *Trailhead: off Generals Hwy. (Rte. 198), near the Giant Forest Museum* ☞ *Shuttle: Giant Forest.*

★ Congress Trail

HIKING/WALKING | This 2-mile trail, arguably the best hike in the parks in terms of natural beauty, is a paved loop that begins near General Sherman Tree. You'll get close-up views of more big trees here than on any other Sequoia hike. Watch for the clusters known as the House and Senate. The President Tree, also on the trail, supplanted the General Grant Tree in 2012 as the world's second largest in volume (behind the General Sherman). An offshoot of the Congress Trail leads to Crescent Meadow, where in summer you can catch a free shuttle back to the Sherman parking lot. *Easy.* ✉ *Sequoia National Park* ✣ *Trailhead: off Generals Hwy. (Rte. 198), 2 miles north of Giant Forest* ☞ *Shuttle: Giant Forest.*

Crescent Meadow Trails

HIKING/WALKING | A 1-mile trail loops around lush Crescent Meadow to Tharp's Log, a cabin built from a fire-hollowed sequoia. From there you can embark on a 60-mile trek to Mt. Whitney, if you're prepared and have the time. Brilliant wildflowers bloom here in midsummer. *Easy.* ✉ *Sequoia National Park* ✣ *Trailhead: the end of Moro Rock–Crescent Meadow Rd., 2.6 miles east off Generals Hwy. (Rte. 198)* ☞ *Shuttle: Moro Rock–Crescent Meadow.*

Little Baldy Trail

HIKING/WALKING | Climbing 700 vertical feet in 1.75 miles of switchbacking, this trail ends at a granite dome with a great view of the peaks of the Mineral King area and the Great Western Divide. The walk to the summit and back takes about four hours. *Moderate.* ✉ *Sequoia National Park* ✣ *Trailhead: Little Baldy Saddle, Generals Hwy. (Rte. 198), 9 miles north of General Sherman Tree* ☞ *Shuttle: Lodgepole-Wuksachi-Dorst.*

Marble Falls Trail

HIKING/WALKING | The 3.7-mile trail to Marble Falls crosses through the rugged foothills before reaching the cascading water. Plan on three to four hours one-way. *Moderate.* ✉ *Sequoia National Park* ✣ *Trailhead: off dirt road across from concrete ditch near site 17 at Potwisha Campground, off Generals Hwy. (Rte. 198).*

Mineral King Trails

HIKING/WALKING | Many trails to the high country begin at Mineral King. Two popular day hikes are Eagle Lake (6.8 miles round-trip) and Timber Gap (4.4 miles round-trip). At the Mineral King Ranger Station (☎ *559/565–3768*) you can pick up maps and check about conditions from late May to late September. *Difficult.* ✉ *Sequoia National Park* ✣ *Trailheads: at end of Mineral King Rd., 25 miles east of Generals Hwy. (Rte. 198).*

Muir Grove Trail

HIKING/WALKING | You will attain solitude and possibly see a bear or two on this unheralded gem of a hike, a 4-mile round-trip from the Dorst Creek Campground. The remote grove is small but lovely, its sound track provided solely by nature. The trailhead is subtly marked. In summer, park in the amphitheater lot and walk down toward the group campsite area. *Easy.* ✉ *Sequoia National Park* ✣ *Trailhead: Dorst Creek Campground, Generals Hwy. (Rte. 198), 8 miles north of Lodgepole Visitor Center* ☞ *Shuttle: Lodgepole-Wuksachi-Dorst.*

Tokopah Falls Trail

HIKING/WALKING | This trail with a 500-foot elevation gain follows the Marble Fork of the Kaweah River for 1.75 miles one-way and dead-ends below the impressive granite cliffs and cascading waterfall of Tokopah Canyon. The trail passes through a mixed-conifer forest. It takes 2½ to 4 hours to make the round-trip journey. *Moderate.* ✉ *Sequoia National Park* ✣ *Trailhead: off Generals Hwy. (Rte. 198), ¼ mile north of Lodgepole Campground* ☞ *Shuttle: Lodgepole-Wuksachi-Dorst.*

HORSEBACK RIDING

Trips take you through forests and flowering meadows and up mountain slopes.

Grant Grove Stables

HORSEBACK RIDING | Grant Grove Stables isn't too far from parts of Sequoia National Park, and is perfect for short rides from June to September. Reservations are recommended. ☎ *559/335–9292 summer* 🌐 *www.nps.gov/seki/planyourvisit/horseride.htm* 🎟 *From $40.*

Horse Corral Packers

HORSEBACK RIDING | One- and two-hour trips through Sequoia are available for beginning and advanced riders. ✉ *Big Meadow Rd., 12 miles east of Generals Hwy. (Rte. 198) between Sequoia and Kings Canyon national parks* ☎ *559/565–3404 summer, 559/565–6429 off-season,* 🌐 *hcpacker.com* 🎟 *From $45.*

SLEDDING AND SNOWSHOEING

The Wolverton area, on Route 198 near Giant Forest, is a popular sledding spot, where sleds, inner tubes, and platters are allowed. You can buy sleds and saucers, with prices starting at $15, at the Alta Market and Ski Shop (☎ *559/565–3301*), at the Lodgepole Visitor Center.

You can rent snowshoes for $18–$24 at the Alta Market and Ski Shop, at the Lodgepole Visitor Center. Naturalists lead snowshoe walks around Giant Forest and Wuksachi Lodge, conditions permitting, on Saturday and holidays. Make reservations and check schedules at Giant

Did You Know?

Sequoias once grew throughout the Northern Hemisphere, until they were almost wiped out by glaciers. Some of the fossils in Arizona's Petrified Forest National Park are extinct sequoia species.

Forest Museum (☏ *559/565–3341*) or Wuksachi Lodge.

SWIMMING

Drowning is the number-one cause of death in both Sequoia and Kings Canyon parks. Though it is sometimes safe to swim in the parks' rivers in the late summer and early fall, it is extremely dangerous to do so in the spring and early summer, when the snowmelt from the high country causes swift currents and icy temperatures. Stand clear of the water when the rivers are running, and stay off wet rocks to avoid falling in. Check with rangers for safety information.

Kings Canyon National Park

Sights

SCENIC DRIVES

★ Kings Canyon Scenic Byway

SCENIC DRIVE | The 30-mile stretch of Route 180 between Grant Grove Village and Zumwalt Meadow delivers eye-popping scenery—granite cliffs, a roaring river, waterfalls, and Kings River canyon itself—much of which you can experience at vista points or on easy walks. The canyon comes into view about 10 miles east of the village at **Junction View.** Five miles beyond, at **Yucca Point,** the canyon is thousands of feet deeper than the more famous Grand Canyon. **Canyon View,** a special spot 1 mile east of the Cedar Grove Village turnoff, showcases evidence of the area's glacial history. Here, perhaps more than anywhere else, you'll understand why John Muir compared Kings Canyon vistas with those in Yosemite. Driving the byway takes about an hour each way without stops. ✉ *Kings Canyon National Park* ✣ *Rte. 180 north and east of Grant Grove village.*

HISTORIC SITES

Fallen Monarch

TOUR—SIGHT | This toppled sequoia's hollow base was used in the second half of the 19th century as a home for settlers, a saloon, and even to stable U.S. Cavalry horses. As you walk through it (assuming entry is permitted, which is not always possible), notice how little the wood has decayed, and imagine yourself tucked safely inside, sheltered from a storm or protected from the searing heat. ✉ *Kings Canyon National Park* ✣ *Grant Grove Trail, 1 mile north of Kings Canyon Park Visitor Center.*

Gamlin Cabin

BUILDING | Despite being listed on the National Register of Historic Places, this replica of a modest 1872 pioneer cabin is only borderline historical. The structure, which was moved and rebuilt several times over the years, once served as U.S. Cavalry storage space and, in the early 20th century, a ranger station. ✉ *Grant Grove Trail.*

SCENIC STOPS

Kings Canyon National Park consists of two sections that adjoin the northern boundary of Sequoia National Park. The western portion, covered with sequoia and pine forest, contains the park's most visited sights, such as Grant Grove. The vast eastern portion is remote high country, slashed across half its southern breadth by the deep, rugged Kings River canyon. Separating the two is Sequoia National Forest, which encompasses Giant Sequoia National Monument. The Kings Canyon Scenic Byway (Route 180) links the major sights within and between the park's two sections.

General Grant Tree

LOCAL INTEREST | President Coolidge proclaimed this to be the "nation's Christmas tree," and 30 years later President Eisenhower designated it as a living shrine to all Americans who have died in wars. Bigger at its base than the General Sherman Tree, it tapers more quickly. It's estimated to be the world's third-largest

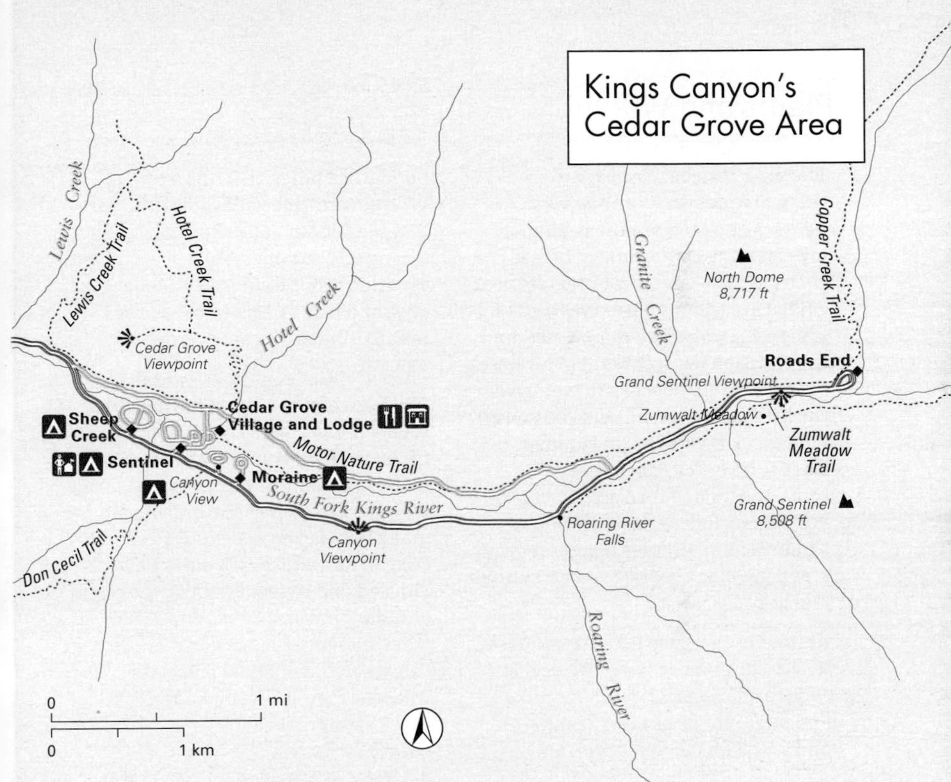

sequoia by volume. A spur trail winds behind the tree, where scars from a long-ago fire remain visible. ✉ *Kings Canyon National Park* ✣ *Trailhead: 1 mile north of Grant Grove Visitor Center.*

Redwood Mountain Sequoia Grove

FOREST | One of the world's largest sequoia groves, Redwood contains within its 2,078 acres nearly 2,200 sequoias whose diameters exceed 10 feet. You can view the grove from afar at an overlook or hike 6 to 10 miles down into the richest regions, which include 2 of the world's 25 heaviest trees. ✉ *Kings Canyon National Park* ✣ *Drive 6 miles south of Grant Grove on Generals Hwy. (Rte. 198), then turn right at Quail Flat; follow it 2 miles to the Redwood Canyon trailhead.*

Activities

The siren song of beauty, challenge, and relative solitude (by national parks standards) draws hard-core outdoors enthusiasts to the Kings River canyon and the backcountry of the park's eastern section. Backpacking, rock-climbing, and extreme-kayaking opportunities abound, but the park also has day hikes for all ability levels. Winter brings sledding, skiing, and snowshoeing fun. No off-road driving or bicycling is allowed in the park, and snowmobiling is also prohibited.

BICYCLING

Bicycles are allowed only on the paved roads in Kings Canyon. Cyclists should be extremely cautious along the steep highways and narrow shoulders.

Plants and Wildlife in Sequoia and Kings Canyon 

The parks can be divided into three distinct zones. In the west (1,500–4,500 feet) are the rolling, lower-elevation foothills, covered with shrubby chaparral vegetation or golden grasslands dotted with oaks. Chamise, red-barked manzanita, and the occasional yucca plant grow here. Fields of white popcorn flower cover the hillsides in spring, and the yellow fiddleneck flourishes. In summer, intense heat and absence of rain cause the hills to turn golden brown. Wildlife includes the California ground squirrel, noisy blue-and-gray scrub jay, black bears, coyotes, skunks, and gray fox.

At middle elevation (5,000–9,000 feet), where the giant sequoia belt resides, rock formations mix with meadows and huge stands of evergreens—red and white fir, incense cedar, and ponderosa pines, to name a few. Wildflowers like yellow blazing star and red Indian paintbrush bloom in spring and summer. Mule deer, golden-mantled ground squirrels, Steller's jays, and black bears (most active in fall) inhabit the area, as does the chickaree.

The high alpine section of the parks is extremely rugged, with a string of rocky peaks reaching above 13,000 feet to Mt. Whitney's 14,494 feet. Fierce weather and scarcity of soil make vegetation and wildlife sparse. Foxtail and whitebark pines have gnarled and twisted trunks, the result of high wind, heavy snowfall, and freezing temperatures. In summer you can see yellow-bellied marmots, pikas, weasels, mountain chickadees, and Clark's nutcrackers.

CROSS-COUNTRY SKIING

Roads to Grant Grove are accessible even during heavy snowfall, making the trails here a good choice over Sequoia's Giant Forest when harsh weather hits.

FISHING

There is limited trout fishing in the park from late April to mid-November, and catches are minor. Still, Kings River is a popular spot. Some of the park's secluded backcountry lakes have good fishing. Licenses are available, along with fishing tackle, in Grant Grove and Cedar Grove. *See Activities, in Sequoia National Park, above, for more information about licenses.*

HIKING

You can enjoy many of Kings Canyon's sights from your car, but the giant gorge of the Kings River canyon and the sweeping vistas of some of the highest mountains in the United States are best seen on foot. Carry a hiking map—available at any visitor center—and plenty of water. Check with rangers for current trail conditions, and be aware of rapidly changing weather. Except for one trail to Mt. Whitney, permits are not required for day hikes.

Big Baldy

HIKING/WALKING | This hike climbs 600 feet and 2 miles up to the 8,209-foot summit of Big Baldy. Your reward is the view of Redwood Canyon. Round-trip the hike is 4 miles. *Moderate.* ✉ *Kings Canyon National Park* ✣ *Trailhead: 8 miles south of Grant Grove on Generals Hwy. (Rte. 198).*

Big Stump Trail

HIKING/WALKING | From 1883 until 1890, logging was done here, complete with a mill. The 1-mile loop trail, whose unmarked beginning is a few yards west of the Big Stump entrance, passes by many enormous stumps. *Easy.* ✉ *Kings Canyon National Park* ✥ *Trailhead: near Big Stump Entrance, Generals Hwy. (Rte. 180).*

Buena Vista Peak

HIKING/WALKING | For a 360-degree view of Redwood Canyon and the High Sierra, make the 2-mile ascent to Buena Vista. *Difficult.* ✉ *Kings Canyon National Park* ✥ *Trailhead: off Generals Hwy. (Rte. 198), south of Kings Canyon Overlook, 7 miles southeast of Grant Grove.*

★ Grant Grove Trail

HIKING/WALKING | Grant Grove is only 128 acres, but it's a big deal. More than 120 sequoias here have a base diameter that exceeds 10 feet, and the **General Grant Tree** is the world's third-largest sequoia by volume. Nearby, the Confederacy is represented by the **Robert E. Lee Tree,** recognized as the world's 11th-largest sequoia. Also along the easy-to-walk trail are the **Fallen Monarch** and the **Gamlin Cabin,** built by 19th-century pioneers. *Easy.* ✉ *Kings Canyon National Park* ✥ *Trailhead: off Generals Hwy. (Rte. 180), 1 mile north of Kings Canyon Park Visitor Center.*

Hotel Creek Trail

HIKING/WALKING | For gorgeous canyon views, take this trail from Cedar Grove up a series of switchbacks until it splits. Follow the route left through chaparral to the forested ridge and rocky outcrop known as Cedar Grove Overlook, where you can see the Kings River canyon stretching below. This strenuous 5-mile round-trip hike gains 1,200 feet and takes three to four hours to complete. *Difficult.* ✉ *Kings Canyon National Park* ✥ *Trailhead: at Cedar Grove Pack Station, 1 mile east of Cedar Grove Village.*

Mist Falls Trail

TRAIL | This sandy trail follows the glaciated South Fork Canyon through forest and chaparral, past several rapids and cascades, to one of the largest waterfalls in the two parks. Nine miles round-trip, the hike is relatively flat, but climbs 600 feet in the last 2 miles. It takes from four to five hours to complete. *Moderate.* ✉ *Kings Canyon National Park* ✥ *Trailhead: at end of Kings Canyon Scenic Byway, 5½ miles east of Cedar Grove Village.*

Panoramic Point Trail

HIKING/WALKING | You'll get a nice view of whale-shape Hume Lake from the top of this Grant Grove path, which is paved and only 300 feet long. It's fairly steep—strollers might work here, but not wheelchairs. Trailers and RVs are not permitted on the steep and narrow road that leads to the trailhead parking lot. *Moderate.* ✉ *Kings Canyon National Park* ✥ *Trailhead: at end of Panoramic Point Rd., 2.3 miles from Grant Grove Village.*

Redwood Canyon Trails

HIKING/WALKING | Two main trails lead into Redwood Canyon grove, the world's largest sequoia grove. The 6.5-mile **Hart Tree and Fallen Goliath Loop** passes by a 19th-century logging site, pristine Hart Meadow, and the hollowed-out Tunnel Tree before accessing a side trail to the grove's largest sequoia, the 277.9-foot-tall Hart Tree. The 6.4-mile **Sugar Bowl Loop** provides views of Redwood Mountain and Big Baldy before winding down into its namesake, a thick grove of mature and young sequoias. *Moderate.* ✉ *Kings Canyon National Park* ✥ *Trailhead: off Quail Flat. Drive 5 miles south of Grant Grove on Generals Hwy. (Rte. 198), turn right at Quail Flat and proceed 1½ miles to trailhead.*

Roads End Permit Station

HIKING/WALKING | You can obtain wilderness permits, maps, and information about the backcountry at this station, where bear canisters, a must for campers, can be rented or purchased. When the station is closed (typically October–mid-May), complete a self-service permit form. ✉ *Kings Canyon National Park* ✥ *Eastern end of Kings Canyon Scenic Byway, 6 miles east of Cedar Grove Visitor Center.*

Mount Whitney

At 14,494 feet, Mt. Whitney is the highest point in the contiguous United States and the crown jewel of Sequoia National Park's wild eastern side. The peak looms high above the tiny, high-mountain desert community of Lone Pine, where numerous Hollywood Westerns have been filmed. The high mountain ranges, arid landscape, and scrubby brush of the eastern Sierra are beautiful in their vastness and austerity.

Despite the mountain's scale, you can't see it from the more traveled west side of the park because it is hidden behind the Great Western Divide. The only way to access Mt. Whitney from the main part of the park is to circumnavigate the Sierra Nevada via a 10-hour, nearly 400-mile drive outside the park. No road ascends the peak; the best vantage point from which to catch a glimpse of the mountain is at the end of Whitney Portal Road. The 13 miles of winding road leads from U.S. 395 at Lone Pine to the trailhead for the hiking route to the top of the mountain. Whitney Portal Road is closed in winter.

Mt. Whitney Trail The most popular route to the summit, the Mt. Whitney Trail can be conquered by very fit and experienced hikers. If there's snow on the mountain, this is a challenge for expert mountaineers only. All overnighters must have a permit, as must day hikers on the trail beyond Lone Pine Lake, about 2½ miles from the trailhead. From May through October, permits are distributed via a lottery run each February by *recreation.gov*. The Eastern Sierra Interagency Visitor Center (*760/876–6200*), on Route 136 at U.S. 395 about a mile south of Lone Pine, is a good resource for information about permits and hiking. *Kings Canyon National Park 760/873–2483 trail reservations www.fs.usda.gov/inyo.*

Roaring River Falls Walk

HIKING/WALKING | Take a shady five-minute walk to this forceful waterfall that rushes through a narrow granite chute. The trail is paved and mostly accessible. *Easy.* *Kings Canyon National Park Trailhead: 3 miles east of Cedar Grove Village turnoff from Kings Canyon Scenic Byway.*

★ Zumwalt Meadow Trail

HIKING/WALKING | Rangers say this is the best (and most popular) day hike in the Cedar Grove area. Just 1.5 miles long, it offers three visual treats: the South Fork of the Kings River, the lush meadow, and the high granite walls above, including those of Grand Sentinel and North Dome. *Easy.* *Kings Canyon National Park Trailhead: 4½ miles east of Cedar Grove Village turnoff from Kings Canyon Scenic Byway.*

HORSEBACK RIDING

One-day destinations by horseback out of Cedar Grove include Mist Falls and Upper Bubb's Creek. In the backcountry, many equestrians head for Volcanic Lakes or Granite Basin, ascending trails that reach elevations of 10,000 feet. Costs per person range from $40 for a one-hour guided ride to around $300 per day for fully guided trips for which the packers do all the cooking and camp chores.

Cedar Grove Pack Station

HORSEBACK RIDING | Take a day ride or plan a multiday adventure along the Kings River canyon with Cedar Grove Pack Station. Popular routes include the Rae Lakes Loop and Monarch Divide. Closed early

September–late May. ✉ *Kings Canyon National Park* ✣ *Kings Canyon Scenic Byway, 1 mile east of Cedar Grove Village* ☎ *559/565–3464 summer, 559/337–2413 off-season* 🌐 *www.nps.gov/seki/planyourvisit/horseride.htm* 🎫 *From $40 per hr or $100 per day.*

Grant Grove Stables

HORSEBACK RIDING | A one- or two-hour trip through Grant Grove leaving from the stables provides a taste of horseback riding in Kings Canyon. Closed October–early June. ✉ *Kings Canyon National Park* ✣ *Rte. 180, ½ mile north of Grant Grove Visitor Center* ☎ *559/335–9292* 🌐 *www.nps.gov/seki/planyourvisit/horseride.htm* 🎫 *From $40.*

SLEDDING AND SNOWSHOEING

In winter, Kings Canyon has a few great places to play in the snow. Sleds, inner tubes, and platters are allowed at both the Azalea Campground area on Grant Tree Road, ¼ mile north of Grant Grove Visitor Center, and at the Big Stump picnic area, 2 miles north of the lower Route 180 entrance to the park.

Snowshoeing is good around Grant Grove, where you can take occasional naturalist-guided snowshoe walks from mid-December through mid-March as conditions permit. Grant Grove Market rents sleds and snowshoes.

Nearby Towns

Numerous towns and cities tout themselves as "gateways" to the parks, with some more deserving of the title than others. One that certainly merits the name is frisky **Three Rivers,** a Sierra foothills hamlet (population 2,200) along the Kaweah River. Close to Sequoia's Ash Mountain and Lookout Point entrances, Three Rivers is a good spot to find a room when park lodgings are full. Either because Three Rivers residents appreciate their idyllic setting or because they know that tourists are their bread and butter, you'll find them almost uniformly pleasant and eager to share tips about the best spots for "Sierra surfing" the Kaweah's smooth, moss-covered rocks or where to find the best cell phone reception.

Visalia, a Central Valley city of about 128,000 people, lies 58 miles southwest of Sequoia's Wuksachi Village and 56 miles southwest of the Kings Canyon Park Visitor Center. Its vibrant downtown contains several good restaurants. If you're into Victorian and other old houses, drop by the visitor center and pick up a free map of them. A clear day's view of the Sierra from Main Street is spectacular, and even Sunday night can find the streets bustling with pedestrians. Visalia provides easy access to grand Sequoia National Park and the serene Kaweah Oaks Preserve.

Closest to Kings Canyon's Big Stump entrance, **Fresno,** the main gateway to the southern Sierra region, is about 55 miles west of Kings Canyon and about 85 miles northwest of Wuksachi Village. This Central Valley city of nearly a half-million people is sprawling and unglamorous, but it has all the cultural and other amenities you'd expect of a major crossroads.

GETTING HERE AND AROUND

Sequoia Shuttle

In summer the Sequoia Shuttle connects Three Rivers to Visalia and Sequoia National Park. ☎ *877/287–4453* 🌐 *www.sequoiashuttle.com* 🎫 *$15 round-trip.*

VISITOR INFORMATION

Fresno/Clovis Convention & Visitors Bureau ✉ *1550 E. Shaw Ave., Suite 101, Fresno* ☎ *559/981–5500, 800/788–0836* 🌐 *www.playfresno.org.* **Sequoia Foothills Chamber of Commerce** ✉ *42268 Sierra Dr., Three Rivers* ☎ *559/561–3300.* **Visalia Convention & Visitors Bureau** ✉ *Kiosk, 303 E. Acequia Ave., at S. Bridge St., Visalia* ☎ *559/334–0141, 800/524–0303* 🌐 *www.visitvisalia.org.*

Sights

★ Colonel Allensworth State Historic Park

HISTORIC SITE | It's worth the slight detour off Highway 99 to learn about and pay homage to the dream of Allen Allensworth and other black pioneers who in 1908 founded Allensworth, the only California town settled, governed, and financed by African Americans. At its height, the town prospered as a key railroad transfer point, but after cars and trucks reduced railroad traffic and water was diverted for Central Valley agriculture, the town declined and was eventually deserted. Today the restored and rebuilt schoolhouse, library, and other structures commemorate Allensworth's heyday, as do festivities that take place each October. ✉ *4129 Palmer Ave., off Hwy. 43; from Hwy. 99 at Delano, take Garces Hwy. west to Hwy. 43 north; from Earlimart, take County Rd. J22 west to Hwy. 43 south, Allensworth* ☎ *661/849–3433* 🌐 *www.parks.ca.gov* 🎫 *$6 per car.*

Exeter Murals

PUBLIC ART | More than two dozen murals in the Central Valley city of Exeter's cute-as-a-button downtown make it worth a quick detour if you're traveling on Route 198. Several of the murals, which depict the area's agricultural and social history, are quite good. All adorn buildings within a few blocks of the intersection of Pine and E streets. If you're hungry, the **Wildflower Cafe,** at 121 South E Street, serves inventive salads and sandwiches. Shortly after entering Exeter head west on Pine Street (it's just before the water tower) to reach downtown. ✉ *Exeter* ✢ *Rte. 65, 2 miles south of Rte. 198, about 11 miles east of Visalia* 🌐 *cityofexeter.com/galleries/exeter-murals.*

★ Forestiere Underground Gardens

GARDEN | **FAMILY** | Sicilian immigrant Baldassare Forestiere spent four decades (1906–46) carving out an odd, subterranean realm of rooms, tunnels, grottoes, alcoves, and arched passageways that once extended for more than 10 acres between Highway 99 and busy, mall-pocked Shaw Avenue. Though not an engineer, Forestiere called on his memories of the ancient Roman structures he saw as a youth and on techniques he learned digging subways in New York and Boston. Only a fraction of his prodigious output is on view, but you can tour his underground living quarters, including bedrooms (one with a fireplace), the kitchen, living room, and bath, as well as a fishpond and auto tunnel. Skylights allow exotic full-grown fruit trees to flourish more than 20 feet belowground. ✉ *5021 W. Shaw Ave., 2 blocks east of Hwy. 99, Fresno* ☎ *559/271–0734* 🌐 *www.undergroundgardens.com* 🎫 *$17* 🕒 *Closed Dec.–Mar.*

Kaweah Oaks Preserve

NATURE PRESERVE | Trails at this 344-acre wildlife sanctuary off the main road to Sequoia National Park lead past majestic valley oak, sycamore, cottonwood, and willow trees. Among the 134 bird species you might spot are hawks, hummingbirds, and great blue herons. Bobcats, lizards, coyotes, and cottontails also live here. The Sycamore Trail has digital signage with QR codes you can scan with your smartphone to access plant and animal information. ✉ *Follow Hwy. 198 for 7 miles east of Visalia, turn north on Rd. 182, and proceed ½ mile to gate on left side, Visalia* ☎ *559/738–0211* 🌐 *www.sequoiariverlands.org* 🎫 *Free.*

Project Survival's Cat Haven

ZOO | Take the rare opportunity to glimpse a Siberian lynx, a clouded leopard, a Bengal tiger, and other endangered wild cats at this conservation facility that shelters more than 30 big cats. A guided hour-long tour along a quarter mile of walkway leads to fenced habitat areas shaded by trees and overlooking the Central Valley. ✉ *38257 E. Kings Canyon Rd. (Rte. 180), 15 miles west of Kings Canyon National Park, Dunlap* ☎ *559/338–3216* 🌐 *www.cathaven.com* 🎫 *$15.*

Sequoia National Forest and Giant Sequoia National Monument

FOREST | Delicate spring wildflowers, cool summer campgrounds, and varied winter-sports opportunities—not to mention more than half of the world's giant sequoia groves—draw outdoorsy types year-round to this sprawling district surrounding the national parks. Together, the forest and monument cover nearly 1,700 square miles, south from the Kings River and east from the foothills along the San Joaquin Valley. The monument's groves are both north and south of Sequoia National Park. One of the most popular is the **Converse Basin Grove,** home of the Boole Tree, the forest's largest sequoia. The grove is accessible by car on an unpaved road.

The Hume Lake Forest Service District Office, at 35860 Kings Canyon Scenic Byway (Route 180), has information about the groves, along with details about recreational activities. In springtime, diversions include hiking among the wildflowers that brighten the foothills. The floral display rises with the heat as the mountain elevations warm up in summer, when hikers, campers, and picnickers become more plentiful. The abundant trout supply attracts anglers to area waters, including 87-acre **Hume Lake,** which is also ideal for swimming and nonmotorized boating. By fall the turning leaves provide the visual delights, particularly in the Western Divide, Indian Basin, and the Kern Plateau. Winter activities include downhill and cross-country skiing, snowshoeing, and snowmobiling. ✉ *Sequoia National Park* ✣ *Northern Entrances: Generals Hwy. (Rte. 198), 7 miles southeast of Grant Grove; Hume Lake Rd. between Generals Hwy. (Rte. 198) and Kings Canyon Scenic Byway (Rte. 180); Kings Canyon Scenic Byway (Rte. 180) between Grant Grove and Cedar Grove. Southern Entrances: Rte. 190 east of Springville; Rte. 178 east of Bakersfield* ☎ *559/784–1500 forest and monument, 559/338–2251 Hume Lake* 🌐 *www.fs.usda.gov/sequoia.*

Activities

BOATING AND RAFTING

Hume Lake

BODY OF WATER | This reservoir, built by loggers in the early 1900s, is now the site of several church-affiliated camps, a gas station, and a public campground. Outside Kings Canyon's borders, Hume Lake offers intimate views of the mountains. Summer lodge room rentals start at $160. ✉ *Hume Lake Rd., off Kings Canyon Hwy., 8 miles northeast of Grant Grove, 64144 Hume Lake Rd., Hume* ☎ *559/305–7770* 🌐 *www.humelake.org, visitsequoia.com.*

Kaweah White Water Adventures

BOATING | Kaweah's trips include a two-hour excursion (good for families) through Class III rapids, a longer paddle through Class IV rapids, and an extended trip (typically Class IV and V rapids). ✉ *40443 Sierra Dr., Three Rivers* ☎ *559/740–8251* 🌐 *www.kaweah-whitewater.com* 🎫 *From $50 per person.*

Kings River Expeditions

TOUR—SPORTS | This outfit arranges one- and two-day white-water rafting trips on the Kings River. The office is in Clovis, but all trips depart from Twin Pines Camp, 60 miles east of Fresno. ✉ *Twin Pines Camp, Clovis* ☎ *559/233–4881, 800/846–3674* 🌐 *www.kingsriver.com* 🎫 *From $145.*

HORSEBACK RIDING

Wood 'n' Horse Training Stables

HORSEBACK RIDING | For hourly horseback rides, riding lessons, or trail rides in the foothills, contact this outfit. From $45 for lessons; from $65 for trail rides. ✉ *42846 N. Fork Dr., Three Rivers* ☎ *559/561–4268* 🌐 *www.wdnhorse.com.*

Performing Arts

Fresno Philharmonic Orchestra

CONCERTS | The orchestra performs classical concerts from September through

June. ✉ *Saroyan Theatre, 730 M St., near Inyo St., Fresno* ☎ *559/261–0600* 🌐 *fresnophil.org.*

Roger Rocka's Dinner Theater
THEATER | This Tower District venue stages Broadway-style musicals. ✉ *1226 N. Wishon Ave., at E. Olive Ave., Fresno* ☎ *559/266–9494* 🌐 *www.rogerrockas.com.*

Shopping

Cedar Grove Gift Shop and Market
GIFTS/SOUVENIRS | This place is small, but it's stocked with the essentials for RV and auto travelers. ✉ *Cedar Grove Village, Kings Canyon National Park* ☎ *559/565–3096* ⏲ *Closed late Oct.–mid-May.*

Grant Grove Gift Shop
GIFTS/SOUVENIRS | This shop sells park-related gifts and souvenirs. ✉ *Grant Grove Village, Kings Canyon National Park* ☎ *559/335–5500.*

Lodgepole Market Center
GIFTS/SOUVENIRS | You'll find gifts, toys, books, souvenirs, and outdoor equipment in Sequoia National Park's largest store. Its grocery department has a fairly wide selection of items, some of them organic, including grab-and-go items for hikes and picnics. Across the hall is a café with various dishes for breakfast, lunch, and dinner. ✉ *63204 Lodgepole Rd., next to Lodgepole Visitor Center, Sequoia National Park* ☎ *559/565–3301* 🌐 *www.visitsequoia.com.*

Wuksachi Gift Shop
GIFTS/SOUVENIRS | Souvenir clothing, Native American crafts, postcards, and snacks are for sale at this tasteful shop off the Wuksachi Lodge lobby. ✉ *Wuksachi Village* ☎ *559/625–7700.*

Restaurants

IN THE PARKS

SEQUOIA

Lodgepole Market and Grill
$$ | **CAFÉ** | The choices here run the gamut from simple to very simple, with several counters only a few strides apart in a central eating complex. The café also sells fresh and prepackaged salads, sandwiches, and wraps. **Known for:** quick and convenient dining; many healthful options; grab-and-go items for picnics. 💲 *Average main: $12* ✉ *Next to Lodgepole Visitor Center, Sequoia National Park* ☎ *559/565–3301.*

The Peaks
$$$ | **MODERN AMERICAN** | Huge windows run the length of the Wuksachi Lodge's high-ceilinged dining room, and a large fireplace on the far wall warms both body and soul. The diverse dinner menu—by far the best at both parks—reflects a commitment to locally sourced and sustainable products. **Known for:** seasonal menus with fresh local ingredients; great views of sequoia grove; box lunches. 💲 *Average main: $28* ✉ *Wuksachi Lodge, 64740 Wuksachi Way, Wuksachi Village* ☎ *559/625–7700* 🌐 *www.visitsequoia.com/dine/the-peaks-restaurant.*

PICNIC AREAS

Take care to dispose of your food scraps properly (the bears might not appreciate this short-term, but the practice helps ensure their long-term survival).

Crescent Meadow
RESTAURANT—SIGHT | A mile or so past Moro Rock, this comparatively remote picnic area has meadow views and is close to a lovely hiking trail. Tables are under the giant sequoias, off the parking area. There are restrooms and drinking water. Fires are not allowed. ✉ *Sequoia National Park* ✥ *End of Moro Rock–Crescent Rd., 2.6 miles east off Generals Hwy. (Rte. 198).*

Foothills Picnic Area

RESTAURANT—SIGHT | Near the parking lot at the southern entrance of the park, this area has tables, drinking water, and restrooms. ✉ *Sequoia National Park* ✣ *Across Generals Hwy. from Foothills Visitor Center.*

Hospital Rock

RESTAURANT—SIGHT | Native Americans once ground acorns into meal at this site; outdoor exhibits tell the story. The picnic area's name, however, stems from a hunter/trapper who was treated for a leg wound here in 1873. Look up, and you'll see Moro Rock. Grills, drinking water, and restrooms are available. ✉ *Sequoia National Park* ✣ *Generals Hwy. (Rte. 198), 6 miles north of Ash Mountain entrance.*

Pinewood Picnic Area

RESTAURANT—SIGHT | Picnic in Giant Forest, in the vicinity of sequoias if not actually under them. Drinking water, restrooms, grills, and wheelchair-accessible spots are provided in this expansive setting near Sequoia National Park's most popular attractions. ✉ *Sequoia National Park* ✣ *Generals Hwy. (Rte. 198), 2 miles north of Giant Forest Museum, halfway between Giant Forest Museum and General Sherman Tree.*

Wolverton Meadow

RESTAURANT—SIGHT | At a major trailhead to the backcountry, this is a great place to stop for lunch before a hike. The area sits in a mixed-conifer forest adjacent to parking. Drinking water, grills, and restrooms are available. ✉ *Sequoia National Park* ✣ *Wolverton Rd., 1½ miles northeast off Generals Hwy. (Rte. 198).*

KINGS CANYON

Cedar Grove Snack Bar

$$ | **AMERICAN** | The menu here is surprisingly extensive, with dinner entrées such as pasta, pork chops, trout, and steak. For breakfast, try the egg burrito, French toast, or pancakes; sandwiches, wraps, burgers (including vegetarian patties) and hot dogs dominate the lunch and dinner choices. **Known for:** scenic river views; extensive options; alfresco dining on balcony overlooking the Kings River. $ *Average main: $16* ✉ *Cedar Grove Village, Kings Canyon National Park* ☎ *559/565–3096* 🌐 *www.visitsequoia.com/dine/cedar-grove-snack-bar* ⏲ *Closed Oct.–May.*

Grant Grove Restaurant

$$ | **AMERICAN** | Gaze at giant sequoias and a verdant meadow while dining in this eco-friendly restaurant's spacious dining room with fireplace, or outdoors on the expansive deck. The menu centers around locally sourced natural and organic ingredients and offers standard American fare. **Known for:** takeout service year-round; walk-up window for pizza, sandwiches, coffee, ice cream; picnic tables on outdoor deck. $ *Average main: $16* ✉ *Grant Grove Village, Kings Canyon National Park* ☎ *559/335–5500.*

PICNIC AREAS

Big Stump

RESTAURANT—SIGHT | Some trees still stand at this site at the edge of a logged sequoia grove. Near the park's entrance, the area is paved and next to the road. It's the only picnic area in either park that is plowed in the wintertime. Restrooms (portable toilets), grills, and drinking water are available, and the area is entirely accessible. ✉ *Kings Canyon National Park* ✣ *Generals Hwy. (Rte. 180), just inside Big Stump entrance.*

Grizzly Falls

RESTAURANT—SIGHT | This little gem is worth a pull-over, if not a picnic at the roadside tables. A less-than-a-minute trek from the parking lot delivers you to the base of the delightful, 100-foot-plus falls. On a hot day, nothing feels better than dipping your feet in the cool water. An outhouse is on-site, but grills are not, and water is not available. ✉ *Kings Canyon National Park* ✣ *Off Rte. 180, 2½ miles west of Cedar Grove entrance.*

OUTSIDE THE PARKS

Antoinette's Coffee and Goodies

$ | **CAFÉ** | For smoothies, well-crafted espresso drinks, breakfast bowls, and pumpkin chocolate-chip muffins and other homemade baked goods, stop for a spell at this convivial coffee shop. Antoinette's is known as the town's hub for vegan and gluten-free items. **Known for:** plentiful vegan and gluten-free items; Wi-Fi on-site; all organic, locally roasted coffee. *Average main: $7 41727 Sierra Dr., Three Rivers 559/561–2253 www.antoinettescoffeeandgoodies.com Closed Tues. No dinner.*

Buckaroo Diner

$$ | **AMERICAN** | Set on a bluff overlooking the Kaweah River, the boho-chic Buckaroo serves fresh, house-made dishes made with seasonal organic ingredients. The restaurant's main dining room occupies a building that housed the original restaurant ('Ol Buckaroo) for decades; you can also sit in the cozy sun room or outdoor terrace overlooking the river. **Known for:** weekend beer garden; smoked foods; daily specials. *Average main: $18 41695 Sierra Dr., Three Rivers 559/465–5088 theolbuckaroo.com Closed Tues. and Wed. No lunch weekdays.*

Café 225

$$$ | **MODERN AMERICAN** | High ceilings and contemporary decor contribute to the relaxed and sophisticated atmosphere at this popular downtown restaurant. Meats and fish grilled on a wood-fired rotisserie figure prominently on the menu, which also includes pastas and unusual treats such as artichoke fritters and goat cheese and roast lamb pizza. **Known for:** wood-fired rotisserie menu items; fresh local ingredients; sophisticated vibe. *Average main: $22 225 W. Main St., Visalia 559/733–2967 www.cafe225.com Closed Sun.*

Gateway Restaurant and Lodge

$$$ | **AMERICAN** | The view's the draw at this roadhouse that overlooks the Kaweah River as it plunges out of the high country. The Gateway serves everything from osso buco and steaks to shrimp in Thai chili sauce; dinner reservations are essential on summer weekends. **Known for:** scenic riverside setting; fine dining in otherwise casual town; popular bar. *Average main: $30 45978 Sierra Dr., Three Rivers 559/561–4133 www.gateway-sequoia.com.*

School House Restaurant & Tavern

$$$ | **MODERN AMERICAN** | A Wine Country–style establishment that sources ingredients from the on-site gardens and surrounding farms and orchards, this popular restaurant occupies a redbrick 1921 schoolhouse in the town of Sanger. Chef Ryan Jackson, who grew up on local fruit farms, creates seasonal menus from the bounty of familiar backyards, mostly filled with classic American dishes with a contemporary twist. **Known for:** fresh ingredients from neighboring farms and orchards; historic country setting; convenient stop between Kings Canyon and Fresno. *Average main: $29 1018 S. Frankwood Ave., at Hwy. 180 (King's Canyon Rd.), 20 miles east of Fresno, Sanger 559/787–3271 schoolhousesanger.com Closed Mon. and Tues.*

Sierra Subs and Salads

$ | **AMERICAN** | This well-run sandwich joint satisfies carnivores and vegetarians alike with crispy-fresh ingredients prepared with panache. Depending on your preference, the centerpiece of the Bull's Eye sandwich, for instance, will be roast beef or a portobello mushroom, but whichever you choose, the accompanying flavors—of ciabatta bread, horseradish-and-garlic mayonnaise, roasted red peppers, Havarti cheese, and spinach—will delight your palate. **Known for:** many vegetarian, vegan, and gluten-free options; weekly specials; Wi-Fi. *Average main: $9 41717 Sierra Dr., Three Rivers 559/561–4810 www.sierrasubsandsalads.com Closed Mon. No dinner.*

★ The Vintage Press

$$$$ | **EUROPEAN** | Built in 1966, this is one of the best restaurants in the Central Valley. The California–Continental cuisine includes dishes such as crispy veal sweetbreads with a port-wine sauce and filet mignon with a cognac-mustard sauce. **Known for:** wine list with more than 900 selections; chocolate Grand Marnier cake and other homemade desserts; sophisticated vibe. *Average main: $32 ✉ 216 N. Willis St., Visalia ☎ 559/733–3033 ⊕ www.thevintage-press.com.*

IN THE PARKS

SEQUOIA

Silver City Mountain Resort

$$$ | **RESORT** | High on Mineral King Road, this privately owned resort has rustic cabins and deluxe chalets—all with a stove, refrigerator, and sink—plus three hotel rooms with private baths. **Pros:** rustic setting; friendly staff; great location for hikers. **Cons:** long, winding road is not for everybody; not much entertainment except hiking; some units have shared baths. *Rooms from: $165 ✉ Sequoia National Park ✣ Mineral King Rd., 21 miles southeast of Rte. 198 ☎ 559/561–3223 ⊕ www.silvercityresort.com ⏲ Closed Nov.–late May 13 cabins, 3 hotel rooms No meals.*

★ Wuksachi Lodge

$$$$ | **HOTEL** | The striking cedar-and-stone main building is a fine example of how a structure can blend effectively with lovely mountain scenery. **Pros:** best place to stay in the parks; lots of wildlife; easy access to hiking and snowshoe/ski trails. **Cons:** rooms can be small; main lodge is a few-minutes' walk from guest rooms; slow Wi-Fi. *Rooms from: $229 ✉ 64740 Wuksachi Way, Wuksachi Village ☎ 559/625–7700, 888/252–5757 reservations ⊕ www.visitsequoia.com/lodging/wuksachi-lodge 102 rooms No meals.*

KINGS CANYON

Cedar Grove Lodge

$$ | **HOTEL** | Backpackers like to stay here on the eve of long treks into the High Sierra wilderness, so bedtimes tend to be early. **Pros:** a definite step up from camping in terms of comfort; great base camp for outdoor adventures; on-site snack bar. **Cons:** impersonal; not everybody agrees it's clean enough; remote location. *Rooms from: $147 ✉ Kings Canyon Scenic Byway, Kings Canyon National Park ☎ 866/807–3598 ⊕ www.visitsequoia.com/lodging/cedar-grove-lodge ⏲ Closed mid-Oct.–mid-May 21 rooms No meals.*

Grant Grove Cabins

$$ | **HOTEL** | Some of the wood-panel cabins here have heaters, electric lights, and private baths, but most have woodstoves, battery lamps, and shared baths. **Pros:** warm, woodsy feel; clean; walk to Grant Grove Restaurant. **Cons:** can be difficult to walk up to if you're not in decent physical shape; costly for what you get; only basic amenities. *Rooms from: $135 ✉ Kings Canyon Scenic Byway in Grant Grove Village, Kings Canyon National Park ☎ 866/807–3598 ⊕ www.visitsequoia.com/Grant-Grove-Cabins.aspx 33 cabins, 9 with bath; 17 tent cabins No meals.*

John Muir Lodge

$$$$ | **HOTEL** | In a wooded area in the hills above Grant Grove Village, this modern, timber-sided lodge has rooms and suites with queen- or king-size beds and private baths. **Pros:** open year-round; common room stays warm; quiet. **Cons:** check-in is down in the village; spotty Wi-Fi; remote location. *Rooms from: $210 ✉ Kings Canyon Scenic Byway, ¼ mile north of Grant Grove Village, 86728 Hwy. 180, Kings Canyon National Park ☎ 866/807–3598 ⊕ www.visitsequoia.com/john-muir-lodge.aspx 36 rooms No meals.*

OUTSIDE THE PARKS

The only lodging immediately outside the parks is in Three Rivers. Options include inns, chain and mom-and-pop motels, and riverside cabins. Numerous chain properties operate in Visalia or Fresno (your favorite is likely represented in one or both cities), about an hour from the south and north entrances, respectively.

Montecito-Sequoia Lodge

$$$$ | **HOTEL** | **FAMILY** | Outdoor activities are what this year-round family resort is all about, including many that are geared toward teenagers and small children. **Pros:** friendly staff; great for kids; lots of fresh air and planned activities. **Cons:** can be noisy with all the activity; no TVs or phones in rooms; not within national park. *Rooms from: $229 63410 Generals Hwy., 11 miles south of Grant Grove, Sequoia National Forest 559/565–3388, 800/227–9900 www.mslodge.com Closed 1st 2 wks of Dec. 52 rooms All meals.*

★ Rio Sierra Riverhouse

$$$ | **B&B/INN** | Guests at Rio Sierra come for the river views, the sandy beach, and the proximity to Sequoia National Park (6 miles away), but invariably end up raving equally about the warm, laid-back hospitality of proprietress Mars Roberts. **Pros:** seductive beach; add-on breakfast option; river views from all rooms; contemporary ambience. **Cons:** books up quickly in summer; some road noise audible in rooms; long walk or drive to restaurants. *Rooms from: $200 41997 Sierra Dr., Hwy. 198, Three Rivers 559/561–4720 www.rio-sierra.com 5 rooms No meals 2-night min stay on summer weekends. Closed Jan.–mid-Feb.*

Chapter 5

MONTEREY BAY AREA

Updated by
Cheryl Crabtree

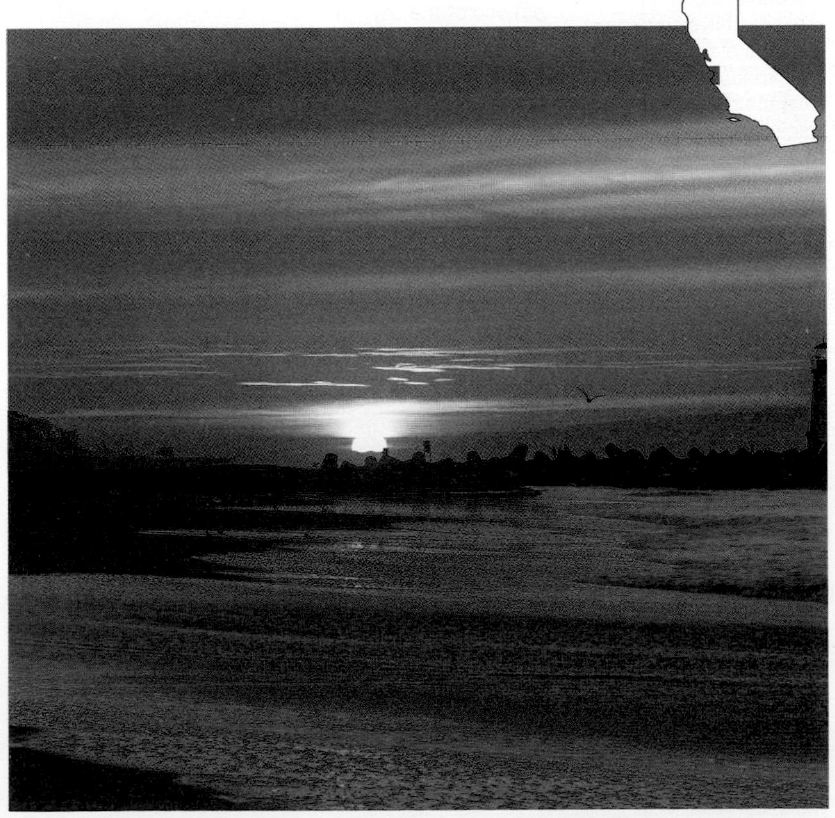

Sights ★★★★★ | Restaurants ★★★★☆ | Hotels ★★★★★ | Shopping ★☆☆☆☆ | Nightlife ★☆☆☆☆

WELCOME TO MONTEREY BAY AREA

TOP REASONS TO GO

★ **Marine life:** Monterey Bay is the location of the world's third-largest marine sanctuary, home to whales, otters, and other underwater creatures.

★ **Getaway central:** For more than a century, urbanites have come to the Monterey Bay area to unwind, relax, and have fun. It's a great place to browse unique shops and galleries, ride a giant roller coaster, or play a round of golf on a world-class course.

★ **Nature preserves:** More than the sea is protected here: the region boasts nearly 30 state parks, beaches, and preserves—fantastic places for walking, jogging, hiking, and biking.

★ **Wine and dine:** The area's rich agricultural bounty translates into abundant fresh produce, great wines, and fabulous dining. It's no wonder more than 300 culinary events take place here every year.

★ **Small-town vibes:** Even the cities here are friendly, walkable places where you'll feel like a local.

North of Big Sur the coastline softens into lower bluffs, windswept dunes, pristine estuaries, and long, sandy beaches, bordering one of the world's most amazing marine environments—Monterey Bay. On the Monterey Peninsula, at the southern end of the bay, are Carmel-by-the-Sea, Pacific Grove, and Monterey; Santa Cruz sits at the northern tip of the crescent. In between, Highway 1 cruises along the coastline, passing windswept beaches piled high with sand dunes. Along the route are wetlands and artichoke and strawberry fields.

1 **Carmel-by-the-Sea.**

2 **Carmel Valley.**

3 **Pebble Beach.**

4 **Pacific Grove.**

5 **Monterey.**

6 **Salinas.**

7 **Pinnacles National Park.**

8 **San Juan Bautista.**

9 **Moss Landing.**

10 **Aptos.**

11 **Capitola and Soquel.**

12 **Santa Cruz.**

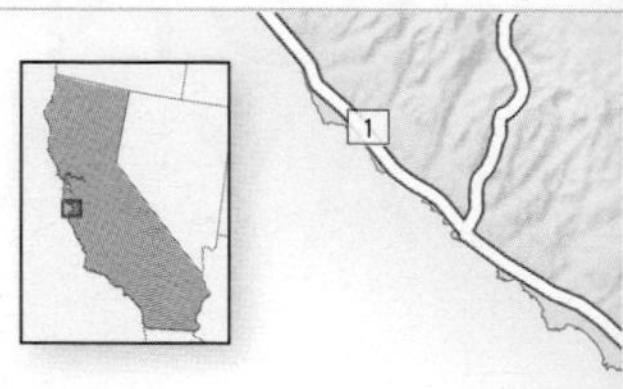

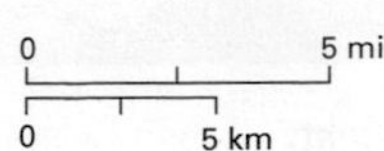

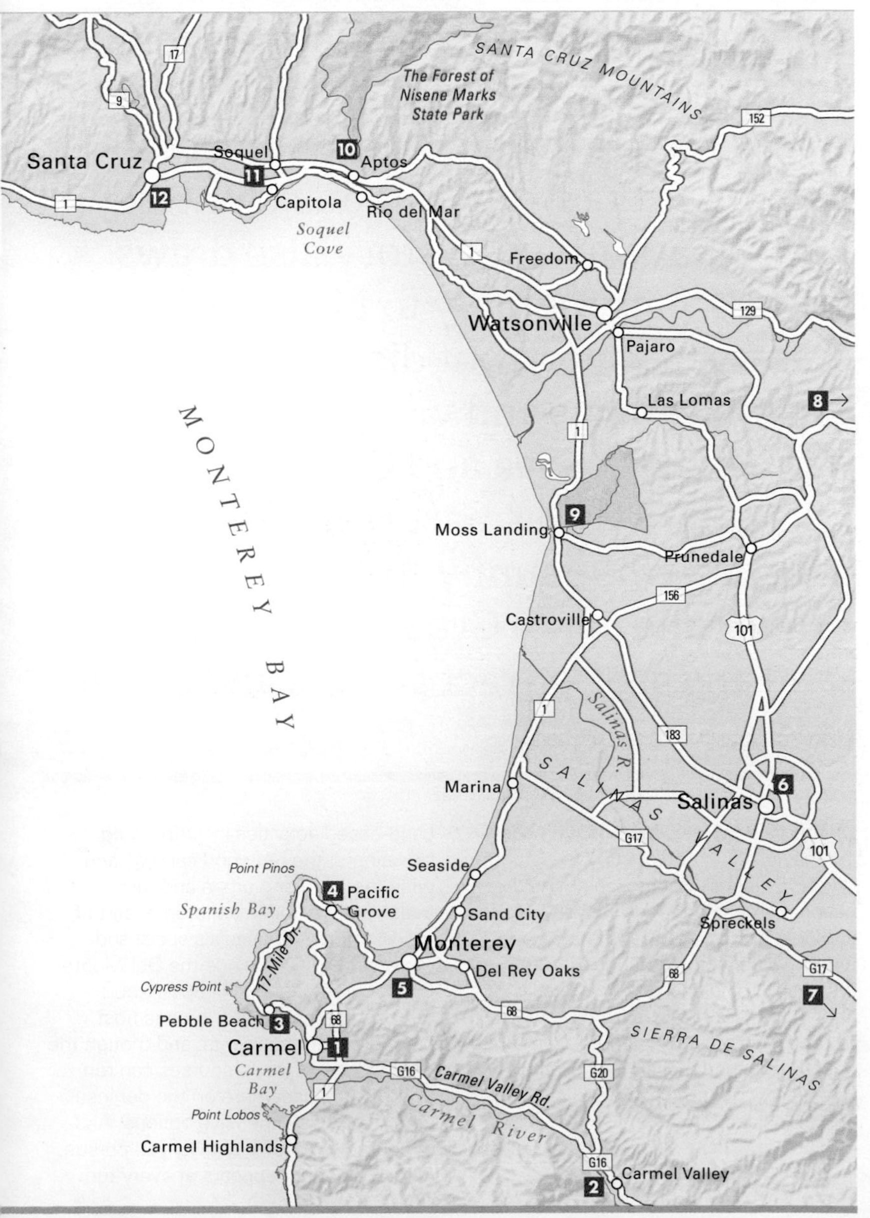
SANTA CRUZ MOUNTAINS
The Forest of Nisene Marks State Park
Santa Cruz
Soquel
Aptos
Capitola
Rio del Mar
Soquel Cove
Freedom
Watsonville
Pajaro
Las Lomas
MONTEREY BAY
Moss Landing
Prunedale
Castroville
Salinas R.
SALINAS VALLEY
Marina
Salinas
Spreckels
Seaside
Point Pinos
Pacific Grove
Spanish Bay
Sand City
Monterey
Del Rey Oaks
17-Mile Dr.
Cypress Point
Pebble Beach
Carmel
Carmel Bay
Carmel Valley Rd.
Carmel River
Point Lobos
Carmel Highlands
Carmel Valley
SIERRA DE SALINAS
1
9
17
152
129
156
101
183
G17
68
G16
G20
1
2
3
4
5
6
7
8
9
10
11
12

Natural beauty is at the heart of the Monterey Bay area's enormous appeal—it's everywhere, from the redwood-studded hillsides to the pristine shoreline with miles of walking paths and bluff-top vistas. Nature even takes center stage indoors at the world-famous Monterey Bay Aquarium, but history also draws visitors, most notably to Monterey's well-preserved waterfront district. Quaint, walkable towns and villages such as Carmel-by-the-Sea and Carmel Valley Village lure with smart restaurants and galleries, while sunny Aptos, Capitola, Soquel, and Santa Cruz, with miles of sand and surf, attract surfers and beach lovers.

Monterey Bay life centers on the ocean. The bay itself is protected by the Monterey Bay National Marine Sanctuary, the nation's largest undersea canyon—bigger and deeper than the Grand Canyon. On-the-water activities abound, from whale-watching and kayaking to sailing and surfing. Bay cruises from Monterey and Moss Landing almost always encounter other enchanting sea creatures, among them sea otters, sea lions, and porpoises.

Land-based activities include hiking, zip-lining in the redwood canopy, and wine tasting along urban and rural trails. Golf has been an integral part of the Monterey Peninsula's social and recreational scene since the Del Monte Golf Course opened in 1897. Pebble Beach's championship courses host prestigious tournaments, and though the greens fees at these courses can run up to $500, elsewhere on the peninsula you'll find less expensive options. And, of course, whatever activity you pursue, natural splendor appears at every turn.

Planning

When to Go

Summer is peak season; mild weather brings in big crowds. In this coastal region a cool breeze generally blows and fog often rolls in from offshore; you will frequently need a sweater or windbreaker. Off-season, from November through April, fewer people visit and the mood is mellower. Rainfall is heaviest in January and February. Fall and spring days are often clearer than those in summer.

Getting Here and Around

AIR TRAVEL

Monterey Regional Airport, 3 miles east of downtown Monterey off Highway 68, is served by Alaska, Allegiant, American, and United. Taxi service costs from $14 to $16 to downtown, and from $23 to $25 to Carmel. Monterey Airbus service between the region and the San Jose and San Francisco airports starts at $42; the Early Bird Airport Shuttle costs from $100 to $235 ($250 from Oakland).

AIRPORT CONTACTS Monterey Regional Airport (*MRY*) ✉ *200 Fred Kane Dr., at Olmsted Rd., off Hwy. 68, Monterey* ☎ *831/648–7000* 🌐 *www.montereyairport.com*.

GROUND TRANSPORTATION Central Coast Cab Company ☎ *831/626–3333* 🌐 *www.centralcoastcab.com*. **Early Bird Airport Shuttle** ☎ *831/462–3933* 🌐 *www.earlybirdairportshuttle.com*. **Monterey Airbus** ☎ *831/373–7777* 🌐 *www.montereyairbus.com*. **Yellow Cab** ☎ *831/333–1234*.

BUS TRAVEL

Greyhound serves Santa Cruz and Salinas from San Francisco and San Jose. The trips take about 3 and 4½ hours, respectively. Monterey-Salinas Transit (MST) provides frequent service in Monterey County (from $1.75 to $3.50; day pass $10), and Santa Cruz METRO ($2; day pass from $6 to $14) buses operate throughout Santa Cruz County. You can switch between the lines in Watsonville.

BUS CONTACTS Greyhound ☎ *800/231–2222* 🌐 *www.greyhound.com*. **Monterey-Salinas Transit** ☎ *888/678–2871* 🌐 *mst.org*. **Santa Cruz METRO** ☎ *831/425–8600* 🌐 *scmtd.com*.

CAR TRAVEL

Highway 1 runs south–north along the coast, linking the towns of Carmel-by-the-Sea, Monterey, and Santa Cruz; some sections have only two lanes. The freeway, U.S. 101, lies to the east, roughly parallel to Highway 1. The two roads are connected by Highway 68 from Pacific Grove to Salinas; Highway 156 from Castroville to Prunedale; Highway 152 from Watsonville to Gilroy; and Highway 17 from Santa Cruz to San Jose. **■ TIP→ Traffic near Santa Cruz can crawl to a standstill during commuter hours. In the morning, avoid traveling between 7 and 9; in the afternoon, avoid traveling between 4 and 7.**

The drive south from San Francisco to Monterey can be made comfortably in three hours or less. The most scenic way is to follow Highway 1 down the coast. A generally faster route is Interstate 280 south to Highway 85 to Highway 17 to Highway 1. The drive from the Los Angeles area takes five or six hours. Take U.S. 101 to Salinas and head west on Highway 68. You can also follow Highway 1 up the coast.

TRAIN TRAVEL

Amtrak's *Coast Starlight* runs between Los Angeles, Oakland, and Seattle. You can also take the *Pacific Surfliner* to San Luis Obispo and connect to Amtrak buses to Salinas or San Jose. From the train station in Salinas you can connect with buses serving Carmel and Monterey, and from the train station in San Jose with buses to Santa Cruz.

TRAIN CONTACTS Amtrak ☎ *800/872–7245* 🌐 *amtrak.com.*

Restaurants

The Monterey Bay area is a culinary paradise. The surrounding waters are full of fish, wild game roams the foothills, and the inland valleys are some of the most fertile in the country—local chefs draw on this bounty for their fresh, truly Californian cuisine. Except at beachside stands and inexpensive eateries, where anything goes, casual but neat dress is the norm. *Restaurant reviews have been shortened. For full information, visit Fodors.com.*

Hotels

Accommodations in the Monterey area range from no-frills motels to luxurious hotels. Pacific Grove, amply endowed with ornate Victorian houses, is the region's bed-and-breakfast capital; Carmel also has charming inns. Lavish resorts cluster in exclusive Pebble Beach and pastoral Carmel Valley.

High season runs from May through October. Rates in winter, especially at the larger hotels, may drop by 50% or more, and smaller inns often offer midweek specials. Whatever the month, some properties require a two-night stay on weekends. *Hotel reviews have been shortened. For full information, visit Fodors.com.* ■ **TIP→ Many of the fancier accommodations aren't suitable for children; if you're traveling with kids, ask before you book.**

WHAT IT COSTS

	$	$$	$$$	$$$$
RESTAURANTS				
	under $16	$16–$22	$23–$30	over $30
HOTELS				
	under $120	$120–$175	$176–$250	over $250

Tour Options

Ag Venture Tours & Consulting
GUIDED TOURS | Crowd-pleasing half- and full-day wine tasting, sightseeing, and agricultural tours are Ag Venture's specialty. Tastings are at Monterey and Santa Cruz Mountains wineries; sightseeing opportunities include the Monterey Peninsula, Big Sur, and Santa Cruz; and the agricultural forays take in the Salinas and Pajaro valleys. Customized itineraries can be arranged. ☎ *831/761–8463* 🌐 *agventuretours.com* 🎫 *From $105 (day).*

California Pacific Excursions
BUS TOURS | This outfit operates motorcoach tours from San Francisco that include one or two days in Monterey and Carmel. The company's three-day San Francisco–Los Angeles tours include stops in Monterey and Carmel. ☎ *415/228–9865* 🌐 *www.californiaparlorcar.com* 🎫 *From $95 (day) and $300 (overnight).*

Monterey Guided Wine Tours
SPECIAL-INTEREST | The company's guides lead customized wine tours in Monterey, Carmel, and Carmel Valley, along with the Santa Lucia Highlands, the Santa Cruz Mountains, and the Paso Robles area. Tours, which typically last from four to six hours, take place in a town car, a stretch limo, or a party bus. ☎ *831/920–2792* 🌐 *montereyguidedwinetours.com* 🎫 *From $125.*

Visitor Information

CONTACTS Monterey County Convention & Visitors Bureau ☎ *888/221–1010* 🌐 *www.seemonterey.com.* **Monterey Wine Country** ☎ *831/375–9400* 🌐 *www.montereywines.org.* **Santa Cruz Mountains Winegrowers Association** ✉ *335 spreckels Dr., #B, Aptos* ☎ *831/685–8463* 🌐 *www.scmwa.com.* **Visit Santa Cruz County** ✉ *303 Water St., No. 100, Santa Cruz* ☎ *831/425–1234, 800/833–3494* 🌐 *visitsantacruz.org.*

Carmel-by-the-Sea

26 miles north of Big Sur.

Even when its population quadruples with tourists on weekends and in summer, Carmel-by-the-Sea, commonly referred to as Carmel, retains its identity as a quaint village. Self-consciously charming, the town is populated by many celebrities, major and minor, and has its share of quirky ordinances. For instance, women wearing high heels do not have the right to pursue legal action if they trip and fall on the cobblestone streets, and drivers who hit a tree and leave the scene are charged with hit-and-run.

Buildings have no street numbers—street names are written on discreet white posts—and consequently no mail delivery. One way to commune with the locals: head to the post office. Artists started this community, and their legacy is evident in the numerous galleries.

GETTING HERE AND AROUND

From north or south follow Highway 1 to Carmel. Head west at Ocean Avenue to reach the main village hub.

TOURS

Carmel Food Tours

WALKING TOURS | Taste your way through Carmel-by-the-Sea culinary delights on this guided walking tour to restaurants and shops serving small portions of standout offerings, from empanadas and ribs to honey and chocolate. Along the way, the guide shares colorful tales about local culture, history, and architecture. The Classic Tour includes seven tasting stops and lasts three hours. Tickets must be purchased in advance. Tours depart from the Sunset Cultural Center at 9th Avenue and San Carlos Street. ✉ *Sunset Cultural Center, 9th Ave. at San Carlos St., Carmel* ☎ *831/256–3007* 🌐 *www.carmelfoodtour.com* 🎟 *From $94.*

Carmel Walks

WALKING TOURS | For insight into Carmel's history and culture, join one of these guided two-hour ambles through hidden courtyards, gardens, and pathways. Tours depart from the Pine Inn courtyard, on Lincoln Street. Call to reserve a spot. ✉ *Lincoln St. at 6th Ave., Carmel* ☎ *831/223–4399* 🌐 *carmelwalks.com* 🎟 *From $30.*

ESSENTIALS

VISITOR INFORMATION Carmel Chamber of Commerce ✉ *Visitor Center, in Carmel Plaza, Ocean Ave. between Junipero and Mission Sts., Carmel* ☎ *831/624–2522, 800/550–4333* 🌐 *carmelchamber.org.*

Sights

Carmel Mission

RELIGIOUS SITE | Long before it became a shopping and browsing destination, Carmel was an important religious center during the establishment of Spanish California. That heritage is preserved in the Mission San Carlos Borroméo del Rio Carmelo, more commonly known as the Carmel Mission. Founded in 1771, it served as headquarters for the mission system in California under Father Junípero Serra. Adjoining the stone church is a tranquil garden planted with California poppies. Museum rooms at the mission include an early kitchen, Serra's spartan sleeping quarters and burial shrine, and the first college library in California. ✉ *3080 Rio Rd., at Lasuen Dr., Carmel* ☎ *831/624–1271* 🌐 *carmelmission.org* 🎟 *$10.*

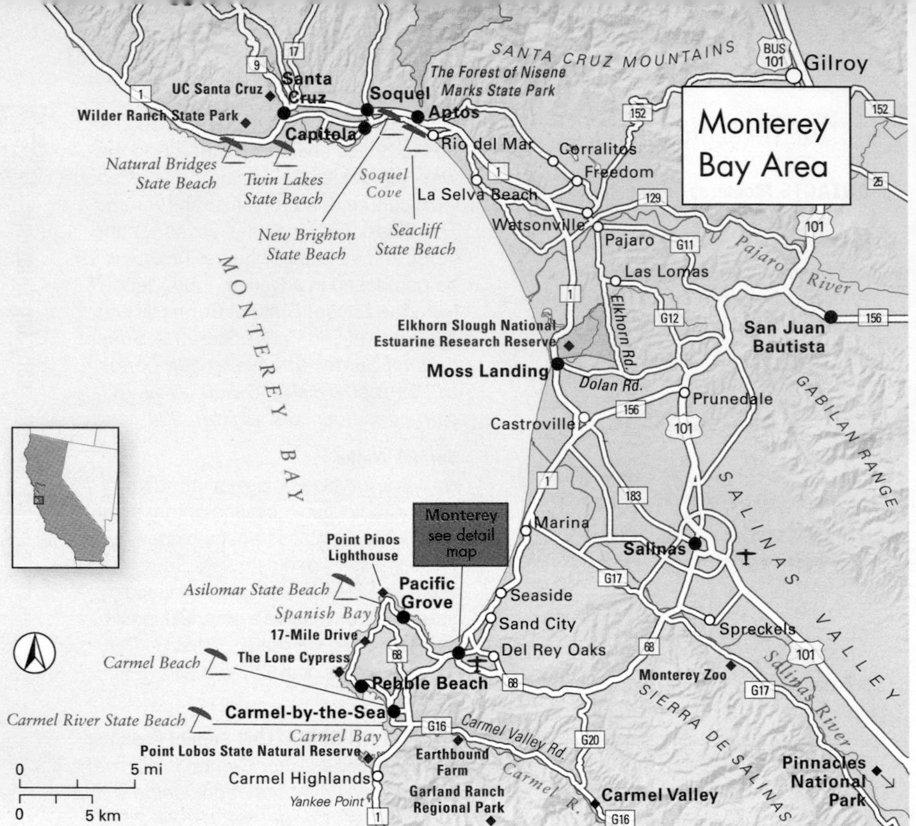

Carmel Wine Walk By-the-Sea

TOUR—SIGHT | If you purchase a Wine Walk Passport, you can park the car and sample local wines at any 10 of 13 tasting rooms, all within a few blocks of each other in downtown Carmel. Individual passports can be used by two or more people at the same tasting room, and they entitle holders to free corkage at some local restaurants. ✉ *Carmel Chamber of Commerce Visitor Center, San Carlos St., between 5th and 6th Aves., Carmel* ☎ *831/624–2522, 800/550–4333* 🌐 *winewalkcarmel.com* 🎫 *$100.*

Dawson Cole Fine Art

MUSEUM | Amazing images of dancers, athletes, and other humans in motion come to life in this gallery that is devoted to the artworks of Monterey Bay resident Richard MacDonald, one of the most famed figurative sculptors of our time. ✉ *Lincoln St., at 6th Ave., Carmel* ☎ *800/972–5528* 🌐 *dawsoncolefineart.com* 🎫 *Free.*

★ Ocean Avenue

NEIGHBORHOOD | Downtown Carmel's chief lure is shopping, especially along its main street, Ocean Avenue, between Junipero Avenue and Camino Real. The architecture here is a mishmash of ersatz Tudor, Mediterranean, and other styles. ✉ *Carmel.*

★ Point Lobos State Natural Reserve

NATIONAL/STATE PARK | A 350-acre headland harboring a wealth of marine life, the reserve lies a few miles south of Carmel. The best way to explore here is to walk along one of the many trails. The Cypress Grove Trail leads through a forest of Monterey cypress (one of only two natural groves remaining) that clings to the rocks above an emerald-green cove.

Sea Lion Point Trail is a good place to view sea lions. From those and other trails, you might also spot otters, harbor seals, and (in winter and spring) migrating whales. An additional 750 acres of the reserve is an undersea marine park open to qualified scuba divers. No pets are allowed. **■ TIP→ Arrive early (or in late afternoon) to avoid crowds; the parking lots fill up.** ✉ *Hwy. 1, Carmel* ☎ *831/624–4909, 831/624–8413 water sports reservations* 🌐 *www.pointlobos.org* 🎫 *$10 per vehicle.*

Tor House

HOUSE | Scattered throughout the pines of Carmel-by-the-Sea are houses and cottages originally built for the writers, artists, and photographers who discovered the area decades ago. Among the most impressive dwellings is Tor House, a stone cottage built in 1919 by poet Robinson Jeffers on a craggy knoll overlooking the sea. Portraits, books, and unusual art objects fill the low-ceilinged rooms. The highlight of the small estate is Hawk Tower, a detached edifice set with stones from the Carmel coastline—as well as one from the Great Wall of China. The docents who lead tours (six people maximum) are well informed about the poet's work and life. Reservations are required. Call the reservation line or click on the reservation link on the website. ✉ *26304 Ocean View Ave., Carmel* ☎ *831/624–1813 direct docent office line, Fri. and Sat. only* 🌐 *www.torhouse.org* 🎫 *$12* ☞ *No children under 12.*

Beaches

Carmel Beach

BEACH—SIGHT | Carmel-by-the-Sea's greatest attraction is its rugged coastline, with pine and cypress forests and countless inlets. Carmel Beach, an easy walk from downtown shops, has sparkling white sands and magnificent sunsets. **■ TIP→ Dogs are allowed to romp off-leash here.** **Amenities:** parking (no fee); toilets. **Best for:** sunset; surfing; walking. ✉ *End of Ocean Ave., Carmel.*

Carmel River State Beach

NATURE PRESERVE | This sugar-white beach, stretching 106 acres along Carmel Bay, is adjacent to a bird sanctuary, where you might spot pelicans, kingfishers, hawks, and sandpipers. Dogs are allowed on leash. **Amenities:** parking (no fee); toilets. **Best for:** sunrise; sunset; walking. ✉ *Off Scenic Rd., south of Carmel Beach, Carmel* ☎ *831/649–2836* 🌐 *www.parks.ca.gov* 🎫 *Free.*

Restaurants

Anton and Michel

$$$$ | **AMERICAN** | Carefully prepared California cuisine is the draw at this airy restaurant. The rack of lamb is carved at the table, the grilled halloumi cheese and tomatoes are meticulously stacked and served with basil and Kalamata olive tapenade, and the desserts are set aflame before your eyes. **Known for:** romantic courtyard with fountain; elegant interior with fireplace lounge; flambé desserts. 💲 *Average main: $32* ✉ *Mission St. and 7th Ave., Carmel* ☎ *831/624–2406* 🌐 *antonandmichel.com.*

★ Aubergine

$$$$ | **AMERICAN** | To eat and sleep at luxe L'Auberge Carmel is an experience in itself, but even those staying elsewhere can splurge at the inn's intimate restaurant. Chef Justin Cogley's nine-course prix-fixe tasting menu (your only option at dinner, $185 per person) is a gastronomical experience unrivaled in the region. **Known for:** exceptional chef's choice tasting menu; expert wine pairings; intimate nine-table dining room. 💲 *Average main: $185* ✉ *Monte Verde at 7th Ave., Carmel* ☎ *831/624–8578* 🌐 *auberginecarmel.com* 🕑 *No lunch.*

★ Basil

$$$ | **MODERN AMERICAN** | Eco-friendly Basil was Monterey County's first restaurant to achieve a green dining certification, recognition of chef-owner Soerke Peters's commitment to using organic,

Point Lobos State Natural Reserve offers stunning vistas of sea and sky.

sustainably cultivated ingredients in his cuisine. Peters grows many of his own herbs, which find their way into creative dishes such as black squid linguine with sea urchin sauce, charred octopus, and smoked venison and other house-made charcuterie. **Known for:** organic ingredients; creative cocktails; year-round patio dining. *Average main: $25 Paseo Square, San Carlos St., between Ocean Ave. and 7th Ave., Carmel 831/626–8226 basilcarmel.com.*

Casanova

$$$$ | **MEDITERRANEAN** | This restaurant inspires European-style celebration and romance in an intimate French Country setting and serves authentic dishes from southern France and northern Italy—think beef tartare and veal sweetbreads. Private dining and a special tasting menu are offered at Van Gogh's Table, a relic from France's Auberge Ravoux, the artist's final residence. **Known for:** house-made pastas and gnocchi; private dining at antique Van Gogh's table; romantic candlelight dining room and outdoor patio. *Average main: $32 5th Ave., between San Carlos and Mission Sts., Carmel 831/625–0501 www.casanovarestaurant.com.*

The Cottage Restaurant

$ | **AMERICAN** | This family-friendly spot serves sandwiches, pizzas, and homemade soups at lunch, but the best meal is breakfast (good thing it's served all day). The menu offers six variations on eggs Benedict, and all kinds of sweet and savory crepes. **Known for:** artichoke soup; eggs Benedict and crepes; daily specials. *Average main: $15 Lincoln St. between Ocean and 7th Aves., Carmel 831/625–6260 cottagerestaurant.com No dinner.*

Flying Fish Grill

$$$ | **SEAFOOD** | Simple in appearance yet bold with its flavors, this Japanese–California seafood restaurant is one of Carmel's most inventive eateries. The warm, wood-lined dining room is broken up into very private booths. **Known for:** almond-crusted sea bass served with Chinese cabbage and rock shrimp stir-fry;

clay pot dinners for two cooked at the table; authentic Asian decor. *Average main: $30 ✉ Carmel Plaza, Mission St. between Ocean and 7th Aves., Carmel ☎ 831/625–1962 ⊕ flyingfishgrill.com ⊙ No lunch.*

Grasing's Coastal Cuisine

$$$$ | **AMERICAN** | Chef Kurt Grasing draws from fresh Carmel Coast and Central Valley ingredients to whip up contemporary adaptations of European-provincial and American cooking. Longtime menu favorites include artichoke lasagna in a roasted tomato sauce, duck with fresh cherries in a red wine sauce, a savory paella, and grilled steaks and chops. **Known for:** artichoke heart lasagna; grilled steaks; bar, patio lounge, and rooftop deck. *Average main: $39 ✉ 6th Ave. and Mission St., Carmel ☎ 831/624–6562 ⊕ grasings.com.*

L'Escargot

$$$$ | **FRENCH** | Chef-owner Kericos Loutas personally sees to each plate of food served at this romantic, unpretentious French restaurant. Order the pan-roasted duck breast or the veal medallions with wild mushrooms or white wine sauce; or, if you can't decide, choose the three-course prix-fixe dinner. **Known for:** authentic French Country dishes; prix-fixe dinner option; locally sourced ingredients. *Average main: $35 ✉ Mission and 4th Ave., Carmel ☎ 831/620–1942 ⊕ escargot-carmel.com ⊙ No lunch.*

Lugano Swiss Bistro

$$$ | **SWISS** | Fondue is the centerpiece here—the house specialty is a version made with Gruyère, Emmentaler, and Appenzeller. Rotisserie-broiled meats are also popular, and include rosemary chicken, plum-basted duck, and fennel pork loin. **Known for:** schnitzel, fondue, and other Swiss specialties; alpine-style heated patio; back room with a hand-painted street scene of Lugano. *Average main: $29 ✉ Barnyard Shopping Center, Hwy. 1 and Carmel Valley Rd., Carmel ☎ 831/626–3779 ⊕ www.swissbistro.com ⊙ Closed Mon.*

Tuck Box

$ | **AMERICAN** | This bright little restaurant is in a cottage right out of a fairy tale, complete with stone fireplace. Handmade scones, good for breakfast or afternoon tea, are the specialty. **Known for:** traditional English afternoon tea; fairy-tale atmosphere; handmade scones. *Average main: $14 ✉ Dolores St., between Ocean and 7th Aves., Carmel ☎ 831/624–6365 ⊕ tuckbox.com ▭ No credit cards ⊙ No dinner.*

Vesuvio

$$$ | **ITALIAN** | Chef and restaurateur Rich Pèpe heats up the night with this lively trattoria downstairs and swinging rooftop terrace, the Starlight Lounge 65°. Pèpe's elegant take on traditional Italian cuisine yields dishes such as wild-boar Bolognese pappardelle, lobster ravioli, and velvety limoncello mousse cake. **Known for:** traditional cuisine of Campania, Italy; two bars with pizzas and small plates; live music on rooftop terrace in summer. *Average main: $30 ✉ 6th and Junipero Aves., Carmel ☎ 831/625–1766 ⊕ vesuviocarmel.com ⊙ No lunch.*

Hotels

Cypress Inn

$$$$ | **B&B/INN** | This luxurious inn has a fresh Mediterranean ambience with Moroccan touches. **Pros:** luxury without snobbery; popular lounge and restaurant; British-style afternoon tea on Saturdays. **Cons:** not for the pet-phobic; some rooms and baths are tiny; basic amenities. *Rooms from: $279 ✉ Lincoln St. and 7th Ave., Carmel ☎ 831/624–3871, 800/443–7443 ⊕ cypress-inn.com ⇨ 44 rooms 🍽 Breakfast.*

The Hideaway

$$$$ | **HOTEL** | On a quiet street with a residential vibe, The Hideaway is a peaceful haven for those seeking stylish comfort in the heart of town. **Pros:** easy walk to

shops, restaurants, galleries; short walk to Carmel Beach; pet-friendly amenities. **Cons:** street parking only; no pool or hot tub; some rooms are tiny. *Rooms from: $295 Junipero St. at 8th Ave., Carmel 831/625–5222 hideawaycarmel.com 24 rooms Breakfast.*

Hyatt Carmel Highlands
$$$$ | **HOTEL** | High on a hill overlooking the Pacific, this place has superb views; accommodations include king rooms with fireplaces, suites with personal Jacuzzis, and full town houses with many perks. **Pros:** killer views; romantic getaway; great food. **Cons:** thin walls; must drive to the center of town; some rooms and buildings need update. *Rooms from: $399 120 Highlands Dr., Carmel 831/620–1234, 800/233–1234 www.hyatt.com 48 rooms.*

★ L'Auberge Carmel
$$$$ | **B&B/INN** | Stepping through the doors of this elegant inn is like being transported to a little European village. **Pros:** in town but off the main drag; four blocks from the beach; full-service luxury. **Cons:** touristy area; not a good choice for families; no air-conditioning. *Rooms from: $465 Monte Verde at 7th Ave., Carmel 831/624–8578 www.laubergecarmel.com 20 rooms Breakfast.*

La Playa Carmel
$$$$ | **HOTEL** | A historic complex of lush gardens and Mediterranean-style buildings, La Playa has light and airy interiors done in Carmel Bay beach-cottage style. **Pros:** residential neighborhood; manicured gardens; two blocks from the beach. **Cons:** four stories (no elevator); busy lobby; some rooms are on the small side. *Rooms from: $449 Camino Real at 8th Ave., Carmel 831/293–6100, 800/582–8900 laplayahotel.com 75 rooms Breakfast.*

Mission Ranch
$$ | **HOTEL** | Movie star Clint Eastwood owns this sprawling property whose accommodations include rooms in a converted barn, and several cottages, some with fireplaces. **Pros:** farm setting; pastoral views; great for tennis buffs. **Cons:** busy parking lot; must drive to the heart of town; old buildings. *Rooms from: $175 26270 Dolores St., Carmel 831/624–6436, 800/538–8221, 831/625–9040 restaurant www.missionranchcarmel.com 31 rooms Breakfast.*

Pine Inn
$$$ | **HOTEL** | A favorite with generations of visitors, the Pine Inn is four blocks from the beach and has Victorian-style furnishings, complete with grandfather clock, padded fabric wall panels, antique tapestries, and marble tabletops. **Pros:** elegant; close to shopping and dining; full breakfast included weekdays. **Cons:** on the town's busiest street; public areas a bit dark; limited parking. *Rooms from: $189 Ocean Ave. and Monte Verde St., Carmel 831/624–3851, 800/228–3851 pineinn.com 49 rooms Breakfast.*

Tally Ho Inn
$$$ | **B&B/INN** | This inn is nearly all suites, many of which have fireplaces and floor-to-ceiling glass walls that open onto ocean-view patios. **Pros:** within walking distance of shops, restaurants, beach; free parking; spacious rooms. **Cons:** small property; busy area; basic breakfast. *Rooms from: $229 Monte Verde St. and 6th Ave., Carmel 831/624–2232, 800/652–2632 tallyho-inn.com 12 rooms Breakfast.*

Tickle Pink Inn
$$$$ | **B&B/INN** | Atop a towering cliff, this inn has views of the Big Sur coastline, which you can contemplate from your private balcony. **Pros:** close to great hiking; intimate; dramatic views. **Cons:** close to a big hotel; lots of traffic during the day; basic breakfast. *Rooms from: $329 155 Highland Dr., Carmel 831/624–1244, 800/635–4774 ticklepink.com 33 rooms, 1 cottage Breakfast.*

Tradewinds Carmel

$$$ | B&B/INN | This converted motel with sleek decor inspired by the South Seas encircles a courtyard with waterfalls, a meditation garden, and a fire pit. **Pros:** serene; within walking distance of restaurants; friendly service. **Cons:** no pool; long walk to the beach; thin walls. *Rooms from: $250 Mission St. at 3rd Ave., Carmel 831/624–2776 tradewindscarmel.com 28 rooms Breakfast.*

Nightlife

BARS AND PUBS

Barmel

BARS/PUBS | Al Capone and other Prohibition-era legends once sidled up to this hip nightspot's carved wooden bar. Rock to DJ music and sit indoors, or head out to the pet-friendly patio. Some menu items pay homage to California's early days, and you can order Baja-style dishes from the adjacent Pescadero restaurant, which is under the same ownership. *San Carlos St., between Ocean and 7th Aves., Carmel 831/626–2095.*

Mulligan Public House

BARS/PUBS | A sports bar with seven TV screens, 12 beers on tap, and extensive menu packed with hearty American pub food, Mulligan usually stays open until midnight. *5 Dolores St., at Ocean 831/250–5910 mulliganspublichouse.com.*

Shopping

ART GALLERIES

Carmel Art Association

ART GALLERIES | Carmel's oldest gallery, established in 1927, exhibits original paintings and sculptures by local artists. *Dolores St., between 5th and 6th Aves., Carmel 831/624–6176 carmel-art.org.*

Galerie Plein Aire

ART GALLERIES | The gallery showcases the oil paintings of a group of local artists. *Dolores St., between Ocean and 6th Aves., Carmel 831/250–5698, 831/277–6165 after hrs galeriepleinaire.com Closed Tues.*

Gallery Sur

ART GALLERIES | Fine art photography of the Big Sur Coast and the Monterey Peninsula, including scenic shots and golf images, is the focus here. *6th Ave., between Dolores and Lincoln Sts., Carmel 831/626–2615 gallerysur.com.*

★ **Weston Gallery**

ART GALLERIES | Run by the family of the late Edward Weston, this is hands down the best photography gallery around, with contemporary color photography and classic black-and-whites. *6th Ave., between Dolores and Lincoln Sts., Carmel 831/624–4453 westongallery.com Closed Mon.*

MALLS

Carmel Plaza

SHOPPING CENTERS/MALLS | Tiffany & Co. and J. Crew are among the name brands doing business at this mall on Carmel's east side, but what makes it worth a stop are homegrown enterprises such as Carmel Honey Company,for local honey harvested and packaged by a high school student and his family; Madrigal for women's fashion; and J. Lawrence Khaki's for debonair menswear. Flying Fish Grill and several other restaurants are here, along with the Wrath Wines tasting room (Chardonnay and Pinot Noir). The Carmel Chamber of Commerce Visitor Center (open daily) is on the second floor. *Ocean Ave. and Mission St., Carmel 831/624–1385 carmelplaza.com.*

SPECIALTY SHOPS

Bittner

SPECIALTY STORES | The shop carries collectible and vintage pens from around the world. *Ocean Ave., between*

Mission and San Carlos Sts., Carmel ☎ 831/626–8828 🌐 bittner.com.

elizabethW

GIFTS/SOUVENIRS | Named after the designer and owner's pioneering great-grandmother, elizabethW handcrafts fragrances, essential oils, candles, silk eye pillows, and other soul-soothing goods for bath, body, and home. ✉ *Ocean Ave., between Monte Verde and Lincoln, Carmel* ☎ *831/626–3892* 🌐 *elizabethw.com.*

Foxy Couture

CLOTHING | Shop for one-of-a-kind treasures at this curated collection of gently used luxury couture and vintage clothes and accessories—think Chanel, Hermes, and Gucci—without paying a hefty price tag. ✉ *San Carlos St., in Vanervort Court, between Ocean and 7th Aves., Carmel* ☎ *831/625–9995* 🌐 *foxycouturecarmel.com.*

Intima

SPECIALTY STORES | The European lingerie ranges from lacy to racy. ✉ *San Carlos St., between Ocean and 6th Aves., Carmel* ☎ *831/625–0599* 🌐 *www.intimacarmel.com.*

Jan de Luz

SPECIALTY STORES | This shop monograms and embroiders fine linens (including bathrobes) while you wait. ✉ *Dolores St., between Ocean and 7th Aves., Carmel* ☎ *831/622–7621* 🌐 *jandeluzlinens.com.*

Carmel Valley

10 miles east of Carmel.

Carmel Valley Road, which heads inland from Highway 1 south of Carmel, is the main thoroughfare through this valley, a secluded enclave of horse ranchers and other well-heeled residents who prefer the area's sunny climate to coastal fog and wind. Once thick with dairy farms, the valley has evolved into an esteemed wine appellation. Carmel Valley Village has crafts shops, art galleries, and the tasting rooms of numerous local wineries.

GETTING HERE AND AROUND

From U.S. 101 north or south, exit at Highway 68 and head west toward the coast. Scenic, two-lane Laureles Grade winds west over the mountains to Carmel Valley Road north of the village.

TOURS

Carmel Valley Grapevine Express

BUS TOURS | An incredible bargain, the express—aka MST's Bus 24—travels between downtown Monterey and Carmel Valley Village, with stops near wineries, restaurants, and shopping centers. ☎ *888/678–2871* 🌐 *mst.org* 🎟 *$10 all-day pass.*

Sights

Bernardus Tasting Room

WINERY/DISTILLERY | At the tasting room of Bernardus, known for its Bordeaux-style red blend, called Marinus, and Chardonnays, you can sample current releases and library and reserve wines. ✉ *5 W. Carmel Valley Rd., at El Caminito Rd.* ☎ *831/298–8021, 800/223–2533* 🌐 *bernardus.com* 🎟 *Tastings from $12.*

Cowgirl Winery

WINERY/DISTILLERY | Cowgirl chic prevails in the main tasting building here, and it's just plain rustic at the outdoor tables, set amid chickens, a tractor, and a flatbed truck. The wines include Chardonnay, Cabernet Sauvignon, Malbec, Pinot Noir, Rosé, and some blends. You can order a wood-fired pizza from sister business Corkscrew Café, and play boccie ball, horseshoes, or corn hole until your food arrives. ✉ *25 Pilot Rd., off W. Carmel Valley Rd.* ☎ *831/298–7030* 🌐 *cowgirlwinery.com* 🎟 *Tastings from $15.*

Earthbound Farm

FARM/RANCH | **FAMILY** | Pick up fresh vegetables, ready-to-eat meals, gourmet groceries, flowers, and gifts at Earthbound

Farm, the world's largest grower of organic produce. You can also take a romp in the kids' garden, cut your own herbs, and stroll through the chamomile aromatherapy labyrinth. Special events, on Saturday from April through December, include bug walks and garlic-braiding workshops. ✉ *7250 Carmel Valley Rd., Carmel* ☎ *831/625–6219* 🌐 *www.ebfarm.com* 🎟 *Free.*

★ Folktale Winery & Vineyards

WINERY/DISTILLERY | The expansive winery on a 15-acre estate (formerly Chateau Julienne) offers daily tastings, live music on weekends (plus Friday in summer and fall), and special events and programs such as Saturday yoga in the vineyard. Best-known wines include the estate Pinot Noir, Sparkling Rosé, and Le Mistral Joseph's Blend. Chefs in the on-site restaurant cook up small plates with wine pairing suggestions. Tours of the winery and organically farmed vineyards are available by appointment. ✉ *8940 Carmel Valley Rd.* ✣ *At Schetter Rd.* ☎ *831/293–7500* 🌐 *folktalewinery.com* 🎟 *Tastings from $20; tours $40 (includes tasting).*

Garland Ranch Regional Park

NATIONAL/STATE PARK | Hiking trails stretch across much of this park's 4,500 acres of meadows, forested hillsides, and creeks. ✉ *700 W. Carmel Valley Rd., 9 miles east of Carmel-by-the-Sea* ☎ *831/372–3196* 🌐 *www.mprpd.org.*

Restaurants

Café Rustica

$$$ | EUROPEAN | European country cooking is the focus at this lively roadhouse, where specialties include roasted meats, seafood, pastas, and thin-crust pizzas from the wood-fired oven. It can get noisy inside; for a quieter meal, request a table outside. **Known for:** Tuscan-flavored dishes from Alsace; open kitchen with wood-fired oven; outdoor patio seating. Ⓢ *Average main: $25* ✉ *10 Delfino Pl., at Pilot Rd., off Carmel Valley Rd.* ☎ *831/659–4444* 🌐 *caferusticavillage.com* ⏲ *Closed Mon.*

Corkscrew Café

$$$ | MODERN AMERICAN | Farm-fresh food is the specialty of this casual, Old Monterey–style bistro. Herbs and seasonal produce come from the Corkscrew's own organic gardens; the catch of the day comes from local waters; and the meats are hormone-free. **Known for:** wood-fired pizzas; fish tacos and chicken salad; garden patio. Ⓢ *Average main: $24* ✉ *55 W. Carmel Valley Rd., at Pilot Rd.* ☎ *831/659–8888* 🌐 *corkscrewcafe.com* ⏲ *Closed Jan. Closed Tues. and Wed.*

Wagon Wheel Coffee Shop

$ | AMERICAN | This local hangout decorated with wagon wheels, cowboy hats, and lassos serves terrific hearty breakfasts, including oatmeal and banana pancakes, eggs Benedict, and biscuits and gravy. The lunch menu includes a dozen different burgers and other sandwiches. **Known for:** traditional American breakfast; cowboy-theme setting; lively local clientele. Ⓢ *Average main: $15* ✉ *Valley Hill Center, 7156 Carmel Valley Rd., next to Quail Lodge, Carmel* ☎ *831/624–8878* ▭ *No credit cards* ⏲ *No dinner.*

Hotels

★ Bernardus Lodge & Spa

$$$$ | RESORT | The spacious guest rooms at this luxury spa resort have vaulted ceilings, French oak floors, featherbeds, fireplaces, patios, and bathrooms with heated-tile floors and soaking tubs for two. **Pros:** exceptional personal service; outstanding food and wine; huge suites. **Cons:** hefty rates; some guests can seem snooty; resort fee. Ⓢ *Rooms from: $475* ✉ *415 W. Carmel Valley Rd.* ☎ *831/658–3400* 🌐 *bernarduslodge.com* 🛏 *73 rooms and villas.*

★ Carmel Valley Ranch

$$$$ | RESORT | The activity options at this luxury ranch are so varied that the resort provides a program director to guide you through them. **Pros:** stunning natural setting; tons of activities; River Ranch center with a pool, splash zone, boccie courts, and fitness center. **Cons:** must drive several miles to shops and nightlife; high rates. *$ Rooms from: $400 ✉ 1 Old Ranch Rd., Carmel ☎ 831/625–9500, 855/687–7262 toll-free reservations 🌐 carmelvalleyranch.com 181 suites 🍽 No meals.*

Quail Lodge & Golf Club

$$$ | HOTEL | FAMILY | A sprawling collection of ranch-style buildings on 850 acres of meadows, fairways, and lakes, Quail Lodge offers luxury rooms and outdoor activities at surprisingly affordable rates. **Pros:** on the golf course; on-site restaurant; spacious rooms. **Cons:** service sometimes spotty; 5 miles from the beach and Carmel Valley Village; basic amenities. *$ Rooms from: $225 ✉ 8205 Valley Greens Dr., Carmel ☎ 866/675–1101 reservations, 831/624–2888 🌐 www.quaillodge.com 93 rooms 🍽 No meals.*

★ Stonepine Estate

$$$$ | RESORT | Set on 330 pastoral acres, the former estate of the Crocker banking family has been converted to a luxurious inn. **Pros:** supremely exclusive; close to Carmel Valley Village; attentive, personalized service. **Cons:** difficult to get a reservation; far from the coast; expensive rates. *$ Rooms from: $500 ✉ 150 E. Carmel Valley Rd. ☎ 831/659–2245 🌐 www.stonepineestate.com 12 rooms, 3 cottages.*

Activities

GOLF

Quail Lodge & Golf Club

GOLF | Robert Muir Graves designed this championship semiprivate 18-hole course next to Quail Lodge that provides challenging play for golfers of all skill levels. The scenic course, which incorporates five lakes and edges the Carmel River, was completely renovated in 2015 by golf architect Todd Eckenrode to add extra challenge to the golf experience, white sand bunkers, and other enhancements. For the most part flat, the walkable course is well maintained, with stunning views, lush fairways, and ultrasmooth greens. *✉ 8000 Valley Greens Dr., Carmel ☎ 831/620–8808 golf shop, 831/620–8866 club concierge 🌐 www.quaillodge.com $185 18 holes, 6500 yards, par 71.*

Shopping

★ Refuge

SPA/BEAUTY | At this co-ed, European-style center on 2 serene acres you can recharge without breaking the bank. Heat up in the eucalyptus steam room or cedar sauna, plunge into cold pools, and relax indoors in zero-gravity chairs or outdoors in Adirondack chairs around fire pits. Repeat the cycle a few times, then lounge around the thermal waterfall pools. Talk is not allowed, and bathing suits are required. *✉ 27300 Rancho San Carlos Rd., south off Carmel Valley Rd., Carmel ☎ 831/620–7360 🌐 refuge.com $44 ☞ $52 admission; $125 50-min massage (includes Refuge admission), $12 robe rental, hot tubs (outdoor), sauna, steam room. Services: aromatherapy, hydrotherapy, massage.*

Pebble Beach

Off North San Antonio Ave. in Carmel-by-the-Sea or off Sunset Dr. in Pacific Grove.

In 1919 the Pacific Improvement Company acquired 18,000 acres of prime land on the Monterey Peninsula, including the entire Pebble Beach coastal region and much of Pacific Grove. Pebble Beach Golf Links and The Lodge at Pebble Beach opened the same year, and the private enclave evolved into a world-class golf destination with three posh lodges, five golf courses, hiking and riding trails, and some of the West Coast's ritziest homes. Pebble Beach has hosted major international golf tournaments, including the U.S. Open in 2019. The annual Pebble Beach Food & Wine, a four-day event in late April with 100 celebrity chefs, is one of the West Coast's premier culinary festivals.

GETTING HERE AND AROUND

If you drive south from Monterey on Highway 1, exit at 17-Mile Drive/Sunset Drive in Pacific Grove to find the northern entrance gate. Coming from Carmel, exit at Ocean Avenue and follow the road almost to the beach; turn right on North San Antonio Avenue to the Carmel Gate. You can also enter through the Highway 1 Gate off Highway 68. Monterey–Salinas Transit buses provide regular service in and around Pebble Beach.

Sights

★ The Lone Cypress

FOREST | The most-photographed tree along 17-Mile Drive is the weather-sculpted Lone Cypress, which grows out of a precipitous outcropping above the waves about 1½ miles up the road from Pebble Beach Golf Links. You can't walk out to the tree, but you can stop for a view of it at a small parking area off the road.

★ 17-Mile Drive

SCENIC DRIVE | Primordial nature resides in quiet harmony with palatial, mostly Spanish Mission–style estates along 17-Mile Drive, which winds through an 8,400-acre microcosm of the Pebble Beach coastal landscape. Dotting the drive are rare Monterey cypresses, trees so gnarled and twisted that Robert Louis Stevenson described them as "ghosts fleeing before the wind." The most famous of these is the **Lone Cypress**. Other highlights include **Bird Rock** and **Seal Rock,** home to harbor seals, sea lions, cormorants, and pelicans and other sea creatures and birds, and the **Crocker Marble Palace,** inspired by a Byzantine castle and easily identifiable by its dozens of marble arches.

Enter 17-Mile Drive at the Highway 1 Gate, at Highway 68; the Carmel Gate, off North San Antonio Avenue; the Pacific Grove Gate, off Sunset Drive; S.F.B. Morse Gate, Morse Drive off Highway 68; and Country Club Gate, at Congress Avenue and Forest Lodge Road. ■ **TIP→ If you spend $35 or more on dining in Pebble Beach and show a receipt upon exiting, you'll receive a refund off the drive's $10.25 per car fee.** ✉ *Hwy. 1 Gate, 17-Mile Dr., west of Hwy. 1 and Hwy. 68 intersection* 🎟 *$11 per car, free for bicyclists.*

Hotels

★ Casa Palmero

$$$$ | **RESORT** | This exclusive boutique hotel evokes a stately Mediterranean villa. **Pros:** ultimate in pampering; sumptuous decor; more private than sister resorts. **Cons:** rates out of reach for most visitors; not the best views compared to sister lodges *too* posh for some; some showers on the small side. *$ Rooms from: $1100* ✉ *1518 Cypress Dr.* ☎ *831/622–6650, 800/877–0597 reservations* 🌐 *www.pebblebeach.com* *24 rooms* 🍴 *Breakfast.*

The Inn at Spanish Bay

$$$$ | **RESORT** | This resort sprawls across a breathtaking stretch of shoreline, and has lush, 600-square-foot rooms. **Pros:** attentive service; many amenities; spectacular views. **Cons:** huge hotel; 4 miles from other Pebble Beach Resorts facilities; atmosphere too snobbish for some. *$ Rooms from: $820* ✉ *2700 17-Mile Dr.* ☎ *831/647–7500, 800/877–0597* 🌐 *www.pebblebeach.com* *269 rooms.*

The Lodge at Pebble Beach

$$$$ | **RESORT** | Most rooms have wood-burning fireplaces and many have wonderful ocean views at this circa-1919 resort, which expanded to include Fairway One, an additional 38-room complex, in 2017. **Pros:** world-class golf; borders the

Did You Know?

The Lone Cypress has stood on this rock for more than 250 years. The tree is the official symbol of the Pebble Beach Company.

ocean and fairways; fabulous facilities. **Cons:** some rooms are on the small side; very pricey; not many activities if you don't golf. *Rooms from: $940* *1700 17-Mile Dr.* *831/624–3811, 800/877–0597* *www.pebblebeach.com* *199 rooms* *No meals.*

Activities

GOLF

Links at Spanish Bay

GOLF | This course, which hugs a choice stretch of shoreline, was designed by Robert Trent Jones Jr., Tom Watson, and Sandy Tatum in the rugged manner of traditional Scottish links, with sand dunes and coastal marshes interspersed among the greens. A bagpiper signals the course's closing each day. **TIP→ Nonguests of the Pebble Beach Resorts can reserve tee times up to two months in advance.** *17-Mile Dr., north end* *800/877–0597* *www.pebblebeach.com* *$290* *18 holes, 6821 yards, par 72.*

★ Pebble Beach Golf Links

GOLF | Each February, show-business celebrities and golf pros team up at this course, the main site of the glamorous AT&T Pebble Beach National Pro-Am tournament. On most days the rest of the year, tee times are available to guests of the Pebble Beach Resorts who book a minimum two-night stay. Nonguests can reserve a tee time only one day in advance on a space-available basis; resort guests can reserve up to 18 months in advance. *17-Mile Dr., near The Lodge at Pebble Beach* *800/877–0597* *www.pebblebeach.com* *$550* *18 holes, 6828 yards, par 72.*

Peter Hay

GOLF | The only 9-hole, par-3 course on the Monterey Peninsula open to the public, Peter Hay attracts golfers of all skill levels. It's an ideal place for warm-ups, practicing short games, and for those who don't have time to play 18 holes. *17-Mile Dr. and Portola Rd.* *800/877–0597* *www.pebblebeach.com* *$30* *9 holes, 725 yards, par 27.*

Poppy Hills

GOLF | An 18-hole course designed in 1986 by Robert Trent Jones Jr., Poppy Hills reopened in 2014 after a yearlong renovation that Jones supervised. Each hole has been restored to its natural elevation along the forest floor, and all 18 greens have been rebuilt with bent grass. Individuals may reserve up to a month in advance. **TIP→ Poppy Hills, owned by a golfing nonprofit, represents good value for this area.** *3200 Lopez Rd., at 17-Mile Dr.* *831/250–1819* *poppyhillsgolf.com* *$250* *18 holes, 7002 yards, par 73.5.*

Spyglass Hill

GOLF | With three holes rated among the toughest on the PGA tour, Spyglass Hill, designed by Robert Trent Jones Sr. and Jr., challenges golfers with its varied terrain but rewards them with glorious views. The first 5 holes border the Pacific, and the other 13 reach deep into the Del Monte Forest. Reservations are essential and may be made up to one month in advance (18 months for resort guests). *Stevenson Dr. and Spyglass Hill Rd.* *800/877–0597* *www.pebblebeach.com* *$395* *18 holes, 6960 yards, par 72.*

Pacific Grove

3 miles north of Carmel-by-the-Sea.

This picturesque town, which began as a summer retreat for church groups more than a century ago, recalls its prim and proper Victorian heritage in its host of tiny board-and-batten cottages and stately mansions. However, long before the church groups flocked here the area received thousands of annual pilgrims—in the form of bright orange-and-black monarch butterflies. They still come, migrating south from Canada and the

Pacific Northwest to take residence in pine and eucalyptus groves from October through March. In Butterfly Town USA, as Pacific Grove is known, the sight of a mass of butterflies hanging from the branches like a long, fluttering veil is unforgettable.

A prime way to enjoy Pacific Grove is to walk or bicycle the 3 miles of city-owned shoreline along Ocean View Boulevard, a cliff-top area landscaped with native plants and dotted with benches meant for sitting and gazing at the sea. You can spot many types of birds here, including the web-footed cormorants that crowd the massive rocks rising out of the surf. Two Victorians of note along Ocean View are the Queen Anne–style Green Gables, at No. 301—erected in 1888, it's now an inn—and the 1909 Pryor House, at No. 429, a massive, shingled, private residence with a leaded- and beveled-glass doorway.

GETTING HERE AND AROUND

Reach Pacific Grove via Highway 68 off Highway 1, just south of Monterey. From Cannery Row in Monterey, head north until the road merges with Ocean Boulevard and follow it along the coast. MST buses travel within Pacific Grove and surrounding towns.

Sights

Lovers Point Park

CITY PARK | FAMILY | The coastal views are gorgeous from this waterfront park whose sheltered beach has a children's pool and a picnic area. The main lawn has a volleyball court and a snack bar. ✉ *Ocean View Blvd. northwest of Forest Ave.* 🌐 *www.cityofpacificgrove.org/living/recreation/parks/lovers-point-park.*

Monarch Grove Sanctuary

NATURE PRESERVE | FAMILY | The sanctuary is a reliable spot for viewing monarch butterflies between November and February. ■ **TIP→ The best time to visit is between noon and 3 pm.** ✉ *250 Ridge Rd., off Lighthouse Ave.* 🌐 *www.pgmuseum.org/monarch-viewing.*

Pacific Grove Museum of Natural History

MUSEUM | The museum, a good source for the latest information about monarch butterflies, has permanent exhibitions about the butterflies, birds of Monterey County, biodiversity, and plants. There's a native plant garden, and a display documents life in Pacific Grove's 19th-century Chinese fishing village. ✉ *165 Forest Ave., at Central Ave.* ☎ *831/648–5716* 🌐 *pgmuseum.org* 🎟 *$9* 🕒 *Closed Mon.*

Point Pinos Lighthouse

LIGHTHOUSE | FAMILY | At this 1855 structure, the West Coast's oldest continuously operating lighthouse, you can learn about the lighting and foghorn operations and wander through a small museum containing U.S. Coast Guard memorabilia. ✉ *Asilomar Ave., between Lighthouse Ave. and Del Monte Blvd.* ☎ *831/648–3176* 🌐 *pointpinoslighthouse.org* 🎟 *$2* 🕒 *Closed Tues. and Wed.*

Beaches

Asilomar State Beach

BEACH—SIGHT | A beautiful coastal area, Asilomar State Beach stretches between Point Pinos and the Del Monte Forest. The 100 acres of dunes, tidal pools, and pocket-size beaches form one of the region's richest areas for marine life—including surfers, who migrate here most winter mornings. Leashed dogs are allowed on the beach. **Amenities:** none. **Best for:** sunrise; sunset; surfing; walking. ✉ *Sunset Dr. and Asilomar Ave.* ☎ *831/646–6440* 🌐 *www.parks.ca.gov.*

Restaurants

Beach House

$$$ | MODERN AMERICAN | Patrons of this bluff-top perch sip classic cocktails, sample California fare, and watch the otters frolic on Lovers Point Beach below. The sunset discounts between 4 and 6 (reservations recommended) are a great value. **Known for:** sweeping bluff-top views; sunset discounts; seafood and organic pastas. *$ Average main: $24 ✉ 620 Ocean View Blvd. ☎ 831/375–2345 🌐 beachhousepg.com ⏲ No lunch.*

★ Fandango

$$$$ | **MEDITERRANEAN** | The menu here is mostly Mediterranean and southern French, with such dishes as osso buco and paella. The decor follows suit: stone walls and country furniture lend the restaurant the earthy feel of a European farmhouse. **Known for:** wood-fire-grilled rack of lamb, seafood, and beef; convivial residential vibe; traditional European flavors. *$ Average main: $34 ✉ 223 17th St., south of Lighthouse Ave. ☎ 831/372–3456 🌐 fandangorestaurant.com.*

Fishwife

$$ | **SEAFOOD** | Fresh fish with a Latin accent makes this a favorite of locals for lunch or a casual dinner. Standards are the sea garden salads topped with your choice of fish and the fried seafood plates. **Known for:** fisherman's bowls with fresh local seafood; house-made desserts; crab cakes and New Zealand mussels. *$ Average main: $22 ✉ 1996½ Sunset Dr., at Asilomar Blvd. ☎ 831/375–7107 🌐 fishwife.com.*

Jennini Kitchen + Wine Bar

$$$ | **MEDITERRANEAN** | Sommelier Thamin Saleh named his lively restaurant and wine bar after his hometown in Palestine, and designed a menu that showcases his favorite dishes from the region, especially southern Spain and the eastern Mediterranean and the islands. The menu (small plates and entrées) changes seasonally, but usually includes faves like chicken and merguez tagine, crispy lamb shanks, hummus and baba ghanoush, and filone bread with goat butter. **Known for:** daily happy hour 4 to 6; eclectic, value-driven wine list with 180 selections; creative twists on classic dishes. *$ Average main: $25 ✉ 542 Lighthouse Ave. ☎ 831/920–2662 🌐 www.jeninni.com ⏲ Closed Wed. No lunch.*

La Mia Cucina

$$$ | **ITALIAN** | Pasta, fish, steaks, and veal dishes are the specialties at this modern trattoria, the best in town for Italian food. The look is spare and clean, with colorful antique wine posters decorating the white walls. **Known for:** house-made gnocchi, ravioli, and sausage; festive dining room; menu centers around Italian family recipes. *$ Average main: $27 ✉ 208 17th St., at Lighthouse Ave. ☎ 831/373–2416 🌐 lamiacucinaristorante.com ⏲ Closed Mon. and Tues. No lunch.*

★ Passionfish

$$$ | **MODERN AMERICAN** | South American artwork and artifacts decorate Passionfish, and Latin and Asian flavors infuse the dishes. The chef shops at local farmers' markets several times a week to find the best produce, fish, and meat available, then pairs it with creative sauces like a caper, raisin, and walnut relish. **Known for:** sustainably sourced seafood and organic ingredients; reasonably priced wine list that supports small producers; slow-cooked meats. *$ Average main: $26 ✉ 701 Lighthouse Ave., at Congress Ave. ☎ 831/655–3311 🌐 passionfish.net ⏲ No lunch.*

Peppers Mexicali Cafe

$$ | **MEXICAN** | This cheerful white-walled storefront serves traditional dishes from Mexico and Latin America, with an emphasis on fresh seafood. Excellent red and green salsas are made throughout the day, and there's a large selection of beers, along with fresh lime margaritas. **Known for:** traditional Latin American dishes; fresh lime margaritas; daily specials. *$ Average main: $18 ✉ 170 Forest Ave., between Lighthouse and Central Aves. ☎ 831/373–6892 🌐 peppersmexicalicafe.com ⏲ Closed Tues. No lunch Sun.*

Red House Café

$$ | **AMERICAN** | When it's nice out, sun pours through the big windows of this

cozy restaurant and across tables on the porch; when fog rolls in, the fireplace is lit. The American menu changes with the seasons but grilled lamb chops atop mashed potatoes are often on offer for dinner, and a grilled calamari steak might be served for lunch, either in a salad or as part of a sandwich. **Known for:** cozy homelike dining areas; comfort food; stellar breakfast and brunch. *Average main: $21 ✉ 662 Lighthouse Ave., at 19th St. ☎ 831/643–1060 🌐 redhousecafe.com ⏲ No dinner Mon.*

Taste Café and Bistro
$$ | **AMERICAN** | **FAMILY** | Grilled marinated rabbit, roasted half chicken, filet mignon, and other meats are the focus at Taste, which serves hearty European-inspired food in a casual, open-kitchen setting. **Known for:** grilled meats; house-made desserts; kids' menu. *Average main: $22 ✉ 1199 Forest Ave., at Prescott La. ☎ 831/655–0324 🌐 tastecafebistro.com ⏲ Closed Sun. and Mon.*

Hotels

Asilomar Conference Grounds
$$$ | **RESORT** | On 107 acres in a state park, Asilomar stands among evergreen woods on the edge of a wild beach. **Pros:** general public can book individual rooms up to six months in advance; tasteful and modern rooms; many activities. **Cons:** basic amenities and furnishings; some rooms aging and need updating; service sometimes disorganized. *Rooms from: $225 ✉ 800 Asilomar Ave. ☎ 831/372–8016, 888/635–5310 🌐 visitasilomar.com 312 rooms.*

Gosby House Inn
$$ | **B&B/INN** | Though in the town center, this turreted butter-yellow Queen Anne Victorian has an informal feel. **Pros:** peaceful; homey; within walking distance of shops and restaurants. **Cons:** too frilly for some; area is busy during the day; limited parking. *Rooms from: $155 ✉ 643 Lighthouse Ave. ☎ 831/375–1287 🌐 gosbyhouseinn.com 22 rooms, 21 with bath Breakfast.*

★ Green Gables Inn
$$ | **B&B/INN** | Stained-glass windows and ornate interior details compete with spectacular ocean views at this Queen Anne–style mansion. **Pros:** exceptional views; impeccable attention to historic detail; afternoon wine and cheese served in the parlor. **Cons:** some rooms are small; thin walls; breakfast room can be crowded. *Rooms from: $169 ✉ 301 Ocean View Blvd. ☎ 831/375–2095 🌐 www.greengablesinnpg.com 11 rooms, 8 with bath Breakfast.*

Martine Inn
$$$ | **B&B/INN** | The glassed-in parlor and many guest rooms at this 1899 Mediterranean-style villa have stunning ocean views. **Pros:** romantic; exquisite antiques; ocean views. **Cons:** not child-friendly; sits on a busy thoroughfare; inconvenient parking. *Rooms from: $229 ✉ 255 Ocean View Blvd. ☎ 831/373–3388 🌐 martineinn.com 25 rooms Breakfast.*

Monterey

2 miles southeast of Pacific Grove, 2 miles north of Carmel.

Monterey is a scenic city filled with early California history: adobe buildings from the 1700s, Colton Hall, where California's first constitution was drafted in 1849, and Cannery Row, made famous by author John Steinbeck. Thousands of visitors come each year to mingle with otters and other sea creatures at the world-famous Monterey Bay Aquarium and in the protected waters of the national marine sanctuary that hugs the shoreline.

GETTING HERE AND AROUND

From San Jose or San Francisco, take U.S. 101 south to Highway 156 West at Prunedale. Head west about 8 miles to Highway 1 and follow it about 15 miles south. From San Luis Obispo, take U.S. 101 north to Salinas and drive west on Highway 68 about 20 miles.

Many MST bus lines connect at the Monterey Transit Center, at Pearl Street and Munras Avenue. In summer (daily from 10 until at least 7) and on weekends and holidays the rest of the year, the free MST Monterey Trolley travels from downtown Monterey along Cannery Row to the Aquarium and back.

TOURS

Monterey Movie Tours

SPECIAL-INTEREST | Board a customized motor coach and relax while a film-savvy local takes you on a scenic tour of the Monterey Peninsula enhanced by film clips from the more than 200 movies shot in the area. The three-hour adventure travels a 32-mile loop through Monterey, Pacific Grove, and Carmel. ✉ *Departs from Monterey Conference Center, 1 Portola Plaza* ☎ *831/372–6278, 800/343–6437* 🌐 *montereymovietours.com* 🎫 *$55.*

Old Monterey Walking Tour

WALKING TOURS | Learn all about Monterey's storied past by joining a guided walking tour through the historic district. Tours begin at the Custom House in Custom House Plaza, across from Fisherman's Wharf and are typically offered Thursday through Sunday at 10:30, 12:30, and 2. **■TIP→ Tours are free for everyone on the last Sunday of the month.** ✉ *Monterey* 🌐 *www.parks.ca.gov/?page_id=951* 🎫 *Tours $10.*

The Original Monterey Walking Tours

WALKING TOURS | Learn more about Monterey's past, primarily the Mexican period until California statehood, on a guided tour through downtown Monterey. You can also join a guided walking tour of Cannery Row in the afternoon. Tours last 1½ to 2 hours and are offered Thursday–Sunday at 10 am and 2. Reservations are essential. ✉ *Monterey* ☎ *831/521–4884* 🌐 *www.walkmonterey.com* 🎫 *From $25.*

ESSENTIALS

VISITOR INFORMATION Monterey County Convention & Visitors Bureau ✉ *Visitor center, 401 Camino El Estero* ☎ *888/221–1010* 🌐 *seemonterey.com.*

Sights

California's First Theatre

MUSEUM | This adobe began its life in 1846 as a saloon and lodging house for sailors. Four years later stage curtains were fashioned from army blankets, and some U.S. officers staged plays to the light of whale oil lamps. The building is open only for private tours and events, but you can stroll in the garden. ✉ *Monterey State Historic Park, Scott and Pacific Sts.* ☎ *831/649–2907* 🌐 *www.parks.ca.gov/mshp* 🎫 *Free.*

Cannery Row

NEIGHBORHOOD | When John Steinbeck published the novel *Cannery Row* in 1945, he immortalized a place of rough-edged working people. The waterfront street, edging a mile of gorgeous coastline, once was crowded with sardine canneries processing, at their peak, nearly 200,000 tons of the smelly silver fish a year. During the mid-1940s, however, the sardines disappeared from the bay, causing the canneries to close. Through the years the old tin-roof canneries have been converted into restaurants, art galleries, and malls with shops selling T-shirts, fudge, and plastic sea otters. Recent tourist development along the row has been more tasteful, however, and includes stylish inns and hotels, wine tasting rooms, and upscale specialty shops. ✉ *Cannery Row, between Reeside and David Aves.* 🌐 *canneryrow.com.*

Casa Soberanes

HOUSE | A classic low-ceiling adobe structure built in 1842, this was once a Custom House guard's residence. Exhibits at the house survey life in Monterey from the era of Mexican rule to the present. The building is open only for private tour

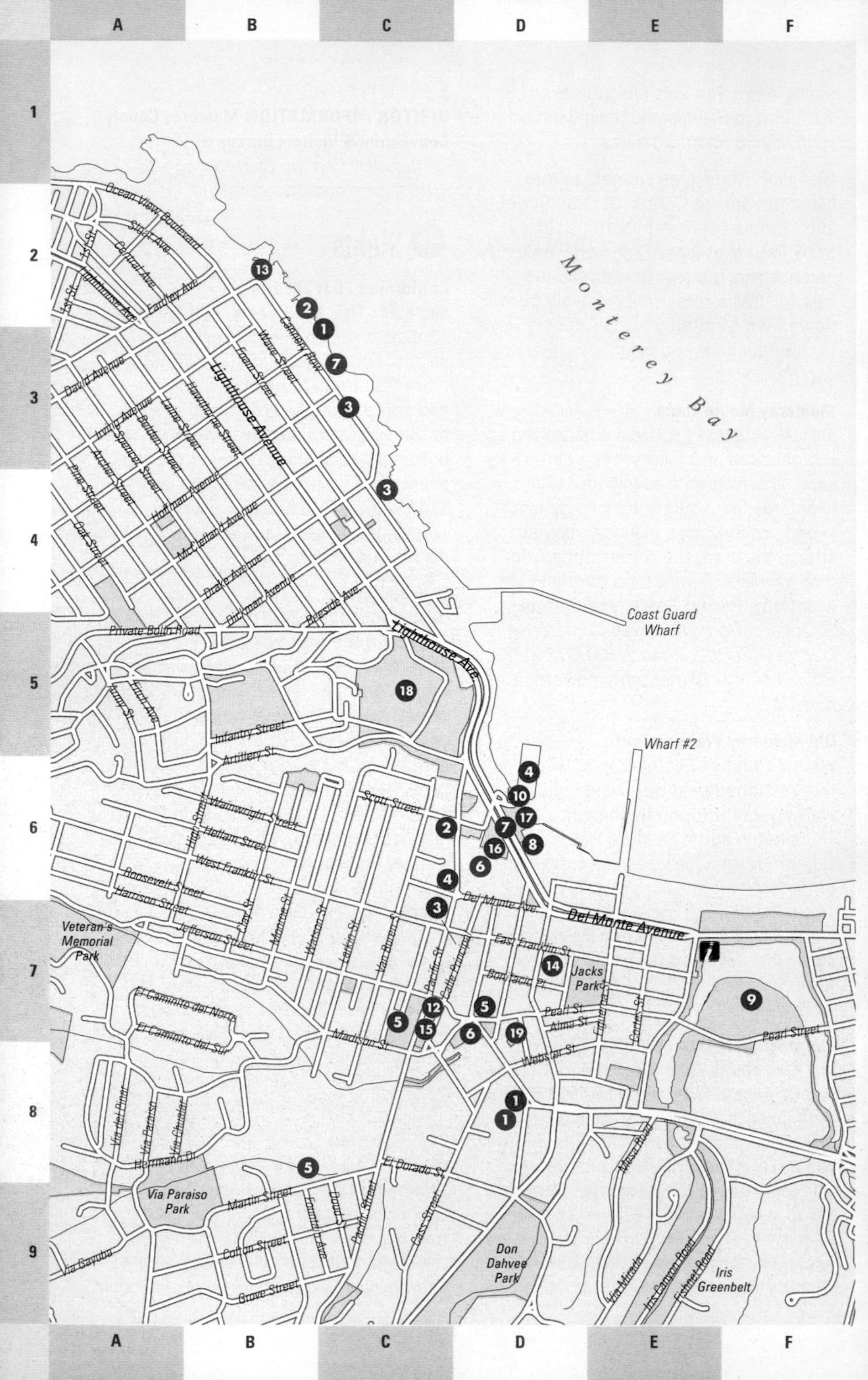

A
B
C
D
E
F
1
2
3
4
5
6
7
8
9
Monterey Bay
Ocean View Boulevard
Cannery Row
Wave Street
Foam Street
Lighthouse Avenue
David Avenue
Irving Avenue
Hoffman Avenue
McClelland Avenue
Drake Avenue
Dickman Avenue
Reeside Ave
Private Bolio Road
Lighthouse Ave
Coast Guard Wharf
Wharf #2
Infantry Street
Artillery St.
Scott Street
Wainwright Street
Hellam Street
West Franklin St.
Roosevelt Street
Harrison Street
Jefferson Street
Del Monte Ave
Del Monte Avenue
East Franklin St.
Bonifacio Pl.
Jacks Park
Pearl St.
Alma St.
Webster St.
Pearl Street
Madison St.
Veteran's Memorial Park
El Caminito del Norte
El Caminito del Sur
Via del Pinar
Via Paraiso
Herrmann Dr.
Via Paraiso Park
Martin Street
Cotton Street
Grove Street
Via Gayuba
El Dorado St.
Pacific Street
Cass Street
Don Dahvee Park
Mesa Road
Via Mirada
Iris Canyon Road
Fishnet Road
Iris Greenbelt
Pacific St.
Calle Principal
Van Buren St.
Larkin St.
Watson St.
Monroe St.
Clay St.
Figueroa St.
Camino El Estero

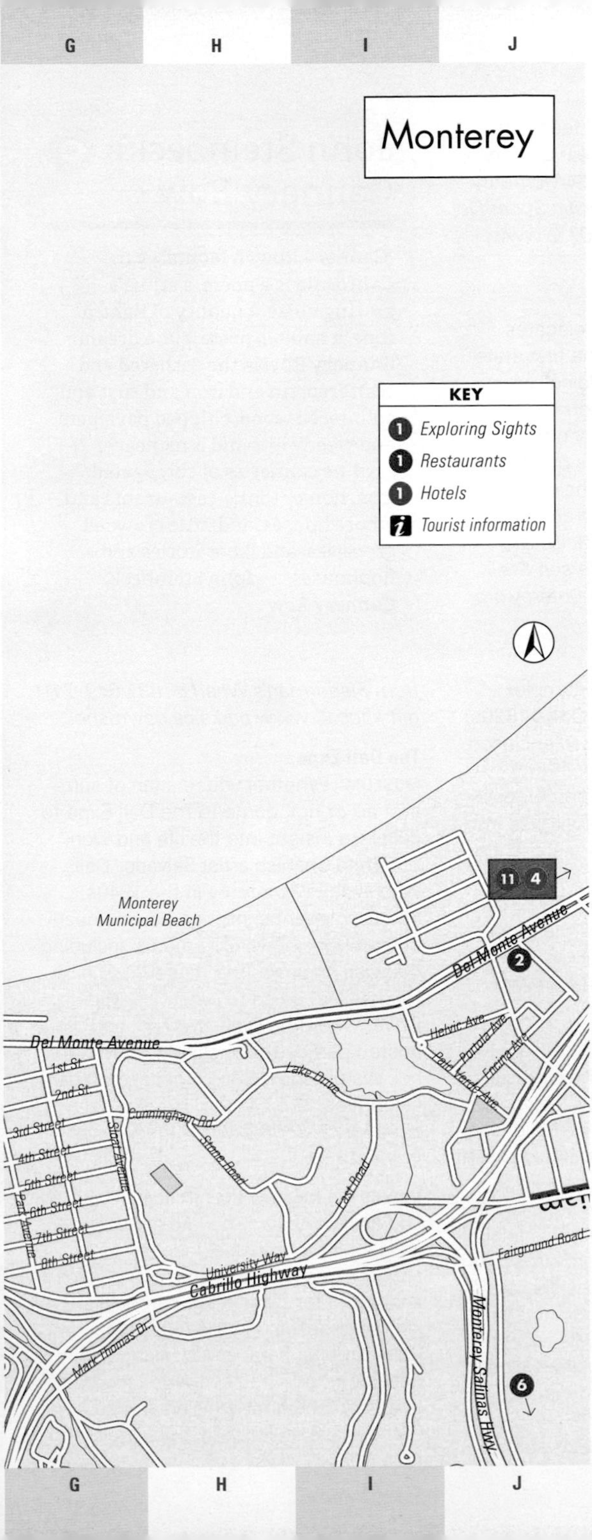

G H I J

Monterey

KEY
1 *Exploring Sights*
1 *Restaurants*
1 *Hotels*
i *Tourist information*

Monterey Municipal Beach
Del Monte Avenue
1st St.
2nd St.
3rd Street
4th Street
5th Street
6th Street
7th Street
8th Street
Park Avenue
Sloat Avenue
Cunningham Rd.
Stone Road
Lake Drive
East Road
Helvic Ave.
Portola Ave.
Palo Verde Ave.
Encina Ave.
University Way
Cabrillo Highway
Mark Thomas Dr.
Fairground Road
Monterey Salinas Hwy.

Sights

1 A Taste of Monterey................C3
2 California's First Theatre.......... D6
3 Cannery Row........................C3
4 Casa Soberanes....................C6
5 Colton Hall...........................C7
6 Cooper-Molera Adobe............ D7
7 Custom House D6
8 The Dali Expo....................... D6
9 Dennis The Menace Playground F7
10 Fisherman's Wharf D6
11 Fort Ord National Monument...... J6
12 Larkin House C7
13 Monterey Bay Aquarium.......... B2
14 Monterey County Youth Museum (MY Museum)........... D7
15 Monterey Museum of Art at Pacific Street.....................C7
16 Monterey State Historic Park D6
17 Pacific House Museum........... D6
18 Presidio of Monterey Museum....C5
19 Stevenson House.................. D7

Restaurants

1 Estéban Restaurant D8
2 Monterey's Fish House.............J6
3 Montrio Bistro...................... D7
4 Old Fishermen's Grotto........... D6
5 Old Monterey Café D7
6 Tarpy's Roadhouse J9

Hotels

1 Casa Munras Garden Hotel & Spa......................... D8
2 InterContinental The Clement Monterey B2
3 Monterey Plaza Hotel & Spa C4
4 Monterey Tides J6
5 Old Monterey Inn B8
6 Portola Hotel & Spa at Monterey Bay........................ D6
7 Spindrift Inn C3

G H I J

requests (call for times and fees), but you can visit the peaceful rear garden and its rose-covered arbor. ⊠ *Monterey State Historic Park, 336 Pacific St., at Del Monte Ave.* ☎ *831/649–2907* 🌐 *www.parks.ca.gov/mshp* 🎟 *Free.*

Colton Hall

MUSEUM | A convention of delegates met here in 1849 to draft the first state constitution. The stone building, which has served as a school, a courthouse, and the county seat, is a city-run museum furnished as it was during the constitutional convention. The extensive grounds outside the hall surround the Old Monterey Jail. ⊠ *570 Pacific St., between Madison and Jefferson Sts.* ☎ *831/646–5640* 🌐 *www.monterey.org/museums* 🎟 *Free.*

Cooper-Molera Adobe

HOUSE | The restored 2-acre complex includes a house dating from the 1820s, a gift shop, and a large garden enclosed by a high adobe wall. The mostly Victorian-era antiques and memorabilia that fill the house provide a glimpse into the life of a prosperous sea merchant's family. If the house is closed, you can still stop by the Cooper Store and pick up walking-tour maps and stroll the grounds. ⊠ *Monterey State Historic Park, Polk and Munras Sts.* ☎ *831/649–7118* 🌐 *www.parks.ca.gov/mshp* 🎟 *$5 tour.*

Custom House

MUSEUM | **FAMILY** | Built by the Mexican government in 1827 and now California's oldest standing public building, the Custom House was the first stop for sea traders whose goods were subject to duties. In 1846 Commodore John Sloat raised the American flag over this adobe structure and claimed California for the United States. The lower floor displays cargo from a 19th-century trading ship. The Custom House Store sells Monterey-themed items. If the house is closed, you can visit the cactus gardens and stroll the plaza. ⊠ *Monterey State Historic Park, 1 Custom House Plaza, across from Fisherman's Wharf* ☎ *831/649–7111 gift shop* 🌐 *www.parks.ca.gov/mshp.*

The Dali Expo

MUSEUM | Whether you're a fan of surrealist art or not, come to The Dali Expo to gain rare insight into the life and work of famed Spanish artist Salvador Dali, who lived in Monterey in the 1940s. The permanent exhibition houses nearly 600 artworks in various media, including 400 Dali originals. The museum's name reflects Dali's ties to nearby 17-Mile Drive, where he lived, worked, and hosted parties that included Andy Warhol, Walt Disney, Bob Hope, and other celebrities, ⊠ *5 Custom House Plaza* ☎ *831/372–2608* 🌐 *www.thedaliexpo.com* 🎟 *$20.*

Dennis the Menace Playground

CITY PARK | **FAMILY** | The late cartoonist Hank Ketcham designed this play area. Its equipment is on a grand scale and made for Dennis-like daredevils: kid favorites include the roller slide, rock-climbing area, and clanking suspension bridge. You can rent a rowboat or a paddleboat for cruising around U-shape Lake El Estero, populated with

John Steinbeck's Cannery Row

"Cannery Row in Monterey in California is a poem, a stink, a grating noise, a quality of light, a tone, a habit, a nostalgia, a dream. Cannery Row is the gathered and scattered, tin and iron and rust and splintered wood, chipped pavement and weedy lots and junk heaps, sardine canneries of corrugated iron, honky tonks, restaurants and whore houses, and little crowded groceries, and laboratories and flophouses." —John Steinbeck, *Cannery Row* an assortment of ducks, mud hens, and geese. ✉ *El Estero Park, Pearl St. and Camino El Estero* ☎ *831/646–3866* 🌐 *www.monterey.org/parks* ⏲ *Closed Tues., Sept.–May.*

Fisherman's Wharf

PEDESTRIAN MALL | **FAMILY** | The mournful barking of sea lions provides a steady sound track all along Monterey's waterfront, but the best way to actually view the whiskered marine mammals is to walk along one of the two piers across from Custom House Plaza. Lined with souvenir shops, the wharf is undeniably touristy, but it's lively and entertaining. At Wharf No. 2, a working municipal pier, you can see the day's catch being unloaded from fishing boats on one side and fishermen casting their lines into the water on the other. The pier has a couple of low-key restaurants, from whose seats lucky customers might spot otters and harbor seals. ✉ *At end of Calle Principal* 🌐 *www.montereywharf.com.*

Fort Ord National Monument

NATIONAL/STATE PARK | Scenic beauty, biodiversity, and miles of trails make this former U.S. Army training grounds a haven for nature lovers and outdoor enthusiasts. The 7,200-acre park, which stretches east over the hills between Monterey and Salinas, is also protected habitat for 35 species of rare and endangered plants and animals. There are 86 miles of single-track, dirt, and paved trails for hiking, biking, and horseback riding. The main trailheads are the Creekside, off Creekside Terrace near Portola Road, and Badger Hills, off Highway 68 in Salinas. Maps are available at the various trail-access points and on the park's website. **■TIP→ Dogs are permitted on trails, but should be leashed when other people are nearby.** ✉ *Bordered by Hwy. 68 and Gen. Jim Moore and Reservation Rds.* ☎ *831/582–2200* 🌐 *www.blm.gov/programs/national-conservation-lands/california/fort-ord-national-monument* 🎟 *Free.*

Larkin House

HOUSE | A veranda encircles the second floor of this 1835 adobe, whose design bears witness to the Mexican and New England influences on the Monterey style. The building's namesake, Thomas O. Larkin, an early California statesman, brought many of the antiques inside from New Hampshire. Tours are available by special appointment only. If the building is closed, you can peek in the windows and stroll the gardens. ✉ *Monterey State Historic Park, 464 Calle Principal, between Jefferson and Pacific Sts.* ☎ *831/649–2907* 🌐 *www.parks.ca.gov/mshp.*

★ Monterey Bay Aquarium

ZOO | **FAMILY** | Sea creatures surround you the minute you hand over your ticket at this extraordinary facility: right at the entrance dozens of them swim in a three-story-tall, sunlit kelp-forest tank. All the exhibits here provide a sense of what it's like to be in the water with the animals—sardines swim around your head in a circular tank, and jellyfish drift in and out of view in dramatically lighted spaces that suggest the ocean depths. A petting pool puts you literally in touch with bat rays, and the million-gallon Open Seas tank illustrates the variety of creatures, from sharks to placid-looking turtles, that live in the eastern Pacific. At the Splash Zone, which has 45 interactive bilingual exhibits, kids can commune with African black-footed penguins, potbellied seahorses, and other creatures. The only drawback to the aquarium experience is that it must be shared with the throngs that congregate daily, but most visitors think it's worth it. ✉ *886 Cannery Row, at David Ave.* ☎ *831/648–4800 info, 866/963–9645 for advance tickets* 🌐 *montereybayaquarium.org* 🎟 *$50.*

Monterey County Youth Museum (MY Museum)

MUSEUM | **FAMILY** | Monterey Bay comes to life from a child's perspective in this fun-filled, interactive indoor exploration

California sea lions are intelligent, social animals that live (and sleep) close together in groups.

center. The seven exhibit galleries showcase the science and nature of the Big Sur coast, theater arts, Pebble Beach golf, and beaches. Also here are a live performance theater, a creation station, a hospital emergency room, and an agriculture corner where kids follow artichokes, strawberries, and other fruits and veggies on their evolution from sprout to harvest to farmers' markets. ✉ *425 Washington St., between E. Franklin St. and Bonifacio Pl.* ☎ *831/649–6444* 🌐 *mymuseum.org* 🎟 *$8* ⏲ *Closed Mon.*

Monterey Museum of Art at Pacific Street

MUSEUM | Photographs by Ansel Adams and Edward Weston and works by other artists who have spent time on the peninsula are on display here, along with international folk art, from Kentucky hearth brooms to Tibetan prayer wheels. ✉ *559 Pacific St., across from Colton Hall* ☎ *831/372–5477* 🌐 *montereyart.org* 🎟 *$10* ⏲ *Closed Wed.*

★ Monterey State Historic Park

NATIONAL/STATE PARK | You can glimpse Monterey's early history in several well-preserved adobe buildings downtown. Some of the structures have gardens that are themselves worthy sights, and they're visitable even if the buildings—among them **Casa Soberanes,** the **Larkin House,** and the **Stevenson House**—are closed. ■ **TIP→ If buildings are closed when you visit you can access a cell phone tour 24/7 at 831/998–9458 or download a mobile app.** ✉ *Pacific House Museum visitor center, 10 Custom House Plaza* ☎ *831/649–7118* 🌐 *www.parks.ca.gov/mshp* 🎟 *Free–$5, 1-hr history walk $10.*

Pacific House Museum

MUSEUM | Once a hotel and saloon, this facility, also a visitor center, commemorates life in pioneer-era California with gold-rush relics and photographs of old Monterey. On the upper floor are Native American artifacts, including gorgeous baskets and pottery. ✉ *Monterey State Historic Park, 10 Custom House Plaza* ☎ *831/649–2907* 🌐 *www.parks.ca.gov/mshp* 🎟 *Free.*

Presidio of Monterey Museum

MUSEUM | This spot has been significant for centuries. Its first incarnation was as a Native American village for the Rumsien tribe. The Spanish explorer Sebastián Vizcaíno landed here in 1602, and Father Junípero Serra arrived in 1770. Notable battles fought here include the 1818 skirmish in which the corsair Hipólito Bruchard conquered the Spanish garrison that stood on this site and claimed part of California for Argentina. The indoor museum tells the stories; plaques mark the outdoor sites. ✉ *Presidio of Monterey, Corporal Ewing Rd., off Lighthouse Ave.* ☎ *831/646–3456* 🌐 *www.monterey.org/museums* 🎟 *Free* ⏲ *Closed Tues. and Wed.*

Stevenson House

HOUSE | This house was named in honor of author Robert Louis Stevenson, who boarded here briefly in a tiny upstairs room. Items from his family's estate furnish Stevenson's room; period-decorated chambers elsewhere in the house include a gallery of memorabilia and a children's nursery stocked with Victorian toys and games. Visit the website or call for tour times and fees. If the building is closed, you can stroll around the gardens. ✉ *Monterey State Historic Park, 530 Houston St., near Pearl St.* ☎ *831/649–2907* 🌐 *www.parks.ca.gov/mshp.*

A Taste of Monterey

WINERY/DISTILLERY | Without driving the back roads, you can taste the wines of nearly 100 area vintners (craft beers, too) while taking in fantastic bay views. Bottles are available for purchase, and food is served from 11:30 until closing. ✉ *700 Cannery Row, Suite KK* ☎ *831/646–5446* 🌐 *atasteofmonterey.com* 🎟 *Tastings $15.*

Restaurants

Estéban Restaurant

$$$ | **SPANISH** | In a festive fireplace dining room at Casa Munras hotel, Estéban serves modern and classic versions of Spanish cuisine: empanadas, Moorish chickpea stew, and three types of paella. Midweek specials abound: on Tuesday nights, feast on a four-course prix-fixe paella dinner ($54 per couple), bottles of wine are half off on Monday, and Wednesday wine flights are just $14 for three tastes. **Known for:** daily tapas happy hour from 4:30 to 6; outdoor patio with fire pit; special menus for kids and pups. $ *Average main: $30* ✉ *700 Munras Ave.* ☎ *831/375–0176* 🌐 *www.estebanrestaurant.com* ⏲ *No lunch.*

Former Capital of California

In 1602 Spanish explorer Sebastián Vizcaíno stepped ashore on a remote California peninsula. He named it after the viceroy of New Spain—Count de Monte Rey. Soon the Spanish built a military outpost, and the site was the capital of California until the state came under American rule.

Monterey's Fish House

$$ | **SEAFOOD** | Casual yet stylish and always packed, this seafood restaurant is removed from the hubbub of the wharf. The bartenders and waitstaff will gladly advise you on the perfect wine to go with your poached, blackened, or oak-grilled seafood. **Known for:** seafood, steaks, house-made pasta; festive atmosphere; oyster bar. $ *Average main: $22* ✉ *2114 Del Monte Ave., at Dela Vina Ave.* ☎ *831/373–4647* 🌐 *montereyfishhouse.com* ⏲ *No lunch weekends.*

★ Montrio Bistro

$$$ | **AMERICAN** | This quirky converted firehouse, with its rawhide walls and iron indoor trellises, has a wonderfully sophisticated menu. Organic produce and meats and sustainably sourced seafood are used in imaginative dishes that reflect the area's agriculture—crispy artichoke hearts with Mediterranean baba ghanoush, for instance, and scallop crudo with avocado-jalapeño panna cotta. **Known for:** green-certified restaurant; extensive international wine list; inventive cocktails. *Average main: $30 414 Calle Principal, at W. Franklin St. 831/648–8880 montrio.com No lunch.*

Old Fisherman's Grotto
$$$ | **SEAFOOD** | Otters and seals frolic in the water just below this nautical-theme Fisherman's Wharf restaurant famous for its creamy clam chowder. Seafood paella, sand dabs, filet mignon, teriyaki chicken, and several pastas are among the many entrée options. **Known for:** Monterey-style clam chowder and calamari; Monterey Bay views; full bar and carefully curated wine list. *Average main: $29 39 Fisherman's Wharf 831/375–4604 oldfishermansgrotto.com.*

Old Monterey Café
$ | **AMERICAN** | Breakfast here gets constant local raves—its fame rests on familiar favorites: a dozen kinds of omelets, and pancakes from blueberry to cinnamon-raisin-pecan. For lunch are good soups, salads, and sandwiches. *Average main: $15 489 Alvarado St., at Munras Ave. 831/646–1021 oldmontereycafeca.com No dinner.*

Tarpy's Roadhouse
$$$ | **AMERICAN** | Fun, dressed-up American favorites—a little something for everyone—are served in this renovated early-1900s stone farmhouse several miles east of town. The kitchen cranks out everything from Cajun-spiced prawns to meat loaf with marsala–mushroom gravy to grilled ribs and steaks. **Known for:** American comfort food with a California twist; rustic dining: indoor fireplace or garden courtyard; generous portions. *Average main: $29 2999 Monterey–Salinas Hwy., Hwy. 68 831/647–1444 tarpys.com.*

Hotels

Casa Munras Garden Hotel & Spa
$$$ | **HOTEL** | **FAMILY** | A Spanish-theme cluster of buildings in the heart of downtown, Casa Munras pays homage to Monterey's historic roots and the legacy of Spanish diplomat Don Estéban Munras, who built a residence on the site in 1824. **Pros:** full-service spa, heated swimming pool, hot tub, and fitness room; on-site tapas restaurant; walk to downtown sights and restaurants; excellent on-site tapas restaurant. **Cons:** $15 parking fee; pool area can get noisy; thin walls. *Rooms from: $199 700 Munras Ave. 831/375–2411, 800/222–2446 www.hotelcasamunras.com 163 rooms No meals.*

InterContinental The Clement Monterey
$$$$ | **HOTEL** | **FAMILY** | Spectacular bay views, upscale amenities, assiduous service, and a superb location next to the aquarium propelled this luxury hotel to immediate stardom. **Pros:** a block from the aquarium; fantastic waterfront views from some rooms; great for families. **Cons:** a tad formal; not budget; Cannery Row crowds everywhere on busy weekends and holidays. *Rooms from: $269 750 Cannery Row 831/375–4500, 866/781–2406 toll-free www.icthe-clementmonterey.com 208 rooms No meals.*

Monterey Plaza Hotel & Spa
$$$$ | **HOTEL** | Guests at this waterfront Cannery Row hotel can see frolicking sea otters from its wide outdoor patio and many room balconies. **Pros:** on the ocean; many amenities; attentive service. **Cons:** touristy area; heavy traffic; resort fee. *Rooms from: $289 400 Cannery Row 831/920–6710, 877/862–7552 www.montereyplazahotel.com 290 rooms.*

Monterey Tides
$$$ | **RESORT** | One of the area's best values, this hotel has a great waterfront location—2 miles north of Monterey,

The Monterey Bay National Marine Sanctuary

Although Monterey's coastal landscapes are stunning, their beauty is more than equaled by the wonders that lie offshore. The Monterey Bay National Marine Sanctuary—which stretches 276 miles, from north of San Francisco almost down to Santa Barbara—teems with abundant life, and has topography as diverse as that aboveground.

The preserve's 5,322 square miles include vast submarine canyons, which reach down 10,663 feet at their deepest point. They also encompass dense forests of giant kelp—a kind of seaweed that can grow more than a hundred feet from its roots on the ocean floor. These kelp forests are especially robust off Monterey.

The sanctuary was established in 1992 to protect the habitat of the many species that thrive in the bay. Some animals can be seen quite easily from land. In summer and winter you might glimpse the offshore spray of gray whales as they migrate between their summer feeding grounds in Alaska and their breeding grounds in Baja. Clouds of marine birds—including white-faced ibis, three types of albatross, and more than 15 types of gull—skim the waves, or roost in the rock islands along 17-Mile Drive. Sea otters dart and gambol in the calmer waters of the bay; and of course, you can watch the sea lions—and hear their round-the-clock barking—on the wharves in Santa Cruz and Monterey.

The sanctuary supports many other creatures, however, that remain unseen by most on-land visitors. Some of these are enormous, such as the giant blue whales that arrive to feed on plankton in summer; others, like the more than 22 species of red algae in these waters, are microscopic. So whether you choose to visit the Monterey Bay Aquarium, take a whale-watch trip, or look out to sea with your binoculars, remember you're seeing just a small part of a vibrant underwater kingdom.

with views of the bay and the city skyline—and offers a surprising array of amenities. **Pros:** on the beach; great value; family-friendly. **Cons:** several miles from major attractions; big-box mall neighborhood; most rooms on the small side. *Rooms from: $206* ⊠ *2600 Sand Dunes Dr.* ☎ *831/394–3321, 800/242–8627* 🌐 *montereytides.com* *196 rooms* *No meals.*

★ Old Monterey Inn

$$$$ | **B&B/INN** | This three-story manor house was the home of Monterey's first mayor, and today it remains a private enclave within walking distance of downtown, set off by lush gardens shaded by huge old trees and bordered by a creek. **Pros:** gorgeous gardens; spa room with treatments by the fireplace; extensive breakfast served in the dining room or in the rooms. **Cons:** must drive to attractions and sights; fills quickly; no pool or hot tub. *Rooms from: $379* ⊠ *500 Martin St.* ☎ *831/652–8999* 🌐 *www.oldmontereyinn.com* *9 rooms, 1 cottage* *Breakfast.*

Portola Hotel & Spa at Monterey Bay

$$$$ | **HOTEL** | One of Monterey's largest hotels and locally owned and operated for more than 40 years, the nautical-theme Portola anchors a prime city block between Custom House Plaza and the Monterey Conference Center. **Pros:** walk to Fisherman's Wharf, Custom House Plaza, and downtown restaurants and shops; three on-site restaurants and coffee shop; pet- and family-friendly. **Cons:** crowded when conferences convene; no air-conditioning; parking fee. *Rooms from: $269* *2 Portola Plaza* *831/649–4511, 888/222–5851* *379 rooms* *No meals.*

Spindrift Inn

$$$ | **HOTEL** | This boutique hotel on Cannery Row has beach access and a rooftop garden that overlooks the water. **Pros:** close to aquarium; steps from the beach; friendly staff. **Cons:** throngs of visitors outside; can be noisy; not good for families. *Rooms from: $216* *652 Cannery Row* *831/646–8900, 800/841–1879* *spindriftinn.com* *45 rooms* *Breakfast.*

Nightlife

BARS

Alvarado Street Brewery & Grill

BREWPUBS/BEER GARDENS | Housed in an historic Beaux Arts building that dates back to 1916, this craft brewery lures locals and visitors alike with a full bar and 20 craft beers on tap, decent gastropub menu, beer garden, and shaded sidewalk patio. *426 Alvarado St.* *831/655–2337* *www.alvaradostreetbrewery.com.*

Cibo

MUSIC CLUBS | An Italian restaurant and event venue with a big bar area, Cibo brings live jazz and other music to downtown from Tuesday through Sunday. *301 Alvarado St., at Del Monte Ave.* *831/649–8151* *cibo.com.*

Crown & Anchor

BARS/PUBS | An authentic British pub, downtown Crown & Anchor has 20 beers on tap, classic cocktails, and a full menu, including 18 daily specials available in the restaurant and heated patio until midnight. *150 W. Franklin St.* *831/649–6496* *crownandanchor.net.*

Peter B's Brewpub

BREWPUBS/BEER GARDENS | House-made beers, 18 HDTVs, a decent pub menu, and a pet-friendly patio ensure lively crowds at this craft brewery in back of the Portola Plaza Hotel. *2 Portola Plaza* *831/649–2699* *www.peterbsbrewpub.com.*

Turn 12 Bar & Grill

BARS/PUBS | The motorcycles and vintage photographs at this downtown watering hole pay homage to nearby 11-turn Laguna Seca Raceway. The large-screen TVs, heated outdoor patio, happy-hour specials, and live entertainment keep the place jumpin' into the wee hours. *400 Tyler St., at E. Franklin St.* *831/372–8876* *turn12barandgrill.com.*

MUSIC FESTIVALS

Jazz Bash by the Bay

FESTIVALS | Traditional jazz bands play early jazz, big band, swing, ragtime, blues, zydeco, and gypsy jazz at waterfront venues during this festival, held on the first full weekend of March. *888/349–6879, 831/754–8786* *jazzbashmonterey.com.*

Monterey International Blues Festival

FESTIVALS | Blues fans flock to the Monterey Fairgrounds for this festival, held the last weekend in June. *montereyinternationalbluesfestival.com.*

Monterey Jazz Festival

FESTIVALS | The world's oldest jazz festival attracts top-name performers to the Monterey Fairgrounds on the third full weekend of September. *888/248–6499 ticket office, 831/373–3366* *montereyjazzfestival.org.*

Activities

Monterey Bay waters never warm to the temperatures of their Southern California counterparts—the warmest they get is the low 60s. That's one reason why the marine life here is so diverse, which in turn brings out the fishers, kayakers, and whale-watchers. During the rainy winter, the waves grow larger, and surfers flock to the water. On land pretty much year-round, bikers find opportunities to ride, and walkers have plenty of waterfront to stroll.

BIKING

Adventures by the Sea

BICYCLING | You can rent surreys plus tandem, standard, and electric bicycles from this outfit that also conducts bike and kayak tours, and rents kayaks and stand-up paddleboards. There are multiple locations along Cannery Row and Custom House Plaza as well as branches at Lovers Point in Pacific Grove and 17-Mile Drive in Pebble Beach. ✉ *299 Cannery Row* ☎ *831/372–1807, 800/979–3370 reservations* 🌐 *adventuresbythesea.com.*

FISHING

J&M Sport Fishing

FISHING | This outfit takes beginning and experienced fishers out to sea to catch rock cod, ling cod, sand dabs, mackerel, halibut, salmon (in season), albacore, squid, Dungeness crab, and other species. ✉ *66 Fisherman's Wharf* ☎ *831/372–7440* 🌐 *jmsportfishing.com.*

KAYAKING

★ Monterey Bay Kayaks

KAYAKING | For many visitors the best way to see the bay is by kayak. This company rents equipment and conducts classes and natural-history tours. ✉ *693 Del Monte Ave.* ☎ *831/373–5357* 🌐 *www.montereybaykayaks.com.*

WALKING

Monterey Bay Coastal Recreation Trail

HIKING/WALKING | From Custom House Plaza, you can walk along the coast in either direction on this 29-mile-long trail and take in spectacular views of the sea. The trail runs from north of Monterey in Castroville south to Pacific Grove, with sections continuing around Pebble Beach. Much of the path follows an old Southern Pacific Railroad route. ☎ *888/221–1010* 🌐 *seemonterey.com/things-to-do/parks/coastal-trail/.*

WHALE-WATCHING

Thousands of gray whales pass close by the Monterey Coast on their annual migration between the Bering Sea and Baja California, and a whale-watching cruise is the best way to see these magnificent mammals close up. The migration south takes place from December through March; January is prime viewing time. The whales migrate north from March through June. Blue whales and humpbacks also pass the coast; they're most easily spotted in late summer and early fall.

Fast Raft Ocean Safaris

TOUR—SPORTS | Naturalists lead whale-watching and sightseeing tours of Monterey Bay aboard the 33-foot *Ranger,* a six-passenger, rigid-hull inflatable boat. The speedy craft slips into coves inaccessible to larger vessels; its quiet engines enable intimate marine experiences without disturbing wildlife. Children ages eight and older are welcome to participate. ✉ *32 Cannery Row, Suite F2* ☎ *408/659–3900* 🌐 *www.fastraft.com* 🎫 *From $165.*

Monterey Bay Whale Watch

WHALE-WATCHING | The marine biologists here lead three- to five-hour whale-watching tours. ✉ *84 Fisherman's Wharf* ☎ *831/375–4658* 🌐 *montereybaywhalewatch.com.*

Princess Monterey Whale Watching

WHALE-WATCHING | Tours are offered daily on a 100-passenger high-speed cruiser and a large 100-foot boat. ✉ *96 Fisherman's Wharf* ☎ *831/372–2203* 🌐 *montereywhalewatching.com.*

Shopping

Alvarado and nearby downtown streets are good places to start a Monterey shopping spree, especially if you're interested in antiques and collectibles.

Boston Store

ANTIQUES/COLLECTIBLES | Antiques and reproductions of 1850s merchandise—linens, crockery, preserves, soaps, and so forth—are available here. ✉ *Monterey State Historic Park, 1 Custom House Plaza, across from Fisherman's Wharf* ☎ *831/277–0343* 🌐 *www.historicgarden-league.org.*

Cannery Row Antique Mall

ANTIQUES/COLLECTIBLES | Bargain hunters can sometimes find little treasures at the mall, which houses more than 100 local vendors under one roof. ✉ *471 Wave St.* ☎ *831/655–0264* 🌐 *canneryrowantique-mall.com.*

The Custom House Gift Shop

SPECIALTY STORES | This store sells 1800s-theme items such as toys, as well as books related to Monterey and California heritage. ✉ *Custom House Plaza, in the Custom House bldg.* ☎ *831/649–7111.*

Old Monterey Book Co.

BOOKS/STATIONERY | Antiquarian books and prints are this shop's specialties. ✉ *136 Bonifacio Pl., off Alvarado St.* ☎ *831/372–3111* ⏲ *Closed Mon.*

Salinas

17 miles east of Monterey on Hwy. 68.

Salinas, a hardworking city surrounded by vineyards and fruit and vegetable fields, honors the memory and literary legacy of John Steinbeck, its most famous native, with the National Steinbeck Center. The facility is in Old Town Salinas, where renovated turn-of-the-20th-century stone buildings house shops and restaurants.

ESSENTIALS

TRAIN INFORMATION Salinas Amtrak Station ✉ *11 Station Pl., at W. Market St.* ☎ *800/872–7245* 🌐 *www.amtrak.com.*

VISITOR INFORMATION California Welcome Center ✉ *1213 N. Davis Rd., west of U.S. 101, exit 330* ☎ *831/757–8687* 🌐 *visitcalifornia.com/attraction/california-welcome-center-salinas.*

Sights

Monterey Zoo

ZOO | **FAMILY** | Exotic animals, many of them retired from film, television, and live production work or rescued from less than ideal environments, find sanctuary here. The zoo offers daily tours (1 pm and 3 pm June–August, 1 pm September–May), but for an in-depth experience, stay in a safari bungalow on-site at Vision Quest Safari B&B, where guests can join the elephants in their enclosures for breakfast. The inn's room rate includes a complimentary zoo tour. ✉ *400 River Rd., off Hwy. 68* ☎ *831/455–1901* 🌐 *www.montereyzoo.com* 🎟 *From $20.*

National Steinbeck Center

MUSEUM | The center's exhibits document the life of Pulitzer- and Nobel-prize winner John Steinbeck and the history of the nearby communities that inspired novels such as *East of Eden*. Highlights include reproductions of the green pickup-camper from *Travels with Charley* and the bunk room from *Of Mice and Men*. **Steinbeck House,** the author's Victorian birthplace, at 132 Central Avenue, is two blocks from the center. Now a decent restaurant (only open for lunch) and gift shop with docent-led tours, it displays memorabilia. ✉ *1 Main St., at Central Ave.* ☎ *831/775–4721* 🌐 *steinbeck.org* 🎟 *$13.*

Pinnacles National Park

38 miles southeast of Salinas.

Pinnacles may be the nation's newest national park, but Teddy Roosevelt recognized the uniqueness of this ancient volcano—its jagged spires and monoliths thrusting upward from chaparral-covered mountains—when he made it a national monument in 1908. Though only about two hours from the bustling Bay Area, the outside world seems to recede even before you reach the park's gates.

GETTING HERE AND AROUND

One of the first things you need to decide when visiting Pinnacles is which entrance—east or west—you'll use, because there's no road connecting the two rugged peaks separating them. Entering from Highway 25 on the east is straightforward. The gate is only a mile or so from the turnoff. From the west, once you head east out of Soledad on Highway 146, the road quickly becomes narrow and hilly, with many blind curves. Drive slowly and cautiously along the 10 miles or so before you reach the west entrance.

ESSENTIALS

Pinnacles Visitor Center

At the park's main visitor center, located at the eastern entrance, you can purchase admission passes, get maps, browse books, and buy gifts. The adjacent campground store sells snacks and drinks. ✉ *Hwy. 146, 2 miles west of Hwy. 25, Paicines* ☎ *831/389–4485* 🌐 *www.nps.gov/pinn.*

West Pinnacles Visitor Contact Station

This station is just past the park's western entrance, about 10 miles east of Soledad. Here you can get maps and information, watch a 13-minute film about Pinnacles, and view some displays. Food and drink aren't available here. ✉ *Hwy. 146, off U.S. 101, Soledad* ☎ *831/389–4427* 🌐 *www.nps.gov/pinn.*

Sights

Pinnacles National Park

NATIONAL/STATE PARK | **FAMILY** | The many attractions at Pinnacles include talus caves, 30 miles of hiking trails, and hundreds of rock-climbing routes. A mosaic of diverse habitats supports an amazing variety of wildlife species: 185 birds, 49 mammals, 70 butterflies, and nearly 400 bees. The park is also home to some of the world's remaining few hundred condors in captivity and release areas. Fourteen of California's 25 bat species live in caves and other habitats in the park. President Theodore Roosevelt declared this remarkable 26,000-acre geologic and wildlife preserve a national monument in 1908. President Barack Obama officially designated it a national park in 2013.

The pinnacles are believed to have been created when two major tectonic plates collided and pushed a smaller plate down beneath the earth's crust, spawning volcanoes in what's now called the Gabilan Mountains, southeast of Salinas and Monterey. After the eruptions ceased, the San Andreas Fault split the volcanic field in two, carrying part of it northward to what is now Pinnacles National Park. Millions of years of erosion left a rugged landscape of rocky spires and crags, or pinnacles. Boulders fell into canyons and valleys, creating talus caves and a paradise for modern-day rock climbers. Spring is the most popular time to visit, when colorful wildflowers blanket the meadows; the light and scenery can be striking in fall and winter; the summer heat is often brutal. The park has two entrances—east and west—but they are not connected. The Pinnacles Visitor Center, Bear Gulch Nature Center, Park Headquarters, the Pinnacles Campground, and the Bear Gulch Cave and Reservoir are on the east side. The Chaparral Parking Area is on the west side, where you can feast on fantastic views of the Pinnacles High Peaks from the parking area. Dogs are not allowed on hiking trails. **■TIP→ The east entrance is 32 miles southeast of Hollister via Highway 25. The west entrance is about 12 miles east of Soledad via Highway 146.** ✉ *5000 Hwy. 146, Paicines* ☎ *831/389–4486, 831/389–4427 Westside* 🌐 *www.nps.gov/pinn* 🎫 *$10 per vehicle, $5 per visitor if biking or walking.*

Activities

HIKING

Hiking is the most popular activity at Pinnacles, with more than 30 miles of trails for every interest and level of fitness. Because there isn't a road through the park, hiking is also the only way to experience its interior, including the High Peaks, the talus caves, and the reservoir.

Balconies Cliffs-Cave Loop

HIKING/WALKING | Grab your flashlight before heading out from the Chaparral Trailhead parking lot for this 2.4-mile loop that takes you through the Balconies Caves. This trail is especially beautiful in spring, when wildflowers carpet the canyon floor. About 0.6 mile from the start of the trail, turn left to begin ascending the Balconies Cliffs Trail, where you'll be rewarded with close-up views of Machete Ridge and other steep, vertical formations; you may run across rock climbers testing their skills before rounding the loop and descending back through the cave. *Easy.* ✉ *West side of park* ✥ *Trailhead: from West Pinnacles Visitor Contact Station, drive about 2 miles to Chaparral Trailhead parking lot. Trail picks up on west side of lot.*

Moses Spring-Rim Trail Loop

HIKING/WALKING | **FAMILY** | Perhaps the most popular hike at Pinnacles, this relatively short (2.2 miles) trail is fun for kids and adults. It leads to the Bear Gulch cave system, and if your timing is right, you'll pass by several seasonal waterfalls inside the caves (flashlights are required). If it has been raining, check with a ranger, as the caves could be flooded. The upper side of the cave is usually closed in spring and early summer to protect the Townsend's big-ear bats and their pups. *Easy.* ✉ *East side of park* ✥ *Trailhead: just past Bear Gulch Nature Center, on south side of overflow parking lot.*

San Juan Bautista

20 miles northeast of Salinas.

Much of the small town that grew up around Mission San Juan Bautista, still a working church, has been protected from development since 1933, when a state park was established here. Small antiques shops and restaurants occupy the Old West and art-deco buildings that line 3rd Street.

GETTING HERE AND AROUND

From Highway 1 north or south, exit east onto Highway 156. MST buses do not serve San Juan Bautista.

Sights

San Juan Bautista State Historic Park

HISTORIC SITE | With the low-slung, colonnaded **Mission San Juan Bautista** as its drawing card, this park 20 miles northeast of Salinas is about as close to early-19th-century California as you can get. Historic buildings ring the wide green plaza, among them an adobe home furnished with Spanish-colonial antiques, a hotel frozen in the 1860s, a blacksmith shop, a pioneer cabin, and a jailhouse. The mission's cemetery contains the unmarked graves of more than 4,300 Native American converts. **■ TIP→ On the first Saturday of the month, costumed volunteers engage in quilting bees, tortilla making, and other frontier activities; and sarsaparilla and other nonalcoholic drinks are served in the saloon.** ✉ *19 Franklin St., off Hwy. 156, east of U.S. 101* ☎ *831/623–4881* 🌐 *www.parks.ca.gov* 🎫 *$3 park, $4 mission.*

Moss Landing

17 miles north of Monterey, 12 miles north of Salinas.

Moss Landing is not much more than a couple of blocks of cafés and restaurants, art galleries, and studios, plus a busy fishing port, but therein lies its charm. It's a fine place to overnight or stop for a meal and get a dose of nature.

GETTING HERE AND AROUND

From Highway 1 north or south, exit at Moss Landing Road on the ocean side. MST buses serve Moss Landing.

TOURS

Elkhorn Slough Safari Nature Boat Tours
This outfit's naturalists lead two-hour tours of Elkhorn Sough aboard a 27-foot pontoon boat. Reservations are required. *Moss Landing Harbor* *831/633–5555* *elkhornslough.com* *$39.*

ESSENTIALS

VISITOR INFORMATION Moss Landing Chamber of Commerce *831/633–4501* *mosslandingchamber.com.*

Sights

Elkhorn Slough National Estuarine Research Reserve
NATURE PRESERVE | The reserve's 1,700 acres of tidal flats and salt marshes form a complex environment that supports some 300 species of birds. A walk along the meandering waterways and wetlands can reveal hawks, white-tailed kites, owls, herons, and egrets. Also living or visiting here are sea otters, sharks, rays, and many other animals. **■TIP→ On weekends, guided walks from the visitor center begin at 10 and 1. On the first Saturday of the month, an early-bird tour departs at 8:30.** *1700 Elkhorn Rd., Watsonville* *831/728–2822* *elkhornslough.org* *$4 day-use fee (credit card only)* *Closed Mon. and Tues.*

Restaurants

Haute Enchilada
$$$ | SOUTH AMERICAN | Part of a complex that includes art galleries and an events venue, the Haute adds bohemian character to the seafaring village of Moss Landing. The inventive Latin American–inspired dishes include shrimp and black corn enchiladas topped with a citrus cilantro cream sauce, and roasted *pasilla* chilies stuffed with mashed plantains and caramelized onions. **Known for:** extensive cocktail and wine list; many vegan and gluten-free options; artsy atmosphere. *Average main: $25* *7902 Moss Landing Rd.* *831/633–5843* *hauteenchilada.com.*

Phil's Fish Market & Eatery
$$ | SEAFOOD | Exquisitely fresh, simply prepared seafood (try the cioppino) is on the menu at this warehouselike restaurant on the harbor; all kinds of glistening fish are for sale at the market in the front. **Known for:** cioppino; clam chowder; myriad artichoke dishes. *Average main: $22* *7600 Sandholdt Rd.* *831/633–2152* *philsfishmarket.com.*

Hotels

Captain's Inn
$$$ | B&B/INN | Commune with nature and pamper yourself with upscale creature comforts at this green-certified complex in the heart of town. **Pros:** walk to restaurants and shops; tranquil natural setting; free Wi-Fi and parking. **Cons:** rooms in historic building don't have water views; far from urban amenities; not appropriate for young children. *Rooms from: $197* *8122 Moss Landing Rd.* *831/633–5550* *www.captainsinn.com* *10 rooms* *Breakfast.*

Activities

KAYAKING

Monterey Bay Kayaks
KAYAKING | Rent a kayak to paddle out into Elkhorn Slough for up-close wildlife encounters. *2390 Hwy. 1, at North Harbor* *831/373–5357* *montereybaykayaks.com.*

Aptos

17 miles north of Moss Landing.

Backed by a redwood forest and facing the sea, downtown Aptos—known as Aptos Village—is a place of wooden walkways and false-fronted shops. Antiques dealers cluster along Trout Gulch Road, off Soquel Drive east of Highway 1.

GETTING HERE AND AROUND

Use Highway 1 to reach Aptos from Santa Cruz or Monterey. Exit at State Park Drive to reach the main shopping hub and Aptos Village. You can also exit at Freedom Boulevard or Rio del Mar. Soquel Drive is the main artery through town.

ESSENTIALS

VISITOR INFORMATION Aptos Chamber of Commerce ✉ *7605–A Old Dominion Ct.* ☎ *831/688–1467* 🌐 *aptoschamber.com.*

Beaches

★ Seacliff State Beach

BEACH—SIGHT | FAMILY | Sandstone bluffs tower above popular Seacliff State Beach. The 1.5-mile walk north to adjacent New Brighton State Beach in Capitola is one of the nicest on the bay. Leashed dogs are allowed on the beach. **Amenities:** food and drink; lifeguards; parking (fee); showers; toilets. **Best for:** sunset; swimming; walking. ✉ *201 State Park Dr., off Hwy. 1* ☎ *831/685–6500* 🌐 *www.parks.ca.gov* *$10 per vehicle.*

Restaurants

Bittersweet Bistro

$$$ | MEDITERRANEAN | A large old tavern with cathedral ceilings houses this popular bistro, where the Mediterranean-California menu changes seasonally, but regular highlights include paella, seafood puttanesca, and pepper-crusted rib-eye steak with Cabernet demi-glace. Breakfast and lunch are available in the casual Bittersweet Café. **Known for:** value-laden happy hour; seafood specials; house-made desserts. *$ Average main: $29* ✉ *787 Rio Del Mar Blvd., off Hwy. 1* ☎ *831/662–9799* 🌐 *www.bittersweetbistro.com* *Closed Mon. and Tues.*

Hotels

Best Western Seacliff Inn

$$$ | HOTEL | FAMILY | Families and business travelers like this 6-acre property near Seacliff State Beach that's more resort than hotel. **Pros:** walking distance to the beach; family-friendly; hot breakfast buffet. **Cons:** close to freeway; occasional nighttime bar noise; no elevator. *$ Rooms from: $230* ✉ *7500 Old Dominion Ct.* ☎ *831/688–7300, 800/367–2003* 🌐 *seacliffinn.com* *158 rooms* *Breakfast.*

Rio Sands Hotel

$$$ | HOTEL | A property-wide makeover completed in 2015 has made this casual two-building complex near the beach an even more exceptional value. **Pros:** two-minute walk to Rio Del Mar Beach (Seacliff State Beach is also nearby); free parking and Wi-Fi; close to a deli and restaurants. **Cons:** some rooms and suites are small; neighborhood becomes congested in summer. *$ Rooms from: $179* ✉ *116 Aptos Beach Dr.* ☎ *831/688–3207, 800/826–2077* 🌐 *riosands.com* *50 rooms* *Breakfast.*

Seascape Beach Resort

$$$$ | RESORT | FAMILY | It's easy to unwind at this full-fledged resort on a bluff overlooking Monterey Bay. The spacious suites sleep from two to eight people. **Pros:** time share–style apartments; access to miles of beachfront; superb views. **Cons:** far from city life; most bathrooms are small; some rooms need updating. *$ Rooms from: $387* ✉ *1 Seascape Resort Dr.* ☎ *831/662–7171, 866/867–0976* 🌐 *seascaperesort.com* *285 suites* *No meals.*

Capitola and Soquel

4 miles northwest of Aptos.

On the National Register of Historic places as California's first seaside resort town, the village of Capitola has been in a holiday mood since the late 1800s. Casual eateries, surf shops, and ice cream parlors pack its walkable downtown. Inland, across Highway 1, antiques shops line Soquel Drive in the town of Soquel. Wineries dot the Santa Cruz Mountains beyond.

GETTING HERE AND AROUND

From Santa Cruz or Monterey, follow Highway 1 to the Capitola/Soquel (Bay Avenue) exit about 7 miles south of Santa Cruz and head west to reach Capitola and east to access Soquel Village. On summer weekends, park for free in the lot behind the Crossroads Center, a block west of the freeway, and hop aboard the free Capitola Shuttle to the village.

ESSENTIALS

VISITOR INFORMATION Capitola-Soquel Chamber of Commerce ✉ *716-G Capitola Ave., Capitola* ☎ *831/475–6522* 🌐 *capitolachamber.com.*

★ New Brighton State Beach

BEACH—SIGHT | FAMILY | Once the site of a Chinese fishing village, New Brighton is now a popular surfing and camping spot. Its Pacific Migrations Visitor Center traces the history of the Chinese and other peoples who settled around Monterey Bay. It also documents the migratory patterns of the area's wildlife, such as monarch butterflies and gray whales. Leashed dogs are allowed in the park. New Brighton connects with Seacliff Beach, and at low tide you can walk or run along this scenic stretch of sand for nearly 16 miles south (though you might have to wade through a few creeks). **■TIP→ The 1½-mile stroll from New Brighton to Seacliff's concrete ship is a local favorite. Amenities:** parking (fee); showers; toilets. **Best for:** sunset; swimming; walking. ✉ *1500 State Park Dr., off Hwy. 1, Capitola* ☎ *831/464–6329* 🌐 *www.parks.ca.gov* *$10 per vehicle.*

Carpo's

$ | SEAFOOD | FAMILY | Locals love this casual counter where seafood predominates, but you can also order burgers, salads, and steaks. Baskets of battered snapper are among the favorites, along with calamari, prawns, seafood kebabs, fish and chips, and homemade olallieberry pie. **Known for:** large portions of healthy comfort food; lots of options under $10; soup and salad bar. *Average main: $14* ✉ *2400 Porter St., at Hwy. 1, Soquel* ☎ *831/476–6260* 🌐 *carposrestaurant.com.*

Gayle's Bakery & Rosticceria

$$ | CAFÉ | FAMILY | Whether you're in the mood for an orange-olallieberry muffin, a wild rice and chicken salad, or tri-tip on garlic toast, this bakery-deli's varied menu is likely to satisfy. Munch on your lemon meringue tartlet or chocolate brownie on the shady patio, or dig into the daily blue-plate dinner—teriyaki grilled skirt steak with edamame-shiitake sticky rice, perhaps, or roast turkey breast with Chardonnay gravy—amid the whirl of activity inside. **Known for:** prepared meals to go; on-site bakery and rosticceria; deli and espresso bar. *Average main: $17* ✉ *504 Bay Ave., at Capitola Ave., Capitola* ☎ *831/462–1200* 🌐 *gaylesbakery.com.*

Michael's on Main

$$$ | AMERICAN | Creative variations on classic comfort food and live music five nights a week draw lively crowds to this upscale but casual creek-side eatery. For a quiet conversation spot, ask for a table on the romantic patio overlooking the creek. **Known for:** locally sourced,

Did You Know?

Soquel Cove in Santa Cruz is surrounded by New Brighton State Beach, and Seacliff State Beach, where a WWI concrete ship sits partially submerged in the water.

usually within 50 miles; excellent wine list; romantic patio overlooking Soquel Creek. *Average main: $29* *2591 Main St., at Porter St., Soquel* *831/479–9777* *michaelsonmain.net* *Closed Mon.*

Shadowbrook

$$$$ | **EUROPEAN** | To get to this romantic spot overlooking Soquel Creek, you can take a cable car or walk the stairs down a steep, fern-lined bank beside a running waterfall. Dining room options include the rooftop Redwood Room, the wood-paneled Wine Cellar, the creek-side, glass-enclosed Greenhouse, the Fireplace Room, and the airy Garden Room. **Known for:** romantic creek-side setting; prime rib and grilled seafood; local special-occasion favorite for nearly 70 years. *Average main: $34* *1750 Wharf Rd., at Lincoln Ave., Capitola* *831/475–1511* *www.shadowbrook-capitola.com* *No lunch.*

Hotels

Inn at Depot Hill

$$$$ | **B&B/INN** | This inventively designed bed-and-breakfast in a former rail depot views itself as a link to the era of luxury train travel. **Pros:** short walk to beach and village; historic charm; excellent service. **Cons:** fills quickly; hot-tub conversation audible in some rooms; rooms need updating. *Rooms from: $309* *250 Monterey Ave., Capitola* *831/462–3376, 800/572–2632* *www.innatdepothill.com* *12 rooms* *Breakfast.*

Santa Cruz

5 miles west of Capitola, 48 miles north of Monterey.

The big city on this stretch of the California coast, Santa Cruz (pop. 63,364) is less manicured than Carmel or Monterey. Long known for its surfing and its amusement-filled beach boardwalk, the town is a mix of grand Victorian-era homes and rinky-dink motels. The opening of the University of California campus in the 1960s swung the town sharply to the left politically, and the counterculture more or less lives on here. At the same time, the revitalized downtown and an insane real-estate market reflect the city's proximity to Silicon Valley and to a growing Wine Country in the surrounding mountains. Amble around the downtown Santa Cruz Farmers' Market (Wednesday afternoons year-round) to experience the local culture, which derives much of its character from close connections to food and farming. The market covers a city block and includes not just the expected organic produce, but also live music and booths with local crafts and prepared food.

California's Oldest Resort Town

As far as anyone knows for certain, Capitola is the oldest seaside resort town on the Pacific Coast. In 1856 a pioneer acquired Soquel Landing, the picturesque lagoon and beach where Soquel Creek empties into the bay, and built a wharf. Another man opened a campground along the shore, and his daughter named it Capitola after a heroine in a novel series. After the train came to town in the 1870s, thousands of vacationers began arriving to bask in the sun on the glorious beach.

GETTING HERE AND AROUND

From the San Francisco Bay area, take Highway 17 south over the mountains to Santa Cruz, where it merges with Highway 1. Use Highway 1 to get around the area. The Santa Cruz Transit Center is at 920 Pacific Avenue, at Front Street, a short walk from the wharf and boardwalk, with connections to public transit throughout the Monterey Bay and San Francisco Bay areas. You can purchase day passes for Santa Cruz METRO buses (*see Bus Travel, in Planner*) here.

ESSENTIALS

VISITOR INFORMATION Visit Santa Cruz County ✉ *303 Water St., No. 100* ☎ *831/425–1234, 800/833–3494* 🌐 *visitsantacruz.org.*

Sights

Monterey Bay National Marine Sanctuary Exploration Center

INFO CENTER | FAMILY | The interactive and multimedia exhibits at this fascinating interpretive center reveal and explain the treasures of the nation's largest marine sanctuary. The two-story building, across from the main beach and municipal wharf, has films and exhibits about migratory species, watersheds, underwater canyons, kelp forests, and intertidal zones. The second-floor deck has stellar ocean views and an interactive station that provides real-time weather, surf, and buoy reports. ✉ *35 Pacific Ave., near Beach St.* ☎ *831/421–9993* 🌐 *montereybay.noaa.gov/vc/sec* 🎫 *Free* ⏲ *Closed Mon. and Tues.*

Mystery Spot

LOCAL INTEREST | Hokey tourist trap or genuine scientific enigma? Since 1940, curious throngs baffled by the Mystery Spot have made it one of the most visited attractions in Santa Cruz. The laws of gravity and physics don't appear to apply in this tiny patch of redwood forest, where balls roll uphill and people stand on a slant. ■ **TIP→ On weekends and holidays, it's wise to purchase tickets online in advance.** ✉ *465 Mystery Spot Rd., off Branciforte Dr. (north off Hwy. 1)* ☎ *831/423–8897* 🌐 *mysteryspot.com* 🎫 *$8, parking $5.*

Pacific Avenue

NEIGHBORHOOD | When you've had your fill of the city's beaches and waters, take a stroll in downtown Santa Cruz, especially on Pacific Avenue between Laurel and Water streets. Vintage boutiques and mountain-sports stores, sushi bars, and Mexican restaurants, day spas, and nightclubs keep the main drag and the surrounding streets hopping from midmorning until late evening.

★ Santa Cruz Beach Boardwalk

CAROUSEL | FAMILY | Santa Cruz has been a seaside resort since the mid-19th century. Along one end of the broad, south-facing beach, the boardwalk has entertained holidaymakers for more than a century. Its Looff carousel and classic wooden Giant Dipper roller coaster, both dating from the early 1900s, are surrounded by high-tech thrill rides and easygoing kiddie rides with ocean views. Video and arcade games, a minigolf course, and a laser-tag arena pack one gigantic building, which is open daily even if the rides aren't running. You have to pay to play, but you can wander the entire boardwalk for free while sampling carnival fare such as corn dogs and garlic fries. ✉ *Along Beach St.* ☎ *831/423–5590 info line* 🌐 *beachboardwalk.com* 🎫 *$40 day pass for unlimited rides, or pay per ride* ⏲ *Some rides closed Sept.–May.*

Santa Cruz Mission State Historic Park

HISTORIC SITE | On the northern fringes of downtown is the site of California's 12th Spanish mission, built in the 1790s and destroyed by an earthquake in 1857. A museum in a restored 1791 adobe and a half-scale replica of the mission church are part of the complex. ✉ *144 School St., at Adobe St.* ☎ *831/425–5849* 🌐 *www.parks.ca.gov* 🎫 *Free* ⏲ *Closed Tues. and Wed.*

Santa Cruz Municipal Wharf

MARINA | FAMILY | Jutting half a mile into the ocean near one end of the boardwalk, the century-old Municipal Wharf is lined with seafood restaurants, a wine bar, souvenir shops, and outfitters offering bay cruises, fishing trips, and boat rentals. A salty sound track drifts up from under the wharf, where barking sea lions lounge in heaps on the crossbeams. Docents from the Seymour Marine Discovery Center lead free 30-minute tours on spring and summer weekends at 1 and 3; meet at the stage on the west side of the wharf between Olitas Cantina and Marini's Candies. ✉ *Beach St. and Pacific Ave.* ☎ *831/459–3800 tour information.*

Santa Cruz Surfing Museum

MUSEUM | This museum inside the Mark Abbott Memorial Lighthouse chronicles local surfing history. Photographs show old-time surfers, and a display of boards includes rarities such as a heavy redwood plank predating the fiberglass era and the remains of a modern board chomped by a great white shark. Surfer docents reminisce about the good old days. ✉ *Lighthouse Point Park, 701 W. Cliff Dr. near Pelton Ave.* ☎ *831/420–6289* 🎫 *$2 suggested donation* ⏲ *Closed Tues. and Wed. except open Tues. July–early Sept.*

Seymour Marine Discovery Center

ZOO | FAMILY | Part of the Long Marine Laboratory at the University of California Santa Cruz's Institute of Marine Sciences, the center looks more like a research facility than a slick aquarium. Interactive exhibits demonstrate how scientists study the ocean, and the aquarium displays creatures of interest to marine biologists. The 87-foot blue whale skeleton is one of the world's largest. **■ TIP→ General tours take place in the afternoon, and there's an abbreviated tour at 11 am for families with small children.** ✉ *100 Shaffer Rd., end of Delaware Ave., west of Natural Bridges State Beach* ☎ *831/459–3800* 🌐 *seymourcenter.ucsc.edu* 🎫 *$9* ⏲ *Closed Mon.*

Surf City Vintners

WINERY/DISTILLERY | A dozen tasting rooms of limited-production wineries occupy renovated warehouse spaces west of the beach. MJA, Sones Cellars, Santa Cruz Mountain Vineyard, and Equinox are good places to start. Also here are the Santa Cruz Mountain Brewing Company and El Salchicheroa, popular for its homemade sausages, jams, and pickled and candied vegetables. ✉ *Swift Street Courtyard, 334 Ingalls St., at Swift St., off Hwy. 1 (Mission St.)* 🌐 *surfcityvintners.com.*

UC Santa Cruz

COLLEGE | The 2,000-acre University of California Santa Cruz campus nestles in the forested hills above town. Its sylvan setting, ocean vistas, and redwood architecture make the university worth a visit, as does its **arboretum** ($5, open daily from 9 to 5), whose walking path leads through areas dedicated to the plants of California, Australia, New Zealand, and South Africa. **■ TIP→ Free shuttles help students and visitors get around campus, and you can join a guided tour (online reservation required).** ✉ *Main entrance at Bay and High Sts. (turn left on High for arboretum)* ☎ *831/459–0111* 🌐 *www.ucsc.edu/visit.*

★ West Cliff Drive

SCENIC DRIVE | The road that winds along an oceanfront bluff from the municipal wharf to Natural Bridges State Beach makes for a spectacular drive, but it's even more fun to walk or bike the paved path that parallels the road. Surfers bob and swoosh in Monterey Bay at several points near the foot of the bluff, especially at a break known as **Steamer Lane.** Named for a surfer who died here in 1965, the nearby Mark Abbott Memorial Lighthouse stands at Point Santa Cruz, the cliff's major promontory. From here you can watch pinnipeds hang out, sunbathe, and frolic on Seal Rock. ✉ *Santa Cruz.*

Wilder Ranch State Park

NATIONAL/STATE PARK | In this park's Cultural Preserve you can visit the homes, barns, workshops, and bunkhouse of a 19th-century dairy farm. Nature has reclaimed most of the ranch land, and native plants and wildlife have returned to the 7,000 acres of forest, grassland, canyons, estuaries, and beaches. Hike, bike, or ride horseback on miles of ocean-view trails. Dogs aren't allowed at Wilder Ranch. ✉ *Hwy. 1, 1 mile north of Santa Cruz* ☎ *831/426–0505 Interpretive Center, 831/423–9703 trail information* 🌐 *www.parks.ca.gov* 🎟 *$10 per car* ⏲ *Interpretive center closed Mon.–Wed.*

Beaches

Natural Bridges State Beach

BEACH—SIGHT | **FAMILY** | At the end of West Cliff Drive lies this stretch of soft sand edged with tide pools and sea-sculpted rock bridges. **■ TIP➔ From September to early January a colony of monarch butterflies roosts in the eucalyptus grove. Amenities:** lifeguards; parking (fee); toilets. **Best for:** sunrise; sunset; surfing; swimming. ✉ *2531 W. Cliff Dr.* ☎ *831/423–4609* 🌐 *www.parks.ca.gov* 🎟 *Beach free, parking $10.*

Twin Lakes State Beach

BEACH—SIGHT | **FAMILY** | Stretching a half mile along the coast on both sides of the small-craft jetties, Twin Lakes is one of Monterey Bay's sunniest beaches. It encompasses Seabright State Beach (with access in a residential neighborhood on the upcoast side) and Black's Beach on the downcoast side. Families often come here to sunbathe, picnic, and hike the nature trail around adjacent Schwann Lake. Parking is tricky from May through September—you need to pay for an $8 day-use permit at a kiosk and the lot fills quickly—but you can park all day in the harbor pay lot and walk here. Leashed dogs are allowed. **Amenities:** food and drink; lifeguards (seasonal); parking; showers; toilets; water sports (seasonal). **Best for:** sunset; surfing; swimming; walking. ✉ *7th Ave., at East Cliff Dr.* ☎ *831/427–4868* 🌐 *www.parks.ca.gov.*

Restaurants

Crow's Nest

$$$ | **SEAFOOD** | **FAMILY** | A classic California beachside restaurant, the Crow's Nest sits right on the water in Santa Cruz Harbor–vintage surfboards and local surf photography line the walls in the main dining room, and nearly every table overlooks sand and surf. For sweeping ocean views and fish tacos, burgers, and other casual fare, head upstairs to the Breakwater Bar & Grill. **Known for:** house-smoked salmon and calamari apps; crab-cake eggs Benedict and olallieberry pancakes; on-site market with pizzas, sandwiches, soups, and salads. [$] *Average main: $24* ✉ *2218 E. Cliff Dr., west of 7th Ave.* ☎ *831/476–4560* 🌐 *crowsnest-santacruz.com.*

Gabriella Café

$$$ | **ITALIAN** | The work of local artists hangs on the walls of this petite, romantic café in a tile-roof cottage. Featuring organic produce from area farms, the seasonal Italian menu has included wild-mushroom risotto; bouillabaisse; marinated chicken with apricots, currants, and olives; and roasted beet salad with wild arugula, goat cheese, and pistachios. **Known for:** nearly all produce comes from local organic farmers; romantic interior with Moorish arches; weekend brunch. [$] *Average main: $26* ✉ *910 Cedar St., at Church St.* ☎ *831/457–1677* 🌐 *www.gabriellacafe.com.*

★ Laili Restaurant

$$ | **MEDITERRANEAN** | Exotic Mediterranean flavors with an Afghan twist take center stage at this artsy, stylish space with soaring ceilings. Evenings are especially lively, when locals come to relax over wine and soft jazz at the blue-concrete bar, the heated patio with twinkly lights, or at a communal table near the open kitchen. **Known for:** house-made pastas and numerous vegetarian and vegan options; fresh naan, chutneys and dips with every meal; traditional dishes like pomegranate eggplant and maush-awa soup. *Average main: $22* *101–B Cooper St., near Pacific Ave.* *831/423–4545* *lailirestaurant.com* *Closed Mon.*

La Posta

$$$ | **ITALIAN** | Authentic Italian fare made with fresh local produce lures diners into cozy, modern-rustic La Posta. Nearly everything is made in-house, from the pizzas and breads baked in the brick oven to the pasta and the vanilla-bean gelato. **Known for:** seasonal wild-nettle lasagna; braised lamb shank; in the heart of the Seabright neighborhood. *Average main: $24* *538 Seabright Ave., at Logan St.* *831/457–2782* *lapostarestaurant.com* *Closed Mon. No lunch.*

Oswald

$$$$ | **EUROPEAN** | Sophisticated yet unpretentious European-inspired California cooking is the order of the day at this intimate and stylish bistro with a seasonal menu, which might include such items as seafood risotto or crispy duck breast in a pomegranate reduction sauce. The creative concoctions poured at the slick marble bar include whiskey mixed with apple and lemon juice, and tequila with celery juice and lime. **Known for:** house-made pork sausage; craft cocktails; local art displays that changes monthly. *Average main: $32* *121 Soquel Ave., at Front St.* *831/423–7427* *oswaldrestaurant.com* *Closed Mon. No lunch Sun. and Tues.*

★ Soif

$$$ | **MEDITERRANEAN** | Wine reigns at this sleek bistro and wineshop that takes its name from the French word for thirst—the selections come from near and far, and you can order many of them by the taste or glass. Mediterranean-inspired small plates and entrées are served at the copper-top bar, the big communal table, and private tables. **Known for:** Mediterranean-style dishes; well-stocked wineshop; jazz combo or solo pianist plays on some evenings. *Average main: $28* *105 Walnut Ave., at Pacific Ave.* *831/423–2020* *soifwine.com* *Closed Sun. No lunch.*

Zachary's

$ | **AMERICAN** | This noisy café filled with students and families defines the funky essence of Santa Cruz. It also dishes up great breakfasts: stay simple with sourdough pancakes, or go for Mike's Mess—eggs scrambled with bacon, mushrooms, and home fries, then topped with sour cream, melted cheese, and fresh tomatoes. **Known for:** nearly everything made in house; "Mike's Mess" egg dishes; local organic ingredients. *Average main: $14* *819 Pacific Ave.* *831/427–0646* *www.zacharyssantacruz.com* *Closed Mon. No dinner.*

Hotels

Babbling Brook Inn

$$$$ | **B&B/INN** | Though it's in the middle of Santa Cruz, this bed-and-breakfast has lush gardens, a running stream, and tall trees that make you feel like you're in a secluded wood. **Pros:** close to UCSC; within walking distance of downtown shops; woodsy feel. **Cons:** near a high school; some rooms close to a busy street; many stairs and no elevator. *Rooms from: $280* *1025 Laurel St.* *831/427–2437, 800/866–1131* *babblingbrookinn.com* *13 rooms* *Breakfast.*

Carousel Beach Inn

$$ | **HOTEL** | This basic but comfy motel, decorated in bold, retro seaside style and across the street from the boardwalk, is ideal for travelers who want easy access to the sand and the amusement park rides without spending a fortune. **Pros:** steps from Santa Cruz Main Beach; affordable lodging rates and ride packages; free parking and Wi-Fi. **Cons:** no pool or spa; no exercise room; not pet-friendly. *Rooms from: $159* *110 Riverside Ave.* *831/425–7090* *santacruzmotels.com/carousel.html* *34 rooms* *Breakfast.*

Chaminade Resort & Spa

$$$$ | **RESORT** | Secluded on 300 hilltop acres of redwood and eucalyptus forest with hiking trails, this Mission-style complex commands expansive views of Monterey Bay. Guest rooms are furnished in an eclectic, bohemian style that pays homage to the artsy local community and the city's industrial past, while incorporating vintage game elements throughout. **Pros:** far from city life; spectacular property; ideal spot for romance and rejuvenation. **Cons:** must drive to attractions and sights; near a major hospital; resort fee. *Rooms from: $280* *1 Chaminade La.* *800/283–6569 reservations, 831/475–5600* *www.chaminade.com* *156 rooms* *No meals.*

★ **Dream Inn Santa Cruz**

$$$$ | **HOTEL** | A short stroll from the boardwalk and wharf, this full-service luxury hotel is the only lodging in Santa Cruz directly on the beach. **Pros:** on-site restaurant with sweeping south-facing views of Monterey Bay; easy parking; walk to boardwalk and downtown. **Cons:** expensive; area gets congested on summer weekends; pool area and hallways can be noisy. *Rooms from: $369* *175 W. Cliff Dr.* *831/740–8141, 844/510–1746* *dreaminnsantacruz.com* *165 rooms* *No meals.*

Hotel Paradox

$$$$ | **HOTEL** | About a mile from the ocean and two blocks from Pacific Avenue, this stylish, forest-theme complex (part of the Marriott Autograph Collection) is among the few full-service hotels in town. **Pros:** close to downtown and main beach; spacious pool area with cabanas, fire pits, hot tub, and dining and cocktail service; on-site farm-to-table restaurant. **Cons:** pool area can get crowded on warm-weather days; some rooms on the small side; thin walls. *Rooms from: $279* *611 Ocean St.* *831/425–7100, 855/425–7200* *hotelparadox.com* *172 rooms* *No meals.*

Hyatt Place Santa Cruz

$$$ | **HOTEL** | Displays of vintage surfboards and local art grace the walls of the spacious ocean-theme lobby at this new downtown hotel, which opened in 2018. **Pros:** close to downtown restaurants and shops; outdoor pool and hot tub and 24-hour fitness center; on-site restaurant and bar. **Cons:** not on the beach; valet parking only; fronts busy road. *Rooms from: $219* *407 Broadway* *831/226–2304* *hyattplace.com* *106 rooms* *No meals.*

Pacific Blue Inn

$$$ | **B&B/INN** | Green themes predominate in this three-story, eco-friendly bed-and-breakfast, on a sliver of prime downtown property. **Pros:** free parking; free bicycles; downtown location. **Cons:** tiny property; not suitable for children; parking lot is a block away. *Rooms from: $189* *636 Pacific Ave.* *831/600–8880* *pacificblueinn.com* *9 rooms* *No meals.*

Sea & Sand Inn

$$$ | **HOTEL** | Location is the main appeal of this motel atop a waterfront bluff where all rooms have an ocean view and the boardwalk is just down the street. **Pros:** beach is steps away; friendly staff; tidy landscaping. **Cons:** tight parking lot; fronts a busy road; can be noisy. *Rooms from: $229* *201 W. Cliff Dr.* *831/427–3400* *santacruzmotels.com* *20 rooms, 2 cottages* *Breakfast.*

★ **West Cliff Inn**

$$$$ | **B&B/INN** | With views of the boardwalk and Monterey Bay, the West Cliff perches on the bluffs across from Cowell Beach. **Pros:** killer views; walking distance of the beach; close to downtown. **Cons:** boardwalk noise; street traffic. *Rooms from: $279* *174 West Cliff Dr.* *831/457–2200* *www.westcliffinn.com* *9 rooms, 1 cottage* *Breakfast.*

O'Neill: A Santa Cruz Icon

O'Neill wet suits and beachwear weren't exactly born in Santa Cruz, but as far as most of the world is concerned, the O'Neill brand is synonymous with Santa Cruz and surfing legend.

The O'Neill wet-suit story began in 1952, when Jack O'Neill and his brother Robert opened their first Surf Shop in a garage across from San Francisco's Ocean Beach. While shaping balsa surfboards and selling accessories, the O'Neills experimented with solutions to a common surfer problem: frigid waters. Tired of being forced back to shore, blue-lipped and shivering, after just 20 or 30 minutes riding the waves, they played with various materials and eventually designed a neoprene vest.

In 1959 Jack moved his Surf Shop 90 miles south to Cowell's Beach in Santa Cruz. It quickly became a popular surf hangout, and O'Neill's new wet suits began to sell like hotcakes. In the early 1960s, the company opened a warehouse for manufacturing on a larger scale. Santa Cruz soon became a major surf city, attracting wave riders to prime breaks at Steamer Lane, Pleasure Point, and the Hook. In 1965 O'Neill pioneered the first wet-suit boots, and in 1971 Jack's son invented the surf leash. By 1980, O'Neill stood at the top of the world wet-suit market. On June 2, 2017, Jack O'Neill passed away at the age of 94, in his longtime Pleasure Point residence overlooking the surf.

Nightlife

Catalyst

DANCE CLUBS | This huge, grimy, and fun club books rock, indie rock, punk, death-metal, reggae, and other acts. ✉ *1011 Pacific Ave.* ☎ *877/987–6487* 🌐 *catalystclub.com.*

Kuumbwa Jazz Center

MUSIC CLUBS | The center draws top performers such as the Lee Ritenour and Dave Grusin, Chris Potter, and the Dave Holland Trio; the café serves meals an hour before most shows. ✉ *320–2 Cedar St.* ☎ *831/427–2227* 🌐 *kuumbwajazz.org.*

Moe's Alley

MUSIC CLUBS | Blues, salsa, reggae, funk: delightfully casual Moe's presents it all (and more). ✉ *1535 Commercial Way* ☎ *831/479–1854* 🌐 *moesalley.com* 🕒 *Closed Mon.*

Performing Arts

Tannery Arts Center

ARTS CENTERS | The former Salz Tannery now contains nearly 30 studios and live-work spaces for artists whose disciplines range from ceramics and glass to film and digital media; most have public hours of business. The social center is the **Bistro One Twelve,** which in the late afternoons and evenings hosts poets, all types of performers, and live music. Performances also take place at the on-site Colligan Theater. The center also hosts assorted arts events on weekends and occasionally on weekdays. ✉ *1060 River St., at intersection of Hwys. 1 and 9* 🌐 *tanneryartscenter.org/.*

ADVENTURE TOURS

Mount Hermon Adventures

TOUR—SPORTS | Zip-line through the redwoods at this adventure center in the Santa Cruz Mountains. On some summer weekends there's an aerial adventure course with obstacles and challenges in the redwoods. **■TIP→ To join a tour (reservations essential), you must be at least 10 years old and at least 54 inches tall, and weigh between 75 and 250 pounds.** ✉ *17 Conference Dr., 9 miles north of downtown Santa Cruz near Felton, Mount Hermon* ☎ *831/430–4357* 🌐 *mounthermonadventures.com* 🎫 *From $65.*

BICYCLING

Another Bike Shop

BICYCLING | Mountain bikers should head here for tips on the best area trails and to browse cutting-edge gear made and tested locally. ✉ *2361 Mission St., at King St.* ☎ *831/427–2232* 🌐 *www.anotherbikeshop.com.*

BOATS AND CHARTERS

Chardonnay II Sailing Charters

BOATING | The 70-foot *Chardonnay II* departs year-round from Santa Cruz yacht harbor on whale-watching, sunset, and other cruises around Monterey Bay. Most regularly scheduled excursions cost $68; food and drink are served on many of them. Reservations are essential. ✉ *Santa Cruz West Harbor, 790 Mariner Park Way* ☎ *831/423–1213* 🌐 *chardonnay.com.*

Stagnaro Sport Fishing, Charters & Whale Watching Cruises

BOATING | Stagnaro operates salmon, albacore, and rock-cod fishing expeditions; the fees include bait. The company (aka Santa Cruz Whale Watching) also runs whale-watching, dolphin, and sea-life cruises year-round. ✉ *1718 Brommer St., near Santa Cruz Harbor* ☎ *831/427–0230* 🌐 *stagnaros.com* 🎫 *From $52.*

GOLF

DeLaveaga Golf Course

GOLF | Woodsy DeLaveaga, a public course set in a hilly park, overlooks Santa Cruz and the bay. With its canyons, tree-lined fairways, and notoriously difficult par-5, dogleg 10th hole, the course challenges novices and seasoned golfers. ✉ *401 Upper Park Rd.* ☎ *831/423–7214* 🌐 *www.delaveagagolf.com* 🎫 *$49 weekdays, $64 weekends/holidays* ⛳ *18 holes, 5700 yards, par 70.*

Pasatiempo Golf Club

GOLF | Designed by famed golf architect Dr. Alister MacKenzie in 1929, this semiprivate course, set amid undulating hills just above the city, is among the nation's top championship courses. Golfers rave about the spectacular views and challenging terrain. According to the club, MacKenzie, who designed Pebble Beach's exclusive Cypress Point course and Augusta National in Georgia, the home of the Masters Golf Tournament, declared this his favorite layout. ✉ *20 Clubhouse Rd.* ☎ *831/459–9155* 🌐 *www.pasatiempo.com* 🎫 *From $260* ⛳ *18 holes, 6125 yards, par 72.*

KAYAKING

Kayak Connection

KAYAKING | From March through May, participants in this outfit's tours mingle with gray whales and their calves on their northward journey to Alaska. Throughout the year, the company rents kayaks and paddleboards and conducts tours of Natural Bridges State Beach, Capitola, and Elkhorn Slough. ✉ *Santa Cruz Harbor, 413 Lake Ave., No. 3* ☎ *831/479–1121* 🌐 *kayakconnection.com* 🎫 *From $60 for scheduled tours.*

Venture Quest Kayaking

KAYAKING | Explore hidden coves and kelp forests on guided two-hour kayak tours that depart from Santa Cruz Wharf. The tours include a kayaking lesson. Venture Quest also rents kayaks (and wet suits and gear), and arranges tours at other Monterey Bay destinations, including

Elkhorn Slough. ✉ *2 Santa Cruz Wharf* ☎ *831/427–2267 kayak hotline, 831/425–8445 rental office* 🌐 *kayaksantacruz.com* 🎟 *From $35 for rentals, $60 for tours.*

SURFING

EQUIPMENT AND LESSONS

Club-Ed Surf School and Camps

SURFING | Find out what all the fun is about at Club-Ed. Your first private or group lesson ($100 and up) includes all equipment. ✉ *Cowell's Beach, at Dream Inn Santa Cruz* ☎ *831/464–0177* 🌐 *club-ed.com.*

Cowell's Beach Surf Shop

SURFING | This shop sells gear, clothing, and swimwear; rents surfboards, stand-up paddle boards, and wet suits; and offers lessons. ✉ *30 Front St.* ☎ *831/427–2355* 🌐 *cowellssurfshop.com.*

Richard Schmidt Surf School

SURFING | Since 1978 Richard Schmidt has shared the stoke of surfing and the importance of ocean awareness and conservation with legions of students of all ages. Today the outfit offers surfing and stand-up paddleboard lessons (equipment provided) and marine adventure tours in Santa Cruz and elsewhere on the bay. Locations depend on where the waves are breaking or the wind's a'blowing, but typically convene at Cowell's Beach or Pleasure Point. ✉ *Santa Cruz* ☎ *831/423–0928* 🌐 *www.richardschmidt.com* 🎟 *From $90.*

Shopping

Bookshop Santa Cruz

BOOKS/STATIONERY | In 2016 the town's best and most beloved independent bookstore celebrated its 50th anniversary of selling new, used, and remaindered titles. The children's section is especially comprehensive, and the shop's special events calendar is packed with readings, social mixers, book signings, and discussions. ✉ *1520 Pacific Ave.* ☎ *831/423–0900* 🌐 *bookshopsantacruz.com.*

O'Neill Surf Shop

SPORTING GOODS | Local surfers get their wetties (wet suits) and other gear at this O'Neill store or the one in Capitola, at 1115 41st Avenue. There's also a satellite shop on the Santa Cruz Boardwalk. ✉ *110 Cooper St.* ☎ *831/469–4377* 🌐 *www.oneill.com.*

Santa Cruz Downtown Farmers' Market

OUTDOOR/FLEA/GREEN MARKETS | FAMILY | Santa Cruz is famous for its long tradition of organic growing and sustainable living, and its downtown market (one of five countywide) especially reflects the incredible diversity and quality of local agriculture and synergistic daily life of community-minded residents. The busy market, which always has live music, happens every Wednesday from 1:30 to 5:30 (6:30 in summer), rain or shine. The stalls cover much of an entire city block near Pacific Avenue and include fresh produce plus everything from oysters, beer, bread, and charcuterie, to arts and crafts and hot prepared foods made from ingredients sourced from on-site vendors. ✉ *Cedar St. at Lincoln St.* ☎ *831/454–0566* 🌐 *www.santacruzfarmersmarket.org.*

The True Olive Connection

FOOD/CANDY | Taste your way through boutique extra-virgin olive oils and balsamic vinegars from around the world at this family-run shop. You can also pick up gourmet food products and olive oil–based gift items. There's another location in Aptos, at 7960 Soquel Drive. ✉ *106 Lincoln St., at. Pacific Ave.* ☎ *831/458–6457* 🌐 *trueoliveconnection.com.*

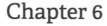

Chapter 6

YOSEMITE NATIONAL PARK

Updated by
Cheryl Crabtree

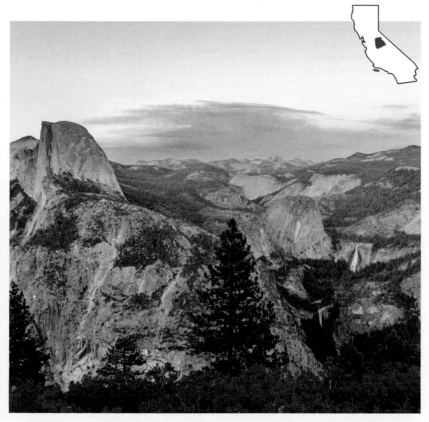

Sights ★★★★★

Restaurants ★★★★☆

Hotels ★★★★★

Shopping ★☆☆☆☆

Nightlife ★☆☆☆☆

WELCOME TO YOSEMITE NATIONAL PARK

TOP REASONS TO GO

★ **Scenic falls:** An easy stroll brings you to the base of Lower Yosemite Fall, where roaring springtime waters make for misty lens caps and lasting memories.

★ **Tunnel vision:** Approaching Yosemite Valley, Wawona Road passes through a mountainside and emerges before one of the park's most heart-stopping vistas.

★ **Inhale the beauty:** Pause to take in the light, pristine air as you travel about the High Sierra's Tioga Pass and Tuolumne Meadows, where 10,000-foot granite peaks just might take your breath away.

★ **Walk away:** Leave the crowds behind—but do bring along a buddy—and take a hike somewhere along Yosemite's 800 miles of trails.

★ **Winter wonder:** Observe the snowflakes and stillness of winter in the park.

1 Yosemite Valley. At an elevation of 4,000 feet, in roughly the center of the park, beats Yosemite's heart. This is where you'll find the park's most famous sights and biggest crowds.

2 Wawona and Mariposa Grove. The park's southern tip holds Wawona, with its grand old hotel and pioneer history center, and the Mariposa Grove of Giant Sequoias. These are closest to the south entrance, 35 miles (a one-hour drive) south of Yosemite Village.

3 Tuolumne Meadows. The highlight of east-central Yosemite is this wildflower-strewn valley with hiking trails, nestled among sharp, rocky peaks. It's a 1½-hour drive northeast of Yosemite Valley along Tioga Road (closed mid-October–late May).

4 Hetch Hetchy. The most remote, least visited part of Yosemite accessible by automobile, this glacial valley is dominated by a reservoir and veined with wilderness trails. It's near the park's western boundary, about a half-hour drive north of the Big Oak Flat entrance.

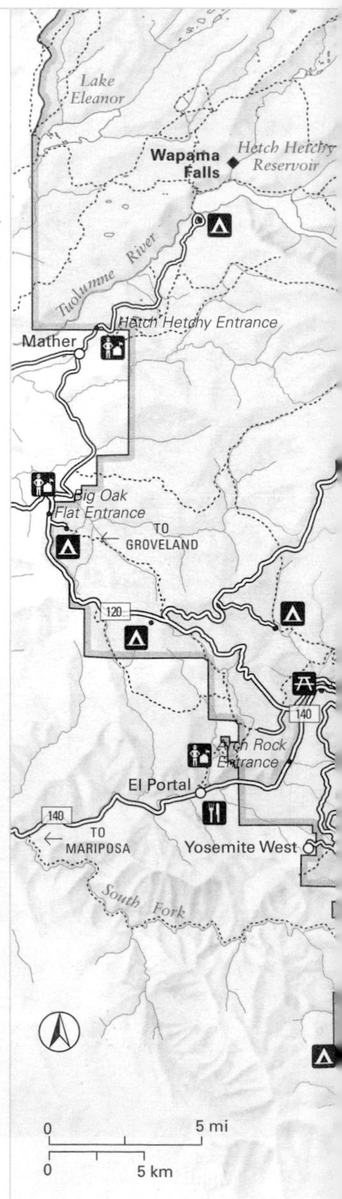

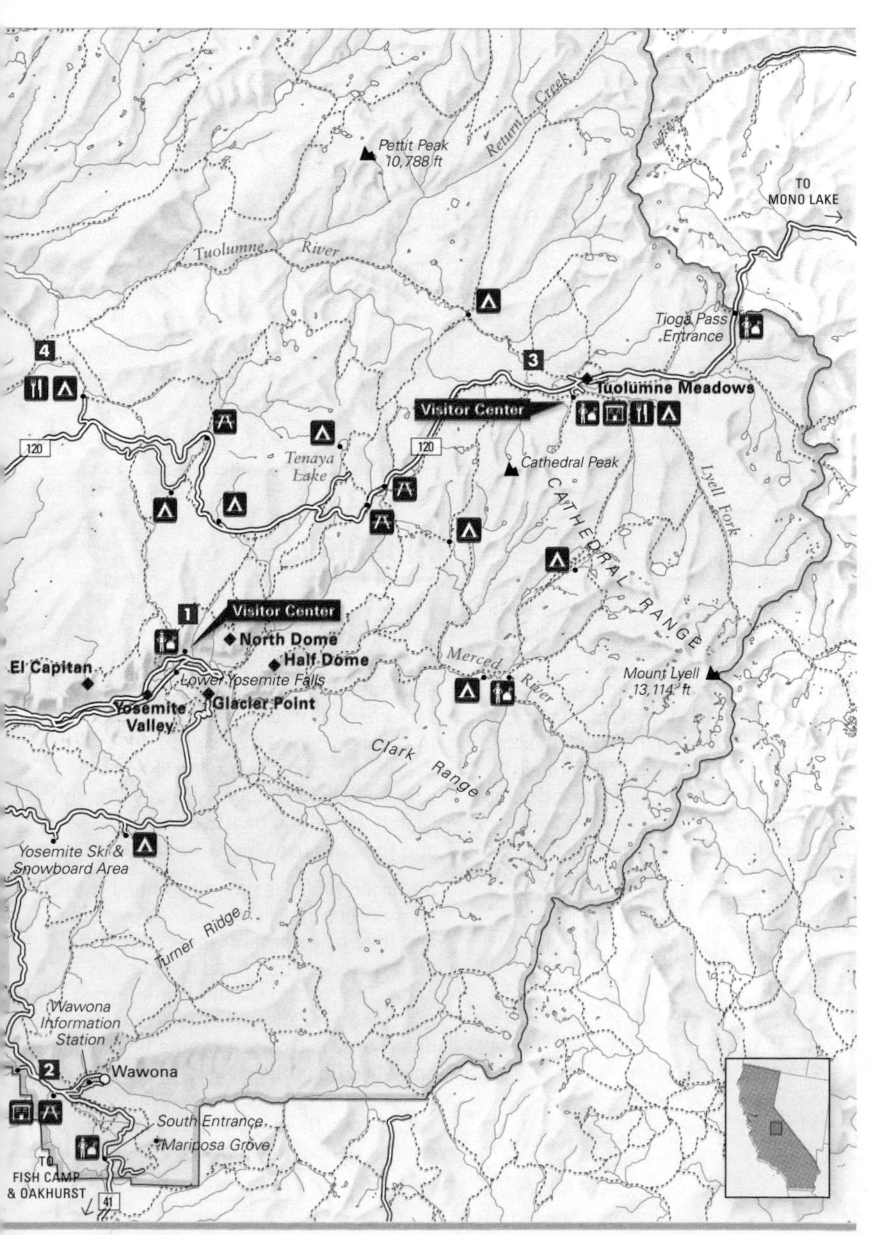
Pettit Peak
10,788 ft
Return Creek
TO
MONO LAKE
Tuolumne River
Tioga Pass
Entrance
4
3
Tuolumne Meadows
Visitor Center
120
Tenaya
Lake
120
Cathedral Peak
CATHEDRAL RANGE
Lyell Fork
1
Visitor Center
North Dome
Half Dome
El Capitan
Lower Yosemite Falls
Merced River
Mount Lyell
13,114 ft
Yosemite
Valley
Glacier Point
Clark Range
Yosemite Ski &
Snowboard Area
Turner Ridge
Wawona
Information
Station
2
Wawona
South Entrance
Mariposa Grove
TO
FISH CAMP
& OAKHURST
41

By merely standing in Yosemite Valley and turning in a circle, you can see more natural wonders in a minute than you could in a full day pretty much anywhere else. Half Dome, Yosemite Falls, El Capitan, Bridalveil Fall, Sentinel Dome, the Merced River, white-flowering dogwood trees, maybe even bears ripping into the bark of fallen trees or sticking their snouts into beehives—it's all in Yosemite Valley.

In the mid-1800s, when tourists were arriving to the area, the valley's special geologic qualities and the giant sequoias of Mariposa Grove 30 miles to the south so impressed a group of influential Californians that they persuaded President Abraham Lincoln to grant those two areas to the state for protection on June 30, 1864. On October 1, 1890—thanks largely to lobbying efforts by naturalist John Muir and Robert Underwood Johnson, the editor of *Century Magazine*—Congress set aside an additional 1,500 square miles for Yosemite National Park; the valley and Mariposa Grove remained under state control until 1906, when they merged with the national park.

Planning

When to Go

During extremely busy periods—such as weekends and holidays throughout the year—you will experience delays at the entrance gates. For smaller crowds, visit midweek. Or come January through March, when the park is a bit less busy and the days usually are sunny and clear.

Summer rainfall is rare. In winter, heavy snows occasionally cause road closures, and tire chains or four-wheel drive may be required on the roads that remain open. The road to Glacier Point beyond the turnoff for Yosemite Ski & Snowboard Area is closed after the first major snowfall; Tioga Road is closed from late October through May or mid-June. Mariposa Grove Road is typically closed for a shorter period in winter.

Festivals and Events

Bluesapalooza

FESTIVAL | The first weekend of every August, Mammoth Lakes hosts a blues and beer festival—with an emphasis on the beer tasting. ✉ *Mammoth Lakes* ☎ *888/992–7397* 🌐 *www.mammoth-bluesbrewsfest.com.*

The Bracebridge Dinner at Yosemite

FESTIVAL | Held at The Majestic Yosemite Hotel (formerly The Ahwahnee) in Yosemite Village every Christmas since 1928, this 17th-century-theme madrigal dinner is so popular that most seats are booked months in advance. Dinner costs $380; lodging packages start at $1,019, or $1,219 if you want to stay at The Majestic Yosemite Hotel. ✉ *The Majestic Yosemite Hotel, 1 Ahwahnee Dr., Yosemite Village* ☎ *888/413–8869, 602/278–8888 international* 🌐 *www.travelyosemite.com.*

Fireman's Muster

FESTIVAL | North of Sonora in the old mining town of Columbia, history springs to life at this festival of antique fire engines, with hose-spraying contests and a parade of the old pumpers. ✉ *Columbia* ☎ *209/533–4420, 800/446–1333.*

The Grand Grape Celebration

FESTIVAL | Some of California's most prestigious vintners hold two- and three-day midweek seminars in the Great Room of The Majestic Yosemite Hotel (formerly The Ahwahnee) in Yosemite Village. They culminate with an elegant—albeit pricey—banquet dinner. Arrive early for seats; book early for dinner ($208) and lodging and dining packages (from $317). ✉ *Yosemite Village* ☎ *888/413–8869, 602/278–8888 international* 🌐 *www.travelyosemite.com.*

Mammoth Jazzfest

FESTIVAL | This weekend festival funded by the town of Mammoth Lakes features free jazz performances at The Village at Mammoth. ✉ *Mammoth Lakes* ☎ *760/934–2712, 888/466–2666* 🌐 *www.mammothjazzfest.org.*

Mother Lode Roundup Parade and Rodeo

FESTIVAL | On Mother's Day weekend, the town of Sonora celebrates its gold-mining, agricultural, and lumbering heritage with a parade, rodeo, entertainment, and food. ✉ *Sonora* ☎ *209/533–4420, 800/446–1333* 🌐 *www.motherloderoundup.com.*

Sierra Art Trails

FESTIVAL | The work of more than 100 artists is on display in studios and galleries throughout eastern Madera and Mariposa counties. Purchase the catalog of locations and hours at area shops. ☎ *559/658–8844* 🌐 *www.sierraarttrails.org.*

A Taste of Yosemite

FESTIVAL | Celebrated chefs present cooking demonstrations and multicourse meals at The Majestic Yosemite Hotel in Yosemite Village from mid-January to early February. Dinner-only costs $208. Two-night packages start at $297 per person; three- and four-night packages are also available. Space is limited. ✉ *Yosemite Village* ☎ *888/413–8869, 602/278–8888 international* 🌐 *www.travelyosemite.com.*

Planning Your Time

YOSEMITE IN ONE DAY

Begin at the **Valley Visitor Center,** where you can watch the documentary *Spirit of Yosemite.* A minute's stroll from there is the **Native American village of the Ahwahnee,** which recalls Native American life circa 1870. Take another 20 minutes to see the **Yosemite Museum.** Then, hop aboard the free shuttle to Yosemite Falls and hike the **Lower Yosemite Fall Trail** to the base of the falls. Have lunch at **Yosemite Valley Lodge,** which you can access by shuttle or walk to from the falls in 20 minutes.

You can either leisurely explore **Half Dome Village (formerly Curry Village)**—by

AVERAGE HIGH/LOW TEMPERATURES					
JAN.	**FEB.**	**MAR.**	**APR.**	**MAY**	**JUNE**
48/29	53/30	55/32	61/36	69/43	78/49
JULY	**AUG.**	**SEPT.**	**OCT.**	**NOV.**	**DEC.**
85/55	84/55	79/49	70/42	56/34	47/29

swimming or ice-skating, shopping, renting a bike, or having a beer on the deck; check out family-friendly **Happy Isles Art and Nature Center** and the adjacent nature trail; or hike up the **Mist Trail** to the Vernal Fall footbridge to admire the view.

Hop back on the shuttle, then disembark at **The Majestic Yosemite Hotel (formerly The Ahwahnee).** The Great Lounge here has a magnificent fireplace and Native American artwork; have a meal in the Dining Room if you're up for a splurge. Or, take the shuttle to **Yosemite Village** where you can grab some fixings, then drive to **El Capitan picnic area** and enjoy an outdoor evening meal. At this time of day, "El Cap" should be sun-splashed. (You will have also gotten several good looks at world-famous **Half Dome** throughout the day.) If the sun hasn't set yet, drive to the base of **Bridalveil Fall** to take a short hike.

Getting Here and Around

AIR TRAVEL

The closest airport to the south and west entrances is Fresno Yosemite International Airport (FAT). Mammoth Yosemite Airport (MMH) is closest to the east entrance. Sacramento International Airport (SMF) is also close to the north and west entrances.

BUS AND TRAIN TRAVEL

Amtrak's daily San Joaquin train stops in Merced and connects with YARTS buses that travel to Yosemite Valley along Highway 140 from Merced. Seasonal YARTS buses (typically mid-May to late September) also travel along Highway 41 from Fresno, Highway 120 from Sonora, and Highway 395 and Tioga Road from Mammoth Lakes with scheduled stops at towns along the way. Once you're in Yosemite Valley you can take advantage of the free shuttle buses, which operate on low emissions, have 21 stops, and run from 7 am to 10 pm year-round. Buses run about every 10 minutes in summer, a bit less frequently in winter. A separate (but also free) summer-only shuttle runs out to El Capitan. Also in summer, you can pay to take the "hikers' bus" from Yosemite Valley to Tuolumne or to ride a tour bus up to Glacier Point. During the snow season, buses run regularly between Yosemite Valley and Yosemite Ski & Snowboard Area.

CAR TRAVEL

Roughly 200 miles from San Francisco, 300 miles from Los Angeles, and 500 miles from Las Vegas, Yosemite takes a while to reach—and its many sites and attractions merit much more time than what rangers say is the average visit: four hours.

Of the park's four entrances, Arch Rock is the closest to Yosemite Valley. The road that goes through it, Route 140 from Merced and Mariposa, is a scenic western approach that snakes alongside the boulder-packed Merced River. Route 41, through Wawona, is the way to come from Los Angeles (or Fresno, if you've flown in and rented a car). Route 120, through Crane Flat, is the most direct route from San Francisco. The only way in from the east is Tioga Road, which may be the best route in terms of scenery—though due to snow accumulation it's open for a frustratingly short amount of time each year (typically early June through mid-October). Once you enter

Yosemite Valley, park your car in one of the two main day parking areas, at Yosemite Village and Yosemite Falls, then visit the sights via the free shuttle bus system. Or walk or bike along the valley's 12 miles of paved paths.

There are few gas stations within Yosemite (Crane Flat and Wawona; none in the valley), so fuel up before you reach the park. From late fall until early spring, the weather is especially unpredictable, and driving can be treacherous. You should carry chains during this period as they are required when roads are icy and when it snows.

Park Essentials

ACCESSIBILITY

Yosemite's facilities are continually being upgraded to make them more accessible. Many of the valley floor trails—particularly at Lower Yosemite Fall, Bridalveil Fall, and Mirror Lake—are wheelchair accessible, though some assistance may be required. The Valley Visitor Center is fully accessible, as are the park shuttle buses. A sign-language interpreter is available for ranger programs. Visitors with respiratory difficulties should take note of the park's high elevations—the valley floor is approximately 4,000 feet above sea level, but Tuolumne Meadows and parts of the high country hover around 10,000 feet.

PARK FEES AND PERMITS

The admission fee, valid for seven days, is $35 per vehicle, $30 per motorcycle, or $20 per individual.

If you plan to camp in the backcountry or climb Half Dome, you must have a wilderness permit. Availability of permits depends upon trailhead quotas. It's best to make a reservation, especially if you will be visiting May through September. You can reserve two days to 24 weeks in advance by phone, mail, or fax (preferred method) (✉ *Box 545, Yosemite, CA* ☎ *209/372–0740* 📠 *209/372–0739*); you'll pay $5 per person plus $5 per reservation if and when your reservations are confirmed. You can download the reservation forms from 🌐 *www.nps.gov/yose/planyourvisit/upload/wildpermitform.pdf*. Without a reservation, you may still get a free permit on a first-come, first-served basis at wilderness permit offices at Big Oak Flat, Hetch Hetchy, Tuolumne Meadows, Wawona, the Wilderness Center in Yosemite Village, and Yosemite Valley in summer. From fall to spring, visit the Valley Visitor Center.

PARK HOURS

The park is open 24/7 year-round. All entrances are open at all hours, except for Hetch Hetchy entrance, which is open roughly dawn to dusk. Yosemite is in the Pacific time zone.

CELL PHONE RECEPTION

Cell phone reception depends on the service provider and can be hit or miss everywhere in the park. There are public telephones at park entrance stations, visitor centers, all restaurants and lodging facilities in the park, gas stations, and in Yosemite Village.

Educational Offerings

CLASSES AND SEMINARS

Art Classes

ARTS VENUE | Professional artists conduct workshops in watercolor, etching, drawing, and other mediums. Bring your own materials or purchase the basics at the Happy Isles Art and Nature Center. Children under 12 must be accompanied by an adult. The center also offers beginner art workshops and children's art and family craft programs ($5–$20 per person). ✉ *Happy Isles Art and Nature Center* ☎ *209/372–1442* 🌐 *www.yosemiteconservancy.org* 💵 *$20* ⏲ *No classes Sun. Closed Dec.–Feb.*

Yosemite Outdoor Adventures

TOUR—SIGHT | Naturalists, scientists, and park rangers lead multihour to multiday educational outings on topics from woodpeckers to fire management to pastel painting. Most sessions take place spring through fall, but a few focus on winter phenomena. ✉ *Yosemite National Park* ☎ *209/379–2317* 🌐 *www.yosemiteconservancy.org* 🎫 *From $99.*

MUSEUMS

Happy Isles Art and Nature Center

MUSEUM | FAMILY | This family-focused center has a rotating selection of hands-on, kid-friendly exhibits that teach tykes and their parents about the park's ecosystem. Books, toys, T-shirts, and water bottles are stocked in the small gift shop. ✉ *Yosemite National Park* ✣ *Off Southside Dr., about ¾ mile east of Half Dome Village* ☎ *209/372–0631* 🎫 *Free* ⏲ *Closed Oct.–Apr.*

Yosemite Museum

MUSEUM | This small museum consists of a permanent exhibit that focuses on the history of the area and the people who once lived here. An adjacent gallery promotes contemporary and historic Yosemite art in revolving gallery exhibits. A docent demonstrates traditional Native American basket-weaving techniques a few days a week. ✉ *Yosemite Village* ☎ *209/372–0299* 🎫 *Free.*

RANGER PROGRAMS

Junior Ranger Program

TOUR—SIGHT | FAMILY | Children ages seven and up can participate in the informal, self-guided Junior Ranger program. A park activity handbook is available at the Valley Visitor Center, the Happy Isles Art and Nature Center, and the Wawona Visitor Center. Once kids complete the book, rangers present them with a badge and, in some cases, a certificate. ✉ *Valley Visitor Center or the Happy Isles Art & Nature Center* ☎ *209/372–0299.*

Ranger-Led Programs

TOUR—SIGHT | Rangers lead entertaining walks and give informative talks several times a day from spring to fall. The schedule is more limited in winter, but most days you can find a program somewhere in the park. In the evenings at Yosemite Valley Lodge and Half Dome Village, lectures, slide shows, and documentary films present unique perspectives on Yosemite. On summer weekends, campgrounds at Half Dome Village and Tuolumne Meadows host sing-along campfire programs. Schedules and locations are posted on bulletin boards throughout the park as well as in the indispensable *Yosemite Guide,* which is distributed to visitors as they arrive at the park. ✉ *Yosemite National Park* 🌐 *nps.gov/yose.*

Restaurants

Yosemite National Park has a couple of moderately priced restaurants in lovely (which almost goes without saying) settings: the Mountain Room at Yosemite Valley Lodge and Big Trees Lodge's dining room. The Majestic Yosemite Hotel (formerly The Ahwahnee) provides one of the finest dining experiences in the country.

Otherwise, food service is geared toward satisfying the masses as efficiently as possible. Yosemite Valley Lodge's Base Camp Eatery is the valley's best lower-cost, hot-food option, with Italian, classic American, and world flavor counter options; Half Dome Village Pavilion's offerings are overpriced and usually fairly bland, but you can get decent pizzas on the adjacent outdoor deck. In Yosemite Valley Village, the Village Grill whips up burgers and fries, Degnan's Kitchen has made-to-order sandwiches, and The Loft at Degnan's has a chalet-like open dining area in which you can enjoy pizza, salads, rice bowls, and desserts.

The White Wolf Lodge and Tuolumne Meadows Lodge—both off Tioga Road and therefore guaranteed open only from early June through September—have small restaurants where meals are competently prepared. Tuolumne Meadows also has a grill, and the gift shop at Glacier Point sells premade sandwiches, snacks, and hot dogs. During the ski season you'll also find one at Yosemite Ski & Snowboard Area, off Glacier Point Road.

Hotels

Indoor lodging options inside the park appear more expensive than initially seems warranted, but that premium pays off big-time in terms of the time you'll save—unless you are bunking within a few miles of a Yosemite entrance, you will face long commutes to the park when you stay outside its borders (though the Yosemite View Lodge, on Route 140, is within a reasonable half-hour's drive of Yosemite Valley).

Because of Yosemite National Park's immense popularity—not just with tourists from around the world but with Northern Californians who make weekend trips here—reservations are all but mandatory. Book up to one year ahead. **■ TIP→ If you're not set on a specific hotel or camp but just want to stay somewhere inside the park, call the main reservation number to check for availability and reserve (888/413–8869 or 602/278–8888 international). Park lodgings have a seven-day cancellation policy, so you may be able to snag last-minute reservations.**

⚠ A trademark dispute with the former park concessioner, Delaware North, has resulted in Yosemite National Park changing the names of several historic park lodges and properties, including the iconic Ahwahnee. This guide uses the new names: Yosemite Lodge at the Falls is now Yosemite Valley Lodge; The Ahwahnee is now The Majestic Yosemite Hotel; Curry Village is now Half Dome Village; Wawona Hotel is now Big Trees Lodge; and Badger Pass Ski Area is now Yosemite Ski & Snowboard Area. For the latest information visit the Yosemite National Park website.

Hotel reviews have been shortened. For full information, visit Fodors.com.

What It Costs

	$	$$	$$$	$$$$
RESTAURANTS	under $12	$12–$20	$21–$30	over $30
HOTELS	under $100	$100–$150	$151–$200	over $200

Tours

★ Ansel Adams Camera Walks
SPECIAL-INTEREST | Photography enthusiasts shouldn't miss these 90-minute guided camera walks offered four mornings (Monday, Tuesday, Thursday, and Saturday) each week by professional photographers. All are free, but participation is limited to 15 people. Meeting points vary, and advance reservations are essential. ✉ *Yosemite National Park* ☎ *209/372–4413* 🌐 *www.anseladams.com* 🎫 *Free.*

Discover Yosemite
GUIDED TOURS | This outfit operates daily tours to Yosemite Valley, Mariposa Grove, and Glacier Point in 14- and 29-passenger vehicles. The tour travels along Highway 41 with stops in Bass Lake, Oakhurst, and Fish Camp; rates include lunch. Sunset tours to Sentinel Dome are additional summer options. ☎ *559/642–4400* 🌐 *www.discoveryosemite.com* 🎫 *From $152.*

Glacier Point Tour
GUIDED TOURS | This four-hour trip takes you from Yosemite Valley to the Glacier Point vista, 3,214 feet above the valley floor. Some people buy a $26 one-way ticket and hike down. Shuttles depart from the Yosemite Valley Lodge three times a day. ✉ *Yosemite National Park* ☎ *888/413–8869* 🌐 *www.travelyosemite.com* 🎫 *From $52* ⏲ *Closed Nov.–late May* ✍ *Reservations essential.*

Grand Tour
TOUR—SIGHT | For a full-day tour of Yosemite Valley, the Mariposa Grove of Giant Sequoias and Glacier Point, try the Grand Tour, which departs from the Yosemite Valley Lodge in the valley. The tour stops for a picnic lunch (included) at the historic Big Trees Lodge. ✉ *Yosemite National Park* ☎ *209/372–1240* 🌐 *www.yosemitepark.com* 🎫 *$102* ✍ *Reservations essential.*

Moonlight Tour
TOUR—SIGHT | This after-dark version of the Valley Floor Tour takes place on moonlit nights from June through September, depending on weather conditions. ✉ *Yosemite National Park* ☎ *209/372–4386* 🌐 *www.travelyosemite.com* 🎫 *$37.*

Tuolumne Meadows Hikers Bus
BUS TOURS | For a full day's outing to the high country, opt for this ride up Tioga Road to Tuolumne Meadows. You'll stop at several overlooks, and you can connect with another shuttle at Tuolumne Lodge. This service is mostly for hikers and backpackers who want to reach high-country trailheads, but everyone is welcome. ✉ *Yosemite National Park* ☎ *209/372–1240* 🌐 *www.travelyosemite.com* 🎫 *$15 one-way, $23 round-trip* ⏲ *Closed Labor Day–mid-June* ✍ *Reservations essential.*

Valley Floor Tour
GUIDED TOURS | Take a two-hour tour of Yosemite Valley's highlights, complete with narration on the area's history, geology, and flora and fauna. Tours are either in trams or enclosed motor coaches, depending on weather conditions. Tours run year-round. ✉ *Yosemite National Park* ☎ *209/372–1240, 888/413–8869 reservations* 🌐 *www.travelyosemite.com* 🎫 *From $37.*

Wee Wild Ones
TOUR—SIGHT | **FAMILY** | Designed for kids under 10, this 45-minute program includes naturalist-led games, songs, stories, and crafts about Yosemite wildlife, plants, and geology. The event is held outdoors before the regular Yosemite Valley Lodge evening programs in summer and fall. All children must be accompanied by an adult. ✉ *Yosemite National Park* ☎ *209/372–1153* 🌐 *www.travelyosemite.com* 🎫 *Free.*

Visitor Information

PARK CONTACT INFORMATION Yosemite National Park ☎ *209/372–0200* 🌐 *www.nps.gov/yose.*

VISITOR CENTERS

Valley Visitor Center
INFO CENTER | Learn about Yosemite Valley's geology, vegetation, and human inhabitants at this visitor center, which is also staffed with helpful rangers and contains a bookstore with a wide selection of books and maps. Two films, including one by Ken Burns, alternate on the half hour in the theater behind the visitor center. ✉ *Yosemite Village* ☎ *209/372–0200* 🌐 *www.nps.gov/yose.*

Yosemite Conservation Heritage Center
INFO CENTER | This small but striking National Historic Landmark (formerly Le Conte Memorial Lodge), with its granite walls and steeply pitched shingle roof, is Yosemite's first permanent public information center. Step inside to see the cathedral-like interior, which contains a library and environmental exhibits. To find out about evening programs, check the kiosk out front. ✉ *Southside Dr., about ½ mile west of Half Dome Village* 🌐 *sierraclub.org/yosemite-heritage-center* ⏲ *Closed Mon., Tues., and Oct.–Apr.*

Sights

SCENIC DRIVE

Tioga Road
SCENIC DRIVE | Few mountain drives can compare with this 59-mile road, especially its eastern half between Lee Vining and Olmstead Point. As you climb 3,200

Did You Know?

A "firefall" appears once a year in February at Horsetail Falls when the sun illuminates the water at the perfect angle.

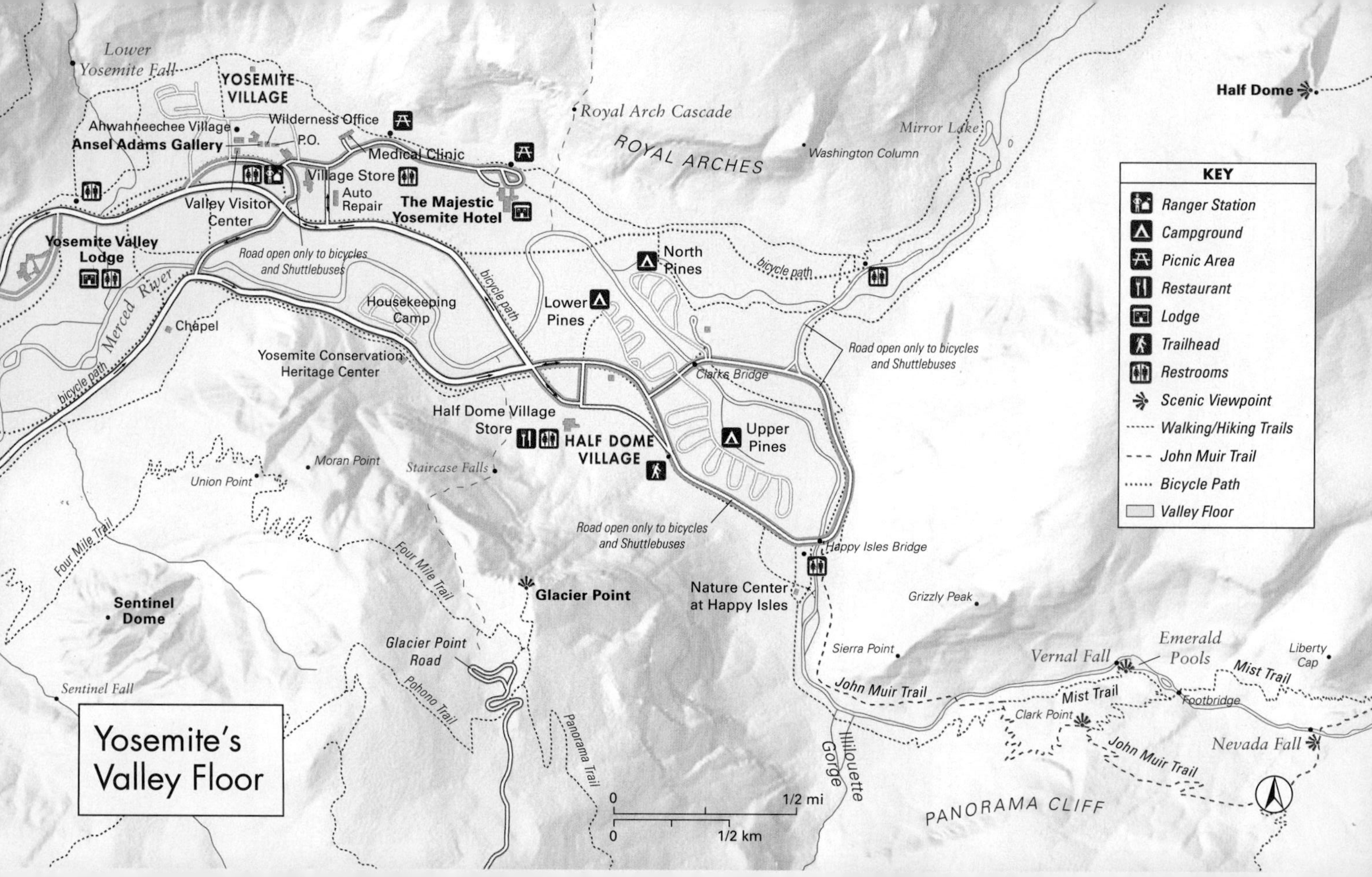
Yosemite's Valley Floor
KEY
Ranger Station
Campground
Picnic Area
Restaurant
Lodge
Trailhead
Restrooms
Scenic Viewpoint
Walking/Hiking Trails
John Muir Trail
Bicycle Path
Valley Floor
Lower Yosemite Fall
YOSEMITE VILLAGE
Ahwahneechee Village
Ansel Adams Gallery
Wilderness Office
P.O.
Medical Clinic
Village Store
Auto Repair
Valley Visitor Center
The Majestic Yosemite Hotel
Yosemite Valley Lodge
Road open only to bicycles and Shuttlebuses
Merced River
Chapel
bicycle path
Housekeeping Camp
Yosemite Conservation Heritage Center
Royal Arch Cascade
ROYAL ARCHES
Washington Column
Mirror Lake
Half Dome
North Pines
Lower Pines
Clarks Bridge
Upper Pines
Half Dome Village Store
HALF DOME VILLAGE
Happy Isles Bridge
Nature Center at Happy Isles
Grizzly Peak
Sierra Point
Vernal Fall
Emerald Pools
Liberty Cap
Mist Trail
Footbridge
Clark Point
John Muir Trail
Nevada Fall
Illilouette Gorge
PANORAMA CLIFF
Moran Point
Staircase Falls
Union Point
Four Mile Trail
Glacier Point
Sentinel Dome
Glacier Point Road
Pohono Trail
Panorama Trail
Sentinel Fall
0
1/2 mi
1/2 km

feet to the 9,945-foot summit of Tioga Pass (Yosemite's sole eastern entrance for cars), you'll encounter broad vistas of the granite-splotched High Sierra and its craggy but hearty trees and shrubs. Past the bustling scene at Tuolumne Meadows, you'll see picturesque Tenaya Lake and then Olmstead Point, where you'll get your first peek at Half Dome. Driving Tioga Road one way takes approximately 1½ hours. Wildflowers bloom here in July and August. By November, the high-altitude road closes for the winter; it sometimes doesn't reopen until early June. ✉ *Yosemite National Park.*

HISTORIC SITES

Big Trees Lodge

HOTEL—SIGHT | Imagine a white-bearded Mark Twain relaxing in a rocking chair on one of the broad verandas of one of the park's first lodges (formerly the Wawona Hotel), a whitewashed series of two-story buildings from the Victorian era. Plop down in one of the dozens of white Adirondack chairs on the sprawling lawn and look across the road at the area's only golf course, one of the few links in the world that does not employ fertilizers or other chemicals. ✉ *Rte. 41, Wawona* ☎ *209/375–1425* 🌐 *www.travelyosemite.com/lodging/big-trees-lodge/* ⏲ *Closed Dec.–Mar. except 2 wks around Christmas and New Year's.*

Half Dome Village

HOTEL—SIGHT | A couple of schoolteachers from Indiana founded Camp Curry in 1899 as a low-cost option for staying in the valley, which it remains today. Half Dome Village's 400-plus lodging options (formerly Curry Village), many of them tent cabins, are spread over a large chunk of the valley's southeastern side. This is one family-friendly place, but it's more functional than attractive. ✉ *Southside Dr., about ½ mile east of Yosemite Village.*

Indian Village of Ahwahnee

MUSEUM VILLAGE | This solemn smattering of structures, accessed by a short loop trail behind the Yosemite Valley Visitor Center, is a look at what Native American life might have been like in the 1870s. One interpretive sign points out that the Miwok people referred to the 19th-century newcomers as "Yohemite" or "Yohometuk," which have been translated as meaning "some of them are killers." ✉ *Northside Dr., Yosemite Village* 🎟 *Free.*

The Majestic Yosemite Hotel

HOTEL—SIGHT | Gilbert Stanley Underwood, architect of the Grand Canyon Lodge, also designed The Majestic Yosemite Hotel (formerly The Ahwahnee hotel). Opened in 1927, it is generally considered his best work. You can stay here (for about $500 a night), or simply explore the first-floor shops and perhaps have breakfast or lunch in the bustling and beautiful Dining Room or more casual bar. The Great Lounge, 77 feet long with magnificent 24-foot-high ceilings and all manner of artwork on display, beckons with big, comfortable chairs and relative calm. ✉ *Ahwahnee Rd., about ¾ mile east of Yosemite Valley Visitor Center, Yosemite Village* ☎ *209/372–1489* 🌐 *www.travelyosemite.com/lodging/the-majestic-yosemite-hotel/.*

Pioneer Yosemite History Center

MUSEUM | **FAMILY** | These historic buildings reflect different eras of Yosemite's history, starting in the 1850s through the early 1900s. They were moved to Wawona (the largest stage stop in Yosemite in the late 1800s) from various areas of Yosemite in the '50s and '60s. There is a self-guided-tour pamphlet available for 50¢. Weekends and some weekdays in the summer, costumed docents conduct free blacksmithing and "wet-plate" photography demonstrations, and for a small fee you can take a stagecoach ride. ✉ *Rte. 41, Wawona* ☎ *209/375–9531* 🌐 *www.nps.gov/yose/planyourvisit/waw.htm* 🎟 *Free* ⏲ *Closed Mon., Tues., and mid-Sept.–early June.*

Plants and Wildlife in Yosemite

Dense stands of incense cedar and Douglas fir—as well as ponderosa, Jeffrey, lodgepole, and sugar pines—cover much of the park, but the stellar standout, quite literally, is the *Sequoiadendron giganteum*, the giant sequoia. Sequoias grow only along the west slope of the Sierra Nevada between 4,500 and 7,000 feet in elevation. Starting from a seed the size of a rolled-oat flake, each of these ancient monuments assumes remarkable proportions in adulthood; you can see them in the Mariposa Grove of Giant Sequoias. In late May the valley's dogwood trees bloom with white, starlike flowers. Wildflowers, such as black-eyed Susan, bull thistle, cow parsnip, lupine, and meadow goldenrod, peak in June in the valley and in July at higher elevations.

The most visible animals in the park—aside from the omnipresent western gray squirrels, which fearlessly attempt to steal your food at every campground and picnic site—are the mule deer. Though sightings of bighorn sheep are infrequent in the park itself, you can sometimes see them on the eastern side of the Sierra Crest, just off Route 120 in Lee Vining Canyon. You may also see the American black bear, which often has a brown, cinnamon, or blond coat. The Sierra Nevada is home to thousands of bears, and you should take all necessary precautions to keep yourself—and the bears—safe. Bears that acquire a taste for human food can become very aggressive and destructive and often must be destroyed by rangers, so store all your food and even scented toiletries in the bear lockers located at many campgrounds and trailheads, or use bear-resistant canisters if you'll be hiking in the backcountry.

Watch for the blue Steller's jay along trails, near public buildings, and in campgrounds, and look for golden eagles soaring over Tioga Road.

SCENIC STOPS

El Capitan

NATURE SITE | Rising 3,593 feet—more than 350 stories—above the valley, El Capitan is the largest exposed-granite monolith in the world. Since 1958, people have been climbing its entire face, including the famous "nose." You can spot adventurers with your binoculars by scanning the smooth and nearly vertical cliff for specks of color. ✉ *Yosemite National Park* ⊕ *Off Northside Dr., about 4 miles west of Valley Visitor Center.*

★ Glacier Point

VIEWPOINT | If you lack the time, desire, or stamina to hike more than 3,200 feet up to Glacier Point from the Yosemite Valley floor, you can drive here—or take a bus from the valley—for a bird's-eye view. You are likely to encounter a lot of day-trippers on the short, paved trail that leads from the parking lot to the main overlook. Take a moment to veer off a few yards to the Geology Hut, which succinctly explains and illustrates what the valley looked like 10 million, 3 million, and 20,000 years ago. ✉ *Yosemite National Park* ⊕ *Glacier Point Rd., 16 miles northeast of Rte. 41* ☎ *209/372–0200* ⊙ *Closed late Oct.–mid-May.*

★ Half Dome

NATURE SITE | Visitors' eyes are continually drawn to this remarkable granite formation that tops out at more than 4,700 feet above the valley floor. Despite its name, the dome is actually about three-quarters intact. You can hike to the top of Half Dome on an 8.5-mile (one-way) trail whose last 400 feet must be ascended while holding onto a steel cable. Permits are required (and checked on the trail), and available only by lottery. Call ☎ *877/444–6777* or visit 🌐 *www.recreation.gov* well in advance of your trip for details. Back down in the valley, see Half Dome reflected in the Merced River by heading to Sentinel Bridge just before sundown. The brilliant orange light on Half Dome is a stunning sight. ✉ *Yosemite National Park* 🌐 *www.nps.gov/yose/planyourvisit/halfdome.htm.*

Hetch Hetchy Reservoir

BODY OF WATER | When Congress approved the O'Shaughnessy Dam in 1913, pragmatism triumphed over aestheticism. Some 2.5 million residents of the San Francisco Bay Area continue to get their water from this 117-billion-gallon reservoir. Although spirited efforts are being made to restore the Hetch Hetchy Valley to its former, pristine glory, three-quarters of San Francisco voters in 2012 ultimately opposed a measure to even consider draining the reservoir. Eight miles long, the reservoir is Yosemite's largest body of water, and one that can be seen up close from several trails. ✉ *Hetch Hetchy Rd., about 15 miles north of Big Oak Flat entrance station.*

High Country

NATURE PRESERVE | The above-tree-line, high-alpine region east of the valley—a land of alpenglow and top-of-the-world vistas—is often missed by crowds who come to gawk at the more publicized splendors. Summer wildflowers, which usually pop up mid-July through August, carpet the meadows and mountainsides with pink, purple, blue, red, yellow, and orange. On foot or on horseback are the only ways to get here. For information on trails and backcountry permits, check with the visitor center. ✉ *Yosemite National Park.*

Mariposa Grove of Giant Sequoias

FOREST | Of Yosemite's three sequoia groves—the others being Merced and Tuolumne, both near Crane Flat well to the north—Mariposa is by far the largest and easiest to walk around. Grizzly Giant, whose base measures 96 feet around, has been estimated to be one of the largest in the world. Perhaps more astoundingly, it's about 1,800 years old. Park at the grove's welcome plaza and ride the free shuttle (required most of the year). Summer weekends are usually crowded here. ✉ *Yosemite National Park* ✣ *Rte. 41, 2 miles north of south entrance station* 🌐 *www.nps.gov/yose/planyourvisit/mg.htm.*

Sentinel Dome

VIEWPOINT | The view from here is similar to that from Glacier Point, except you can't see the valley floor. A moderately steep 1.1-mile path climbs to the viewpoint from the parking lot. Topping out at an elevation of 8,122 feet, Sentinel is more than 900 feet higher than Glacier Point. ✉ *Glacier Point Rd., off Rte. 41.*

Tuolumne Meadows

MOUNTAIN—SIGHT | The largest subalpine meadow in the Sierra (at 8,600 feet) is a popular way station for backpack trips along the Pacific Crest and John Muir trails. The setting is not as dramatic as Yosemite Valley, 56 miles away, but the almost perfectly flat basin, about 2½ miles long, is intriguing, and in July it's resplendent with wildflowers. The most popular day hike is up Lembert Dome, atop which you'll have breathtaking views of the basin below. Keep in mind that Tioga Road rarely opens before June and usually closes by mid-October. ✉ *Tioga Rd. (Rte. 120), about 8 miles west of Tioga Pass entrance station.*

WATERFALLS

Yosemite's waterfalls are at their most spectacular in May and June. When the snow starts to melt (usually peaking in May), streaming snowmelt spills down to meet the Merced River. By summer's end, some falls, including the mighty Yosemite Falls, trickle or dry up. Their flow increases in late fall, and in winter they may be hung dramatically with ice. Even in drier months, the waterfalls can be breathtaking. If you choose to hike any of the trails to or up the falls, be sure to wear shoes with no-slip soles; the rocks can be extremely slick. Stay on trails at all times.

■ TIP→ Visit the park during a full moon and you can stroll without a flashlight and still make out the ribbons of falling water, as well as silhouettes of the giant granite monoliths.

Bridalveil Fall

BODY OF WATER | This 620-foot waterfall is often diverted dozens of feet one way or the other by the breeze. It is the first marvelous site you will see up close when you drive into Yosemite Valley. ✉ *Yosemite Valley, access from parking area off Wawona Rd.*

Nevada Fall

BODY OF WATER | Climb Mist Trail from Happy Isles for an up-close view of this 594-foot cascading beauty. If you don't want to hike (the trail's final approach is quite taxing), you can see it—albeit distantly—from Glacier Point. Stay safely on the trail, as there have been fatalities in recent years after visitors have fallen and been swept away by the water. ✉ *Yosemite Valley, access via Mist Trail from Nature Center at Happy Isles.*

Ribbon Fall

BODY OF WATER | At 1,612 feet, this is the highest single fall in North America. It's also the first waterfall to dry up in summer; the rainwater and melted snow that create the slender fall evaporate quickly at this height. Look just west of El Capitan for the best view of the fall from the base of Bridalveil Fall. ✉ *Yosemite Valley, west of El Capitan Meadow.*

Vernal Fall

BODY OF WATER | Fern-covered black rocks frame this 317-foot fall, and rainbows play in the spray at its base. You can get a distant view from Glacier Point, or hike to see it close up. You'll get wet, but the view is worth it. ✉ *Yosemite Valley, access via Mist Trail from Nature Center at Happy Isles.*

★ Yosemite Falls

BODY OF WATER | Actually three falls, they together constitute the highest combined waterfall in North America and the fifth highest in the world. The water from the top descends a total of 2,425 feet, and when the falls run hard, you can hear them thunder across the valley. If they dry up—that sometimes happens in late summer—the valley seems naked without the wavering tower of spray. If you hike the mile-long loop trail (partially paved) to the base of the Lower Fall in spring, prepare to get wet. You can get a good full-length view of the falls from the lawn of Yosemite Chapel, off Southside Drive. ✉ *Yosemite Valley, access from Yosemite Valley Lodge or trail parking area.*

Activities

BIKING

One enjoyable way to see Yosemite Valley is to ride a bike beneath its lofty granite monoliths. The eastern valley has 12 miles of paved, flat bicycle paths across meadows and through woods, with bike racks at convenient stopping points. For a greater challenge but at no small risk, you can ride on 196 miles of paved park roads—but bicycles are not allowed on hiking trails or in the backcountry. Kids under 18 must wear a helmet.

Yosemite bike rentals

BICYCLING | You can arrange for rentals from Yosemite Valley Lodge and Half Dome Village bike stands. Bikes with child trailers, baby-jogger strollers, and wheelchairs are also available. The cost for bikes is $12 per hour, or $33.50 a day. ✉ *Yosemite Valley Lodge or Half Dome*

Half Dome at sunset.

Village ☎ *209/372–4386* 🌐 *www.travelyosemite.com.*

BIRD-WATCHING

More than 250 bird species have been spotted in the park, including the sage sparrow, pygmy owl, blue grouse, and mountain bluebird. Park rangers lead free bird-watching walks in Yosemite Valley a few days each week in summer; check at a visitor center or information station for times and locations. Binoculars sometimes are available for loan.

Birding seminars

BIRD WATCHING | The Yosemite Conservancy organizes day- and weekend-long seminars for beginner and intermediate birders, as well as bird walks a few times a week. They can also arrange private naturalist-led walks any time of year. ✉ *Yosemite National Park* ☎ *209/379–2321* 🌐 *www.yosemiteconservancy.org* 🎫 *From $99.*

FISHING

The waters in Yosemite are not stocked; trout, mostly brown and rainbow, live here but are not plentiful. Yosemite's fishing season begins on the last Saturday in April and ends on November 15. Some waterways are off-limits at certain times; be sure to inquire at the visitor center about regulations.

A California fishing license is required; licenses cost around $16 for one day, $24 for two days, and $48 for 10 days. Full-season licenses cost $48 for state residents and $130 for nonresidents (costs fluctuate year to year). Buy your license in season at **Yosemite Mountain Shop in Half Dome Village** (☎ *209/372–1286*) or at the **Big Trees General Store** (☎ *209/375–6574*).

HIKING

Wilderness Center

HIKING/WALKING | This facility provides free wilderness permits, which are required for overnight camping (advance reservations are available for $5 per person plus $5 per reservation and are highly recommended for popular trailheads in summer and on weekends). The staff here also provides maps and advice to hikers heading into the backcountry, and rents and sells bear-resistant canisters, which are required if you don't have your own. ✉ *Between Ansel Adams Gallery and post office, Yosemite Village* ☎ *209/372–0308.*

Yosemite Mountaineering School and Guide Service

HIKING/WALKING | From April to November, you can learn to climb, hire a guide, or join a two-hour to full-day trek with Yosemite Mountaineering School. They also rent gear and lead backpacking and overnight excursions. Reservations are recommended. In winter, cross-country ski programs are available at Yosemite Ski & Snowboard Area. ✉ *Yosemite Mountain Shop, Half Dome Village* ☎ *209/372–8344* 🌐 *yosemitemountaineering.com.*

Cook's Meadow Loop

HIKING/WALKING | **FAMILY** | Take this 1-mile, wheelchair-accessible, looped path around Cook's Meadow to see and learn the basics about Yosemite Valley's past, present, and future. A self-guiding trail guide (available at a kiosk just outside the entrance) explains how to tell oaks, cedars, and pines apart; how fires help keep the forest floor healthy; and how pollution poses significant challenges to the park's inhabitants. *Easy.* ✉ *Yosemite National Park* ✣ *Trailhead: across from Valley Visitor Center.*

Chilnualna Falls Trail

HIKING/WALKING | This Wawona-area trail runs 4 miles one way to the top of the falls, then leads into the backcountry, connecting with miles of other trails. This is one of the park's most inspiring and secluded—albeit strenuous—trails. Past the tumbling cascade, and up through forests, you'll emerge before a panoramic vista at the top. *Difficult.* ✉ *Wawona* ✣ *Trailhead: at Chilnualna Falls Rd., off Rte. 41.*

★ John Muir Trail to Half Dome

HIKING/WALKING | Ardent and courageous trekkers continue on from Nevada Fall to the top of Half Dome. Some hikers attempt this entire 10- to 12-hour, 16¾-mile round-trip trek in one day; if you're planning to do this, remember that the 4,800-foot elevation gain and the 8,842-foot altitude will cause shortness of breath. Another option is to hike to a campground in Little Yosemite Valley near the top of Nevada Fall the first day, then climb to the top of Half Dome and hike out the next day. Get your wilderness permit (required for a one-day hike to Half Dome, too) at least a month in advance. Be sure to wear hiking boots and bring gloves. The last pitch up the back of Half Dome is very steep—the only way to climb this sheer rock face is to pull yourself up using the steel cable handrails, which are in place only from late spring to early fall. Those who brave the ascent will be rewarded with an unbeatable view of Yosemite Valley below and the high country beyond. Only 300 hikers per day are allowed atop Half Dome, and they all must have permits, which are distributed by lottery, one in the spring before the season starts and another two days before the climb. Contact 🌐 *www.recreation.gov* for details. *Difficult.* ✉ *Yosemite National Park* ✣ *Trailhead: at Happy Isles* 🌐 *www.nps.gov/yose/planyourvisit/halfdome.htm.*

Mist Trail

HIKING/WALKING | Except for Lower Yosemite Fall, more visitors take this trail (or portions of it) than any other in the park. The trek up to and back from Vernal Fall is 3 miles. Add another 4 miles total by continuing up to 594-foot Nevada Fall; the trail becomes quite steep and

Ansel Adams's Black-and-White Yosemite 

What John Muir did for Yosemite with words, Ansel Adams did with photographs. His photographs have inspired millions of people to visit Yosemite, and his persistent activism helped to ensure the park's conservation.

Born in 1902, Adams first came to the valley when he was 14, photographing it with a Box Brownie camera. He later said his first visit "was a culmination of experience so intense as to be almost painful. From that day in 1916 my life has been colored and modulated by the great earth gesture of the Sierra." By 1919 he was working in the valley, as custodian of LeConte Memorial Lodge (now called Yosemite Conservation Heritage Center), the Sierra Club headquarters in Yosemite National Park.

Adams had harbored dreams of a career as a concert pianist, but the park sealed his fate as a photographer in 1928, the day he shot *Monolith: The Face of Half Dome,* which remains one of his most famous works. Adams also married Virginia Best in 1928, in her father's studio in the valley (now the Ansel Adams Gallery).

As Adams's photographic career took off, Yosemite began to sear itself into the American consciousness. David Brower, first executive director of the Sierra Club, later said of Adams's impact, "That Ansel Adams came to be recognized as one of the great photographers of this century is a tribute to the places that informed him."

In 1934 Adams was elected to the Sierra Club's board of directors; he would serve until 1971. As a representative of the conservation group, he combined his work with the club's mission, showing his photographs of the Sierra to influential officials such as Secretary of the Interior Harold L. Ickes, who showed them to President Franklin Delano Roosevelt. The images were a key factor in the establishment of Kings Canyon National Park.

In 1968, the Department of the Interior granted Adams its highest honor, the Conservation Service Award, and in 1980 he received the Presidential Medal of Freedom in recognition of his conservation work. Until his death in 1984, Adams continued not only to record Yosemite's majesty on film but to urge the federal government and park managers to do right by the park.

In one of his many public pleas on behalf of Yosemite, Adams said, "Yosemite Valley itself is one of the great shrines of the world and—belonging to all our people—must be both protected and appropriately accessible." As an artist and an activist, Adams never gave up on his dream of keeping Yosemite wild yet within reach of every visitor who wants to experience that wildness.

Did You Know?

Yosemite's Merced River formed roughly 10 million years ago as the surrounding Sierra Nevada Mountain range rose up.

slippery in its final stages. The elevation gain to Vernal Fall is 1,000 feet, and to Nevada Fall an additional 1,000 feet. The Merced River tumbles down both falls on its way to a tranquil flow through the valley. *Moderate.* ✉ *Yosemite National Park* ✣ *Trailhead: at Happy Isles.*

★ Panorama Trail

HIKING/WALKING | Few hikes come with the visual punch that this 8½-mile trail provides. It starts from Glacier Point and descends to Yosemite Valley. The star attraction is Half Dome, visible from many intriguing angles, but you also see three waterfalls up close and walk through a manzanita grove. *Moderate.* ✉ *Yosemite National Park* ✣ *Trailhead: at Glacier Point.*

★ Yosemite Falls Trail

HIKING/WALKING | Yosemite Falls is the highest waterfall in North America. The upper fall (1,430 feet), the middle cascades (675 feet), and the lower fall (320 feet) combine for a total of 2,425 feet, and when viewed from the valley appear as a single waterfall. The ¼-mile trail leads from the parking lot to the base of the falls. Upper Yosemite Fall Trail, a strenuous 7.2-mile round-trip climb rising 2,700 feet, takes you above the top of the falls. Lower trail: *Easy.* Upper trail: *Difficult.* ✉ *Yosemite National Park* ✣ *Trailhead: off Camp 4, north of Northside Dr.*

HORSEBACK RIDING

Reservations for guided trail rides must be made in advance at the hotel tour desks or by phone. Scenic trail rides range from two hours to a half day; four- and six-day High Sierra saddle trips are also available.

Big Trees Stable

HORSEBACK RIDING | Two-hour rides at these stables start at $67, and a challenging full-day ride to the Mariposa Grove of Giant Sequoias (for experienced riders in good physical condition only) costs $140. Reservations are recommended. ✉ *Rte. 41, Wawona* ☎ *209/375–6502* 🌐 *www.travelyosemite.com/things-to-do/horseback-mule-riding/* 🎫 *From $67.*

RAFTING

Rafting is permitted only on designated areas of the Middle and South forks of the Merced River. Check with the Valley Visitor Center for closures and other restrictions.

Half Dome Village Recreation Center

WHITE-WATER RAFTING | The per-person rental fee ($33) at Half Dome Village Recreation Center covers the four- to six-person raft, two paddles, and life jackets, plus a return shuttle at the end of your trip. ✉ *South side of Southside Dr., Half Dome Village* ☎ *209/372–4386* 🌐 *www.travelyosemite.com/things-to-do/rafting/* 🎫 *From $33.*

ROCK CLIMBING

The granite canyon walls of Yosemite Valley are world renowned for rock climbing. El Capitan, with its 3,593-foot vertical face, is the most famous, but there are many other options here for all skill levels.

Yosemite Mountaineering School & Guide Service

CLIMBING/MOUNTAINEERING | The one-day basic lesson at Yosemite Mountaineering School and Guide Service includes some bouldering and rappelling, and three or four 60-foot climbs. Climbers must be at least 10 years old and in reasonably good physical condition. Intermediate and advanced classes include instruction in first aid, anchor building, multipitch climbing, summer snow climbing, and big-wall climbing. There's a Nordic program in the winter. ✉ *Yosemite Mountain Shop, Half Dome Village* ☎ *209/372–8444* 🌐 *www.travelyosemite.com* 🎫 *From $172.*

SWIMMING

The pools at **Half Dome Village** (☎ *209/372–8324* 🌐 *www.travelyosemite.com*) and **Yosemite Valley Lodge** (☎ *209/372–1250* 🌐 *www.*

travelyosemite.com) are open to nonguests for $5, late May through early or mid-September. Additionally, several swimming holes with small sandy beaches can be found in midsummer along the Merced River at the eastern end of Yosemite Valley. Find gentle waters to swim; currents are often stronger than they appear, and temperatures are chilling. To conserve riparian habitats, step into the river at sandy beaches and other obvious entry points. **■TIP→ Do not attempt to swim above or near waterfalls or rapids; people have died trying.**

WINTER ACTIVITIES

The beauty of Yosemite under a blanket of snow has long inspired poets and artists, as well as ordinary folks. Skiing and snowshoeing activities in the park center on Yosemite Ski & Snowboard Area, California's oldest snow-sports resort, which is about 40 minutes away from the valley on Glacier Point Road. Here you can rent equipment, take a lesson, have lunch, join a guided excursion, and take the free shuttle back to the valley after a drink in the lounge.

ICE-SKATING

Half Dome Village Ice Rink

ICE SKATING | Winter visitors have skated at this outdoor rink for decades, and there's no mystery why: it's a kick to glide across the ice while soaking up views of Half Dome and Glacier Point. ✉ *South side of Southside Dr., Half Dome Village* ☎ *209/372–8319* 🌐 *www.travelyosemite.com* 🎫 *$10 per session, $4 skate rental.*

SKIING AND SNOWSHOEING

Yosemite Ski & Snowboard Area

SKIING/SNOWBOARDING | California's first ski resort has five lifts and 10 downhill runs, as well as 90 miles of groomed cross-country trails. Free shuttle buses from Yosemite Valley operate between December and the end of March, weather permitting. Lessons, backcountry guiding, and cross-country and snowshoeing tours are also available. You can rent downhill, telemark, and cross-country skis, plus snowshoes and snowboards. **Facilities:** 10 trails; 90 acres; 800-foot vertical drop; 5 lifts. ✉ *Yosemite National Park* ✥ *Badger Pass Rd., off Glacier Point Rd., 18 miles from Yosemite Valley* ☎ *209/372–8430* 🌐 *www.travelyosemite.com/winter/yosemite-ski-snowboard-area/* 🎫 *Lift ticket: from $55.*

Yosemite Cross-Country Ski School

SKIING/SNOWBOARDING | The highlight of Yosemite's cross-country skiing center is a 21-mile loop from Yosemite Ski & Snowboard Area to Glacier Point. You can rent cross-country skis for $28 per day at the Cross-Country Ski School, which also rents snowshoes ($23 per day) and telemarking equipment ($28). ☎ *209/372–8444* 🌐 *www.travelyosemite.com.*

Yosemite Mountaineering School

SKIING/SNOWBOARDING | This branch of the Yosemite Mountaineering School, open at the Yosemite Ski & Snowboard Area during ski season only, conducts snowshoeing, cross-country skiing, telemarking, and skate-skiing classes starting at $44. ✉ *Yosemite Ski & Snowboard Area* ☎ *209/372–8444* 🌐 *www.travelyosemite.com.*

Yosemite Ski & Snowboard Area School

SKIING/SNOWBOARDING | The gentle slopes of Yosemite Ski & Snowboard Area make the ski school an ideal spot for children and beginners to learn downhill skiing or snowboarding for as little as $75 for a group lesson. ☎ *209/372–8430* 🌐 *www.travelyosemite.com.*

Nightlife

Vintage Music of Yosemite

MUSIC CLUBS | A pianist-singer performs four hours of live old-time music at the Big Trees Lodge (formerly Wawona Hotel); call for schedule of performances. ✉ *Big Trees Lodge, Rte. 41, Wawona* ☎ *209/375–6556* 🎫 *Free.*

Performing Arts

Yosemite Theatre

THEATER | Various theater and music programs are held throughout the year, and one of the best loved is Lee Stetson's portrayal of John Muir in *Conversation with a Tramp* and other Muir-theme shows. Purchase tickets in advance at the Conservancy Store at the Valley Visitor Center or the Tour and Activity Desk at Yosemite Valley Lodge. Unsold seats are available at the door at performance time, 7 pm. ✉ *Valley Visitor Center, Yosemite Village* ☎ *209/372–0299* 🎫 *$10.*

Shopping

Ansel Adams Gallery

ART GALLERIES | Framed prints of the famed nature photographer's best works are on sale here, as are affordable posters. New works by contemporary artists are available, along with Native American jewelry and handicrafts. The gallery's elegant camera shop conducts photography workshops, from free camera walks a few mornings a week to five-day workshops. ✉ *Northside Dr., Yosemite Village* ☎ *209/372–4413* 🌐 *anseladams.com/ansel-adams-gallery-in-yosemite/.*

Majestic Hotel Gift Shop

GIFTS/SOUVENIRS | This shop sells more upscale items, such as Native American crafts, photographic prints, handmade ceramics, and elegant jewelry. For less expensive gift items, browse the small book selection, which includes writings by John Muir. ✉ *The Majestic Yosemite Hotel, Ahwahnee Rd.* ☎ *209/372–1409.*

Yosemite Mountain Shop

SPECIALTY STORES | A comprehensive selection of camping, hiking, backpacking, and climbing equipment, along with experts who can answer all your questions, make this store a valuable resource for outdoors enthusiasts. This is the best place to ask about climbing conditions and restrictions around the park, as well as purchase almost any kind of climbing gear. ✉ *Half Dome Village* ☎ *209/372–8436.*

Nearby Towns

Marking the southern end of the Sierra's gold-bearing mother lode, **Mariposa** is the last town before you enter Yosemite on Route 140 to the west of the park. In addition to a fine mining museum, Mariposa has numerous shops, restaurants, and service stations.

Motels and restaurants dot both sides of Route 41 as it cuts through the town of **Oakhurst,** a boomtown during the gold rush that is now an important regional refueling station in every sense of the word, including organic foods and a full range of lodging options. Oakhurst has a population of about 3,000 and sits 15 miles south of the park.

Almost surrounded by the Sierra National Forest, **Bass Lake** is a warm-water reservoir whose waters can reach 80 degrees F in summer. Created by a dam on a tributary of the San Joaquin River, the lake is owned by Pacific Gas and Electric Company and is used to generate electricity as well as for recreation.

As you climb in elevation along Highway 41 northbound, you see nothing but trees until you get to **Fish Camp,** where there's a post office and general store, but no gasoline. (For gas, head 7 miles north to Wawona, in Yosemite, or 14 miles south to Oakhurst.)

Near the park's eastern entrance, the tiny town of **Lee Vining** is home to the eerily beautiful, salty Mono Lake, where millions of migratory birds nest. Visit **Mammoth Lakes,** about 40 miles southeast of Yosemite's Tioga Pass entrance, for excellent skiing and snowboarding in winter, with fishing, mountain biking, hiking, and horseback riding in summer. Nine deep-blue lakes form the Mammoth

Lakes Basin, and another hundred dot the surrounding countryside. Devils Postpile National Monument sits at the base of Mammoth Mountain.

VISITOR INFORMATION Mammoth Lakes Tourism ✉ *2510 Main St., Mammoth Lakes* ☎ *760/934–2712, 888/466–2666* 🌐 *www.visitmammoth.com.* **Mono Lake Information Center and Bookstore** ☎ *760/647–6595* 🌐 *www.leevining.com.* **Tuolumne County Visitors Bureau** ✉ *193 S. Washington St., Sonora* ☎ *209/533–4420, 800/446–1333* 🌐 *www.visittuolumne.com.* **Visit Yosemite/Madera County** ✉ *40343 Hwy. 41, Oakhurst* ☎ *559/683–4636* 🌐 *www.yosemitethisyear.com.* **Yosemite Mariposa County Tourism Bureau** ✉ *5158 Hwy. 140, Suite E, Mariposa* ☎ *209/742–4567, 866/425–3366 visitor center toll-free, 209/966–7081 visitor center* 🌐 *www.yosemite.com.*

Sights

California State Mining and Mineral Museum

MUSEUM | **FAMILY** | A California state park, the museum has displays on gold-rush history including a replica hard-rock mine shaft to walk through, a miniature stamp mill, and a 13-pound chunk of crystallized gold. ✉ *5005 Fairground Rd., off Hwy. 49, Mariposa* ☎ *209/742–7625* 🌐 *www.parks.ca.gov/miningandmineralmuseum* 🎫 *$4* ⏲ *Closed Mon.–Wed.*

★ Devils Postpile National Monument

NATURE SITE | Volcanic and glacial forces sculpted this formation of smooth, vertical basalt columns. For a bird's-eye view, take the short, steep trail to the top of a 60-foot cliff. To see the monument's second scenic wonder, **Rainbow Falls,** hike 2 miles past Devils Postpile. A branch of the San Joaquin River plunges more than 100 feet over a lava ledge here. When the water hits the pool below, sunlight turns the resulting mist into a spray of color. From mid-June to early September, day-use visitors must ride the shuttle bus from the Mammoth Mountain Ski Area to the monument. ✉ *Mammoth Lakes* ✣ *13 miles southwest of Mammoth Lakes off Minaret Rd. (Hwy. 203)* ☎ *760/934–2289, 760/872–1901 shuttle* 🌐 *www.nps.gov/depo* 🎫 *$10 per vehicle (allowed when the shuttle isn't running, usually early Sept.–mid-Oct.), $8 per person shuttle.*

Hot Creek Geologic Site

NATURE SITE | Forged by an ancient volcanic eruption, the Hot Creek Geologic Site is a landscape of boiling hot springs, fumaroles, and geysers about 10 miles southeast of the town of Mammoth Lakes. You can stroll along boardwalks through the canyon to view the steaming volcanic features. Fly-fishing for trout is popular upstream from the springs. ✉ *Hot Creek Hatchery Rd. east of U.S. 395, Mammoth Lakes* ☎ *760/873–2400* 🌐 *www.fs.usda.gov/recarea/inyo/recarea/?recid=20414* 🎫 *Free.*

Yosemite Mountain Sugar Pine Railroad

TRANSPORTATION SITE (AIRPORT/BUS/FERRY/TRAIN) | **FAMILY** | Travel back to a time when powerful steam locomotives hauled massive log trains through the Sierra. This 4-mile, narrow-gauge railroad excursion takes you near Yosemite's south gate. There's a moonlight special ($58), with dinner and entertainment, and you can pan for gold ($10) and visit the free museum. ✉ *56001 Hwy. 41, 8 miles south of Yosemite, Fish Camp* ☎ *559/683–7273* 🌐 *www.ymsprr.com* 🎫 *$24* ⏲ *Closed Nov.–Mar. Closed some weekdays Apr. and Oct.*

Activities

RAFTING

Zephyr Whitewater Expeditions

BOATING | This outfitter conducts half-day to three-day white-water trips on the Tuolumne, Merced, and American rivers for paddlers of all experience levels. ☎ *800/431–3636 reservations, 209/532–6249* 🌐 *www.zrafting.com* 🎫 *From $112.*

SKIING

★ Mammoth Mountain Ski Area

SKIING/SNOWBOARDING | One of the West's largest and best ski areas, Mammoth has more than 3,500 acres of skiable terrain and a 3,100-foot vertical drop. The views from the 11,053-foot summit are some of the most stunning in the Sierra. Below, you'll find a 6½-mile-wide swath of groomed boulevards and canyons, as well as pockets of tree-skiing and a dozen vast bowls. Snowboarders are everywhere on the slopes; there are seven outstanding freestyle terrain parks of varying difficulty, with jumps, rails, tabletops, and giant super pipes—this is the location of several international snowboarding competitions, and, in summer, mountain-bike meets. Mammoth's season begins in November and often lingers into July. Lessons and equipment are available, and there's a children's ski and snowboard school. Mammoth runs free shuttle-bus routes around town and to the ski area, and the Village Gondola runs from the Village complex to Canyon Lodge. However, only overnight guests are allowed to park at the Village for more than a few hours. **Facilities:** 155 trails; 3,500 acres; 3,100-foot vertical drop; 25 lifts. ✉ *Minaret Rd., west of Mammoth Lakes, Rte. 203, off U.S. 395, Mammoth Lakes* ☎ *760/934–2571, 800/626–6684, 760/934–0687 shuttle* 🌐 *www.mammothmountain.com* 🎫 *From $99.*

Restaurants

IN THE PARK

In addition to the dining options listed here, you'll find fast-food grills and cafeterias, plus temporary snack bars, hamburger stands, and pizza joints lining park roads in summer. Many dining facilities in the park are open summer only.

Base Camp Eatery

$$ | **AMERICAN** | The design of this modern food court, open for breakfast, lunch, and dinner, honors the history of rock climbing in Yosemite. Choose from a wide range of menu options, from hamburgers, salads, and pizzas, to rice and noodle bowls. **Known for:** grab-and-go selections; best casual dining venue in the park; automated ordering kiosks to speed up service. [$] *Average main: $12* ✉ *Yosemite Valley Lodge, about ¾ mile west of visitor center, Yosemite Village* ☎ *209/372–1265* 🌐 *www.travelyosemite.com.*

Big Trees Lodge Dining Room

$$$ | **AMERICAN** | Watch deer graze on the meadow while you dine in the romantic, candlelit dining room of the whitewashed Big Trees Lodge (formerly the Wawona Hotel), which dates from the late 1800s. The American-style cuisine favors fresh ingredients and flavors; trout and flatiron steaks are menu staples. **Known for:** Saturday-night barbecues on the lawn; historic ambience; Mother's Day and other Sunday holiday brunches. [$] *Average main: $28* ✉ *8308 Wawona Rd., Wawona* ☎ *209/375–1425* ⏲ *Closed most of Dec., Jan., Feb., and Mar.*

Half Dome Village Pavilion

$$ | **AMERICAN** | Formerly Curry Village Pavilion, this cafeteria-style eatery serves everything from roasted meats and salads to pastas, burritos, and beyond. Alternatively, order a pizza from the stand on the deck, and take in the views of the valley's granite walls. **Known for:** convenient eats; Saturday evening chuck wagon barbecues mid-June–August; additional venues: Meadow Grill, Pizza Patio, Coffee Corner and Village Bar. [$] *Average main: $18* ✉ *Half Dome Village* ☎ *209/372–8303* ⏲ *Closed mid-Oct.–mid-Apr. No lunch.*

★ The Majestic Yosemite Hotel Dining Room

$$$$ | **EUROPEAN** | Formerly The Ahwahnee Hotel Dining Room, rave reviews about the dining room's appearance are fully justified—it features towering windows, a 34-foot-high ceiling with interlaced sugar-pine beams, and massive chandeliers. Reservations are always advised, and

Did You Know?

In the Sierra's mixed-conifer forests, telling the many types of pines apart can be difficult if you don't know the trick: sizing up the cones and examining the branches to count how many needles are in discrete clusters. If the needles are paired, you're likely looking at a lodgepole pine. If the needles are long and come in threes, chances are you've come upon a ponderosa pine.

the attire is "resort casual." **Known for:** lavish $56 Sunday brunch; finest dining in the park; bar menu with lighter lunch and dinner fare at more affordable prices. *Average main: $39 ✉ The Majestic Yosemite Hotel, Ahwahnee Rd., about ¾ mile east of Yosemite Valley Visitor Center, Yosemite Village ☎ 209/372–1489 🌐 www.travelyosemite.com.*

★ Mountain Room

$$$ | **AMERICAN** | Gaze at Yosemite Falls through this dining room's wall of windows—almost every table has a view—as you nosh on steaks, seafood, and classic California salads and desserts. The Mountain Room Lounge, a few steps away in the Yosemite Lodge complex, has about 10 beers on tap. **Known for:** locally sourced, organic ingredients; usually there is a wait for a table (no reservations); vegetarian and vegan options. *Average main: $29 ✉ Yosemite Valley Lodge, Northside Dr., about ¾ mile west of visitor center, Yosemite Village ☎ 209/372–1403 🌐 www.travelyosemite.com ⏲ No lunch except Sun. brunch.*

Tuolumne Meadows Grill

$ | **FAST FOOD** | Serving continuously throughout the day until 5 or 6 pm, this fast-food eatery cooks up basic breakfast, lunch, and snacks. It's possible that ice cream tastes better at this altitude. **Known for:** soft serve ice cream; crowds; fresh local ingredients. *Average main: $8 ✉ Tioga Rd. (Rte. 120), 1½ miles east of Tuolumne Meadows Visitor Center ☎ 209/372–8426 🌐 www.travelyosemite.com ⏲ Closed Oct.–Memorial Day. No dinner.*

Tuolumne Meadows Lodge

$$$ | **AMERICAN** | In a central dining tent beside the Tuolumne River, this restaurant serves a menu of hearty American fare at breakfast and dinner. The red-and-white-checkered tablecloths and a handful of communal tables give it the feeling of an old-fashioned summer camp. **Known for:** box lunches; communal tables; small menu. *Average main: $24 ✉ Tioga Rd. (Rte. 120) ☎ 209/372–8413 🌐 www.travelyosemite.com ⏲ Closed late Sept.–mid-June. No lunch.*

Village Grill Deck

$$ | **FAST FOOD** | If a burger joint is what you've been missing, head to this bustling eatery in Yosemite Village that serves veggie, salmon, and a few other burger varieties in addition to the usual beef patties. Order at the counter, then take your tray out to the deck and enjoy your meal under the trees. **Known for:** burgers, sandwiches, and hot dogs; crowds; outdoor seating on expansive deck. *Average main: $12 ✉ Yosemite Village ⊕ 100 yards east of Yosemite Valley Visitor Center ☎ 209/372–1207 🌐 www.travelyosemite.com ⏲ Closed Oct.–May. No dinner.*

PICNIC AREAS

Considering how large the park is and how many visitors come here—some 5 million people every year, most of them just for the day—it is somewhat surprising that Yosemite has few formal picnic areas, though in many places you can find a smooth rock to sit on and enjoy breathtaking views along with your lunch. The convenience stores all sell picnic supplies, and prepackaged sandwiches and salads are widely available. Those options can come in especially handy during the middle of the day, when you might not want to spend precious daylight hours in such a spectacular setting sitting in a restaurant for a formal meal. *None of the below options has drinking water available; most have some type of toilet.*

Cathedral Beach. You may have some solitude picnicking here, as this spot usually has fewer people than picnic areas at the eastern end of the valley. *Southside Dr. underneath spirelike Cathedral Rocks.*

Church Bowl. Tucked behind The Majestic Yosemite Hotel, this picnic area nearly abuts the granite walls below the Royal Arches. If you're walking from the village with your supplies, this is the shortest trek to a picnic area. *Behind The Majestic Yosemite Hotel, Yosemite Valley.*

El Capitan. Come here for great views that look straight up the giant granite wall above. *Northside Dr., at western end of valley.*

Sentinel Beach. Usually crowded in season, this area is right alongside a running creek and the Merced River. *Southside Dr., just south of Swinging Bridge.*

Swinging Bridge. This picnic area is just before the little wooden footbridge that crosses the Merced River, which babbles pleasantly by. *Southside Dr., east of Sentinel Beach.*

OUTSIDE THE PARK

Ducey's on the Lake/Ducey's Bar & Grill

$$$$ | **AMERICAN** | With elaborate chandeliers sculpted from deer antlers, the lodge-style restaurant at Ducey's attracts boaters, locals, and tourists with its lake views and standard lamb, beef, seafood, and pasta dishes. It's also open for breakfast: try the Bass Lake seafood omelet, huevos rancheros, or the Rice Krispies–crusted French toast. **Known for:** steaks and fresh fish; lake views; upstairs bar and grill with more affordable eats. *Average main: $32 ✉ Pines Resort, 54432 Rd. 432, Bass Lake ☎ 559/642–3131 🌐 www.basslake.com.*

★ Erna's Elderberry House

$$$$ | **EUROPEAN** | Erna Kubin-Clanin, the grande dame of Château du Sureau, created this culinary oasis, stunning for its understated elegance, gorgeous setting, and impeccable service. Earth-tone walls and wood beams accent the dining room's high ceilings, and arched windows reflect the glow of candles. **Known for:** elite waitstaff; romantic setting; seasonal prix-fixe and à la carte menus. *Average main: $48 ✉ Château du Sureau, 48688 Victoria La., off Hwy. 41, Oakhurst ☎ 559/683–6800 🌐 www.elderberryhouse.com ⏲ No lunch Mon.–Sat.*

★ South Gate Brewing Company

$$ | **AMERICAN** | Locals pack this family-friendly, industrial-chic restaurant to socialize and savor small-lot beers, crafted on-site, along with tasty meals. The creative pub fare runs a wide gamut, from thin-crust brick-oven pizzas to fish tacos, fish-and-chips, and vegan black-bean burgers. **Known for:** craft beer; homemade desserts; live-music calendar. *Average main: $16 ✉ 40233 Enterprise Dr., off Hwy. 49, north of Von's shopping center, Oakhurst ☎ 559/692–2739 🌐 southgatebrewco.com.*

Hotels

At this writing, a still-ongoing trademark dispute with a former park concessioner resulted in Yosemite National Park changing the names of several historic park lodges and properties, including the iconic Ahwahnee. This guide has changed the historic names, with some references to the former. The changes include: Yosemite Lodge at the Falls is Yosemite Valley Lodge, The Ahwahnee is The Majestic Yosemite Hotel, Curry Village is Half Dome Village, Wawona Hotel is Big Trees Lodge, and Badger Pass Ski Area is Yosemite Ski & Snowboard Area.

IN THE PARK

Big Trees Lodge

$$ | **HOTEL** | This 1879 National Historic Landmark at Yosemite's southern end (formerly Wawona Hotel) is a Victorian-era mountain resort, with whitewashed buildings, wraparound verandas, and pleasant, no-frills rooms decorated with period pieces. **Pros:** lovely building; peaceful atmosphere; historic photos in public areas. **Cons:** few modern amenities, such as phones and TVs; an hour's drive from Yosemite Valley; shared bathrooms in half the rooms. *Rooms from: $148 ✉ 8308 Wawona Rd., Wawona ☎ 888/413–8869 🌐 www.travelyosemite.com ⏲ Closed Dec.–Mar., except mid-Dec.–Jan. 2 104 rooms, 50 with bath Breakfast.*

Half Dome Village

$$ | **HOTEL** | Opened in 1899 as a place for budget-conscious travelers, Half Dome Village (formerly Curry Village) has plain accommodations: standard motel rooms, simple cabins with either private or shared baths, and tent cabins with shared baths. **Pros:** close to many activities; family-friendly atmosphere; surrounded by iconic valley views. **Cons:** community bathrooms need updating; can be crowded; sometimes a bit noisy. *Rooms from: $143 South side of Southside Dr. 888/413–8869, 602/278–8888 international www.travelyosemite.com 583 rooms and cabins No meals.*

★ The Majestic Yosemite Hotel

$$$$ | **HOTEL** | Formerly The Ahwahnee, this National Historic Landmark is constructed of sugar-pine logs and features Native American design motifs; public spaces are enlivened with art-deco flourishes, Persian rugs, and elaborate iron- and woodwork. **Pros:** best lodge in Yosemite; helpful concierge; in the historic heart of the valley. **Cons:** expensive rates; some reports that service has slipped in recent years. *Rooms from: $581 Ahwahnee Rd., about ¾ mile east of Yosemite Valley Visitor Center, Yosemite Village 801/559–4884 www.travelyosemite.com 125 rooms and suites No meals.*

Redwoods in Yosemite

$$$$ | **RENTAL** | This collection of more than 125 homes in the Wawona area is a great alternative to the overcrowded valley. **Pros:** sense of privacy; peaceful setting; full kitchens. **Cons:** 45-minute drive from the valley; some have no air-conditioning; cell phone service can be spotty. *Rooms from: $260 8038 Chilnualna Falls Rd., off Rte. 41, Wawona 209/375–6666 international, 888/225–6666 www.redwoodsinyosemite.com 125 units No meals.*

White Wolf Lodge

$$ | **HOTEL** | Set in a subalpine meadow, the rustic accommodations at White Wolf Lodge make it an excellent base camp for hiking the backcountry. **Pros:** quiet location; near some of Yosemite's most beautiful, less crowded hikes; good restaurant. **Cons:** far from the valley; tent cabins share bathhouse; remote setting. *Rooms from: $138 Yosemite National Park Off Tioga Rd. (Rte. 120), 25 miles west of Tuolumne Meadows and 15 miles east of Crane Flat 801/559–4884 Closed mid-Sept.–mid-June 28 cabins No meals.*

Yosemite Valley Lodge

$$$$ | **HOTEL** | This 1915 lodge near Yosemite Falls (formerly Yosemite Lodge at the Falls) is a collection of numerous two-story, glass-and-wood structures tucked beneath the trees. **Pros:** centrally located; dependably clean rooms; lots of tours leave from out front. **Cons:** can feel impersonal; high prices; no in-room air-conditioning. *Rooms from: $260 9006 Yosemite Valley Lodge Dr., Yosemite Village 888/413–8869 www.travelyosemite.com 245 rooms No meals.*

OUTSIDE THE PARK

Best Western Plus Yosemite Gateway Inn

$$$$ | **HOTEL** | **FAMILY** | Perched on 11 hillside acres, Oakhurst's best motel has carefully tended landscaping and rooms with stylish contemporary furnishings and hand-painted murals of Yosemite. **Pros:** close to park's southern entrance; on-site restaurant; indoor and outdoor swimming pools; frequent deer and wildlife sightings. **Cons:** some rooms on the small side; Internet connection can be slow; some rooms need updating. *Rooms from: $249 40530 Hwy. 41, Oakhurst 559/683–2378 www.yosemitegatewayinn.com 149 rooms No meals.*

Camping in Bear Country

The national parks' campgrounds and some campgrounds outside the parks provide food-storage boxes that can keep bears from pilfering your edibles (portable canisters for backpackers can be rented in most park stores). It's imperative that you move all food, coolers, and items with a scent (including toiletries, toothpaste, chewing gum, and air fresheners) from your car (including the trunk) to the storage box at your campsite; day-trippers should lock food in bear boxes provided at parking lots. If you don't, a bear may break into your car by literally peeling off the door or ripping open the trunk, or ransack your tent. The familiar tactic of hanging your food from high tree limbs is not an effective deterrent, as bears easily can scale trees. In the southern Sierra, bear canisters are the only effective and proven method for preventing bears from getting human food. Details on bears and food storage are posted on the park website, 🌐 *www.nps.gov/yose/planyourvisit/bears.htm.*

★ Château du Sureau
$$$$ | **RESORT** | The inn here is straight out of a children's book: every room is impeccably styled with European antiques, sumptuous fabrics, fresh-cut flowers, and oversize soaking tubs. **Pros:** luxurious; great views; sumptuous spa facility. **Cons:** expensive; cost might not seem worth it to guests not spa-oriented; can seem pretentious to some. Ⓢ *Rooms from: $420* ✉ *48688 Victoria La., Oakhurst* ☎ *559/683–6860* 🌐 *www.chateausureau.com* 🛏 *11 rooms* 🍴 *Breakfast.*

Evergreen Lodge at Yosemite
$$$$ | **RESORT** | **FAMILY** | Amid the trees near Yosemite National Park's Hetch Hetchy entrance, this sprawling property is perfect for families. **Pros:** cabin complex includes amphitheater, pool, and more; guided tours available; great roadhouse-style restaurant. **Cons:** no TVs; long, winding access road; spotty cell service. Ⓢ *Rooms from: $280* ✉ *33160 Evergreen Rd., 30 miles east of town of Groveland, Groveland* ☎ *209/379–2606* 🌐 *www.evergreenlodge.com* 🛏 *88 cabins.*

Homestead Cottages
$$$ | **B&B/INN** | Set on 160 acres of rolling hills that once held a Miwok village, these cottages (the largest sleeps six) have gas fireplaces, fully equipped kitchens, and queen-size beds. **Pros:** remote location; quiet setting; friendly owners. **Cons:** might be too quiet for some; breakfasts on the simple side; 7 miles from center of Oakhurst. Ⓢ *Rooms from: $189* ✉ *41110 Rd. 600, 2½ miles off Hwy. 49, Ahwahnee* ☎ *559/683–0495* 🌐 *www.homesteadcottages.com* 🛏 *7 cottages* 🍴 *Breakfast.*

Narrow Gauge Inn
$$$$ | **HOTEL** | The well-tended rooms at this family-owned property have balconies with views of the surrounding woods and mountains. **Pros:** close to Yosemite's south entrance; nicely appointed rooms; wonderful balconies. **Cons:** rooms can be a bit dark; dining options are limited, especially for vegetarians; housekeeping service can be spotty. Ⓢ *Rooms from: $229* ✉ *48571 Hwy. 41, Fish Camp* ☎ *559/683–7720, 888/644–9050* 🌐 *www.narrowgaugeinn.com* 🛏 *27 rooms* 🍴 *No meals.*

Best Campgrounds in Yosemite

If you are going to concentrate solely on valley sites and activities, you should endeavor to stay in one of the "Pines" campgrounds, which are clustered near Half Dome Village and within an easy stroll from that busy complex's many facilities. For a more primitive and quiet experience, and to be near many backcountry hikes, try one of the Tioga Road campgrounds.

National Park Service Reservations Office
Reservations are required at many of Yosemite's campgrounds. You can book a site up to five months in advance, starting on the 15th of the month. Unless otherwise noted, book your site through the central National Park Service Reservations Office. If you don't have reservations when you arrive, many sites, especially those outside Yosemite Valley, are available on a first-come, first-served basis. ☎ *877/444–6777 reservations, 518/885–3639 international, 888/448–1474 customer service* 🌐 *www.recreation.gov.*

Bridalveil Creek. This campground sits among lodgepole pines at 7,200 feet, above the valley on Glacier Point Road. From here, you can easily drive to Glacier Point's magnificent valley views. ✉ *From Rte. 41 in Wawona, go north to Glacier Point Rd. and turn right; entrance to campground is 25 miles ahead on right side.*

Camp 4. Formerly known as Sunnyside Walk-In, and extremely popular with rock climbers, who don't mind that a total of six are assigned to each campsite; no matter how many are in your group, this is the only valley campground available on a first-come, first-served basis. ✉ *Base of Yosemite Falls Trail, just west of Yosemite Valley Lodge on Northside Dr., Yosemite Village.*

Housekeeping Camp. Composed of three concrete walls and covered with two layers of canvas, each unit has an open-ended fourth side that can be closed off with a heavy white canvas curtain. You can rent "bedpacks," consisting of blankets, sheets, and other comforts. ✉ *Southside Dr., ½ mile west of Half Dome Village.*

Porcupine Flat. Sixteen miles west of Tuolumne Meadows, this campground sits at 8,100 feet. If you want to be in the high country, this is a good bet. ✉ *Rte. 120, 16 miles west of Tuolumne Meadows.*

Tuolumne Meadows. In a wooded area at 8,600 feet, just south of its namesake meadow, this is one of the most spectacular and sought-after campgrounds in Yosemite. ✉ *Rte. 120, 46 miles east of Big Oak Flat entrance station.*

Upper Pines. This is one of the valley's largest campgrounds and the closest one to the trailheads. Expect large crowds in the summer—and little privacy. ✉ *At east end of valley, near Half Dome Village.*

Wawona. Near the Mariposa Grove, just downstream from a popular fishing spot, this year-round campground has larger, less densely packed sites than campgrounds in the valley. ✉ *Rte. 41, 1 mile north of Wawona.*

White Wolf. Set in the beautiful high country at 8,000 feet, this is a prime spot for hikers from early July to mid-September. ✉ *Tioga Rd., 15 miles east of Big Oak Flat entrance.*

★ Rush Creek Lodge

$$$$ | **RESORT** | **FAMILY** | This sleek, nature-inspired complex occupies 20 acres on a wooded hillside and includes a saltwater pool and hot tubs, a restaurant and tavern with indoor/outdoor seating, a guided recreation program, massage studios and wellness program, and a general store. **Pros:** close to Yosemite's Big Oak Flat entrance; YARTS bus stops here and connects with Yosemite Valley and Sonora spring; year-round evening s'mores. **Cons:** no TVs; pricey in high season; spotty cell service. *Rooms from: $410 ✉ 34001 Hwy. 120, Groveland ✣ 25 miles east of Groveland, 23 miles north of Yosemite Valley ☎ 209/379–2373 ⊕ www.rushcreeklodge.com ⇆ 143 rooms and suites ꟾ⊚ꟾ No meals.*

Sierra Sky Ranch

$$$$ | **HOTEL** | Off Highway 41 just 10 miles south of the Yosemite National Park, this 19th-century cattle ranch near a hidden grove of giant sequoia trees provides a restful, rustic retreat. **Pros:** peaceful setting; historic property; short drive to giant sequoias. **Cons:** some rooms on the small side; not in town; basic breakfast. *Rooms from: $249 ✉ 50552 Rd. 632, Oakhurst ☎ 559/683–8040 ⊕ www.sierraskyranch.com ⇆ 26 rooms ꟾ⊚ꟾ Breakfast.*

Tamarack Lodge Resort

$$$ | **RESORT** | Tucked away on the edge of the John Muir Wilderness Area, where cross-country ski trails loop through the woods, this 1924 lodge looks like something out of a snow globe. **Pros:** rustic but not run-down; tons of nearby outdoor activities; excellent wine list in restaurant. **Cons:** thin walls; some shared bathrooms; some cabins are tiny. *Rooms from: $169 ✉ Lake Mary Rd., off Rte. 203, Mammoth Lakes ☎ 760/934–2442, 800/237–6879 ⊕ www.tamaracklodge.com ⇆ 45 rooms and cabins ꟾ⊚ꟾ Free Breakfast.*

★ Tenaya Lodge

$$$$ | **RESORT** | **FAMILY** | One of the region's largest hotels, Tenaya Lodge is ideal for people who enjoy wilderness treks by day but prefer creature comforts at night. **Pros:** close to Yosemite and Mariposa Grove of Giant Sequoias; exceptional spa and exercise facility, 36 miles of mountain bike trails; activities for all ages. **Cons:** so big it can seem impersonal; pricey during summer; daily resort fee. *Rooms from: $379 ✉ 1122 Hwy. 41, Fish Camp ☎ 559/683–6555, 888/514–2167 ⊕ www.tenayalodge.com ⇆ 352 rooms ꟾ⊚ꟾ No meals.*

Yosemite View Lodge

$$$$ | **HOTEL** | Two miles outside Yosemite's Arch Rock entrance, this modern property is the most convenient place to spend the night if you are unable to secure lodgings in the valley. **Pros:** great location; good views; lots of on-site amenities. **Cons:** somewhat pricey; it can be a challenge to get the dates you want; rooms could use an update. *Rooms from: $239 ✉ 11136 Hwy. 140, El Portal ☎ 209/379–2681, 888/742–4371 ⊕ www.stayyosemiteviewlodge.com ⇆ 335 rooms ꟾ⊚ꟾ No meals.*

Chapter 7

EASTERN SIERRA

Updated by
Cheryl Crabtree

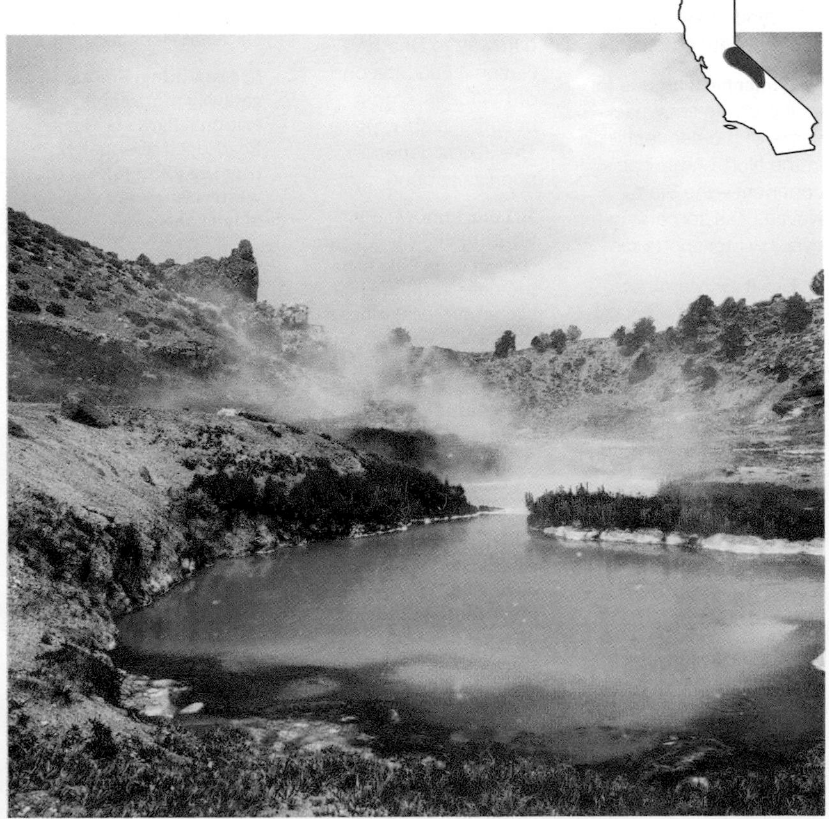

Sights ★★★★★ | Restaurants ★★★★☆ | Hotels ★★★★★ | Shopping ★☆☆☆☆ | Nightlife ★☆☆☆☆

WELCOME TO EASTERN SIERRA

TOP REASONS TO GO

★ **Hiking:** Whether you walk the paved loops in the national parks or head off the beaten path into the backcountry, a hike through groves and meadows or alongside streams and waterfalls will allow you to see, smell, and feel nature up close.

★ **Winter fun:** Famous for its incredible snowpack—some of the deepest in the North American continent—the Sierra Nevada has something for every winter-sports fan.

★ **Live it up:** Mammoth Lakes is eastern California's most exciting resort area.

★ **Road trip heaven:** Legendary Highway 395 is one of California's most scenic byways, and stops in Independence, Lone Pine, Bishop, and Bodie Ghost Town give you a glimpse of Old West history.

★ **Go with the flow:** Fish, float, raft, and row in the abundant lakes, hot springs, creeks, and rivers.

The transition between Los Angeles and the Mojave Desert and the rugged Eastern Sierra may be the most dramatic in California sightseeing. U.S. 395 is the main north–south road on the eastern side of the Sierra Nevada, at the western edge of the Great Basin, and a gateway to Death Valley National Park. It's one of California's most beautiful highways. The 395 is generally open year-round.

1 Lone Pine. Mount Whitney and the Alabama Hills in Lone Pine have provided authentic backdrops for hundreds of films and TV shows for nearly a century, as evidenced in the town's Museum of Western Film History.

2 Independence. The moving Manzanar National Historic Site, where 11,000 Japanese-Americans were interned during World War II, lies 6 miles south of Independence, a tiny Old West town.

3 Bishop. One of the largest towns along Highway 395, Bishop is an excellent road stop and base camp for exploration in the surrounding mountains.

4 Mammoth Lakes. Easy access to year-round outdoor adventures has made Mammoth Lakes one of the Sierra Nevada's most popular destinations. The bustling town's many attractions include sprawling Mammoth Mountain Ski and Bike Area and nearby Mammoth Lakes Basin and Devil's Postpile National Monument.

5 Lee Vining. The eastern gateway to Yosemite National Park via Tioga Road (open seasonally), tiny Lee Vining sits at the western shores of vast Mono Lake.

6 Bodie State Historic Park. The town of Bridgeport is the main portal to Bodie State Historic Park and the well-preserved Bodie Ghost Town.

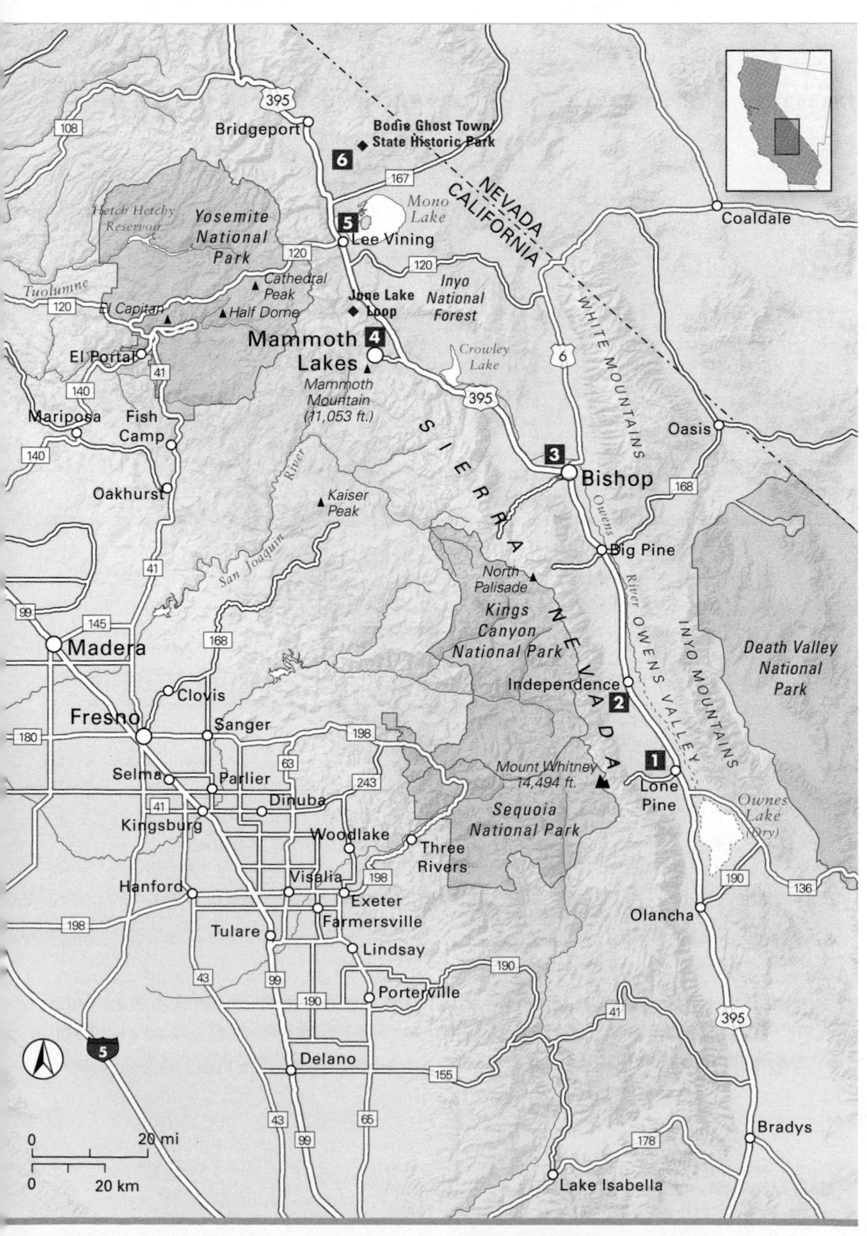

Bridgeport
Bodie Ghost Town/ State Historic Park
Mono Lake
NEVADA
CALIFORNIA
Hetch Hetchy Reservoir
Yosemite National Park
Lee Vining
Coaldale
Tuolumne
Cathedral Peak
Half Dome
El Capitan
June Lake Loop
Inyo National Forest
Mammoth Lakes
Crowley Lake
El Portal
Mammoth Mountain (11,053 ft.)
WHITE MOUNTAINS
Mariposa
Fish Camp
Oasis
Oakhurst
SIERRA NEVADA
Bishop
Kaiser Peak
San Joaquin River
Owens River
Big Pine
North Palisade
Kings Canyon National Park
Madera
Death Valley National Park
INYO MOUNTAINS
OWENS VALLEY
Independence
Clovis
Fresno
Sanger
Selma
Parlier
Mount Whitney 14,494 ft.
Lone Pine
Dinuba
Kingsburg
Sequoia National Park
Owens Lake (Dry)
Woodlake
Three Rivers
Hanford
Visalia
Exeter
Farmersville
Olancha
Tulare
Lindsay
Porterville
Delano
Bradys
Lake Isabella
0 20 mi
0 20 km

The Eastern Sierra's granite peaks and ancient pines bedazzle heart and soul so completely that for many visitors the experience surpasses that at more famous urban attractions. Most of the Sierra's wonders lie within national parks, but outside them deep-blue Mono Lake and its tufa towers never cease to astound. The megaresort Mammoth Lakes, meanwhile, lures skiers and snowboarders in winter and hikers and mountain bikers in summer.

The Eastern Sierra is accessed most easily via Highway 395, which travels the length of the region from the Mojave Desert in the south to Bridgeport in the north. Main towns along the route include Lone Pine, Independence, Bishop, Mammoth Lakes, June Lake, and Lee Vining, a small town at the eastern endpoint of Tioga Road from Yosemite National Park. Pristine lakes and rolling hills outside the parks offer year-round opportunities for rest and relaxation. Or not. In winter the thrill of the slopes—and their relative isolation compared to busy Lake Tahoe—draws a hearty breed of outdoor enthusiasts. In summer a hike through groves and meadows or alongside streams and waterfalls allows you to see, smell, and feel nature up close.

Planning

Getting Here and Around

AIR TRAVEL

Three main airports provide access to the Eastern Sierra: Fresno Yosemite International (FAT), on the western side, and, on the eastern side, Mammoth–Yosemite (MMH), 6 miles east of Mammoth Lakes, and Reno–Tahoe (RNO), 130 miles north of Mammoth Lakes via U.S. 395. Alaska, Allegiant, American, Delta, Frontier, United, and a few other carriers serve Fresno and Reno. United and JetSuiteX serve Mammoth Lakes.

AIRPORTS Fresno Yosemite International Airport *(FAT) ⊠ 5175 E. Clinton Ave., Fresno ☎ 800/244–2359 automated information, 559/454–2052 terminal info desk ⊕ www.flyfresno.com.* **Mammoth–Yosemite Airport** *⊠ 1200 Airport*

Rd., Mammoth Lakes ☎ *760/934–2712, 888/466–2666* 🌐 *www.visitmammoth.com/getting-mammoth-lakes.* **Reno–Tahoe International Airport** ✉ *2001 E. Plumb La., Reno* ☎ *775/328–6400* 🌐 *www.renoairport.com.*

BUS TRAVEL

Eastern Sierra Transit Authority buses serve Mammoth Lakes, Bishop, and other Eastern Sierra towns along Highway 395, from Reno in the north to Lancaster in the south. In summer YARTS (Yosemite Area Regional Transportation System) connects Yosemite National Park with Mammoth Lakes, June Lake, and Lee Vining in the Eastern Sierra, and Central Valley cities and towns in the west, including Fresno and Merced. This is a good option during summer, when parking in Yosemite Valley and elsewhere in the park can be difficult.

BUS CONTACTS Eastern Sierra Transit Authority ☎ *760/872–1901 general, 800/922–3190 toll-free, 760/924–3184 Mammoth Lakes* 🌐 *www.estransit.com.* **YARTS** ☎ *877/989–2787* 🌐 *www.yarts.com.*

CAR TRAVEL

Interstate 5 and Highway 99 travel north–south along the western side of the Sierra Nevada. U.S. 395 follows a roughly parallel route on the eastern side. In summer, Tioga Pass Road in Yosemite National Park opens to car and bus travel, intersecting with U.S. 395 at Lee Vining.

From San Francisco: Head east on Interstate 80 to Sacramento, then continue on Interstate 80 to U.S. 395, east of Lake Tahoe's north shore, or take U.S. 50 to Lake Tahoe's south shore and continue on 207E to U.S. 395, then head south.

From Los Angeles: Head north on Interstate 5, exiting and continuing north onto Highway 14 and later onto U.S. 395.

■ **TIP→ Gas stations are few and far between in the Sierra, so fill your tank when you can.** Between October and May heavy snow may cover mountain roads. Always check road conditions before driving. Carry tire chains, and know how to install them. On Interstate 80 and U.S. 50, and at the Mammoth Lakes exit off U.S. 395 chain installers assist travelers (for $40), but elsewhere you're on your own.

TRAVEL REPORTS Caltrans Current Highway Conditions ☎ *800/427–7623* 🌐 *www.dot.ca.gov.*

TRAIN TRAVEL

Amtrak's daily *San Joaquin* train stops in Fresno and Merced, where you can connect to YARTS for travel to Yosemite National Park and in summer to smaller gateway towns, including Mammoth Lakes, June Lake, and Lee Vining.

TRAIN CONTACT Amtrak ☎ *800/872–7245, 215/856–7924 international* 🌐 *www.amtrak.com.*

Restaurants

Most small towns in the Sierra Nevada have at least one restaurant. Standard American fare is the norm, but you'll also find sophisticated cuisine. With few exceptions, dress is casual. Local grocery stores and delis stock picnic fixings, good to have on hand should the opportunity for an impromptu meal under giant trees emerge. *Restaurant reviews have been shortened. For full information, visit Fodors.com.*

Hotels

The lodgings in Mammoth Lakes and nearest Yosemite National Park generally fill up the quickest; book hotels everywhere in the Eastern Sierra well in advance in summer. *Hotel reviews have been shortened. For full information, visit Fodors.com.*

What It Costs

	$	$$	$$$	$$$$
RESTAURANTS	under $16	$16–$22	$23–$30	over $30
HOTELS	under $120	$120–$175	$176–$250	over $250

Tours

MAWS Transportation

BUS TOURS | This outfit (aka Mammoth All Weather Shuttle) operates summer tours from Mammoth Lakes to Yosemite; north to June Lake, Mono Lake, and Bodie Ghost Town; and around the lakes region. The company also transfers passengers from the Mammoth–Yosemite Airport into town, drops off and picks up hikers at trailheads, and runs charters to Bishop, Los Angeles, Reno, and Las Vegas airports—useful when inclement weather causes flight cancellations at Mammoth's airport. ✉ *Mammoth Lakes* ☎ *760/709–2927* 🌐 *www.mawshuttle.com* 🎫 *From $60.*

Visitor Information

Eastern Sierra Visitor Center

Pull off the 395 at this one-stop, interagency center for visitor, wilderness, and highway information, plus views of Mt. Whitney. You can also pick up wilderness permits, rent or buy bear-resistant food containers, and picnic on the grounds. It's open year-round from 9 to 5 (8 to 5 May–October). ✣ *2 miles south of Lone Pine, at junctions of U.S. Hwy. 395 and CA Hwy. 136* ☎ *760/876–6200, 760/876–6222* 🌐 *www.fs.usda.gov/recarea/inyo/recarea/?recid=20698.*

Mammoth Lakes Tourism

✉ *Mammoth Lakes* ☎ *760/934–2712, 888/466–2666* 🌐 *www.visitmammoth.com.*

Mono County Tourism

✉ *Mammoth Lakes* ☎ *800/845–7922* 🌐 *monocounty.org.*

Lone Pine

30 miles west of Panamint Valley.

Mt. Whitney towers majestically over this tiny community, which supplied nearby gold- and silver-mining outposts in the 1860s, and for the past century the town has been touched by Hollywood glamour: several hundred movies, TV episodes, and commercials have been filmed here.

GETTING HERE AND AROUND

Arrive by car via U.S. 395 from the north or south, or Highway 190 or Highway 138 from Death Valley National Park. Eastern Sierra Transit buses connect Lone Pine to Reno in the north and Lancaster in the south.

ESSENTIALS

VISITOR INFORMATION Lone Pine Chamber of Commerce ✉ *120 S. Main St., at Whitney Portal Rd.* ☎ *760/876–4444* 🌐 *www.lonepinechamber.org.*

Alabama Hills

MOUNTAIN—SIGHT | Drop by the Lone Pine Visitor Center for a map of the Alabama Hills and take a drive up Whitney Portal Road (turn west at the light) to this wonderland of granite boulders. Erosion has worn the rocks smooth; some have been chiseled to leave arches and other formations. The hills have become a popular location for rock climbing. Tuttle Creek Campground sits among the rocks, with a nearby stream for fishing. The area has served as a scenic backdrop for hundreds of films; ask about the self-guided tour of the various movie locations at the Museum of Western Film History. ✉ *Whitney Portal Rd., 4½ miles west of Lone Pine.*

Mt. Whitney
MOUNTAIN—SIGHT | Straddling the border of Sequoia National Park and Inyo National Forest–John Muir Wilderness, Mt. Whitney (14,496 feet) is the highest mountain in the contiguous United States. A favorite game for travelers passing through Lone Pine is trying to guess which peak is Mt. Whitney. Almost no one gets it right, because Mt. Whitney is hidden behind other mountains. There is no road that ascends the peak, but you can catch a glimpse of the mountain by driving curvy Whitney Portal Road west from Lone Pine into the mountains. The pavement ends at the trailhead to the top of the mountain, which is also the start of the 211-mile John Muir Trail from Mt. Whitney to Yosemite National Park. Day and overnight permits are required to ascend Mt. Whitney. The highly competitive lottery for these permits opens on February 1st. At the portal, a restaurant (known for its pancakes) and a small store cater to hikers and campers staying at Whitney Portal Campground. You can see a waterfall from the parking lot and go fishing in a small trout pond. The portal area is closed from mid-October to early May; the road closes when snow conditions require. ✉ *Whitney Portal Rd., west of Lone Pine* 🌐 *www.fs.usda.gov/attmain/inyo.*

Museum of Western Film History
MUSEUM | Hopalong Cassidy, Barbara Stanwyck, Roy Rogers, John Wayne—even Robert Downey Jr.—are among the stars who have starred in Westerns and other films shot in the Alabama Hills and surrounding dusty terrain. The marquee-embellished museum relates this Hollywood-in-the-desert tale via exhibits and a rollicking 20-minute documentary. ✉ *701 S. Main St., U.S. 395* ☎ *760/876–9909* 🌐 *www.museumofwesternfilmhistory.org* 🎟 *$5.*

Alabama Hills Café & Bakery
$ | **AMERICAN** | The extensive breakfast and lunch menus at this eatery just off the main drag include many vegetarian items. Sandwiches are served on homemade bread; choose from up to six varieties baked fresh daily, and get a homemade pie, cake, or loaf to go. **Known for:** house-roasted turkey and beef; huge portions; on-site bakery. 💲 *Average main: $13* ✉ *111 W. Post St., at S. Main St.* ☎ *760/876–4675.*

The Grill
$$ | **AMERICAN** | **FAMILY** | Open for three meals a day, this small restaurant next to the Dow Villa Motel is a convenient place to stop for a break while driving along Highway 395. The extensive menu includes an array of options, from omelets and French toast for breakfast and sandwiches and burgers for lunch, to grilled steaks and fish for dinner. **Known for:** hearty meals with large portions; friendly service; house-made desserts. 💲 *Average main: $21* ✉ *446 S. Main St.* ☎ *760/876–4240.*

Seasons Restaurant
$$$ | **AMERICAN** | **FAMILY** | This inviting, country-style diner serves all kinds of traditional American fare. For a special treat, try the medallions of Cervena elk, smothered in port wine, dried cranberries, and toasted walnuts; finish with the Baileys Irish Cream cheesecake or the Grand Marnier crème brûlée for dessert. **Known for:** high-end dining in remote area; steaks and wild game; children's menu. 💲 *Average main: $27* ✉ *206 S. Main St.* ☎ *760/876–8927* 🌐 *www.seasonslonepine.com* 🕒 *Closed Mon. Nov.–Mar. No lunch.*

Dow Villa Motel and Dow Hotel
$$ | **HOTEL** | Built in 1923 to cater to the film industry, the Dow Villa Motel and

the historic Dow Hotel sit in the center of Lone Pine. **Pros:** clean rooms; great mountain views; in-room whirlpool tubs in some motel rooms. **Cons:** some rooms in hotel share bathrooms; sinks in some rooms are in the bedroom, not the bath; on busy highway. *Rooms from: $119* ✉ *310 S. Main St.* ☎ *760/876–5521, 800/824–9317* 🌐 *www.dowvillamotel.com* *92 rooms* *No meals.*

Independence

17 miles north of Lone Pine.

Named for a military outpost that was established near here in 1862, sleepy Independence has some wonderful historic buildings and is worth a stop for two other reasons. The Eastern California Museum provides a marvelous overview of regional history, and 6 miles south of the small downtown lies the Manzanar National Historic Site, one of 10 camps in the West where people of Japanese descent were confined during the Second World War.

GETTING HERE AND AROUND

Eastern Sierra Transit buses pass through town, but most travelers arrive by car on U.S. 395.

Sights

Ancient Bristlecone Pine Forest

FOREST | FAMILY | About an hour's drive from Independence or Bishop you can view some of the oldest living trees on Earth, some of which date back more than 40 centuries. The world's largest bristlecone pine can be found in Patriarch Grove, while the world's oldest known living tree is along Methusula Trail in Schulman Grove. Getting to Patriarch Grove is slow going along the narrow dirt road, especially for sedans with low clearance, but once there you'll find picnic tables, restrooms, and self-guided interpretive trails. ✉ *Schulman Grove Visitor Center, White Mountain Rd., Bishop* ✣ *From U.S. 395, turn east onto Hwy. 168 and follow signs for 23 miles* 🌐 *www.fs.usda.gov/main/inyo/home* *$3.*

Eastern California Museum

MUSEUM | FAMILY | The highlights of this museum dedicated to Inyo County and the Eastern Sierra's history include photos and artifacts from the Manzanar War Relocation Center, Paiute and Shoshone baskets, and exhibits on the Los Angeles Aqueduct and mountaineer Norman Clyde. ✉ *155 N. Grant St., at W. Center St.* ☎ *760/878–0258* 🌐 *www.inyocounty.us/ecmsite* *Free.*

★ Manzanar National Historic Site

HISTORIC SITE | A reminder of an ugly episode in U.S. history, the former Manzanar War Relocation Center is where more than 11,000 Japanese-Americans were confined behind barbed-wire fences between 1942 and 1945. A visit here is both deeply moving and inspiring—the former because it's hard to comprehend that the United States was capable of confining its citizens in such a way, the latter because those imprisoned here showed great pluck and perseverance in making the best of a bad situation. Most of the buildings from the 1940s are gone, but two sentry posts, the auditorium, and numerous Japanese rock gardens remain. One of eight guard towers, two barracks, and a women's latrine have been reconstructed, and a mess hall has been restored. Interactive exhibits inside the barracks include audio and video clips from people who were incarcerated in Manzanar during WWII. You can drive the one-way road on a self-guided tour past various ruins to a small cemetery, where a monument stands. Signs mark where the barracks, a hospital, a school, and the fire station once stood. An outstanding 8,000-square-foot interpretive center has exhibits and documentary photographs and screens a short film. ✉ *Independence* ✣ *West side of U.S. 395 between*

Independence and Lone Pine ☎ *760/878–2194* 🌐 *www.nps.gov/manz* 🎟 *Free.*

Mt. Whitney Fish Hatchery

FISH HATCHERY | FAMILY | A delightful place for a family picnic, the hatchery was one of California's first trout farms. The Tudor Revival–style structure, completed in 1917, is an architectural stunner, its walls nearly 3 feet thick with locally quarried granite. Fish production ceased in 2007 after a fire and subsequent mudslide, but dedicated volunteers staff the facility and raise trout for display purposes in a large pond out front. Bring change for the fish-food machines. ✉ *1 Golden Trout Circle, 2 miles north of town* ☎ *760/279–1592* 🌐 *www.mtwhitneyfishhatchery.org* 🎟 *Free (donations welcome)* ⏲ *Closed mid-Dec.–mid-Apr. Closed Tues. and Wed.*

Bishop

43 miles north of Independence.

One of the biggest towns along U.S. 395, bustling Bishop has views of the Sierra Nevada and the White and Inyo mountains. First settled by the Northern Paiute Indians, the area was named in 1861 for cattle rancher Samuel Bishop, who established a camp here. Paiute and Shoshone people reside on four reservations in the area. Bishop kicks off the summer season with its Mule Days Celebration. Held over Memorial Day weekend, the five-day event includes mule races, a rodeo, an arts-and-crafts show, and country-music concerts.

GETTING HERE AND AROUND

To fully enjoy the many surrounding attractions, you should get here by car. Arrive and depart via U.S. 395 or, from Nevada, U.S. 6. Local transit provides limited service to nearby tourist sites.

ESSENTIALS

BUS INFORMATION Eastern Sierra Transit Authority ☎ *760/872–1901* 🌐 *www.estransit.com.*

VISITOR INFORMATION Bishop Chamber of Commerce ✉ *690 N. Main St., at Park St.* ☎ *760/873–8405, 888/395–3952* 🌐 *www.bishopvisitor.com.*

Sights

Laws Railroad Museum

MUSEUM | FAMILY | The laid-back and wholly nostalgic railroad museum celebrates the Carson and Colorado Railroad Company, which set up a narrow-gauge railroad yard here in 1883. Among the exhibits are a self-propelled car from the Death Valley Railroad, a stamp mill from an area mine, and a full village of rescued buildings, including a post office, the original 1883 train depot, and a restored 1900 ranch house. Many of the buildings are full of "modern amenities" of days gone by. ✉ *200 Silver Canyon Rd., off U.S. 6, 4.5 miles north of town* ☎ *760/873–5950* 🌐 *www.lawsmuseum.org* 🎟 *$5 suggested donation.*

Mule Days Celebration

FESTIVAL | For five days around Memorial Day weekend more than 30,000 tourists and locals pack into Bishop to celebrate the humble mule. Activities include what organizers bill as the longest nonmotorized parade in the world, a rodeo, and good old-fashioned country-and-western concerts. ✉ *1141 N. Main St.* ☎ *760/872–4263* 🌐 *www.muledays.org.*

Restaurants

Erick Schat's Bakkerÿ

$ | BAKERY | A bustling stop for motorists traveling to and from Mammoth Lakes, this shop is crammed with delicious pastries, cookies, rolls, and other baked goods. The biggest draw, though, is the sheepherder bread, a hand-shaped and stone hearth–baked sourdough that was introduced during the gold rush by immigrant Basque sheepherders in 1907. **Known for:** sheepherder bread and pastries; convenient place to stock up; hefty sandwiches. $ *Average main: $10* ✉ *763 N. Main St., near Park St.* ☎ *760/873–7156* 🌐 *www.erickschatsbakery.com.*

Great Basin Bakery

$ | **AMERICAN** | Stop at this small, old-world-style community bakery for fresh and healthy salads, sandwiches (made all day), bagels, artisan breads, cookies, pies, and pastries. Savor your goodies indoors and listen to local banter (it's a favorite gathering spot), or take them along to eat at a picnic spot while adventuring nearby. **Known for:** sandwiches on fresh-baked, house-made bread; all items made and packaged by hand; stellar pies and other desserts. $ *Average main: $13* ✉ *275 S. Main St.* ☎ *760/873–9828* 🌐 *greatbasinbakerybishop.com.*

Hotels

Bishop Creekside Inn

$$ | **B&B/INN** | The nicest spot to stay in Bishop, this clean and comfortable mountain-style hotel is a good base from which to explore the town or go skiing and trout fishing nearby. **Pros:** nice pool; spacious and modern rooms; on-site restaurant. **Cons:** pets not allowed; hotel fronts busy road; basic breakfast. $ *Rooms from: $170* ✉ *725 N. Main St.* ☎ *760/872–3044, 800/273–3550* 🌐 *www.bishopcreeksideinn.com* *89 rooms* *Breakfast.*

Activities

The Owens Valley is trout country; its glistening alpine lakes and streams are brimming with feisty rainbow, brown, brook, and golden trout. Good spots include Owens River, the Owens River gorge, and Pleasant Valley Reservoir. Although you can fish year-round here, some fishing is catch-and-release. Bishop is the site of fishing derbies throughout the year, including the Blake Jones Blind Bogey Trout Derby in March. Rock-climbing, mountain biking, and hiking are also popular Owens Valley outdoor activities.

FISHING

Reagan's Sporting Goods

FISHING | Stop at Reagan's to pick up bait, tackle, and fishing licenses and to find out where the fish are biting. They can also recommend guides. ✉ *963 N. Main St.* ☎ *760/872–3000* 🌐 *www.reaganssportinggoods.com.*

TOURS

Sierra Mountain Center

TOUR—SPORTS | The guided experiences Sierra Mountain offers include hiking, skiing, snowshoeing, rock-climbing, and mountain-biking trips for all levels of expertise. ✉ *200 S. Main St.* ☎ *760/873–8526* 🌐 *www.sierramountaincenter.com* *From $140.*

Sierra Mountain Guides

TOUR—SPORTS | Join expert guides on custom and scheduled alpine adventures, from backcountry skiing and mountaineering to backpacking and mountain running. Programs range from half-day forays to treks that last several weeks. ✉ *312 N. Main St.* ☎ *760/648–1122* 🌐 *www.sierramtnguides.com* *From $150.*

Mammoth Lakes

30 miles south of the eastern edge of Yosemite National Park.

International real-estate developers joined forces with Mammoth Mountain Ski Area to transform the once sleepy town of Mammoth Lakes (elevation 7,800 feet) into an upscale ski destination. Relatively sophisticated dining and lodging options can be found at the Village at Mammoth complex, and multimillion-dollar renovations to tired motels and restaurants have revived the "downtown" area of Old Mammoth Road. Also here is

Twin Lakes, in the Mammoth Lakes region, is a great place to unwind.

the hoppin' Mammoth Rock 'n' Bowl, a two-story activity, dining, and entertainment complex. Winter is high season at Mammoth; in summer, the room rates drop.

GETTING HERE AND AROUND

The best way to get to Mammoth Lakes is by car. The town is about 2 miles west of U.S. 395 on Highway 203, signed as Main Street in Mammoth Lakes and Minaret Road west of town. In summer and early fall (until the first big snow) you can drive to Mammoth Lakes east through Yosemite National Park on scenic Tioga Pass Road; signed as Highway 120 outside the park, the road connects to U.S. 395 north of Mammoth. In summer YARTS provides once-a-day public-transit service between Mammoth Lakes and Yosemite Valley. The shuttle buses of Eastern Sierra Transit Authority serve Mammoth Lakes and nearby tourist sites.

ESSENTIALS

VISITOR INFORMATION Mammoth Lakes Visitor Center ✉ *Welcome Center, 2510 Main St., near Sawmill Cutoff Rd.* ☎ *760/934–2712, 888/466–2666* 🌐 *www.visitmammoth.com.*

HOTEL CONTACTS Mammoth Reservations ☎ *800/223–3032* 🌐 *www.mammothreservations.com.*

Sights

★ Devils Postpile National Monument

NATURE SITE | Volcanic and glacial forces sculpted this formation of smooth, vertical basalt columns. For a bird's-eye view, take the short, steep trail to the top of a 60-foot cliff. To see the monument's second scenic wonder, **Rainbow Falls,** hike 2 miles past Devils Postpile. A branch of the San Joaquin River plunges more than 100 feet over a lava ledge here. When the water hits the pool below, sunlight turns the resulting mist into a spray of color. From mid-June to early September, day-use visitors must ride the shuttle bus from the Mammoth Mountain Ski Area to the monument. ✉ *Mammoth Lakes ✣ 13 miles southwest of Mammoth Lakes off Minaret Rd. (Hwy. 203)* ☎ *760/934–2289, 760/872–1901 shuttle* 🌐 *www.nps.gov/depo* 🎫 *$10 per vehicle (allowed when the shuttle isn't running, usually early Sept.–mid-Oct.), $8 per person shuttle.*

Hot Creek Geological Site

NATURE SITE | Forged by an ancient volcanic eruption, the geological site is a landscape of boiling hot springs, fumaroles, and occasional geysers. Swimming is prohibited—the water can go from warm to boiling in a short time—but you can look down from the parking area into the canyon to view the steaming volcanic features, a very cool sight indeed. You can also hike the foot path along the creek shores. Fly-fishing for trout is popular upstream from the springs. ✉ *Hot Creek Hatchery Rd., off U.S. 395 (airport exit), about 10 miles southeast of Mammoth Lakes* ☎ *760/924–5501* 🌐 *www.fs.usda.gov/inyo* 🎫 *Free.*

Hot Creek Trout Hatchery

FISH HATCHERY | **FAMILY** | This outdoor fish hatchery has the breeding ponds for many of the fish—typically from 3 to 5 million annually—with which the state stocks Eastern Sierra lakes and rivers. In recent years budget cuts have reduced these numbers, but locals have formed foundations to keep the hatchery going. For more details, take the worthwhile self-guided tour. **■ TIP→ Kids enjoy feeding the fish here.** ✉ *121 Hot Creek Hatchery Rd., off U.S. 395 (airport exit), about 10 miles southeast of Mammoth Lakes* ☎ *760/934–2664* 🎫 *Free.*

June Lake Loop

SCENIC DRIVE | Heading south from Lee Vining, U.S. 395 intersects the June Lake Loop. This gorgeous 17-mile drive follows an old glacial canyon past Grant, June, Gull, and Silver lakes before reconnecting with U.S. 395 on its way to Mammoth Lakes. **■ TIP→ The loop is especially colorful in fall.** ✉ *Hwy. 158 W, Lee Vining.*

★ Mammoth Lakes Basin

BODY OF WATER | Mammoth's seven main lakes are popular for fishing and boating in summer, and a network of multiuse paths connects them to the North Village. First comes Twin Lakes, at the far end of which is Twin Falls, where water cascades 300 feet over a shelf of volcanic rock. Also popular are Lake Mary, the largest lake in the basin; Lake Mamie; and Lake George. **■ TIP→ Horseshoe Lake is the only lake in which you can swim.** ✉ *Lake Mary Rd., off Hwy. 203, southwest of town.*

Mammoth Rock 'n' Bowl

RESTAURANT—SIGHT | **FAMILY** | A sprawling complex with sweeping views of the Sherwin Mountains, Mammoth Rock 'n' Bowl supplies one-stop recreation, entertainment, and dining. Downstairs are 12 bowling lanes, lounge areas, Ping-Pong and foosball tables, dartboards, and a casual bar-restaurant ($$) serving burgers, pizzas, and small plates. The upstairs floor has three golf simulators, a pro shop, and Mammoth Rock Brasserie ($$$), an upscale dining room and lounge. **■ TIP→ If the weather's nice, sit on the outdoor patio or the upstairs deck and enjoy the unobstructed vistas.** ✉ *3029 Chateau Rd., off Old Mammoth Rd.* ☎ *760/934–4200* 🌐 *mammothrocknbowl.com* 🎫 *Bowling: from $16.*

Minaret Vista

NATURE SITE | The glacier-carved sawtooth spires of the Minarets, the remains of an ancient lava flow, are best viewed from the Minaret Vista. Pull off the road, park your car in the visitors' viewing area, and walk along the path, which has interpretive signs explaining the spectacular peaks, ridges, and valleys beyond. ✉ *Off Hwy. 203, 1¼ mile west of Mammoth Mountain Ski Area.*

★ Panorama Gondola

MOUNTAIN—SIGHT | **FAMILY** | Even if you don't ski, ride the gondola to see Mammoth Mountain, the aptly named dormant volcano that gives Mammoth

Lakes its name. Gondolas serve skiers in winter and mountain bikers and sightseers in summer. The high-speed, eight-passenger gondolas whisk you from the chalet to the summit, where you can learn about the area's volcanic history in the interpretive center, have lunch in the café, and take in top-of-the-world views. Standing high above the tree line, you can look west 150 miles across the state to the Coastal Range; to the east are the highest peaks of Nevada and the Great Basin beyond. You won't find a better view of the Sierra High Country without climbing. ⚠ **The air is thin at the 11,053-foot summit; carry water, and don't overexert yourself.** ✉ *Boarding area at Main Lodge, off Minaret Rd. (Hwy. 203), west of village center* ☎ *760/934–0745, 800/626–6684* 🌐 *www.mammothmountain.com* 🎫 *From $34.*

Village at Mammoth

TOWN | This huge complex of shops, restaurants, and luxury accommodations is the town's tourist center, and the venue for many special events—check the website for the weekly schedule. The complex is also the transfer hub for the free public transit system, with fixed routes throughout the Mammoth Lakes area. The free village gondola starts here and travels up the mountain to Canyon Lodge and back. ■ **TIP→ Unless you're staying in the village and have access to the on-site lots, parking can be very difficult here.** ✉ *100 Canyon Blvd.* 🌐 *villageatmammoth.com.*

Restaurants

Black Velvet

$$ | CAFÉ | Start your day the way scores of locals do—with a stop at the slick Black Velvet espresso bar for Belgian waffles, baked treats, and coffee drinks made from small batches of beans roasted on-site. Then return in the afternoon or evening to hang out with friends in the upstairs wine bar (open 4 to 9). **Known for:** small-batch coffee roasting; small-lot wines by the glass; Belgian waffles. 💲 *Average main: $16* ✉ *3343 Main St., Suite F* ☎ 🌐 *www.blackvelvetcoffee.com.*

Bleu Handcrafted Foods

$$ | WINE BAR | Handcrafted artisanal cheeses and meats, wine and beer tastings, bread baked on-site, and specialty meats and seafood draw patrons to Bleu, a combination market, restaurant (lunch and dinner), and wine bar. Bleu also cooks up savory pub fare at The Eatery at Mammoth Brewing Company. **Known for:** organic, locally sourced ingredients; bar and lounge with wine and craft beer tastings; on-site deli, butchery, bakery, and market. 💲 *Average main: $20* ✉ *106 Old Mammoth Rd.* ☎ *760/914–2538* 🌐 *www.bleufoods.com.*

Burgers

$ | AMERICAN | Don't even think about coming to this bustling restaurant unless you're hungry. Burgers is known, appropriately enough, for its burgers and sandwiches, and everything comes in mountainous portions. **Known for:** great service; hefty portions; burgers and seasoned fries. 💲 *Average main: $15* ✉ *6118 Minaret Rd., across from the Village* ☎ *760/934–6622* 🌐 *www.burgersrestaurant.com* ⏲ *Closed 2 wks in May and 4–6 wks in Oct. and Nov.*

Mammoth Brewing Company

$$ | AMERICAN | Steps from the Village gondola and main bus transfer hub, this brewery lures hungry patrons with about a dozen craft beers on tap, tasty grub from the on-site restaurant, tasting flights, a contemporary vibe at two spacious bar areas, and a beer garden. The dining menu changes constantly, but reflects a locals' twist on pub food, for example, wild game sausages, fig-and-house-made-ricotta flatbread, or house-made "hopped tots." **Known for:** craft beer made on-site; upscale pub food; popular après-ski hangout. 💲 *Average main: $16* ✉ *18 Lake Mary Rd.* ✥ *At intersection of Main St. and Minaret Rd.*

☎ *760/934–7141* 🌐 *mammothbrewingco.com.*

The Mogul

$$$ | **STEAKHOUSE** | **FAMILY** | Come here for straightforward steaks—top sirloin, New York, filet mignon, and T-bone. The only catch is that the waiters cook them, and the results vary depending on their skill level; but generally things go well, and kids love the experience. **Known for:** traditional alpine atmosphere; servers custom-grill your order; all-you-can-eat salad bar. *Average main: $30* ✉ *1528 Tavern Rd., off Old Mammoth Rd.* ☎ *760/934–3039* 🌐 *www.themogul.com* ⏲ *No lunch.*

Petra's Bistro & Wine Bar

$$$ | **AMERICAN** | The ambience at Petra's—quiet, dark, and warm (there's a great fireplace)—complements its seductive meat and seafood entrées and smart selection of wines from California and around the world. With its pub grub, whiskies, and craft beers and ales, the downstairs Clocktower Cellar bar provides a lively, if sometimes rowdy, alternative. **Known for:** romantic atmosphere; top-notch service; lively downstairs bar. *Average main: $30* ✉ *Alpenhof Lodge, 6080 Minaret Rd.* ☎ *760/934–3500* 🌐 *www.petrasbistro.com* ⏲ *Closed Mon. No lunch.*

★ Restaurant at Convict Lake

$$$$ | **AMERICAN** | The lake is one of the most spectacular spots in the Eastern Sierra, and the food here lives up to the view. The woodsy room has a vaulted knotty-pine ceiling and a copper-chimney fireplace; natural light abounds in the daytime, but if it's summer, opt for a table outdoors under the white-barked aspens. **Known for:** beef wellington, rack of lamb, and pan-seared local trout; exceptional service; extensive wine list with reasonably priced European and California bottlings. *Average main: $36* ✉ *Convict Lake Rd. off U.S. 395, 4 miles south of Mammoth Lakes* ☎ *760/934–3800* 🌐 *www.convictlake.com* ⏲ *No lunch early Sept.–mid-June.*

Toomey's

$$ | **MODERN AMERICAN** | **FAMILY** | A passionate baseball fan, chef Matt Toomey designed this casual space near the Village Gondola to resemble a dugout, and decorated it with baseball memorabilia. Fill up on coconut mascarpone pancakes or a smoked trout bagel in the morning before heading outdoors; relax later over buffalo meat loaf, seafood jambalaya, or a New Zealand elk rack chop. **Known for:** lobster taquitos and fish tacos; curbside take-out delivery to your car; homemade organic and gluten-free desserts. *Average main: $20* ✉ *6085 Minaret Rd., at the Village* ☎ *760/924–4408* 🌐 *toomeysmammoth.com.*

★ The Warming Hut

$ | **AMERICAN** | **FAMILY** | Warm up by a crackling fire in the stone fireplace while fueling up on healthy, made-from-scratch breakfast and lunch dishes at this ski-lodge-style eatery. The flexible menu allows for lots of choice, including a DIY breakfast with more than 20 mix-and-match items, five types of hash, keto selections, grab-and-go sandwiches, salads, burgers, and soups. **Known for:** nearly everything made in-house, including ketchup; build-your-own pancake stack (batters, mix-ins, toppings); family-owned and operated. *Average main: $15* ✉ *343 Old Mammoth Rd.* ☎ *760/965–0549* ⏲ *No dinner.*

Hotels

Alpenhof Lodge

$$ | **HOTEL** | Across from the Village at Mammoth, this mom-and-pop motel offers basic comforts and a few niceties such as the attractive pine furniture. **Pros:** convenient for skiers; reasonable rates; excellent dinner at on-site restaurant, Petra's. **Cons:** some bathrooms are small; rooms above pub can be noisy; no elevator. *Rooms from: $159* ✉ *6080*

Minaret Rd., Box 1157 ☎ 760/934–6330, 800/828–0371 🌐 www.alpenhof-lodge.com ⇨ 54 rooms, 3 cabins 🍽 Breakfast.

★ Convict Lake Resort

$$$ | **RESORT** | The cabins at this resort a 10-minute drive south from Mammoth Lakes range from rustic to modern and come with fully equipped kitchens, including coffeemakers and premium coffee. **Pros:** great views; tranquil atmosphere; wildlife galore. **Cons:** the smallest quarters feel cramped; spotty Wi-Fi and cell service; too remote for some. $ *Rooms from: $189 ✉ Convict Rd., 2 miles off U.S. 395 ☎ 760/934–3800, 800/992–2260 🌐 www.convictlake.com ⇨ 28 cabins, 3 houses 🍽 No meals.*

★ Double Eagle Resort and Spa

$$$ | **RESORT** | Lofty pines tower over this very fine spa retreat on the June Lake Loop. **Pros:** pretty setting; spectacular indoor pool; 1½ miles from June Mountain Ski Area. **Cons:** expensive; remote; no in-room air-conditioning. $ *Rooms from: $249 ✉ 5587 Hwy. 158, Box 736, June Lake ☎ 760/648–7004 🌐 www.doubleeagle.com ⇨ 17 2-bedroom cabins, 16 rooms, 1 3-bedroom house 🍽 No meals.*

Holiday Haus

$$ | **HOTEL** | A short walk from the Village, Holiday Haus is a collection of contemporary mountain-activity-theme rooms and suites—many with full kitchens—at relatively affordable prices. **Pros:** free parking and Wi-Fi; good option for groups and families; walk to the Village. **Cons:** showers, no tubs in most rooms; no 24-hour desk; basic breakfast. $ *Rooms from: $149 ✉ 3905 Main St. ☎ 760/934–2414 🌐 holidayhausmotelandhostel.com ⇨ 23 rooms, 1 cabin, 1 26-bed hostel.*

Juniper Springs Resort

$$$ | **RESORT** | Tops for slope-side comfort, these condominium-style units have full kitchens and ski-in ski-out access to the mountain. **Pros:** bargain during summer; direct access to the slopes in winter; free shuttle to town in winter. **Cons:** no nightlife within walking distance; no air-conditioning; property needs updating. $ *Rooms from: $199 ✉ 4000 Meridian Blvd. ☎ 760/924–1102, 800/626–6684 🌐 www.mammothmountain.com ⇨ 184 studios and apartments 🍽 No meals.*

Mammoth Mountain Inn

$$$ | **RESORT** | If you want to be within walking distance of the Mammoth Mountain Main Lodge, this is the place. **Pros:** great location; big rooms; a traditional place to stay. **Cons:** can be crowded in ski season; needs updating; not in the heart of town. $ *Rooms from: $179 ✉ 1 Minaret Rd. ☎ 760/934–2581, 800/626–6684 🌐 www.mammothmountain.com ⇨ 216 rooms, 50 condos.*

Sierra Nevada Resort & Spa

$$$ | **RESORT** | A full-service resort in the heart of Old Mammoth, the Sierra Nevada has it all: Old Mammoth rustic elegance, three restaurants, four bars, a dedicated spa facility, on-site ski and snowboard rentals, a seasonal pool and Jacuzzi, seasonal miniature golf, and room and suite options in three buildings. **Pros:** kids' club on weekends from 4 to 9; walk to restaurants on property or downtown; complimentary shuttle service. **Cons:** must drive or ride a bus or shuttle to the slopes; thin walls in older rooms; resort fee. $ *Rooms from: $199 ✉ 164 Old Mammoth Rd. ☎ 760/934–2515, 800/824–5132 🌐 thesierranevadaresort.com ⇨ 143 rooms, 6 townhomes 🍽 No meals.*

★ Tamarack Lodge Resort & Lakefront Restaurant

$$$ | **RESORT** | On the edge of the John Muir Wilderness Area, where cross-country ski trails lace the woods, this 1924 lodge looks like something out of a snow globe. **Pros:** rustic; eco-sensitive; many nearby outdoor activities. **Cons:** high price tag; shared bathrooms for some main lodge rooms; spartan furnishings in lodge rooms. $ *Rooms from: $239 ✉ Lake Mary Rd., off Hwy. 203 ☎ 760/934–2442, 800/626–6684 🌐 www.tamaracklodge.*

com 🛏 *46 rooms and cabins* 🍽 *No meals.*

The Village Lodge

$$$ | **RESORT** | With their exposed timbers and peaked roofs, these four-story condo buildings at the epicenter of Mammoth's dining and nightlife scene pay homage to Alpine style. **Pros:** central location; big rooms; good restaurants nearby. **Cons:** pricey; can be noisy outside; somewhat sterile decor. 💲 *Rooms from: $239* ✉ *1111 Forest Trail* ☎ *760/934–1982, 800/626–6684* 🌐 *www.mammothmountain.com* 🛏 *277 units* 🍽 *No meals.*

★ Westin Monache Resort

$$$$ | **RESORT** | On a hill just steps from the Village at Mammoth, the Westin provides full-service comfort and amenities close to restaurants, entertainment, and free public transportation. **Pros:** full bar, pool, 24-fitness center; prime location; free gondola to the slopes is across the street. **Cons:** long, steep stairway down to village; added resort fee. 💲 *Rooms from: $359* ✉ *50 Hillside Dr.* ☎ *760/934–0400, 888/627–8154 reservations, 760/934–4686* 🌐 *www.marriott.com/mmhwi* 🛏 *230 rooms and suites* 🍽 *No meals.*

Activities

Mammoth Mega Zip

ZIP LINING | In summer 2019, Mammoth Mountain opened a zip-line tour with the tallest vertical drop (2,100 feet) in North America. Ride the Panoramic Gondola up to the summit of Mammoth Mountain, then descend side by side on parallel cables that run more than a mile back down to the base, at speeds of up to 60 mph (minimum weight 75 lbs). ✉ *Mammoth Adventure Center, 10001 Minaret Rd.* ☎ *800/626–6684* 🌐 *www.mammothmountain.com.*

Via Ferrata

CLIMBING/MOUNTAINEERING | In Europe, a Via Ferrata is a protected climbing network that allows people to experience the thrills of rock climbing and mountaineering without as much risk. Mammoth's version has six different routes of varying ability, with steel cables, iron rungs, and a suspended bridge, all permanently affixed to the rock. The fully guided tour begins with a gondola ride up the mountain. Clip yourself into a cable and climb securely to sweeping views of the Sierra Nevada range. If time and group ability allow, you can follow multiple routes during a session. No climbing experience is required. ✉ *Mammoth Mountain, 10001 Minaret Rd.* ☎ *800/626–6684* 🌐 *www.mammothmountain.com* 🎫 *From $359.*

BIKING

★ Mammoth Bike Park

BICYCLING | The park opens when the snow melts, usually by July, and has 80 miles of single-track trails—from mellow to super-challenging. Chairlifts and shuttles provide trail access, and rentals are available. ✉ *Mammoth Mountain Ski Area* ☎ *760/934–0677, 800/626-6684* 🌐 *www.mammothmountain.com* 🎫 *$55 day pass.*

FISHING

The main fishing season runs from the last Saturday in April until November 15; there are opportunities for catch-and-release fishing in winter. Crowley Lake is the top trout-fishing spot in the area; Convict Lake, June Lake, and the lakes of the Mammoth Basin are other prime spots. One of the best trout rivers is the super-scenic Upper Owens River, near the east side of Crowley Lake. Hot Creek, a designated Wild Trout Stream, is renowned for fly-fishing (catch-and-release only).

Kittredge Sports

FISHING | This outfit rents rods and reels and conducts guided trips. ✉ *3218 Main St., at Forest Trail* ☎ *760/934–7566* 🌐 *kittredgesports.com.*

Sierra Drifters Guide Service

FISHING | To maximize your time on the water, get tips from local anglers, or

Camping in the Eastern Sierra

Camping in the Sierra Nevada means gazing up at awe-inspiring constellations and awakening to the sights of nearby meadows and streams and the unforgettable landscape of giant granite. More than a hundred campgrounds, from remote, tents-only areas to full-service facilities with RV hookups close to the main attractions, operate in the Eastern Sierra. Be aware that Yosemite National Park's most accessible campgrounds can be jam-packed and claustrophobic in the summer. Luckily, there are many options to the east, including calm and beautiful sites such as Lake Mary Campground in the Mammoth Lakes area. The following campsites are recommended. Reserve sites at *www.recreation.gov.*

Convict Lake Campground A 10-minute drive south of Mammoth, this campground near the Convict Lake Resort is run by the U.S. Forest Service. **Pros:**. **Cons:**. *Convict Lake Rd., 2 miles off U.S. 395* *760/924–5500* *88 campsites.*

Lake Mary Campground There are few sites as beautiful as this lakeside campground at 8,900 feet, open from June to September. **Pros:**. **Cons:**. *Lake Mary Loop Dr., off Hwy. 203* *760/924–5500* *No credit cards* *48 sites (tent or RV)* *No meals.*

better yet, book a guided fishing trip, contact Sierra Drifters. *Mammoth Lakes* *760/935–4250* *www.sierradrifters.com.*

HIKING

Hiking in Mammoth is stellar, especially along the trails that wind through alpine scenery around the Lakes Basin. Carry lots of water; and remember, the air is thin at 8,000-plus feet.

Visit the Mammoth Lakes Trail System website (*www.mammothtrails.org*) for descriptions of more than 300 miles of trails, maps, and a wealth of information on recreation in Mammoth Lakes and the Inyo National Forest in all seasons.

Mammoth Lakes Welcome Center

HIKING/WALKING | Stop at the Mammoth Lakes Welcome Center, just east of the town of Mammoth Lakes, for an area trail map and permits for backpacking in wilderness areas. *2510 Main St., Hwy. 203* *760/924–5501* *www.visitmammoth.com.*

EASY

Convict Lake Loop

HIKING/WALKING | This 2.8-mile trail loops gently around deep blue Convict Lake, a popular site for anglers. Feast your eyes on stunning views of tall peaks, glistening water, and aspen and cottonwood groves while you hike. *Easy.* *Trailhead: at Convict Lake, 9 miles south of Mammoth Lakes.*

Minaret Falls

HIKING/WALKING | **FAMILY** | Hike along portions of both the Pacific Crest and John Muir trails on this scenic trail (3 miles round-trip) that leads to Devil's Postpile, Minaret Falls, and natural volcanic springs. This is a good family hike, especially in late summer when the water has receded a bit and kids can climb boulders and splash around. *Easy.* *Trailhead: At Devil's Postpile National Monument.*

MODERATE

Emerald Lake and Sky Meadows

HIKING/WALKING | The first part of this trail travels through shady pine forest along Coldwater Creek to bright-green Emerald

Lake (1.8 miles round-trip). Extend the hike by climbing up a trail along an inlet stream up to Gentian Meadow and Sky Meadows (4 miles round-trip), especially beautiful in July and August when various alpine wildflowers, fed by snowmelt, are at their peak splendor. *Moderate.* ✉ *Trailhead: Coldwater Campground, Mammoth Lakes.*

DIFFICULT

Duck Lake

HIKING/WALKING | This popular and busy trail (11 miles round-trip) heads up Coldwater Canyon along Mammoth Creek, past a series of spectacular lakes and wildflower meadows over 10,797-foot Duck Pass to dramatic Duck Lake, which eventually links up with the John Muir Trail. *Difficult.* ✉ *Trailhead: Coldwater Campground.*

HORSEBACK RIDING

Stables around Mammoth are typically open from June through September.

Mammoth Lakes Pack Outfit

HORSEBACK RIDING | This company runs day and overnight horseback and mule trips and will shuttle you to the high country. ✉ *Lake Mary Rd., between Twin Lakes and Lake Mary* ☎ *888/475–8747, 760/934–2434* 🌐 *www.mammothpack.com.*

McGee Creek Pack Station

HORSEBACK RIDING | These folks customize pack trips or will shuttle you to camp alone. ✉ *2990 McGee Creek Rd., Crowley Lake* ☎ *760/935–4324 summer, 760/878–2207, 800/854–7407* 🌐 *www.mcgeecreekpackstation.com.*

SKIING

In winter, check the On the Snow website or call the Snow Report for information about Mammoth weather conditions.

June Mountain Ski Area

SKIING/SNOWBOARDING | **FAMILY** | Snowboarders especially dig June Mountain, a compact, low-key resort north of Mammoth Mountain. Three beginner-to-intermediate terrain areas—the Surprise Fun Zone, and Mambo Playground—are for both skiers and boarders. There's rarely a line for the lifts here: if you must ski on a weekend and want to avoid the crowds, this is the place to come, and in a storm it's better protected from wind and blowing snow than Mammoth is. (If it starts to storm, you can use your Mammoth ticket at June.) The services include a rental-and-repair shop, a ski school, and a sports shop. There's food, but the options are better at Mammoth. **■ TIP→ Kids 12 and under ski and ride free.** ✉ *3819 Hwy. 158/June Lake Loop, off U.S. 395, 22 miles northwest of Mammoth, June Lake* ☎ *760/648–7733, 888/586–3686* 🌐 *www.junemountain.com* 🎟 *From $99* ☞ *35 trails on 1,400 acres, rated 35% beginner, 45% intermediate, 20% advanced. Longest run 2 miles, base 7,545 feet, summit 10,190 feet. Lifts: 7.*

★ Mammoth Mountain Ski Area

SKIING/SNOWBOARDING | One of the West's largest and best ski areas, Mammoth has more than 3,500 acres of skiable terrain and a 3,100-foot vertical drop. The views from the 11,053-foot summit are some of the most stunning in the Sierra. Below, you'll find a 6½-mile-wide swath of groomed boulevards and canyons, as well as pockets of tree-skiing and a dozen vast bowls. Snowboarders are everywhere on the slopes; there are seven outstanding freestyle terrain parks of varying difficulty, with jumps, rails, tabletops, and giant super pipes—this is the location of several international snowboarding competitions, and, in summer, mountain-bike meets. Mammoth's season begins in November and often lingers into July. Lessons and equipment are available, and there's a children's ski and snowboard school. Mammoth runs free shuttle-bus routes around town and to the ski area, and the Village Gondola runs from the Village complex to Canyon Lodge. However, only overnight guests are allowed to park at the Village for more

Why Is There So Much Snow?

The Sierra Nevada receives some of the deepest snow anywhere in North America. In winter, houses literally get buried, and homeowners have to build tunnels to their front doors (though many install enclosed wooden walkways). In the high country, it's not uncommon for a single big storm to bring 10 feet of snow and for 30 feet of snow to accumulate at the height of the season. In the enormous bowls of Mammoth Mountain, you might ski past a tiny pine that looks like a miniature Christmas tree—until you remember that more than 30 feet of tree is under the snow.

To understand the weather, you have to understand the terrain. The Sierra Nevada are marked by a gentle western rise from sea level to the Sierra crest, which tops out at a whopping 14,494 feet at Sequoia National Park's Mt. Whitney, the highest point in the continental United States. On the eastern side of the crest, at the escarpment, the mountains drop sharply—as much as 5,000 feet—giving way to the Great Basin and the high-mountain deserts of Nevada and Utah.

When winter storms blow in off the Pacific, carrying vast stores of water with them, they race across the relatively flat, 100-mile-wide Central Valley. As they ascend the wall of mountains, though, the decrease in temperature and the increase in pressure on the clouds force them to release their water. Between October and April, that means snow—lots of it. Storms can get hung up on the peaks for days, dumping foot after foot of the stuff. By the time they finally cross over the range and into the Great Basin, there isn't much moisture left for the lower elevations on the eastern side. This is why, if you cross the Sierra eastward on your way to U.S. 395, you'll notice that brightly colored wildflowers and forest-green trees give way to pale-green sagebrush and brown sand as you drop out of the mountains.

The coastal cities and farmlands of the rest of the state depend heavily on the water from the Sierra snowpack. Most of the spring and summer runoff from the melting snows is caught in reservoirs in the foothills and routed to farmlands and cities throughout the state via a complex system of levees and aqueducts, which you'll no doubt see in the foothills and Central Valley, to the west of the range. But much of the water remains in the mountains, forming lakes, most notably giant Lake Tahoe to the north, Mono Lake to the east, and the thousands of little lakes along the Sierra Crest. The lakes are an essential part of the ecosystem, providing water for birds, fish, and plant life.

than a few hours. **Facilities:** 155 trails; 3,500 acres; 3,100-foot vertical drop; 25 lifts. ✉ *Minaret Rd., west of Mammoth Lakes, Rte. 203, off U.S. 395* ☎ *760/934–2571, 800/626–6684, 760/934–0687 shuttle* 🌐 *www.mammothmountain.com* 🎫 *From $99.*

Tamarack Cross Country Ski Center
SKIING/SNOWBOARDING | Trails at the center, adjacent to Tamarack Lodge, meander around several lakes. Rentals are available. ✉ *Lake Mary Rd., off Hwy. 203* ☎ *760/934–5293, 760/934–2442* 🌐 *tamaracklodge.com* 🎫 *$58 all-inclusive day rate.*

SKI RENTALS AND RESOURCES

★ Black Tie Ski Rentals

SKIING/SNOWBOARDING | Skiers and snowboarders love this rental outfit whose staffers will deliver and custom-fit equipment for free. They also offer slope-side assistance. ✉ *501 Old Mammoth Rd.* ☎ *760/934–7009* 🌐 *mammothskis.com.*

Footloose

SKIING/SNOWBOARDING | When the U.S. Ski Team visits Mammoth and needs boot adjustments, everyone heads to Footloose, the best place in town—and possibly all California—for ski-boot rentals and sales, as well as custom insoles. ✉ *3043 Main St., at Mammoth Rd.* ☎ *760/934–2400* 🌐 *www.footloosesports.com.*

Kittredge Sports

SKIING/SNOWBOARDING | Advanced skiers should consider this outfit, which has been around since the 1960s. ✉ *3218 Main St.* ☎ *760/934–7566* 🌐 *kittredgesports.com.*

Snow Report

SKIING/SNOWBOARDING | For information on winter conditions around Mammoth, call the Snow Report. ✉ *Mammoth Lakes* ☎ *760/934–7669, 888/766–9778* 🌐 *www.mammothmountain.com/winter/mountain-information.*

Woolly's Tube Park & Snow Play

SNOW SPORTS | **FAMILY** | Ride a lift to the top of the hill and whoosh down in a high-speed snow tube as often as you like during a 1¼-hour session. The park has six lanes, a heated deck, and snack shop. Discounts available for a second session if you're not ready to stop riding. Little ones can hang out in the snow play area with sleds and saucers. ✉ *9000 Minaret Rd.* ☎ *800/626–6684 reservations, 760/934–7533 direct line* 🌐 *www.mammothmountain.com* 🎫 *From $39, play area $20.*

SNOWMOBILING

Mammoth Snowmobile Adventures

SNOW SPORTS | Mammoth Snowmobile Adventures conducts guided tours along wooded trails. ✉ *Mammoth Mountain Main Lodge* ☎ *760/934–9645, 800/626–6684* 🌐 *www.mammothmountain.com* 🎫 *From $119.*

Lee Vining

20 miles east of Tuolumne Meadows, 30 miles north of Mammoth Lakes.

Tiny Lee Vining is known primarily as the eastern gateway to Yosemite National Park (summer only) and the location of vast and desolate Mono Lake. Pick up supplies at the general store year-round, or stop here for lunch or dinner before or after a drive through the high country. In winter the town is all but deserted, except for the ice climbers who come to scale frozen waterfalls.

GETTING HERE AND AROUND

Lee Vining is on U.S. 395, north of the road's intersection with Highway 120 and on the south side of Mono Lake. In summer YARTS public transit (🌐 *yarts.com*) can get you here from Yosemite Valley, but you'll need a car to explore the area.

ESSENTIALS

VISITOR INFORMATION Lee Vining Chamber of Commerce ☎ *760/647–6629* 🌐 *www.leevining.com.* **Mono Basin National Forest Scenic Area Visitor Center** ✉ *Visitor Center Dr., off U.S. 395, 1 mile north of Hwy. 120* ☎ *760/647–3044* 🌐 *www.monolake.org/visit/vc.*

Sights

June Lake Loop

SCENIC DRIVE | Heading south from Lee Vining, U.S. 395 intersects the June Lake Loop. This gorgeous 17-mile drive follows an old glacial canyon past Grant, June, Gull, and Silver lakes before reconnecting with U.S. 395 on its way to Mammoth Lakes. **■TIP→ The loop is especially colorful in fall.** ✉ *Hwy. 158 W.*

Did You Know?

These "tufa" towers on the shores Mono Lake are essentially made of limestone and form over decades. Some can be as tall as 30 feet.

Did You Know?

The town of Bodie offers ghost tours of its abandoned village at night.

★ Mono Lake

BODY OF WATER | Since the 1940s Los Angeles has diverted water from this lake, exposing striking towers of tufa, or calcium carbonate. Court victories by environmentalists have meant fewer diversions, and the lake is rising again. Although to see the lake from U.S. 395 is stunning, make time to visit South Tufa, whose parking lot is 5 miles east of U.S. 395 off Highway 120. There in summer you can join the naturalist-guided **South Tufa Walk,** which lasts about 90 minutes. The **Scenic Area Visitor Center,** off U.S. 395, is a sensational stop for its interactive exhibits and sweeping Mono Lake views (closed in winter). In town at U.S. 395 and 3rd Street, the **Mono Lake Committee Information Center & Bookstore**, open from 9 to 5 daily (extended hours in summer), has more information about this beautiful area. ✉ *Hwy. 120, east of Lee Vining* ☎ *760/647–3044 visitor center, 760/647–6595 info center* 🌐 *www.monolake.org* 🎫 *Free.*

Restaurants

Epic Cafe

$ | **AMERICAN** | **FAMILY** | Hungry travelers and locals feast on fresh, healthy, cooked-to-order comfort food at this casual café at Lakeview Lodge, near the Tioga Road and Highway 395 junction. The menu changes daily, but you can count on items like waffles and frittatas for breakfast; paninis, sandwiches, salads, rice bowls, and soups for lunch; and three special dinner entrées, perhaps locally caught fish, chicken potpie, or braised short ribs. **Known for:** local and organic food sources; cozy indoor dining room and garden patio; fresh-baked scones, muffins, desserts, and other goodies. $ *Average main: $15* ✉ *349 Lee Vining Ave.* ☎ *760/965–6282* 🌐 *epiccafesierra.com* ⏲ *Closed Nov.–early May. Closed Sun.*

Mono Cone

$ | **AMERICAN** | Get soft-serve ice cream, burgers, and fries at this hopping shack in the middle of Lee Vining, but be prepared to do what's rare in these uncrowded parts: wait in line. There's some indoor seating, but unless the clouds are leaking, take your food to nearby (and quiet) Hess Park, whose views of Mono Lake make it one of the best picnic spots in eastern California. $ *Average main: $9* ✉ *51508 U.S. 395* ☎ *760/647–6606* 💳 *No credit cards* ⏲ *Closed in winter.*

Tioga Gas Mart & Whoa Nelli Deli

$$ | **AMERICAN** | This might be the only gas station in the United States serving craft beers and lobster taquitos, but its appeal goes beyond novelty. Order at the counter and grab a seat inside, or sit at one of the picnic tables on the lawn outside and take in the distant view of Mono Lake. **Known for:** fish tacos and barbecued ribs; regular live music; convenient location. $ *Average main: $16* ✉ *Hwy. 120 and U.S. 395* ☎ *760/647–1088* 🌐 *www.whoanelliedeli.com* ⏲ *Closed early Nov.–late Apr.*

Hotels

Lake View Lodge

$$ | **B&B/INN** | Enormous rooms and landscaping that includes several shaded sitting areas set this motel apart from its competitors in town. **Pros:** convenient access to Yosemite, Mono Lake, Bodie State Historic Park; peaceful setting; on-site restaurant. **Cons:** could use updating; slow Wi-Fi in some areas; no views from some rooms. $ *Rooms from: $143* ✉ *51285 U.S. 395* ☎ *760/647–6543, 800/990–6614* 🌐 *www.lakeviewlodgeyosemite.com* 🛏 *76 rooms, 12 cottages.*

Bodie State Historic Park

31 miles northeast of Lee Vining.

Bodie State Historic Park's scenery is spectacular, with craggy, snowcapped peaks looming over vast prairies. The town of Bridgeport is the gateway to the park, and the only supply center for miles around. Bridgeport's claims to fame include an historic courthouse that's been in continuous use since 1880 and the excellent fishing—the California state record brown trout, at 26 pounds 12 ounces, was caught in Bridgeport's Twin Lakes. In winter, much of Bridgeport shuts down.

GETTING HERE AND AROUND

A car is the best way to reach this area. Bodie is on Highway 270 about 13 miles east of U.S. 395.

Sights

★ Bodie Ghost Town

GHOST TOWN | The mining village of Rattlesnake Gulch, abandoned mine shafts, and the remains of a small Chinatown are among the sights at this fascinating ghost town. The town boomed from about 1878 to 1881, but by the late 1940s all its residents had departed. A state park was established here in 1962, with a mandate to preserve everything in a state of "arrested decay." Evidence of Bodie's wild past survives at an excellent museum, and you can tour an old stamp mill where ore was crushed into fine powder to extract gold and silver. Bodie lies 13 miles east of U.S. 395 off Highway 270. The last 3 miles are unpaved, and snow may close the highway from late fall through early spring. No food, drink, or lodging is available in Bodie. ✉ *Bodie Rd., off Hwy. 270, Bodie* ☎ *760/616–5040* 🌐 *www.parks.ca.gov/bodie* 🎫 *$8.*

Chapter 8

SAN FRANCISCO

Updated by
Rebecca Flint
Marx, Denise Leto,
Andrea Powell, and
Trevor Felch

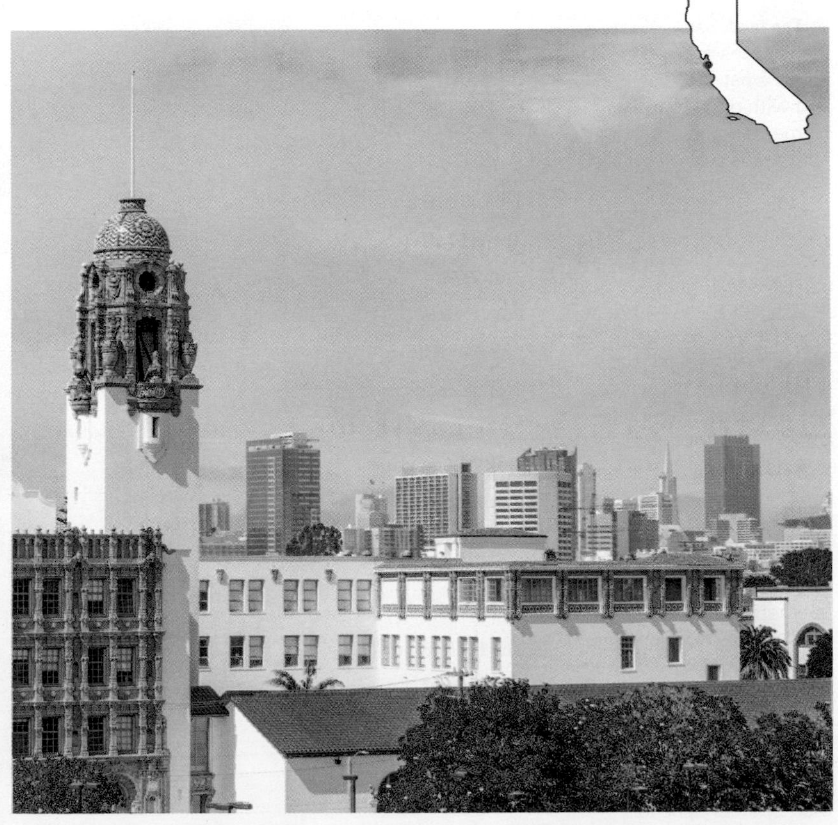

Sights	Restaurants	Hotels	Shopping	Nightlife
★★★★★	★★★★☆	★★★★★	★☆☆☆☆	★☆☆☆☆

WELCOME TO SAN FRANCISCO

TOP REASONS TO GO

★ **The bay:** It's hard not to gasp as you catch sight of sunlight dancing on the water when you crest a hill, or watch the Golden Gate Bridge vanish and reemerge in the summer fog.

★ **The food:** San Franciscans are serious about what they eat, and with good reason. Home to some of the nation's best chefs, top restaurants, and finest local produce, it's hard not to eat well here.

★ **The shopping:** Shopaholics visiting the city will not be disappointed—San Francisco is packed with browsing destinations, everything from quirky boutiques to massive malls.

★ **The good life:** A laid-back atmosphere, beautiful surroundings, and oodles of cultural, culinary, and aesthetic pleasures … if you spend too much time here, you might not leave.

★ **The great outdoors:** From Golden Gate Park to sidewalk cafés in North Beach, San Franciscans relish their outdoor spaces.

San Francisco is a compact city; just 46.7 square miles. Essentially a tightly packed cluster of extremely diverse neighborhoods, the city dearly rewards walking. The areas that most visitors cover are easy (and safe) to reach on foot, but many have steep—make that steep—hills.

1 **Union Square.**

2 **Chinatown.**

3 **Financial District.**

4 **SoMa.**

5 **Civic Center.**

6 **Hayes Valley.**

7 **Nob Hill.**

8 **Polk Gulch.**

9 **Russian Hill.**

10 **North Beach.**

11 **Fisherman's Wharf.**

12 **Embarcadero.**

13 **The Marina.**

14 **Cow Hollow.**

15 **Presidio.**

16 **Golden Gate Park.**

17 **The Richmond.**

18 **The Sunset.**

19 **The Haight.**

20 **The Castro.**

21 **Noe Valley.**

22 **Mission District.**

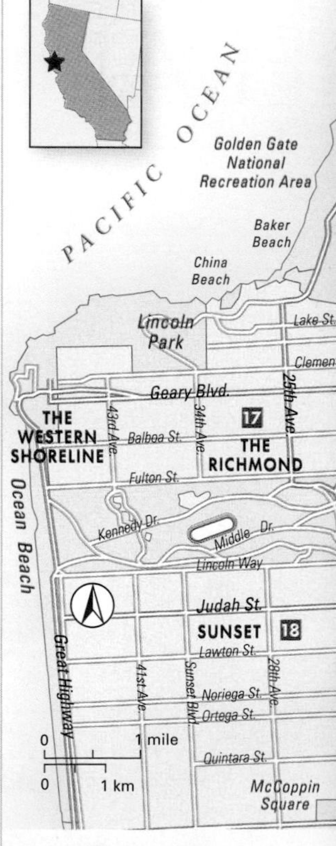

23 **Pacific Heights.**

24 **Japantown.**

25 **Western Addition.**

26 **The Tenderloin.**

27 **Potrero Hill.**

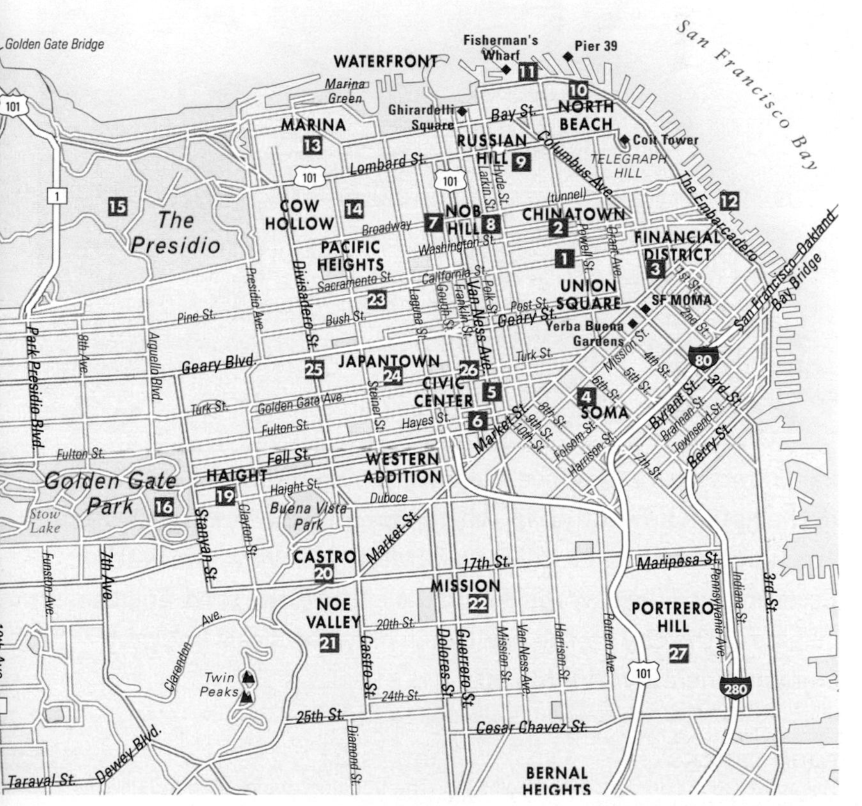
Golden Gate Bridge
San Francisco Bay
WATERFRONT
Fisherman's Wharf
Pier 39
Marina Green
Ghirardelli Square
Bay St.
NORTH BEACH
MARINA
RUSSIAN HILL
Columbus Ave.
Coit Tower
TELEGRAPH HILL
Lombard St.
The Embarcadero
The Presidio
COW HOLLOW
NOB HILL
CHINATOWN
(tunnel)
Broadway
Washington St.
FINANCIAL DISTRICT
PACIFIC HEIGHTS
California St.
Sacramento St.
UNION SQUARE
SF MOMA
San Francisco-Oakland Bay Bridge
Pine St.
Bush St.
Post St.
Geary St.
Yerba Buena Gardens
Presidio Ave.
Divisadero St.
Laguna St.
Gough St.
Franklin St.
Van Ness Ave.
Polk St.
Hyde St.
Larkin St.
Powell St.
Grant Ave.
1st St.
2nd St.
Park Presidio Blvd.
8th Ave.
Arguello Blvd.
Geary Blvd.
JAPANTOWN
Turk St.
CIVIC CENTER
Mission St.
4th St.
5th St.
6th St.
SOMA
Bryant St.
3rd St.
Golden Gate Ave.
Steiner St.
Hayes St.
Market St.
8th St.
9th St.
10th St.
Folsom St.
Harrison St.
Brannan St.
Townsend St.
Berry St.
Fulton St.
Fell St.
WESTERN ADDITION
7th St.
Golden Gate Park
HAIGHT
Haight St.
Buena Vista Park
Duboce
Stow Lake
Stanyan St.
Clayton St.
CASTRO
17th St.
Mariposa St.
Funston Ave.
7th Ave.
MISSION
NOE VALLEY
20th St.
PORTRERO HILL
Pennsylvania Ave.
Indiana St.
Clarendon Ave.
Castro St.
Dolores St.
Guerrero St.
Mission St.
Van Ness Ave.
Harrison St.
Potrero Ave.
Twin Peaks
24th St.
25th St.
Cesar Chavez St.
Dewey Blvd.
Diamond St.
Taraval St.
BERNAL HEIGHTS
101
1
80
280
1 2 3 4 5 6 7 8 9 10 11 12 13 14 15 16 19 20 21 22 23 24 25 26 27

HOW TO EAT LIKE A LOCAL

Several farmers' markets occupy the Ferry Building

San Francisco may well be the most piping-red-hot dining scene in the nation now. After all, with a booming tech industry, there are mouths to feed. Freedom to do what you want. Innovation. Eccentricity. These words define the culture, the food, and the cuisine of the city by the bay. Get in on what locals know by enjoying their favorite foods.

FOOD TRUCKS

This is where experimentation begins, where the overhead is low, and risk-taking is fun. From these mobile kitchens careers are launched. A food meet-up called "Off the Grid" happens in season at Fort Mason where you can have a progressive dinner among the 25 or so trucks. Year-round the convoy roams to different locations, selling things like Korean poutine, Indian burritos, and Vietnamese burgers. Each dish seems to reflect a refusal to follow the norm.

DIM SUM

The tradition of dim sum took hold in San Francisco when Chinese immigrants from Guangdong Province arrived with Cantonese cuisine. These earlier settlers eventually established teahouses and bakeries that sold dim sum, like the steamed dumplings stuffed with shrimp (*har gow*) or pork (*shao mai*). Now carts roll from table to table in Chinatown restaurants—and other parts of the city. Try the grilled and fried bite-size savories but also the sweets like *dan tat,* an egg custard tart.

BARBECUE

Whaaa? San Francisco barbecue? And what would that be? You can bet it's meat from top purveyors nearby. The city is surrounded by grazing lands, where the animals and their minders, the ranchers, are king. Until now, meats came simply plated. Now it's messy, with smokiness, charred crusts, and gorgeous marbling. But you may never hear of a San-Fran-style barbecue because, in the words of one chef, we're "nondenominational." You'll see it all: Memphis, Texas, Carolina, and Kansas City.

ICE CREAM

How ice cream became so popular in a place that spends many of its 365 days below the 75 degree mark is a mystery. But the lines attest to the popularity of the frozen dessert that gets its own San Francisco twist. This is the vanilla-bean vanilla and Tcho chocolate crowd. Bourbon and cornflakes? Reposado tequila? Cheers to that. Diversity and local produce is blended into flavors like ube (purple yam), yuzu, and Thai latte.

BURRITOS

This stuffed tortilla got its Bay Area start in the 1960s in the Mission District. Because the size and fillings distinguish it from other styles, it became known as the Mission burrito. Look for rice (Southern Californians are cringing), beans, salsa, and enough meat in the burrito for two meals. The aluminum foil keeps the interior neat, in theory. Popular choices are *carne asada* (beef) and *carnitas* (pork). But then there's *lengua* (beef tongue) and *birria* (goat). This is a hands-on meal.

Dim sum

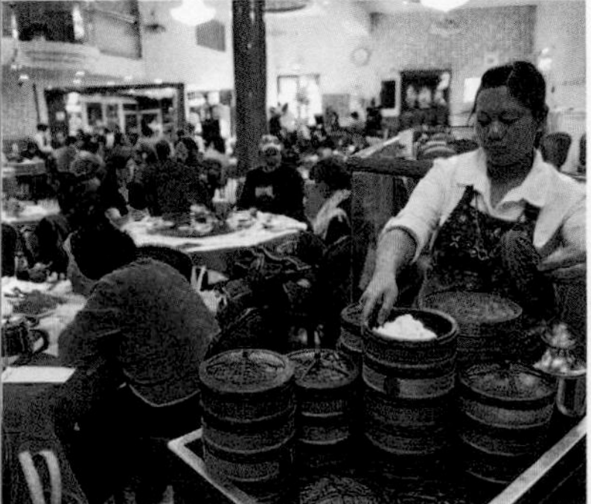

The food truck

COFFEE

Coffee roasters here are like sports teams in other cities. You pick one of the big five or six to be loyal to, and defend it tirelessly. San Francisco favorites source impeccably and blend different beans as if they were wine making. In addition, a few of the big names—Four Barrel, Sightglass, Ritual, Blue Bottle—roast their own to control what they grind and pour at their outlets across the city—and now nationally and internationally.

FARMERS' MARKETS

These are our new grocery stores. They're the places to discover the latest in fruits, vegetables, and dried beans—much of it grown within a 60-mile radius. Cheeses, cured salami, breads, and nuts are sampled. Then there are the local ready-to-eat snacks, like pizza and *huevos rancheros*. The most popular market is the one on Saturday at the Ferry Plaza.

On a 46½-square-mile strip of land between San Francisco Bay and the Pacific Ocean, San Francisco has charms great and small. Residents cherish their city for the same reasons visitors do: the proximity to the bay, rows of Victorian homes clinging precariously to the hillsides, the sun setting behind the Golden Gate Bridge, the world-class cuisine. Locals and visitors alike spend hours exploring downtown, Chinatown, North Beach, the northern and western waterfronts, and Golden Gate Park, along with colorful neighborhoods like the Haight, the Mission murals, and the Castro.

The city's attraction, though, goes much deeper than its alluring physical space, from the diversity of its neighborhoods to its free-spirited tolerance. Take all these things together and you'll understand why many San Franciscans—despite the dizzying cost of living and the chilly summers—can't imagine calling any place else home.

You won't want to miss the City by the Bay's highlights, whether it's a cable car ride over Nob Hill; a walk down the Filbert Street Steps; gazing at the thundering Pacific from the cliffs of Lincoln Park; cheering the San Francisco Giants to *beat L.A.* in lively Oracle Park; or eating freshly shucked oysters at the Ferry Building. San Francisco is a beautiful metropolis packed with diverse wonders that inspire at every turn.

Planning

When to Go

You can visit San Francisco comfortably any time of year. Possibly the best time is September and October, when the city's summerlike weather brings outdoor concerts and festivals. The climate here always feels Mediterranean and moderate, with a foggy, sometimes chilly bite. The temperature rarely drops below 40°F, and anything warmer than 80°F is considered a heat wave. Be prepared for rain in winter, especially December and January. Winds off the ocean can add to the chill factor. That old joke about summer in San Francisco feeling like winter is true at heart, but once you move inland, it gets warmer. (And some locals swear that the thermostat has inched up in recent years.)

Getting Here and Around

AIR TRAVEL

The major gateway to San Francisco is San Francisco International Airport (SFO), 15 miles south of the city. It's off U.S. 101 near Millbrae and San Bruno. Oakland International Airport (OAK) is across the bay, not much farther away from downtown San Francisco (via Interstate 80 east and Interstate 880 south), but rush-hour traffic on the Bay Bridge may lengthen travel times considerably. San Jose International Airport (SJC) is about 40 miles south of San Francisco; travel time depends largely on traffic flow, but plan on an hour and a half with moderate traffic.

AIRPORTS San Francisco International Airport (*SFO*). ✉ *McDonnell and Links Rds., San Francisco* ☎ *800/435–9736, 650/821–8211* 🌐 *www.flysfo.com.* **Oakland International Airport** (*OAK*). ✉ *1 Airport Dr., Oakland* ☎ *510/563–3300* 🌐 *www.oaklandairport.com.* **San Jose International Airport** (*SJC*). ✉ *1701 Airport Blvd., San Jose* ☎ *408/392–3600* 🌐 *www.flysanjose.com.*

AIRPORT TRANSFERS Marin Airporter. ☎ *415/461–4222* 🌐 *www.marinairporter.com.* **Marin Door to Door.** ☎ *415/457–2717* 🌐 *www.marindoortodoor.com.* **SamTrans.** ☎ *800/660–4287* 🌐 *www.samtrans.com.*

BART TRAVEL

BART (Bay Area Rapid Transit) trains, which run until midnight, travel under the bay via tunnel to connect San Francisco with Oakland, Berkeley, and other cities and towns beyond. Within San Francisco, stations are limited to downtown, the Mission, and a couple of outlying neighborhoods.

Trains travel frequently from early morning until evening on weekdays. After 8 pm weekdays and on weekends there's often a 20-minute wait between trains on the same line. Trains also travel south from San Francisco as far as Millbrae. BART trains connect downtown San Francisco to San Francisco International Airport; the ride costs $8.95.

Intracity San Francisco fares are $1.95; intercity fares are $3.20 to $11.45. BART bases its ticket prices on miles traveled and doesn't offer price breaks by zone. The easy-to-read maps posted in BART stations list fares based on destination, radiating out from your starting point of the current station.

During morning and evening rush hour, trains within the city are crowded—even standing room can be hard to come by. Cars at the far front and back of the train are less likely to be filled to capacity. Smoking, eating, and drinking are prohibited on trains and in stations.

CONTACTS Bay Area Rapid Transit (*BART*). ☎ *510/465-2278* 🌐 *www.bart.gov.*

BOAT TRAVEL

Several ferry lines run out of San Francisco. Blue & Gold Fleet operates a number of routes, including service to Sausalito ($11.50 one-way) and Tiburon ($11.50 one-way). Tickets are sold at Pier 39; boats depart from Pier 41 nearby. Alcatraz Cruises, owned by Hornblower Cruises and Events, operates the ferries to Alcatraz Island ($35.50 including audio tour and National Park Service ranger-led programs) from Pier 33, about a half-mile east of Fisherman's Wharf.

Boats leave 14 times a day (more in summer), and the journey itself takes 30 minutes. Allow at least 2½ hours for a round-trip jaunt. Golden Gate Ferry runs daily to and from Sausalito and Larkspur ($11.75 and $11 one-way), leaving from Pier 1, behind the San Francisco Ferry Building. The Alameda/Oakland Ferry operates daily between Alameda's Main Street Terminal, Oakland's Jack London Square, and San Francisco's Pier 41 and the Ferry Building ($6.60 one-way); some ferries go only to Pier 41 or the Ferry Building, so ask when you board. Purchase tickets on board.

INFORMATION Alameda/Oakland Ferry. ☎ *877/643–3779* 🌐 *sanfranciscobayferry.com.* **Alcatraz Cruises.** ☎ *415/981–7625* 🌐 *www.alcatrazcruises.com.* **Blue & Gold Fleet.** ☎ *415/705–8200* 🌐 *www.blueandgoldfleet.com.* **Ferry Building Marketplace.** ✉ *1 Ferry Bldg., at foot of Market St. on Embarcadero, San Francisco* ☎ *415/983–8030* 🌐 *www.ferrybuildingmarketplace.com.* **Golden Gate Ferry.** ☎ *415/923–2000* 🌐 *www.goldengateferry.org.*

CABLE-CAR TRAVEL

Don't miss the sensation of moving up and down some of San Francisco's steepest hills in a clattering cable car. Jump aboard as it pauses at a designated stop, and wedge yourself into any available space. Then just hold on.

The fare (for one direction) is $7. You can buy tickets on board (exact change isn't required but operators can only make change up to $20) or at the kiosks at the cable-car turnarounds at Hyde and Beach streets and at Powell and Market streets.

The heavily traveled Powell–Mason and Powell–Hyde lines begin at Powell and Market streets near Union Square and terminate at Fisherman's Wharf; lines for these routes can be long, especially in summer. The California Street line runs east and west from Market and California streets to Van Ness Avenue; there's often no wait to board this route.

CAR TRAVEL

Driving in San Francisco can be a challenge because of the one-way streets, snarly traffic, and steep hills. The first two elements can be frustrating enough, but those hills are tough for unfamiliar drivers. ■**TIP→ Remember to curb your wheels when parking on hills—turn wheels away from the curb when facing uphill, toward the curb when facing downhill. You can get a ticket if you don't do this.**

MUNI TRAVEL

The San Francisco Municipal Railway, or Muni, operates light-rail vehicles, the historic F-line streetcars along Fisherman's Wharf and Market Street, buses, and the world-famous cable cars. Light rail travels along Market Street to the Mission District and Noe Valley (J line), the Ingleside District (K line), and the Sunset District (L, M, and N lines) while also passing through the West Portal, Glen Park, and Castro neighborhoods. The N line continues around the Embarcadero to the Caltrain station at 4th and King streets; the T-line light rail runs from the Castro, down Market Street, around the Embarcadero, and south past Mission Bay and Hunters Point to Sunnydale Avenue and Bayshore Boulevard. Muni provides 24-hour service on select lines to all areas of the city.

On buses and streetcars the fare is $2.50. Exact change is required, and dollar bills are accepted in the fare boxes. For all Muni vehicles other than cable cars, 90-minute transfers are issued free upon request at the time the fare is paid. These are valid for unlimited transfers in any direction until they expire (time is indicated on the ticket). Cable cars cost $7 and include no transfers *(see Cable-Car Travel)*.

One-day ($21), three-day ($32), and seven-day ($42) Passports valid on the entire Muni system can be purchased at several outlets, including the cable-car ticket booth at Powell and Market streets and the visitor information center downstairs in Hallidie Plaza. A monthly ticket is available for $80, and can be used on all Muni lines (including cable cars) and on BART within city limits. The San Francisco CityPass ($86), a discount ticket booklet to several major city attractions, also covers all Muni travel for seven consecutive days.

The San Francisco Municipal Transit and Street Map ($5) is a useful guide to the extensive transportation system. You can buy the map at most bookstores and at the San Francisco Visitor Information Center, on the lower level of Hallidie Plaza at Powell and Market streets.

BUS OPERATORS

Outside the city, AC Transit serves the East Bay, and Golden Gate Transit serves Marin County and a few cities in southern Sonoma County.

BUS AND MUNI INFORMATION San Francisco Municipal Transportation Agency (*Muni*). ☎ *311, 415/701–3000* 🌐 *www.sfmta.com.*

TAXI TRAVEL

Taxi service is notoriously bad in San Francisco, and finding a cab can be frustratingly difficult. Popular nightspots such as the Mission, SoMa, North Beach, and the Castro are the easiest places to hail a cab off the street; hotel taxi stands are also an option. If you're going to the airport, make a reservation or book a shuttle instead. Taxis in San Francisco charge $3.50 for the first 0.5 mile (one of the highest base rates in the United States), 55¢ for each additional 0.2 mile, and 55¢ per minute in stalled traffic; a $4 surcharge is added for trips from the airport. There's no charge for additional passengers; there's no surcharge for luggage. For trips farther than 15 miles outside city limits, multiply the metered rate by 1.5; tolls and tip are extra.

That said, San Francisco's poor taxi service was a direct factor in the creation of ride-sharing services such as Uber and Lyft, which are easy to use and prominent throughout the city and its surrounding areas. San Franciscans generally regard taxis as a thing of the past and use ride-sharing on a day-to-day basis. If you're willing to share a car with strangers, a trip within the city can run as low as $4; rates go up for private rides and during peak demand times. These services are especially economical when going to or from the airport, where a shared ride will run you about $25—half the cost of a cab.

TAXI COMPANIES Flywheel Taxi. ☎ *415/970–1303* 🌐 *flywheeltaxi.com.* **Luxor Cab.** ☎ *415/282–4141* 🌐 *www.luxorcab.com.* **National Veterans Cab.** ☎ *415/321–8294* 🌐 *sfnationalcab.sftaxischool.com/index.html.* **Yellow Cab.** ☎ *415/333–3333* 🌐 *yellowcabsf.com.*

COMPLAINTS San Francisco Police Department Taxi Complaints. ☎ *415/701–4400.*

TRAIN TRAVEL

Amtrak trains travel to the Bay Area from some cities in California and the United States. The *Coast Starlight* travels north from Los Angeles to Seattle, passing the Bay Area along the way, but contrary to its name, the train runs inland through the Central Valley for much of its route through Northern California; the most scenic stretch is in Southern California, between San Luis Obispo and Los Angeles. Amtrak also has several routes between San Jose, Oakland, and Sacramento. The *California Zephyr* travels from Chicago to the Bay Area, and has spectacular alpine vistas as it crosses the Sierra Nevada range. San Francisco doesn't have an Amtrak train station but does have an Amtrak bus stop at the Ferry Building, from which shuttle buses transport passengers to trains in Emeryville, just over the Bay Bridge. Shuttle buses also connect the Emeryville train station with BART and other points in downtown San Francisco. You can buy a California Rail Pass, which gives you 7 days of travel in a 21-day period for $159.

Caltrain connects San Francisco to Palo Alto, San Jose, Santa Clara, and many smaller cities en route. In San Francisco, trains leave from the main depot, at 4th and Townsend streets, and a rail-side stop at 22nd and Pennsylvania streets. One-way fares are $3.75 to $13.75, depending on the number of zones through which you travel; tickets are valid for four hours after purchase time. A ticket is $7.75 from San Francisco to Palo Alto, at least $9.75 to San Jose. You can also buy a day pass ($7.50–$27.50) for unlimited travel in a 24-hour period. It's worth waiting for an express train for trips that last from 1 to 1¾ hours. On weekdays, trains depart three or four times per hour during the morning and evening, only once or twice per hour during daytime non-commute hours and late night. Weekend trains run once per hour, though there are two bullet trains per day, one in late morning and one in early evening. The system shuts down after midnight. There are no onboard ticket sales. You must buy tickets before boarding the train or risk paying up to $250 for fare evasion.

INFORMATION Amtrak. ☎ *800/872–7245* 🌐 *www.amtrak.com.* **Caltrain.** ☎ *800/660–4287* 🌐 *www.caltrain.com.* **San Francisco Caltrain station.** ✉ *700 4th St., near Townsend St., San Francisco* ☎ *800/660–4287.*

Restaurants

Make no mistake, San Francisco is one of America's top food cities. Some of the biggest landmarks are restaurants. In fact, on a Saturday, the Ferry Building—a temple to local eating—may attract more visitors than the Golden Gate Bridge: cheeses, breads, "salty pig parts," homemade delicacies, and sensory-perfect vegetables and fruits attract rabidly dedicated aficionados. You see, San Franciscans are a little loco about their edibles. If you ask them what their favorite season is, don't be surprised if they respond, "tomato season."

Some renowned restaurants are booked weeks or even months in advance. But you can get lucky at the last minute if you're flexible—and friendly. Most restaurants keep a few tables open for walk-ins and VIPs. Show up for dinner early (5:30 pm) or late (after 9 pm) and politely inquire about any last-minute vacancies or cancellations.

What It Costs

	$	$$	$$$	$$$$
RESTAURANTS	under $16	$16–$22	$23–$30	over $30

Hotels

San Francisco accommodations are diverse, ranging from cozy inns and kitschy motels, to chic little inns and true grande dames, housed in century-old structures and sleek high-rises. While the tech boom has skyrocketed the prices of even some of the most dependable low-cost options, luckily, some Fodor's faves still offer fine accommodations without the jaw-dropping prices to match those steep hills. In fact, the number of reasonably priced accommodations is impressive.

Hotel reviews have been shortened. For full information, visit Fodors.com.

What It Costs

	$	$$	$$$	$$$$
HOTELS	under $150	$150–$249	$250–$350	over $350

Nightlife

After hours, business folk and the working class give way to costume-clad partygoers, hippies and hipsters, downtown divas, frat boys, and those who prefer something a little more clothing-optional.

Entertainment information is printed in the "Datebook" section and the more calendar-based "96 Hours" section of the *San Francisco Chronicle* (🌐 *www.sfgate.com*). Also consult any of the free alternative weeklies, notably the *SF Weekly* (🌐 *www.sfweekly.com*), which blurbs nightclubs and music, and the *San Francisco Bay Guardian* (🌐 *www.sfbg.com*), which lists neighborhood, avant-garde, and budget events. SF Station (🌐 *www.sfstation.com*; online only) has an up-to-date calendar of entertainment goings-on.

You're better off taking public transportation or taxis on weekend nights, unless you're heading downtown (Financial District or Union Square) and are willing to park in a lot. There's only street parking in North Beach, the Mission, Castro, and the Haight, and finding a spot can be practically impossible. Muni stops running between 1 am and 5 am but has its limited Owl Service on a few lines—including the K, N, L, 90, 91, 14, 24, 38, and 22—every 30 minutes. Service cuts have put a dent in frequency; check 🌐 *www.sfmuni.com* for current details. You can sometimes hail a taxi on the street in well-trodden nightlife locations like North Beach or the Mission, but you can also call for one (☎ *415/626–2345 Yellow Cab, 415/648–3181 Arrow*). The best option by far is booking a taxi with a smartphone-based app (🌐 *www.uber.com*, 🌐 *www.lyft.com*). **■TIP→ Cabs in San Francisco are more expensive than in other areas of the United States; expect to pay at least $15 to get anywhere within the city. Keep in mind that BART service across the bay stops shortly after midnight.**

Performing Arts

Sophisticated, offbeat, and often ahead of the curve, San Francisco's performing arts scene supports world-class opera, ballet, and theater productions, along with alternative-dance events, avant-garde plays, groundbreaking documentaries, and a slew of spoken-word and other literary happenings.

The best guide to the arts is printed in the "Datebook" section and the "96 Hours" section of the *San Francisco Chronicle* (🌐 *www.sfgate.com*). Also check out the city's free alternative weeklies, including *SF Weekly* (🌐 *www.sfweekly.com*) and the *San Francisco Bay Guardian* (🌐 *www.sfbg.com*).

Online, SF Station (🌐 *www.sfstation.com*) has a frequently updated arts and nightlife calendar. *San Francisco Arts Monthly* (🌐 *www.sfarts.org*), which is published at the end of the month, has arts features and events listings, plus a helpful "Visiting San Francisco?" section. For offbeat, emerging-artist performances, consult CounterPULSE (🌐 *www.counterpulse.org*).

Shopping

With its grand department stores and funky secondhand boutiques, San Francisco summons a full range of shopping experiences. From the anarchist bookstore to the mouthwatering specialty-food purveyors at the gleaming Ferry Building, the local shopping opportunities reflect the city's various personalities. Visitors with limited time often focus their energies on the high-density Union Square area, where several major department stores tower over big-name boutiques. But if you're keen to find unique local shops, consider moving beyond the square's radius.

Each neighborhood has its own distinctive finds, whether it's 1960s housewares, cheeky stationery, or vintage Levi's. If shopping in San Francisco has a downside, it's that real bargains can be few and far between. Sure, neighborhoods such as the Lower Haight and the Mission have thrift shops and other inexpensive stores, but you won't find many discount outlets in the city, where rents are sky-high and space is at a premium.

Visitor Information

The San Francisco Convention and Visitors Bureau can mail you brochures, maps, and events listings. Once in town, you can stop by the bureau's info center near Union Square.

CONTACTS San Francisco Visitor Information Center. ✉ *Hallidie Plaza, lower level, 900 Market St., at Powell St., Union Sq.* ☎ *415/391–2000* 🌐 *www.sftravel.com.*

Union Square

The Union Square area bristles with big-city bravado. The crowds zigzag among international brands, trailing glossy shopping bags.

Maiden Lane

BUILDING | Known as Morton Street in the raffish Barbary Coast era, this former red-light district reported at least one murder a week during the late 19th century. Things cooled down after the 1906 fire destroyed the brothels, and these days Maiden Lane is a chic, designer-boutique-lined pedestrian mall stretching two blocks, between Stockton and Kearny streets. Wrought-iron gates close the street to traffic most days between 11 and 5, when the lane becomes an alfresco hot spot dotted with a patchwork of umbrella-shaded tables. At **140 Maiden Lane** is the only Frank Lloyd Wright building in San Francisco, fronted by a large brick archway. The graceful, curving ramp and skylights of the interior, which houses exclusive Italian menswear boutique Isaia, are said to have been his model for the Guggenheim Museum in New York. ✉ *Between Stockton and Kearny Sts., Union Sq.*

Union Square

PLAZA | Ground zero for big-name shopping in the city and within walking distance of many hotels, Union Square is home base for many visitors. The Westin St. Francis Hotel and Macy's line two of the square's sides, and Saks, Neiman-Marcus, and Tiffany & Co. edge the other two. Four globular contemporary lamp sculptures by the artist R. M. Fischer preside over the landscaped, 2½-acre park, which has a café with outdoor seating, an open-air stage, and a visitor-information booth—along with a familiar kaleidoscope of characters: office workers sunning and brown-bagging, street musicians, shoppers taking a rest, kids chasing pigeons, and a fair number of homeless people. The constant clang of cable cars traveling up and down Powell Street helps maintain a festive mood. ✉ *Bordered by Powell, Stockton, Post, and Geary Sts., Union Sq.*

Westin St. Francis Hotel

HOTEL—SIGHT | Built in 1904 and barely established as the most sumptuous hotel in town before it was ravaged by fire following the 1906 earthquake, this grande-dame hotel designed by Walter Danforth Bliss and William Baker Faville reopened in 1907 with the addition of a luxurious Italian Renaissance–style residence designed to attract loyal clients from among the world's rich and powerful. The hotel's checkered past includes the ill-fated 1921 bash in the suite of the silent-film superstar Fatty Arbuckle, at which a woman became ill and later died. Arbuckle endured three sensational trials for rape and murder before being acquitted, by which time his career was

The epicenter of high-end shopping, Union Square is lined with department stores.

kaput. In 1975, Sara Jane Moore, standing among a crowd outside the hotel, attempted to shoot then-President Gerald Ford. Of course, the grand lobby contains no plaques commemorating these events. **■ TIP→ Some visitors make the St. Francis a stop whenever they're in town, soaking up the lobby ambience or enjoying a cocktail at the Clock Bar or lunch at the Oak Room Restaurant.** *✉ 335 Powell St., at Geary St., Union Sq. ☎ 415/397–7000 🌐 westinstfrancis.com.*

Restaurants

★ Liholiho Yacht Club

$$$$ | MODERN AMERICAN | Inspired but not defined by the chef's native Hawaii, Ravi Kapur's lively restaurant is known for big-hearted, high-spirited cooking, including contemporary riffs on poke and Spam, but also squid served with crispy tripe, and beef ribs with kimchi chili sauce. The dining room and front bar area are perpetually packed, and dominated by an enormous photo of a beaming woman who happens to be none other than the chef's mother. **Known for:** Hawaiian-inspired food; giant mains that serve two to four people; lively buzz. *$ Average main: $40 ✉ 871 Sutter St., Union Sq. ☎ 415/440–5446 🌐 www.lycsf.com ⏲ Closed Sun. No lunch.*

Hotels

★ Golden Gate Hotel

$$ | B&B/INN | FAMILY | Budget seekers looking for accommodations around Union Square will enjoy this four-story Edwardian with bay windows, an original birdcage elevator, hallways lined with historical photographs, and rooms decorated with antiques, wicker pieces, and Laura Ashley bedding and curtains. **Pros:** friendly staff; spotless rooms; good location if you're a walker. **Cons:** some rooms share a bath; resident cat and dog, so not good for guests with allergies; some rooms on small side. *$ Rooms from: $185 ✉ 775 Bush St., Union Sq. ☎ 415/392–3702, 800/835–1118 🌐 www.goldengatehotel.com 23 rooms 🍽 Breakfast.*

Sights

1 Chinatown Gate C4
2 Golden Gate Fortune Cookie Factory C2
3 Maiden Lane D5
4 Portsmouth Square C2
5 Tin How Temple C3
6 Union Square C5
7 Westin St. Francis Hotel B5

Restaurants

1 Cotogna D2
2 Liholiho Yacht Club A5
3 Mister Jiu's C3
4 Perbacco E3
5 R & G Lounge C3
6 Yank Sing E4

Hotels

1 Golden Gate Hotel B4
2 Hotel Diva B5
3 Hotel Emblem San Francisco B4
4 Hotel Triton C4
5 Westin St Francis B5

Hotel Diva

$$ | **HOTEL** | Entering this magnet for urbanites craving modern decor requires stepping over footprints, handprints, and autographs embedded in the sidewalk by visiting stars; in the rooms, designer carpets complement mid-century-modern chairs and brushed-steel headboards whose shape mimics that of ocean waves. **Pros:** contemporary design; in the heart of the theater district; accommodating staff. **Cons:** few frills; tiny bathrooms (but equipped with eco-friendly bath products); many rooms are small. *Rooms from: $209 ✉ 440 Geary St., Union Sq. ☎ 415/885–0200, 800/553–1900 🌐 www.hoteldiva.com 130 rooms No meals.*

Hotel Emblem

$$$ | **HOTEL** | Inspiration is everywhere at intimate Hotel Emblem, refurbished and rebranded in 2019 with a literary theme that celebrates San Francisco's Beat poets, from its lobby wall of books and poetry-laced carpet to in-room libraries and typewriters. **Pros:** fun, creative vibe; excellent Union Square location; amenities available by request include essential oil diffusers, coloring books, and bath bombs. **Cons:** $25 nightly amenity fee; expensive parking; some rooms on the small side. *Rooms from: $295 ✉ 562 Sutter St., Union Sq. ☎ 415/433–4434 🌐 www.viceroyhotelsandresorts.com/en/emblem 96 rooms No meals.*

Hotel Triton

$$$ | **HOTEL** | With a fresh top-to-bottom 2018 redesign and a location at the convergence of Chinatown, the Financial District, and Union Square, this boutique anchor attracts a design-conscious crowd. **Pros:** arty environs; good location; room service from next-door Café de la Presse. **Cons:** rooms and baths are on the small side; hallways feel cramped; $25 obligatory fee for fitness center access, Wi-Fi, and lobby beverages. *Rooms from: $279 ✉ 342 Grant Ave., Union Sq. ☎ 415/394–0500, 877/793–9931 🌐 www.hoteltriton.com 140 rooms No meals.*

Cable Car Terminus

Two of the three cable-car lines begin and end their runs at Powell and Market streets, a couple blocks south of Union Square. These two lines are the most scenic, and both pass near Fisherman's Wharf, so they're usually clogged with first-time sightseers. The wait to board a cable car at this intersection is longer than at any other stop in the system. If you'd rather avoid the mob, board the less-touristy California line at the bottom of Market Street, at Drumm Street.

Westin St. Francis

$$$$ | **HOTEL** | The survivor of two major earthquakes, some headline-grabbing scandals, and even an attempted presidential assassination, this richly appointed and superbly located grande dame dating to 1904 is comprised of the landmark building, renovated in 2018, and a modern 32-story tower whose glass elevators reveal Union Square views from the upper floors. **Pros:** prime Union Square location; great views from some rooms; Chateau Montelena wine-tasting room. **Cons:** rooms in original building can be small; public spaces lack the panache of days gone by; no dinner at on-site Oak Room Restaurant. *Rooms from: $356 ✉ 335 Powell St., Union Sq. ☎ 415/397–7000, 800/917–7458 🌐 www.westinstfrancis.com 1,195 rooms No meals.*

Nightlife

Harry Denton's Starlight Room

BARS/PUBS | Forget low-key drinks—the only way to experience Harry Denton's is to cough up the cover charge and enjoy the opulent, over-the-top decor. Red velvet booths and romantic lighting help re-create the 1950s high life on the 21st floor of the Sir Francis Drake Hotel. Sunday brunch brings a popular drag show, and the small dance floor is packed on Friday and Saturday nights. Jackets are preferred for men. ✉ *Sir Francis Drake Hotel, 450 Powell St., between Post and Sutter Sts., Union Sq.* ☎ *415/395–8595* 🌐 *starlightroomsf.com.*

Pacific Cocktail Haven

BARS/PUBS | PCH for short, this neighborhood hangout with a convivial aura and industrial-chic decor hits all the right notes. Plus the well-chosen and unique ingredients mean there's a little something for everyone, and the glassware is as dazzling as the elixirs inside. **■TIP→ The must-try cocktail is the Oh Snap!, a concoction of gin, sugar snap peas, citrus, and absinthe.** ✉ *580 Sutter St., at Mason St., Union Sq.* ☎ *415/398–0195* 🌐 *pacificcocktailsf.com* 🕒 *Closed Sun.*

Performing Arts

TIX Bay Area

TICKETS | Half-price, same-day tickets for many local and touring shows go on sale (cash only) at the TIX booth in Union Square, which is open daily from 10 to 6. Discount purchases can also be made online. ✉ *350 Powell St., at Geary St., Union Sq.* ☎ *415/433–7827* 🌐 *www.tixbayarea.org.*

THEATER

American Conservatory Theater

THEATER | One of the nation's leading regional theater companies presents about eight plays a year, from classics to contemporary works, often in repertory. The season runs from early fall to late spring. In December ACT stages a beloved version of Charles Dickens's *A Christmas Carol.* ✉ *415 Geary St., Union Sq.* ☎ *415/749–2228* 🌐 *www.act-sf.org.*

Shopping

ART GALLERIES

★ Berggruen Gallery

ART GALLERIES | Twentieth-century European and American paintings, including Bay Area figurative works, are displayed throughout two airy floors at this well-respected gallery established in 1970. Some recent exhibitions have included the works of Robert Kelly and Isca Greenfield-Sanders. Look for thematic shows here, too; past exhibits have had titles such as Summer Highlights and Four Decades. ✉ *10 Hawthorne St., at Howard St., SoMa* ☎ *415/781–4629* 🌐 *www.berggruen.com.*

CLOTHING: MEN AND WOMEN

★ Margaret O'Leary

CLOTHING | If you can only buy one piece of clothing in San Francisco, make it a hand-loomed cashmere sweater by this Irish-born local legend. The perfect antidote to the city's wind and fog, the sweaters are so beloved by San Franciscans that some of them never wear anything else. Pick up an airplane wrap for your trip home. Another store is in Pacific Heights, at 2400 Fillmore Street. ✉ *1 Claude La., at Sutter St., just west of Kearny St., Union Sq.* ☎ *415/391–1010* 🌐 *www.margaretoleary.com.*

Chinatown

A few blocks uphill from Union Square is the abrupt beginning of dense and insular Chinatown—the oldest such community in the country. When the street signs have Chinese characters, produce stalls crowd pedestrians off the sidewalk, and whole roast ducks hang in deli windows, you'll know you've arrived. (The neighborhood huddles together in the 17 blocks and 41 alleys bordered roughly by Bush, Kearny, and Powell streets and Broadway.) Chinatown has been attracting the curious for more than 100 years, and no other

Continued on page 205

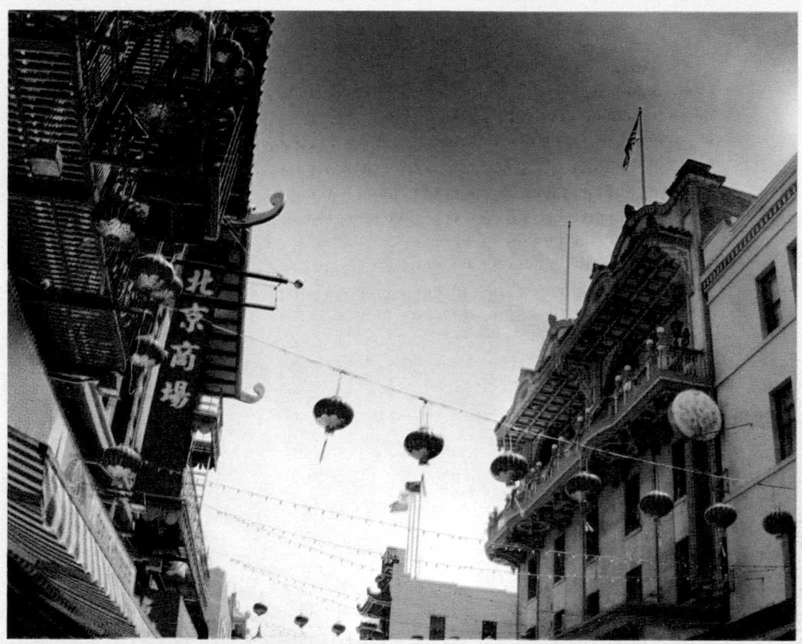

CHINATOWN

Chinatown's streets flood the senses. Incense and cigarette smoke mingle with the scents of briny fish and sweet vanilla. Rooflines flare outward, pagoda-style. Loud Cantonese bargaining and honking car horns rise above the sharp clack of mah-jongg tiles and the eternally humming cables beneath the street.

Most Chinatown visitors march down Grant Avenue, buy a few trinkets, and call it a day. Do yourself a favor and dig deeper. This is one of the largest Chinese communities outside Asia, and there is far more to it than buying a back-scratcher near Chinatown Gate. To get a real feel for the neighborhood, wander off the main drag. Step into a temple or an herb shop and wander down a flag-draped alley. And don't be shy: residents welcome guests warmly, though rarely in English.

Whatever you do, don't leave without eating something. Noodle houses, bakeries, tea houses, and dim sum shops seem to occupy every other storefront. There's a feast for your eyes as well: in the market windows on Stockton and Grant, you'll see hanging whole roast ducks, fish, and shellfish swimming in tanks, and strips of shiny, pink-glazed Chinese-style barbecued pork.

CHINATOWN'S HISTORY

Sam Brannan's 1848 cry of "Gold!" didn't take long to reach across the world to China. Struggling with famine, drought, and political upheaval at home, thousands of Chinese jumped at the chance to try their luck in California. Most came from the Pearl River Delta region, in the Guangdong province, and spoke Cantonese dialects. From the start, Chinese businesses circled around Portsmouth Square, which was conveniently central. Bachelor rooming houses sprang up, since the vast majority of new arrivals were men. By 1853, the area was called Chinatown.

The Street of Gamblers (Ross Alley), 1898 (top). The first Chinese telephone operator in Chinatown (bottom).

COLD WELCOME

The Chinese faced discrimination from the get-go. Harrassment became outright hostility as first the gold rush, then the work on the Transcontinental Railroad petered out. Special taxes were imposed to shoulder aside competing "coolie labor." Laws forbidding the Chinese from moving outside Chinatown kept the residents packed in like sardines, with nowhere to go but up and down—thus the many basement establishments in the neighborhood. State and federal laws passed in the 1870s deterred Chinese women from immigrating, deeming them prostitutes. In the late 1870s, looting and arson attacks on Chinatown businesses soared.

The coup de grace, though, was the Chinese Exclusion Act, passed by the U.S. Congress in 1882, which slammed the doors to America for "Asiatics." This was

Chinatown's Grant Avenue.

Women and children flooded into the neighborhood after the Great Quake.

the country's first significant restriction on immigration. The law also prevented the existing Chinese residents, including American-born children, from becoming naturalized citizens. With a society of mostly men (forbidden, of course, from marrying white women), San Francisco hoped that Chinatown would simply die out.

OUT OF THE ASHES

When the devastating 1906 earthquake and fire hit, city fathers thought they'd seize the opportunity to kick the Chinese out of Chinatown and get their hands on that desirable piece of downtown real estate. Then Chinatown businessman Look Tin Eli had a brainstorm of Disneyesque proportions.

He proposed that Chinatown be rebuilt, but in a tourist-friendly, stylized, "Oriental" way. Anglo-American architects would design new buildings with pagoda roofs and dragon-covered columns. Chinatown would attract more tourists—the curious had been visiting on the sly for decades—and add more tax money to the city's coffers. Ka-ching: the sales pitch worked.

PAPER SONS

For the Chinese, the 1906 earthquake turned the virtual "no entry" sign into a flashing neon "welcome!" All the city's immigration records went up in smoke, and the Chinese quickly began to apply for passports as U.S. citizens, claiming their old ones were lost in the fire. Not only did thousands of Chinese become legal overnight, but so did their sons in China, or "sons," if they weren't really related. Whole families in Chinatown had passports in names that weren't their own; these "paper sons" were not only a windfall but also an uncomfortable neighborhood conspiracy. The city caught on eventually and set up an immigration center on Angel Island in 1910. Immigrants spent weeks or months being inspected and interrogated while their papers were checked. Roughly 250,000 people made it through. With this influx, including women and children, Chinatown finally became a more complete community.

A GREAT WALK THROUGH CHINATOWN

■ Start at the Chinatown Gate and walk ahead on Grant Avenue, entering the souvenir gauntlet. (You'll also pass Old St. Mary's Cathedral.)

■ Make a right on Clay Street and walk to Portsmouth Square. Sometimes it feels like the whole neighborhood's here, playing chess and exercising.

■ Head up Washington Street to the Old Chinese Telephone Exchange building, now the EastWest Bank. Across Grant, look left for Waverly Place. Here Free Republic of China (Taiwanese) flags flap over some of the neighborhood's most striking buildings, including Tin How Temple.

■ At the Sacramento Street end of Waverly Place stands the First Chinese Baptist Church of 1908. Just across the way, the Clarion Music Center is full of unusual instruments, as well as exquisite lion-dance sets.

■ Head back to Washington Street and check out the many herb shops.

■ Follow the scent of vanilla down Ross Alley (entrance across from Superior Trading Company) to the Golden Gate Fortune Cookie Factory. Then head across the alley to Sam Bo Trading Co., where religious items are stacked in the narrow space. Tell the owners your troubles and they'll prepare a package of joss papers, joss sticks, and candles, and tell you how and when to offer them up.

■ Turn left on Jackson Street; ahead is the real Chinatown's main artery, Stockton Street, where most residents do their grocery shopping. Vegetarians will want to avoid Luen Fat Market (No. 1135), with tanks of live frogs, turtles, and lobster as well as chickens and ducks. Look toward the back of stores for Buddhist altars with offerings of oranges and grapefruit. From here you can loop one block east back to Grant.

neighborhood in the city absorbs as many tourists without seeming to forfeit its character. Join the flow and step into another world. Good-luck banners of crimson and gold hang beside dragon-entwined lampposts and pagoda roofs, while honking cars chime in with shoppers bargaining loudly in Cantonese or Mandarin.

Look Up!

When wandering around Chinatown, don't forget to look up! Above the chintziest souvenir shop might loom an ornate balcony or a curly pagoda roof. The best examples are on the 900 block of Grant Avenue (at Washington Street) and at Waverly Place.

Sights

Chinatown Gate

BUILDING | This is the official entrance to Chinatown. Stone lions flank the base of the pagoda-topped gate; the lions, dragons, and fish up top symbolize wealth, prosperity, and other good things. The four Chinese characters immediately beneath the pagoda represent the philosophy of Sun Yat-sen (1866–1925), the leader who unified China in the early 20th century. Sun Yat-sen, who lived in exile in San Francisco for a few years, promoted the notion of friendship and peace among all nations based on equality, justice, and goodwill. The vertical characters under the left pagoda read "peace" and "trust," the ones under the right pagoda "respect" and "love." The whole shebang telegraphs the internationally understood message of "photo op." Immediately beyond the gate, dive into souvenir shopping on Grant Avenue, Chinatown's tourist strip. ✉ *Grant Ave. at Bush St., Chinatown.*

Golden Gate Fortune Cookie Factory

FACTORY | **FAMILY** | Follow your nose down Ross Alley to this tiny but fragrant cookie factory. Two workers sit at circular motorized griddles and wait for dollops of batter to drop onto a tiny metal plate, which rotates into an oven. A few moments later out comes a cookie that's pliable and ready for folding. It's easy to peek in for a moment, and hard to leave without a few free samples. A bagful of cookies—with mildly racy "adult" fortunes or more benign ones—costs less than $5. ✉ *56 Ross Alley, between Washington and Jackson Sts., west of Grant Ave., Chinatown* ☎ *415/781–3956* 🎫 *Free.*

Portsmouth Square

PLAZA | Chinatown's living room buzzes with activity. The square, with its pagoda-shape structures, is a favorite spot for morning tai chi; by noon dozens of men huddle around Chinese chess tables, engaged in competition. Kids scamper about the square's two grungy playgrounds. Back in the late 19th century this land was near the waterfront. The square is named for the USS *Portsmouth*, the ship helmed by Captain John Montgomery, who in 1846 raised the American flag here and claimed the then-Mexican land for the United States. A couple of years later, Sam Brannan kicked off the gold rush at the square when he waved his loot and proclaimed, "Gold from the American River!" Robert Louis Stevenson, the author of *Treasure Island,* often dropped by, chatting up the sailors who hung out here. Some of the information he gleaned about life at sea found its way into his fiction. A bronze galleon sculpture, a tribute to Stevenson, anchors the square's northwest corner. A plaque marks the site of California's first public school, built in 1847. ✉ *Bordered by Walter Lum Pl. and Kearny, Washington, and Clay Sts., Chinatown.*

★ Tin How Temple

RELIGIOUS SITE | Duck into the inconspicuous doorway, climb three flights of stairs, and be assaulted by the aroma of incense in this tiny, altar-filled room. In 1852, Day Ju, one of the first three Chinese to arrive in San Francisco, dedicated this temple to the Queen of the Heavens and the Goddess of the Seven Seas, and the temple looks largely the same today as it did more than a century ago. In the entryway, elderly ladies can often be seen preparing "money" to be burned as offerings to various Buddhist gods or as funds for ancestors to use in the afterlife. Hundreds of red-and-gold lanterns cover the ceiling; the larger the lamp, the larger its donor's contribution to the temple. Gifts of oranges, dim sum, and money left by the faithful, who kneel mumbling prayers, rest on altars to different gods. Tin How presides over the middle back of the temple, flanked by one red and one green lesser god. Take a good look around, since taking photographs is not allowed. ✉ *125 Waverly Pl., between Clay and Washington Sts., Chinatown* 🎫 *Free, donations accepted.*

Mister Jiu's

$$$$ | **CHINESE** | Brandon Jew's ambitious, graceful restaurant offers the chef's contemporary, farm-to-table interpretation of Chinese cuisine, including options such as hot-and-sour soup garnished with nasturtiums and pot stickers made with Swiss chard and local chicken. The elegant dining room—accented with plants and a chrysanthemum chandelier—provides beautiful views of Chinatown, while the menu breathes new life into it. **Known for:** modern Chinese food; cocktails; one Michelin star. $ *Average main: $36* ✉ *28 Waverly Pl., Chinatown* ☎ *415/857–9688* 🌐 *www.misterjius.com* ⏲ *Closed Sun. and Mon. No lunch.*

R&G Lounge

$$ | **CHINESE** | **FAMILY** | Salt-and-pepper Dungeness crab is a delicious draw at this bright, three-level Cantonese eatery that draws a packed crowd for its crustacean specialties—crab portions are easily splittable by three—and dim sum. A menu with photographs will help you sort through other HK specialties, including Peking duck and shrimp-stuffed bean curd, and much of the seafood is fresh from the tank. **Known for:** fresh-from-the-tank crab; Cantonese specialties; extensive menu. $ *Average main: $20* ✉ *631 Kearny St., Chinatown* ☎ *415/982–7877* 🌐 *www.rnglounge.com.*

Financial District

Cotogna

$$$ | **ITALIAN** | The draw at this urban trattoria—just as in demand as its fancier big sister, Quince, next door—is chef Michael Tusk's flavorful, rustic, seasonally driven Italian cooking, such as the irresistible raviolo di ricotta, filled with warm house-made ricotta and topped with an egg yolk, and bistecca alla Fiorentina. The look is comfortably chic, with wood tables, quality stemware, and fantastic Italian wines by the bottle and glass. **Known for:** rustic Italian; fantastic wine list; chic space. $ *Average main: $27* ✉ *490 Pacific Ave., Financial District* ☎ *415/775–8508* 🌐 *www.cotognasf.com* ⏲ *No lunch Sun.*

Perbacco

$$$$ | **ITALIAN** | From the complimentary basket of skinny, brittle bread sticks to the pappardelle with short rib ragu, Chef Staffan Terje's entire menu is a delectable paean to northern Italy. With a long marble bar and open kitchen, this brick-lined two-story space oozes big-city charm, attracting business types and Italian food aficionados with such standouts as the house-made cured meats (Terje makes some of the city's finest salumi), burrata with seasonal vegetables, and delicate *agnolotti dal plin* (pasta stuffed with meat and cabbage). **Known for:** pasta stuffed with meat and cabbage; house-made cured meats; authentic northern Italian cuisine. *Average main: $31 230 California St., Financial District 415/955–0663 www.perbaccosf.com Closed Sun. No lunch Sat.*

Yank Sing

$$ | CHINESE | FAMILY | This bustling teahouse serves some of San Francisco's best dim sum to office workers on weekdays and boisterous families on weekends, and the take-out counter makes a meal on the run a satisfying compromise when office duties—or touring—won't wait. The several dozen varieties prepared daily include both the classic and the creative; steamed pork buns, shrimp dumplings, scallion-skewered prawns tied with bacon, and basil seafood dumplings are among the many delights, and the Shanghai soup dumplings are perfection. **Known for:** classic dim sum; Shanghai soup dumplings; energetic room. *Average main: $18 49 Stevenson St., Financial District 415/541–4949 www.yanksing.com No dinner.*

Performing Arts

San Francisco Performances

TICKETS | SFP brings an eclectic array of top-flight global music and dance talents to various venues—mostly the Yerba Buena Center for the Arts, Davies Symphony Hall, and Herbst Theatre. Artists have included Yo-Yo Ma, Edgar Meyer, the Paul Taylor Dance Company, and Midori. Tickets can be purchased in person through City Box Office, online, or by phone. *500 Sutter St., Suite 710, Financial District 415/392–2545 www.sfperformances.org.*

SoMa

SoMa is less a neighborhood than a sprawling area of wide, traffic-heavy boulevards lined with office skyscrapers and ultrachic condo high-rises. Aside from the fact that many of them work in the area, locals are drawn to the cultural offerings, destination restaurants, and concentration of bars and restaurants. In terms of sightseeing, gigantic and impressive SFMOMA tops the list, followed by the specialty museums of the Yerba Buena arts district.

Contemporary Jewish Museum

MUSEUM | Daniel Libeskind designed the postmodern CJM, whose impossible-to-ignore diagonal blue cube juts out of a painstakingly restored power substation. A physical manifestation of the Hebrew phrase *l'chaim* (to life), the cube may have obscure philosophical origins, but Libeskind created a unique, light-filled space that merits a stroll through the lobby even if current exhibits don't entice you into the galleries. **TIP→ San Francisco's best Jewish deli, Wise Sons, operates a counter in the museum, giving you a chance to sample the company's wildly popular smoked trout or a slice of chocolate babka.** *736 Mission St., between 3rd and 4th Sts., SoMa 415/655–7800 www.thecjm.org $14; $5 Thurs. after 5 pm, free 1st Tues. of month Closed Wed.*

Museum of the African Diaspora (MoAD)

MUSEUM | Dedicated to the influence that people of African descent have had all over the world, MoAD focuses on temporary exhibits in its four galleries over three floors. With floor-to-ceiling windows onto Mission Street, the museum fits perfectly into the cultural scene of Yerba Buena and is well worth a 30-minute foray. Most striking is its front-window exhibit: a three-story mosaic, made

A
B
C
D
E
F
1
2
3
4
5
6
7
8
9
CHINATOWN
Cable Car
Cable Car Barn
Broadway
Pacific Avenue
101
Jackson Street
Washington Street
Lafayette Park
Clay Street
Sacramento Street
California Street
Van Ness Avenue
Polk Street
Larkin Street
Hyde Street
Leavenworth Street
Jones Street
Taylor Street
Mason Street
Powell Street
Pleasant St.
Huntington Park
NOB HILL
POLK GULCH
Pine Street
Bush Street
Sutter Street
Post Street
Geary Street
O'Farrell Street
Gough Street
Franklin Street
Ellis Street
Eddy Street
Cleary Ct.
TENDERLOIN
Turk Street
Jefferson Square
Golden Gate Ave.
McAllister Street
Fulton St.
Market Street
6th Street
Jessie St.
Stevenson St.
7th Street
Mission St.
CIVIC CENTER
Grove Street
8th Street
Jullia St.
HAYES VALLEY
Laguna St.
Hayes Street
Linden St.
Fell Street
Hickory St.
Oak St.
Lily St.
Page St.
Rose St.
Octavia Blvd.
9th Street
10th Street
11th Street
Minna St.
Natoma St.
Washburn St.
Grace St.
Howard Street
Tehama St.
Clementina St.
Folsom Street
Ringold St.
Harrison Street
Dore St.
Brady St.
Gough St.
Lafayette St.
12th St.
Kissling St.
Valencia St.
Mission St.
KEY
Exploring Sights
Restaurants
Hotels
BART station
0
300m
0
1,000 ft

Sights ▼

1 Asian Art Museum........ D6
2 City Hall........ C6
3 Contemporary Jewish Museum........ H4
4 Museum of the African Diaspora (MoAD)........ H4
5 SFJAZZ Center........ B7
6 San Francisco Museum of Modern Art........ I4
7 Yerba Buena Center for the Arts........ H4
8 Yerba Buena Gardens........ H4

Restaurants ▼

1 Benu........ I4
2 In Situ........ I4
3 Marlowe........ J7
4 Nojo Ramen Tavern........ B7
5 Rich Table........ B8
6 Trou Normand........ I4
7 Zuni Café........ B8

Hotels ▼

1 Four Seasons Hotel San Francisco........ G4
2 Hotel Zetta San Francisco........ G5
3 Metro Hotel........ A8
4 The St. Regis San Francisco........ H4

from thousands of photographs, that forms the image of a young girl's face. ■ **TIP→ Walk up the stairs inside the museum to view the photographs up close—Malcolm X is there, Muhammad Ali, too, along with everyday folks—but the best view is from across the street.** ✉ *685 Mission St., SoMa* ☎ *415/358–7200* 🌐 *www.moadsf.org* 🎟 *$10* 🕑 *Closed Mon. and Tues.*

★ **San Francisco Museum of Modern Art**

MUSEUM | First opened in 1935, the San Francisco Museum of Modern Art was the first museum on the West Coast dedicated to modern and contemporary art. In 2016, after a major three-year building expansion designed by Snøhetta, SFMOMA emerged as one of the largest modern art museums in the country and the revitalized anchor of the Yerba Buena arts district. Nearly tripling its gallery space over seven floors, the museum displays only a portion of its more than 33,000-work collection, including numerous temporary exhibits. It can be overwhelming—you could easily spend a day taking it all in, but allow at least two hours; three is better. The museum's expanded collection includes a heavy dose of new art from the Doris and Donald Fisher Collection, one of the greatest private collections of modern and contemporary art in the world. Highlights include a deep collection of German abstract expressionist Gerhard Richter, American painter Ellsworth Kelly, and a tranquil gallery of Agnes Martin. Photography has long been one of the museum's strong suits, and the third floor is dedicated to it. Also look for seminal works by Diego Rivera, Alexander Calder, Matisse, and Picasso. Don't miss the new third-floor sculpture terrace with its striking living wall. The first floor is free to the public and contains four large works, as well as the museum's wonderful shop and expensive restaurant. If you don't have hours, save the steep entrance fee and take a spin through here. Ticketing, information, and one gallery are on the second floor; save time and reserve timed tickets online. Daily guided tours—a quick 20 minutes or 45 minutes—are an excellent way to get a foothold in this expansive space. And if you start to fade, grab a cup of Sightglass coffee at the café on the third floor; another café/restaurant is located by the fifth-floor sculpture garden. ✉ *151 3rd St., SoMa* ☎ *415/357–4000* 🌐 *www.sfmoma.org* 🎟 *$25.*

Yerba Buena Center for the Arts

ARTS VENUE | You never know what's going to be on display at this facility in Yerba Buena Gardens, but whether it's an exhibit of Mexican street art (graffiti to laypeople), innovative modern dance, or a baffling video installation, it's likely to be memorable. The productions here, which lean toward the cutting edge, tend to draw a young, energetic crowd. ■ **TIP→ Present any public library card or public transit ticket to receive a 10% discount.** ✉ *701 Mission St., SoMa* ☎ *415/978–2787* 🌐 *www.ybca.org* 🎟 *Galleries $10, free 1st Tues. of month* 🕑 *Closed Mon.*

Yerba Buena Gardens

CONVENTION CENTER | **FAMILY** | There's not much south of Market Street that encourages lingering outdoors—or indeed walking at all—with this notable exception. These two blocks encompass the Yerba Buena Center for the Arts, the Metreon, and newly renovated Moscone Convention Center, but the gardens themselves are the everyday draw. Office workers escape to the green swath of the East Garden, the focal point of which is the memorial to Martin Luther King Jr. Powerful streams of water surge over large, jagged stone columns, mirroring the enduring force of King's words that are carved on the stone walls and on glass blocks behind the waterfall. Moscone North is behind the memorial, and an overhead walkway leads to Moscone South and its rooftop attractions. ■ **TIP→ The gardens are liveliest during the week and especially during the Yerba Buena Gardens Festival, from May**

through October (www.ybgfestival.org), with free performances of everything from Latin music to Balinese dance.

Atop the Moscone Convention Center perch a few lures for kids. The historic Looff carousel (*$4 for two rides*) twirls daily 10–5. The carousel is attached to the Children's Creativity Museum (*415/820–3320, creativity.org*), a high-tech, interactive arts-and-technology center (*$13*) geared to children ages 3–12. Just outside, kids adore the excellent slides, including a 25-foot tube slide, at the play circle. Also part of the rooftop complex are gardens, an ice-skating rink, and a bowling alley. *Bordered by 3rd, 4th, Mission, and Folsom Sts., SoMa yerbabuenagardens.com Free.*

Restaurants

★ Benu

$$$$ | MODERN AMERICAN | Chef Corey Lee's three-Michelin-star fine-dining mecca is a must-stop for those who hop from city to city, collecting memorable meals. Each of the tasting menu's courses is impossibly meticulous, a marvel of textures and flavors. **Known for:** high-end dining; tasting menu; good service. *Average main: $310 22 Hawthorne St., SoMa 415/685–4860 www.benusf.com Closed Sun. and Mon. No lunch.*

★ In Situ

$$$ | CONTEMPORARY | Benu chef Corey Lee's restaurant at SFMOMA is an exhibition of its own, with a rotating menu comprised of dishes from 80 famous chefs around the world. You might taste David Chang's sausage and rice cakes, Rene Redzepi's wood sorrel granita, or Wylie Dufresne's shrimp grits. **Known for:** global influences; originality; museum location. *Average main: $30 151 3rd St., SoMa 415/941–6050 insitu.sfmoma.org Closed Tues. and Wed. No dinner Mon.*

Marlowe

$$$ | AMERICAN | Hearty American bistro fare and hip design draw crowds to this Anna Weinberg–Jennifer Puccio production. The menu boasts one of the city's best burgers, and the dining room gleams with white penny tile floors and marble countertops. **Known for:** burgers; strong drinks; festive atmosphere. *Average main: $27 500 Brannan St., SoMa 415/777–1413 www.marlowesf.com.*

★ Trou Normand

$$$ | MODERN AMERICAN | Thad Vogler's second endeavor (Bar Agricole was the first) delivers a fun boozy evening in stunning surroundings. Located off the lobby of the art deco–era Pacific Telephone building, it excels at house-cured salami and charcuterie and classic cocktails. **Known for:** house-made charcuterie; cocktails. *Average main: $28 140 New Montgomery St., SoMa 415/975–0876 www.trounormandsf.com.*

Hotels

Four Seasons Hotel San Francisco

$$$$ | HOTEL | Occupying floors 5 through 17 of a skyscraper, the Four Seasons delivers subdued elegance in rooms with contemporary artwork, fine linens, floor-to-ceiling windows that overlook Yerba Buena Gardens or downtown, and bathrooms with deep soaking tubs and glass-enclosed showers. **Pros:** near museums, galleries, restaurants, shopping, and clubs; terrific fitness facilities; luxurious rooms and amenities. **Cons:** pricey; rooms can feel sterile. *Rooms from: $569 757 Market St., SoMa 415/633–3000 www.fourseasons.com/sanfrancisco 277 rooms No meals.*

★ Hotel Zetta San Francisco

$$$ | HOTEL | With a playful lobby lounge, the London-style Cavalier brasserie, and slick-yet-homey tech-friendly rooms, this trendy redo behind a stately 1913 neoclassical facade is a leader in the

SoMa hotel scene. **Pros:** tech amenities and arty design; in-room spa services; noteworthy fitness center. **Cons:** lots of hubbub and traffic; no bathtubs; aesthetic too frenetic for some guests. *Rooms from: $315* *55 5th St., SoMa* *415/543–8555* *hotelzetta.com* *116 rooms* *No meals.*

★ The St. Regis San Francisco
$$$$ | **HOTEL** | Across from Yerba Buena Gardens and SFMOMA, the luxurious and modern St. Regis is favored by celebrities such as Lady Gaga and Al Gore. **Pros:** excellent views; stunning lap pool; luxe spa. **Cons:** expensive rates; small front-desk area; cramped space for passenger unloading. *Rooms from: $382* *125 3rd St., SoMa* *415/284–4000* *www.stregis.com/sanfrancisco* *260 rooms* *No meals.*

Nightlife

City Beer Store
BARS/PUBS | Called CBS by locals, this friendly tasting room-cum-liquor mart has a wine bar's sensibility. Perfect for connoisseurs and the merely beer curious, CBS stocks hundreds of different bottled beers, and more than a dozen are on tap. The indecisive can mix and match six-packs to go. *1148 Mission St., between 7th and 8th Sts., SoMa* *415/503–1033* *www.citybeerstore.com.*

The Stud
BARS/PUBS | Glam trans women, gay bears, tight-teed pretty boys, ladies and their ladies, and a handful of straight onlookers congregate here to dance to live DJ sounds and watch world-class drag performers on the small stage. The entertainment is often campy, pee-your-pants funny, and downright fantastic. Each night's music is different—from funk, soul, and hip-hop to '80s tunes and disco favorites. *399 9th St, at Harrison St., SoMa* *415/863–6623* *www.studsf.com* *Closed Mon.*

21st Amendment Brewery
BARS/PUBS | This popular brewery is known for its range of beer types, with multiple taps going at all times. In the spring, the Hell or High Watermelon—a wheat beer—gets rave reviews. **■ TIP→ Serious beer drinkers should try the Back in Black, a black IPA-style beer this brewpub helped pioneer.** The space has an upmarket warehouse feel, though exposed wooden ceiling beams, framed photos, whitewashed brick walls, and hardwood floors make it feel cozy. It's a good spot to warm up before a Giants game and an even better place to party after they win. *563 2nd St., between Bryant and Brannan Sts., SoMa* *415/369–0900* *www.21st-amendment.com.*

Performing Arts

Yerba Buena Center for the Arts
ARTS CENTERS | Across the street from the San Francisco Museum of Modern Art and abutting a lovely urban garden, this performing arts complex schedules interdisciplinary art exhibitions, touring and local dance troupes, music, film programs, and contemporary theater events. You can depend on the quality of the productions at Yerba Buena. Film buffs often come here to check out the San Francisco Cinematheque (*www.sfcinematheque.org*), which showcases experimental film and digital media. And dance enthusiasts can attend concerts by a roster of city companies that perform here, including Smuin Ballet/SF (*www.smuinballet.org*), ODC/San Francisco (*www.odcdance.org*), the Margaret Jenkins Dance Company (*www.mjdc.org*), and Alonzo King's Lines Ballet (*www.linesballet.org*). The Lamplighters (*www.lamplighters.org*), an alternative opera that specializes in Gilbert and Sullivan, also performs here. *3rd and Mission Sts., SoMa* *415/978–2787* *www.ybca.org.*

Shopping

BOOKS

★ Chronicle Books

BOOKS/STATIONERY | This local beacon of publishing produces inventively designed fiction, cookbooks, art books, and other titles, as well as diaries, planners, and address books—all of which you can purchase at two different airy and attractive spaces. The other store is located at 680 2nd Street, near Oracle Park. ✉ *Metreon Westfield Shopping Center, 165 4th St., near Howard St., SoMa* ☎ *415/369–6271* 🌐 *www.chroniclebooks.com.*

FOOD AND DRINK

K&L Wine Merchants

WINE/SPIRITS | More than any other wine store, this one has an ardent cult following around town. The friendly staffers promise not to sell what they don't taste themselves, and weekly events—on Friday from 5 pm to 6:30 pm and Saturday from noon to 3 pm—open the tastings to customers. The best-seller list for varietals and regions for both the under- and over-$30 categories appeals to the wine lover in everyone. ✉ *855 Harrison St., near 4th St., SoMa* ☎ *415/896–1734* 🌐 *www.klwines.com.*

Civic Center

The eye-catching, gold-domed City Hall presides over this patchy neighborhood bordered roughly by Franklin, McAllister, Hyde, and Grove streets. The optimistic "City Beautiful" movement of the early 20th century produced the Beaux Arts–style complex for which the area is named, including City Hall, the War Memorial Opera House, the Veterans Building, and the old public library, now the home of the Asian Art Museum. The wonderful Main Library on Larkin Street between Fulton and Grove streets is a modern variation on the Civic Center's architectural theme.

Sights

★ Asian Art Museum

MUSEUM | You don't have to be a connoisseur of Asian art to appreciate a visit to this museum whose monumental exterior conceals a light, open, and welcoming space. The fraction of the Asian's collection on display (about 2,500 pieces out of 18,000-plus total) is laid out thematically and by region, making it easy to follow historical developments.

Begin on the third floor, where highlights of Buddhist art in Southeast Asia and early China include a large, jewel-encrusted, exquisitely painted 19th-century Burmese Buddha, and clothed rod puppets from Java. On the second floor you can find later Chinese works, as well as pieces from Korea and Japan. The joy here is all in the details: on a whimsical Korean jar, look for a cobalt tiger jauntily smoking a pipe, or admire the delicacy of the Japanese tea implements. The ground floor is devoted to temporary exhibits and the museum's wonderful gift shop. During spring and summer, visit the museum on Thursday evenings for extended programs and sip drinks while a DJ spins tunes. ✉ *200 Larkin St., between McAllister and Fulton Sts., Civic Center* ☎ *415/581–3500* 🌐 *www.asianart.org* 🎟 *$25, free 1st Sun. of month; $10 Thurs. 5–9* ⏲ *Closed Mon.*

City Hall

GOVERNMENT BUILDING | This imposing 1915 structure with its massive gold-leaf dome—higher than the U.S. Capitol's—is about as close to a palace as you're going to get in San Francisco. The classic granite-and-marble behemoth was modeled after St. Peter's Basilica in Rome. Architect Arthur Brown Jr., who also designed Coit Tower and the War Memorial Opera House, designed an interior with grand columns and a sweeping central staircase. San Franciscans were thrilled, and probably a bit surprised, when his firm built City Hall in just a few years. The 1899 structure it replaced had taken 27 years to erect, as corrupt builders and politicians lined their pockets with funds earmarked for it. That building collapsed in about 27 seconds during the 1906 earthquake, revealing trash and newspapers mixed into the construction materials.

City Hall was spruced up and seismically retrofitted in the late 1990s, but the sense of history remains palpable. Some note-worthy events that have taken place here include the marriage of Marilyn Monroe and Joe DiMaggio (1954); the hosing—down the central staircase—of civil-rights and freedom-of-speech protesters (1960); the murders of Mayor George Moscone and openly gay supervisor Harvey Milk (1978); the torching of the lobby by angry members of the gay community in response to the light sentence given to the former supervisor who killed both men (1979); and the registrations of scores of gay couples in celebration of the passage of San Francisco's Domestic Partners Act (1991). In 2004, Mayor Gavin Newsom took a stand against then-current state and federal law by issuing marriage licenses to same-sex partners.

On display in the South Light Court are city artifacts including maps, documents, and photographs. That enormous, 700-pound iron head once crowned the *Goddess of Progress* statue, which topped the old City Hall building until it crumbled during the 1906 earthquake.

Across Polk Street from City Hall is **Civic Center Plaza,** with lawns, walkways, seasonal flower beds, a playground, and an underground parking garage. This sprawling space is generally clean but somewhat grim. Many homeless people hang out here, so the plaza can feel dodgy. ✉ *Bordered by Van Ness Ave. and Polk, Grove, and McAllister Sts., Civic Center* ☎ *415/554–6023 recorded tour info, 415/554–6139 tour reservations* 🌐 *sfgov.org/cityhall/city-hall-tours* 🎫 *Free* ⏲ *Closed weekends.*

Performing Arts

City Box Office

TICKETS | This charge-by-phone service sells tickets for many performances and lectures. You can also buy tickets online, or in person on weekdays from 9:30 to 5:30. ✉ *180 Redwood St., Suite 100, off Van Ness Ave., between Golden Gate Ave. and McAllister St., Civic Center* ☎ *415/392–4400* 🌐 *www.cityboxoffice.com.*

DANCE

★ San Francisco Ballet

DANCE | For ballet lovers, the nation's oldest professional company is reason alone to visit the Bay Area. SFB's performances, for the past three decades under the direction of Helgi Tomasson, have won critical raves. The primary season runs from February through May. The repertoire includes full-length ballets such as *Don Quixote* and *Sleeping Beauty*; the December presentation of *The Nutcracker* is truly spectacular. The company also performs bold new dances from star choreographers such as William Forsythe and Mark Morris, alongside modern classics by George Balanchine and Jerome Robbins. Tickets are available at the **War Memorial Opera House.** ✉ *War Memorial Opera House, 301 Van Ness Ave., at Grove St., Civic Center* ☎ *415/865–2000* 🌐 *www.sfballet.org.*

MUSIC

★ San Francisco Symphony

MUSIC | One of America's top orchestras performs from September through May, with additional summer performances of light classical music and show tunes. The orchestra and its charismatic music director, Michael Tilson Thomas, known for his daring programming of 20th-century American works, often perform with soloists of the caliber of Andre Watts, Gil Shaham, and Renée Fleming. The symphony's adventurous projects include its collaboration with the heavy-metal band Metallica. ■ **TIP→ Deep discounts on tickets are often available through Travelzoo,**

Groupon, and other vendors. ✉ *Davies Symphony Hall, 201 Van Ness Ave., at Grove St., Civic Center* ☎ *415/864–6000* 🌐 *www.sfsymphony.org.*

OPERA

★ San Francisco Opera

OPERA | Founded in 1923, this internationally recognized organization has occupied the War Memorial Opera House since the building's completion in 1932. From September through December and June through July, the company presents a wide range of operas, from *Carmen* to an operatic take on *It's a Wonderful Life*. The opera also frequently collaborates with European companies and presents unconventional, sometimes edgy projects designed to attract younger audiences. Translations are projected above the stage during most non-English productions. ✉ *War Memorial Opera House, 301 Van Ness Ave., at Grove St., Civic Center* ☎ *415/864–3330 tickets* 🌐 *www.sfopera.com* ☞ *Box office open Mon. 10–5, Tues.–Fri. 10–6.*

★ War Memorial Opera House

ARTS CENTERS | With its soaring vaulted ceilings and marble foyer, this elegant 3,146-seat venue, built in 1932, rivals the old-world theaters of Europe. Part of the San Francisco War Memorial and Performing Arts Center, which also includes Davies Symphony Hall and Herbst Theatre, this is the home of the San Francisco Opera and the San Francisco Ballet. ✉ *301 Van Ness Ave., at Grove St., Civic Center* ☎ *415/621–6600* 🌐 *www.sfwmpac.org.*

Hayes Valley

A chic neighborhood due west of Civic Center, Hayes Valley has terrific eateries, cool watering holes, and great browsing in its funky clothing, home-decor, and design boutiques. Locals love this quarter, but without any big-name draws it remains off the radar for many visitors.

Sights

★ SFJAZZ Center

ARTS VENUE | Devoted entirely to jazz, the center hosts performances by jazz greats such as McCoy Tyner, Joshua Redman, Regina Carter, and Chick Corea. Walk by and the street-level glass walls will make you feel as if you're inside; head indoors and the acoustics will knock your socks off. ✉ *201 Franklin St., at Fell St., Hayes Valley* ☎ *866/920–5299* 🌐 *www.sfjazz.org.*

Restaurants

Nojo Ramen

$$ | JAPANESE | For a little bonhomie before the symphony, it's hard to go wrong with this buzzy (and typically crowded) ramen spot. Noodles are the star of the menu, and deservedly so, but you'll also find izakaya-style small plates and comfort food like chicken teriyaki. **Known for:** ramen with chicken-based (paitan) broth; Japanese comfort foods; long lines. 💲 *Average main: $17* ✉ *231 Franklin St., Hayes Valley* ☎ *415/896–4587* 🌐 *www.nojosf.com* 🕒 *Closed Mon. No lunch.*

★ Rich Table

$$$$ | MODERN AMERICAN | Sardine chips and porcini doughnuts are popular bites at co-chefs Evan and Sarah Rich's lively restaurant—and indicative of its creativity. The mains are also clever stunners: try one of the proteins or pastas, like the sea urchin cacio e pepe. **Known for:** creative food; freshly baked bread; seasonal ingredients. 💲 *Average main: $34* ✉ *199 Gough St., Hayes Valley* ☎ *415/355–9085* 🌐 *www.richtablesf.com* 🕒 *No lunch.*

★ Zuni Café

$$$$ | MEDITERRANEAN | After one bite of Zuni's succulent brick-oven-roasted whole chicken with Tuscan bread salad, you'll understand why the two-floor café is a perennial star. Its long copper bar is a hub for a disparate mix of patrons who commune over oysters on the half shell and cocktails and wine. **Known for:** famous roast chicken; classic San Francisco dining; power lunches. Ⓢ *Average main: $35* ✉ *1658 Market St., Hayes Valley* ☎ *415/552–2522* 🌐 *www.zunicafe.com* ⏲ *Closed Mon.*

Hotels

★ Metro Hotel

$ | HOTEL | These tiny rooms, with simple yet modern decor and equipped with private, if small, bathrooms, are within walking distance to the lively Haight, Hayes Valley, Panhandle, NoPa, and Castro neighborhoods. **Pros:** can't beat the price; out-of-downtown location; friendly staffers. **Cons:** small rooms and bathrooms; street noise; no elevator. Ⓢ *Rooms from: $107* ✉ *319 Divisadero St., Hayes Valley* ☎ *415/861–5364* 🌐 *www.metrohotelsf.com* 🛏 *24 rooms* 🍽 *No meals.*

Nightlife

★ Smuggler's Cove

BARS/PUBS | With the decor of a pirate ship and a slew of rum-based cocktails, you half expect Captain Jack Sparrow to sidle up next to you at this offbeat, Disney-esque hangout. But don't let the kitschy ambience fool you. The folks at Smuggler's Cove take rum so seriously they've even had it made for them from distillers around the world, which you can sample along with more than 550 other offerings, some of them vintage and very hard to find. A punch card is provided so you can try the entire menu (featuring 80-plus cocktails) and remember where you left off without getting shipwrecked. The small space fills up quickly, so arrive early. ✉ *650 Gough St., at McAllister St., Hayes Valley* ☎ *415/869–1900* 🌐 *www.smugglerscovesf.com.*

Performing Arts

★ SFJAZZ Center

MUSIC | Jazz legends Branford Marsalis and Herbie Hancock have performed at the snazzy center, as have Rosanne Cash and world-music favorite Esperanza Spalding. The sight lines and acoustics here impress. Shows often sell out quickly. ✉ *201 Franklin St., Hayes Valley* ☎ *866/920–5299* 🌐 *www.sfjazz.org.*

Shopping

FOOD AND DRINK

Arlequin Wine Merchant

WINE/SPIRITS | If you like the wine list at Absinthe Brasserie, you can walk next door and pick up a few bottles from its highly regarded sister establishment. This small, unintimidating shop carries hard-to-find wines from small producers. Why wait to taste? Crack open a bottle on the patio out back. ✉ *384A Hayes St., near Gough St., Hayes Valley* ☎ *415/863–1104* 🌐 *www.arlequinwinemerchant.com.*

Miette

FOOD/CANDY | There is truly nothing sweeter than a cellophane bag tied with colorful ribbon and filled with malt balls or floral meringues from this Insta-friendly candy and pastry-store. Grab a gingerbread cupcake or a tantalizing macaron or some shortbread. The pastel-color cake stands make even window-shopping a treat. ✉ *449 Octavia Blvd., between Hayes and Linden Sts., Hayes Valley* ☎ *415/626–6221* 🌐 *www.miette.com.*

Nob Hill

Nob Hill was officially dubbed during the 1870s when "the Big Four"—Charles Crocker, Leland Stanford, Mark Hopkins, and Collis P. Huntington, who were involved in the construction of the transcontinental railroad—built their hilltop estates. The lingo is thick from this era: those on the hilltop were referred to as "nabobs" (originally meaning a provincial governor from India) and "swells," and the hill itself was called Snob Hill, a term that survives to this day. By 1882 so many estates had sprung up on Nob Hill that Robert Louis Stevenson called it "the hill of palaces." But the 1906 earthquake and fire destroyed all the palatial mansions except for portions of the James Flood brownstone. History buffs may choose to linger here, but for most visitors, a casual glimpse from a cable car will be enough.

Sights

Cable Car Museum

MUSEUM | FAMILY | One of the city's best free offerings, this museum is an absolute must for kids. You can even ride a cable car here—all three lines stop between Russian Hill and Nob Hill. The facility, which is inside the city's last cable-car barn, takes the top off the system to let you see how it all works. Eternally humming and squealing, the massive powerhouse cable wheels steal the show. You can also climb aboard a vintage car and take the grip, let the kids ring a cable-car bell (briefly), and check out vintage gear dating from 1873. ✉ *1201 Mason St., at Washington St., Nob Hill* ☎ *415/474–1887* 🌐 *www.cablecarmuseum.org* 🎫 *Free.*

Grace Cathedral

RELIGIOUS SITE | Not many churches can boast an altarpiece by Keith Haring and not one but two labyrinths. The seat of the Episcopal Church in San Francisco, this soaring Gothic-style structure, erected on the site of the 19th-century railroad baron Charles Crocker's mansion, took 14 years to build, beginning in 1927 and eventually wrapping up in 1964. The gilded bronze doors at the east entrance were taken from casts of Lorenzo Ghiberti's incredible Gates of Paradise, which are on the Baptistery in Florence, Italy. A sculpture of St. Francis by Beniamino Bufano greets you as you enter. The 34-foot-wide limestone labyrinth is a replica of the 13th-century stone maze on the floor of Chartres Cathedral. All are encouraged to walk the 1/8-mile-long labyrinth, a ritual based on the tradition of meditative walking. There's also a granite outdoor labyrinth on the church's northeast side. The AIDS Interfaith Chapel, to the right as you enter Grace, contains a bronze triptych by the late artist Keith Haring and panels from the AIDS Memorial Quilt. **■ TIP→ Especially dramatic times to view the cathedral are during Thursday-night evensong (5:15 pm) and during special holiday programs.** ✉ *1100 California St., at Taylor St., Nob Hill* ☎ *415/749–6300* 🌐 *www.gracecathedral.org* 🎫 *Free; tours $25.*

Restaurants

★ Sons & Daughters

$$$$ | AMERICAN | The nine-course tasting menu that chef-owner Teague Moriarty serves at his elegant Michelin-starred restaurant serves as a primer for how to do highly seasonal cuisine—and tasting menus—the right way. Each course is nuanced and beautifully executed, whether it's tender grilled squid with a fennel-persimmon mole or a sorrel granita with buckwheat shortbread. **Known for:** changing prix-fixe menu; excellent housemade bread; attentive service. 💲 *Average main: $145* ✉ *708 Bush St., Nob Hill* ☎ *415/391–8311* 🌐 *www.sonsanddaughterssf.com* ⊘ *No lunch.*

Hotels

Fairmont San Francisco

$$$$ | HOTEL | Dominating the top of Nob Hill like a European palace, the Fairmont indulges guests in luxury—rooms in the main building, adorned in sapphire blues with platinum and pewter accents, have high ceilings, decadent beds, and marble bathrooms; rooms in the newer Tower, many with fine views, have a neutral color palette with bright-silver notes. **Pros:** huge bathrooms; stunning lobby; great location. **Cons:** some older rooms are small; hills can be challenging for those on foot. *Rooms from: $459 ✉ 950 Mason St., Nob Hill ☎ 415/772–5000, 800/257–7544 🌐 www.fairmont.com/san-francisco 606 rooms No meals.*

★ The Ritz-Carlton, San Francisco

$$$$ | **HOTEL** | A tribute to beauty and attentive, professional service, the Ritz-Carlton emphasizes luxury and elegance, which is evident in the Ionic columns that grace the neoclassical facade and the crystal chandeliers that illuminate marble floors and walls in the lobby. **Pros:** terrific service; beautiful surroundings; Parallel 37 restaurant and Lobby Lounge. **Cons:** expensive; hilly location; no pool. *Rooms from: $538 ✉ 600 Stockton St., at Pine St., Nob Hill ☎ 415/296–7465, 800/542–8680 🌐 www.ritzcarlton.com/sanfrancisco 336 rooms No meals.*

Polk Gulch

Polk Gulch, the microhood surrounding north–south Polk Street, hugs the western edges of Nob Hill and Russian Hill but is nothing like either. It's actually two microhoods: Upper Polk Gulch, fairly classy in its northern section, runs from about Union Street south to California Street; Lower Polk Gulch, the rougher southern part, continues south from California to Geary or so. Polk Gulch was the Castro before the Castro. It was the city's gay neighborhood into the 1970s, hosting San Francisco's first pride parade in 1972 and several festive Halloween extravaganzas.

Restaurants

★ Acquerello

$$$$ | **ITALIAN** | Chef-co-owner Suzette Gresham has elicited plenty of swoons over the years with her high-end but soulful Italian cooking. Her Parmesan *budino* (pudding) is a star of the menu, which features both classic and cutting-edge dishes. **Known for:** prix-fixe dining; Parmesan budino; extensive Italian wine list. *Average main: $95 ✉ 1722 Sacramento St., Polk Gulch ☎ 415/567–5432 🌐 www.acquerello.com ⏲ Closed Sun. and Mon. No lunch.*

★ Lord Stanley

$$$$ | **AMERICAN** | Husband-and-wife team Carrie and Rupert Blease bring European training and a Californian sensibility to their sophisticated but approachable Michelin-starred cooking, pairing refined technique with earthy and inventive charm. You may find kimchi dip accompanying *brandade* (creamed cod) beignets, or tender roast duck served with sweet-and-sour cabbage heart. **Known for:** excellent wine list; new interpretations of California cooking; attentive service. *Average main: $35 ✉ 2065 Polk St., Polk Gulch ☎ 415/872–5512 🌐 lordstanleysf.com ⏲ Closed Mon. No lunch.*

★ Swan Oyster Depot

$$ | **SEAFOOD** | Half fish market and half diner, this small, slim, family-run seafood operation, open since 1912, has no tables, just a narrow marble counter with about 18 stools. Most people come in to buy perfectly fresh salmon, halibut, crabs, and other seafood to take home. **Known for:** fresh seafood; long lines; rich history. *Average main: $18 ✉ 1517 Polk St., Polk Gulch ☎ 415/673–1101 No credit cards ⏲ Closed Sun. No dinner.*

Russian Hill

Essentially a tony residential neighborhood of spiffy pieds-à-terre, Victorian flats, Edwardian cottages, and boxlike condos, Russian Hill has some of the city's loveliest stairway walks, hidden garden ways, and steepest streets—not to mention those bay views.

Sights

1 Cable Car Museum D4
2 Grace Cathedral D5
3 Lombard Street B2
4 San Francisco Art Institute C1

Restaurants

1 Acquerello.............. A5
2 Lord Stanley............ A4
3 Sons & Daughters E5
4 Swan Oyster Depot..... B5

Hotels

1 Fairmont San Francisco............ E5
2 The Ritz-Carlton, San Francisco............ E5

Sights

Lombard Street

NEIGHBORHOOD | The block-long "Crookedest Street in the World" makes eight switchbacks down the east face of Russian Hill between Hyde and Leavenworth streets. Residents bemoan the traffic jam outside their front doors, but the throngs continue. Join the line of cars waiting to drive down the steep hill, or avoid the whole mess and walk down the steps on either side of Lombard. You take in super views of North Beach and Coit Tower whether you walk or drive—though if you're the one behind the wheel, you'd better keep your eye on the road lest you become yet another of the many folks who ram the garden barriers. **■ TIP→ Can't stand the traffic? Thrill seekers of a different stripe may want to head two blocks south of Lombard to Filbert Street. At a gradient of 31.5%, the hair-raising descent between Hyde and Leavenworth streets is one of the city's steepest. Go slowly!** ✉ *Lombard St. between Hyde and Leavenworth Sts., Russian Hill.*

San Francisco Art Institute

MUSEUM | The number-one reason for a visit is Mexican master Diego Rivera's *The Making of a Fresco Showing the Building of a City* (1931), in the student gallery to your immediate left inside the entrance. Rivera himself is in the fresco—his broad behind is to the viewer—and he's surrounded by his assistants. They in turn are surrounded by a construction scene, laborers, and city notables such as sculptor Robert Stackpole and architect Timothy Pflueger. *Making* is one of three San Francisco murals painted by Rivera. The number-two reason to come here is the café, or more precisely the eye-popping, panoramic view from the café, which serves surprisingly decent food for a song.

The **Walter & McBean Galleries** (*415/749–4563; Tues. 11–7, Wed.–Sat. 11–6*) exhibit the often provocative works of established artists. ✉ *800 Chestnut St., Russian Hill* ☎ *415/771–7020* 🌐 *www.sfai.edu* 🎫 *Galleries free.*

North Beach

San Francisco novelist Herbert Gold calls North Beach "the longest-running, most glorious, American bohemian operetta outside Greenwich Village." Indeed, to anyone who's spent some time in its eccentric old bars and cafés, North Beach evokes everything from the Barbary Coast days to the no-less-rowdy Beatnik era.

Sights

★ City Lights Bookstore

STORE/MALL | Take a look at the exterior of the store: the replica of a revolutionary mural destroyed in Chiapas, Mexico, by military forces; the art banners hanging above the windows. This place isn't just doling out best sellers. Designated a city landmark, the hangout of Beat-era writers and independent publishers remains a vital part of San Francisco's literary scene. Browse the three levels of poetry, philosophy, politics, fiction, history, and local zines, to the tune of creaking wood floors.

Back in the day, writers like Ginsberg and Jack Kerouac would read and even receive mail in the basement. Co-founder Lawrence Ferlinghetti cemented City Lights's place in history by publishing Ginsberg's *Howl and Other Poems* in 1956. The small volume was ignored in the mainstream ... until Ferlinghetti and the bookstore manager were arrested for obscenity and corruption of youth. In the landmark First Amendment trial that followed, the judge exonerated both men, declaring that a work that has "redeeming social significance" can't be obscene. *Howl* went on to become a classic.

Continued on page 225

SAN FRANCISCO'S CABLE CARS

The moment it dawns on you that you severely underestimated the steepness of the San Francisco hills will likely be the same moment you look down and realize those tracks aren't just for show—or just for tourists.

Sure, locals rarely use the cable cars for commuting these days. (That's partially due to the $7 fare—hear that, Muni?) So you'll likely be packed in with plenty of fellow sightseers. You may even be approaching cable-car fatigue after seeing its image on so many souvenirs. But if you fear the magic is gone, simply climb on board, and those jaded thoughts will dissolve. Grab the pole and gawk at the view as the car clanks down an insanely steep grade toward the bay. Listen to the humming cable, the clang of the bell, and the occasional quip from the gripman. It's an experience you shouldn't pass up, whether on your first trip or your fiftieth.

HOW CABLE CARS WORK

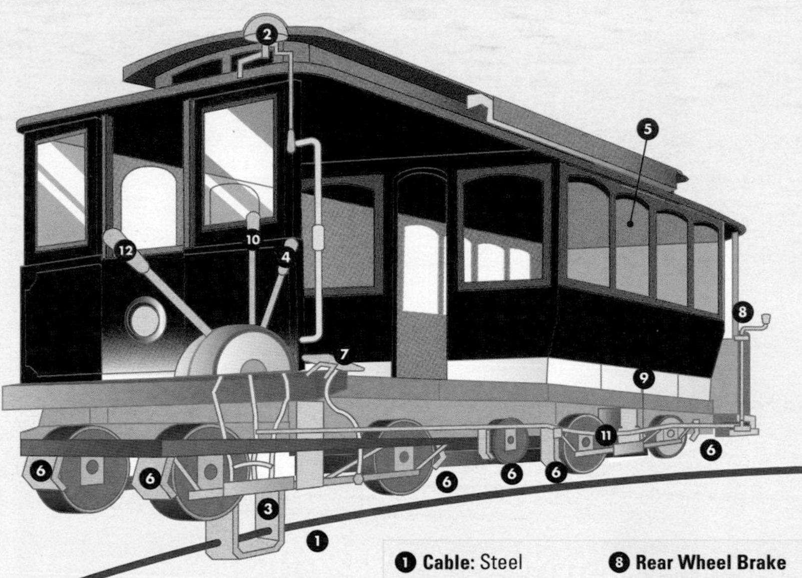

The mechanics are pretty simple: cable cars grab a moving subterranean cable with a "grip" to go. To stop, they release the grip and apply one or more types of brakes. Four cables, totaling 9 miles, power the city's three lines. If the gripman doesn't adjust the grip just right when going up a steep hill, the cable will start to slip and the car will have to back down the hill and try again. This is an extremely rare occurrence—imagine the ribbing the gripman gets back at the cable car barn!

Gripman: Stands in front and operates the grip, brakes, and bell. Favorite joke, especially at the peak of a steep hill: "This is my first day on the job folks . . ."

Conductor: Moves around the car, deals with tickets, alerts the grip about what's coming up, and operates the rear wheel brakes.

❶ **Cable:** Steel wrapped around flexible sisal core; 2 inches thick; runs at a constant 9½ mph.

❷ **Bells:** Used for crew communication; alerts other drivers and pedestrians.

❸ **Grip:** Vice-like lever extends through the center slot in the track to grab or release the cable.

❹ **Grip Lever:** Left-hand lever; operates grip.

❺ **Car:** Entire car weighs 8 tons.

❻ **Wheel Brake:** Steel brake pads on each wheel.

❼ **Wheel Brake Lever:** Foot pedal; operates wheel brakes.

❽ **Rear Wheel Brake Lever:** Applied for extra traction on hills.

❾ **Track Brake:** 2-foot-long sections of Monterey pine push down against the track to help stop the car.

❿ **Track Brake Lever:** Middle lever; operates track brakes.

⓫ **Emergency Brake:** 18-inch steel wedge, jams into street slot to bring car to an immediate stop.

⓬ **Emergency Brake Lever:** Right-hand lever, red; operates emergency brake.

ROUTES

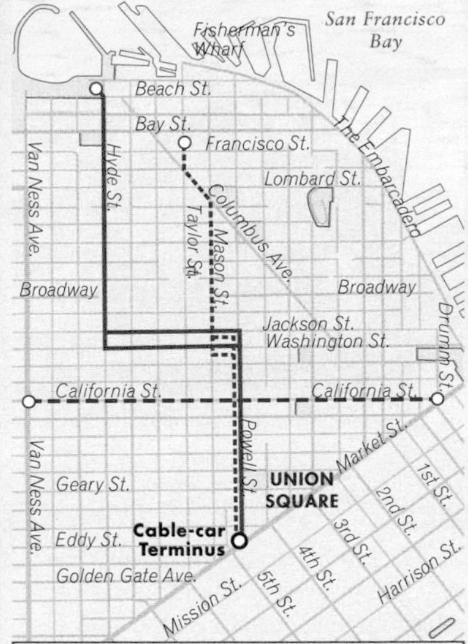

Cars run at least every 15 minutes, from around 6 am to about 1 am.

Powell–Hyde line: Most scenic, with classic Bay views. Begins at Powell and Market streets, then crosses Nob Hill and Russian Hill before a white-knuckle descent down Hyde Street, ending near the Hyde Street Pier.

Powell–Mason line: Also begins at Powell and Market streets, but winds through North Beach to Bay and Taylor streets, a few blocks from Fisherman's Wharf.

California line: Runs from the foot of Market Street, at Drumm Street, up Nob Hill and back. Great views (and aromas and sounds) of Chinatown on the way up. Sit in back to catch glimpses of the Bay. **■TIP➔ Take the California line if it's just the cable-car experience you're after—the lines are shorter, and the grips and conductors say it's friendlier and has a slower pace.**

RULES OF THE RIDE

Tickets. There are ticket booths at all three turnarounds, or you can pay the conductor after you board (they can make change). Try not to grumble about the price—they're embarrassed enough as it is.

■TIP➔ If you're planning to use public transit a few times, or if you'd like to ride back and forth on the cable car without worrying about the price, consider a one-day Muni passport. You can get passports online, at the Powell Street turnaround, the TIX booth on Union Square, or the Fisherman's Wharf cable-car ticket booth at Beach and Hyde streets.

All Aboard. You can board on either side of the cable car. It's legal to stand on the running boards and hang on to the pole, but keep your ears open for the gripman's warnings. **■TIP➔ Grab a seat on the outside bench for the best views.**

Most people wait (and wait) in line at one of the cable car turnarounds, but you can also hop on along the route. Board wherever you see a white sign showing a figure climbing aboard a brown cable car; wave to the approaching driver, and wait until the car stops.

Riding on the running boards can be part of the thrill.

CABLE CAR HISTORY

HALLIDIE FREES THE HORSES

In the 1850s and '60s, San Francisco's streetcars were drawn by horses. Legend has it that the horrible sight of a car dragging a team of horses downhill to their deaths roused Andrew Smith Hallidie to action. The English immigrant had invented the "Hallidie Ropeway," essentially a cable car for mined ore, and he was convinced that his invention could also move people. In 1873, Hallidie and his intrepid crew prepared to test the first cable car high on Russian Hill. The anxious engineer peered down into the foggy darkness, failed to see the bottom of the hill, and promptly turned the controls over to Hallidie. Needless to say, the thing worked . . . but rides were free for the first two days because people were afraid to get on.

SEE IT FOR YOURSELF

The Cable Car Museum is one of the city's best free offerings and an absolute must for kids. (You can even ride a cable car there, since all three lines stop between Russian Hill and Nob Hill.) The museum, which is inside the city's last cable-car barn, takes the top off the system to let you see how it all works. Eternally humming and squealing, the massive powerhouse cable wheels steal the show. You can also climb aboard a vintage car and take the grip, let the kids ring a cable-car bell (briefly, please!), and check out vintage gear dating from 1873.

■ TIP→ The gift shop sells cable car paraphernalia, including an authentic gripman's bell for $600 (it'll sound like Powell Street in your house every day). For significantly less, you can pick up a key chain made from a piece of worn-out cable.

CHAMPION OF THE CABLE CAR BELL

Each September the city's best and brightest come together to crown a bell-ringing champion at Union Square. The crowd cheers gripmen and conductors as they stomp, shake, and riff with the rope. But it's not a popularity contest; the ringers are judged by former bell-ringing champions who take each ping and gong very seriously.

Stroll Kerouac Alley, branching off Columbus Avenue next to City Lights, to read the quotes from Ferlinghetti, Maya Angelou, Confucius, John Steinbeck, and the street's namesake embedded in the pavement. ✉ *261 Columbus Ave., North Beach* ☎ *415/362–8193* 🌐 *www.citylights.com.*

Coit Tower

BUILDING | Among San Francisco's most distinctive skyline sights, this 210-foot tower is often considered a tribute to firefighters because of the donor's special attachment to the local fire company. As the story goes, a young gold rush–era girl, Lillie Hitchcock Coit (known as Miss Lil), was a fervent admirer of her local fire company—so much so that she once deserted a wedding party and chased down the street after her favorite engine, Knickerbocker No. 5, while clad in her bridesmaid finery. She became the Knickerbocker Company's mascot and always signed her name "Lillie Coit 5." When Lillie died in 1929 she left the city $125,000 to "expend in an appropriate manner … to the beauty of San Francisco." You can ride the elevator to the top of the tower—the only thing you have to pay for here—to enjoy the view of the Bay Bridge and the Golden Gate Bridge; due north is Alcatraz Island. Most visitors saunter right past the 27 fabulous Depression-era murals inside the tower that depict California's economic and political life, but take the time to appreciate the first New Deal art project supported by taxpayer money. ✉ *Telegraph Hill Blvd. at Greenwich St. or Lombard St., North Beach* ☎ *415/362–0808* 🌐 *sfrecpark.org* 🎫 *Free; elevator to top $9.*

Grant Avenue

NEIGHBORHOOD | Originally called Calle de la Fundación, Grant Avenue is the oldest street in the city, but it's got plenty of young blood. Here dusty bars such as the Saloon and perennial favorites like the Savoy Tivoli mix with hotshot boutiques, odd curio shops and antique jumbles like the vintage map store Schein & Schein, atmospheric cafés such as the boho haven Caffè Trieste, and authentic Italian delis. While the street runs from Union Square through Chinatown, North Beach, and beyond, the fun stuff in this neighborhood is crowded into the four blocks between Columbus Avenue and Filbert Street. ✉ *North Beach.*

★ Telegraph Hill

NEIGHBORHOOD | Residents here have some of the city's best views, as well as the most difficult ascents to their aeries. The hill rises from the east end of Lombard Street to a height of 284 feet and is capped by Coit Tower. Imagine lugging your groceries up that! If you brave the slope, though, you can be rewarded with a "secret treasure" San Francisco moment. Filbert Street starts up the hill, then becomes the **Filbert Steps** when the going gets too steep. You can cut between the Filbert Steps and another flight, the **Greenwich Steps,** on up to the hilltop. As you climb, you can pass some of the city's oldest houses and be surrounded by beautiful, flowering private gardens. In some places the trees grow over the stairs so it feels like you're walking through a green tunnel; elsewhere, you'll have wide-open views of the bay. The cypress trees that grow on the hill are a favorite roost of local avian celebrities, the wild parrots of Telegraph Hill; you'll hear the cries of the cherry-headed conures if they're nearby. And the telegraphic name? It comes from the hill's status as the first Morse code signal station back in 1853. ✉ *Bordered by Lombard, Filbert, Kearny, and Sansome Sts., North Beach.*

Washington Square

PLAZA | Once the daytime social heart of Little Italy, this grassy patch has changed character numerous times over the years. The Beats hung out here in the 1950s, hippies camped out in the 1960s and early '70s, and nowadays you're more

The Birds

While on Telegraph Hill, you might be startled by a chorus of piercing squawks and a rushing sound of wings. No, you're not about to have a Hitchcock bird-attack moment. These small, vivid green parrots with cherry red heads number in the hundreds; they're descendants of former pets that escaped or were released by their owners. (The birds dislike cages, and they bite if bothered—must've been some disillusioned owners along the way.)

The parrots like to roost high in the aging cypress trees on the hill, chattering and fluttering, sometimes taking wing en masse. They're not popular with some residents, but they did find a champion in local bohemian Mark Bittner, a former street musician. Bittner began chronicling their habits, publishing a book and battling the homeowners who wanted to cut down the cypresses. A documentary, *The Wild Parrots of Telegraph Hill*, made the issue a cause célèbre. In 2007 City Hall, which recognizes a golden goose when it sees one, stepped in and brokered a solution to keep the celebrity birds in town. The city would cover the homeowners' insurance worries and plant new trees for the next generation of wild parrots.

likely to see elderly Asians doing tai chi than Italian folks reminiscing about the old country. You might also see homeless people hanging out on the benches and young locals sunbathing or running their dogs. Lillie Hitchcock Coit, in yet another show of affection for San Francisco's firefighters, donated the statue of two firemen with a child they rescued. ✉ *Bordered by Columbus Ave. and Stockton, Filbert, and Union Sts., North Beach.*

Restaurants

Tony's Pizza Napoletana
$$$ | **PIZZA** | **FAMILY** | Repeatedly crowned the World Champion Pizza Maker at the World Pizza Cup in Naples, Tony Gemignani is renowned here for his flavorful dough and impressive range. The multiple gas, electric, and wood-burning ovens in his casual, modern pizzeria turn out many different pies—the famed Neapolitan-style Margherita, but also Sicilian, Romana, and Detroit styles—while salads, antipasti, homemade pastas, and calzone round out the menu. **Known for:** World Champion Pizza chef; multiple pizza ovens and pie styles; family dining. 💲 *Average main: $27* ✉ *1570 Stockton St., North Beach* ☎ *415/835–9888* 🌐 *www.tonyspizzanapoletana.com* 🕓 *Closed Tues.*

Tosca Cafe
$$$ | **ITALIAN** | The leather booths and chairs are in high demand at this dark and clubby 1919 boho classic, where celebs and local scenesters dine on food that skews Italian. You can eat at the bar, which is first come, first served, or stop by for a cappuccino with local Dandelion chocolate and a shot of bourbon while a jukebox belts out tunes. **Known for:** Italian-American comfort food; tasty cocktails; signature roast chicken for two. 💲 *Average main: $24* ✉ *242 Columbus Ave., North Beach* ☎ *415/986–9651* 🌐 *www.toscacafesf.com* 🕓 *No lunch.*

Hotels

★ San Remo Hotel
$ | **HOTEL** | **FAMILY** | A few blocks from Fisherman's Wharf, this three-story 1906 Italianate Victorian—once home to longshoremen and Beat poets—has a narrow

stairway to the front desk and labyrinthine hallways. **Pros:** inexpensive rates; free Wi-Fi; rooftop penthouse (reserve way ahead) has private bath and deck with Coit Tower views. **Cons:** some rooms are dark; only the penthouse suite has a private bath; parking (discounted fee) is off-site. *Rooms from: $144 ✉ 2237 Mason St., North Beach ☎ 415/776–8688, 800/352–7366 ⊕ www.sanremohotel.com ⇨ 64 rooms 🍽 No meals.*

Nightlife

Bimbo's 365 Club

MUSIC CLUBS | The plush main room and adjacent lounge of this club, here since 1951, retain a retro vibe perfect for the "Cocktail Nation" programming that keeps the crowds entertained. For a taste of the old-school San Francisco nightclub scene, you can't beat it. Indie low-fi and pop bands such as Mustache Harbor and Tainted Love play here. *✉ 1025 Columbus Ave., at Chestnut St., North Beach ☎ 415/474–0365 ⊕ www.bimbos365club.com.*

★ Club Fugazi

CABARET | The claim to fame here is *Beach Blanket Babylon,* an ever-changing wacky musical send-up of San Francisco moods and mores that has been going strong since 1974, making it the longest-running musical revue anywhere. Although the choreography is colorful, the singers brassy, and the satirical songs witty, the real stars are the comically exotic costumes and famous ceiling-high "hats"—which are worth the price of admission alone. The revue sells out as early as a month in advance. *✉ 678 Green St., at Powell St., North Beach ☎ 415/421–4222 ⊕ www.beachblanketbabylon.com.*

★ Vesuvio Cafe

BARS/PUBS | If you're hitting only one bar in North Beach, it should be this one. The low-ceilinged second floor of this raucous boho hangout, little altered since its 1960s heyday (when Jack Kerouac frequented the place), is a fine vantage point for watching the colorful Broadway and Columbus Avenue intersection. Another part of Vesuvio's appeal is its diverse clientele, from older neighborhood regulars and young couples to Bacchanalian posses. *✉ 255 Columbus Ave., at Broadway, North Beach ☎ 415/362–3370 ⊕ www.vesuvio.com.*

SHOPPING

Knitz & Leather

CLOTHING | Local artisans Julia Relinghaus and Katharina Ernst have been producing one-of-a-kind and custom products of extraordinary craftsmanship for 30 years. Ernst's bold knitted sweaters and accessories and Relinghaus's exquisite, high-quality leather jackets for men and women are expensive but made to last. *✉ 1453 Grant Ave., North Beach ☎ 415/391–3480.*

Fisherman's Wharf

The crack of fresh Dungeness crab, the aroma of sourdough warm from the oven, the cry of the gulls—in some ways you can experience Fisherman's Wharf today as it has been for more than 100 years.

Sights

F-line

TRANSPORTATION SITE (AIRPORT/BUS/FERRY/TRAIN) | The city's system of vintage electric trolleys, the F-line, gives the cable cars a run for their money as a beloved mode of transportation. The beautifully restored streetcars—some dating from the 19th century—run from the Castro District down Market Street to the Embarcadero, then north to Fisherman's Wharf. Each car is unique, restored to the colors of its city of origin, from New Orleans and Philadelphia to Moscow and Milan. **■TIP→ Purchase tickets on board; exact change is required.** *✉ San Francisco ⊕ www.streetcar.org 🎟 $3.*

A
B
C
D
E
F
1
2
3
4
5
6
7
8
9
Pier 45
Pier 43
Pier 41
Pier 39
Pier 35
Pier 47
NORTH BEACH
Aquatic Park
Maritime Museum
Ghirardelli Square
Jefferson Street
Beach Street
North Point St.
Bay Street
Columbus Avenue
Mason Street
Powell Street
Taylor Street
Jones Street
Kearny St.
Russian Hill Park
Cable Car
San Francisco Art Institute
Francisco Street
Stockton Street
Pfeiffer St.
TELEGRAPH HILL
Chestnut Street
Lombard Street
Greenwich Street
Hyde Street
Filbert Street
Union Street
Union St.
Grant Ave.
Kearny Street
Van Ness Avenue
Polk Street
Larkin Street
Leavenworth Street
Green Street
Vallejo Street
RUSSIAN HILL
Tunnel
Bernard St.
CHINATOWN
Broadway
John Street
Jackson Street
Washington Street
101
Clay Street
Pleasant St.
Huntington Park
Sacramento Street
POLK GULCH
California Street
NOB HILL
St. Mary's Sq.
Pine Street
Chinatown Gate
Grant Avenue
Bush Street
Sutter Street
Post Street
Geary St.
UNION SQUARE
KEY
Exploring Sights
Restaurants
Hotels
BART station

North Beach, Fisherman's Wharf, and Embarcadero

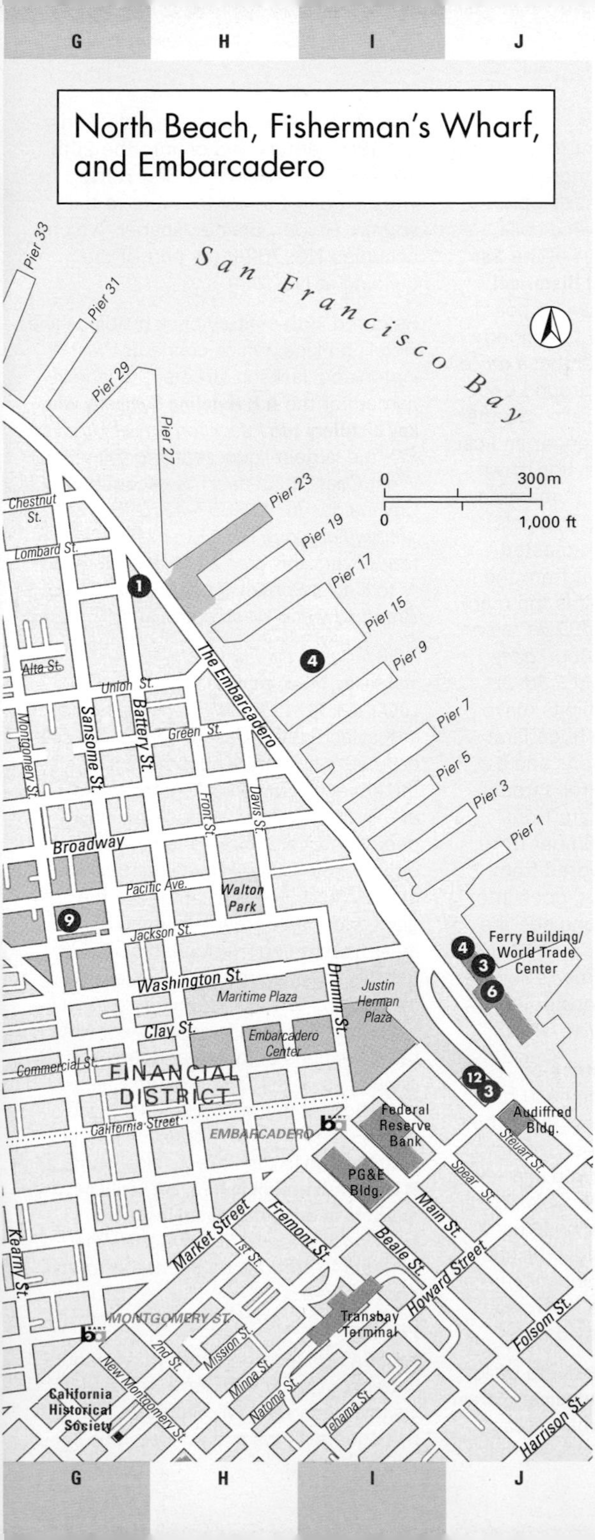

Sights

1 Alcatraz F1
2 City Lights Bookstore F6
3 Coit Tower F4
4 Exploratorium I4
5 F-line C2
6 Ferry Building J6
7 Grant Avenue F6
8 Hyde Street Pier B2
9 Jackson Square Historic District G6
10 Musée Mécanique C2
11 Pier 39 .... E1
12 San Francisco Railway Museum J7
13 Telegraph Hill F4
14 Washington Square E5

Restaurants

1 Fog City G4
2 Gary Danko B3
3 Hog Island Oyster Company J6
4 Slanted Door J6
5 Tony's Pizza Napoletana E5
6 Tosca Cafe F6

Hotels

1 Argonaut Hotel B2
2 Buena Vista Café B3
3 Hotel Vitale J7
4 Hotel Zoe Fisherman's Wharf D3
5 San Remo Hotel D3

★ Hyde Street Pier

MARINA | FAMILY | If you want to get to the heart of the Wharf, there's no better place to do it than at this pier. Don't pass up the centerpiece collection of historic vessels, part of the **San Francisco Maritime National Historical Park,** almost all of which can be boarded. The *Balclutha,* an 1886 full-rigged three-masted sailing vessel that's more than 250 feet long, sailed around Cape Horn 17 times. Kids especially love the *Eureka,* a side-wheel passenger and car ferry, for her onboard collection of vintage cars. The *Hercules* is a steam-powered tugboat, and the *C.A. Thayer* is a beautifully restored three-masted schooner. Across the street from the pier and a museum in itself is the maritime park's **Visitor Center** (*499 Jefferson St., 415/447–5000, June–Aug., daily 9:30–5:30; Sept.–May, daily 9:30–5*), whose fun, large-scale exhibits make it an engaging stop. See a huge First Order Fresnel lighthouse lens and a shipwrecked boat. Then stroll through time in the exhibit "The Waterfront," where you can touch the timber from a gold rush–era ship recovered from below the Financial District, peek into 19th-century storefronts, and see the sails of an Italian fishing vessel. ✉ *Hyde and Jefferson Sts., Fisherman's Wharf* ☎ *415/561–7100* 🌐 *www.nps.gov/safr* 🎫 *Ships $15 (ticket good for 7 days).*

Jackson Square Historic District

NEIGHBORHOOD | This was the heart of the Barbary Coast of the Gay '90s—the 1890s, that is. Although most of the red-light district was destroyed in the fire that followed the 1906 earthquake, the remaining old redbrick buildings, many of them now occupied by advertising agencies, law offices, and antiques firms, retain hints of the romance and rowdiness of San Francisco's early days.

With its gentrified gold rush–era buildings, the 700 block of **Montgomery Street** just barely evokes the Barbary Coast days, but this was a colorful block in the 19th century and on into the 20th. Writers Mark Twain and Bret Harte were among the contributors to the spunky *Golden Era* newspaper, which occupied No. 732 (now part of the building at No. 744).

Restored 19th-century brick buildings line Hotaling Place, which connects Washington and Jackson streets. The lane is named for the **A.P. Hotaling Company whiskey distillery** (*451 Jackson St., at Hotaling Pl.*), the largest liquor repository on the West Coast in its day. The exceptional City Guides (☎ *415/557–4266,* 🌐 *www.sfcityguides.org*) Gold Rush City walking tour covers this area and brings its history to life. ✉ *Bordered by Columbus Ave., Broadway, and Washington and Sansome Sts., San Francisco.*

★ Musée Mécanique

LOCAL INTEREST | FAMILY | Once a staple at Playland-at-the-Beach, San Francisco's early 20th-century amusement park, the antique mechanical contrivances at this time-warped arcade—including peep shows and nickelodeons—make it one of the most worthwhile attractions at the Wharf. Some favorites are the giant and rather creepy "Laffing Sal," an arm-wrestling machine, the world's only steam-powered motorcycle, and mechanical fortune-telling figures that speak from their curtained boxes. Note the depictions of race that betray the prejudices of the time: stoned Chinese figures in the "Opium-Den" and clown-faced African Americans eating watermelon in the "Mechanical Farm." **■ TIP→ Admission is free, but you'll need quarters to bring the machines to life.** ✉ *Pier 45, Shed A, Fisherman's Wharf* ☎ *415/346–2000* 🌐 *museemecaniquesf.com* 🎫 *Free.*

Pier 39

MARINA | FAMILY | The city's most popular waterfront attraction draws millions of visitors each year, who come to browse through its shops and concessions

Thousands of visitors take ferries to Alcatraz each day to walk in the footsteps of the notorious criminals who were held on "The Rock."

hawking every conceivable form of souvenir. The pier can be quite crowded, and the numerous street performers may leave you feeling more harassed than entertained. Arriving early in the morning ensures you a front-row view of the sea lions that bask here, but if you're here to shop—and make no mistake about it, Pier 39 wants your money—be aware that most stores don't open until 9:30 or 10 (later in winter).

Follow the sound of barking to the northwest side of the pier to view the **sea lions** that flop about the floating docks. During the summer, orange-clad naturalists answer questions and offer fascinating facts about the playful pinnipeds—for example, that most of the animals here are males.

At the **Aquarium of the Bay** (☎ *415/623–5300 or 888/732–3483,* 🌐 *www.aquariumofthebay.org, $27.95, hrs vary but at least 10–6 daily*) moving walkways transport you through a space surrounded on three sides by water filled with indigenous San Francisco Bay marine life, from fish and plankton to sharks. ✉ *Beach St. at Embarcadero, Fisherman's Wharf* 🌐 *www.pier39.com.*

Restaurants

Gary Danko

$$$$ | **AMERICAN** | This San Francisco classic has earned a legion of fans—and a Michelin star—for its namesake chef's refined and creative seasonal California cooking, displayed in dishes such as pan-seared scallops with parsnip puree, and juniper-crusted venison. The cost of a meal is pegged to the number of courses, from three to five, the wine list is the size of a small-town phone book, and the banquette-lined rooms, with stunning floral arrangements, are as memorable as the food and impeccable service. **Known for:** prix-fixe menu; fine dining; extensive wine list. [$] *Average main: $92* ✉ *800 N. Point St., Fisherman's Wharf* ☎ *415/749–2060* 🌐 *www.garydanko.com* ⏲ *No lunch* 🧥 *Jacket required.*

Hotels

★ Argonaut Hotel

$$$ | **HOTEL** | **FAMILY** | The nautically themed Argonaut's spacious guest rooms have exposed-brick walls, wood-beam ceilings, and best of all, windows that open to the sea air and the sounds of the waterfront; many rooms enjoy Alcatraz and Golden Gate Bridge views. **Pros:** bay views; near Hyde Street cable car; toys for the kids. **Cons:** nautical theme isn't for everyone; cramped public areas; far from crosstown attractions. *Rooms from: $269 ✉ 495 Jefferson St., at Hyde St., Fisherman's Wharf ☎ 415/563–0800, 866/415–0704 ⊕ www.argonauthotel.com 252 rooms No meals.*

Hotel Zoe Fisherman's Wharf

$$ | **HOTEL** | A smart-looking boutique hotel with guest-room interiors inspired by luxury Mediterranean yachts, the Zoe aims for subtle contemporary elegance in the form of lightly stained woods and soft-brown and cream fabrics and walls. **Pros:** cozy feeling; steps from Fisherman's Wharf; smart-looking contemporary design. **Cons:** congested touristy area; small rooms; resort fee catches some guests off guard. *Rooms from: $249 ✉ 425 N. Point St., at Mason St., Fisherman's Wharf ☎ 415/561–1100, 800/648–4626 ⊕ www.hotelzoesf.com 221 rooms No meals.*

Nightlife

Buena Vista Café

BARS/PUBS | At the end of the Hyde Street cable-car line, the Buena Vista packs 'em in for its famous Irish coffee—which, according to owners, was the first served stateside (in 1952). The place oozes nostalgia, drawing devoted locals as well as out-of-towners relaxing after a day of sightseeing. It's narrow and can get crowded, but this spot provides a fine alternative to the overpriced tourist joints nearby. *✉ 2765 Hyde St., at Beach St., Fisherman's Wharf ☎ 415/474–5044 ⊕ www.thebuenavista.com.*

Embarcadero

Stretching from below the Bay Bridge to Fisherman's Wharf, San Francisco's flat, accessible waterfront invites you to get up close and personal with the bay, the picturesque and constant backdrop to this stunning city. For decades the Embarcadero was obscured by a terrible raised freeway and known best for the giant buildings on its piers that further cut off the city from the bay. With the freeway gone and a few piers restored for public access, the Embarcadero has been given a new lease on life. Millions of visitors may come through the northern waterfront every year, lured by Fisherman's Wharf and Pier 39, but locals tend to stop short of these, opting instead for the gastronomic pleasures of the Ferry Building. Between the two, though, you'll find tourists and San Franciscans alike soaking up the sun, walking out over the water on a long pier to see the sailboats, savoring the excellent restaurants and old-time watering holes, watching the street performers that crowd Embarcadero Plaza on a sunny day—these are the simple joys that make you happy you're in San Francisco, whether for a few days or a lifetime.

Alcatraz

JAIL | **FAMILY** | Thousands of visitors come every day to walk in the footsteps of Alcatraz's notorious criminals. The stories of life and death on "the Rock" may sometimes be exaggerated, but it's almost impossible to resist the chance to wander the cell block that tamed the country's toughest gangsters and saw daring escape attempts of tremendous desperation. Fewer than 2,000 inmates ever did time on the Rock, and though they weren't the worst criminals, they were definitely the worst prisoners, including Al "Scarface" Capone, Robert "The Birdman" Stroud, and George "Machine Gun" Kelly.

Some tips for escaping to Alcatraz: (1) Buy your ticket in advance. Visit the website for Alcatraz Cruises (🌐 *www.alcatrazcruises.com*) to scout out available departure times for the ferry. Prepay by credit card and keep a receipt record; the ticket price covers the boat ride and the audio tour. Pick up your ticket at the "will call" window at Pier 33 up to an hour before sailing. (2) Dress smart. Bring a jacket to ward off the chill from the boat ride and wear comfortable shoes. (3) Go for the evening tour. You'll get even more out of your Alcatraz experience at night. The evening tour has programs not offered during the day, the bridge-to-bridge view of the city twinkles at night, and your "prison experience" will be amplified as darkness falls. (4) Be mindful of scheduled and limited-capacity talks. Some programs are given only once a day (the schedule is posted in the cell house) and have limited seating, so keep an eye out for a cell-house staffer handing out passes shortly before the start time.

The boat ride to the island is brief (15 minutes), but affords beautiful views of the city, Marin County, and the East Bay. The audio tour, highly recommended, includes observations by guards and prisoners about life in one of America's most notorious penal colonies. Plan your schedule to allow at least three hours for the visit and boat rides combined. Not inspired by the prison? Wander around the lovely native plant gardens and (if the tide is cooperating) the tide pools on the north side of the island. ✉ *Pier 33, Embarcadero* ☎ *415/981–7625* 🌐 *www.nps.gov/alca* 🎫 *From $40.*

★ Exploratorium

MUSEUM | FAMILY | Walking into this fascinating "museum of science, art, and human perception" is like visiting a mad-scientist's laboratory. Most of the exhibits are supersize, and you can play with everything. Signature experiential exhibits include the Tinkering Studio and a glass Bay Observatory building, where the exhibits inside help visitors better understand what they see outside. Get an Alice-in-Wonderland feeling in the distorted room, where you seem to shrink and grow as you walk across the slanted, checkered floor. In the shadow room, a powerful flash freezes an image of your shadow on the wall; jumping is a favorite pose. More than 650 other exhibits focus on sea and insect life, computers, electricity, patterns and light, language, the weather, and more. One surefire hit is the pitch-black, touchy-feely Tactile Dome ($15 extra; reservations required): crawl through a course of ladders, slides, and tunnels, relying solely on your sense of touch." ✉ *Piers 15–17, Embarcadero* ☎ *415/528–4444 general information, 415/528–4407 Tactile Dome reservations* 🌐 *www.exploratorium.edu* 🎫 *$30.*

★ Ferry Building

MARKET | The jewel of the Embarcadero, erected in 1896, is topped by a 230-foot clock tower modeled after the campanile of the cathedral in Seville, Spain. On the morning of April 18, 1906, the tower's four clock faces stopped at 5:17—the moment the great earthquake struck—and stayed still for 12 months.

Today San Franciscans flock to the street-level marketplace, stocking up on supplies from local favorites such as Acme Bread, Cowgirl Creamery, Blue Bottle Coffee, and Humphry Slocombe ice cream. Slanted Door, the city's beloved high-end Vietnamese restaurant, is here, along with the well-regarded Hog Island Oyster Company. On the plaza side, the outdoor tables at Gott's Roadside offer great people-watching with their famous burgers. On Saturday morning the plazas outside the building buzz with an upscale farmers' market where you can buy exotic sandwiches and other munchables. Extending south from the piers north of the building all the way to the Bay Bridge, the waterfront promenade out front is a favorite among joggers and picnickers, with a front-row view of sailboats plying the bay. True to its name, the Ferry Building still serves actual ferries: from its eastern flank they sail to Sausalito, Larkspur, Tiburon, and the East Bay. ✉ *Embarcadero at foot of Market St., Embarcadero* ☎ *415/983–8030* 🌐 *www.ferrybuildingmarketplace.com.*

San Francisco Railway Museum
MUSEUM | **FAMILY** | A labor of love brought to you by the same vintage-transit enthusiasts responsible for the F-line's revival, this one-room museum and store celebrates the city's streetcars and cable cars with photographs, models, and artifacts. The permanent exhibit includes the replicated end of a streetcar with a working cab—complete with controls and a bell—for kids to explore; the cool, antique Wiley birdcage traffic signal; and models and display cases to view. Right on the F-line track, just across from the Ferry Building, this is a great quick stop. ✉ *77 Steuart St., Embarcadero* ☎ *415/974–1948* 🌐 *www.streetcar.org* 🎫 *Free* 🕒 *Closed Mon.*

Restaurants

Fog City
$$ | **AMERICAN** | **FAMILY** | All but hidden on a far-flung stretch of the Embarcadero, this 21st-century diner that's well worth the hike is best known for its updated classics, like a short-rib BLT with kimchi mayo and cornbread that emerges hot from the wood-fired oven. An inviting U-shape bar and tables-with-a-view attract a mix of FiDi locals and tourists who've wandered right into a gold mine. **Known for:** updated diner food; excellent cocktails; views of Battery Street and the Embarcadero. [$] *Average main: $22* ✉ *1300 Battery St., Embarcadero* ☎ *415/982–2000* 🌐 *www.fogcitysf.com.*

Hog Island Oyster Company
$$ | **SEAFOOD** | A thriving oyster farm north of San Francisco in Tomales Bay serves up its harvest at this raw bar and restaurant in the Ferry Building, where devotees come for impeccably fresh oysters and clams on the half shell. Other mollusk-centered options include a first-rate seafood stew, baked oysters, clam chowder, and "steamer" dishes, but the bar also turns out one of the city's best grilled-cheese sandwiches, made with three artisanal cheeses on artisanal bread. **Known for:** fresh oysters; first-rate seafood stew; busy raw bar. [$] *Average main: $19* ✉ *Ferry Bldg., Embarcadero at Market St., Embarcadero* ☎ *415/391–7117* 🌐 *www.hogislandoysters.com.*

Slanted Door
$$$$ | **VIETNAMESE** | Celebrated chef-owner Charles Phan has mastered the upmarket, Western-accented Vietnamese menu, showcased in a big space with sleek wooden tables and chairs, a big bar, an enviable bay view, and dedicated clientele. His popular dishes, including green-papaya salad, daikon rice cakes, cellophane crab noodles, chicken clay pot, and shaking beef (tender beef cubes with garlic and onion) don't come cheap, but they're made with quality ingredients. **Known for:** upscale Vietnamese food; some of the city's best cocktails; bustling dining room with great bay views. [$] *Average main: $38* ✉ *Ferry Bldg., Embarcadero at Market St., Embarcadero* ☎ *415/861–8032* 🌐 *www.slanteddoor.com.*

Hotels

★ Hotel Vitale
$$$$ | **HOTEL** | **FAMILY** | The emphasis on luxury and upscale relaxation at this eight-story bay-front property is apparent: limestone-lined baths stocked with top-of-the-line products; the penthouse-level day spa with soaking tubs set in a rooftop bamboo forest; terraces on the fifth, seventh, and eighth

floors with great waterfront views. **Pros:** family-friendly studios; great waterfront views; penthouse spa. **Cons:** some rooms feel cramped; "urban fee" adds further expense to an already pricey property; yet another charge for Wi-Fi beyond basic. *Rooms from: $385* *8 Mission St., Embarcadero* *415/278–3700, 888/890–8688* *www.hotelvitale.com* *200 rooms* *No meals.*

Nightlife

Hard Water

BARS/PUBS | This waterfront restaurant and bar with stunning bay views pays homage to America's most iconic spirit—bourbon—with a wall of whiskeys and a lineup of specialty cocktails. The menu, crafted by Charles Phan of Slanted Door fame, is an ode to New Orleans cuisine and includes spicy pork-belly cracklings, jambalaya, and other fun snacks. *Pier 3, at Embarcadero, Embarcadero* *415/392–3021* *www.hardwaterbar.com.*

Pagan Idol

BARS/PUBS | Giving the Tonga Bar a run for its money as the kitchiest tiki bar in town, Pagan Idol features a secret back room complete with erupting volcano, giant tikis, and a starry night sky. The folks from Bourbon & Branch are behind this faux pirate ship, so even if the cocktails are served in goofy tiki glasses with paper umbrellas—even if they're on fire—rest assured they're top-shelf and on the money. Expect live music Tuesday through Thursday. *375 Bush St., near Kearney St., Financial District* *415/985–6375* *www.paganidol.com.*

Rickhouse

BARS/PUBS | An after-work FiDi crowd fills this brick-walled and dimly lit speakeasy, revered for its extensive whiskey menu and curated list of seasonal cocktails. It's a beautiful space with barrels aplenty, an evening oasis in a neighborhood that traditionally rolls up the sidewalks at sunset. *246 Kearney St., near Bush St., Financial District* *415/398–2827* *www.rickhousebar.com.*

Shopping

FARMERS' MARKETS

★ Ferry Plaza Farmers' Market

OUTDOOR/FLEA/GREEN MARKETS | The partylike Saturday edition of the city's most upscale and expensive farmers' market places baked goods, gourmet cheeses, smoked fish, and fancy pots of jam alongside organic basil, specialty mushrooms, heirloom tomatoes, and juicy-ripe locally grown fruit. Smaller markets also take place on Tuesday and Thursday from April through December. *Ferry Plaza, at Market St., Embarcadero* *415/291–3276* *www.ferrybuildingmarketplace.com.*

The Marina

Well-funded postcollegiates and the nouveau riche flooded the Marina after the 1989 Loma Prieta earthquake had sent many residents running for more-solid ground, changing the tenor of this formerly low-key neighborhood. The number of yuppie coffee emporiums skyrocketed, a bank became a Williams-Sonoma store, and the local grocer gave way to a Pottery Barn. On weekends a young, fairly homogeneous, well-to-do crowd floods the cafés and bars.

Sights

★ Palace of Fine Arts

BUILDING | At first glance this stunning, rosy rococo palace seems to be from another world, and indeed, it's the sole survivor of the many tinted-plaster structures (a temporary classical city of sorts) built for the 1915 Panama-Pacific International Exposition, the world's fair that celebrated San Francisco's recovery from the 1906 earthquake and fire. The expo buildings originally extended about a mile along the shore. Bernard Maybeck designed this faux-Roman classic beauty, which was reconstructed in concrete and reopened in 1967. A victim of the elements, the Palace required a piece-by-piece renovation that was completed in 2008.

The pseudo-Latin language adorning the Palace's exterior urns continues to stump scholars. The massive columns (each topped with four "weeping maidens"), great rotunda, and swan-filled lagoon have been used in countless fashion layouts, films, and wedding photo shoots. After admiring the lagoon, look across the street to the house at 3460 Baker Street. If the maidens out front look familiar, they should—they're original casts of the "garland ladies" you can see in the Palace's colonnade. ✉ *3301 Lyon St., at Beach St., Marina* ☎ *415/563–6504* *Free.*

Restaurants

A16

$$$$ | **ITALIAN** | Named after a highway that runs through southern Italy, this trattoria specializes in the food from that region, done very, very well. The menu is stocked with pizza and rustic pastas like *maccaronara* with *ragu napoletana* and house-made salted ricotta, as well as entrées like roasted chicken with sage salsa verde. **Known for:** equally noteworthy pastas and pizzas; one of the city's best Italian wine lists; meatball Mondays. $ *Average main: $36* ✉ *2355 Chestnut St., Marina* ☎ *415/771–2216* 🌐 *www.a16pizza.com* ⏲ *No lunch Mon.–Thurs.*

Bistro Aix

$$$ | **BISTRO** | In a neighborhood full of trendy minichains, this over-two-decades-old Californian-French spot is the calm elder statesmen for the often rowdy Marina. The food is unfussy (perfect duck leg confit cassoulet; house-smoked salmon and potato galette) and doesn't try to be anything overly ambitious, yet everything is consistently on the mark. **Known for:** honest bistro cooking with quality ingredients; rear courtyard with beautiful olive tree; warm, romantic atmosphere. $ *Average main: $26* ✉ *3340 Steiner St., Marina* ✣ *Between Chestnut St. and Lombard St.* ☎ *415/202–0100* 🌐 *www.bistroaix.com* ⏲ *Closed Sun.*

Causwells

$$$ | **AMERICAN** | There are two personalities to Chestnut Street's sleek grown-up diner—the double-stack burger that draws burgerhounds from dozens of miles away and the rest of the honest, spruced-up comfort food menu. Start with homemade ricotta and a bountiful salad, then go straight after the burger and jerk chicken with creamed corn, before concluding with the must-try doughnut bread pudding. **Known for:** the Americana burger; excellent wine list full of lesser known regions; kitchen open until midnight on weekends. $ *Average main: $25* ✉ *2346 Chestnut St., Marina* ☎ *415/447–6081* 🌐 *www.causwells.com.*

Greens

$$$ | **VEGETARIAN** | Owned and operated by the San Francisco Zen Center, this legendary vegetarian restaurant gets some of its fresh produce from the center's organic Green Gulch Farm. Despite the lack of meat, hearty dishes from chef Annie Somerville—such as green squash curry and chestnut fettuccine with chanterelle mushrooms—really satisfy. **Known for:** unbeatable views; superb vegetarian food; pizza at lunch. $ *Average main: $25* ✉ *Bldg. A, Fort Mason, 2 Marina Blvd., Marina* ☎ *415/771–6222* 🌐 *www.greensrestaurant.com* ⏲ *No lunch Mon.*

Nightlife

California Wine Merchant

WINE BARS—NIGHTLIFE | Part cluttered shop, part cozy bar, Chestnut Street's marquee wine destination is a longtime favorite for grabbing a glass or three. Wines featured always come from some of the state's most highly regarded vintners of all sizes and celebrity status. The neighborhood has many wine bars, but this is where the locals go when the focus is on the wine itself. *2113 Chestnut St., Marina* *415/567–0646* *www.californiawinemerchant.com.*

The Interval at Long Now

BARS/PUBS | Even many locals don't realize that the Fort Mason Center is home to one of the city's most impressive and scene-free cocktail bars. As part of the Long Now Foundation, a nonprofit devoted to long-term thinking, the cocktails reflect that commitment to finding innovative ways to serve tried-and-true libations. The Navy Gimlet with clarified lime juice is a modern day San Francisco classic. *2 Marina Blvd., Landmark Bldg. A, Marina* *415/496–9187* *www.theinterval.org.*

Cow Hollow

Between old-money Pacific Heights and the well-heeled, postcollegiate Marina lies comfortably upscale Cow Hollow. The neighborhood's name harks back to the 19th-century dairy farms whose owners eked out a living here despite the fact that there was more sand than grass.

Sights

Octagon House

HOUSE | This eight-sided home sits across the street from its original site on Gough Street; it's one of two remaining octagonal houses in the city (the other is on Russian Hill), and the only one open to the public. White quoins accent each of the eight corners of the pretty blue-gray exterior, and a colonial-style garden completes the picture. The house is full of antique American furniture, decorative arts (paintings, silver, rugs), and documents from the 18th and 19th centuries, including the contents of a time capsule left by the original owners in 1861 that was discovered during a 1950s renovation. A deck of Revolutionary-era hand-painted playing cards takes an anti-monarchist position: in place of kings, queens, and jacks, the American upstarts substituted American statesmen, Roman goddesses, and Indian chiefs. Note that the home is only open on the second Sunday, and second and fourth Thursday of each month (closed all January). *2645 Gough St., near Union St., Cow Hollow* *415/441–7512* *nscda-ca.org/octagon-house/* *Free, donations encouraged.*

Restaurants

★ Atelier Crenn

$$$$ | **MODERN FRENCH** | Dinner at the spectacularly inventive flagship of San Francisco's most celebrated chef of the moment, Dominique Crenn, starts with the presentation of a poem. Each course is described by a line in the poem, so the "Hidden beneath the bluffs" might be whole grilled Monterey abalone with a purée of its own liver and a grilled mussel sauce. **Known for:** extraordinary, whimsical tasting menu; stratospheric prices; hip-elegant atmosphere. *Average main: $335* *3127 Fillmore St., Cow Hollow* *415/440–0460* *www.ateliercrenn.com* *Closed Sun. and Mon.*

Bar Crenn

$$$$ | **FRENCH** | Dominique Crenn's sumptuous salon decked out with fur-draped bar stools, chandeliers, and lush velvet drapes is really a bar only in name. Yes, there's a bar pouring outstanding wines and it's possible to graze on warm gougères and oysters. **Known for:** Versailles-style furnishings; eggshell filled with bone marrow custard, topped with caviar; fine Champagne. Ⓢ *Average main: $36* ✉ *3131 Fillmore St., Cow Hollow* ☎ *415/440–0460* 🌐 *www.barcrenn.com* ⏲ *Closed Sun. and Mon.*

Kaiyo

$$ | **PERUVIAN** | San Francisco has a handful of Peruvian restaurants, but this uber hip Union Street spot is the first "Nikkei" cuisine (Japanese-Peruvian) restaurant for diners to explore. Skip the pedestrian *pollo a la brasa* and have fun sampling around the *tiraditos* and sushi rolls. **Known for:** creative pisco cocktails; smoked duck and shaved foie gras sushi; street art murals in bathrooms. Ⓢ *Average main: $18* ✉ *1838 Union St., Cow Hollow* ☎ *415/525–4804* 🌐 *www.kaiyosf.com* ⏲ *Closed Mon.*

Rose's Café

$$$ | **ITALIAN** | **FAMILY** | Although it's open morning until night, this cozy café is most synonymous with brunch. Sleepy-headed locals turn up for delights like the smoked ham, fried egg, and Gruyère breakfast sandwich and the French toast bread pudding with caramelized apples. **Known for:** pizzas for the morning and night; house-baked goods; brunch lines. Ⓢ *Average main: $28* ✉ *2298 Union St., Cow Hollow* ☎ *415/775–2200* 🌐 *www.rosescafesf.com.*

Hotels

★ Union Street Inn

$$ | **B&B/INN** | Antiques, unique artwork, and such touches as candles, fresh flowers, wineglasses, and fine linens make rooms in this green-and-cream 1902 Edwardian popular with honeymooners and those looking for a romantic getaway with an English countryside ambience. **Pros:** personal service; excellent full breakfast; beautiful secret garden. **Cons:** parking is pricey; two-night minimum stay on weekends; no elevator. Ⓢ *Rooms from: $249* ✉ *2229 Union St., Cow Hollow* ☎ *415/346–0424* 🌐 *www.unionstreetinn.com* *6 rooms* *Breakfast.*

Shopping

The Caviar Company

FOOD/CANDY | "The Caviar Sisters" Petra and Saskia Bergstein created this sustainability-minded brand that developed a cult following among caviar connoisseurs and chefs in the Bay Area. Their chic above-street level boutique on Union Street allows the public to pick out some of the finest caviar products in town—and feel good about it. ✉ *1954 Union St., Cow Hollow* ☎ *415/300–0299* 🌐 *www.thecaviarco.com* ⏲ *Closed Mon.*

Ginger Elizabeth Chocolates

FOOD/CANDY | **FAMILY** | A Sacramento chocolatier with a nationally known name expanded to San Francisco in 2018. It's already a marquee destination for macarons or a box of chocolate bonbons with atypical flavors like sweet cream chai and buttermilk lime. ✉ *3108 Fillmore St., Cow Hollow* ☎ *415/671–7113* 🌐 *www.gingerelizabeth.com* ⏲ *Closed Mon. and Tues.*

Wrecking Ball Coffee Roasters

FOOD/CANDY | The Instagram set knows this Wi-Fi-free, almost seating-free Union Street roaster and café as the place with the pineapple wallpaper. Everyone enjoys some of the finest lattes and espresso shots around, usually to-go, but sometimes enjoyed on the low bench in front of that famous wallpaper. ✉ *2271 Union St., Cow Hollow* ☎ *415/638–9227* 🌐 *www.wreckingballcoffee.com.*

Nightlife

The Black Horse London Pub

BARS/PUBS | Barely seven stools fit in San Francisco's smallest bar. Plus, there are just as many bottled beers (no taps) as seats and be sure to bring some cash since credit cards aren't accepted. It's as bare-bones as it gets but there's sports on TV, a fun dice game, and most importantly a neighborhood camaraderie that is increasingly hard to find. ✉ *1514 Union St., Cow Hollow* 🌐 *www.blackhorselondon.com.*

West Coast Wine & Cheese

WINE BARS—NIGHTLIFE | Whether you're in the mood for a Mendocino County rosé or an Oregon Pinot Noir, as the name suggests, you'll find it at this narrow, sleek locals' favorite. The kitchen isn't much more than a stove top, but does some pretty impressive work beyond cheese and charcuterie. Take advantage of the ability to order half pours and sample more wines. ✉ *2165 Union St., Cow Hollow* ☎ *415/376–9720* 🌐 *www.westcoastsf.com.*

Presidio

At the foot of the Golden Gate Bridge, one of city residents' favorite in-town getaways is the 1,400-plus-acre Presidio, which combines accessible nature-in-the-raw with a window into the past.

Sights

★ Baker Beach

BEACH—SIGHT | **FAMILY** | West of the Golden Gate Bridge is a mile-long stretch of soft sand beneath steep cliffs, beloved for its spectacular views and laid-back vibe (read: you'll see naked people here on the northernmost end). Its isolated location makes it rarely crowded, but many San Franciscans know that there is no better place to take in the sunset than this beach. Kids love climbing around the old Battery Chamberlin. This is truly one of those places that inspires local pride. ✉ *Baker Beach, Presidio* ✣ *Accessed from Bowley St. off Lincoln Blvd.* 🌐 *www.parksconservancy.org/parks-baker-beach.*

Crissy Field

BEACH—SIGHT | **FAMILY** | One of the most popular places for San Franciscans to get fresh air is a stretch of restored marshland along the sand of the bay. Kids on bikes, folks walking dogs, and joggers share the paved path along the shore, often winding up at the Warming Hut, a combination café and fun gift store at the end of the path, for a hot chocolate in the shadow of the Golden Gate Bridge. Midway along the Golden Gate Promenade that winds along the shore is the Gulf of the Farallones National Marine Sanctuary Visitor Center, where kids can get a close-up view of small sea creatures and learn about the rich ecosystem offshore. Alongside the main green of Crissy Field, there are several renovated airplane hangars and warehouses that are now home to the likes of rock-climbing gyms, an air trampoline park, and a craft brewery. ✉ *Crissy Field, Presidio* 🌐 *www.presidio.gov/places/crissy-field.*

★ Golden Gate Bridge

BRIDGE/TUNNEL | With its simple but powerful art-deco design, the 1.7-mile suspension span that connects San Francisco and Marin County was built to withstand winds of more than 100 mph. It's also not a bad place to be in an earthquake: designed to sway almost 28 feet, the Golden Gate Bridge (unlike the Bay Bridge) was undamaged by the 1989 Loma Prieta quake. If you're walking on the bridge when it's windy, stand still and you can feel it swaying a bit.

Crossing the Golden Gate Bridge under your own power is exhilarating—a little scary, and definitely chilly. From the bridge's eastern-side walkway, the only side pedestrians are allowed on, you can take in the San Francisco skyline and the bay islands; look west for the wild hills of the Marin Headlands, the curving coast south to Lands End, and the Pacific Ocean. On sunny days, sailboats dot the water, and brave windsurfers test the often-treacherous tides beneath the bridge. A vista point on the Marin County side provides a spectacular city panorama.

A structural engineer, dreamer, and poet named Joseph Strauss worked tirelessly for 20 years to make the bridge a reality, first promoting the idea of it and then

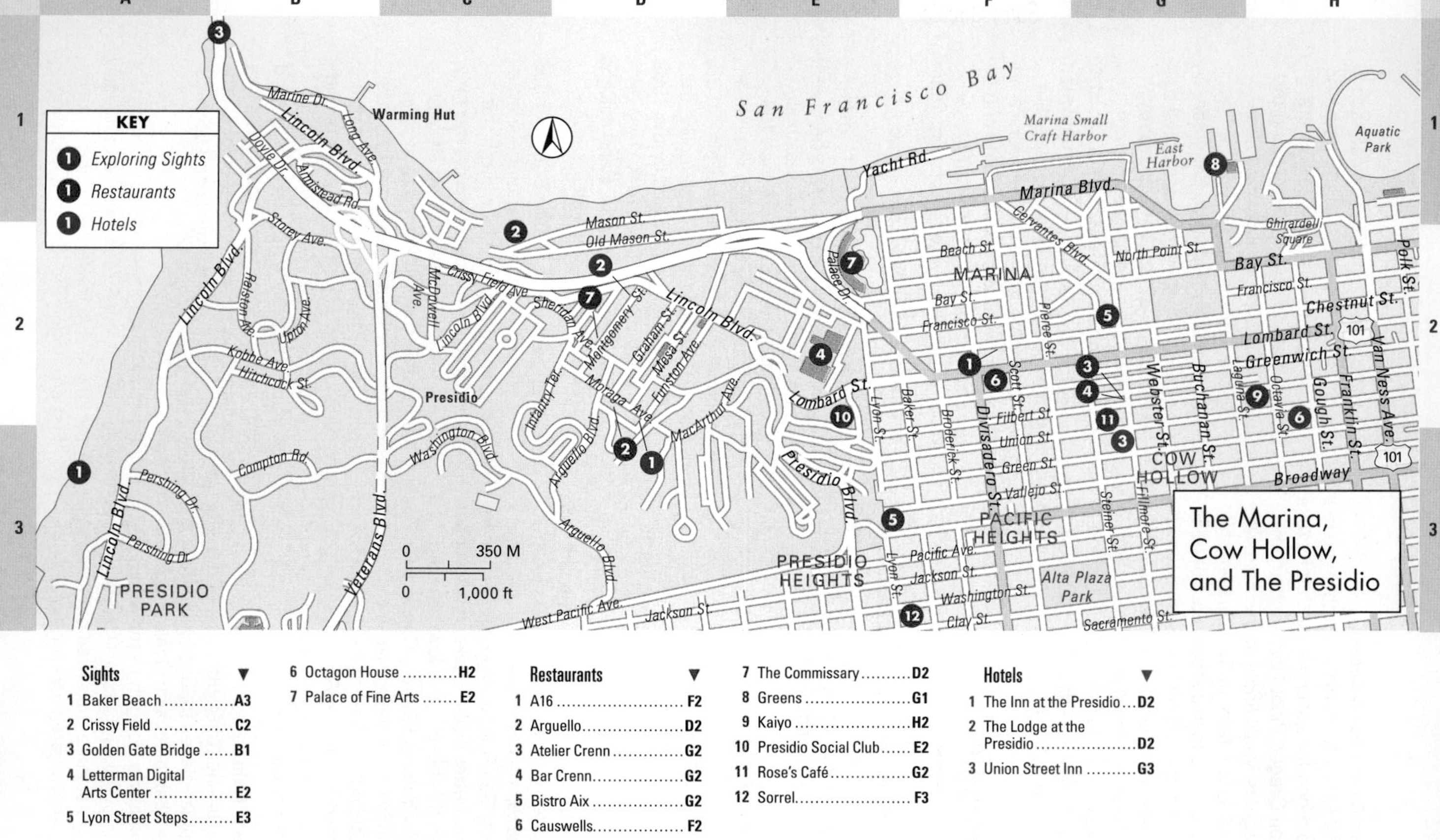

Sights ▼

1 Baker Beach A3
2 Crissy Field C2
3 Golden Gate Bridge B1
4 Letterman Digital Arts Center E2
5 Lyon Street Steps......... E3
6 Octagon House H2
7 Palace of Fine Arts E2

Restaurants ▼

1 A16 .... F2
2 Arguello.................... D2
3 Atelier Crenn G2
4 Bar Crenn.................. G2
5 Bistro Aix G2
6 Causwells.................. F2
7 The Commissary.......... D2
8 Greens G1
9 Kaiyo H2
10 Presidio Social Club...... E2
11 Rose's Café................ G2
12 Sorrel....................... F3

Hotels ▼

1 The Inn at the Presidio ... D2
2 The Lodge at the Presidio D2
3 Union Street Inn G3

overseeing design and construction. Though the final structure bore little resemblance to his original plan, Strauss guarded his legacy jealously, refusing to recognize the seminal contributions of engineer Charles A. Ellis. In 2007, the Golden Gate Bridge district finally recognized Ellis's role, though Strauss, who died less than a year after opening day in 1937, would doubtless be pleased with the inscription on his statue, which stands sentry in the southern parking lot: "The Man Who Built the Bridge."

You won't see it on a T-shirt, but the bridge is perhaps the world's most publicized suicide platform, with an average of one jumper about every 10 days. Signs on the bridge refer the disconsolate to special telephones, and officers patrol the walkway and watch by security camera to spot potential jumpers. A suicide barrier, an unobtrusive net not unlike the one that saved 19 workers during the bridge's construction, is expected to be completed in 2020.

While at the bridge, you can grab a healthy snack at the art deco–style Bridge Café. The Bridge Pavilion sells attractive, high-quality souvenirs and has a small display of historical artifacts. At the outdoor exhibits, you can see the bridge rise before your eyes on hologram panels, learn about the features that make it art deco, and read about the personalities behind its design and construction. City Guides offers free walking tours of the bridge every Thursday and Sunday at 11 am. ✉ *Lincoln Blvd. near Doyle Dr. and Fort Point, Presidio* ☎ *415/921–5858* 🌐 *www.goldengatebridge.org* 🎫 *Free.*

Letterman Digital Arts Center

BUILDING | FAMILY | Bay Area filmmaker George Lucas's 23-acre **Letterman Digital Arts Center,** a digital studio "campus," along the eastern edge of the land, is exquisitely landscaped and largely open to the public. If you have kids in tow or are a *Star Wars* fan yourself, make the pilgrimage to the **Yoda Fountain** (Letterman Drive at Dewitt Road), between two of the arts-center buildings, then take your picture with the life-size Darth Vader statue in the lobby, open to the public on weekdays. ✉ *1 Letterman Dr., Presidio* 🌐 *www.presidio.gov/letterman-digital-arts-center.*

Lyon Street Steps

VIEWPOINT | Get ready for a stairs workout—and a spectacularly rewarding view at the top—when tackling the 332 steps at the eastern edge of the Presidio. There will likely be no shortage of exercise seekers huffing and puffing up the steps, but feel free to conquer the climb slowly. The trimmed hedge landscaping is worthy of its own visit, but there's no doubt that the view of the Presidio forests and the bay are the reason these steps are a top attraction. ✉ *2545 Lyon St., Presidio Heights* ✥ *Between Green St. and Pacific Ave.*

Restaurants

Arguello

$$$ | MODERN MEXICAN | FAMILY | Whether enjoying shrimp tacos at lunch on the beautiful, intimate patio or a perfect margarita with a host of small plates at the bar for a casual dinner, celebrated chef Traci Des Jardins's Californian-Mexican restaurant always hits the right notes. Tortillas and salsas are made in-house, and the tequila and mezcal selection is one of the deepest in San Francisco. **Known for:** intimate outdoor patio; superb pozole verde; various lunch tacos. $ *Average main: $23* ✉ *50 Moraga St., Presidio* ✥ *In Presidio Officers' Club* ☎ *415/561–3650* 🌐 *www.arguellosf.com* ⏲ *Closed Mon. No dinner Tues. and Sun.*

The Commissary

$$$$ | SPANISH | Order a Spanish brandy riff on a Negroni and a few tapas, then get ready for one of the city's top Spanish dining experiences right by the Walt Disney Museum. Chef-owner Traci Des Jardins and her team does a fantastic job incorporating local produce and Bay Area spirit to tapas bar classics like patatas bravas and warm cheese fritters. **Known for:** large format steak dishes; excellent, simple desserts; terrific wine and sherry program but ugly stemless wineglasses. *Average main: $35 ✉ 101 Montgomery St., Presidio ☎ 415/561–3600 🌐 www.thecommissarysf.com ⏲ Closed Sun.*

Presidio Social Club

$$$ | **AMERICAN** | **FAMILY** | Set in an old barracks building at the eastern edge of the Presidio, American comfort classics meet seasonal California cooking. Like the military base/national park itself, the restaurant has a blend of the nostalgic past and the trendy present (beef liver and onions; ahi tuna poke and crisp eggplant fries). **Known for:** weekend brunch; PSC meat loaf; barrel-aged cocktails. *Average main: $24 ✉ 563 Ruger St., Presidio ☎ 415/885–1888 🌐 www.presidiosocialclub.com.*

Sorrel

$$$$ | **MODERN AMERICAN** | After a long run as one of San Francisco's most important dining pop-ups, Alex Hong's refined Californian-Italian cooking finally found a permanent home in 2018. And, what a gorgeous home it is in swanky Laurel Heights! **Known for:** exemplary pastas; dry-aged duck for two; upscale dinner party vibe. *Average main: $33 ✉ 3228 Sacramento St., Presidio Heights ☎ 415/525–3765 🌐 www.sorrelrestaurant.com ⏲ Closed Sun. and Mon.*

Hotels

The Inn at the Presidio

$$$ | **B&B/INN** | **FAMILY** | Built in 1903 and opened as a hotel in 2012, this two-story, Georgian Revival–style structure once served as officers' quarters but now has 26 guest rooms—most of them suites—complete with gas fireplaces and modern-meets-salvage-store finds such as wrought-iron beds, historic black-and-white photos, and Pendleton blankets. **Pros:** beautifully designed rooms; peaceful, away from the frenetic city feel; Presidio's hiking and biking trails, Disney museum, and other attractions. **Cons:** lack of noise blocking because of old building; no elevator; challenging to get a taxi/ride-share. *Rooms from: $310 ✉ 42 Moraga Ave., Presidio ☎ 415/800–7356 🌐 www.innatthepresidio.com 26 rooms Breakfast.*

★ The Lodge at the Presidio

$$$ | **B&B/INN** | The Presidio's hotel population doubled in 2018 with the opening of its second boutique accommodation, a slightly more upscale sibling to The Inn at the Presidio. **Pros:** gorgeous and spacious rooms; charming staff; feels like a vacation from the city within the city. **Cons:** traffic noise is fairly loud in rooms facing Golden Gate Bridge; isolated from many attractions; prices are similar to downtown. *Rooms from: $275 ✉ 105 Montgomery St., Presidio ☎ 415/561–1234 🌐 www.presidiolodging.com/lodge-at-the-presidio 42 rooms Free Breakfast.*

Shopping

Dash Lane

HOUSEHOLD ITEMS/FURNITURE | From longtime landscape designer Katherine Webster, gorgeous outdoor furnishings and accessories are the theme of this beautiful Presidio Heights showroom. While alfresco entertaining is the prominent theme, many of the goods from boutique luxury labels like Janus et Cie and DEDON work just as well indoors. *✉ 3352 B Sacramento St., Presidio Heights ✣ Upstairs from street level at orange door ☎ 415/757–0794 🌐 www.dashlanesf.com.*

Armed with only helmets, safety harnesses, and painting equipment, a full-time crew of 38 painters keeps the Golden Gate Bridge clad in International Orange.

Golden Gate Park

Jogging, cycling, skating, picnicking, going to a museum, checking out a concert, dozing in the sunshine ... Golden Gate Park is the perfect playground for fast-paced types, laid-back dawdlers, and everyone in between.

Sights

★ California Academy of Sciences

MUSEUM | FAMILY | With its native plant–covered living roof, retractable ceiling, three-story rain forest, gigantic planetarium, living coral reef, and frolicking penguins, the California Academy of Sciences is one of the city's most spectacular treasures. Dramatically designed by Renzo Piano, it's an eco-friendly, energy-efficient adventure in biodiversity and green architecture; the roof's large mounds and hills mirror the local topography. Moving away from a restrictive role as a museum that cataloged natural history, the academy these days is all about sustainability and the future, but the locally beloved dioramas in African Hall remain.

By the time you arrive, hopefully you've decided which shows and programs to attend, looked at the academy's floor plan, and designed a plan to cover it all in the time you have. And if not, here's the quick version: Head left from the entrance to the wooden walkway over otherworldly rays in the Philippine Coral Reef, then continue to the Swamp to see Claude, the famous albino alligator. Swing through African Hall and gander at the penguins, take the elevator up to the living roof, then return to the main floor and get in line to explore the Rainforests of the World, ducking free-flying butterflies and watching for other live surprises. You'll end up below ground in the Amazonian Flooded Rainforest, where you can explore the academy's other aquarium exhibits. Phew. The academy's popular adult-only NightLife event, held every Thursday evening, includes after-dark access to all exhibits, as well as special programming and a full bar. ■ **TIP→ Considering the hefty price of admission here, start out early and take advantage of in-and-out privileges to take a break.** ✉ *55 Music Concourse Dr., Golden Gate Park* ☎ *415/379–8000* 🌐 *www.calacademy.org* 🎟 *$36, save $3 if you bike, walk, or take public transit here.*

Conservatory of Flowers

GARDEN | Whatever you do, be sure to at least drive by the Conservatory of Flowers—it's too darn pretty to miss. The gorgeous, white-framed 1878 glass structure is topped with a 14-ton glass dome. Stepping inside the giant greenhouse is like taking a quick trip to the rain forest, with its earthy smell and humid warmth. The undeniable highlight is the Aquatic Plants section, where lily pads float and carnivorous plants dine on bugs to the sounds of rushing water. On the east side of the conservatory (to the right as you face the building), cypress, pine, and redwood trees surround the **Dahlia Garden,** which blooms in summer and fall. Adding to the allure are temporary exhibits such as a past one devoted to prehistoric plants; a recurring holiday-season model-train display punctuated with mini buildings, found objects, and dwarf plants; and a butterfly garden that returns periodically. To the west is the **Rhododendron Dell,** which contains 850 varieties, more than any other garden in the country. It's a favorite local Mother's Day picnic spot. ✉ *John F. Kennedy Dr. at Conservatory Dr., Golden Gate Park* ☎ *415/831–2090* 🌐 *conservatoryofflowers.org* 🎟 *$9, free 1st Tues. of month* ☞ *No strollers allowed inside.*

de Young Museum

MUSEUM | It seems that everyone in town has a strong opinion about the de Young Museum: some adore its striking copper facade, while others just hope that the green patina of age will mellow the effect. Most maligned is the 144-foot tower, but the view from its ninth-story observation room, ringed by floor-to-ceiling windows and free to the public, is worth a trip here by itself. The building almost overshadows the de Young's respected collection of American, African, and Oceanic art. The museum also plays host to major international exhibits, such as 100 works from Paris's Musée National Picasso and a collection of the work of Jean Paul Gaultier from the Montreal Museum of Fine Arts; there's often an extra admission charge for these. The annual Bouquets to Art is a fanciful tribute to the museum's collection by notable Bay Area floral designers. On many Friday evenings in the fall, admission is free and the museum hosts fun events, with live music and a wine and beer bar (the café stays open late, too). ✉ *50 Hagiwara Tea Garden Dr., Golden Gate Park* ☎ *415/750–3600* 🌐 *deyoung.famsf.org* 🎟 *$15, good for same-day admittance to the Legion of Honor; free 1st Tues. of month* ⏲ *Closed Mon.*

The Richmond

In the mid-19th century, the western section of town just north of Golden Gate Park was known as the Outer Lands, covered in sand dunes and seen fit for cemeteries and little else. Today it's the Richmond, comprised of two distinct neighborhoods: the Inner Richmond, from Arguello Boulevard to about 20th Avenue, and the Outer Richmond, from 20th to the ocean.

Sights

Cliff House

LOCAL INTEREST | Spectacular ocean views have been bringing diners to its several restaurants for more than a century—you can see 30 miles or more on a clear day. Three buildings have occupied this site—today owned by the National Park Service—since 1863, and the current building dates from 1909. Sitting on the observation deck is the **Giant Camera,** a camera obscura with its lens pointing skyward housed in a cute yellow-painted wooden shack. Built in the 1940s and threatened many times with demolition, it's now on the National Register of Historic Places. To the north of the Cliff House lie the ruins of the once grand glass-roof **Sutro Baths.** Adolph Sutro, eccentric onetime San Francisco mayor and Cliff House owner, built the bath complex in 1896, so that everyday folks could enjoy the benefits of swimming. Six enormous baths—freshwater and seawater—more than 500 dressing rooms, and several restaurants covered 3 acres north of the Cliff House and accommodated 25,000 bathers. Likened to Roman baths in a European glass palace, the baths were for decades a favorite destination of San Franciscans. The complex fell into disuse after World War II, was closed in 1952, and burned down (under questionable circumstances) during demolition in 1966. ✉ *1090 Point Lobos Ave., Richmond* ☎ *415/386–3330* 🌐 *www.cliffhouse.com* 🎟 *Free.*

Legion of Honor

MUSEUM | Built to commemorate Californian soldiers who died in World War I, and set atop cliffs overlooking the ocean, the Golden Gate Bridge, and the Marin Headlands, this beautiful Beaux Arts building in Lincoln Park displays an impressive collection of 4,000 years of ancient and European art. A pyramidal glass skylight in the entrance court illuminates the lower-level galleries, which exhibit prints and drawings, English and European porcelain, and ancient Assyrian, Greek, Roman, and Egyptian art. The 20-plus galleries on the upper level display the permanent collection of European art (paintings, sculpture, decorative arts, and tapestries) from the 14th century to the present day. The noteworthy Auguste Rodin collection includes two galleries devoted to the master and a third with works by Rodin and other 19th-century sculptors. An original cast of Rodin's *The Thinker* welcomes you as you walk through the courtyard. As fine as the museum is, the setting and view outshine the collection and also make a trip here worthwhile. ✉ *34th Ave. at Clement St., Richmond* ☎ *415/750–3600* 🌐 *legionofhonor.famsf.org* 🎟 *$15, free 1st Tues. of month* ⏲ *Closed Mon.*

★ Lincoln Park

CITY PARK | Although many of the city's green spaces are gentle and welcoming, Lincoln Park is a wild, 275-acre park in the Outer Richmond with windswept cliffs and panoramic views. The Coastal Trail, the park's most dramatic one, leads out to **Lands End**; pick it up west of the Legion of Honor (at the end of El Camino del Mar) or from the parking lot at Point Lobos and El Camino del Mar. Time your hike to hit Mile Rock at low tide, and you might catch a glimpse of two wrecked ships peeking up from their watery graves. ⚠ **Be careful if you hike here; landslides are frequent, and people have fallen into the sea by standing too close to the edge of a crumbling bluff top.**

Lincoln Park's 18-hole golf course is on land that in the 19th century was the Golden Gate Cemetery. In 1900 the Board of Supervisors voted to ban burials within city limits, and all but two city cemeteries (at Mission Dolores and the Presidio) were moved to Colma, a small town just south of San Francisco. When digging has to be done in the park, bones occasionally surface again. ✉ *Entrance at 34th Ave. at Clement St., Richmond.*

Restaurants

Burma Superstar

$ | **ASIAN** | Locals make the trek to the "Avenues" for this perennially crowded spot's flavorful, well-prepared Burmese food, including its extraordinary signature tea leaf salad, a combo of spicy, salty, crunchy, and sour that is mixed

Sights

1 California Academy of Sciences G4
2 Cliff House A2
3 Conservatory of Flowers H3
4 de Young Museum G4
5 Legion of Honor C1
6 Lincoln Park B1

Restaurants

1 Burma Superstar H2
2 Nopalito G5

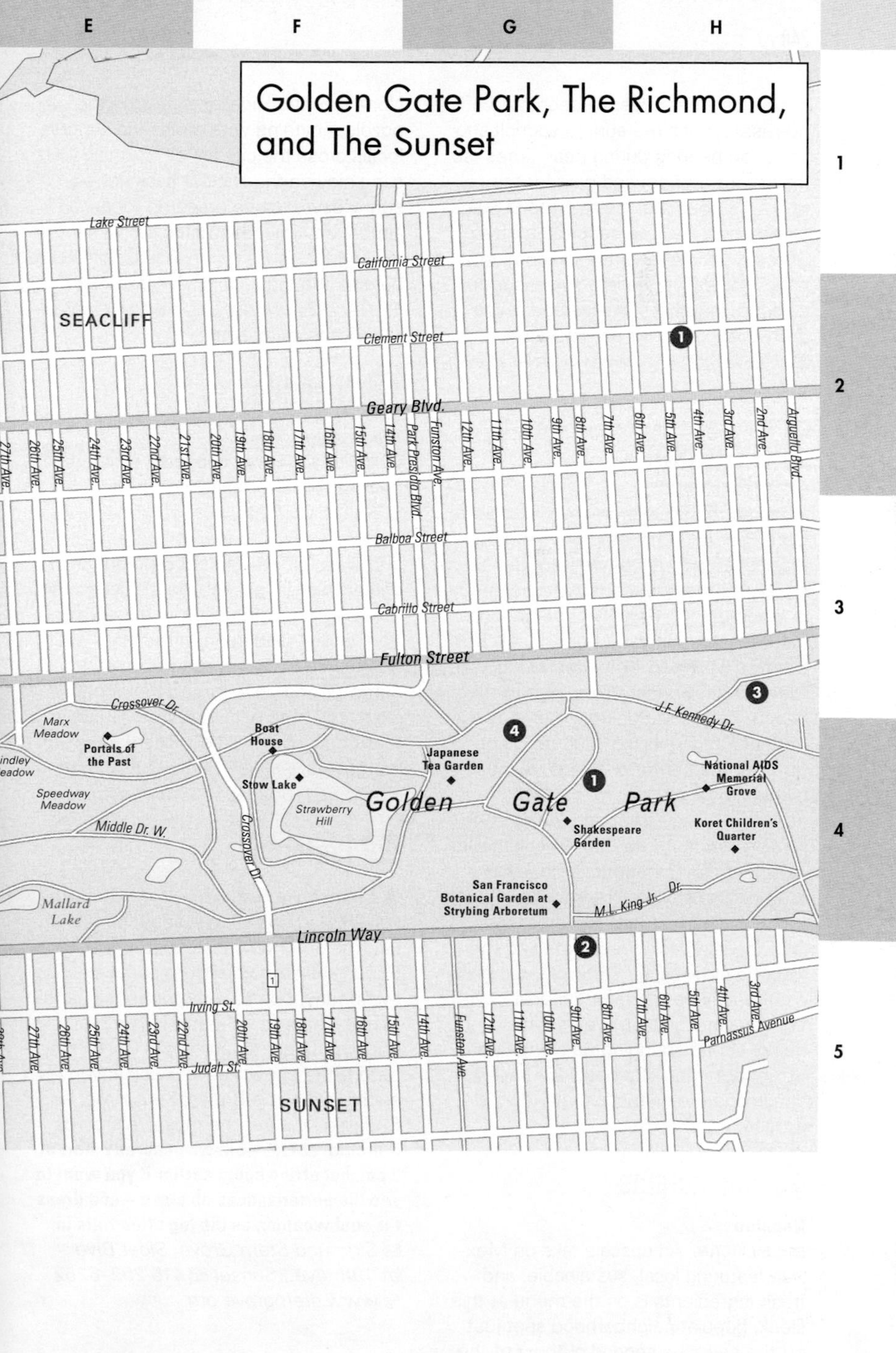
E
F
G
H
Golden Gate Park, The Richmond, and The Sunset
1
2
3
4
5
Lake Street
California Street
SEACLIFF
Clement Street
Geary Blvd.
27th Ave.
26th Ave.
25th Ave.
24th Ave.
23rd Ave.
22nd Ave.
21st Ave.
20th Ave.
19th Ave.
18th Ave.
17th Ave.
16th Ave.
15th Ave.
14th Ave.
Park Presidio Blvd.
Funston Ave.
12th Ave.
11th Ave.
10th Ave.
9th Ave.
8th Ave.
7th Ave.
6th Ave.
5th Ave.
4th Ave.
3rd Ave.
2nd Ave.
Arguello Blvd.
Balboa Street
Cabrillo Street
Fulton Street
Crossover Dr.
J.F. Kennedy Dr.
Marx Meadow
Portals of the Past
Boat House
Japanese Tea Garden
Stow Lake
Strawberry Hill
Golden Gate Park
Speedway Meadow
Middle Dr. W.
Crossover Dr.
Shakespeare Garden
National AIDS Memorial Grove
Koret Children's Quarter
Mallard Lake
San Francisco Botanical Garden at Strybing Arboretum
M.L. King Jr. Dr.
Lincoln Way
Irving St.
Judah St.
Parnassus Avenue
SUNSET

table-side. The modestly decorated, no-reservations restaurant is small and lines can be long during peak times, so leave your number and wait for the call or walk a couple blocks east to B-Star, owned by the same people but often less crowded and with a welcoming patio. **Known for:** tea leaf salad; samusa soup; long lines. $ *Average main: $15* ✉ *309 Clement St., Richmond* ☎ *415/387–2147* 🌐 *www.burmasuperstar.com.*

The Sunset

Hugging the southern edge of Golden Gate Park and built atop the sand dunes that covered much of western San Francisco into the 19th century, the Sunset is made up of two distinct neighborhoods— the popular Inner Sunset, from Stanyan Street to 19th Avenue, and the foggy Outer Sunset, from 19th to the beach. The Inner Sunset is perhaps the perfect San Francisco "suburb": not too far from the center of things, reachable by public transit, and home to main streets—Irving Street and 9th Avenue just off Golden Gate Park—packed with excellent dining options, with Asian food particularly well represented. Long the domain of surfers and others who love the laid-back beach vibe and the fog, the slow-paced Outer Sunset finds itself newly on the radar of locals, with high-quality cafés and restaurants and quirky shops springing up along Judah Street between 42nd and 46th avenues. The zoo is the district's main tourist attraction.

Restaurants

Nopalito

$$ | **MEXICAN** | An upscale take on Mexican featuring local, sustainable, and fresh ingredients is on the menu at this sleek, popular neighborhood spot just off the park, the second outpost of the Nopa favorite. Highlights include the pozole, anything with mole, and carnitas locals cross the city for, all of which you can enjoy on the front or back patio on sunny days, but be prepared for a wait almost anytime. **Known for:** carnitas worth waiting for; focus on freshness; Mexican beyond the taqueria. $ *Average main: $22* ✉ *1224 9th Ave., Sunset* ☎ *415/233–9966* 🌐 *nopalitosf.com.*

Nightlife

The Riptide

BARS/PUBS | A cozy cabin bar that's the perfect finale for beachgoers, Riptide is a surfer favorite, but you don't have to own a board to feel at home. You'll find classic beers and good food, all at wallet-friendly prices. There's live music most nights, often country, bluegrass, honky-tonk, and open mike. Many tourists fooled by San Francisco's version of summer end up warming their popsicle toes at the bar's fireplace. Sunday features a bacon Bloody Mary, great for hangovers. ✉ *3639 Taraval St, Sunset* ☎ *415/681–8433* 🌐 *www.riptidesf.com.*

Performing Arts

★ Stern Grove Festival

FESTIVALS | The nation's oldest continual free summer music festival hosts Sunday-afternoon performances of symphony, opera, jazz, pop music, and dance. The amphitheater is in a beautiful eucalyptus grove, perfect for picnicking before the show. World-music favorites such as Ojos de Brujas, Seu Jorge, and Shuggie Otis get the massive crowds dancing. **■ TIP→ Shows generally start at 2 pm, but arrive hours earlier if you want to see the performances up close—and dress for cool weather, as the fog often rolls in.** ✉ *Sigmund Stern Grove, Sloat Blvd. at 19th Ave., Sunset* ☎ *415/252–6252* 🌐 *www.sterngrove.org.*

The Haight

During the 1960s the siren song of free love, peace, and mind-altering substances lured thousands of young people to the Haight, a neighborhood just east of Golden Gate Park. By 1966 the area had become a hot spot for rock artists, including the Grateful Dead, Jefferson Airplane, and Janis Joplin. Some of the most infamous flower children, including Charles Manson and People's Temple founder Jim Jones, also called the Haight home.

Sights

Haight-Ashbury Intersection

NEIGHBORHOOD | On October 6, 1967, hippies took over the intersection of Haight and Ashbury streets to proclaim the "Death of Hip." If they thought hip was dead then, they'd find absolute confirmation of it today, what with the only tie-dye in sight on the famed corner being Ben & Jerry's storefront. ✉ *Haight.*

Restaurants

Parada 22

$$ | **PUERTO RICAN** | A small, colorful space sandwiched between larger restaurants on either side, Parada 22 serves up heaping plates of Puerto Rican cuisine—think plantains, seafood, and slow-roasted pork. This still being the Haight, there's plenty of vegetarian fare on offer, and the yuca fries will be devoured by everyone. **Known for:** home-style Puerto Rican cuisine; marinated meats and vegetables; lunch specials. *Average main: $17* ✉ *1805 Haight St., near Shrader St., Haight* ☎ *415/750–1111* 🌐 *parada22.com.*

Nightlife

Magnolia Brewing Company

BREWPUBS/BEER GARDENS | Known for its food as much as its beers, Magnolia is a San Francisco institution, thanks in part to its prime location one block away from the famous Haight-Ashbury intersection. Come for the smoked trout croquettes, falafel salad, and famed burgers, or just grab any one of the over a dozen beers on tap, many made right there in the in-house brewery. ✉ *1398 Haight St., Haight* ✥ *At Masonic St.* ☎ *415/864–7468* 🌐 *magnoliabrewing.com.*

Shopping

MUSIC

★ Amoeba Music

MUSIC STORES | With well over a million new and used CDs, DVDs, and records at bargain prices, this warehouselike offshoot of the Berkeley original carries titles you likely can't find on Amazon. No niche is ignored—from electronica and hip-hop to jazz and classical—and the stock changes frequently. **■ TIP→ Weekly in-store performances attract large crowds.** ✉ *1855 Haight St., between Stanyan and Shrader Sts., Haight* ☎ *415/831–1200* 🌐 *www.amoeba.com.*

The Castro

The Castro district—the social, political, and cultural center of San Francisco's thriving gay community— stands at the western end of Market Street. This neighborhood is one of the city's liveliest and most welcoming, especially on weekends. Streets teem with folks out shopping, pushing political causes, heading to art films, and lingering in bars and cafés. It's also one of the city's most expensive neighborhoods to live in, with an influx of tech money exacerbating an identity crisis that's been simmering for a couple of decades.

Sights

★ Castro Theatre

ARTS VENUE | Here's a classic way to join in a beloved Castro tradition: grab some popcorn and catch a flick at this

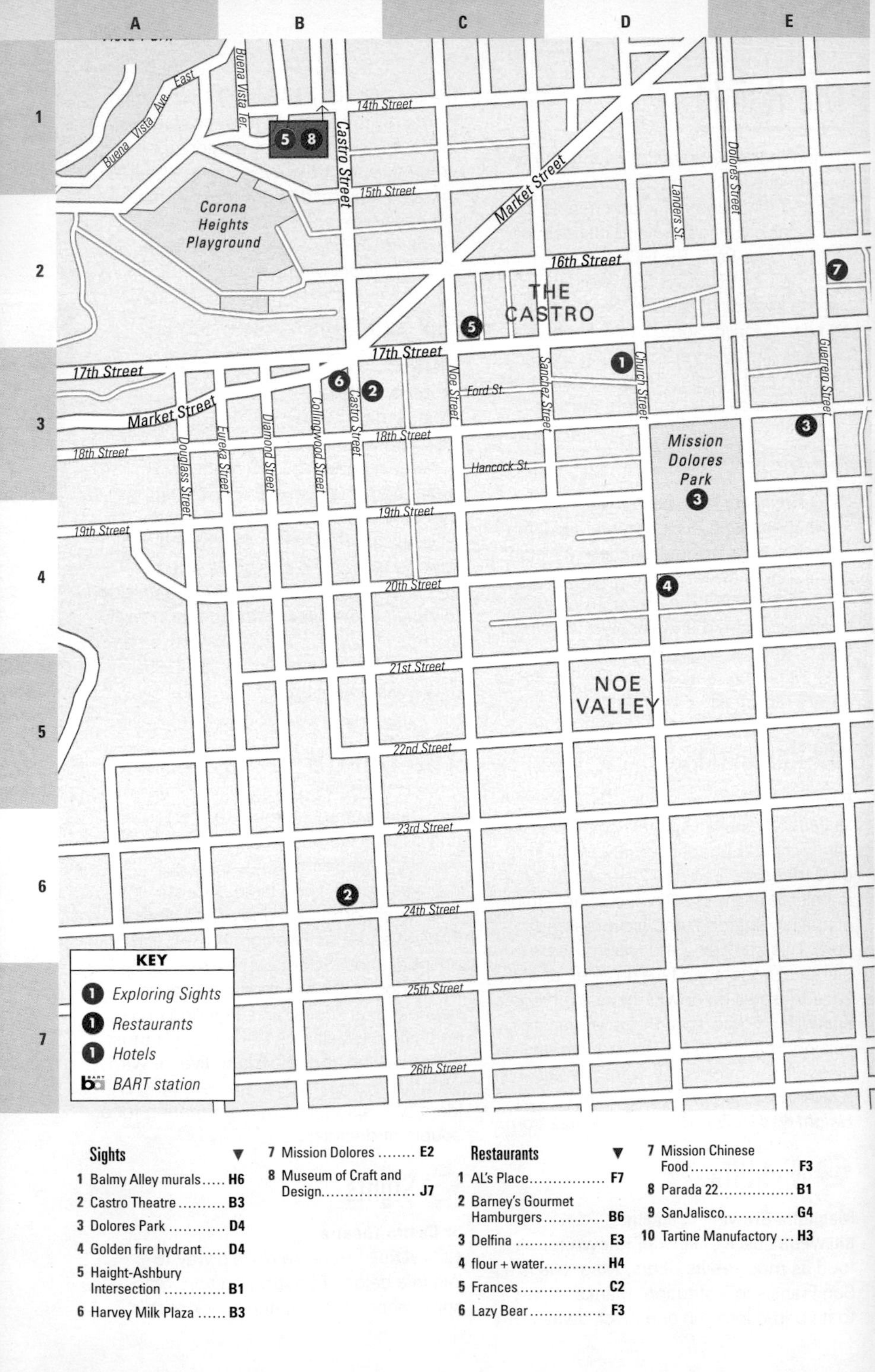

Sights

1 Balmy Alley murals **H6**

2 Castro Theatre **B3**

3 Dolores Park **D4**

4 Golden fire hydrant..... **D4**

5 Haight-Ashbury Intersection **B1**

6 Harvey Milk Plaza **B3**

7 Mission Dolores **E2**

8 Museum of Craft and Design.................... **J7**

Restaurants

1 AL's Place................ **F7**

2 Barney's Gourmet Hamburgers............ **B6**

3 Delfina **E3**

4 flour + water............ **H4**

5 Frances **C2**

6 Lazy Bear **F3**

7 Mission Chinese Food **F3**

8 Parada 22................ **B1**

9 SanJalisco................ **G4**

10 Tartine Manufactory ... **H3**

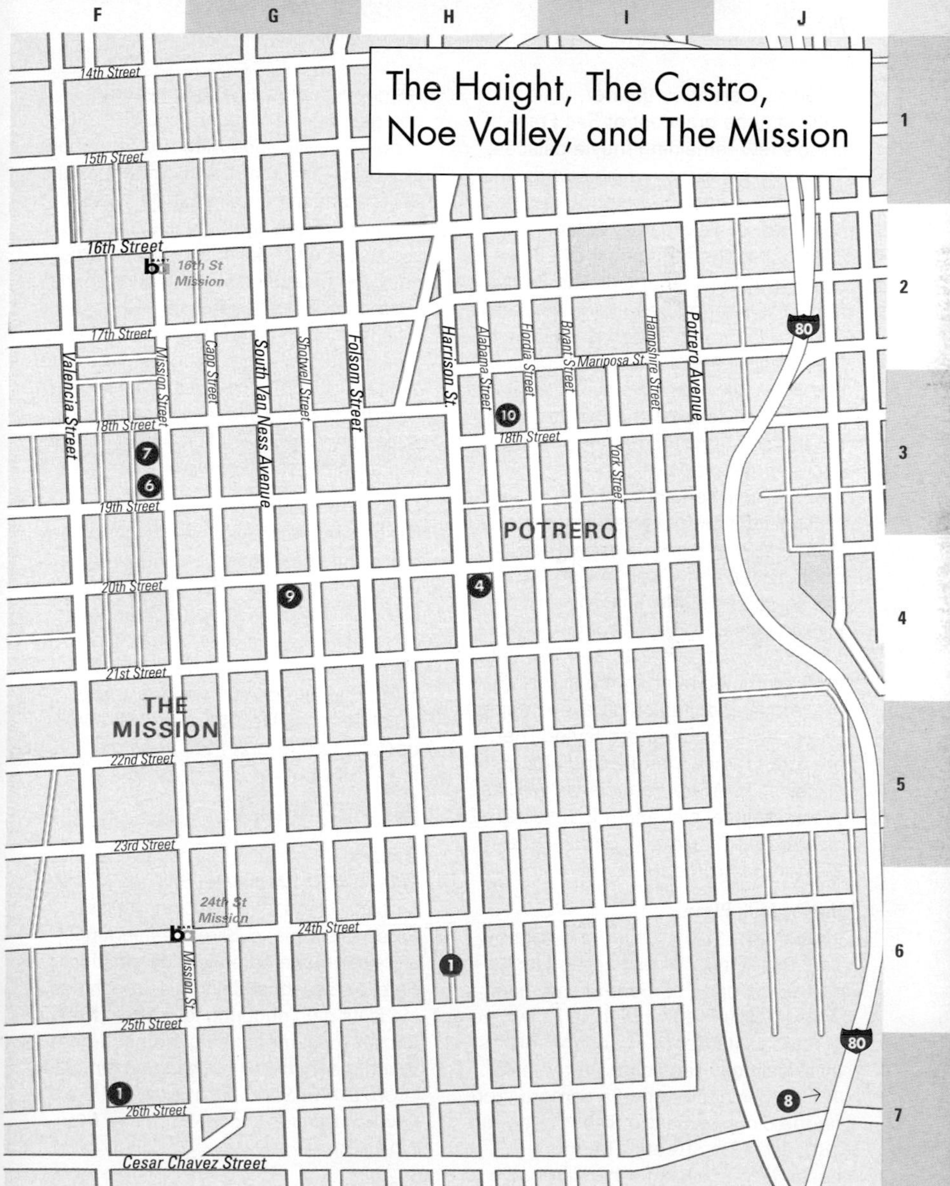

The Haight, The Castro, Noe Valley, and The Mission
F
G
H
I
J
1
2
3
4
5
6
7
14th Street
15th Street
16th Street
16th St Mission
17th Street
18th Street
19th Street
20th Street
21st Street
22nd Street
23rd Street
24th St Mission
24th Street
25th Street
26th Street
Cesar Chavez Street
Valencia Street
Mission Street
Capp Street
South Van Ness Avenue
Shotwell Street
Folsom Street
Harrison St.
Alabama Street
Florida Street
Bryant Street
Mariposa St.
Hampshire Street
Potrero Avenue
York Street
18th Street
Mission St.
THE MISSION
POTRERO
80

Hotels ▼

1 The Parker Guest House D3

1,500-seat art-deco theater; built in 1922, it's the grandest of San Francisco's few remaining movie palaces. The neon marquee, which stands at the top of the Castro strip, is the neighborhood's great landmark. The Castro was the fitting host of 2008's red-carpet preview of Gus Van Sant's film *Milk*, starring Sean Penn as openly gay San Francisco supervisor Harvey Milk. The theater's elaborate Spanish baroque interior is fairly well preserved. Before many shows the theater's pipe organ rises from the orchestra pit and an organist plays pop and movie tunes, usually ending with the Jeanette McDonald standard "San Francisco" (go ahead, sing along). The crowd can be enthusiastic and vocal, talking back to the screen as loudly as it talks to them. Flicks such as *Who's Afraid of Virginia Woolf?* take on a whole new life, with the assembled beating the actors to the punch and fashioning even snappier comebacks for Elizabeth Taylor. There are often family-friendly sing-alongs to classics like *Mary Poppins*, as well as the occasional niche film festival. ✉ *429 Castro St., Castro* ☎ *415/621–6120* 🌐 *www.castrotheatre.com.*

Harvey Milk Plaza

HISTORIC SITE | An 18-foot-long rainbow flag, the symbol of gay pride, flies above this plaza named for the man who electrified the city in 1977 by being elected to its Board of Supervisors as an openly gay candidate. In the early 1970s Milk had opened a camera store on the block of Castro Street between 18th and 19th streets. The store became the center for his campaign to open San Francisco's social and political life to gays and lesbians.

The liberal Milk hadn't served a full year of his term before he and Mayor George Moscone, also a liberal, were shot in November 1978 at City Hall. The murderer was a conservative ex-supervisor named Dan White, who had recently resigned his post and then became enraged when Moscone wouldn't reinstate him. Milk and White had often been at odds on the board, and White thought Milk had been part of a cabal to keep him from returning to his post. Milk's assassination shocked the gay community, which became infuriated when the infamous "Twinkie defense"—that junk food had led to diminished mental capacity—resulted in a manslaughter verdict for White. During the so-called White Night Riot of May 21, 1979, gays and their allies stormed City Hall, torching its lobby and several police cars.

Milk, who had feared assassination, left behind a tape recording in which he urged the community to continue the work he had begun. His legacy is the high visibility of gay people throughout city government; a bust of him was unveiled at City Hall on his birthday in 2008, and the 2008 film *Milk* gives insight into his life. ✉ *Southwest corner of Castro and Market Sts., Castro.*

Restaurants

Frances

$$$ | **MODERN AMERICAN** | Still one of the hottest tickets in town, chef Melissa Perello's simple, sublime restaurant is a consummate date-night destination. Perello's seasonal California-French cooking is its own enduring love affair. **Known for:** seasonal menu; neighborhood gem; tough reservation. $ *Average main: $34* ✉ *3870 17th St., Castro* ☎ *415/621–3870* 🌐 *www.frances-sf.com* ⊙ *Closed Mon. No lunch.*

Performing Arts

FILM

★ Castro Theatre

FILM | A large neon sign marks the exterior of this 1,400-plus-seat art-deco movie palace whose exotic interior transports you back to 1922, when the theater first opened. High-profile festivals present

A colorful mosaic mural in the Castro

films here, along with classic revivals and foreign flicks. There are a few cult-themed drag shows every month. **■TIP→ Lines for the Castro's popular sing-along movie musicals often trail down the block.** ✉ *429 Castro St., near Market St., Castro* ☎ *415/621–6120* 🌐 *www.castrotheatre.com.*

Noe Valley

This upscale but relaxed enclave just south of the Castro is among the city's most desirable places to live, with laid-back cafés, kid-friendly restaurants, and comfortable, old-time shops along Church Street and 24th Street, its main thoroughfares. You can also see remnants of Noe Valley's agricultural beginnings: Billy Goat Hill (at Castro and 30th streets), a wild-grass hill often draped in fog and topped by one of the city's best rope-swinging trees, is named for the goats that grazed here right into the 20th century.

Sights

Golden fire hydrant

LOCAL INTEREST | When all the other fire hydrants went dry during the fire that followed the 1906 earthquake, this one kept pumping. Noe Valley and the Mission District were thus spared the devastation wrought elsewhere in the city, which explains the large number of prequake homes here. Every year on April 18 (the anniversary of the quake), folks gather here to share stories about the earthquake, and the famous hydrant gets a fresh coat of gold paint. ✉ *Church and 20th Sts., southeastern corner, across from Dolores Park, Noe Valley.*

Restaurants

Barney's Gourmet Hamburgers

$ | **AMERICAN** | **FAMILY** | The Noe Valley location of this family-friendly California burger chain offers a cozy indoor-outdoor dining area, the latter really a patio encased in glass windows for watching foot traffic along 24th Street. The menu

Castro and Noe Walk

The Castro and Noe Valley are both neighborhoods that beg to be walked—or ambled through, really, without time pressure or an absolute destination. Hit the Castro first, beginning at **Harvey Milk Plaza** under the gigantic rainbow flag. If you're going on to Noe Valley, first head east down **Market Street** for the cafés, bistros, and shops, then go back to **Castro Street** and head south, past the glorious art-deco **Castro Theatre,** checking out boutiques and cafés along the way (Cliff's Variety, at 479 Castro Street, is a must). To tour Noe Valley, go east down **18th Street** to Church (at Dolores Park), and then either strap on your hiking boots and head south over the hill or hop the J-Church to **24th Street,** the center of this rambling neighborhood.

is loaded with fancier versions of diner classics—think the "gastropub" burger with a fried egg, blackened potato chips, and a pretzel bun, or the "maui waui," with a teriyaki glaze and grilled pineapple. **Known for:** diverse menu selection; vegetarian options; milk shakes. [$] *Average main: $14* ✉ *4138 24th St., near Castro St., Noe Valley* ☎ *415/282–7770* 🌐 *www.barneyshamburgers.com.*

Mission District

The Mission has a number of distinct personalities: it's the Latino neighborhood, where working-class folks raise their families and where gangs occasionally clash; it's the hipster hood, where tattooed and pierced twenty- and thirtysomethings hold court in the coolest cafés and bars in town; it's a culinary epicenter, with the strongest concentration of destination restaurants and affordable ethnic cuisine; it's the face of gentrification, where high-tech money prices out longtime commercial and residential renters; and it's the artists' quarter, where murals adorn literally blocks of walls long after the artists have moved to cheaper digs. It's also the city's equivalent of the Sunshine State—this neighborhood's always the last to succumb to fog.

Sights

Balmy Alley murals

PUBLIC ART | Mission District artists have transformed the walls of their neighborhood with paintings, and Balmy Alley is one of the best-executed examples. Many murals adorn the one-block alley, with newer ones continually filling in the blank spaces. In 1971, artists began teaming with local children to create a space to promote peace in Central America, community spirit, and (later) AIDS awareness; since then dozens of artists have added their vibrant works. ⚠ **Be alert here: the 25th Street end of the alley adjoins a somewhat dangerous area.** ✉ *24th St. between and parallel to Harrison and Treat Sts., alley runs south to 25th St., Mission District.*

★ Dolores Park

LOCAL INTEREST | A two-square-block microcosm of life in the Mission, Dolores Park is one of San Francisco's liveliest green spaces: dog lovers and their pampered pups congregate, kids play at the extravagant playground, and hipsters hold court, drinking beer on sunny days. During the summer, the park hosts movie nights; performances by Shakespeare in the Park, the San Francisco Mime Troupe, and the San Francisco Symphony; and any number of pop-up events and impromptu parties. Spend a warm day here—maybe sitting at the top of the park with a view of the city and the Bay Bridge—surrounded by locals and that laid-back San Francisco energy, and you may well find yourself plotting your move to the city. ✉ *Between 18th and 20th Sts. and Dolores and Church Sts., Mission District.*

Mission Dolores

RELIGIOUS SITE | Two churches stand side by side here, including the small adobe **Mission San Francisco de Asís,** which, along with the Presidio's Officers' Club, is the oldest standing structure in San Francisco. Completed in 1791, it's the sixth of the 21 California missions founded by Franciscan friars in the 18th and early 19th centuries. Its ceiling depicts original Ohlone Indian basket designs, executed in vegetable dyes. The tiny chapel includes frescoes and a hand-painted wooden altar.

There's a hidden treasure here, too, a mural forgotten and rediscovered over more than 200 years. In 2004 an archaeologist and an artist crawled along the ceiling's rafters and opened a trapdoor behind the altar in an attempt to finally document the mission's original mural, painted with natural dyes by Native Americans in 1791. The centuries have taken their toll, so the team photographed the 20-by-22-foot mural and began digitally restoring the photographic version. Among the images is a dagger-pierced Sacred Heart of Jesus.

The small museum here covers the mission's founding and history, and the pretty little cemetery—which appears in Alfred Hitchcock's film *Vertigo*—contains the graves of mid-19th-century European immigrants. The remains of an estimated 5,000 Native Americans who died at the mission lie in unmarked graves. Services are held in both the old mission and next door in the handsome multidome basilica. ✉ *Dolores and 16th Sts., Mission District* ☎ *415/621–8203* 🌐 *www.missiondolores.org* 🎟 *Suggested donation $7.*

Museum of Craft and Design

MUSEUM | Right at home in this once-industrial neighborhood now bursting with creative energy, this small, four-room space—definitely a quick view—mounts temporary art and design exhibitions. The focus might be sculpture, metalwork, furniture, or jewelry—or industrial design, architecture, or other topics. The MakeArt Lab gives kids (and grown-ups) the opportunity to create their own exhibit-inspired work, and the beautifully curated shop sells tempting textiles, housewares, jewelry, and other well-crafted items. ✉ *2569 3rd St., near 22nd St., Dogpatch* ☎ *415/773–0303* 🌐 *sfmcd.org* 🎟 *$8, free 1st Tues. of month* ⏲ *Closed Mon.*

Restaurants

AL's Place

$$ | **MODERN AMERICAN** | AL is chef Aaron London, and his place is a sunny, whitewashed corner spot that serves inventive, Michelin-starred vegetable-forward cooking. London's menu changes frequently, but some dishes, like lightly cured trout and grits with seasonal produce, stick around, and the fries have a cult following. **Known for:** seasonal cooking; inventive vegetable-heavy menu; fries with cult following. 💲 *Average main: $18* ✉ *1499 Valencia St., Mission* ☎ *415/416–6136* 🌐 *www.alsplacesf.com* ⏲ *Closed Mon. and Tues. No lunch.*

★ Delfina

$$$ | **ITALIAN** | Crowds are a constant fixture at Craig and Annie Stoll's cultishly adored northern Italian spot, where aluminum-topped tables are squeezed into an urban interior, with hardwood floors and a tile bar that seems to radiate with happiness. Deceptively simple, exquisitely flavored dishes include the signature spaghetti with plum tomatoes and consistently great roast chicken, and the panna cotta is best in class. **Known for:** signature spaghetti with plum tomatoes; long waits; much-lauded panna cotta. *Average main: $24 ✉ 3621 18th St., Mission District ☎ 415/552–4055 🌐 www.delfinasf.com ⏲ No lunch.*

flour + water

$$$ | **ITALIAN** | This handsome and boisterous hot spot with slate-gray walls, sturdy wooden tables, and a taxidermy cabinet in the bathroom is synonymous with pasta, though its blistery thin-crust Neapolitan pizzas are also top notch, but the grand experience here is the seven-course pasta-tasting menu (extra for wine pairings). The homemade rutabaga tortelli with candy cap mushrooms is a crowd-pleaser, as is the toasted sourdough rigatoni. **Known for:** difficult-to-get reservations; delicious pizzas and pastas; noisy scene. *Average main: $25 ✉ 2401 Harrison St., Mission District ☎ 415/826–7000 🌐 www.flourandwater.com ⏲ No lunch.*

Lazy Bear

$$$$ | **MODERN AMERICAN** | There's no end to the buzz around chef David Barzelay's 14-plus-course prix-fixe modern American dinners, which might include sweet pea custard lamb with dates, or charred onion broth with country ham. An ode to the Western lodge, the two-level dining room, which includes a fireplace, charred wood walls, wooden rafters, and tables made of American elm, hosts what is essentially a dinner party for 40, with cocktails and bites enjoyed upstairs and dinner downstairs at two communal tables. **Known for:** hot-ticket often resold; communal dining; dinner party setup. *Average main: $185 ✉ 3416 19th St., Mission District ☎ 415/874–9921 🌐 www.lazybearsf.com ⏲ Closed Sun. and Mon. No lunch.*

Mission Chinese Food

$$ | **CHINESE** | While the setting is somewhat one-star, the food draws throngs for its bold, cheerfully inauthentic riffs on Chinese cuisine made with quality meats and ingredients, including the fine and super-fiery kung pao pastrami, salt cod fried rice with mackerel confit, and sour chili chicken. Some of the food spikes hot (mapo tofu) while milder dishes (Westlake rice porridge) are homey and satisfying. **Known for:** kung pao pastrami; salt cod fried rice; to-go spot due to long waits. *Average main: $16 ✉ 2234 Mission St., Mission District ☎ 415/863–2800 🌐 www.missionchinesefood.com ⏲ No lunch Tues. and Wed.*

SanJalisco

$ | **MEXICAN** | **FAMILY** | This colorful old-time, sun-filled, family-run restaurant has been a neighborhood favorite for more than 30 years, and not only because it serves breakfast all day—though the hearty *chilaquiles* hit the spot. On weekends, adventurous eaters may opt for *birria,* a spicy barbecued goat stew, or *menudo,* a tongue-searing soup made from beef tripe, complemented by beer and sangria. **Known for:** breakfast all day; beef-tripe menudo; delicious sangria. *Average main: $13 ✉ 901 S. Van Ness Ave., Mission District ☎ 415/648–8383.*

Tartine Manufactory

$$$ | **MODERN AMERICAN** | **FAMILY** | At this sunny, cathedral-like space in the Heath Ceramics building, you'll find Chad Robertson's bread and Liz Prueitt's pastries, but also breakfast, lunch, and dinner, with seasonal salads front and center, as well as a porchetta sandwich that tends to sell out early. As with the original bakery, you can expect to spend some time

Did You Know?

These pastel Victorian homes in Pacific Heights are closer to the original hues sported back in the 1900s. It wasn't until the 1960s that the bold, electric colors now seen around San Francisco gained popularity. Before that, the most typical house paint color was a standard gray.

in line—and to be rewarded for your troubles. **Known for:** Chad Robertson's bread; Liz Prueitt's pastries; seasonal salads. *Average main: $28 ✉ 595 Alabama St., Mission District ☎ 415/757–0007 🌐 www.tartinemanufactory.com.*

Hotels

★ The Parker Guest House

$$ | **B&B/INN** | Two yellow 1909 Edwardian houses enchant travelers wanting an authentic San Francisco experience; dark hallways and steep staircases lead to bright earth-toned rooms with private tiled baths (most with tubs), comfortable sitting areas, and cozy linens. **Pros:** handsome affordable rooms; just steps from Dolores Park and the vibrant Castro District on a Muni line; elaborate gardens. **Cons:** stairs can be challenging for those with limited mobility; parking can be difficult if garage is full; standard rooms are a little tight. *Rooms from: $249 ✉ 520 Church St., Mission District ☎ 415/621–4139 🌐 parkerguesthouse.com 21 rooms Breakfast.*

Nightlife

ABV

BARS/PUBS | One of the city's top cocktail bars offers elevated small plates—think pork belly with peanut mole, burgers, and meat and cheese boards—until 1 am to pair with the excellent cocktail menu, which features such favorites as the Mumbai Mule with saffron vodka. A knowledgeable and friendly staff serves a hipster crowd that knows their drinks in a smart modern setting, with hard surfaces, bar-stool seating, and a giant mural. The sidewalk tables are popular on sunny days. *✉ 3174 16th St., near Guerrero St., Mission District ☎ 415/400–4748 🌐 www.abvsf.com.*

★ El Rio

MUSIC CLUBS | A dive bar in the best sense, El Rio has a calendar chock-full of events, from free bands and films to Salsa Sunday (seasonal), all of which keep Mission kids coming back. Bands play several nights a week, and there are plenty of other events. No matter what day you attend, expect to find a diverse gay-straight crowd. When the weather's warm, the large patio out back is especially popular, and the midday dance parties are *the* place to be. *✉ 3158 Mission St., between César Chavez and Valencia Sts., Mission District ☎ 415/282–3325 🌐 www.elriosf.com.*

Martuni's

BARS/PUBS | A mixed crowd enjoys cocktails in the semi-refined environment of this piano bar where the Castro, the Mission, and Hayes Valley intersect; variations on the martini are a specialty. In the intimate back room a pianist plays nightly, and patrons take turns boisterously singing show tunes. Martuni's often gets busy after symphony and opera performances—Davies Hall and the Opera House are both within walking distance. **■ TIP→ The Godiva Chocolate Martini is a crowd favorite.** *✉ 4 Valencia St., at Market St., Mission District ☎ 415/241–0205.*

Zeitgeist

BARS/PUBS | It's a dive but one of the city's best beer bars—there are almost 50 on tap—a great place to relax with a cold one or an ever-popular Bloody Mary in the large "garden" (there's not much greenery) on a sunny day. Burgers and brats are available, and if you own a trucker hat, a pair of Vans, and a Pabst Blue Ribbon T-shirt, you'll fit right in. *✉ 199 Valencia St., at Duboce Ave., Mission District ☎ 415/255–7505.*

Shopping

FURNITURE, HOUSEWARES, AND GIFTS

★ Paxton Gate

GIFTS/SOUVENIRS | Elevating gardening to an art, this serene shop offers beautiful earthenware pots, amaryllis and narcissus bulbs, decorative garden items, and coffee-table books such as *An Inordinate Fondness for Beetles.* The collection of taxidermy and preserved bugs provides more unusual gift ideas. A couple of storefronts away is too-cute Paxton Gate Curiosities for Kids, jam-packed with retro toys, books, and other stellar finds. ✉ *824 Valencia St., between 19th and 20th Sts., Mission District* ☎ *415/824–1872* 🌐 *www.paxton-gate.com.*

Pacific Heights

Pacific Heights defines San Francisco's most expensive and dramatic real estate. Grand Victorians line the streets, mansions and town houses are priced in the millions, and there are magnificent views from almost any point in the neighborhood. Old money and new, personalities in the limelight and those who prefer absolute media anonymity live here, and few outsiders see anything other than the pleasing facades of Queen Anne charmers, English Tudor imports, and baroque bastions. Nancy Pelosi and Dianne Feinstein, Larry Ellison, and Gordon Getty all own impressive homes here, but not even pockets as deep as those can buy a large garden—space in the city is simply at too much of a premium. Luckily, two of the city's most spectacular parks are located in the area. The boutiques and restaurants along Fillmore Street, which range from glam to funky, are a draw for the whole city as well.

Sights

Haas-Lilienthal House

HOUSE | A small display of photographs on the bottom floor of this elaborate, gray 1886 Queen Anne house makes clear that despite its lofty stature and striking, round third-story tower, the house was modest compared with some of the giants that fell victim to the 1906 earthquake and fire. San Francisco Heritage, a foundation to preserve San Francisco's architectural history, operates the home, whose carefully kept rooms provide a glimpse into late-19th-century life through period furniture, authentic details (antique dishes in the kitchen built-in), and photos of the Haas family who occupied the house for three generations until 1972. **■ TIP→ You can admire hundreds of gorgeous San Francisco Victorians from the outside, but this is the only one that's open to the public, and it's worth a visit.** Volunteers conduct one-hour house tours three days a week, and informative two-hour walking tours of Pacific Heights on Sunday afternoon (call or check website for schedule). ✉ *2007 Franklin St., between Washington and Jackson Sts., Pacific Heights* ☎ *415/441–3004* 🌐 *www.haaslilienthal-house.org* 🎫 *Tours $10.*

Restaurants

True Laurel

$$$ | **MODERN AMERICAN** | A great Plan B for those who didn't book far enough ahead to score a table at Lazy Bear, this excellent cocktail bar and small-plates restaurant by the same people offers intriguing combinations and endless conversation starters in a cool modern setting. Menu standouts include the Dungeness-crab-and-aged-cheddar fondue and fried hen-of-the-woods mushrooms, while don't-misses on the cocktail side include the Top Dawg, a house-fermented sparkling concoction, and aquavit-based A-Dilla. **Known for:** equal focus on food and cocktails; unusual ingredients; innovative combinations. 💲 *Average main: $24* ✉ *753 Alabama St., Mission District* ☎ *415/341–0020* 🌐 *truelaurelsf.com* 🕑 *No lunch.*

Hotels

★ Hotel Drisco

$$$$ | HOTEL | Pretend you're a denizen of one of San Francisco's wealthiest residential neighborhoods while you stay at this understated, elegant 1903 Edwardian hotel. **Pros:** terrific recent renovation of rooms and public spaces; great service and many amenities; quiet residential retreat. **Cons:** not an easy walk to nearby restaurants and bars; room prices are as steep as nearby hill; no complimentary chauffeur service in the afternoon or evening. *Rooms from: $499* *2901 Pacific Ave., Pacific Heights* *415/346–2880, 800/634–7277* *www.hoteldrisco.com* *64 rooms* *Breakfast.*

Nightlife

The Snug

BARS/PUBS | Open since late 2017, this Lower Pac Heights bar is exactly the welcoming yet refined drinking destination the well-heeled and fun-loving neighborhood needed. It's the rare bar that emphasizes clever cocktails, in-high-demand local craft beer, and smartly selected wine in equal parts. Come hungry, as well, because elevated takes on bar bites like seabream poke and fresh-from-the-tandoor sesame naan with shiitake mushroom hummus are created by a chef formerly at some of the country's gastronomic heavyweights (Benu, Alinea). *2301 Fillmore St., Lower Pacific Heights* *Near Clay St.* *www.thesnugsf.com.*

Shopping

Browser Books

BOOKS/STATIONERY | FAMILY | One of the city's most beloved independent bookstores resides quietly among the chic fashion boutiques lining Fillmore Street. Opened in 1976, all ages will find ample choices for their next reading material from contemporary fiction to children's books to a large selection of Buddhist Dharma literature. *2195 Fillmore St., Lower Pacific Heights* *415/567–8027* *www.browserbookstore.com.*

★ Verve Wine

WINE/SPIRITS | Wine nerds will fall in love with this trendy, upscale destination from one of the country's few Master Sommeliers, Dustin Wilson. High-quality, smaller producers from prominent and lesser known regions share wall space in this exceptionally organized boutique. *Verve Wine, 2358 Fillmore St., Lower Pacific Heights* *Between Washington St. and Jackson St.* *415/896–4935* *www.vervewine.com/about/san-francisco.*

Japantown

Though still the spiritual center of San Francisco's Japanese American community, Japantown feels somewhat adrift. The Japan Center mall, for instance, comes across as rather sterile, and whereas Chinatown is densely populated and still largely Chinese, Japantown struggles to retain its unique character.

Sights

Japan Center

HISTORIC SITE | FAMILY | Cool and curious trinkets, noodle houses and sushi joints, a destination bookstore, and a peek at Japanese culture high and low await at this 5-acre complex designed in 1968 by noted American architect Minoru Yamasaki. The Japan Center includes the shop- and restaurant-filled Kintetsu and Kinokuniya buildings; the excellent Kabuki Springs & Spa; the Hotel Kabuki; and the AMC Kabuki reserved-seating cinema/restaurant complex.

The Kinokuniya Bookstore, in the Kinokuniya Building, has an extensive selection of Japanese-language books, *manga* (graphic novels), books on design, English-language translations, and books on Japanese topics. Just outside, follow the Japanese teenagers to Pika Pika, where you and your friends can step into a photo booth and then use special effects and stickers to decorate your creation. On the bridge connecting the buildings, check out Shige Antiques for *yukata* (lightweight cotton kimonos) for kids and lovely silk kimonos, and Asakichi and its tiny incense shop for tinkling wind chimes and display-worthy teakettles. Continue into the Kintetsu Building for a selection of Japanese restaurants.

Between the West Mall and the East Mall are the five-tier, 100-foot-tall **Peace Pagoda** and the Peace Plaza, where seasonal festivals are held. The pagoda, which draws on the 1,200-year-old tradition of miniature round pagodas dedicated to eternal peace, was designed in the late 1960s by Yoshiro Taniguchi to convey the "friendship and goodwill" of the Japanese people to the people of the United States. ✉ *Bordered by Geary Blvd. and Fillmore, Post, and Laguna Sts., Japantown* 🌐 *www.japancentersf.com.*

★ Kabuki Springs & Spa

SPA—SIGHT | This serene spa is one Japantown destination that draws locals from all over town, from hipster to grandma, Japanese American or not. Balinese urns decorate the communal bath area of this house of tranquility.

The extensive service menu includes facials, salt scrubs, and mud and seaweed wraps, in addition to massage. You can take your massage in a private room with a bath or in a curtained-off area.

The communal baths ($30) contain hot and cold tubs, a large Japanese-style bath, a sauna, a steam room, and showers. Bang the gong for quiet if your fellow bathers are speaking too loudly. The clothing-optional baths are open for men only on Monday, Thursday, and Saturday; women bathe on Wednesday, Friday, and Sunday. Bathing suits are required on Tuesday, when the baths are coed.

Men and women can reserve private rooms daily. ✉ *1750 Geary Blvd., Japantown* ☎ *415/922–6000* 🌐 *www.kabukisprings.com.*

Restaurants

Marufuku Ramen

$ | **RAMEN** | Hakata style *tonkotsu* (pork) or extra intense chicken *paitan* ramen are the specialties of this modern-looking Japan Center restaurant that serves what many San Franciscans consider the city's finest bowl of ramen. As a result, long lines can be daunting, but luckily prospective guests can join an online wait list. **Known for:** rich bowls of ramen; more "al dente" style noodles; lively, contemporary vibe. *Average main: $13* ✉ *1581 Webster St. #235, Japantown* ✣ *In Kinokuniya Bldg.* ☎ *415/872–9786* 🌐 *www.marufukuramen.com* ⊙ *Closed Mon.*

Mifune Don

$ | **JAPANESE** | **FAMILY** | Homemade thin soba and thick udon, served either hot or cold with various toppings, are the stars of this low-key, charming restaurant with a wooden facade that looks like it was imported directly from the countryside. Seating is at wooden tables, where diners of every age can be heard slurping down big bowls of traditional Japanese combinations. **Known for:** bowls of noodles; savory Japanese pancakes (okonomiyaki); bargain lunch deals. *Average main: $12* ✉ *22 Peace Plaza, Suite 560, Japantown* ✣ *2nd fl. of East Mall* ☎ *415/346–1993* ⊙ *Closed Tues.*

A
B
C
D
E
F
1
2
3
4
5
6
7
8
9
PACIFIC HEIGHTS
FILLMORE
WESTERN ADDITION
HAIGHT ASHBURY
Green Street
Vallejo Street
Broadway
Pacific Avenue
Jackson Street
Washington Street
Washington St.
Baker St.
Clay Street
Sacramento Street
California Street
Pine Street
Bush Street
Sutter Street
Post Street
Geary Blvd.
Geary Street
O'Farrell Street
Ellis Street
Ellis St.
Eddy Street
Willow St.
Hollis
Cleary Ct.
Elm St.
Turk St.
Golden Gate Ave.
McAllister St.
Fulton St.
Grove St.
Hayes Street
Fell Street
Oak Street
Page Street
Haight Street
Haight St.
Waller St.
Germania St.
Herman St.
Divisadero Street
Scott Street
Pierce St.
Pierce Street
Steiner Street
Fillmore Street
Webster St.
Buchanan Street
Laguna Street
Broderick Street
Baker Street
Lyon Street
Lyon St.
Presidio Avenue
Terra Vista Ave.
Encanto Ave.
Fortuna Ave.
Baker St.
Josephs Ave.
Anza Vista Ave.
Alta Plaza
Pacific Med. Center
Lafayette Park
Mt. Zion Hosp.
Hamilton Square
Kimball Playground
St. Francis Square
Kaiser Med. Ctr.
Western Addition Cultural Center
Alamo Square
Panhandle
0
300 m
0
1,000 ft

Sights

1 Alamo Square Park D7
2 Cathedral Of Saint Mary Of The Assumption G5
3 Haas-Lilienthal House G1
4 Japan Center E4
5 Kabuki Springs & Spa D4

Restaurants

1 Avery D5
2 Che Fico C7
3 4505 Burgers & BBQ C7
4 Marufuku Ramen E4
5 Merchant Roots D5
6 Mifune Don E4
7 The Mill C7
8 Nopa C8
9 Octavia F3
10 The Snug D2
11 State Bird Provisions D5
12 True Laurel I9

Hotels

1 Hotel Drisco Pacific Heights A2
2 Phoenix Hotel I5

Shopping

BOOKS

Kinokuniya Bookstore

BOOKS/STATIONERY | The selection of English-language books about Japanese culture—everything from medieval history to origami instructions—is one of the finest in the country. Kinokuniya is the city's biggest seller of Japanese-language books. Dozens of glossy Asian fashion magazines attract the young and trendy; the manga and anime books and magazines are wildly popular, too. ✉ *Kinokuniya Bldg., 1581 Webster St., at Geary Blvd., Japantown* ☎ *415/567–7625* 🌐 *www.kinokuniya.com/us.*

Western Addition

Part of the Western Addition, the Lower Fillmore in its post–World War II heyday was known as the Harlem of the West for its profusion of jazz night spots, where such legends as Billie Holliday, Duke Ellington, and Charlie Parker would play. These days the neighborhood tries to maintain its African American core and its link to that heritage; one success is the annual Fillmore Jazz Festival in June. More live music rings at the Fillmore Auditorium, made famous in the 1960s by Bill Graham and the iconic bands he booked there, and at the blues-centric Boom Boom Room.

Sights

★ Alamo Square Park

CITY PARK | FAMILY | Whether you've seen them on postcards or on the old TV show "Full House," the colorful "Painted Ladies" Victorians are some of San Francisco's world-renowned icons. The signature view of them with the downtown skyline in the background is from the east side of this hilly park that reopened in 2017 after an extensive renovation. Tourists love the photo opportunities, but locals also adore the park's tennis courts, dog-playing area, and ample picnic area—with great views, of course. After taking plenty of photos, swing by the park's northwest corner and admire the William Westerfeld House (*1198 Fulton St.*), a splendid five-story late-19th-century Victorian mansion. ✉ *Western Addition* ✥ *Between Steiner St., Hayes St., Fulton St., and Hayes St.*

Cathedral of Saint Mary of the Assumption

RELIGIOUS SITE | Residing at the prominent intersection of two busy thoroughfares (Geary Boulevard and Gough Street), there's no missing this striking cathedral and its sweeping contemporary design. Opened in 1971, Italian architects Pietro Belluschi and Pier Luigi Nervi intended to create a spectacular cathedral that reflects the Catholic faith and modern technology. It was controversial at first, yet now is applauded for its grand, curving roof that rises to a height of 190 feet, meeting to form a cross. Don't miss the ceiling's intricate stained glass work. The cathedral is open daily for visitors other than during Mass times and usually has docents on duty in the late morning hours. ✉ *1111 Gough St., Western Addition* ✥ *At Geary St.* 🌐 *smcsf.org.*

Restaurants

Avery

$$$$ | MODERN AMERICAN | With caviar bumps, a cheese course in buckwheat tartlet form, and dazzling crispy shrimp "aebelskivers" (Danish beignet), the solo debut of wunderkind chef Rodney Wages is definitely not your average proper fine dining destination. Then again, with its triple-digit price tags and liberal use of luxe ingredients, it very much fits right into the exclusive San Francisco lavish spectacle dining club. **Known for:** captivating tasting menu with distinct Japanese influences; minimalist elegant decor; strong sake roster. $ *Average main: $130* ✉ *1552 Fillmore*

St., Western Addition ⊕ By Geary St. ☎ 415/817–1187 ⊕ www.averysf.com ⊙ Closed Mon. and Tues.

Che Fico

$$$ | **MODERN ITALIAN** | This red-hot Divisadero spot on the second floor of a revamped auto body shop was San Francisco's biggest restaurant debut of 2018. In a city full of Italian restaurants, it sets itself apart with homemade charcuterie, antipasti, pastas, and pizza that effortlessly blur the line between modern and traditional. **Known for:** pineapple pizza; hard-to-get reservations; Roman Jewish specialties. *$ Average main: $28 ✉ 838 Divisadero St., Western Addition ☎ 415/416–6959 ⊕ www.chefico.com ⊙ Closed Sun. and Mon.*

4505 Burgers & BBQ

$$ | **BARBECUE** | The smoker works overtime from noon to night at this hipster-chic barbecue shack, churning out an array of succulent meats that can be had by the plate, the pound, or as a sandwich. Every plate comes with two sides, and you should certainly make the frankaroni one of them. **Known for:** smoked meats; decadent sides; self-named "Best Damn Cheeseburger". *$ Average main: $17 ✉ 705 Divisadero St., Western Addition ⊕ Between Grove St. and Fulton St. ☎ 415/231–6993 ⊕ www.4505burgersandbbq.com.*

Merchant Roots

$ | **CAFÉ** | It's hard to look past the vintage pasta machine by the sidewalk window, cranking out fresh pastas all day. However, the Fillmore café/craft grocer is so much more than pastas with salads, sandwiches, baked goods, and a noteworthy wineshop in the back. **Known for:** chocolate chip cookies; excellent pasta; photogenic chocolate cannolis. *$ Average main: $13 ✉ 1365 Fillmore St., Western Addition ☎ 530/574–7365 ⊕ www.merchantroots.com ⊙ Closed Sun. and Mon.*

★ The Mill

$ | **BAKERY** | "Four-dollar toast" is a phrase used around San Francisco referring to gentrification—and it was inspired by this sun-drenched, Wi-Fi-less café. It's a project between one of the city's leading bakers, Josey Baker (yes, that's really his last name and profession!), and the Mission's Four Barrel Coffee. **Known for:** toast in various forms; stellar loaves of bread; a precious, post-yoga vibe. *$ Average main: $8 ✉ 736 Divisadero St., Western Addition ☎ 415/345–1953 ⊕ www.themillsf.com.*

★ Nopa

$$$ | **AMERICAN** | This is the good-food granddaddy of the hot corridor of the same name (it's hard to tell which came first—Nopa the restaurant or NoPa the North of the Panhandle neighborhood). The Cali-rustic fare here draws dependable crowds regardless of the night. **Known for:** high-quality comforting food with smart twists; actually good food after 11 pm; a constant and diverse crowd. *$ Average main: $27 ✉ 560 Divisadero St., Western Addition ☎ 415/864–8643 ⊕ www.nopasf.com ⊙ No lunch weekdays.*

★ Octavia

$$$$ | **MODERN AMERICAN** | Regardless of the time of year, Melissa Perello's second and more upscale restaurant (Frances) is a perennial favorite for diners seeking out what "California cuisine" really tastes like. The warm, immaculate dining room is a perfect setting for edgier dishes like the popular chilled squid ink noodles starter, along with more comforting produce-driven small plates and entrées. **Known for:** exciting preparations with peak-of-season produce; spicy deviled egg starter; truly professional service. *$ Average main: $32 ✉ 1701 Octavia St., Lower Pacific Heights ⊕ At Bush St. ☎ 415/408–7507 ⊕ www.octavia-sf.com.*

★ State Bird Provisions

$$$ | MODERN AMERICAN | It's more or less impossible to score a reservation for a normal dinner hour at husband-and-wife Stuart Brioza and Nicole Krasinski's game-changing restaurant. But once you nab a golden ticket for one of the 80 dining room and chef counter seats, you'll be rewarded with fascinating bites served from roving carts and an à la carte printed menu. **Known for:** dim sum–style dining; long lines at opening time; "State Bird" namesake buttermilk fried quail. *Average main: $23* ✉ *1529 Fillmore St., Western Addition* ☎ *415/795–1272* 🌐 *www.statebirdsf.com* ⊗ *No lunch.*

Nightlife

Boom Boom Room

MUSIC CLUBS | One of San Francisco's liveliest music spots is this Fillmore blues favorite, opened in 1997 by the "King of Boogie" John Lee Hooker. The club has a fun blend of blues, funk, and hip-hop shows most nights of the week. ✉ *1601 Fillmore St., Western Addition* ✣ *At Geary Blvd.* ☎ *415/673–8000* 🌐 *www.boomboomroom.com.*

Fat Angel

BARS/PUBS | Part of San Francisco knows this intimate, dimly lit Fillmore spot as the unofficial waiting room for State Bird Provisions. However, its many regulars know this gastropub is one of the finest craft beer bars in the entire city. Belgian beers and hard-to-find West Coast small-batch brews share space on the tap list and bottle roster. On the food front, spicy mac 'n' cheese and SF's best chicken potpie are crowd favorites for soaking up multiple rounds. ✉ *1740 O'Farrell St., Western Addition* ✣ *Near Fillmore St.* ☎ *415/525–3013* 🌐 *www.fatangelsf.com.*

The Fillmore

MUSIC CLUBS | This is *the* club that all the big names, from Coldplay to Clapton, want to play. San Francisco's most famous rock-music hall presents national and local acts: rock, reggae, grunge, jazz, folk, acid house, and more. Go upstairs to view the amazing collection of rock posters lining the walls. At the end of each show, free apples are set near the door, and staffers hand out collectible posters. **■ TIP→ Avoid steep service charges by purchasing tickets at the club's box office on Sunday from 10 to 4.** ✉ *1805 Geary Blvd., at Fillmore St., Western Addition* ☎ *415/346–6000* 🌐 *www.thefillmore.com.*

Horsefeather

BARS/PUBS | Creative produce-driven cocktails and a chic, low-key vibe make this Divisadero drinking destination a locals' frequent top choice for a fun night out. The always interesting (but never too bizarre) cocktails range from a breezy "California Cooler" with celery juice to the rum-and-whiskey-based "Breakfast Punch" featuring clarified Cinnamon Toast Crunch-infused milk. Weekend brunch is excellent as is the delightfully messy double cheeseburger. As an added bonus, the kitchen stays open until 1 am nightly. ✉ *528 Divisadero St., Western Addition* ☎ *415/817–1939* 🌐 *www.horsefeatherbar.com.*

Indian Paradox

WINE BARS—NIGHTLIFE | This festive, tiny Divisadero spot is hardly your average "wine bar." Cheese and charcuterie plates are swapped out here for Indian street food and chaat. With an eye-catching bar background made of milk crates and murals of the colorful delivery trucks in India, it also certainly doesn't look like your typical wine bar. Most of all, the quirky but beautiful wines work wonders with the exciting small bites offered à la carte or in a very reasonably priced tasting menu. ✉ *258 Divisadero St., Western Addition* ☎ *415/593–5386* 🌐 *www.indianparadoxsf.com.*

The Tenderloin

Hotels

Phoenix Hotel

$$ | **HOTEL** | A magnet for the boho crowd, the Phoenix is retro and low-key, with colorful furniture, white bedspreads, and original pieces by local artists, as well as modern amenities like flat-screen TVs. **Pros:** mellow staffers set boho tone; cheeky design, hip restaurant/bar; free parking. **Cons:** somewhat seedy location; no elevators; can be loud in the evening. *Rooms from: $230* ✉ *601 Eddy St., Tenderloin* ☎ *415/776–1380, 800/248–9466* 🌐 *www.phoenixsf.com* *44 rooms* *No meals.*

Nightlife

★ Bourbon & Branch

BARS/PUBS | Bourbon & Branch reeks of Prohibition-era speakeasy cool. It's not exclusive, though: everyone is granted a password. The place has sex appeal, with tin ceilings, bordello-red silk wallpaper, intimate booths, and low lighting; loud conversations and cell phones are not allowed. The menu of expertly mixed cocktails and quality bourbon and whiskey is substantial, though the servers aren't always authorities. ■ **TIP→ Your reservation dictates your exit time, which is strictly enforced.** There's also a speakeasy within the speakeasy called Wilson & Wilson, which is more exclusive, but just as funky. ✉ *501 Jones St., at O'Farrell St., Tenderloin* ☎ *415/346–1735* 🌐 *www.bourbonandbranch.com.*

Great American Music Hall

MUSIC CLUBS | You can find top-drawer entertainment at this eclectic concert venue. Acts range from the best in blues, folk, and jazz to up-and-coming college-radio and American-roots artists to indie rockers such as OK Go, Mates of State, and Cowboy Junkies. The colorful marble-pillared emporium (built in 1907 as a bordello) also accommodates dancing at some shows. Pub grub is available on most nights. ✉ *859 O'Farrell St., between Polk and Larkin Sts., Tenderloin* ☎ *415/885–0750* 🌐 *www.slimspresents.com.*

Potrero Hill

Nightlife

Bottom of the Hill

MUSIC CLUBS | This is a great live-music dive—in the best sense of the word—and truly the epicenter of Bay Area indie rock. The club has hosted some great acts over the years, including the Strokes and the Throwing Muses. Rap and hip-hop acts occasionally make it to the stage. ✉ *1233 17th St., at Texas St., Potrero Hill* ☎ *415/621–4455* 🌐 *www.bottomofthehill.com.*

Chapter 9

THE BAY AREA

Updated by
Monique Peterson

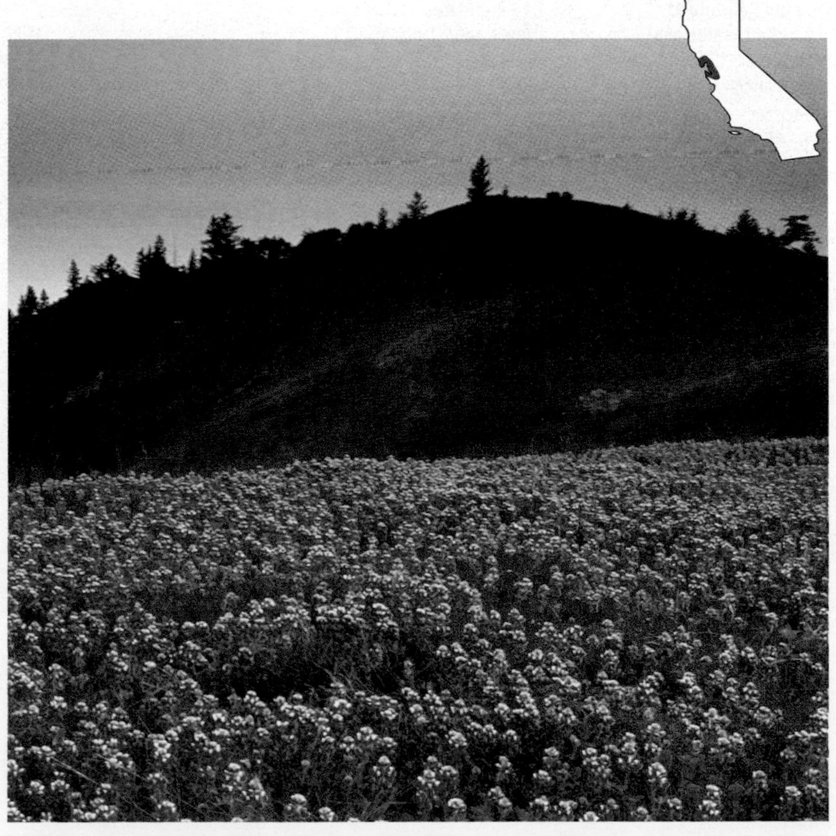

Sights	Restaurants	Hotels	Shopping	Nightlife
★★★★☆	★★★★☆	★★☆☆☆	★★☆☆☆	★★★★☆

WELCOME TO THE BAY AREA

TOP REASONS TO GO

★ **Bite into the "Gourmet Ghetto":** Eat your way through this area of North Berkeley, starting with a slice of perfect pizza from Cheese Board Pizza (just look for the line).

★ **Find solitude at Point Reyes National Seashore:** Hike beautifully rugged—and often deserted—beaches at one of the most beautiful places on Earth, period.

★ **Sit on a dock by the bay:** Admire the beauty of the Bay Area from the rocky, picturesque shores of Sausalito or Tiburon.

★ **Go barhopping in Oakland's hippest hood:** Spend an evening swinging through the watering holes of Uptown, Oakland's artsy-hip and fast-rising corner of downtown.

★ **Walk among giants:** Walking into Muir Woods, a mere 12 miles north of the Golden Gate Bridge, is like entering a cathedral built by God.

1 Berkeley. Independent bookstores, coffee spots, and cyclists.

2 Oakland. Lively arts, nightlife, and food scene.

3 The Marin Headlands. From the Golden Gate Bridge to Muir Beach, these headlands offer spectacular views.

4 Sausalito. Stunning views and a bohemian feel.

5 Tiburon. This scenic, quaint town has lots of good dining and hiking.

6 Mill Valley. A superb natural setting with a lively downtown area.

7 Muir Woods National Monument. Home to some of the most majestic redwoods in the world.

8 Mt. Tamalpais State Park. This park offers views of the entire Bay Area and the Pacific Ocean to the west.

9 Muir Beach. A quiet beach has a distinctly local feel.

10 Stinson Beach. Expect a nonchalant surfer vibe.

11 Point Reyes National Seashore. A dramatic rocky coastline with miles of sandy beaches.

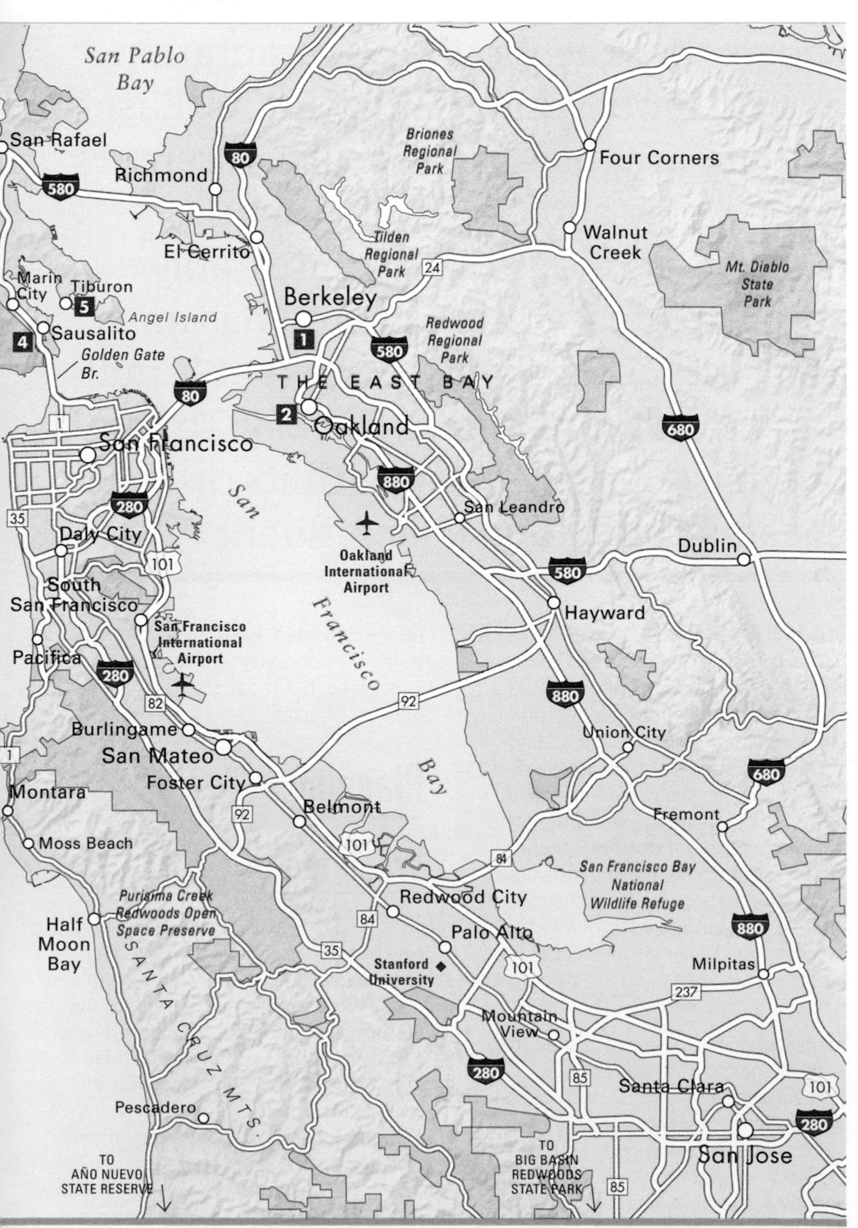
San Pablo Bay
San Rafael
Richmond
El Cerrito
Briones Regional Park
Tilden Regional Park
Four Corners
Walnut Creek
Mt. Diablo State Park
Marin City
Tiburon
Angel Island
Sausalito
Golden Gate Br.
Berkeley
Redwood Regional Park
THE EAST BAY
Oakland
San Francisco
San Francisco Bay
San Leandro
Daly City
Oakland International Airport
Dublin
South San Francisco
San Francisco International Airport
Hayward
Pacifica
Burlingame
San Mateo
Foster City
Union City
Montara
Belmont
Fremont
Moss Beach
San Francisco Bay National Wildlife Refuge
Purisima Creek Redwoods Open Space Preserve
Redwood City
Half Moon Bay
Palo Alto
Stanford University
Milpitas
SANTA CRUZ MTS.
Mountain View
Santa Clara
Pescadero
San Jose
TO AÑO NUEVO STATE RESERVE
TO BIG BASIN REDWOODS STATE PARK

It's rare for a metropolis to compete with its suburbs for visitors, but the view from any of San Francisco's hilltops shows that the Bay Area's temptations extend far beyond the city limits. East of the city are the energetic urban centers of Berkeley and Oakland. Famously radical Berkeley is also comfortably sophisticated, while Oakland has an arts and restaurant scene so hip that it pulls San Franciscans across the bay. To the north is Marin County with its dramatic coastal beauty and chic, affluent villages.

MAJOR REGIONS

The East Bay. The college town of Berkeley has long been known for its liberal ethos, stimulating university community (and perhaps even more stimulating coffee shops), and activist streak. But these days, the lively restaurant and arts scenes are luring even those who wouldn't be caught dead in Birkenstocks. Meanwhile, life in the diverse, harbor-front city of Oakland is strongly defined by a turbulent history. Today, progressive Oakland is an incubator for artisans of all kinds, and the thriving culinary and art scenes are taking off.

Marin County. Marin is considered the prettiest of the Bay Area counties, primarily because of its wealth of open space. Anchored by water on three sides, the county is mostly parkland, including long stretches of undeveloped coastline. The picturesque small towns here—Sausalito, Tiburon, Mill Valley, and Bolinas among them—may sometimes look rustic, but most are in a dizzyingly high tax bracket.

Planning

When to Go

As with San Francisco, you can visit the rest of the Bay Area any time of year, and it's especially nice in late spring and fall. Unlike San Francisco, though, the surrounding areas are reliably sunny in summer—it gets hotter as you head inland. Even the rainy season has its charms, as otherwise golden hills turn a rich green and wildflowers become plentiful. Precipitation is usually the heaviest between November and March. Berkeley is a university town, so it's easier to navigate the streets and find parking near the university between semesters, but there's also less buzz around town.

Getting Here and Around

Seamless travel from train to ferry to bus with one fare card is possible—and often preferable to driving on congested freeways and over toll bridges. For trips from one city to the next across the bay, take a tip from locals and save time and money with a Clipper card. They work with BART, Muni, buses, and ferries. ■ **TIP→ Order a Clipper card before you travel:** 🌐 *www.clippercard.com.*

BART TRAVEL

Using public transportation to reach Berkeley or Oakland is ideal. The under- and aboveground BART (Bay Area Rapid Transit) trains make stops in both cities as well as other East Bay destinations. Trips to either take about a half hour one-way from the center of San Francisco. BART does not serve Marin County.

CONTACTS BART ☎ *510/465–2278* 🌐 *www.bart.gov.*

BOAT AND FERRY TRAVEL

For sheer romance, nothing beats the ferry; there's service from San Francisco to Sausalito, Tiburon, and Larkspur in Marin County, and to Alameda and Oakland in the East Bay.

The Golden Gate Ferry crosses the bay to Larkspur and Sausalito from San Francisco's Ferry Building (✉ *Market St. and the Embarcadero*). Blue & Gold Fleet ferries depart daily for Sausalito and Tiburon from Pier 41 at Fisherman's Wharf; weekday commuter ferries leave from the Ferry Building for Tiburon. The trip to either Sausalito or Tiburon takes from 25 minutes to an hour. Purchase tickets from terminal vending machines.

The Angel Island–Tiburon Ferry sails to the island daily from April through October and on weekends the rest of the year.

The San Francisco Bay Ferry runs several times daily between San Francisco's Ferry Building or Pier 41 and Oakland's Jack London Square by way of Alameda. The trip lasts from 25 to 45 minutes, and leads to Oakland's waterfront shopping and restaurant district. Purchase tickets on board.

BOAT AND FERRY LINES Angel Island–Tiburon Ferry ☎ *415/435–2131* 🌐 *www.angelislandferry.com.* **Blue & Gold Fleet** ☎ *415/705–8200* 🌐 *www.blueandgold-fleet.com.* **Golden Gate Ferry** ☎ *415/921–5858* 🌐 *www.goldengateferry.org.* **San Francisco Bay Ferry** ☎ *707/643–3779, 877/643–3779* 🌐 *sanfranciscobayferry.com.*

BUS TRAVEL

Golden Gate Transit buses travel north to Sausalito, Tiburon, and elsewhere in Marin County from the Transbay Temporary Terminal (located at Howard and Main, two blocks south of Market) and other points in San Francisco. For Mt. Tamalpais State Park and West Marin (Stinson Beach, Bolinas, and Point Reyes Station), take any route to Marin City and then transfer to the West Marin Stagecoach. San Francisco Muni buses primarily serve the city, though the 76X does cross the Golden Gate and end at the Marin Headlands Visitors Center on weekends. ■ **TIP→ Several other bus options exist for local and regional travel throughout the Bay Area, including Amtrak, Greyhound, California Shuttle, and more (www.bayareatransit.net/regional).**

Though less speedy than BART, more than 30 AC Transit bus lines provide service to and from the Transbay Temporary Terminal and throughout the East Bay, even after BART shuts down. The F and FS lines will get you to Berkeley, while lines C, P, B, and O take you to Oakland and Piedmont.

BUS LINES AC Transit ☎ *510/891–4777* 🌐 *www.actransit.org.* **Golden Gate Transit** ☎ *511* 🌐 *www.goldengatetransit.org.* **SamTrans** ☎ *800/660–4287* 🌐 *www.samtrans.com.* **San Francisco Muni** ☎ *311* 🌐 *www.sfmta.com.* **West Marin Stagecoach** ☎ *511* 🌐 *www.marintransit.org.*

CAR TRAVEL

To reach the East Bay from San Francisco, take Interstate 80 East across the San Francisco–Oakland Bay Bridge. For U.C. Berkeley, merge onto Interstate 580 West and take Exit 11 for University Avenue. For Oakland, merge onto Interstate 580 East. To reach downtown, take Interstate 980 West from Interstate 580 East and exit at 14th Street. Travel time varies depending on traffic, but should take about 30 minutes (or more than an hour if it's rush hour).

For all points in Marin, head north on U.S. 101 and cross the Golden Gate Bridge. Sausalito, Tiburon, the Marin Headlands, and Point Reyes National Seashore are all accessed off U.S. 101. The scenic coastal route, Highway 1, also called Shoreline Highway and Panoramic for certain stretches, can be accessed off U.S. 101 as well. Follow this road to Muir Woods, Mt. Tamalpais State Park, Muir Beach, Stinson Beach, and Bolinas. From Bolinas, you can continue north on Highway 1 to Point Reyes.

Restaurants

The Bay Area is home to many popular and innovative restaurants, such as Chez Panisse in Berkeley and Commis in Oakland—for which reservations must be made well in advance. There are also countless casual but equally tasty eateries to test out; expect an emphasis on organic seasonal produce, locally raised meats, craft cocktails, and curated wine menus. Marin's dining scene trends toward the sleepy side, so be sure to check hours ahead of time. *Restaurant reviews have been shortened. For full information, visit Fodors.com.*

Hotels

With a few exceptions, hotels in Berkeley and Oakland tend to be standard-issue, but many Marin hotels package themselves as cozy retreats. Summer in Marin is often booked well in advance, despite weather that can be downright chilly. Check for special packages during this season. *Hotel reviews have been shortened. For full information, visit Fodors.com.*

WHAT IT COSTS

	$	$$	$$$	$$$$
RESTAURANTS	under $16	$16–$22	$23–$30	over $30
HOTELS	under $150	$150–$199	$200–$250	over $250

Tours

★ **Best Bay Area Tours**

SPECIAL-INTEREST | Morning and afternoon tours of Muir Woods and Sausalito include at least 90 minutes in the redwoods before heading on to Sausalito. On returning to the city, tours make a scenic stop in the Marin Headlands to enjoy fantastic views. Knowledgeable guides lead small tours in comfortable vans, and hotel pickup is included, though park entrance is not. Another tour option includes a visit to Muir Woods and Wine Country exploration. ☎ *877/705–8687* 🌐 *bestbayareatours.com* 🎫 *From $60.*

Berkeley

2 miles northeast of Bay Bridge.

Berkeley is the birthplace of the Free Speech Movement, the radical hub of the 1960s, the home of arguably the nation's top public university, and a frequent site of protests and political movements. The city of 115,000 is also a culturally diverse breeding ground for social trends, a bastion of the counterculture, and an important center for Bay Area writers, artists, and musicians. Berkeley residents, students, and faculty spend hours nursing coffee concoctions while they read, discuss, and debate at the dozens of cafés that surround campus. It's the quintessential university town, with numerous independent bookstores, countless casual eateries, myriad meetups, and thousands of cyclists.

Oakland may have Berkeley beat when it comes to ethnic diversity and cutting-edge arts, but unless you're accustomed to sipping hemp milk lattes while planning a protest prior to yoga, you'll likely find Berkeley charmingly offbeat.

GETTING HERE AND AROUND

BART is the easiest way to get to Berkeley from San Francisco. Exit at the Downtown Berkeley station, and walk a block up Center Street to get to the western edge of campus. AC Transit buses F and FS lines stop near the university and 4th Street shopping. By car, take Interstate 80 East across the Bay Bridge, merge onto Interstate 580 West, and take the University Avenue exit through downtown Berkeley or take the Ashby Avenue exit and turn left on Telegraph Avenue. Once you arrive, explore on foot. Berkeley is very pedestrian-friendly.

ESSENTIALS

VISITOR INFORMATION Koret Visitor Center ✉ *2227 Piedmont Ave., at California Memorial Stadium, Downtown* ☎ *510/642–5215* 🌐 *visit.berkeley.edu.* **Visit Berkeley** ✉ *2030 Addison St., Suite 102, Downtown* ☎ *510/549–7040, 800/847–4823* 🌐 *www.visitberkeley.com.*

A Tasting Tour 

For an unforgettable foodie experience, book a **Culinary Walking Tour** with Edible Excursions (☎ *415/806–5970,* 🌐 *www.edible-excursions.net*). Come hungry for knowledge and noshing. Tours ($110) take place on Thursday at 11 and Saturday at 10.

 Sights

BAMPFA (Berkeley Art Museum and Pacific Film Archive)

MUSEUM | This combined art museum and repertory movie theater and film archive contains more than 19,000 works of art and 16,000 films and videos. Art works span five centuries and include modernist notables Mark Rothko, Jackson Pollock, David Smith, and Hans Hofmann. The Pacific Film Archive specializes in international films and offers regular screenings, programs, and performances. ✉ *2155 Center St., Downtown* ☎ *510/642–0808* 🌐 *bampfa.org* 🎫 *$13; free 1st Thurs. of month* ⏲ *Closed Mon. and Tues.*

4th Street

NEIGHBORHOOD | Once an industrial area, this walkable stretch of 4th Street north of University Avenue has transformed into the busiest few blocks of refined shopping and eating in Berkeley. For lovers of design, curated taste experiences, artful living, and fashion, the vibrant district boasts more than 70 shops, specialty stores, cafés, and restaurants. See creation and inspiration at Castle in the Air, Builders Booksource, and The Stained Glass Garden, or sip a "live roast" at Artis, where you can watch small-batch coffee roasting in progress. ✉ *4th St.*

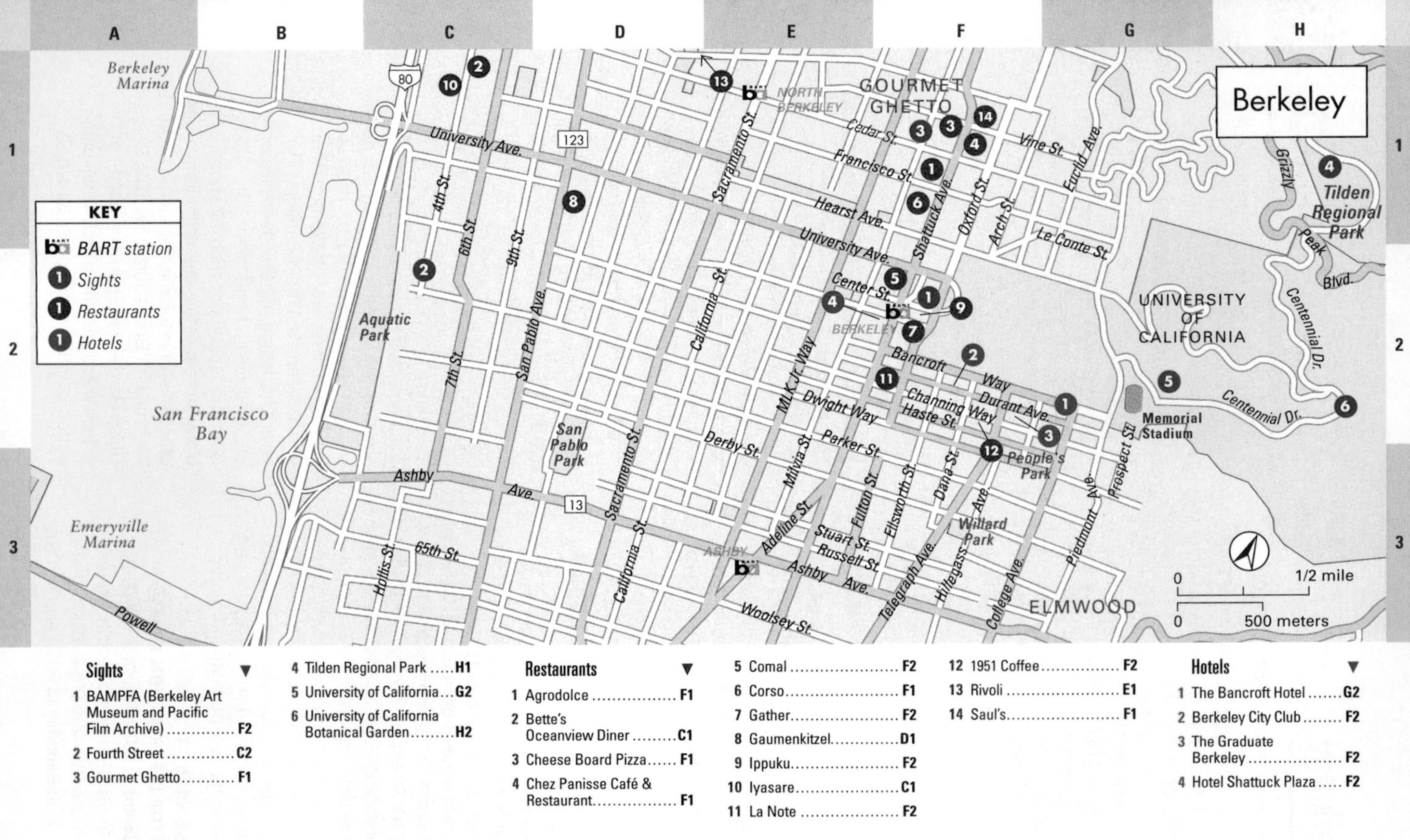

Sights ▼

1 BAMPFA (Berkeley Art Museum and Pacific Film Archive) F2
2 Fourth Street C2
3 Gourmet Ghetto F1
4 Tilden Regional Park H1
5 University of California ... G2
6 University of California Botanical Garden H2

Restaurants ▼

1 Agrodolce F1
2 Bette's Oceanview Diner C1
3 Cheese Board Pizza F1
4 Chez Panisse Café & Restaurant F1
5 Comal F2
6 Corso F1
7 Gather F2
8 Gaumenkitzel D1
9 Ippuku F2
10 Iyasare C1
11 La Note F2
12 1951 Coffee F2
13 Rivoli E1
14 Saul's F1

Hotels ▼

1 The Bancroft Hotel G2
2 Berkeley City Club F2
3 The Graduate Berkeley F2
4 Hotel Shattuck Plaza F2

between University Ave. and Virginia St. 🌐 *www.fourthstreet.com.*

★ Gourmet Ghetto

NEIGHBORHOOD | The success of Alice Waters's Chez Panisse defined California cuisine and attracted countless food-related enterprises to a stretch of Shattuck Avenue now known as the Gourmet Ghetto. Foodies will do well here poking around the shops, grabbing a quick bite, or indulging in a feast.

César (*1515 Shattuck*) wine bar provides afternoon tapas and late-night drinks, while the **Epicurious Garden** (*1509–1513 Shattuck*) food stands sell everything from sushi to gelato. A small terraced garden winds up to the **Imperial Tea Court**, a Zen-like teahouse rife with imports and tea ware.

Across Vine, the **Vintage Berkeley** (*2113 Vine*) wineshop offers regular tastings and reasonably priced bottles within the walls of a historic former pump house. Coffee lovers can head to the original **Peet's Coffee & Tea** at the corner of Walnut and Vine (*2124 Vine*).

South of Cedar Street, the **Local Butcher Shop** (*No. 1600*) sells locally sourced meat and hearty sandwiches of the day. For high-end food at takeout prices, try the salads, sandwiches, and signature potato puffs at **Grégoire**, around the corner on Cedar Street (*No. 2109*). **Masse's Pastries** (*No. 1469 Shattuck*) is a museum of edible artwork. We could go on, but you get the idea. ✉ *Shattuck Ave. between Delaware and Rose Sts., North Berkeley* 🌐 *www.gourmetghetto.org.*

★ Tilden Regional Park

NATIONAL/STATE PARK | **FAMILY** | Stunning bay views, a scaled-down steam train, and a botanic garden that boasts the nation's most complete collection of California plant life are the hallmarks of this 2,000-acre park in the hills just east of the U.C. Berkeley campus. The garden's visitor center offers tours, as well as information about Tilden's other attractions, including its picnic spots, Lake Anza swimming site, golf course, and hiking trails (the paved **Nimitz Way,** at Inspiration Point, is a popular hike with wonderful sunset views). **■ TIP→ Children love Tilden's interactive Little Farm and vintage carousel.** ✉ *Tilden Regional Park, 2501 Grizzly Peak Blvd., Tilden Park* ☎ *510/544–2747 park office* 🌐 *www.ebparks.org/parks/tilden* 🎟 *Free parking and botanic garden.*

University of California

COLLEGE | Known simply as "Cal," the founding campus of California's university system is one of the leading intellectual centers in the United States and a major site for scientific research. Chartered in 1868, the university sits on 178 oak-covered acres split by Strawberry Creek; it's bound by Bancroft Way to the south, Hearst Avenue to the north, Oxford Street to the west, and Gayley Road to the east. Campus highlights include bustling and historic **Sproul Plaza** (*Bancroft Way and Sather Rd.*), the seven floors and 61-bell carillon of **Sather Tower** (*Campanile Esplanade*), the nearly 3 million artifacts in the **Phoebe A. Hearst Museum of Anthropology** (Kroeber Hall), hands-on **Lawrence Hall of Science** (*1 Centennial Dr.*), the vibrant 34-acre **Botanical Gardens** (*200 Centennial Dr.*), and the historic **Hearst Greek Theatre** (*2001 Gayley Rd.*), the classic outdoor amphitheater designed by John Galen Howard. ✉ *Downtown* ☎ *510/642–6000* 🌐 *www.berkeley.edu.*

University of California Botanical Garden

GARDEN | **FAMILY** | Thanks to Berkeley's temperate climate, more than 10,000 types of plants from all corners of the world flourish in the 34-acre University of California Botanical Garden. Free garden tours are given regularly with paid admission. Benches and shady picnic tables make this a relaxing place for a snack with a breathtaking view. ✉ *200 Centennial Dr., Downtown* ☎ *510/643–2755*

The University of California is the epicenter of Berkeley's energy and activism.

botanicalgarden.berkeley.edu *$12*
Closed 1st Tues. every month.

Restaurants

Dining in Berkeley may be low-key when it comes to dress, but it's top-of-class in quality, even in less-refined spaces. Late diners beware: Berkeley is an "early to bed" kind of town.

Agrodolce

$$ | **ITALIAN** | **FAMILY** | Angelo D'Alo's family brings Sicilian flavors and their love for preparing them freshly to the heart of the Gourmet Ghetto, where black-and-white photos and Italian home decor add to the old-world atmosphere. The menu features local, sustainable, and organic ingredients in such dishes as house-made orecchiette, seafood risotto, and free-range *pollo scarpariello*. **Known for:** braised pork pappardelle; homemade sauces; antipasti specialties. *Average main: $17* *1730 Shattuck Ave., North Berkeley* *510/848–8748* *www.agrodolceberkeley.com* *Closed Tues.*

Bette's Oceanview Diner

$ | **DINER** | **FAMILY** | Checkered floors, vintage burgundy booths, and an old-time jukebox set the scene at this retro-chic diner in the heart of Berkeley's fashionable 4th Street shopping district. The wait for a seat at breakfast can be quite long; luckily Bette's To Go is always an option. **Known for:** soufflé pancakes; poached egg specialties; meat loaf and gravy. *Average main: $13* *1807 4th St., near Delaware St., 4th Street* *510/644–3230* *www.bettesdiner.com* *No dinner.*

★ Cheese Board Pizza

$ | **PIZZA** | A jazz combo entertains the line that usually snakes down the block outside Cheese Board Pizza; it's that good. The cooperatively owned takeout spot and restaurant draws devoted customers with the smell of just-baked garlic on the pie of the day. **Known for:** vegetarian pizza by the slice or slab; live music performances; green sauce. *Average main: $11* *1504–1512 Shattuck Ave., at Vine St., North Berkeley* *510/549–3183* *cheeseboardcollective.coop/pizza*

⏲ *Pizza closed Sun. and Mon., bakery closed Sun.*

★ Chez Panisse Café & Restaurant

$$$$ | **MODERN AMERICAN** | Alice Waters's legendary eatery is known for its locally sourced ingredients, formal prix-fixe menus, and personal service, while its upstairs café offers simpler fare in a more casual setting. Both menus change daily and legions of loyal fans insist that Chez Panisse lives up to its reputation. **Known for:** sustainably sourced meats; inventive use of seasonal ingredients; attention to detail. $ *Average main: $125 ✉ 1517 Shattuck Ave., at Vine St., North Berkeley ☎ 510/548–5525 restaurant, 510/548–5049 café 🌐 www.chezpanisse.com ⏲ Closed Sun. No lunch in restaurant.*

★ Comal

$$ | **MODERN MEXICAN** | Relaxed yet trendy, Comal's cavernous indoor dining space and intimate back patio and fire pit draw a diverse, decidedly casual crowd for creative Oaxacan-inspired fare and well-crafted cocktails. The modern Mexican menu centers on small dishes that lend themselves to sharing and are offered alongside more than 100 tequilas and mezcals. **Known for:** margaritas and mezcal; house-made chicharrones; wood-fired entrées. $ *Average main: $16 ✉ 2020 Shattuck Ave., near University Ave., Downtown ☎ 510/926–6300 🌐 www.comalberkeley.com ⏲ No lunch.*

Corso

$$$ | **MODERN ITALIAN** | This lively spot serves up a seasonal menu of excellent Tuscan cuisine and Italian wines in a sparse but snazzy space. The open kitchen dominates a room, which includes closely spaced tables and festive flickering candles. **Known for:** handcrafted pastas; house-cured salumi; daily butcher's specials. $ *Average main: $24 ✉ 1788 Shattuck Ave., at Delaware St., North Berkeley ☎ 510/704–8004 🌐 www.corsoberkeley.com ⏲ No lunch.*

Gather

$$$ | **MODERN AMERICAN** | All things local, organic, seasonal, and sustainable reside harmoniously under one roof at Gather. This haven for vegans, vegetarians, and carnivores alike is a vibrant, well-lit space that boasts funky light fixtures, shiny wood furnishings, and banquettes made of recycled leather belts. **Known for:** heirloom varietals; wood-fired pizzas; house-made liqueurs. $ *Average main: $24 ✉ 2200 Oxford St., at Allston Way, Downtown ☎ 510/809–0400 🌐 www.gatherrestaurant.com.*

Gaumenkitzel

$$ | **GERMAN** | **FAMILY** | This convivial locale for organic, slow-food German fare is also the spot for the Bay Area's best variety of German beers. With dishes like spätzle and caramelized onions, house-made *brezel* with bratwurst, *jägerschnitzel* with braised red cabbage, and panfried rainbow trout, this kitchen puts a fresh stamp on traditional German favorites. **Known for:** German wine and beer selection; house-made German breads; fresh, sustainable ingredients. $ *Average main: $20 ✉ 2121 San Pablo Ave., Downtown ☎ 510/647–5016 🌐 www.gaumenkitzel.net ⏲ Closed Mon.*

★ Ippuku

$$$ | **JAPANESE** | More Tokyo street chic than standard sushi house, this *izakaya*—the Japanese equivalent of a bar with appetizers—is decked with bamboo-screen booths. Servers pour an impressive array of sakes and *shōchū* and serve up surprising fare. **Known for:** shōchū selection; charcoal-grilled yakitori skewers; selection of small dishes. $ *Average main: $28 ✉ 2130 Center St., Downtown ☎ 510/665–1969 🌐 www.ippukuberkeley.com ⏲ Closed Mon. No lunch.*

Iyasare

$$$ | **JAPANESE** | Reservations are recommended at this 4th Street hot spot where the outdoor seating is ideal for people-watching and the Japanese country

food is uniquely prepared. Locals come back for seasonally changing eclectic dishes made with a blend of local ingredients, such as burdock root tempura and ume-cured sashimi or miso-bell pepper puree with Dungeness crab. **Known for:** Japanese whiskey and specialty sakes; donburi and small plates; cured salads. *Average main: $23 ✉ 1830 4th St., 4th Street ☎ 510/845–8100 🌐 iyasare-berkeley.com.*

★ La Note

$$ | **FRENCH** | A charming taste of Provence in a 19th-century locale with stone floors, country tables, and a seasonal flowering patio, La Note's rustic French food is as thoughtfully prepared as the space is lovely. Enjoy breakfast and brunch outdoors with fresh crusty breads and pastries, eggs *Lucas* with house-roasted tomatoes, and lemon gingerbread pancakes or romantic dinners with mussels *mouclade,* ratatouille, and homemade fondue. **Known for:** sandwiches; house-made Merguez sausage; brioche pan perdu. *Average main: $18 ✉ 2377 Shattuck Ave., Downtown ✥ Between Channing and Durant ☎ 510/843–1525 🌐 www.lanoterestaurant.com ⏲ No dinner Sun.–Wed.*

1951 Coffee

$ | **CAFÉ** | Taking its name from the 1951 Refugee Convention at which the United Nations first set guidelines for refugee protections, 1951 Coffee Company is a nonprofit coffee shop inspired and powered by refugees. In addition to crafting high-caliber coffee drinks and dishing out local pastries and savory bites, this colorful café also serves as an inspiring advocacy space and training center for refugees. Just three blocks south of campus, it's a favorite meet-up spot for locals and students alike. **Known for:** 1951 hand-roasted blends; Third Culture Bakery Mochi doughnuts and muffins; chai latte. *Average main: $7 ✉ 2410 Channing Way, at Dana St., Downtown ☎ 510/280–6171 🌐 1951coffee.com.*

Rivoli

$$$$ | **MODERN AMERICAN** | Italian-inspired dishes using fresh California ingredients star on a menu that changes regularly. Inventive offerings are served in a Zen-like modern dining room with captivating views of the lovely back garden. **Known for:** line-caught fish and sustainably sourced meats; curated wine list; thoughtfully combined ingredients. *Average main: $32 ✉ 1539 Solano Ave., at Neilson St., North Berkeley ☎ 510/526–2542 🌐 www.rivolirestaurant.com ⏲ No lunch.*

★ Saul's

$$ | **AMERICAN** | **FAMILY** | High ceilings and red-leather booths add to the friendly, retro atmosphere of Saul's deli, a Berkeley institution that is well known for its homemade celery tonic sodas and enormous sandwiches made with Acme bread. Locals swear by the pastrami sandwiches, stuffed-cabbage rolls, and challah French toast. **Known for:** hand-rolled organic bagels; matzo ball soup; Niman Ranch grass-fed beef and Monterey Fish Company seafood. *Average main: $16 ✉ 1475 Shattuck Ave., near Vine St., North Berkeley ☎ 510/848–3354 🌐 www.saulsdeli.com.*

Hotels

For inexpensive lodging, investigate University Avenue, west of campus. The area can be noisy, congested, and somewhat dilapidated, but it does include a few decent motels and chain properties. All Berkeley lodgings are strictly mid-range.

The Bancroft Hotel

$$ | **HOTEL** | This eco-friendly boutique hotel—across from the U.C. campus—is quaint, charming, and completely green. **Pros:** closest hotel in Berkeley to U.C. campus; friendly staff; many rooms have good views. **Cons:** some rooms are quite small; despite renovation, the building shows its age with thin walls; no elevator. *Rooms from: $160 ✉ 2680*

Famed Berkeley restaurant Chez Panisse focuses on seasonal local ingredients.

Bancroft Way, Downtown ☎ 510/549–1000, 800/549–1002 toll-free 🌐 bancrofthotel.com 22 rooms 🍽 Breakfast.

★ Berkeley City Club

$$$ | HOTEL | Moorish design and Gothic architecture meet modern amenities at this historic locale steps from campus, arts, and eateries. **Pros:** art gallery and courtyard seating; laundry facilities; on-site salon and skin care. **Cons:** no nonservice pets allowed; limited, fee-only parking; no televisions in rooms. *$ Rooms from: $245 ✉ 2315 Durant Ave., Downtown ☎ 🌐 www.berkeleycityclub.com 38 rooms 🍽 Free Breakfast.*

The Graduate Berkeley

$$$ | HOTEL | Fresh, colorful design and Bohemian flair set the tone at this historically renovated hotel just steps from campus and downtown eating, shopping, and entertainment. **Pros:** convenient location; pet-friendly; complimentary bikes. **Cons:** rooms can be noisy; rooms can be small; fee parking only. *$ Rooms from: $239 ✉ 2600 Durant Ave., Downtown ☎ 510/845–8981 🌐 www.graduatehotels.com/berkeley 144 rooms 🍽 No meals.*

★ Hotel Shattuck Plaza

$$$ | HOTEL | This historic boutique hotel sits amid Berkeley's downtown arts district, just steps from the U.C. campus and a short walk from the Gourmet Ghetto. **Pros:** central location near public transit; special date night and B&B packages; modern facilities. **Cons:** public and street parking only; limited on-site fitness center; street-facing rooms may be loud. *$ Rooms from: $246 ✉ 2086 Allston Way, at Shattuck Ave., Downtown ☎ 510/845–7300 🌐 www.hotelshattuck-plaza.com 199 rooms 🍽 No meals.*

Nightlife

★ The Freight & Salvage Coffeehouse

MUSIC CLUBS | For more than 50 years, the Freight has been a venue for some of the world's finest practitioners of folk, jazz, gospel, blues, world-beat, bluegrass, and storytelling. The nonprofit organization grew from an 87-seat coffee house to a thriving, 500-seat venue in the heart of Berkeley's Art District. Many tickets cost less than $30. ✉ *2020 Addison St., between Shattuck Ave. and Milvia St., Downtown* ☎ *510/644–2020* 🌐 *www.thefreight.org.*

★ Tupper & Reed
BARS/PUBS | Housed in the former music shop of John C. Tupper and Lawrence Reed, this music-inspired cocktail haven features a symphony of carefully crafted libations, which are mixed with live music performed by local musicians. The historic 1925 building features a balcony bar, cozy nooks, antique fixtures, a pool table, and romantic fireplaces. ✉ *2271 Shattuck Ave., at Kitteredge St., Downtown* ☎ *510/859–4472* 🌐 *www.tupperandreed.com.*

Performing Arts

Berkeley Repertory Theatre
THEATER | One of the region's most highly respected and innovative repertory theaters, Berkeley Rep performs the work of classic and contemporary playwrights. Well-known pieces such as *Tartuffe* and *Macbeth* mix with world premieres and edgier fare like Green Day's *American Idiot* and Lemony Snicket's *The Composer Is Dead.* The theater's complex is in the heart of downtown Berkeley's arts district, near BART's Downtown Berkeley station. ✉ *2025 Addison St., near Shattuck Ave., Downtown* ☎ *510/647–2949* 🌐 *www.berkeleyrep.org.*

Cal Performances
CONCERTS | Based out of U.C. Berkeley, this series runs from September through May. It features a varied bill of internationally acclaimed artists ranging from classical soloists to the latest jazz, world-music, theater, and dance ensembles. Past performers include Alvin Ailey American Dance Theater, the National Ballet of China, and Yo-Yo Ma. ✉ *101 Zellerbach Hall, Suite 4800, Dana St. and Bancroft Way, Downtown* ☎ *510/642–9988* 🌐 *calperformances.org.*

Shopping

★ Acci Gallery
ART GALLERIES | The Arts and Crafts Cooperative, Inc., a collective of Berkeley artists and artisans, has been a stalwart gallery and retail store showcasing ceramics, textiles, paintings, photography, jewelry, and various media for more than 60 years. Explore the amazing range of local talent in a well-lit historic space, and find truly one-of-a-kind gems to take home. ✉ *1652 Shattuck Ave., North Berkeley* ✥ *At Lincoln* ☎ *510/843–2527* 🌐 *www.accigallery.com.*

★ Amoeba Music
MUSIC STORES | Heaven for audiophiles and movie collectors, this legendary Berkeley favorite is *the* place to head for new and used CDs, vinyl, cassettes, VHS tapes, Blu-ray discs, and DVDs. The massive and ever-changing stock includes thousands of titles for all music tastes, as well as plenty of Amoeba merch. There are branches in San Francisco and Hollywood, but this is the original. ✉ *2455 Telegraph Ave., at Haste St., Downtown* ☎ *510/549–1125* 🌐 *www.amoeba.com.*

Kermit Lynch Wine Merchant
WINE/SPIRITS | Credited with taking American appreciation of old-world wines to a higher level, this small shop is a great place to peruse as you educate your palate. The friendly salespeople will happily direct you to the latest French and Italian bargains. ✉ *1605 San Pablo Ave., at Cedar St.* ☎ *510/524–1524* 🌐 *www.kermitlynch.com* ⏲ *Closed Sun. and Mon.*

Moe's Books
BOOKS/STATIONERY | The spirit of Moe—the creative, cantankerous, cigar-smoking late proprietor—lives on in this world-famous four-story house of new and used books. Students and professors come here to browse the large selection, which includes literary and cultural criticism, art

titles, and literature in foreign languages. ✉ *2476 Telegraph Ave., near Haste St., Downtown* ☎ *510/849–2087* 🌐 *www.moesbooks.com.*

Oakland

East of Bay Bridge.

In contrast to San Francisco's buzz and beauty and Berkeley's storied counterculture, Oakland's allure lies in its amazing diversity. Here you can find a Nigerian clothing store, a Gothic revival skyscraper, a Buddhist meditation center, and a lively salsa club, all within the same block.

Oakland's multifaceted nature reflects its colorful and tumultuous history. Once a cluster of Mediterranean-style homes and gardens that served as a bedroom community for San Francisco, the town had a major rail terminal and port city by the turn of the 20th century. Already a hub of manufacturing, Oakland became a center for shipbuilding and industry when the United States entered World War II. New jobs in the city's shipyards, railroads, and factories attracted thousands of laborers from across the country, including sharecroppers from the Deep South, Mexican Americans from the Southwest, and some of the nation's first female welders. Neighborhoods were imbued with a proud but gritty spirit, along with heightened racial tension. In the wake of the civil rights movement, racial pride gave rise to militant groups like the Black Panther Party, but they were little match for the economic hardships and racial tensions that plagued Oakland. In many neighborhoods the reality was widespread poverty and gang violence—subjects that dominated the songs of such Oakland-bred rappers as the late Tupac Shakur. The highly publicized protests of the Occupy Oakland movement in 2011 and 2012 and the #BlackLivesMatter movement of 2014 and 2015 illustrate just how much Oakland remains a mosaic of its past.

Oakland's affluent reside in the city's hillside homes and wooded enclaves like Claremont, Piedmont, and Montclair, which provide a warmer, more spacious alternative to San Francisco, while a constant flow of newcomers ensures continued diversity, vitality, and growing pains. Many neighborhoods to the west and south of the city center have yet to be touched by gentrification, but a renovated downtown and vibrant arts scene has injected new energy into the city. Even San Franciscans, often loath to cross the Bay Bridge, come to Uptown and Temescal for the nightlife, arts, and restaurants.

Everyday life here revolves around the neighborhood. In some areas, such as Piedmont and Rockridge, you'd swear you were in Berkeley or San Francisco's Noe Valley. Along Telegraph Avenue just south of 51st Street, Temescal is littered with hipsters and pulsing with creative culinary and design energy. These are perfect places for browsing, eating, or relaxing between sightseeing trips to Oakland's architectural gems, rejuvenated waterfront, and numerous green spaces.

GETTING HERE AND AROUND

Driving from San Francisco, take Interstate 80 East across the Bay Bridge, then take Interstate 580 East to the Grand Avenue exit for Lake Merritt. To reach downtown and the waterfront, take Interstate 980 West from Interstate 580 East and exit at 12th Street; exit at 18th Street for Uptown. For Temescal, take Interstate 580 East to Highway 24 and exit at 51st Street.

By BART, use the Lake Merritt Station for the Oakland Museum and southern Lake Merritt; the Oakland City Center–12th Street Station for downtown, Chinatown, and Old Oakland; and the 19th Street

Station for Uptown, the Paramount Theatre, and the north side of Lake Merritt.

By bus, take the AC Transit's C and P lines to get to Piedmont in Oakland. The O bus stops at the edge of Chinatown near downtown Oakland.

Oakland's Jack London Square is an easy hop on the ferry from San Francisco. Those without cars can take advantage of the free Broadway Shuttle, which runs from the Jack London Square to 27th Street via downtown on weekdays and Friday and Saturday nights.

Be aware of how quickly neighborhoods can change. Walking is generally safe downtown and in the Piedmont and Rockridge areas, but be mindful when walking west and southeast of downtown, especially at night.

SHUTTLE CONTACT Broadway Shuttle 🌐 *www.oaklandca.gov.*

ESSENTIALS

VISITOR INFORMATION Visit Oakland ✉ *481 Water St., near Broadway, Jack London Square* ☎ *510/839–9000* 🌐 *www.visitoakland.com.*

Sights

Lake Merritt

NATURE PRESERVE | This lagoon with its unique habitat for more than 100 bird species became the nation's first wildlife refuge in 1870. Today the 3.1-mile path around the lake is also a refuge for walkers, bikers, joggers, and nature lovers. **Lakeside Park** has **Children's Fairyland** (*699 Bellevue*) and the **Rotary Nature Center** (*600 Bellevue*), where monthly bird walks commence every fourth Wednesday. For views from the water, the **Lake Merritt Boating Center** (*568 Bellevue*) rents kayaks and rowboats (🌐 *www.lakemerritt.org*). Venetian gondolas cruise from the Oakland Boathouse (*$60 for 30 mins for 2,* 🌐 *gondolaservizio.com*).

On the lake's south side, the **Camron-Stanford House** (*1418 Lakeside Dr.*), is the last of the grand Victorians that once dominated the area; it's open Sundays for tours. Nearby bold **Oakland mural art** offers a more modern feast for the eyes (*between Madison and Webster Strs. and 7th and 11th Sts.*).

The lake's necklace of lights adds allure for dinner-goers to the art-deco **Terrace Room** (*1800 Madison St.*) or **Lake Chalet** (*1520 Lakeside Dr.*), as well as to a host of tasty spots along Grand Avenue, from **Enssaro** Ethiopian (*357a*) and Korean BBQ at **Jong Ga House** (*372*) to comfort gourmet at **Grand Lake Kitchen** (*576*). ✉ *Lake Merritt.*

★ Oakland Museum of California

MUSEUM | FAMILY | This museum, designed by Kevin Roche, is one of the country's quintessential examples of mid-century modern architecture. Explore the robust collection of nearly 2 million objects in three distinct galleries celebrating the state's history, natural sciences, and art. Listen to native species and environmental soundscapes in the Library of Natural Sounds and engage in stories of the state's past and future from Ohlone basket making to emerging technologies and current events. Not to be missed are the photographs from Dorothea Lange's personal archive and a worthy collection of Bay Area figurative painters including David Park and Joan Brown. Take a break at the Blue Oak café for seasonal dishes sourced from local ingredients. **■ TIP→ On Friday evening the museum gets lively, with live music, food trucks, and after-hours gallery access.** ✉ *1000 Oak St., at 10th St., Downtown* ☎ *510/318–8400, 888/625–6873 toll-free* 🌐 *museumca.org* 🎫 *$16, free 1st Sun. of month* ⏲ *Closed Mon. and Tues.*

★ Paramount Theatre

ARTS VENUE | A glorious art-deco specimen, the Paramount operates as a venue for concerts and performances of all kinds, from the Oakland Symphony

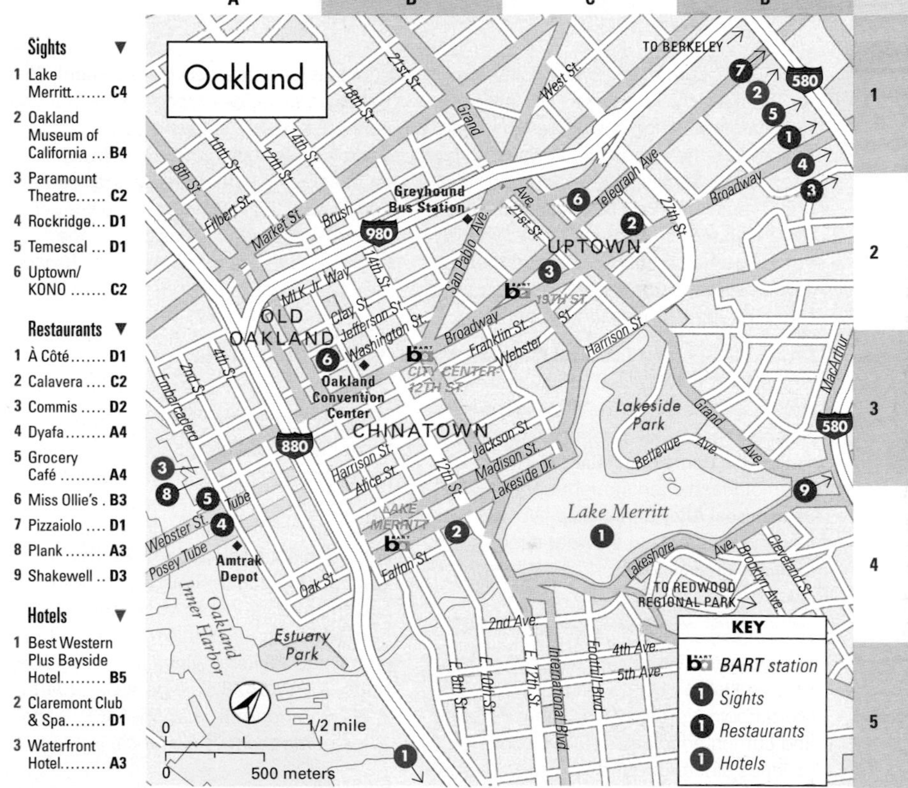

to Jerry Seinfeld and Elvis Costello. The popular classic movie nights start off with a 30-minute Wurlitzer concert. ■ **TIP→ Docent-led tours, offered the first and third Saturday of the month, are fun and informative.** ✉ *2025 Broadway, at 20th St., Uptown* ☎ *510/465–6400* 🌐 *www.paramounttheatre.com* 🎫 *Tour $5.*

★ Rockridge

NEIGHBORHOOD | FAMILY | This fashionable upscale neighborhood is one of Oakland's most desirable places to live. Explore the tree-lined streets that radiate out from **College Avenue** just north and south of the Rockridge BART station for a look at California Craftsman bungalows at their finest. By day College Avenue between Broadway and Alcatraz Avenue is crowded with shoppers buying fresh flowers, used books, and clothing; by night the same folks are back for handcrafted meals, artisan wines, and locally brewed ales. With its specialty-food shops and quick bites to go, **Market Hall,** an airy European-style marketplace at Shafter Avenue, is a hub of culinary activity. ✉ *5655 College Ave., between Alcatraz Ave. and Broadway, Rockridge* 🌐 *www.rockridgedistrict.com.*

★ Temescal

NEIGHBORHOOD | Centering on Telegraph Avenue between 40th and 51st streets, Temescal (the Aztec term for "sweat house") is a low-pretension, mon-eyed-hipster hood with young families and middle-aged folks thrown into the mix. A critical mass of excellent eateries draws folks from around the Bay Area; there's veteran **Doña Tomás** (*5004 Telegraph Ave.*) and favorites **Pizzaiolo** (*5008 Telegraph Ave.*) and **Rose's Taproom** (*4930 Telegraph Ave.*) as well as **Bakesale Betty**

(*5098 Telegraph Ave.*), where folks line up for the fried-chicken sandwich. Old-time dive bars and smog-check stations share space with the trendy children's clothing shop **Ruby's Garden** (*5026 Telegraph Ave.*) and the stalwart **East Bay Depot for Creative Reuse** (*4695 Telegraph Ave.*), where you might find a bucket of buttons or 1,000 muffin wrappers among birdcages, furniture, lunch boxes, and ribbon.

Around the corner, **Temescal Alley** (*49th St.*), a tucked-away lane of tiny storefronts, crackles with the creative energy of local makers. Find botanical wonders at **Crimson Horticultural Rarities** (*No. 470*) or an old-fashioned straight-edge shave at **Temescal Alley Barbershop** (*No. 470B*). Don't miss grabbing a sweet scoop at **Curbside Creamery** (*No. 482*). ✉ *Telegraph Ave., between 40th and 51st Sts., Temescal* 🌐 *www.temescaldistrict.org.*

★ Uptown/KONO

NEIGHBORHOOD | Uptown and KONO (Koreatown-Northgate) is where nightlife and cutting-edge art merge. Dozens of galleries cluster around Telegraph Avenue and north of Grand Avenue into KONO, exhibiting everything from photography and installations to glasswork and fiber arts. The first Friday of each month, upwards of 50,000 descend for **Art Murmur** (🌐 *oaklandartmurmur.org*), a late-night gallery event that has expanded into **First Friday** (🌐 *oaklandfirstfridays.org*), a festival of food trucks, street vendors, and live music along Telegraph Avenue.

Restaurants with a distinctly urban vibe make Uptown/KONO a dining destination every night of the week. Favorites include eclectic Japanese-inspired fare at **Hopscotch** (*1915 San Pablo Ave.*), stylish cuisine at art-deco **Flora** (*1900 Telegraph Ave.*), tasty tapas at trendy **Duende** (*468 19th*), just to name a few.

Toss in the bevy of bars and there's plenty within walking distance to keep you busy all evening: **Bar Three Fifty-Five** (*355 19th St.*), an upscale dive with iconic cocktails; the three-generation **Stork Club Oakland** (*2330 Telegraph Ave.*), a stalwart venue for new music and comedy; **Drake's Dealership** (*2325 Broadway*), with its spacious hipster-friendly beer garden; and **Somar** (*1727 Telegraph Ave.*), a bar, music lounge, and art gallery in one. ✉ *Oakland* ✣ *Telegraph Ave. and Broadway from 14th to 27th Sts.*

Restaurants

À Côté

$$ | **MEDITERRANEAN** | This Mediterranean hot spot is all about seasonal small plates, cozy tables, family-style eating, and excellent wine. Heavy wooden tables, intimate dining nooks, natural light, and a heated patio make this an ideal destination for couples, families, and the after-work crowd. **Known for:** Pernod mussels; exquisite small plates; global and regional wine list. [$] *Average main: $19* ✉ *5478 College Ave., at Taft Ave., Rockridge* ☎ *510/655–6469* 🌐 *acoterestaurant.com* ⏲ *No lunch.*

Calavera

$$$ | **MODERN MEXICAN** | This Oaxacan-inspired hot spot offers inventive and elevated plates in an industrial-chic space with lofty ceilings, warm wooden tables, exposed brick walls, and heated outdoor dining. Innovative cocktails like the salt-air margarita come from a beautiful bar with a library of more than 100 agaves. **Known for:** fresh ceviche; wide selection of tequilas and mezcal; carnitas tacos served in nixtamal heirloom corn tortillas. [$] *Average main: $24* ✉ *2337 Broadway, at 24th St., Uptown* ☎ *510/338–3273* 🌐 *calaveraoakland.com* ⏲ *Closed Mon.*

★ Commis

$$$$ | **AMERICAN** | A slender, unassuming storefront houses the first East Bay restaurant with a Michelin star (two of them, in fact). The room is minimalist and polished: nothing distracts from the artistry of chef James Syhabout, who creates a multicourse dining experience based on the season and his distinctive vision. **Known for:** inventive multicourse tasting menu; Michelin-winning execution; artful precision. $ *Average main: $165 ✉ 3859 Piedmont Ave., at Rio Vista Ave., Piedmont ☎ 510/653–3902 🌐 commisrestaurant.com ⏲ Closed Mon. and Tues. No lunch.*

Dyafa

$$$ | **MIDDLE EASTERN** | **FAMILY** | Reem Assil, one of the Bay Area's best chefs, brings Arabic heritage flavors to Jack London Square at Dyafa, where hot and cold *mezze* dishes such as Hummus Kawarma (served warm with lamb and cured lime) and *suhoon* dishes such as Musakhan (sumac-spiced chicken confit) are best shared family-style. Menus pair cocktails and wine flights with seasonally changing dishes for brunch, lunch, and dinner. **Known for:** freshly baked mana'eesh; house-made dips and pickles; Arabic-inspired cocktails. $ *Average main: $30 ✉ 44 Webster St., Jack London Square ☎ 510/250–9491 🌐 www.dyafaoakland.com.*

Grocery Café

$$ | **BURMESE** | Home-style Burmese food may be one of the best kept secrets in the Jack London Square area, where the bright, cozy Grocery Café serves up savory street food like *khauk swe thoke* (rainbow noodle salad) alongside traditional favorites like *mohinga* (fish chowder soup) and mango chutney pork stew. Vegan and veggie house special tofu and vegetarian hinga soup are among the locals' favorites on the menu. **Known for:** tea leaf salad; pork belly thoke; coconut rice. $ *Average main: $19 ✉ 90 Franklin St., Jack London Square.*

Miss Ollie's

$$ | **CARIBBEAN** | **FAMILY** | Centrally located in the city's historic district, Miss Ollie's is a colorful Afro-Caribbean gem in Swan's Market that packs in mouthwatering flavors. Daily lunch specialties include juicy, crispy fried chicken and waffles, braised oxtails, and creole doughnuts, while hearty dinner fare offers jerk chicken, island-style slow-cooked pork, split-pea and okra fritters, and exceptional pea and pumpkin soups. **Known for:** fried chicken; sweet plantains; jerk shrimp. $ *Average main: $17 ✉ 901 Washington St., Old Oakland ☎ 510/285–6188 🌐 www.realmissolliesoakland.com.*

Pizzaiolo

$$$ | **ITALIAN** | **FAMILY** | Chez Panisse alum Charlie Hallowell helms the kitchen of this rustic-chic Oakland institution. Diners of all ages perch on wooden chairs with red-leather backs and nosh on farm-to-table Italian fare from a daily changing menu. **Known for:** seasonal wood-fired pizza; daily house-made breads; rustic California-Italian entrées. $ *Average main: $23 ✉ 5008 Telegraph Ave., at 51st St., Temescal ☎ 510/652–4888 🌐 www.pizzaiolooakland.com ⏲ No lunch.*

Plank

$$ | **AMERICAN** | **FAMILY** | Plank brings food and entertainment together in an expansive indoor-outdoor space with a waterfront view. Sip from more than 50 handcrafted local beers while playing bocce ball in the beer garden, lunch on Cuban sandwiches and Cajun mahi tacos during a bowling or billiards match, or try your hand at the arcade before biting into baby back ribs. **Known for:** fun outdoor space with fire pits; generous portions; games and activities. $ *Average main: $17 ✉ 98 Broadway, Jack London Square ☎ 510/817–0980 🌐 www.plankoakland.com.*

★ Shakewell

$$$ | **MEDITERRANEAN** | Two *Top Chef* vets opened this stylish Lakeshore restaurant, which serves creative and memorable Mediterranean small plates in a lively setting that features an open kitchen, wood-fired oven, communal tables, and snug seating. As the name implies, well-crafted cocktails are shaken (or stirred) and poured with panache. **Known for:** wood-oven paella; Spanish and Mediterranean small plates; unique cocktails.

$ *Average main: $26* ✉ *3407 Lakeshore Ave., near Mandana Blvd., Grand Lake* ☎ *510/251–0329* 🌐 *www.shakewelloakland.com* ⏲ *Closed Mon. No lunch Tues.*

Hotels

Best Western Plus Bayside Hotel

$$ | HOTEL | Sandwiched between the serene Oakland Estuary and an eight-lane freeway, this all-suites property has handsome accommodations with balconies or patios, many overlooking the water. **Pros:** attractive, budget-conscious choice; free parking; free shuttle to and from airport, Jack London Square, and downtown locations. **Cons:** few shops or restaurants in walking distance; freeway-side rooms can be loud; some rooms have no views or patios/balconies. $ *Rooms from: $189* ✉ *1717 Embarcadero, off I–880, at 16th St. exit* ☎ *510/356–2450* 🌐 *www.baysidehoteloakland.com* *81 rooms* *Breakfast.*

★ Claremont Club & Spa

$$$$ | HOTEL | FAMILY | Straddling the Oakland–Berkeley border, this amenities-rich Fairmont property—which is more than 100 years old—beckons like a gleaming white castle in the hills. **Pros:** amazing spa; supervised child care; solid business amenities. **Cons:** parking is pricey; mandatory facilities charge; remote from shops or restaurants. $ *Rooms from: $338* ✉ *41 Tunnel Rd., at Ashby and Domingo Aves.* ☎ *510/843–3000, 800/257–7544 reservations* 🌐 *www.fairmont.com/claremont-berkeley* *276 rooms* *No meals.*

Waterfront Hotel

$$$ | HOTEL | FAMILY | This thoroughly modern, pleasantly appointed Joie de Vivre property sits among the many high-caliber restaurants of Jack London Square. **Pros:** complimentary wine-and-cheese hour weekdays; lovely views; free shuttle service to downtown. **Cons:** passing trains can be noisy on city side; parking is pricey; limited amenities. $ *Rooms from: $209* ✉ *10 Washington St., Jack London Square* ☎ *510/836–3800 front desk, 888/842–5333 reservations* 🌐 *www.jdvhotels.com* *145 rooms* *No meals.*

Nightlife

Back when rent was still relatively cheap, artists flocked to Oakland, giving rise to a cultural scene—visual arts, indie music, spoken word, film—that's still buzzing, especially in Uptown. Trendy new spaces pop up regularly and the beer-garden renaissance is already well established. Whether you're a self-proclaimed beer snob or just someone who enjoys a cold drink on a sunny day, there's something for everyone. Oakland's nightlife scene is less crowded and more intimate than what you'll find in San Francisco. Music is just about everywhere, though the most popular venues are downtown.

BARS

★ Café Van Kleef

BARS/PUBS | Long before Uptown got hot, the late Peter Van Kleef was serving stiff fresh-squeezed greyhounds, telling tales about his collection of pop-culture mementos, and booking live music at Café Van Kleef, a funky café-bar that crackles with creative energy—there's still live music every weekend. This local favorite still serves some of the stiffest drinks in town. ✉ *1621 Telegraph Ave., between 16th and 17th Sts., Uptown* ☎ *510/763–7711* 🌐 *cafevankleef.net.*

★ Heinold's First and Last Chance Saloon

BARS/PUBS | Arguably California's longest continuously active saloon since it opened in 1884, this watering hole, built from the hull of a flat-bottomed stern-wheeler, is the famous place where young Jack London got his start as a writer. Historic photos, artifacts, and turn-of-the-20th-century curios hang from the crooked walls and ceilings, which have been atilt since the 1906 earthquake. Sit at the slanted bar for beers on tap and bottomless stories of Oakland history or take drinks outside and enjoy the marina view. ✉ *48 Webster St., Jack London Square* ☎ *510/839–6761* 🌐 *oaklandsaloon.com.*

The Layover Music Bar and Lounge
BARS/PUBS | Bright, bold, and unabashedly bohemian, this hangout filled with recycled furniture is constantly evolving because everything is for sale, from the artwork to the pillows, rugs, and lamps. The busy bar serves up signature organic cocktails, and live entertainment includes comedy shows, storytelling, and local DJs. ✉ *1517 Franklin St., near 15th St., Uptown* ☎ *510/834–1517* 🌐 *www.oaklandlayover.com.*

Make Westing
BARS/PUBS | Named for a short story by Oakland native Jack London, this sprawling industrial-chic space is always abuzz with hipsters playing bocce, the postwork crowd sipping old-fashioneds, or pretheater couples passing Mason jars of unexpected delectables like Cajun shrimp boil. The patio's your best bet for a conversation on a busy evening. ✉ *1741 Telegraph Ave., at 18th St., Uptown* ☎ *510/251–1400* 🌐 *makewesting.com.*

BREWPUBS AND BEER GARDENS

Beer Revolution
BREWPUBS/BEER GARDENS | Hard-core beer geeks: with hundreds of bottled beers and 50 taps, this craft beer and bottle shop is for you. When you're done salivating over the extensive beer lists, grab a table on the patio. ✉ *464 3rd St., at Broadway, Jack London Square* ☎ *510/452–2337* 🌐 *www.beer-revolution.com.*

Diving Dog Brewhouse
BARS/PUBS | The brewing scene is alive and hopping in Oakland, and among the dozens of stops on the Oakland Ale Trail, the Diving Dog is one craft locale where folks can brew their own alongside the masters (and bottle it in two-weeks' time). With more than 100 rare and unusual bottled beers and 30 flavors on tap, this modern space is an ideal place to improve your brew IQ and sample what's fresh before a show at the Fox or other Uptown venue. ✉ *1802 Telegraph Ave., Uptown* ☎ *510/306–1914* 🌐 *www.divingdogbrew.com.*

★ Lost & Found
BREWPUBS/BEER GARDENS | **FAMILY** | The diversions on the spacious, succulent-filled patio include Ping-Pong, cornhole, and communal tables full of chilled-out locals. The beer selection ranges from blue collar to Belgian, and a seasonal menu focuses on internationally inspired small bites. ✉ *2040 Telegraph Ave., at 21st St., Uptown* ☎ *510/763–2040* 🌐 *www.lostandfound510.com* ⏲ *Closed Mon.*

The Trappist
BREWPUBS/BEER GARDENS | Brick walls, dark wood, soft lighting, and a buzz of conversation set a warm and mellow tone inside this Old Oakland Victorian space that's been renovated to resemble a traditional Belgian pub. The setting (which includes two bars and a back patio) is definitely a draw, but the real stars are the artisan beers—more than 100 Belgian, Dutch, and North American brews. Light fare includes bar snacks and meat and cheese boards. ✉ *460 8th St., near Broadway, Old Oakland* ☎ *510/238–8900* 🌐 *www.thetrappist.com.*

ROCK, POP, HIP-HOP, FOLK, AND BLUES CLUBS

Fox Theater
MUSIC CLUBS | This renovated 1928 theater, Oakland's favorite performance venue, is a remarkable feat of Mediterranean Moorish architecture and has seen the likes of Willie Nelson, Magnetic Fields, Rebelution, and B.B. King, to name a few. The venue boasts good sight lines, a state-of-the-art sound system, brilliant acoustics, and a restaurant and bar, among other amenities. ✉ *1807 Telegraph Ave., between 18th and 19th*

Sts., Uptown ☎ *510/302–2250* 🌐 *thefox-oakland.com.*

★ Yoshi's

MUSIC CLUBS | Opened in 1972 as a sushi bar, Yoshi's has evolved into one of the area's best jazz and live music venues. The full Yoshi's experience includes traditional Japanese and Asian fusion cuisine in the adjacent restaurant. ✉ *510 Embarcadero W, between Washington and Clay Sts., Jack London Square* ☎ *510/238–9200* 🌐 *www.yoshis.com.*

Shopping

Pop-up shops and stylish, locally focused stores are scattered throughout the funky alleys of Old Oakland, Uptown, Rockridge, and Temescal, while the streets around Lake Merritt and Grand Lake offer more modest boutiques.

Maison d'Etre

GIFTS/SOUVENIRS | Close to the Rockridge BART station, this store epitomizes the Rockridge neighborhood's funky-chic shopping scene. Look for high-end housewares and impulse buys like whimsical watches, imported fruit-tea blends, and funky slippers. ✉ *5640 College Ave., at Keith Ave., Rockridge* ☎ *510/658–2801* 🌐 *maisondetre.com.*

★ Oaklandish

CLOTHING | This is the place for Oaktown swag. What started in 2000 as a public art project of local pride has become a celebrated brand around the bay, and a portion of the proceeds from hip Oaklandish brand T-shirts and accessories supports grassroots nonprofits committed to bettering the local community. It's good-looking stuff for a good cause. ✉ *1444 Broadway, near 15th St., Uptown* ☎ *510/251–9500* 🌐 *oaklandish.com.*

Viscera

JEWELRY/ACCESSORIES | Urban planning meets fashion in this atypical men's and women's boutique. With 3D printing technology and custom-made items in house, the creators behind this Oakland flagship brand achieve artful, innovative functionality in their American-made clothing, gifts, and accessories. Ask about their in-house DIY workshops. ✉ *1542 Broadway, Uptown* ☎ *510/500–5376* 🌐 *shopviscera.com* 🕓 *Closed Sun. and Mon. (open by appt. only).*

The Marin Headlands

Due west of the Golden Gate Bridge's northern end.

The term *Golden Gate* has become synonymous with the world-famous bridge, but it was first given to the narrow waterway that connects the Pacific and the San Francisco Bay. To the north of the Golden Gate Strait lies the Marin Headlands, part of the Golden Gate National Recreation Area (GGNRA), which boasts some of the area's most dramatic scenery.

GETTING HERE AND AROUND

Driving from San Francisco, head north on U.S. 101. Just after you cross the Golden Gate Bridge, take Exit 442 for Alexander Avenue. Keep left at the fork and follow signs for "San Francisco/U.S. 101 South," go through the tunnel under the freeway, and turn right up the hill. Muni bus 76X runs hourly from Sutter and Sansome streets to the Marin Headlands Visitor Center on weekends and major holidays only.

Sights

★ Marin Headlands

NATIONAL/STATE PARK | **FAMILY** | The headlands stretch from the Golden Gate Bridge to Muir Beach. Photographers perch on the southern headlands for spectacular shots of the city and bridge. Equally remarkable are the views north along the coast and out to the ocean, where the Farallon Islands are visible on clear days.

The headlands' strategic position at the mouth of San Francisco Bay made them a logical site for military installations from 1890 through the Cold War. Today you can explore the crumbling concrete batteries where naval guns once protected the area. The headlands' main attractions are centered on Fts. Barry and Cronkhite, which are separated by Rodeo Lagoon and Rodeo Beach, a dark stretch of sand that attracts sand-castle builders and dog owners.

The visitor center is a worthwhile stop for its exhibits on the area's history and ecology, and kids enjoy the "please touch" educational sites and small play area inside. You can pick up guides to historic sites and wildlife, and get information about programming and guided walks. ✉ *Golden Gate National Recreation Area, Visitors Center, Fort Barry Chapel, Ft. Barry, Bldg. 948, Field and Bunker Rds., Fort Baker* ☎ *415/331–1540* 🌐 *www.nps.gov/goga/marin-headlands.htm* ⏲ *Closed Tues.*

Point Bonita Lighthouse

LIGHTHOUSE | **FAMILY** | A restored beauty that still guides ships to safety with its original 1855 refractory lens, the lighthouse anchors the southern headlands. Half the fun of a visit is the steep half-mile walk from the parking area through a rock tunnel, across a suspension bridge, and down to the lighthouse. Signposts along the way detail the bravado of surfmen, as the early lifeguards were called, and the tenacity of the "wickies," the first keepers of the light. **■TIP→ Call about 90-minute full-moon tours.** ✉ *End of Conzelman Rd., Ft. Barry, Bldg. 948, Sausalito* ☎ *415/331–1540* 🌐 *www.nps.gov/goga/pobo.htm* ⏲ *Closed Tues.–Sat.*

Sausalito

2 miles north of Golden Gate Bridge.

Bougainvillea-covered hillsides and an expansive yacht harbor give Sausalito the feel of an Adriatic resort. The town sits on the northwestern edge of San Francisco Bay, where it's sheltered from the ocean by the Marin Headlands; the mostly mild weather here is perfect for strolling and outdoor dining. Nevertheless, morning fog and afternoon winds can roll over the hills without warning, funneling through the central part of Sausalito once known as Hurricane Gulch.

South of Bridgeway, which snakes between the bay and the hills, a waterside esplanade is lined with restaurants on piers that lure diners with good seafood and even better views. Stairs along the west side of Bridgeway and throughout town climb into wooded hillside neighborhoods filled with both rustic and opulent homes, while back on the northern portion of the shoreline, harbors shelter a community of more than 400 houseboats. As you amble along Bridgeway past shops and galleries, you'll notice the absence of basic services. Find them and more on Caledonia Street, which runs parallel to Bridgeway and inland a couple of blocks. While ferry-side shops flaunt kitschy souvenirs, smaller side streets and narrow alleyways offer eccentric jewelry and handmade crafts.

■TIP→ The ferry is the best way to get to Sausalito from San Francisco; you get more romance (and less traffic) and disembark in the heart of downtown.

Sausalito developed its bohemian flair in the 1950s and '60s, when creative types, including artist Jean Varda, poet Shel Silverstein, and madam Sally Stanford, established an artists' colony and a houseboat community here (this is Otis Redding's "Dock of the Bay"). Both the spirit of the artists and the neighborhood of floating homes persist. For a close-up view of the quirky community, head north on Bridgeway, turn right on Gate Six Road, park where it dead-ends, and enter through the unlocked gates.

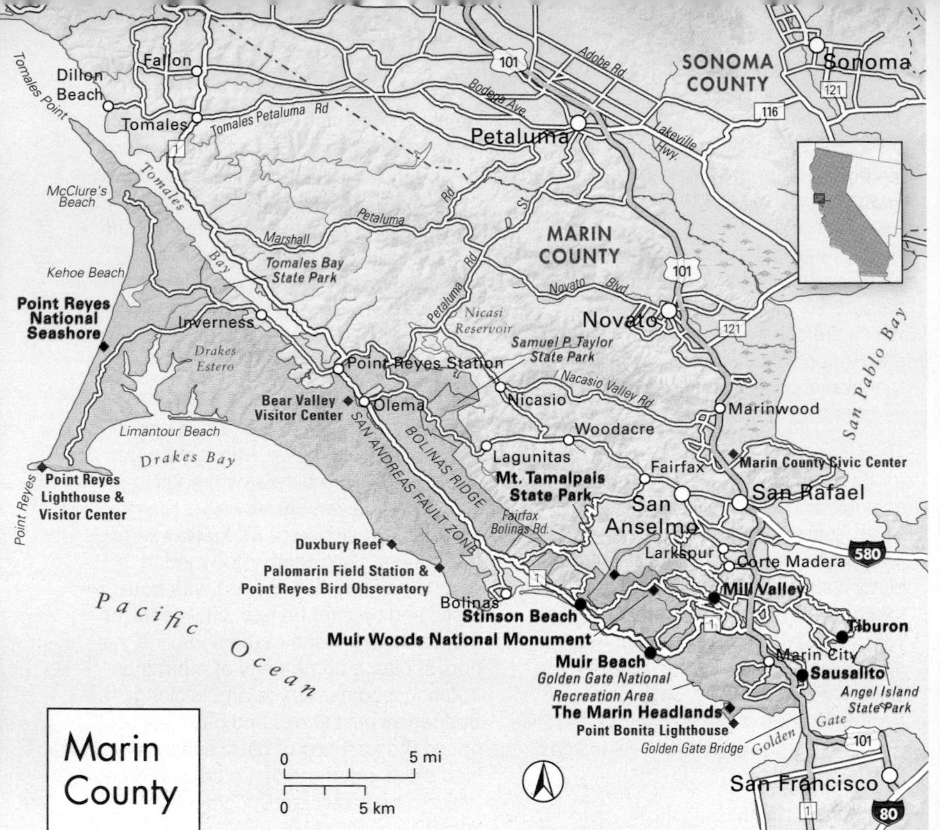

GETTING HERE AND AROUND

From San Francisco by car or bike, follow U.S. 101 north across the Golden Gate Bridge and take Exit 442 for Alexander Avenue, just past Vista Point; continue down the winding hill to the water to where the road becomes Bridgeway. Golden Gate Transit buses will drop you off in downtown Sausalito, and the ferries dock downtown as well. The center of town is flat, with plenty of sidewalks and bay views. It's a pleasure and a must to explore on foot.

ESSENTIALS

VISITOR INFORMATION Sausalito Chamber of Commerce ✉ *1913 Bridgeway* ☎ *415/331–7262* 🌐 *www.sausalito.org.*

Sights

The Marine Mammal Center

COLLEGE | **FAMILY** | This hospital for distressed, sick, and injured marine animals is a leading center for ocean conservancy in the Bay Area and the largest rehabilitation center of its kind. Dedicated to pioneering education, rehabilitation, and research, the center is free and open daily to the public. Tour the facilities and see how elephant seals, sea lions, and pups are cared for and meet the scientists who care for them. Bonus: you'll see some of the best views of the Marin Headlands and San Francisco Bay along the way. ✉ *2000 Bunker Rd., Fort Baker* ☎ *415/289–7325* 🌐 *www.marinemammalcenter.org* 🎫 *Guided tours $10.*

Sally Stanford Drinking Fountain

FOUNTAIN | There's an unusual historic landmark on the Sausalito Ferry Pier—a drinking fountain inscribed "Have a drink on Sally" in remembrance of Sally Stanford, the former San Francisco brothel madam who became Sausalito's mayor in the 1970s. Sassy Sally would have appreciated the fountain's eccentric attachment: a knee-level basin with the inscription "Have a drink on Leland," in memory of her beloved dog. ✉ *Sausalito Ferry Pier, Anchor St. at Humboldt St., off southwest corner of Gabrielson Park* 🌐 *www.oursausalito.com/sausalito-ferry-1.html.*

Sausalito Ice House Visitors Center and Museum

INFO CENTER | The local historical society operates this dual educational exhibit and visitor center, where you can get your bearings, learn some history, and find out what's happening in town. The artifacts of indigenous Miwok peoples and photography of turn-of-the-20th-century Sausalito are worth a peek. ✉ *780 Bridgeway, at Bay St.* ☎ *415/332–0505* 🌐 *www.sausalitohistoricalsociety.com* 🕑 *Closed Mon.*

Viña del Mar Plaza and Park

PLAZA | The landmark Plaza Viña del Mar, named for Sausalito's sister city in Chile, marks the center of town. Adjacent to the parking lot and ferry pier, the plaza is flanked by two 14-foot-tall elephant statues, which were created for the San Francisco Panama–Pacific International Exposition in 1915. It also features a picture-perfect fountain that's great for people-watching. ✉ *Bridgeway and El Portal St.* 🌐 *www.oursausalito.com/parks-in-sausalito/vina-del-mar-park.html.*

Restaurants

Bridgeway Cafe

$ | CAFÉ | The view's the thing at this diner-café on the main drag across the road from the bay. People line up on weekends for great traditional breakfast fare and fresh café lunch items. **Known for:** all-day breakfast fare, including eggs Benedict; Mediterranean-inspired hummus and kabobs; generous burgers. 💵 *Average main: $14* ✉ *633 Bridgeway, at Princess St.* ☎ *415/332–3426* 🌐 *bridgewaycafe.com* 🕑 *No dinner.*

Fast Food Français

$$ | BISTRO | FAMILY | F3 puts a French twist on classic American fast food and dishes up some French nibbles, too, in this casual bistro. The same folks who started Le Garage branch out here with quick-bites like French onion burgers with cheddar fondue and double-cream mac and cheese among servings of Brussels sprouts chips, deviled eggs, and ratatouille. **Known for:** fries and frites; spacious locale; brunch. 💵 *Average main: $17* ✉ *39 Caledonia St.* ☎ *415/887–9047* 🌐 *www.eatf3.com.*

★ Fish

$$ | SEAFOOD | FAMILY | Unsurprisingly, fish—specifically, fresh, sustainably caught fish—is the focus at this gleaming dockside fish house a mile north of downtown. Order at the counter—cash only—and then grab a seat by the floor-to-ceiling windows or at a picnic table on the pier, overlooking the yachts and fishing boats. **Known for:** taco plate; barbecued oysters; sustainably caught, fire-grilled entrées. 💵 *Average main: $21* ✉ *350 Harbor Dr., at Gate 5 Rd., off Bridgeway* ☎ *415/331–3474* 🌐 *www.331fish.com* 💳 *No credit cards.*

★ Hamburgers Sausalito

$ | BURGER | Patrons queue up daily outside this tiny street-side shop for organic Angus beef patties that are made to order on a wheel-shaped grill. Brave the line (it moves fast) and take your food to the esplanade to enjoy fresh air and bayside views. **Known for:** legendary burgers; bay views; local following. 💵 *Average main: $9* ✉ *737 Bridgeway, at Anchor St.* ☎ *415/332–9471* 🕑 *No dinner.*

Le Garage

$$$ | **FRENCH** | Brittany-born Olivier Souvestre serves traditional French bistro fare in a relaxed, bay-side setting that feels more sidewalk café than the converted garage that it is. The restaurant seats only 35 inside and 15 outside, so make reservations or arrive early. **Known for:** PEI mussels and house-cut fries; weekend brunch; balsamic-glazed Brussels sprouts. *Average main: $26 ✉ 85 Liberty Ship Way, Suite 109 ☎ 415/332–5625 🌐 www.legaragebistrosausalito.com ☞ No reservations for weekend brunch.*

Poggio

$$$ | **ITALIAN** | A hillside dining destination, Poggio serves modern Tuscan-style comfort food in a handsome, old-world-inspired space whose charm spills onto the sidewalks. An extensive and ever-changing menu, with ingredients sourced from their own garden and local farms, include house-made capellini, grilled fish, and wood-fired pizzas. **Known for:** fresh local ingredients and traditional northern Italian dishes; rotisserie chicken with property-grown organic herbs and vegetables; lobster-roe pasta. *Average main: $30 ✉ 777 Bridgeway, at Bay St. ☎ 415/332–7771 🌐 www.poggiotrattoria.com.*

Sausalito Seahorse

$$$ | **ITALIAN** | Live music and dancing served alongside Tuscan seafood and pasta specialties make the Seahorse one of Sausalito's most spirited supper clubs. Sample an abundant antipasti menu and homemade focaccia on outdoor patios or enjoy the band inside with traditional seafood stew or lasagna classica. **Known for:** happy hour; Sunday salsa dancing; fun atmosphere. *Average main: $24 ✉ 305 Harbor Dr. ☎ 415/331–2899 🌐 www.sausalitoseahorse.com.*

★ Sushi Ran

$$$ | **JAPANESE** | Sushi aficionados swear that this tiny, stylish restaurant—in business for more than three decades—is the Bay Area's best option for raw fish, but don't overlook the excellent Pacific Rim fusions, a melding of Japanese ingredients and French cooking techniques. Book in advance or expect a wait, which you can soften by sipping one of the bar's 30 by-the-glass sakes. **Known for:** fish imported from Tokyo's famous Tsukiji market; local miso-glazed black cod; outstanding sake and wine list. *Average main: $30 ✉ 107 Caledonia St., at Pine St. ☎ 415/332–3620 🌐 www.sushiran.com ⏲ No lunch weekends.*

Taste of Rome

$$ | **ITALIAN** | **FAMILY** | From early-morning espresso and frittatas to late-night wine and marsalas, there's something just right at the Taste of Rome any time of day. With spacious indoor and outdoor seating and a bountiful menu of fresh and homemade Italian specialties, it's easy to see why this family-owned café is beloved among locals. **Known for:** coffee drinks; desserts; house-made pasta. *Average main: $16 ✉ 1000 Bridgeway ☎ 415/332–7660 🌐 tasteofrome.co.*

Venice Gourmet Deli & Pizza

$ | **ITALIAN** | The Italian deli sandwiches, pizzas made daily, and a shop filled with gourmet delectables, wines, kitchenware, and local flavor here have enticed taste buds along picturesque Bridgeway for more than 50 years. Enjoy a meal alfresco at the sidewalk tables, or take a picnic a few steps away to Yee Toch Chee Park for a waterside bite. **Known for:** picnic-perfect sandwiches; service and quality from family owners; plentiful selections. *Average main: $13 ✉ 625 Bridgeway ☎ 415/332–3544 🌐 www.venicegourmet.com.*

Hotels

Hotel Sausalito

$$$ | **HOTEL** | Handcrafted furniture and tasteful original art and reproductions give this Mission Revival–style inn the feel of a small European hotel. **Pros:**

some rooms have harbor or park views; central location; vouchers to nearby Cafe Tutti provided. **Cons:** no room service; most rooms are small; daily public parking fee. $ *Rooms from: $240* ✉ *16 El Portal, at Bridgeway* ☎ *415/332–0700* 🌐 *www.hotelsausalito.com* *16 rooms* *No meals.*

The Inn Above Tide

$$$$ | B&B/INN | The balconies at the Inn Above Tide literally hang over the water, and each of its rooms has a "perfect 10" view that takes in wild Angel Island as well as the city lights across the bay. **Pros:** generous continental breakfast; free bikes to tour the area; in-room spa services available. **Cons:** costly daily parking; some rooms are on the small side; ferry-side rooms can be noisy. $ *Rooms from: $415* ✉ *30 El Portal* ☎ *415/332–9535, 800/893–8433* 🌐 *www.innabovetide.com* *33 rooms* *Breakfast.*

Shopping

Studio 333 Downtown

ART GALLERIES | There's always something new, interesting, and eye-catching on display at this storefront, including curated collections of handcrafted gifts, housewares, jewelry, and accessories by more than 40 Bay Area artisans. Visit the original art gallery and event space on 333 Caledonia for more delightful creations. ✉ *803 Bridgeway* ☎ *415/332–5483* 🌐 *www.studio333downtown.com.*

Tiburon

7 miles north of Sausalito, 11 miles north of Golden Gate Bridge.

On a peninsula that was named Punta de Tiburon (Shark Point) by 18th-century Spanish explorers, this beautiful Marin County community retains the feel of a village—it's more low-key than Sausalito—despite the encroachment of commercial establishments from the downtown area. The harbor faces Angel Island across Raccoon Strait, and San Francisco is directly south across the bay—which means the views from the decks of harbor restaurants are major attractions. Since 1884, when the San Francisco and North Pacific Railroad relocated their ferry terminal facilities to the harbor town, Tiburon has centered on the waterfront. **■ TIP→ The ferry is the most relaxing (and fastest) way to get here, and allows you to skip traffic and parking problems.**

GETTING HERE AND AROUND

Blue & Gold Fleet ferries travel between San Francisco and Tiburon daily. By car, head north from San Francisco on U.S. 101 and get off at CA 131/Tiburon Boulevard/East Blithedale Avenue (Exit 447). Turn right onto Tiburon Boulevard and drive just over 4 miles to downtown. Golden Gate Transit serves downtown Tiburon from San Francisco; watch for changes during evening rush hour. Tiburon's Main Street is made for wandering, as are the footpaths that frame the water's edge.

ESSENTIALS

VISITOR INFORMATION Tiburon ✉ *Town Hall, 1505 Tiburon Blvd.* ☎ *415/435–7373* 🌐 *www.destinationtiburon.org.*

Sights

Angel Island State Park

NATIONAL/STATE PARK | FAMILY | One of the bay's best secrets in plain sight, its largest natural island was once a favored camp for Coast Miwok (later for the U.S. Army to protect San Francisco Bay), and is now a natural wildlife habitat and historic park favored by bikers, hikers, and picnickers. Thirteen miles of roads and trails from the perimeter up to Mt. Livermore (788 feet) offer magnificent panoramic views. The 12-minute ferry ride to Angel Island from Tiburon ($15 round-trip) includes the cost of the park.

■ **TIP→ To see the sites by bike, rent on the island (angelisland.com/bicycles) or in Tiburon at Pedego Electric Bikes (10 Main Street).** ✉ *Angel Island* ✣ *Accessible only by public ferry or private boat* ☎ *415/435–1915* 🌐 *www.parks.ca.gov.*

Ark Row

STORE/MALL | **FAMILY** | The second block of Main Street is known as historic Ark Row and has a tree-shaded walk lined with antiques, restaurants, and specialty stores. The quaint stretch gets its name from the 19th-century ark houseboats that floated in Belvedere Cove before being beached and transformed into stores. ■ **TIP→ If you're curious about architectural history, the Tiburon Heritage & Arts Commission has a self-guided walking-tour map, available online and at local businesses.** ✉ *Ark Row, Main St., south of Juanita La.* 🌐 *tiburonheritageandarts.org.*

Old St. Hilary's Landmark and John Thomas Howell Wildflower Preserve

NATURE PRESERVE | The architectural centerpiece of this attraction is a stark-white 1888 Carpenter Gothic church that overlooks the town and the bay from its hillside perch. Surrounding the church, which was dedicated as a historical monument in 1959, is a wildflower preserve that's spectacular in May and June, when the rare Tiburon paintbrush or black jewelflower blooms. Expect a steep walk uphill to reach the preserve. The Landmarks Society will arrange guided tours by appointment. ■ **TIP→ The hiking trails behind the landmark wind up to a peak that has views of the entire Bay Area.** ✉ *201 Esperanza St., off Mar West St. or Beach Rd.* ☎ *415/435–1853* 🌐 *landmarkssociety.com/landmarks/st-hilarys/* ⏲ *Church closed Mon.–Sat. and Nov.–Mar.*

Railroad and Ferry Depot Museum

HISTORIC SITE | A short waterfront walk from the ferry landing, this free museum in Shoreline Park is a well-preserved time capsule of the city's industrial history, complete with working trains. The landmark building has a detailed scale model of Tiburon and its 43-acre rail yard at the turn of the 20th century when the city served as a major railroad and ferry hub for the San Francisco Bay. The Depot House Museum on the second floor showcases a restoration of the stationmaster's living quarters. ✉ *1920 Paradise Dr.* ☎ *415/435–1853* 🌐 *landmarkssociety.com/landmarks/railroad-ferry-museum* ⏲ *Closed Nov.–Mar.; Mon. and Tues.*

Restaurants

Caffe Acri

$ | **CAFÉ** | This Italian espresso bar and café at the end of the Tiburon Ferry dock is a sweet spot to enjoy a leisurely breakfast or lunch with a cup of locally roasted coffee while waiting for the ferry. In addition to daily-baked pastries and desserts, the menu ranges from omelets and toasted sandwiches to smoothies and farm-fresh salads. **Known for:** desserts; espresso drinks; soups and paninis. *Average main: $9* ✉ *1 Main St.* ☎ *415/435–8515* 🌐 *www.caffeacri.com.*

Luna Blu

$$$ | **SICILIAN** | Friendly, informative staff serve Sicilian-inspired seafood in this lively sliver of an Italian restaurant just a stone's throw from the ferry. Take a seat on the heated patio overlooking the bay, or cozy up with friends on one of the high-sided booths near the bar. **Known for:** sustainably caught seafood and local, organic ingredients; homemade pastas; rock crab bisque. *Average main: $26* ✉ *35 Main St.* ☎ *415/789–5844* 🌐 *lunablurestaurant.com* ⏲ *Closed Tues. No lunch weekdays.*

New Morning Cafe

$ | **AMERICAN** | **FAMILY** | Omelets, scrambles, and pancakes are served all day long at this homey triangular bay-side café with sunny outdoor seating. If you're past morning treats, this locals' go-to brunch spot offers many soups, salads, and sandwiches, best enjoyed at picnic tables. **Known for:** hearty American breakfast fare; fresh-squeezed orange juice; sour cream waffles. *Average main: $14* *1696 Tiburon Blvd., near Juanita La.* *415/435–4315* *No dinner.*

Salt & Pepper

$$ | **AMERICAN** | **FAMILY** | This bright and welcoming American bistro on Ark Row is known for its seafood starters and salads (think: oyster poppers, crab stacks, and steamers) as well as shareable dishes and burgers, chops, and ribs. The airy, rustic space has a pleasant café-like atmosphere that makes it easy to stay and consider the organic ice cream sundaes and banana splits for dessert. **Known for:** clam chowder; kabocha squash and vegetable curry; Mongolian pork chops. *Average main: $21* *38 Main St.* *415/435–3594* *www.saltandpeppertiburon.com.*

Sam's Anchor Cafe

$$$ | **AMERICAN** | Open since 1920, this casual dockside restaurant, rife with plastic chairs and blue-checked oilcloths, is the town's most famous eatery. Most people flock to the deck for beers, views, sunsets, and exceptionally tasty seafood. **Known for:** raw bar; pink lemonade and margarita "bowls"; hurricane fries. *Average main: $25* *27 Main St.* *415/435–4527* *www.samscafe.com.*

Servino Ristorante

$$ | **SOUTHERN ITALIAN** | **FAMILY** | This family-owned eatery specializes in southern Italian recipes including lobster agnolotti, seafood stew, pork sausage fondue, and pizza made with local, sustainable ingredients. With spacious indoor and outdoor seating and waterfront views, the scene is cozy and welcoming even in cooler weather, when there's heated patio dining. **Known for:** alfresco dining; wines from Italy and California; black truffle raviolacci. *Average main: $22* *9 Main St.* *415/435–2676* *www.servino.com.*

Waypoint Pizza

$ | **PIZZA** | **FAMILY** | A nautical theme and a tasty "between the sheets" pizza-style sandwich are signatures of this creative pizzeria, which is housed in the 19th-century landmark building that was once home to the Pioneer Boat House and is now owned by two sailing aficionados. Booths are brightened with blue-checked tablecloths, and a playful air is added by indoor deck chairs and a picnic table complete with umbrella. **Known for:** pizza-style sandwiches; wild shrimp pesto pizza; soft-serve organic ice cream. *Average main: $13* *15 Main St.* *415/435–3440* *www.waypointpizza.com* *Closed Tues.*

Hotels

Waters Edge Hotel

$$$$ | **B&B/INN** | Checking into this stylish downtown hotel feels like tucking away into an inviting retreat by the water—the views are stunning and the lighting is perfect. **Pros:** complimentary wine and cheese for guests every evening; restaurants/sights are steps away; free bike rentals for guests. **Cons:** downstairs rooms lack privacy and balconies; paid self-parking; fitness center is off-site. *Rooms from: $299* *25 Main St., off Tiburon Blvd.* *415/789–5999, 877/789–5999* *www.marinhotels.com* *23 rooms* *Breakfast.*

Mill Valley

2 miles north of Sausalito, 4 miles north of Golden Gate Bridge.

Chic and woodsy Mill Valley has a dual personality. Here, as elsewhere in the county, the foundation is a superb natural setting. Virtually surrounded by parkland, the town lies at the base of Mt. Tamalpais and contains dense redwood groves traversed by countless creeks. But this is no lumber camp. Smart restaurants and chichi boutiques line streets that have been roamed by more rock stars than one might suspect.

The rustic village flavor isn't a modern conceit, but a holdover from the town's early days as a center for the lumber industry. In 1896, the Mt. Tamalpais Scenic Railroad—dubbed "The Crookedest Railroad in the World" because of its curvy tracks—began transporting visitors from Mill Valley to the top of Mt. Tam and down to Muir Woods, and the town soon became a vacation retreat for city slickers. The trains stopped running in the 1930s, as cars became more popular, but the old railway depot still serves as the center of town: the 1929 building has been transformed into the popular Depot Bookstore & Cafe, at 87 Throckmorton Avenue.

The small downtown area has the constant bustle of a leisure community; even at noon on a Tuesday, people are out shopping for fancy cookware, eco-friendly home furnishings, and boutique clothing.

GETTING HERE AND AROUND

By car from San Francisco, head north on U.S. 101 and get off at CA 131/Tiburon Boulevard/East Blithedale Avenue (Exit 447). Turn left onto East Blithedale Avenue and continue west to Throckmorton Avenue; turn left to reach Depot Plaza, then park. Golden Gate Transit buses serve Mill Valley from San Francisco. Once here, explore the town on foot.

ESSENTIALS

VISITOR INFORMATION Mill Valley Chamber of Commerce and Visitor Center
✉ *85 Throckmorton Ave.* ☎ *415/388–9700*
🌐 *www.millvalley.org.*

Lytton Square

PLAZA | FAMILY | Mill Valley locals congregate on weekends to socialize in the coffeehouses and cafés near the town's central square, but it bustles most of the day. The Mill Valley Book Depot and Cafe at the hub of it all is the place to grab a coffee and sweet treat while reading or playing a game of chess. Shops, restaurants, and cultural venues line the nearby streets. ✉ *Miller and Throckmorton Aves.*

★ Mill Valley Lumber Yard

HISTORIC SITE | FAMILY | The Mill Valley Lumber Yard, once a vital center of the region's logging industry, is now a vibrant micro village of craftsfolk, bakers, makers, and their boutiques and restaurants. The preserved brick-red historic structures are hard to miss along Miller Avenue, and with plenty of parking in the area, plus picnic tables and outdoor space, it's well worth a visit. ✉ *129 Miller Ave.* 🌐 *millvalleylumberyard.com.*

Old Mill Park

CITY PARK | FAMILY | To see one of the numerous outdoor oases that make Mill Valley so appealing, follow Throckmorton Avenue a quarter mile west from Lytton Square to Old Mill Park, a shady patch of redwoods that shelters a playground and reconstructed sawmill and hosts September's annual Mill Valley Arts

Off the Beaten Path

Marin County Civic Center A wonder of arches, circles, and skylights just 10 miles north of Mill Valley, the Civic Center was Frank Lloyd Wright's largest public project and has been designated a national and state historic landmark, as well as a UNESCO World Heritage Site. One-hour docent-led tours leave from the café on the second floor Wednesday and Friday morning at 10:30. ✉ *3501 Civic Center Dr., off N. San Pedro Rd., San Rafael* ☎ *415/473–3762 visitor services office* 🌐 *www.marincounty.org/depts/cu/tours* 🎫 *Free admission; $10 tour fee.*

Festival. From the park, Cascade Way winds its way past creek-side homes to the trailheads of several forest paths. ✉ *Throckmorton Ave. and Cascade Dr.* 🌐 *www.millvalleyrecreation.org.*

Restaurants

Avatar's Restaurant

$ | **INDIAN** | The lines can get long at this hole-in-the-wall kitchen, where Indian curries are served burrito style while you wait (note: it's cash only). Punjabi burritos or rice plates come with savory lamb, chicken, fish, vegetarian, and vegan ingredients flavored with seasonal fruit chutneys, tamarind sauce, and aromatic blends. **Known for:** curried pumpkin; smoked eggplant; lassi drinks. *$ Average main: $8* ✉ *15 Madrona St.* ☎ *415/381–8293* 🌐 *avatars-restaurant-mill-valley.sites.tablehero.com* 💳 *No credit cards.*

Boo Koo

$ | **ASIAN** | Southeast Asian street food with a local flair is fired up in this hip and modern street café, where there's outdoor seating and a 10-tap bar. Summer rolls, satays, and skewers complement pho and wok specialties. **Known for:** green curry noodles; mint salad; Asian brussels sprouts. *$ Average main: $11* ✉ *25 Miller Ave.* ☎ *415/888–8303* 🌐 *eatbookoo.com.*

Buckeye Roadhouse

$$$$ | **AMERICAN** | House-smoked meats and fish, grilled steaks, classic salads, and decadent desserts bring locals and visitors back again and again to this 1937 lodge-style roadhouse. Enjoy a Marin martini at the cozy mahogany bar or sip local wine beside the river-rock fireplace. **Known for:** oysters bingo; chili-lime "brick" chicken; ribs and chops. *$ Average main: $35* ✉ *15 Shoreline Hwy., off U.S. 101* ☎ *415/331–2600* 🌐 *www.buckeyeroadhouse.com.*

Bungalow 44

$$$ | **AMERICAN** | An open, well-lit space with booths and countertop seating from which diners can watch the cooks in action sets the scene at this lively eatery, which serves contemporary Californian cuisine and inventive cocktails. A 2018 remodel revitalized the decor as well as the menu, with its focus on locally sourced veggies and seafood. **Known for:** $1 oyster daily happy hour; tuna carpaccio; kickin' fried chicken. *$ Average main: $25* ✉ *44 E. Blithedale Ave., at Sunnyside Ave.* ☎ *415/381–2500* 🌐 *www.bungalow44.com* 🕑 *No lunch.*

The Dipsea Cafe

$$ | **AMERICAN** | **FAMILY** | Named after the 7-mile trail that winds from Mill Valley to Stinson Beach, this bustling diner serves hearty breakfast favorites, sandwiches, salads, and Mediterranean-inspired lunch plates. Locals crowd the checkered tables, bright yellow booths, and a shiny wooden counter and stools. **Known for:** weekend brunches; huevos rancheros; Mediterranean gyros, calamari, and souvlaki. *$ Average main: $18* ✉ *200 Shoreline Hwy.* ☎ *415/381–0298* 🌐 *www.dipseacafe.com* 🕑 *No dinner.*

Equator Coffees and Teas

$ | **CAFÉ** | This is the prime spot for a pick-me-up (and people-watching) over a picturesque view of downtown Mill Valley and Mt. Tam. The owners are as serious about coffee as they are about social responsibility, from their fair-chain single-origin beans and organic loose teas down to locally recycled metal decor. **Known for:** espresso and cappuccino drinks; breakfast sandwiches; strawberry and chocolate waffles. *$ Average main: $9* ✉ *2 Miller Ave.* ☎ *415/383–1651* 🌐 *www.equatorcoffees.com/pages/mill-valley-1.*

La Ginestra

$$ | **ITALIAN** | **FAMILY** | In business since 1964, La Ginestra—named for the flowers that grow on Mt. Vesuvius, the owners' homeland—is a Mill Valley institution renowned for its no-pretense, family-style Italian meals and impressive wine list. The Sorrento Bar, off the dining room, serves up a delectable array of bar

bites, pizzas, and sweets to enjoy while sipping wines and cocktails inspired by the Aversa's family's homeland. **Known for:** handmade pasta and gnocchi; ravioli; daily fish and small plates. *Average main: $19 127 Throckmorton Ave., off Miller Ave. 415/388–0224 www.laginestramv.com Closed Mon. No lunch.*

Piazza D'Angelo

$$ | **ITALIAN** | **FAMILY** | In the heart of downtown, busy D'Angelo's is known for its authentic and fresh pastas; there even are gluten-free options. Another draw is the scene, especially in the lounge area, which hosts a lively cocktail hour that serves food until 10 or 11 pm—late for Mill Valley. **Known for:** fresh seafood; homemade pasta; tiramisu. *Average main: $20 22 Miller Ave., off Throckmorton 415/388–2000 www.piazzadangelo.com.*

★ Pizza Molina

$$ | **CONTEMPORARY** | A cozy and clean aesthetic, a convivial vibe, and impeccable pizza from a wood-fired oven are central to this neighborhood spot. Chef Justin Bruckert spent months developing the perfect dough with just the right texture, pliability, and flavor as a base for the freshest seasonal ingredients. **Known for:** wood-fired pizzas; house-made meatballs; local beers on tap. *Average main: $16 17 Madrona St., between Lovell and Throckmorton Aves. 415/383–4200 www.pizzamolina.com No lunch.*

Playa

$$ | **MODERN MEXICAN** | Modern Mexican farm-to-table creations and inspired cocktails are the focus of this festive indoor-outdoor space that's popular for its fire pit, made-to-order masa station, and happy hour. An open kitchen serves up locally sourced, organic, and sustainable dishes like ceviche and flautas, grilled octopus tacos, and braised pork tortas. **Known for:** taco Tuesdays; rare tequilas and mezcals; moles and salsas. *Average main: $18 41 Throckmorton Ave. 415/384–8871 www.playamv.com.*

Vasco

$$ | **ITALIAN** | This lovely corner restaurant, with its wood-fired pizza, wine bar, and live music in the evening, has serious neighborhood charm. Authentic Italian specialties include chicken marsala and calamari steak. **Known for:** great atmosphere; tiramisu; pizzas. *Average main: $16 106 Throckmorton Ave. 415/381–3343 vascorestaurantmillvalley.com.*

Hotels

Acqua Hotel

$$$ | **HOTEL** | Astride Richardson Bay, this stylish boutique hotel has modern, elegant rooms decorated in soft Zen-like color schemes. **Pros:** evening wine service; free parking and Wi-Fi; hearty breakfast buffet. **Cons:** next to freeway; traffic audible in rooms facing east; not much within walking distance. *Rooms from: $229 555 Redwood Hwy., off U.S. 101 415/388–9353 www.marinhotels.com 49 rooms Breakfast.*

Mill Valley Inn

$$$$ | **B&B/INN** | The only hotel in downtown Mill Valley is comprised of one of the area's first homes, the Creek House, with smart-looking Victorian rooms, and two small cottages tucked in a grove beyond a creek. **Pros:** steps from local shops and restaurants; some rooms have balconies, soaking tubs, and fireplaces; free mountain bikes. **Cons:** limited room service; dark in winter because of surrounding trees; some rooms are not accessible via elevator. *Rooms from: $369 165 Throckmorton Ave., near Miller Ave. 415/389–6608, 855/334–7946 www.marinhotels.com 25 rooms Breakfast.*

Mountain Home Inn

$$$ | **B&B/INN** | Abutting 40,000 acres of state and national parks, this airy wooden inn sits on the skirt of Mt. Tamalpais, where you can follow hiking trails all the way to Stinson Beach. **Pros:** amazing terrace and views; peaceful, remote

setting; cooked-to-order breakfast. **Cons:** nearest town is a 12-minute drive away; restaurant can get crowded on sunny weekend days; no on-site fitness option. *Rooms from: $210* *810 Panoramic Hwy., at Edgewood Ave.* *415/381–9000* *www.mtnhomeinn.com* *10 rooms* *Breakfast.*

Nightlife

BREWPUS AND BEER GARDENS

Mill Valley Beerworks

BREWPUBS/BEER GARDENS | A great place to rest your feet after shopping or hiking, this neighborhood taproom serves a rotating selection of local and imported drafts and bottles alongside choice house brews on tap. A simple menu of small plates includes locally sourced cheeses and enticing salads. Weekend brunches include fresh recipes like strawberry pepper scones or polenta with roasted beets along with Verve coffee. *173 Throckmorton Ave.* *415/888–8218* *millvalleybeerworks.com.*

MUSIC VENUES

Sweetwater Music Hall

MUSIC CLUBS | With the help of part-owner Bob Weir of the Grateful Dead, this renowned nightclub and café reopened in a historic Masonic Hall in 2012. Famous as well as up-and-coming bands play on most nights, and local stars such as Bonnie Raitt and Huey Lewis have been known to stop in for a pickup session. *19 Corte Madera Ave., between Throckmorton and Lovell Aves.* *415/388–3850, 877/987–6487 tickets* *www.sweetwatermusichall.com.*

Performing Arts

★ Throckmorton Theatre

ART GALLERIES—ARTS | The restored cinema and vaudeville house in Mill Valley is a vibrant cultural hub in the region and is known for fostering exceptional arts and education. The darling playhouse seats upwards of 260 and features live theater, Tuesday night comedy, and concerts. Two smaller street-side halls, the Tivoli and Crescendo feature free classical concerts on Wednesdays, along with Sunday evening sessions, jazz performances, and new art exhibits every month. *142 Throckmorton Ave.* *415/383–9611* *throckmortontheatre.org.*

Shopping

Mill Valley Market

FOOD/CANDY | FAMILY | This family-owned market has been the go-to stop for specialty foods, grocery, deli, and hot food since 1929. Known for their notable beer and wine selection alongside a variety of local and organic produce and healthy grab-and-go foods, this is an ideal stop to prepare for a picnic or to seek out gourmet gifts like imported chocolates and 100-year-old balsamic vinegars. *12 Corte Madera Ave.* *415/388–3222* *millvalleymarket.com.*

Muir Woods National Monument

12 miles northwest of the Golden Gate Bridge.

Climbing hundreds of feet into the sky, *Sequoia sempervirens* are the tallest living things on Earth—some are more than 1,800 years old. One of the last remaining old-growth stands of these redwood behemoths, Muir Woods is nature's cathedral: imposing, awe-inspiring, reverence-inducing, and not to be missed.

Though much of California's 2 million acres of redwood forest were lost to the logging industry, this area was saved from destruction by William and Elizabeth Kent, who purchased the land in 1905, and later gifted it to the federal government. Theodore Roosevelt declared the space a national monument in 1908 and Kent named it after naturalist John Muir,

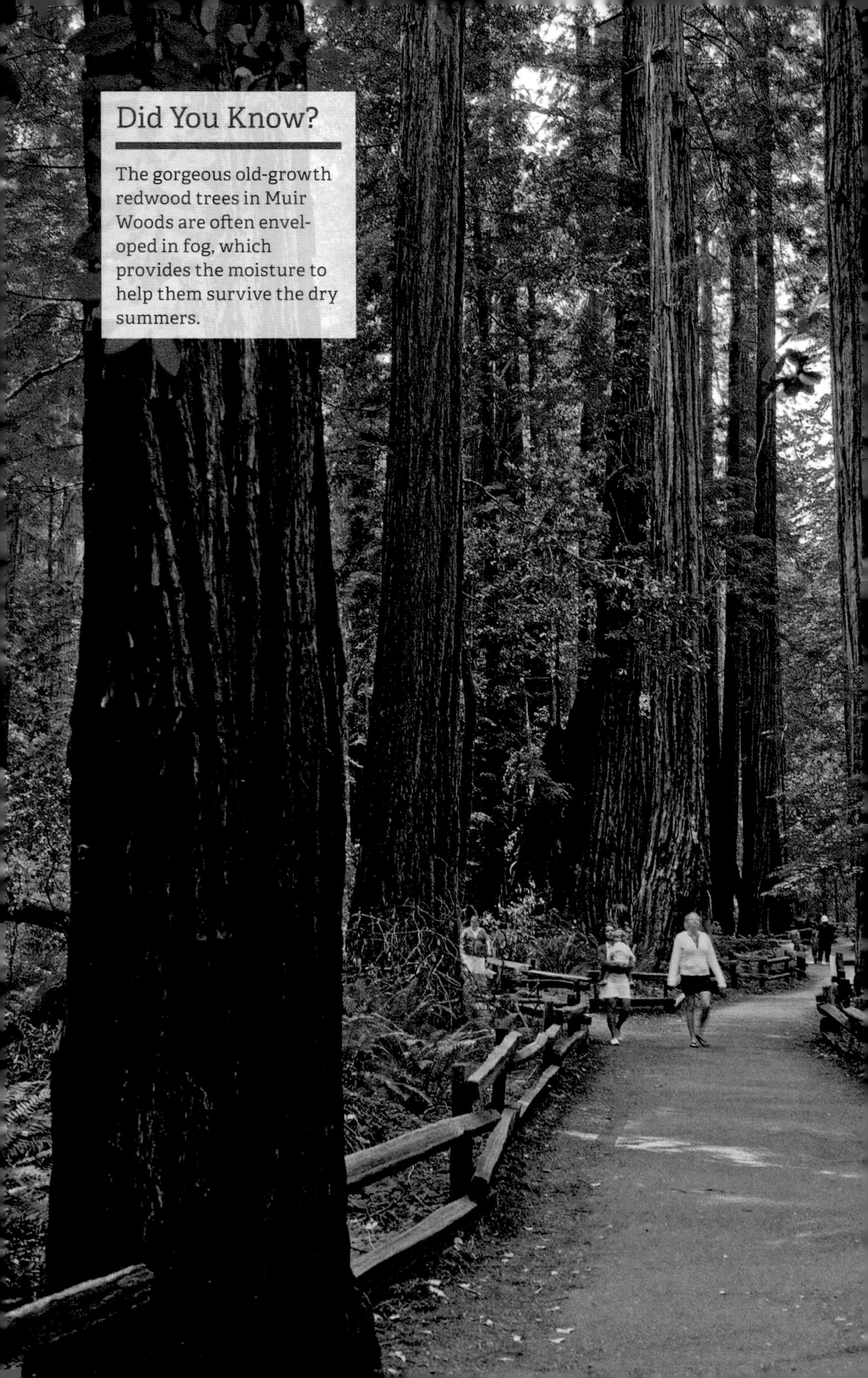

Did You Know?

The gorgeous old-growth redwood trees in Muir Woods are often enveloped in fog, which provides the moisture to help them survive the dry summers.

whose environmental campaigns helped establish the national park system.

GETTING HERE AND AROUND

If you drive to Muir Woods on a weekend or during peak season, expect to find epic traffic jams around the tiny parking areas and adjacent roads. Do yourself a favor and take a shuttle if you can. Reservations are required for parking, so plan ahead. Marin Transit's Route 66 Muir Woods shuttle (*$3 round-trip* 🌐 *www.marintransit.org*) provides weekend and seasonal transport from the Sausalito ferry landing, as well as Marin City, on a seasonal schedule. Private bus tours run year-round. To drive directly from San Francisco by car, take U.S. 101 north across the Golden Gate Bridge to Exit 445B for Mill Valley/Stinson Beach, then follow signs for Highway 1 north and Muir Woods.

Sights

★ Muir Woods National Monument

NATIONAL/STATE PARK | **FAMILY** | Nothing gives perspective like walking among old-growth redwoods. The nearly 560 acres of Muir Woods National Monument contain some of the most majestic redwoods in the world—some more than 250 feet tall.

Part of the Golden Gate National Recreation Area, Muir Woods is a pedestrian's park. The popular 2-mile main trail begins at the park headquarters and provides easy access to streams, ferns, azaleas, and redwood groves. Summer weekends can prove busy, so for a little serenity, consider taking a more challenging route, such as the **Dipsea Trail,** which climbs west from the forest floor to soothing views of the ocean and the Golden Gate Bridge. For a complete list of trails, which vary in difficulty and distance, check with rangers.

Picnicking and camping aren't allowed, and neither are pets. Crowds can be large, especially from May through October, so try to come early in the morning or late in the afternoon. The **Muir Woods Visitor Center** has books and exhibits about redwood trees and the woods' history as well as the latest info on trail conditions; the **Muir Woods Trading Company** serves hot food, organic pastries, and other tasty snacks, and the gift shop offers plenty of souvenirs. **■ TIP→ Muir Woods has no cell service or Wi-Fi, so plan directions and communication ahead of time.** ✉ *1 Muir Woods Rd., off Panoramic Hwy., Mill Valley* ☎ *415/561–2850 park information, 511 Marin transit* 🌐 *www.nps.gov/muwo* 🎟 *$15; free on government holidays.*

Mt. Tamalpais State Park

13 miles northwest of Golden Gate Bridge.

The view of Mt. Tamalpais from all around the bay can be a beauty, but that's nothing compared to the views *from* the mountain, which range from jaw-dropping to spectacular and take in San Francisco, the East Bay, the coast, and beyond—on a clear day, all the way to the Farallon Islands, 25 miles away.

GETTING HERE AND AROUND

By car, take U.S. 101 north across the Golden Gate Bridge and Exit 445B for Mill Valley/Stinson Beach. Continue north on Highway 1, which will turn into Panoramic Highway. By bus, take Golden Gate Transit to Marin City; in Marin City transfer to the West Marin Stagecoach, Route 61, and get off at Pantoll Ranger Station (☎ *415/226–0855* 🌐 *www.marintransit.org/stage.html*). Once here, the only way to explore is on foot or by bike.

★ Mt. Tamalpais State Park

NATIONAL/STATE PARK | **FAMILY** | Although the summit of Mt. Tamalpais is only 2,571 feet high, the mountain rises practically from sea level, dominating the topography of Marin County. Adjacent to Muir Woods National Monument, Mt. Tamalpais State Park affords views of the entire Bay Area and the Pacific Ocean to the west. The name for the sacred mount comes from the Coast Miwok tribe and means "west hill," though some have tied it to a folktale about the "sleeping maiden" in the mountain's profile. For years the 6,300-acre park has been a favorite destination for hikers. There are more than 200 miles of trails, some rugged but many developed for easy walking through meadows, grasslands, and forests and along creeks. Mt. Tam, as it's called by locals, is also the birthplace (in the 1970s) of mountain biking, and today many spandex-clad bikers whiz down the park's winding roads.

The park's major thoroughfare, Panoramic Highway, snakes its way up from U.S. 101 to the **Pantoll Ranger Station** and then drops down to the town of Stinson Beach. Pantoll Road branches off the highway at the station, connecting up with Ridgecrest Boulevard. Along these roads are numerous parking areas, picnic spots, scenic overlooks, and trailheads. Parking is free along the roadside, but there's an $8 fee (cash or check only) to park at the ranger station and additional charges for walk-in campsites and group use.

The **Mountain Theater,** also known as the Cushing Memorial Amphitheatre, is a natural 4,000-seat amphitheater that was reconstructed with stone by the Civilian Conservation Corps in the 1930s. It has showcased summer "Mountain Plays" since 1913.

The **Rock Spring Trail** starts at the Mountain Theater and gently climbs for 1½ miles to the **West Point Inn,** which was once a stop on the Mt. Tam railroad route. Relax at a picnic table and stock up on water before forging ahead, via Old Railroad Grade Fire Road and the Miller Trail, to Mt. Tam's Middle Peak, which is another 1½–2 miles depending on route.

Starting from the Pantoll Ranger Station, the precipitous **Steep Ravine Trail** brings you past stands of coastal redwoods and, in the springtime, small waterfalls. Take the connecting **Dipsea Trail** to reach the town of Stinson Beach and its swath of golden sand. **■TIP→ If you're too weary to make the 3½-mile trek back up, Marin Transit Bus 61 takes you from Stinson Beach back to the ranger station.** ✉ *Pantoll Ranger Station, 3801 Panoramic Hwy., at Pantoll Rd.* ☎ *415/388–2070* 🌐 *www.parks.ca.gov.*

Muir Beach

12 miles northwest of Golden Gate Bridge, 6 miles southwest of Mill Valley.

Except on the sunniest of weekends, Muir Beach is relatively quiet, but the drive here is a scenic adventure.

GETTING HERE AND AROUND

A car is the best way to reach Muir Beach. From Highway 1, follow Pacific Way southwest ¼ mile.

Sights

Green Gulch Farm Zen Center

FARM/RANCH | Giant eucalyptus trees frame the long and winding road that leads to this tranquil Buddhist practice center. Meditation programs, tea instruction, gardening classes, and various other workshops and events take place here; there's also an extensive organic farm. Visitors are welcome to roam the property and walk through the gardens that reach down toward Muir Beach. Public Sunday programs are especially geared toward visitors. ✉ *1601 Shoreline Hwy., at Green Gulch Rd.* ☎ *415/383–3134 welcome center* 🌐 *www.sfzc.org* *Free.*

Beaches

Muir Beach

BEACH—SIGHT | FAMILY | Small but scenic, this beach—a rocky patch of shoreline off Highway 1 in the northern Marin Headlands—is a good place to stretch your legs and gaze out at the Pacific. Locals often walk their dogs here; families and cuddling couples come for picnicking and sunbathing. At the northern end of the beach are waterfront homes (and occasional nude sunbathers) and at the other are the bluffs of the Golden Gate National Recreation Area. A land bridge connects directly from the parking lot to the beach, as well as a short trail that leads to a scenic overlook and connects to other coastal paths. There are no lifeguards on duty and the currents can be challenging so swimming is not advised. **Amenities:** parking (free); toilets. **Best for:** solitude; sunsets; hiking. ✉ *100 Pacific Way, off Shoreline Hwy.* 🌐 *www.nps.gov/goga/planyourvisit/muirbeach.htm.*

Hotels

Pelican Inn

$$$ | B&B/INN | From its slate roof to its whitewashed plaster walls, this inn looks so Tudor that it's hard to believe it was built in the 1970s, but the Pelican is English to the core, with its cozy upstairs guest rooms (no elevator), draped half-tester beds, a sun-filled solarium, and bangers and grilled tomatoes for breakfast. **Pros:** five-minute walk to beach; great bar and restaurant; peaceful setting. **Cons:** 20-minute drive to nearby attractions; rooms are quite small and rustic; workout and steam room access not on-site. $ *Rooms from: $224* ✉ *10 Pacific Way, off Hwy. 1* ☎ *415/383–6000* 🌐 *www.pelicaninn.com* *7 rooms* *Breakfast.*

Stinson Beach

20 miles northwest of Golden Gate Bridge.

This laid-back hamlet is all about the beach, and folks come from all over the Bay Area to walk its sandy, often windswept shore. Ideal day trip: a morning hike at Mt. Tam followed by lunch at one of Stinson's unassuming eateries and a leisurely beach stroll.

GETTING HERE AND AROUND

If you're driving, take U.S. 101 to the Mill Valley/Stinson Beach/Highway 1 exit and follow the road west and then north. By bus, take Golden Gate Transit to Marin City and then transfer to the West Marin Stagecoach (61) for Bolinas.

Beaches

Stinson Beach

BEACH—SIGHT | FAMILY | When the fog hasn't rolled in, this expansive stretch of sand is about as close as you can get in Marin to the stereotypical feel of a Southern California beach. There are several clothing-optional areas, among them a section south of Stinson Beach called Red Rock Beach. ⚠ **Swimming at Stinson Beach can be dangerous; the undertow is strong, and shark sightings, though infrequent, have occurred; lifeguards are on duty May–September.** On any hot summer weekend, roads to Stinson are packed and the parking lot fills, so factor this into your plans. The town itself—population 600, give or take—has a nonchalant surfer vibe, with a few good eating options and pleasant hippie-craftsy browsing. **Amenities:** food and drink; lifeguards (summer); parking (free); showers; toilets. **Best for:** nudists; sunset; surfing; swimming; walking, windsurfing. ✉ *Hwy. 1, 1 Calle Del Sierra* ☎ *415/868–0942 lifeguard tower* 🌐 *www.stinsonbeachonline.com* ☞ *No pets allowed on national park section of beach.*

Restaurants

Parkside Cafe
$$$ | **AMERICAN** | **FAMILY** | The Parkside is popular for its 1950s beachfront snack bar, but the adjoining café, coffee bar, marketplace, and bakery shouldn't be missed either. A full menu serves up fresh ingredients, local seafood, wood-fired pizzas, and just-baked breads. **Known for:** espresso and pastry bar; fish-and-chips; rustic house-made breads. *Average main: $27* ✉ *43 Arenal Ave., off Shoreline Hwy.* ☎ *415/868–1272* 🌐 *www.parksidecafe.com.*

Hotels

Sandpiper Lodging
$$ | **B&B/INN** | **FAMILY** | Recharge, rest, and enjoy the local scenery at this ultrapopular lodging that books up months, even years, in advance. **Pros:** beach chairs, towels, and toys provided; lush gardens with BBQ; minutes from the beach and town. **Cons:** walls are thin; limited amenities; charge for roll-away beds and extra persons. *Rooms from: $185* ✉ *1 Marine Way, off Arenal Ave.* ☎ *415/868–1632* 🌐 *www.sandpiperstinsonbeach.com* *11 rooms* *No meals.*

Point Reyes National Seashore

Bear Valley Visitor Center is 14 miles north of Stinson Beach.

With sandy beaches stretching for miles, a dramatic rocky coastline, a gem of a lighthouse, and idyllic, century-old dairy farms, Point Reyes National Seashore is one of the most varied and strikingly beautiful corners of the Bay Area.

GETTING HERE AND AROUND

From San Francisco, take U.S. 101 north, head west at Sir Francis Drake Boulevard (Exit 450B) toward San Anselmo, and follow the road just under 20 miles to Bear Valley Road. From Stinson Beach or Bolinas, drive north on Highway 1 and turn left on Bear Valley Road. If you're going by bus, take one of several Golden Gate Transit buses to Marin City; in Marin City transfer to the West Marin Stagecoach (you'll switch buses in Olema). Once at the visitor center, the best way to get around is on foot.

Sights

Bear Valley Visitor Center
INFO CENTER | **FAMILY** | A life-size elephant seal model dominates the center's engaging exhibits about the wildlife, history, and ecology of the Point Reyes National Seashore. The rangers at the barnlike facility are fonts of information about beaches, whale-watching, hiking trails, and camping. Restrooms are available, as well as trailhead parking and a picnic area with barbecue grills. Winter hours may be shorter and summer weekend hours may be longer; call or check the website for details. ✉ *Bear Valley Visitor Center, 1 Bear Valley Visitor Center Access Rd., west of Hwy. 1, off Bear Valley Rd., Point Reyes Station* ☎ *415/464–5100* 🌐 *www.nps.gov/pore/planyourvisit.*

★ Duxbury Reef
NATURE PRESERVE | **FAMILY** | Excellent tide pooling can be had along the 3-mile shoreline of Duxbury Reef; it's the most extensive tide pool area near Point Reyes National Seashore, as well as one of the largest shale intertidal reefs in North America. Look for sea stars, barnacles, sea anemones, purple urchins, limpets, sea mussels, and the occasional abalone. But check a tide table (🌐 *tidesandcurrents.noaa.gov*) or the local papers if you plan to explore the reef—it's accessible only at low tide. The reef is a 30-minute drive from the Bear Valley Visitor Center. Take Highway 1 south from the center, turn right at Olema–Bolinas Road (keep an eye peeled; the road is easy to miss),

left on Horseshoe Hill Road, right on Mesa Road, left on Overlook Drive, and then right on Elm Road, which dead-ends at the Agate Beach County Park parking lot. *At Duxbury Point, 1 mile west of Bolinas* *www.ptreyes.org/activities/tidepools.*

Palomarin Field Station & Point Reyes Bird Observatory

NATURE PRESERVE | FAMILY | Birders adore Point Blue Conservation Science, which maintains the Palomarin Field Station and the Point Reyes Bird Observatory (PRBO) that are located in the southernmost part of Point Reyes National Seashore. The Field Station, open daily from sunrise to sunset, has excellent interpretive exhibits, including a comparative display of real birds' talons. The surrounding woods harbor some 200 bird species. As you hike the quiet trails through forest and along ocean cliffs, you're likely to see biologists banding birds to aid in the study of their life cycles. **■TIP→ Visit Point Blue's website for detailed directions and to find out when banding will occur.** *999 Mesa Rd., Bolinas* *415/868–0655 field station, 707/781–2555 headquarters* *www.pointblue.org.*

★ Point Reyes National Seashore

NATIONAL/STATE PARK | FAMILY | One of the Bay Area's most spectacular treasures and the only national seashore on the West Coast, the 71,000-acre Point Reyes National Seashore encompasses hiking trails, secluded beaches, and rugged grasslands as well as Point Reyes itself, a triangular peninsula that juts into the Pacific. The town of **Point Reyes Station** is a one-main-drag affair with some good places to eat and gift shops that sell locally made and imported goods.

When explorer Sir Francis Drake sailed along the California coast in 1579, he allegedly missed the Golden Gate and San Francisco Bay, but he did land at what he described as a convenient harbor. In 2012 the federal government conceded a centuries-long debate and officially recognized Drake's Bay, which flanks the point on the east, as that harbor, designating the spot a National Historic Landmark and silencing competing claims in the 433-year-old controversy. Today Point Reyes's hills and dramatic cliffs attract other kinds of explorers: hikers, whale-watchers, and solitude seekers.

The infamous San Andreas Fault runs along the park's eastern edge and up the center of Tomales Bay; take the short **Earthquake Trail** from the visitor center to see the impact near the epicenter of the 1906 earthquake that devastated San Francisco. A half-mile path from the visitor center leads to **Kule Loklo,** a reconstructed Miwok village that sheds light on the daily lives of the region's first inhabitants. From here, trails also lead to the park's hike-in campgrounds (no car camping).

■TIP→ In late winter and spring, take the short walk at Chimney Rock, just before the lighthouse, to the Elephant Seal Overlook. Even from the cliff, the male seals look enormous as they spar, growling and bloodied, for resident females.

You can experience the diversity of Point Reyes's ecosystems on the scenic **Coast Trail,** which starts at the Palomarin Trailhead, just outside Bolinas. From here, it's a 3-mile trek through eucalyptus groves and pine forests and along seaside cliffs to beautiful and tiny Bass Lake. To reach the Palomarin Trailhead, take Olema–Bolinas Road toward Bolinas, turn right on Mesa Road, follow signs to Point Blue Conservation Science, and then continue until the road dead-ends.

The 4.7-mile-long (one-way) **Tomales Point Trail** follows the spine of the park's northernmost finger of land through a Tule Elk Preserve, providing spectacular ocean views from the high bluffs. Expect to see elk, but keep your distance from the animals. To reach the moderately easy hiking trail, take Sir Francis Drake

Boulevard through the town of Inverness; when you come to a fork, veer right to stay on Pierce Point Road and continue until you reach the parking lot at Pierce Point Ranch. ✉ *Bear Valley Visitor Center, 1 Bear Valley Visitor Center Access Rd., west of Hwy. 1, off Bear Valley Rd., Point Reyes Station* ☎ *415/464–5100* 🌐 *www.nps.gov/pore.*

Restaurants

Café Reyes

$$ | PIZZA | FAMILY | Sunny patio seating, hand-tossed pizza, and organic local ingredients are the selling points of this laid-back café. The semi-industrial dining room, which is built around a brick oven, features glazed concrete floors, warm-painted walls, and ceilings high enough to accommodate full-size market umbrellas. **Known for:** wood-fired pizza; Drake's Bay fresh oysters; outdoor patio dining. $ *Average main: $16* ✉ *11101 Hwy. 1, Point Reyes Station* ☎ *415/663–9493* 🌐 *cafe-reyes.com* ⏲ *Closed Mon. and Tues.*

Due West

$$$ | AMERICAN | Award-winning chef Jonathan Pfluege brings local, sustainable culinary provisions to this classic Point Reyes tavern, a popular horse-and-wagon stop since the 1860s. The seasonal menu includes American classics from burgers and brick-roasted chicken to seafood specialties like Dungeness crab chowder and oysters fried, grilled, or freshly shucked. **Known for:** artisanal cheese plate; steak frites; regional wine list. $ *Average main: $24* ✉ *10021 Coastal Hwy. 1, Olema* ☎ *415/663–1264* 🌐 *olemahouse.com/dine.*

★ Hog Island Oyster Co. Marshall Oyster Farm & the Boat Oyster Bar

$$$ | SEAFOOD | FAMILY | Take a short trek north on Highway 1 to the gritty mecca of Bay Area oysters—the Hog Island Marshall Oyster Farm. For a real culinary adventure, arrange to shuck and barbecue your own oysters on one of the outdoor grills (all tools supplied, reservations required), or for the less adventurous, the Boat Oyster Bar is an informal outdoor café that serves raw and BBQ oysters, local snacks, and tasty beverages. **Known for:** fresh, raw, and BBQ oysters; picnic grills; Hog Shack shellfish to go. $ *Average main: $24* ✉ *20215 Shoreline Hwy.* ☎ *415/663–9218* 🌐 *hogislandoysters.com/locations/marshall* ⏲ *Oyster Bar closed Tues.–Thurs. No dinner.*

★ Osteria Stellina

$$ | ITALIAN | Chef-owner Christian Caiazzo's menu of "Point Reyes Italian" cuisine puts an emphasis on showcasing hyperlocal ingredients like Marin-grown kale and Sonoma cheese. Pastas, pizzas, and a handful of entrées are served in a rustic-contemporary space with a raw bar that serves local oysters all day long. **Known for:** locally sourced produce and seafood; fresh oysters; inventive pizzas. $ *Average main: $22* ✉ *11285 Hwy. 1, at 3rd St., Point Reyes Station* ☎ *415/663–9988* 🌐 *www.osteriastellina.com.*

★ Side Street Kitchen

$$ | AMERICAN | FAMILY | Rotisserie meats and veggies sourced from local farms steal the show at this former mid-century truck stop and diner. It's a go-to for tri-tip and pork belly sandwiches or house-seasoned roasted chicken, best eaten family style with a host of salads, sides, and butterscotch pudding. **Known for:** cold smoked seafood and rotisserie chicken; dog-friendly outdoor patio; apple fritters. $ *Average main: $16* ✉ *60 4th St., Point Reyes Station* ☎ *415/663–0303* 🌐 *sidestreet-prs.com* ⏲ *No dinner.*

Sir and Star at the Olema

$$$$ | AMERICAN | With lovely garden views, creative and cryptically named dishes, and upscale-rustic decor that somehow incorporates taxidermied animals, this historic roadhouse (located within the Olema Inn) elicits both rants and raves, often from diners sharing the same table. The locally focused menu of California cuisine changes seasonally; a special prix fixe is offered by reservation on Saturday evening. **Known for:** great atmosphere; small plates; Saturday Chef's Meal. 💲 *Average main: $35* ✉ *10000 Sir Francis Drake Blvd., at Hwy. 1, Olema* ☎ *415/663–1034* 🌐 *sirandstar.com* 🕓 *Closed Mon.–Wed. No lunch.*

Station House Cafe

$$ | **AMERICAN** | In good weather, hikers fresh from the park fill the Station House's lovely outdoor garden as well as its homey indoor tables, banquettes, and bar stools, so prepare for a wait. The community-centric eatery is locally focused and serves a blend of modern and classic California dishes comprised of organic seasonal ingredients, sustainable hormone-free meats, and wild-caught seafood. **Known for:** signature popovers; hearty breakfast items; local fresh seafood. 💲 *Average main: $22* ✉ *11180 Hwy. 1, at 2nd St., Point Reyes Station* ☎ *415/663–1515* 🌐 *www.stationhousecafe.com* 🕓 *Closed Wed.*

Stinson Beach Breakers Cafe

$$$ | **AMERICAN** | Hard to miss along the tiny stretch of Main Street, this café is an easy prebeach destination for coffee and griddle specialties or postsurf bar bites and cocktails on the heated patio in the afternoon. Beach cottage hardwood floors and a wood stove add to the warmth of the rustic seaside interior, while a mountain view and fire pit adds to the deck. **Known for:** hearty egg breakfast dishes with a Latin twist; fresh oysters; fish tacos. 💲 *Average main: $23* ✉ *3465 Hwy. 1, Stinson Beach* ☎ *415/868–2002* 🌐 *stinsonbeachcafe.com* 🕓 *Closed Tues. and Wed., Nov.–Mar.*

Hotels

★ Olema House

$$$$ | **B&B/INN** | **FAMILY** | Once a historic 1860s stagecoach stopover, this renovated, luxurious getaway offers just as many reasons to stay on property—with its views of Mt. Wittenberg—as to explore the 71,000 acres of national seashore just steps away. **Pros:** lush garden; convenient parking and horse hitching; friendly and informative staff. **Cons:** steps to some rooms may be steep; street-facing rooms above restaurant may be noisy; Wi-Fi and cell service may be spotty. 💲 *Rooms from: $300* ✉ *10021 Coastal Hwy. 1, Olema* ☎ *415/663–9000* 🌐 *olemahouse.com* *25 rooms* *Free Breakfast.*

Shopping

★ Cowgirl Creamery

LOCAL SPECIALTIES | **FAMILY** | In this former hay barn, a couple of Berkeley foodies (from Chez Panisse and Bette's Oceanview Diner) started their original creamery for artisanal cheeses. In addition to more than 200 specialty cheeses—local, regional, and international—you'll find Tomales Bay Foods offerings featuring West Marin farm wares. Cowgirl Creamery cheeses harness flavors unique to Point Reyes, such as their award-winning Red Hawk and Mt. Tam made from Straus Family Dairy milk. Sample seasonal cheeses and see how the cheese is made or order a hot mac and cheese at the cantina and stay for a bite at the picnic tables. Abundant deli items, gourmet goodies, and wine selections make it easy to pack a picnic for the beach or a hike here. ✉ *80 4th St., Point Reyes Station* ☎ *415/663–9335* 🌐 *www.cowgirlcreamery.com/pt-reyes-shop-creamery* 🕓 *Closed Mon. and Tues.*

Gospel Flat Farm Stand

OUTDOOR/FLEA/GREEN MARKETS | **FAMILY** | This combination art gallery, farm stand, and flower shop captures the true essence of the area, with its dedication to community and bounty of local organic vegetables, fruits, and eggs. A must-see when passing through the Bolinas and Olema area, the self-serve site is open 24 hours. What makes it truly special is that the entire stand operates on the honor system. Weigh and log your produce, and slip your payment (cash or check) in the box. The local art on exhibit adds to the allure of this roadside treasure. ✉ *140 Olema-Bolinas Rd., Bolinas* ☎ *415/858–4730* 🌐 *gospelflatfarm.com.*

★ Toby's Feed Barn

LOCAL SPECIALTIES | FAMILY | The heart of the community since 1942, this barn has a bounty of local gifts and produce, plus an art gallery, yoga studio, and Toby's Coffee Bar for espresso drinks and sell-out pastries. See and hear what's happening locally, catch a live band, and explore the garden. The internationally renowned all-local, all-organic Point Reyes Farmers' Market is held here on Saturday for 20 weeks during the growing season. ✉ *11250 Hwy. 1, Point Reyes Station* ☎ *415/663–1223* 🌐 *tobysfeedbarn.com.*

Chapter 10

NAPA AND SONOMA

Updated by
Daniel Mangin

Sights	Restaurants	Hotels	Shopping	Nightlife
★★★★★	★★★★★	★★★★☆	★★★☆☆	★★★☆☆

WELCOME TO NAPA AND SONOMA

TOP REASONS TO GO

★ **Touring wineries:** Let's face it: this is the reason you're here, and the range of excellent sips to sample would make any oenophile (or novice drinker, for that matter) giddy.

★ **Biking:** Gentle hills and vineyard-laced farmland make Napa and Sonoma perfect for combining leisurely back-roads cycling with winery stops.

★ **Browsing the farmers' markets:** Many towns in Napa and Sonoma have seasonal farmers' markets, each rounding up an amazing variety of local produce.

★ **A meal at The French Laundry:** Chef Thomas Keller's Yountville restaurant is one of the country's best. The mastery of flavors and attention to detail are subtly remarkable.

★ **Viewing the art:** Several wineries, among them the Hess Collection in Napa, The Donum Estate in Sonoma, and Hall St. Helena, display museum-quality artworks indoors and on their grounds.

The Napa and Sonoma valleys run parallel, northwest to southeast, and are separated by the Mayacamas Mountains. Southwest of Sonoma Valley are several other important viticultural areas in Sonoma county, including the Dry Creek, Alexander, and Russian River valleys. The Carneros, which spans southern Sonoma and Napa counties, is just north of San Pablo Bay.

1 **Napa.**

2 **Yountville.**

3 **Oakville.**

4 **Rutherford.**

5 **St. Helena.**

6 **Calistoga.**

7 **Sonoma.**

8 **Glen Ellen.**

9 **Kenwood.**

10 **Healdsburg.**

11 **Geyserville**

12 **Forestville.**

13 **Guerneville**

14 **Sebastopol.**

15 **Santa Rosa.**

16 **Pertaluma.**

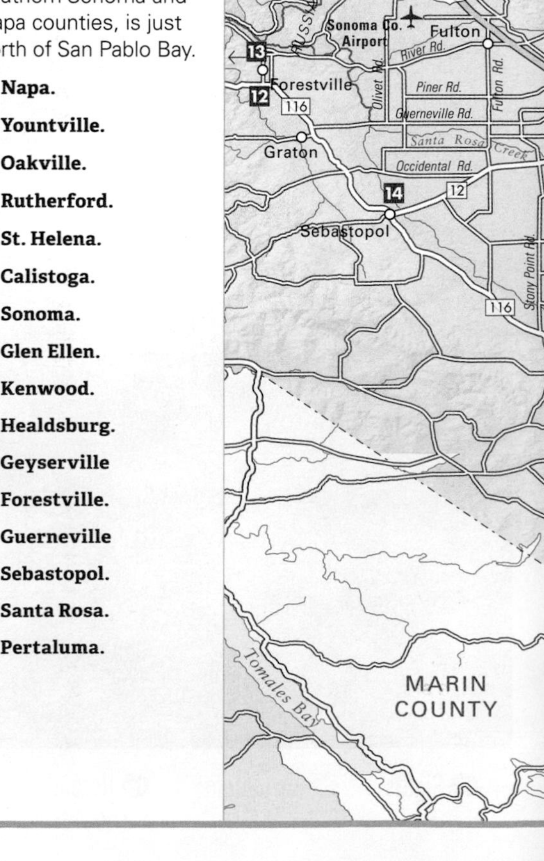

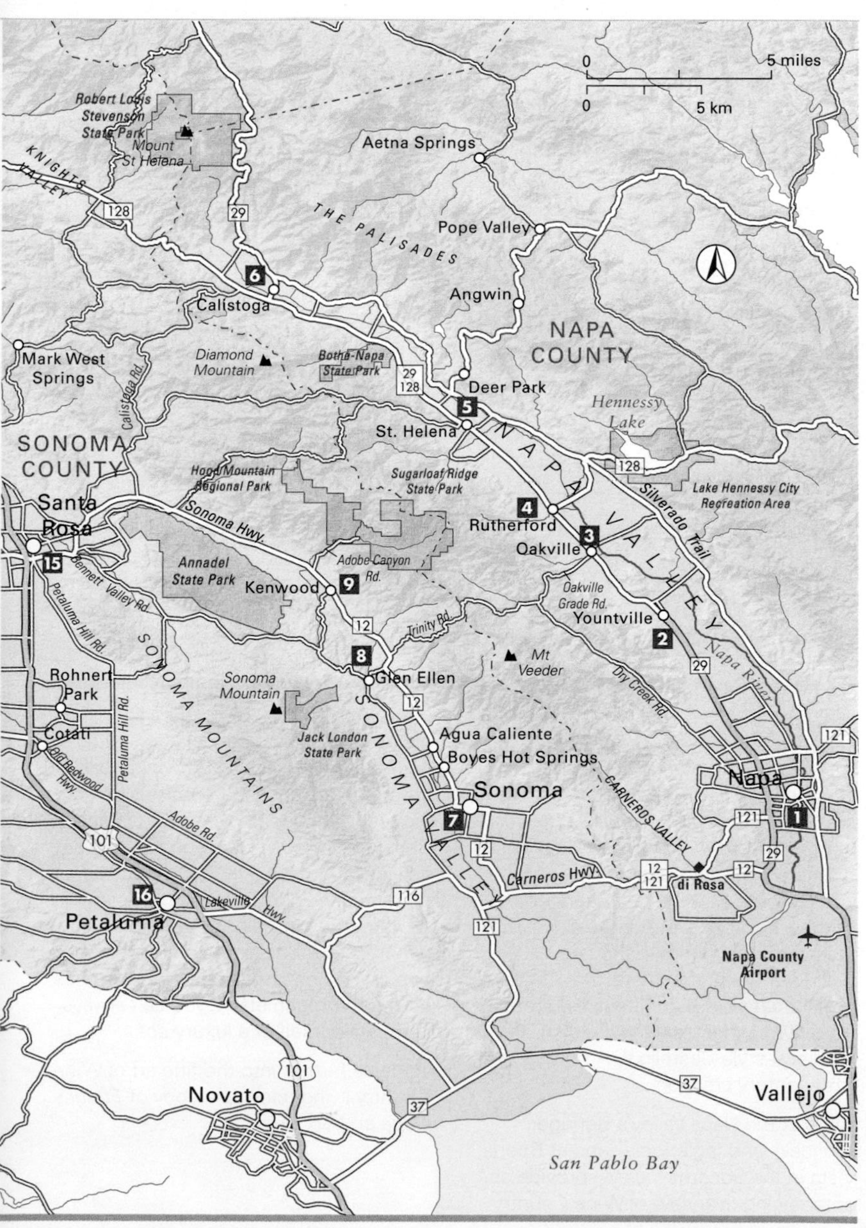
0
5 miles
0
5 km
Robert Louis Stevenson State Park
Mount St Helena
KNIGHTS VALLEY
128
29
Aetna Springs
THE PALISADES
Pope Valley
Angwin
6
Calistoga
NAPA COUNTY
Mark West Springs
Diamond Mountain
Bothe-Napa State Park
29
128
Deer Park
5
St. Helena
Hennessy Lake
NAPA VALLEY
SONOMA COUNTY
Calistoga Rd.
Hood Mountain Regional Park
Sugarloaf Ridge State Park
128
Silverado Trail
Lake Hennessy City Recreation Area
Santa Rosa
Sonoma Hwy.
4
Rutherford
3
Oakville
15
Annadel State Park
Adobe Canyon Rd.
Kenwood
9
Bennett Valley Rd.
Petaluma Hill Rd.
Oakville Grade Rd.
Yountville
2
12
Trinity Rd.
SONOMA MOUNTAINS
8
Mt Veeder
29
Napa River
Rohnert Park
Glen Ellen
Sonoma Mountain
Dry Creek Rd.
Petaluma Hill Rd.
12
Cotati
Jack London State Park
SONOMA VALLEY
Agua Caliente
Boyes Hot Springs
121
Old Redwood Hwy.
Sonoma
CARNEROS VALLEY
Napa
7
121
1
Adobe Rd.
101
12
29
Carneros Hwy.
12
121
12
di Rosa
16
Lakeville Hwy.
116
Petaluma
121
Napa County Airport
101
37
Novato
37
Vallejo
San Pablo Bay

In California's premier wine region, the pleasures of eating and drinking are celebrated daily. It's easy to join in at famous wineries and rising newcomers off country roads, or at trendy in-town tasting rooms. Chefs transform local ingredients into feasts, and gourmet groceries sell perfect picnic fare. Yountville, Healdsburg, and St. Helena have small-town charm as well as luxurious inns, hotels, and spas, yet the natural setting is equally sublime, whether experienced from a canoe on the Russian River or the deck of a winery overlooking endless rows of vines.

The Wine Country is also rich in history. In Sonoma you can explore California's Spanish and Mexican pasts at the Sonoma Mission, and the origins of modern California wine making at Buena Vista Winery. Some wineries, among them St. Helena's Beringer and Rutherford's Inglenook, have cellars or tasting rooms dating to the late 1800s. Calistoga is a flurry of late-19th-century Steamboat Gothic architecture, though the town's oldest-looking building, the medieval-style Castello di Amorosa, is a 21st-century creation.

Tours at the Napa Valley's Beringer, Mondavi, and Inglenook—and at Buena Vista in the Sonoma Valley—provide an entertaining overview of Wine Country history. The tour at the splashy visitor center at St. Helena's Hall winery will introduce you to 21st-century wine-making technology, and over in Glen Ellen's Benziger Family Winery you can see how its vineyard managers apply biodynamic farming principles to grape growing. At numerous facilities you can play winemaker for a day at seminars in the fine art of blending wines. If that strikes you as too much effort, you can always pamper yourself at a luxury spa.

To delve further into the fine art of Wine Country living, pick up a copy of *Fodor's Napa and Sonoma*.

MAJOR REGIONS

Napa Valley. With more than 500 wineries and many of the biggest brands in the business, the Napa Valley is the Wine Country's star. With a population of about 79,000, Napa, the valley's largest town, lures with its cultural attractions and (relatively) reasonably priced accommodations. A few miles farther north, compact **Yountville** is densely packed with top-notch restaurants and hotels, and **Rutherford** and **Oakville** are renowned for their Cabernet Sauvignon–friendly soils. Beyond them, **St. Helena** teems with elegant boutiques and restaurants, and casual **Calistoga**, known for spas and hot springs, has the feel of an Old West frontier town.

The Sonoma Valley. The birthplace of modern California wine making—Count Aragon Haraszthy opened Buena Vista Winery here in 1857—Sonoma Valley seduces with its unpretentious attitude and pastoral landscape. Tasting rooms, restaurants, and historic sites, among the latter the last mission established in California by Franciscan friars, abound near Sonoma Plaza. Beyond downtown Sonoma, the wineries and attractions are spread out along gently winding roads. Sonoma County's half of the Carneros District lies within Sonoma Valley, whose other towns of note include Glen Ellen and Kenwood. Sonoma Valley tasting rooms are often less crowded than those in Napa or northern Sonoma County, especially midweek, and the vibe here, though sophisticated, is definitely less sceney.

Planning

When to Go

High season extends from April through October. In summer, expect the days to be hot and dry, the roads filled with cars, and traffic heavy at the tasting rooms. Hotel rates are highest during the height of harvest, in September and October. Then and in summer book lodgings well ahead. November, except for Thanksgiving week, and December before Christmas are less busy. The weather in Napa and Sonoma is pleasant nearly year-round. Daytime temperatures average from about 55°F during winter to the 80s in summer, when readings in the 90s and higher are common. April, May, and October are milder but still warm. The rainiest months are usually from December through March.

Getting Here and Around

AIR TRAVEL

Wine Country regulars often bypass San Francisco and Oakland and fly into Santa Rosa's Charles M. Schulz Sonoma County Airport (STS), which receives direct flights from San Diego, Las Vegas, Los Angeles, Phoenix, Portland, and Seattle. The airport is 15 miles from Healdsburg. **■ TIP→ Alaska Airlines allows passengers flying out of STS to check up to one case of wine for free.**

BUS TRAVEL

Bus travel is an inconvenient way to explore the Wine Country, though it is possible. Take Golden Gate Transit from San Francisco to connect with Sonoma County Transit buses. VINE connects with BART commuter trains in the East Bay and the San Francisco Bay Ferry in Vallejo. VINE buses serve the Napa Valley.

CAR TRAVEL

A car is the most convenient way to navigate Napa and Sonoma. If you're flying into the area, it's almost always easiest to pick up a car at the airport. You'll also find rental companies in major Wine Country towns. A few rules to note: Smartphone use for any purpose is prohibited, including mapping applications unless the device is mounted to a car's windshield or dashboard and can be activated with a single swipe or finger tap. A right turn after stopping at a red light is legal unless posted otherwise.

If you base yourself in the Napa Valley towns of Napa, Yountville, or St. Helena, or in Sonoma County's Healdsburg or Sonoma, you can visit numerous tasting rooms and nearby wineries on foot or by bicycle on mostly flat terrain. The free Yountville trolley loops through town, and ride-sharing is viable there and in Napa. Sonoma County sprawls more, but except for far west the public transit and ride-sharing generally work well.

■ TIP→ If you're wine tasting, either select a designated driver or be careful of your wine intake—the police keep an eye out for tipsy drivers.

From San Francisco to Napa: Cross the Golden Gate Bridge, then go north on U.S. 101. Head east on Highway 37 toward Vallejo, then north on Highway 121, aka the Carneros Highway. Turn left (north) when Highway 121 runs into Highway 29.

From San Francisco to Sonoma: Cross the Golden Gate Bridge, then go north on U.S. 101, east on Highway 37 toward Vallejo, and north on Highway 121. When you reach Highway 12, take it north to the town of Sonoma. For Sonoma County destinations north of Sonoma Valley stay on U.S. 101, which passes through Santa Rosa and Healdsburg.

From Berkeley and Oakland: Take Interstate 80 north to Highway 37 west, then on to Highway 29 north. For the Napa Valley, continue on Highway 29; to reach Sonoma County, head west on Highway 121.

Restaurants

Farm-to-table Modern American cuisine is the prevalent style in the Napa Valley and Sonoma County, but this encompasses both the delicate preparations of Thomas Keller's highly praised The French Laundry and the upscale comfort food served throughout the Wine Country. The quality (and hype) often means high prices, but you can also find appealing, inexpensive eateries, especially in the towns of Napa, Calistoga, Sonoma, and Santa Rosa, and many high-end delis prepare superb picnic fare. At pricey restaurants you can save money by having lunch instead of dinner. With a few exceptions (noted in individual restaurant listings), dress is informal. *Restaurant reviews have been shortened. For full information, visit Fodors.com.*

Hotels

The fanciest accommodations are concentrated in the Napa Valley towns of Yountville, Rutherford, St. Helena, and Calistoga; Sonoma County's poshest lodgings are in Healdsburg. The spas, amenities, and exclusivity of high-end properties attract travelers with the means and desire for luxury living. The cities of Napa and Santa Rosa are the best bets for budget hotels and inns, but even at a lower price point you'll still find a touch of Wine Country glamour. On weekends, two- or even three-night minimum stays are commonly required at smaller lodgings. Book well ahead for stays at such places during the busy summer or fall season. If your party will include travelers under age 16, inquire about policies regarding younger guests; some smaller lodgings discourage (or discreetly forbid) children. *Hotel reviews have been shortened. For full information, visit Fodors.com.*

What It Costs

	$	$$	$$$	$$$$
RESTAURANTS				
	under $16	$16–$22	$23–$30	over $30
HOTELS				
	under $200	$200–$300	$301–$400	over $400

Napa

46 miles northeast of San Francisco.

After many years as a blue-collar burg detached from the Wine Country scene, the Napa Valley's largest town (population about 80,000) has evolved into one of its shining stars. Masaharu Morimoto and other chefs of note operate restaurants here, swank hotels and inns can be found downtown and beyond, and the nightlife options include the West Coast edition of the famed Blue Note jazz club. A walkway that follows the Napa River has made downtown more pedestrian-friendly, and the Oxbow Public Market, a complex of high-end food purveyors, is popular with locals and tourists. The nearby CIA at Copia, operated by the Culinary Institute of America, hosts cooking demonstrations and other activities open to the public and has a shop and a restaurant. If you establish your base in Napa, plan on spending at least a half day strolling the downtown district.

GETTING HERE AND AROUND

Downtown Napa lies a mile east of Highway 29—take the 1st Street exit and follow the signs. Ample parking, much of it free for the first three hours and some for the entire day, is available on or near Main Street. Several VINE buses serve downtown and beyond.

Sights

Artesa Vineyards & Winery

WINERY/DISTILLERY | From a distance the modern, minimalist architecture of Artesa blends harmoniously with the surrounding Carneros landscape, but up close its pools, fountains, and large outdoor sculptures make a vivid impression. So, too, do the wines: mostly Chardonnay and Pinot Noir but also Cabernet Sauvignon, sparkling, and limited releases like Albariño and Tempranillo. You can sample wines without a reservation in the Foyer Bar, but one is required for single-vineyard flights and food pairings. The latter can be enjoyed in the light-filled Salon Bar or outside on a terrace with views of estate and neighboring vineyards and, on a clear day, San Francisco. ✉ *1345 Henry Rd., Napa* ✣ *Off Old Sonoma Rd. and Dealy La.* ☎ *707/224–1668* 🌐 *www.artesawinery.com* *Tastings from $35, tour $45 (includes tasting).*

★ Ashes & Diamonds

WINERY/DISTILLERY | Barbara Bestor's sleek white design for this appointment-only winery's glass-and-metal tasting space evokes mid-century modern architecture and with it the era and wines before the Napa Valley's rise to prominence. Two much-heralded pros lead the wine-making team assembled by record producer Kashy Khaledi: Steve Matthiasson, known for his classic, restrained style and attention to viticultural detail, and Diana Snowden Seysses, who draws on experiences in Burgundy, Provence, and California. Bordeaux varietals are the focus, most notably Cabernet Sauvignon and Cabernet Franc but also the white blend of Sauvignon Blanc and Sémillon and even the rosé (of Cabernet Franc). With a label designer who was also responsible for a Jay-Z album cover and interiors that recall the *Mad Men* in Palm Springs story arc, the pitch seems unabashedly to millennials, but the wines, low in alcohol and with higher acidity (good for aging), enchant connoisseurs

Continued on page 326

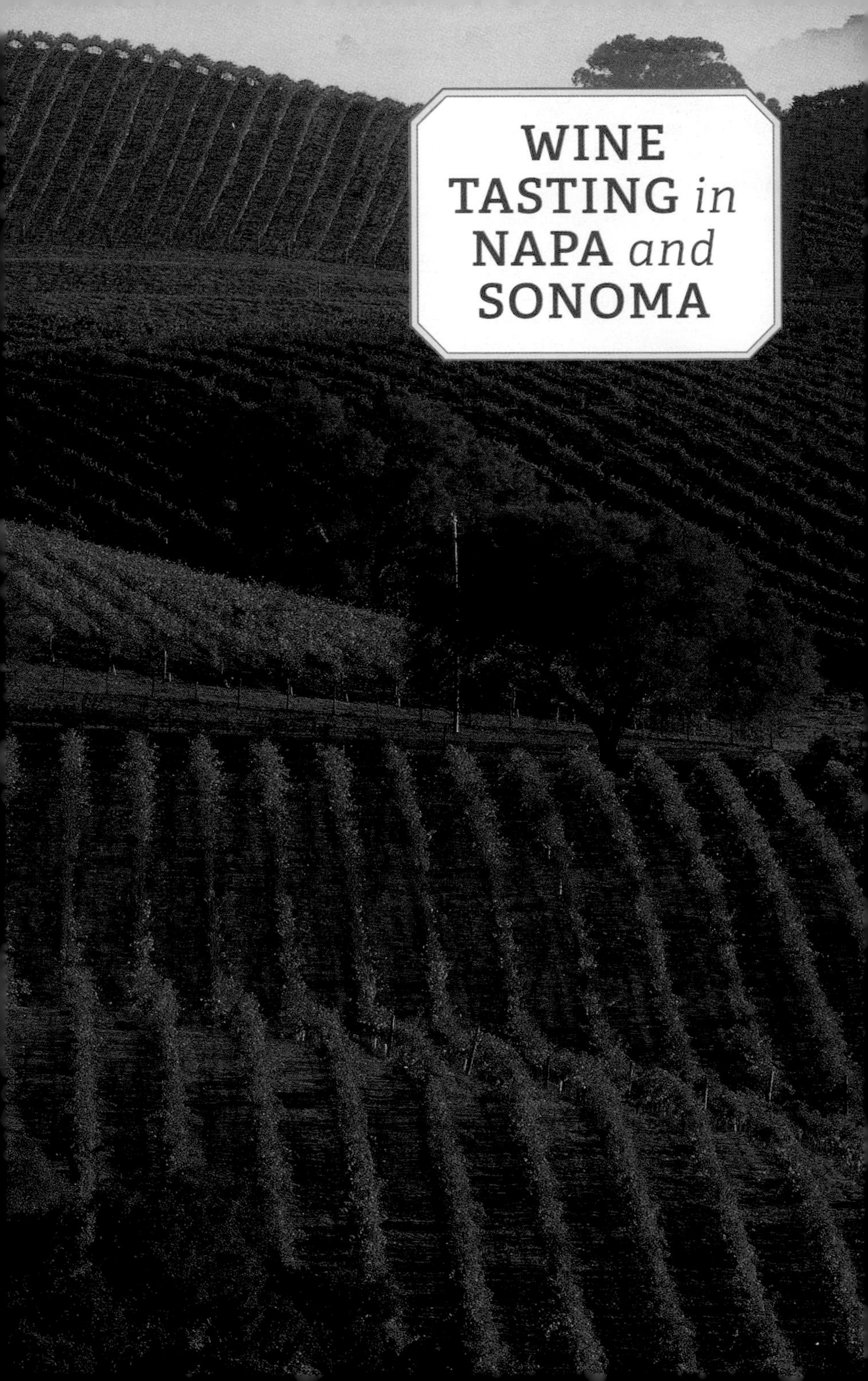
WINE
TASTING in
NAPA and
SONOMA

Whether you're a serious wine collector making your annual pilgrimage to Northern California's Wine Country or a newbie who doesn't know the difference between a Merlot and Mourvèdre but is eager to learn, you can have a great time touring Napa and Sonoma wineries. Your gateway to the wine world is the tasting room, where staff members are happy to chat with curious guests.

(opposite page) Carneros vineyards in autumn, Napa Valley. (top) Pinot Gris grapes. (bottom) Bottles from Far Niente winery.

VISITING WINERIES

Tasting rooms range from the grand to the humble, offering everything from a few sips of wine to in-depth tours of facilities and vineyards. Many are open for drop-in visits, usually daily from around 10 am to 5 pm. Others require guests to make reservations. First-time visitors frequently enjoy the history-oriented tours at Charles Krug and Inglenook, or ones at Mondavi and J Vineyards that highlight the process as well. The environments at some wineries reflect their founders' other interests: art and architecture at Artesa and Hall St. Helena, movie making at Francis Ford Coppola, and medieval history at the Castello di Amorosa.

Many wineries describe their pourers as "wine educators," and indeed some of them have taken online or other classes and have passed an exam to prove basic knowledge of appellations, grape varietals, vineyards, and wine-making techniques. The one constant, however, is a deep, shared pleasure in the experience of wine tasting. To prepare you for winery visits, we've covered the fundamentals: tasting rooms, fees and what to expect, and the types of tours wineries offer.

Fees. In the past few years, tasting fees have skyrocketed. Most Napa wineries charge $25 or $30 to taste a few wines, though $40, $50, or even $75 fees aren't unheard of. Sonoma wineries are often a bit cheaper, in the $15 to $35 range, and you'll still find the occasional freebie.

Some winery tours are free, in which case you're usually required to pay a separate fee if you want to taste the wine. If you've paid a fee for the tour—generally from $20 to $40—your wine tasting is usually included in that price.

MAKING THE MOST OF YOUR TIME

(top) Sipping and swirling in the DeLoach tasting room. (bottom) Learning about barrel aging at Robert Mondavi Winery.

■ **Call ahead.** Some wineries require reservations to visit or tour. It's wise to check before visiting.

■ **Come on weekdays.** Especially between June and October, try to visit on weekdays to avoid traffic-clogged roads and crowded tasting rooms. For more info on the best times of year to visit, see this chapter's Planner.

■ **Get an early start.** Tasting rooms are often deserted before 11 am or so, when most visitors are still lingering over a second cup of coffee. If you come early, you'll have the staff's undivided attention. You'll usually encounter the largest crowds between 3 and 5 pm.

■ **Schedule strategically.** Visit appointment-only wineries in the morning and ones that allow walk-ins in the afternoon. It'll spare you the stress of being "on time" for later stops.

■ **Hit the Trail.** Beringer, Mondavi, and other high-profile wineries line heavily trafficked Highway 29, but the going is often quicker on the Silverado Trail, which runs parallel to the highway to the east. You'll find famous names here, too, among them the sparkling wine house Mumm Napa Valley, but the traffic is often lighter and sometimes the crowds as well.

Domaine Carneros.

AT THE BAR

In most tasting rooms, you'll be handed a list of the wines available that day. The wines will be listed in a suggested tasting order, starting with the lightest-bodied whites, progressing to the most intense reds, and ending with dessert wines. If you can't decide which wines to choose, tell the server what types of wines you usually like and ask for a recommendation.

The server will pour you an ounce or so of each wine you select. As you taste it, feel free to take notes or ask questions. Don't be shy—the staff are there to educate you about the wine. If you don't like a wine, or you've simply tasted enough, feel free to pour the rest into one of the dump buckets on the bar.

TOURS

Tours tend to be the most exciting (and the most crowded) in September and October, when the harvest and crushing are underway. Tours typically last from 30 minutes to an hour and give you a brief overview of the winemaking process. At some of the older wineries, the tour guide might focus on the history of the property.

■ **TIP→** If you plan to take any tours, wear comfortable shoes, since you might be walking on wet floors or dirt or gravel pathways or stepping over hoses or other equipment.

MONEY-SAVING TIPS

■ Many hotels and B&Bs distribute coupons for free or discounted tastings to their guests—don't forget to ask.

■ If you and your travel partner don't mind sharing a glass, servers are happy to let you split a tasting.

■ Some wineries will refund all or part of the tasting fee if you buy a bottle. Usually one fee is waived per bottle purchased, though sometimes you must buy two or three.

■ Almost all wineries will also waive the fee if you join their wine club program. However, this typically commits you to buying a certain number of bottles on a regular basis, so be sure you really like the wines before signing up.

Preston of Dry Creek bottles only estate-grown grapes.

TOP 2-DAY ITINERARIES

First-Timer's Napa Tour

Start: Oxbow Public market, Napa. Get underway by browsing the shops selling wines, spices, locally grown produce, and other fine foods, for a taste of what the Wine Country has to offer.

Inglenook, Rutherford. The tour here is a particularly fun way to learn about the history of Napa winemaking—

and you can see the old, atmospheric, ivy-covered château.

Frog's Leap, Rutherford. Friendly, unpretentious, and knowledgeable staff makes this place great for wine newbies. (Make sure you get that reservation lined up.)

Dinner and Overnight: St. Helena. Splurge at Meadowood Napa Valley and you won't need to leave the property for an extravagant din-

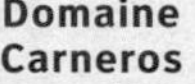

Wine Buff's Tour

Start: Stag's Leap Wine Cellars, Yountville, Napa. Famed for its Cabernet Sauvignon and Bordeaux blends.

Silver Oak, Oakville. Schedule a tour of this celebrated winery and taste the flagship Cabernet Sauvignon.

Mumm Napa, Rutherford. Come for the bubbly—which is available in a variety of tastings—stay for the photography exhibits.

Dinner and Overnight: Yountville. Have dinner at one of the Thomas Keller restaurants. Splurge at Bardessono; save at Maison Fleurie.

Next Day: Robert Mondavi, Oakville. Spring for the reserve room tasting so you can sip the top-of-the-line wines, especially the Cabernet Sauvignon. Head across Highway 29 to the Oakville Grocery to pick up a picnic lunch.

ner at its restaurant. Save at El Bonita Motel with dinner at Gott's.

Next Day: Poke around St. Helena's shops, then drive to Yountville for lunch.

di Rosa, Napa.
Call ahead to book a one- or two-hour tour of the acres of gardens and galleries, which are chock-full of thousands of works of art.

Domaine Carneros, Napa.
Toast your trip with a glass of outstanding bubbly.

Far Niente, Oakville.
You have to make a reservation and the fee for the tasting and tour is steep, but the payoff is an especially intimate winery experience. You'll taste excellent Cabernet and Chardonnay, then end your trip on a sweet note with a dessert wine.

Sonoma Backroads

Start: Iron Horse Vineyards, Russian River Valley.
Soak up a view of vine-covered hills and Mount St. Helena while sipping a sparkling wine or Pinot Noir at this beautifully rustic spot.

Dutton-Goldfield Winery, Russian River Valley.
A terrific source for Pinot Noir and Chardonnay, the stars of this valley.

Dinner and Overnight: Forestville. Go all out with a stay at the Farmhouse Inn, whose award-winning restaurant is one of the best in all of Sonoma.

Next Day: Westside Road, Russian River Valley.
This scenic route, which follows the river, is crowded with worthwhile wineries like Arista and Rochioli—but it's not crowded with visitors. Pinot fans will find a lot to love. Picnic at either winery and enjoy the view.

Balletto Vineyards, Santa Rosa. End on an especially relaxed note with a walk through the vineyards and a patio tasting.

WINE TASTING 101

TAKE A GOOD LOOK.
Hold your glass by the stem, raise it to the light, and take a close look at the wine. Check for clarity and color. (This is easiest to do if you can hold the glass in front of a white background.) Any tinge of brown usually means that the wine is over the hill or has gone bad.

BREATHE DEEP.
1. Sniff the wine once or twice to see if you can identify any smells.

2. Swirl the wine gently in the glass. Aerating the wine this way releases more of its aromas. (It's called "volatilizing the esters," if you're trying to impress someone.)

3. Take another long sniff. You might notice that experienced wine tasters spend more time sniffing the wine than drinking it. This is because this step is where the magic happens. The number of scents you might detect is almost endless, from berries, apricots, honey, and wildflowers to leather, cedar, or even tar. Does the wine smell good to you? Do you detect any "off" flavors, like wet dog or sulfur?

AT LAST! TAKE A SIP.
1. Swirl the wine around your mouth so that it makes contact with all your taste buds and releases more of its aromas. Think about the way the wine feels in your mouth. Is it watery or rich? Is it crisp or silky? Does it have a bold flavor, or is it subtle? The weight and intensity of a wine are called its body.

2. Hold the wine in your mouth for a few seconds and see if you can identify any developing flavors. More complex wines will reveal many different flavors as you drink them.

SPIT OR SWALLOW.
The pros typically spit, since they want to preserve their palate (and sobriety!) for the wines to come, but you'll find that swallowers far outnumber the spitters in the winery tasting rooms. Whether you spit or swallow, notice the flavor that remains after the wine is gone (the finish).

Swirl

Sniff

Sip

DODGE THE CROWDS

To avoid bumping elbows in the tasting rooms, look for wineries off the main drags of Highway 29 in Napa and Highway 12 in Sonoma. The back roads of the Russian River, Dry Creek, and Alexander valleys, all in Sonoma, are excellent places to explore. In Napa, try the northern end. Also look for wineries that are open by appointment only; they tend to schedule visitors carefully to avoid a big crush at any one time.

HOW WINE IS MADE

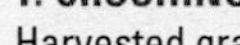

1. CRUSHING
Harvested grapes go into a stemmer-crusher, which separates stems from fruit and crushes the grapes to release "free-run" juice.

2. PRESSING
Remaining juice is gently extracted from grapes. Usually done by pressing grapes against the walls of a tank with an inflatable bladder.

3. FERMENTING
Extracted juice (and also grape skins and pulp, when making red wine) goes into stainless-steel tanks or oak barrels to ferment. During fermentation, sugars convert to alcohol.

4. AGING
Wine is stored in stainless-steel or oak casks or barrels, or sometimes in concrete vessels, to develop flavors.

5. RACKING
Wine is transferred to clean barrels; sediment is removed. Wine may be filtered and fined (clarified) to improve its clarity, color, and sometimes flavor.

6. BOTTLING
Wine is bottled either at the winery or at a special facility, then stored again for bottle-aging.

WHAT'S AN APPELLATION?

American Viticultural Area (AVA) or, more commonly, an appellation. What can be confusing is that some appellations encompass smaller subappellations. The Rutherford, Oakville, and Mt. Veeder AVAs, for instance, are among the Napa Valley AVA's 15 subappellations. Wineries often buy grapes from outside their AVA, so their labels might reference different appellations. A winery in the warmer Napa Valley, for instance, might source Pinot Noir grapes from the cooler Russian River Valley, where they grow better. The appellation listed on a label always refers to where a wine's grapes were grown, not to where the wine was made. By law, if a label bears the name of an appellation, 85% of the grapes must come from it.

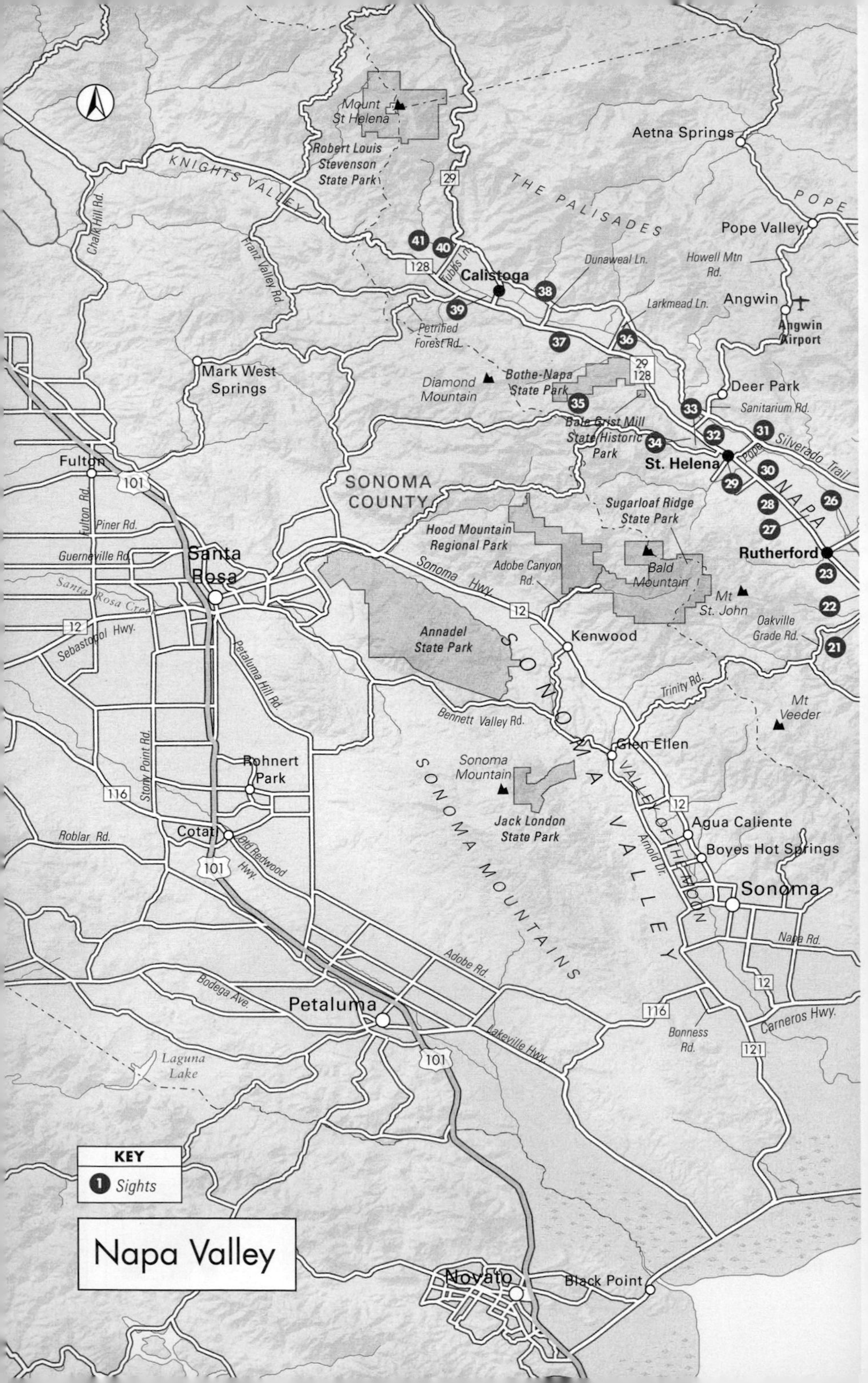

Napa Valley
KEY
1 Sights
Mount St Helena
Robert Louis Stevenson State Park
Knights Valley
The Palisades
Aetna Springs
Pope Valley
Pope
Howell Mtn Rd.
Angwin
Angwin Airport
Chalk Hill Rd.
Franz Valley Rd.
Calistoga
Dunaweal Ln.
Larkmead Ln.
Tubbs Ln.
Petrified Forest Rd.
Mark West Springs
Diamond Mountain
Bothe-Napa State Park
Deer Park
Sanitarium Rd.
Bale Grist Mill State Historic Park
St. Helena
Silverado Trail
Napa
Fulton
Fulton Rd.
Piner Rd.
Guerneville Rd.
Sonoma County
Hood Mountain Regional Park
Sugarloaf Ridge State Park
Santa Rosa
Santa Rosa Creek
Sebastopol Hwy.
Sonoma Hwy
Adobe Canyon Rd.
Bald Mountain
Mt St. John
Rutherford
Oakville Grade Rd.
Annadel State Park
Petaluma Hill Rd.
Kenwood
Trinity Rd.
Mt Veeder
Bennett Valley Rd.
Glen Ellen
Sonoma Mountain
Rohnert Park
Stony Point Rd.
Jack London State Park
Valley of the Moon
Agua Caliente
Boyes Hot Springs
Arnold Dr.
Roblar Rd.
Cotati
Old Redwood Hwy.
Sonoma Valley
Sonoma Mountains
Sonoma
Napa Rd.
Adobe Rd.
Bodega Ave.
Petaluma
Lakeville Hwy.
Bonness Rd.
Carneros Hwy.
Laguna Lake
Novato
Black Point
101
116
12
128
29
121
21
22
23
26
27
28
29
30
31
32
33
34
35
36
37
38
39
40
41

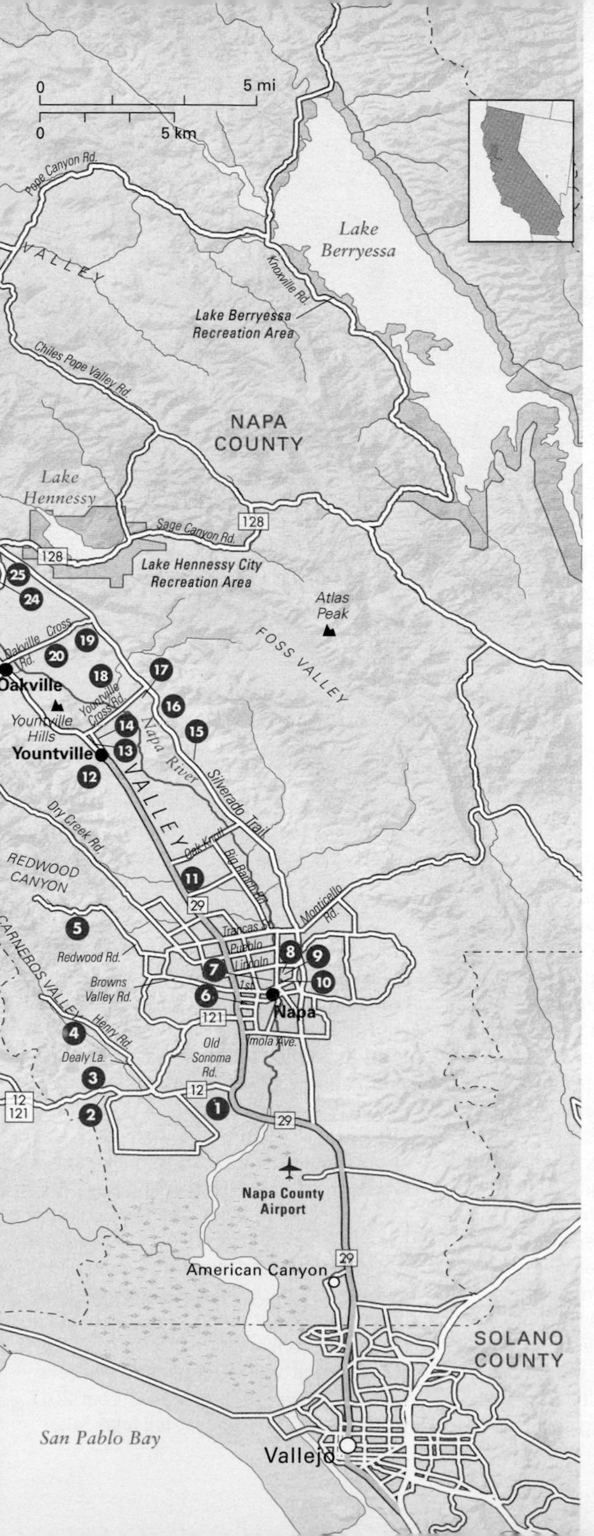

Sights

- Artesa Vineyards & Winery **4**
- Ashes & Diamonds **11**
- B Cellars **19**
- Beringer Vineyards **33**
- Ca' Toga Galleria d'Arte **39**
- Castello di Amorosa **37**
- Charles Krug Winery **32**
- Chateau Montelena **40**
- CIA at Copia **9**
- Cliff Lede Vineyards **17**
- Culinary Institute of America at Greystone **34**
- di Rosa Center for Contemporary Art **3**
- Domaine Carneros **2**
- Domaine Chandon **12**
- Etude Wines **1**
- Far Niente **21**
- Frank Family Vineyards **36**
- Frog's Leap **24**
- Goosecross Cellars **18**
- Hall St. Helena **29**
- Hess Collection **5**
- Honig Vineyard & Winery **26**
- Inglenook **23**
- Joseph Phelps Vineyards **31**
- Mad Fritz Brewing Co. **30**
- Mumm Napa **25**
- Napa Valley Distillery. **6**
- Napa Valley Wine Train **8**
- Oxbow Public Market **10**
- Prager Winery & Port Works .. **28**
- Pride Mountain Vineyards **35**
- The Prisoner Wine Company .. **27**
- RH Yountville **13**
- Robert Mondavi Winery **22**
- Robert Sinskey Vineyards **16**
- Silver Oak **20**
- St Clair Brown Winery & Brewery **7**
- Stag's Leap Winery **15**
- Stewart Cellars **14**
- Tamber Bey Vineyards **41**
- Venge Vineyards **38**

Wine and contemporary art find a home at di Rosa.

of all stripes. ✉ *4130 Howard La., Napa ✣ Off Hwy. 29* ☎ *707/666–4777* 🌐 *ashes-diamonds.com* 🎫 *Tastings from $40.*

★ CIA at Copia

COLLEGE | Full-fledged foodies and the merely curious achieve gastronomical bliss at the Culinary Institute of America's Oxbow District campus, its facade brightened since 2018 by a wraparound mural inspired by the colorful garden that fronts the facility. A restaurant, a shop, a museum, and the Vintners Hall of Fame—not to mention classes and demonstrations involving food-and-wine pairings, sparkling wines, ancient grains, cheeses, pasta, and sauces—make this a spend-a-half-day-here sort of place. One well-attended class for adults explores the Napa Valley's history through eight glasses of wine, and children join their parents for Family Funday workshops about making mac and cheese and nutritious lunches. Head upstairs to the Chuck Williams Culinary Arts Museum. Named for the founder of the Williams-Sonoma kitchenwares chain, it holds a fascinating collection of cooking, baking, and other food-related tools, tableware, gizmos, and gadgets, some dating back more than a century. ✉ *500 1st St., Napa ✣ Near McKinstry St.* ☎ *707/967–2500* 🌐 *www.ciaatcopia.com* 🎫 *Facility free, demonstrations and classes from $15.*

di Rosa Center for Contemporary Art

MUSEUM | The late Rene di Rosa assembled an extensive collection of artworks created by Northern California artists from the 1960s to the present, displaying them on this 217-acre Carneros District property surrounded by Chardonnay and Pinot Noir vineyards. Two galleries at opposite ends of a 35-acre lake show works from the collection and host temporary exhibitions, and the Sculpture Meadow behind the second gallery holds a few dozen large outdoor pieces. As 2019 dawned, di Rosa's residence, previously a highlight of a visit here, remained closed as conservation efforts continued to restore artworks damaged by smoke during the Wine Country's October 2017 wildfires. ■ **TIP→ Docent-led tours take**

place daily at 11 and 1. ✉ *5200 Sonoma Hwy./Hwy. 121, Napa* ✣ *Near Duhig Rd.* ☎ *707/226–5991* 🌐 *www.dirosaart.org* 🎫 *$18* ⏲ *Closed Mon. and Tues.*

★ Domaine Carneros

WINERY/DISTILLERY | A visit to this majestic château is an opulent way to enjoy the Carneros District—especially in fine weather, when the vineyard views are spectacular. The château was modeled after an 18th-century French mansion owned by the Taittinger family. Carved into the hillside beneath the winery, the cellars produce sparkling wines reminiscent of those made by Taittinger, using only Los Carneros AVA grapes. The winery sells flights and glasses of its sparklers, Chardonnay, Pinot Noir, and other wines. Enjoy them all with cheese and charcuterie plates, caviar, or smoked salmon. Seating is in the Louis XV–inspired salon or on the terrace overlooking the vines. The tour covers traditional methods of making sparkling wines. Tours and tastings are by appointment only. ✉ *1240 Duhig Rd., Napa* ✣ *At Hwy. 121* ☎ *707/257–0101, 800/716–2788* 🌐 *www.domainecarneros.com* 🎫 *Tastings from $12, tour $50.*

Etude Wines

WINERY/DISTILLERY | You're apt to see or hear hawks, egrets, Canada geese, and other wildlife on the grounds of Etude, known for sophisticated Pinot Noirs. Although the winery and its light-filled tasting room are in Napa County, the grapes for its flagship Carneros Estate Pinot Noir come from the Sonoma portion of Los Carneros, as do those for the rarer Heirloom Carneros Pinot Noir. Hosts pour Chardonnay, Pinot Blanc, Pinot Noir, and other wines daily at the tasting bar and in good weather on the patio. Carneros, Sonoma Coast, Willamette Valley, Santa Barbara County, and New Zealand Pinots, all crafted by winemaker Jon Priest, are compared at Study of Pinot Noir sessions (reservations required). **■ TIP→ Etude also excels at single-vineyard Napa Valley Cabernets; these can be sampled by appointment at seated tastings overlooking the production facility.** ✉ *1250 Cuttings Wharf Rd., Napa* ✣ *1 mile south of Hwy. 121* ☎ *707/257–5782* 🌐 *www.etudewines.com* 🎫 *Tastings from $25.*

Hess Collection

WINERY/DISTILLERY | About 9 miles northwest of Napa, up a winding road ascending Mt. Veeder, this winery is a delightful discovery. The limestone structure, rustic from the outside but modern and airy within, contains Swiss owner Donald Hess's world-class art collection, including large-scale works by contemporary artists such as Andy Goldsworthy, Anselm Kiefer, and Robert Rauschenberg. Cabernet Sauvignon is a major strength, with Chardonnays, Albariño, and Grüner Veltliner among the whites. Tastings outdoors in the garden and the courtyard take place from spring to fall, with cheese or nuts and other nibbles accompanying the wines. **■ TIP→ Among the wine-and-food pairings offered year-round, most of which involve a guided tour of the art collection, is a fun one showcasing locally made artisanal chocolates.** ✉ *4411 Redwood Rd., Napa* ✣ *West off Hwy. 29 at Trancas St./Redwood Rd. exit* ☎ *707/255–1144* 🌐 *www.hesscollection.com* 🎫 *Tastings from $25, art gallery free.*

Napa Valley Distillery

WINERY/DISTILLERY | Entertaining educators keep the proceedings light and lively at this distillery, which bills itself as Napa's first since Prohibition. NVD makes gin, rum, whiskey, and the flagship grape-based vodka, along with brandies and barrel-aged bottled cocktails that include Manhattans (the top seller), mai tais, and negronis. Visits, always by appointment, begin with a tasting upstairs in the "art-deco speakeasy with a tiki twist" Grand Salon, where lesson number one is how to properly sip spirits (spoiler: don't swirl your glass like you would with wine). Back downstairs in the production facility, you'll learn the basics of alcohol and distilling. ■ **TIP→ If you just want to sample the wares, the distillery operates a tasting bar in the main Oxbow Public Market building.** ✉ *2485 Stockton St., Napa* ✣ *Off California Blvd.* ☎ *707/265–6272* 🌐 *www.napadistillery.com* 🎫 *Tastings $30* ⏲ *Closed Wed.*

Napa Valley Wine Train

TOUR—SIGHT | Guests on this Napa Valley attraction, a fixture since 1989, ride the same rails along which, from the 1860s to the 1930s, trains transported passengers as far north as Calistoga's spas and hauled wine and other agricultural freight south toward San Francisco. The rolling stock includes restored Pullman railroad cars and a two-story Vista Dome car with a curved glass roof that travel a leisurely, scenic route between Napa and St. Helena. Patrons on the Quattro Vino tour enjoy a four-course lunch and tastings at four wineries, with stops at one or more wineries incorporated into other tours. Some rides involve no winery stops, and themed trips are scheduled throughout the year. ■ **TIP→ It's best to make this trip during the day, when you can enjoy the vineyard views.** ✉ *1275 McKinstry St., Napa* ✣ *Off 1st St.* ☎ *707/253–2111, 800/427–4124* 🌐 *www.winetrain.com* 🎫 *From $149.*

★ Oxbow Public Market

MARKET | The market's two dozen stands provide an introduction to Northern California's diverse artisanal food products. Swoon over decadent charcuterie at the Fatted Calf (great sandwiches, too), slurp oysters at Hog Island, or chow down on vegetarian, duck, or salmon tacos at C Casa. You can sample wine (and cheese) at the Oxbow Cheese & Wine Merchant, ales at Fieldwork Brewery's taproom, and barrel-aged cocktails at the Napa Valley Distillery. Napa Bookmine is among the few nonfood vendors here. ■ **TIP→ If you don't mind eating at the counter, you can select a steak at the Five Dot Ranch meat stand and pay $10 above market price ($14 with two sides) to have it grilled on the spot, a real deal for a quality slab.** ✉ *610 and 644 1st St., Napa* ✣ *At McKinstry St.* 🌐 *www.oxbowpublicmarket.com.*

Stags' Leap Winery

WINERY/DISTILLERY | A must for history buffs, this winery was established in 1893 in a bowl-shaped micro valley at the base of the Stags Leap Palisades. Three years earlier its original owners erected the Manor House, which reopened in 2016 after restoration of its castlelike stone facade and redwood-paneled interior. The home, whose open-air porch seems out of a flapper-era movie set, hosts elegant, appointment-only seated tastings of equally refined wines by the Bordeaux-born Christophe Paubert. Estate Cabernet Sauvignons, Merlot, and Petite Sirah, one bottling of the last varietal from vines planted in 1929, are the calling cards. Paubert also makes a blend of these three red grapes, along with Viognier, Chardonnay, and rosé. Some tastings take place on the porch, others inside; all require an appointment and include a tour of the property and tales of its storied past. ✉ *6150 Silverado Trail, Napa* ✣ *¾ mile south of Yountville Cross Rd.* ☎ *707/257–5790* 🌐 *stagsleap.com* 🎫 *Tastings from $65.*

★ St. Clair Brown Winery & Brewery

WINERY/DISTILLERY | Tastings at this women-run "urban winery"—and, since 2017, nanobrewery—a few blocks north of downtown take place in an intimate, light-filled greenhouse or a colorful culinary garden. Winemaker Elaine St. Clair, well regarded for stints at Domaine Carneros and Black Stallion, produces elegant wines—crisp yet complex whites and smooth, French-style reds whose stars include Cabernet Sauvignon and Syrah. While pursuing her wine-making degree, St. Clair also studied brewing; a few of her light-, medium-, and full-bodied brews are always on tap. You can taste the wines or beers by the glass or flight or enjoy them paired with appetizers that might include pork rillette with pickled tomatoes from the garden or addictive almonds roasted with rosemary, lemon zest, and lemon olive oil. Tuesday and Wednesday visits are by appointment only. ✉ *816 Vallejo St., Napa* ✣ *Off Soscol Ave.* ☎ *707/255–5591* 🌐 *www.stclairbrown.com* 🎫 *Tastings from $12 flights, from $4 by the glass.*

Restaurants

★ Compline

$$$ | MODERN AMERICAN | The full name of the three-in-one enterprise masterminded by master sommelier Matt Stamp and restaurant wine vet Ryan Stetins is Compline Wine Bar, Restaurant, and Merchant, and indeed you can just sip wine or purchase it here. The place evolved into a hot spot, though, for its youthful vibe and chef Yancy Windsperger's eclectic small and large plates that might include poached egg and polenta or gnocchi vegetable Bolognese. **Known for:** youthful vibe; by-the-glass wines; knowledgeable staff. $ *Average main: $25* ✉ *1300 1st St., Suite 312, Napa* ☎ *707/492–8150* 🌐 *complinewine.com* ⏲ *Closed Tues.*

Grace's Table

$$$ | ECLECTIC | A dependable, varied, three-squares-a-day menu makes this modest corner restaurant occupying a brick-and-glass storefront many Napans' go-to choice for a simple meal. Iron-skillet corn bread with lavender honey and butter shows up at all hours, with chilaquiles scrambled eggs a breakfast favorite, savory fish tacos a lunchtime staple, and cassoulet and roasted young chicken popular for dinner. **Known for:** congenial staffers; good beers on tap; eclectic menu focusing on France, Italy, and the Americas. $ *Average main: $24* ✉ *1400 2nd St., Napa* ✣ *At Franklin St.* ☎ *707/226–6200* 🌐 *www.gracestable.net.*

Gran Eléctrica

$$ | MEXICAN | A neon sign toward the back of Gran Eléctrica translates to "badass bar," but the same goes for the restaurant and its piquant lineup of *botanas* (snacks), tacos, tostadas, quesadillas, entrées, and sides. Ceviche tostadas, fish and carnitas tacos, the chile relleno, and duck-confit mole are among the year-round favorites, with dishes like grilled street-style corn with chipotle mayo appearing in-season. **Known for:** zippy decor; outdoor patio; tequila and mescal flights, specialty cocktails. $ *Average main: $19* ✉ *1313 Main St., Napa* ✣ *Near Clinton St.* ☎ *707/258–1313* 🌐 *www.granelectrica.com/about-napa* ⏲ *No lunch Mon.–Sat.*

★ La Toque

$$$$ | MODERN AMERICAN | Chef Ken Frank's La Toque is the complete package: his imaginative French cuisine, served in a formal brown-hued dining space, is complemented by a wine lineup that earned the restaurant a coveted *Wine Spectator* Grand Award. Signature dishes that might appear on the prix-fixe four- or five-course tasting menu include rösti potato with Kaluga caviar, Angus beef tenderloin with grilled king trumpet mushrooms, and New York strip loin with Fiscalini cheddar pearl tapioca and Rutherford red-wine sauce. **Known for:** chef's table menu for entire party; astute wine pairings; vegetarian tasting menu. $ *Average main: $110* ✉ *Westin Verasa Napa, 1314 McKinstry St., Napa* ✣ *Off Soscol Ave.* ☎ *707/257–5157* 🌐 *www.latoque.com* ⏲ *No lunch.*

★ Miminashi

$$$ | JAPANESE | Japanese *izakaya*—gastropubs that serve appetizers downed with sake or cocktails—inspired chef Curtis Di Fede's buzz-worthy downtown Napa restaurant, where two peaks in the slatted poplar ceiling echo Shinto and Buddhist temple designs. Ramen, fried rice, and yakitori anchor the menu, whose highlights include wok-fried edamame and the ooh-inspiring *okonomiyaki* pancake with bacon, cabbage, and dried fermented tuna flakes; wines and sakes selected by Jessica Pinzon, formerly of Thomas Keller's Yountville restaurants Bouchon and Ad Hoc, further elevate Di Fede's dishes. **Known for:** distinctive design; wine and sake selection; soft-serve ice cream for dessert and from to-go window. *Average main: $29 821 Coombs St., Napa Near 3rd St. 707/254–9464 mimi-nashi.com No lunch.*

Morimoto Napa

$$$$ | **JAPANESE** | *Iron Chef* star Masaharu Morimoto is the big name behind this downtown Napa restaurant where everything is delightfully overdone, right down to the desserts. Organic materials such as twisting grapevines above the bar and rough-hewn wooden tables seem simultaneously earthy and modern, creating a fitting setting for the gorgeously plated Japanese fare, from sashimi served with grated fresh wasabi to elaborate concoctions that include sea-urchin carbonara made with Inaniwa udon noodles. **Known for:** elaborate concoctions; gorgeous plating; chef's choice omakase menu (from $130). *Average main: $37 610 Main St., Napa At 5th St. 707/252–1600 www.morimotonapa.com.*

Oenotri

$$$ | **ITALIAN** | Often spotted at local farmers' markets and his restaurant's gardens, Oenotri's ebullient chef-owner and Napa native Tyler Rodde is ever on the lookout for fresh produce to incorporate into his rustic southern-Italian cuisine. His restaurant, a brick-walled contemporary space with tall windows and wooden tables, is a lively spot to sample house-made salumi and pastas, thin-crust pizzas, and entrées that might include roasted squab, Atlantic salmon, or pork sausage. **Known for:** fresh ingredients; Margherita pizza with San Marzano tomatoes; lively atmosphere. *Average main: $27 1425 1st St., Napa At Franklin St. 707/252–1022 www.oenotri.com.*

★ Torc

$$$$ | **MODERN AMERICAN** | *Torc* means "wild boar" in an early Celtic dialect, and owner-chef Sean O'Toole, who formerly helmed kitchens at top Manhattan, San Francisco, and Yountville establishments, occasionally incorporates the restaurant's namesake beast into his eclectic offerings. A recent menu featured sea urchin with Persian melon carpaccio, Maine-lobster risotto, and veal sweetbreads with sweet and sour tomatoes, all prepared by O'Toole and his team with style and precision. **Known for:** gracious service; specialty cocktails; Bengali sweet-potato pakora and deviled-egg appetizers. *Average main: $36 1140 Main St., Napa At Pearl St. 707/252–3292 www.torcnapa.com Closed Tues. No lunch weekdays.*

★ ZuZu

$$$ | **SPANISH** | At festive ZuZu the focus is on cold and hot tapas, paella, and other Spanish favorites often downed with cava or sangria. Regulars revere the paella, made with Spanish *bomba* rice, and small plates that might include grilled octopus, garlic shrimp, jamón Ibérico, and white anchovies with sliced egg and rémoulade on grilled bread. **Known for:** singular flavors and spicing; Latin jazz on the stereo; sister restaurant La Taberna three doors south for beer, wine, and bar bites. *Average main: $30 829 Main St., Napa Near 3rd St. 707/224–8555 www.zuzunapa.com No lunch weekends.*

Hotels

★ Andaz Napa

$$$ | **HOTEL** | Part of the Hyatt family, this boutique hotel with an urban-hip vibe has spacious, luxurious rooms with flat-screen TVs, laptop-size safes, and white-marble bathrooms stocked with high-quality bath products. **Pros:** proximity

to downtown restaurants, theaters, and tasting rooms; access to modern fitness center; complimentary beverage upon arrival; complimentary snacks and nonalcoholic beverages in rooms. **Cons:** parking can be a challenge on weekends; unremarkable views from some rooms; expensive on weekends in high season. *Rooms from: $306 1450 1st St., Napa 707/687–1234 andaznapa.com 141 rooms No meals.*

★ Archer Hotel Napa

$$$ | **HOTEL** | A hybrid of New York City and Las Vegas glamour infused downtown Napa with the 2018 completion of this five-story hotel ideal for travelers seeking design pizzazz, a see-and-be-seen atmosphere, and a slate of first-class amenities. **Pros:** restaurants and room service by chef Charlie Palmer; Sky & Vine rooftop bar; views from upper-floor rooms (especially south and west). **Cons:** not particularly rustic; expensive in high season; occasional service, hospitality lapses. *Rooms from: $374 1230 1st St., Napa 707/690–9800, 855/437–9100 archerhotel.com/napa 183 rooms No meals.*

★ Carneros Resort & Spa

$$$$ | **RESORT** | Freestanding board-and-batten cottages with rocking chairs on each porch are simultaneously rustic and chic at this luxurious property made even more so by a $6.5 million makeover. **Pros:** cottages have lots of privacy; beautiful views from hilltop pool and hot tub; heaters on private patios. **Cons:** long drive to upvalley destinations; least expensive accommodations pick up highway noise; pricey pretty much year-round. *Rooms from: $600 4048 Sonoma Hwy./Hwy. 121, Napa 707/299–4900, 888/400–9000 www.carnerosresort.com 100 rooms No meals.*

★ The Inn on First

$$ | **B&B/INN** | Guests gush over the hospitality at this inn whose painstakingly restored 1905 mansion facing 1st Street contains five rooms, with five additional accommodations, all suites, in a building behind a secluded patio and garden. **Pros:** full gourmet breakfast by hosts-with-the-most owners; gas fireplaces and whirlpool tubs in all rooms; away from downtown but not too far. **Cons:** no TVs; owners "respectfully request no children"; lacks pool, fitness center, and other amenities of larger properties. *Rooms from: $220 1938 1st St., Napa 707/253–1331 www.theinnonfirst.com 10 rooms Breakfast.*

★ Inn on Randolph

$$ | **B&B/INN** | A few calm blocks from the downtown action on a nearly 1-acre lot with landscaped gardens, the Inn on Randolph—with a Gothic Revival–style main house and its five guest rooms plus five historic cottages out back—is a sophisticated haven celebrated for its gourmet gluten-free breakfasts and snacks. **Pros:** quiet residential neighborhood; spa tubs in cottages and two main-house rooms; romantic setting. **Cons:** a bit of a walk from downtown; expensive in-season; weekend minimum-stay requirement. *Rooms from: $299 411 Randolph St., Napa 707/257–2886 www.innonrandolph.com 10 rooms Breakfast.*

Nightlife

Blue Note Napa

MUSIC CLUBS | The famed New York jazz room's West Coast club hosts national headliners such as Brian McKnight, Dee Dee Bridgewater, and Coco Montoya, along with local talents such as Lavay Smith & Her Red Hot Skillet Lickers. There's a full bar, and you can order a meal or small bites from the kitchen. *Napa Valley Opera House, 1030 Main St., Napa At 1st St. 707/880–2300 www.bluenotenapa.com.*

Cadet Wine + Beer Bar

WINE BARS—NIGHTLIFE | Cadet plays things urban-style cool with a long bar, high-top tables, an all-vinyl sound track, and a low-lit, generally loungelike feel. When they opened their bar, the two owners described their outlook as "unabashedly pro-California," but their wine-and-beer lineup circles the globe. The crowd here is youngish, the vibe festive. ⊠ *930 Franklin St., Napa* ✣ *At end of pedestrian alley between 1st and 2nd Sts.* ☎ *707/224–4400* ⊕ *www.cadetbeerandwinebar.com.*

Yountville

9 miles north of the town of Napa.

These days Yountville is something like Disneyland for food lovers. You could stay here for a week and not exhaust all the options—several of them owned by The French Laundry's Thomas Keller—and the tiny town is full of small inns and high-end hotels that cater to those who prefer to walk (not drive) after an extravagant meal. It's also well located for excursions to many big-name Napa wineries, especially those in the Stags Leap District, from which big, bold Cabernet Sauvignons helped make the Napa Valley's wine-making reputation.

GETTING HERE AND AROUND

Downtown Yountville sits just off Highway 29. Approaching from the south take the Yountville exit—from the north take Madison—and proceed to Washington Street, home to the major shops and restaurants. Yountville Cross Road connects downtown to the Silverado Trail, along which many noted wineries do business. The free Yountville Trolley serves the town daily 10 am–7 pm (on-call service until 11 except on Sunday).

Sights

★ Cliff Lede Vineyards

WINERY/DISTILLERY | Inspired by his passion for classic rock, owner and construction magnate Cliff Lede named the blocks in his Stags Leap District vineyard after hits by the Grateful Dead and other bands. The vibe at his efficient, high-tech winery is anything but laid-back, however. Cutting-edge agricultural and enological science informs the vineyard management and wine making here. Architect Howard Backen designed the winery and its tasting room, where Lede's Sauvignon Blanc, Cabernet Sauvignons, and other wines, along with some from sister winery FEL, which produces much-lauded Anderson Valley Pinot Noirs, are poured. **■ TIP→ Walk-ins are welcome at the tasting bar, but appointments are required for the veranda outside and a nearby gallery that displays rock-related art.** ⊠ *1473 Yountville Cross Rd., Yountville* ✣ *Off Silverado Trail* ☎ *707/944–8642* ⊕ *cliffledevineyards.com* 🎫 *Tastings from $35.*

Domaine Chandon

WINERY/DISTILLERY | On a knoll shaded by ancient oak trees, this French-owned maker of sparkling wines claims one of Yountville's prime pieces of real estate. Chandon is best known for bubbles, but the still wines—among them Cabernet Sauvignon, Chardonnay, and Pinot Noir—are also worth a try. You can sip by the flight or by the glass at the bar, or begin there and sit at tables in the lounge and return to the bar as needed; in good weather, tables are set up outside. Bottle service is also available. ⊠ *1 California Dr., Yountville* ✣ *Off Hwy. 29* ☎ *707/204–7530, 888/242–6366* ⊕ *www.chandon.com* 🎫 *Tastings from $10.*

Goosecross Cellars

WINERY/DISTILLERY | When Christi Coors Ficeli purchased this boutique winery in 2013 and commissioned a new barnlike tasting space, she and her architect had one major goal: bring the outside in. Large retractable west-facing windows open up behind the tasting bar to idyllic views of Cabernet vines—in fine weather, guests on the outdoor deck can practically touch them. Goosecross makes Chardonnay and Pinot Noir from Carneros grapes, but the soul of this cordial operation is its 12-acre estate vineyard, its 10 planted acres mostly Cabernet Sauvignon and Merlot with some Cabernet Franc and Petit Verdot. The Cab and Merlot are the stars, along with the Aeros Bordeaux-style blend of the best estate grapes. Aeros isn't usually poured, but a Howell Mountain Petite Sirah with expressive tannins (there's also a Howell Mountain Cabernet) often is. Visits to Goosecross are by appointment only. ✉ *1119 State La., Yountville* ⊕ *Off Yountville Cross Rd.* ☎ *707/944–1986* 🌐 *www.goosecross.com* 🎫 *Tastings from $40.*

RH Yountville

MUSEUM | Gargantuan crystal chandeliers, century-old olive trees, and strategically placed water features provide visual and aural continuity at Restoration Hardware's quadruple-threat food, wine, art, and design compound. An all-day café fronts two steel, glass, and concrete home-furnishings galleries, with a bluestone walkway connecting them to a reboot of the Ma(i)sonry wine salon. Inside a two-story 1904 manor house constructed from Napa River stone and rechristened The Wine Vault at the Historic Ma(i)sonry Building, it remains an excellent tasting choice. Classic and Connoisseur flights focus on small-lot Napa and Sonoma bottlings; hosts at Collector tastings pour Napa Valley wines by elite winemakers like Heidi Barrett and Philippe Melka. In good weather, some tastings take place in outdoor living rooms where patrons can also enjoy coffee, tea, or wine by the glass or bottle. Walk-ins are welcome, but reservations are recommended (and wise on weekends in-season). ✉ *6725 Washington St., Yountville* ⊕ *At Pedroni St.* ☎ *707/339–4654* 🌐 *www.restorationhardware.com* 🎫 *Tastings from $50.*

★ Robert Sinskey Vineyards

WINERY/DISTILLERY | Although the winery produces a well-regarded Stags Leap Cabernet Sauvignon, two Bordeaux-style red blends (Marcien and POV), and white wines, Sinskey is best known for its intense, brambly Carneros District Pinot Noirs. All the grapes are grown in organic, certified biodynamic vineyards. The influence of Robert's wife, Maria Helm Sinskey—a chef and cookbook author and the winery's culinary director—is evident during the tastings, which are accompanied by a few bites of food with each wine. **■TIP→ The Perfect Circle Tour, offered daily, takes in the winery's gardens and ends with a seated pairing of food and wine. Even more elaborate, also by appointment, is the five-course Chef's Table pairing of seasonal dishes with current and older wines.** ✉ *6320 Silverado Trail, Napa* ⊕ *At Yountville Cross Rd.* ☎ *707/944–9090* 🌐 *www.robertsinskey.com* 🎫 *Tastings from $40, tours (with tastings) from $95.*

★ Stewart Cellars

WINERY/DISTILLERY | Three stone structures meant to mimic Scottish ruins coaxed into modernity form this complex that includes public and private tasting spaces, a bright outdoor patio, and a hip, independently run café. The attention to detail in the ensemble's design mirrors that of the wines, whose grapes come from coveted vineyards, most notably all six of the Beckstoffer Heritage Vineyards, among the Napa Valley's most historic sites. Although Cabernet is the focus, winemaker Blair Guthrie, with input from consulting winemaker Paul Hobbs, also makes Sauvignon Blanc, Chardonnay, Pinot Noir, and Merlot. **■TIP→ On sunny days this is a good stop around lunchtime, when you can order a meal from the café and a glass of wine from the tasting room—for permit reasons this must be done separately—and enjoy them on the patio.** ✉ *6752 Washington St., Yountville* ⊕ *Near Pedroni St.* ☎ *707/963–9160* 🌐 *www.stewartcellars.com* 🎫 *Tastings from $30.*

Restaurants

★ Ad Hoc

$$$$ | **MODERN AMERICAN** | At this low-key dining room with zinc-top tables and wine served in tumblers, superstar chef Thomas Keller offers a single, fixed-price, nightly menu that might include smoked beef short ribs with creamy herb rice and charred broccolini or sesame chicken with radish kimchi and fried rice. Ad Hoc also serves a small but decadent Sunday brunch, and Keller's Addendum annex, in a separate small building behind the restaurant, sells boxed lunches to go (beyond moist buttermilk fried chicken) from Thursday to Saturday except in winter. **Known for:** casual cuisine at great prices for a Thomas Keller restaurant; don't-miss buttermilk-fried-chicken night; street-side outdoor seating. *Average main: $55 ✉ 6476 Washington St., Yountville ✣ At Oak Circle ☎ 707/944–2487 ⊕ www.adhocrestaurant.com ⏲ No lunch Mon.–Sat.; no dinner Tues. and Wed. ☞ Call day ahead to find out next day's menu.*

★ Bistro Jeanty

$$$ | FRENCH | Escargots, cassoulet, *daube de boeuf* (beef stewed in red wine), and other French classics are prepared with the utmost precision at this country bistro whose lamb tongue and other obscure delicacies delight daring diners. Regulars often start with the rich tomato soup in a flaky puff pastry before proceeding to sole meunière or coq au vin, completing the French sojourn with a lemon meringue tart or other authentic desserts. **Known for:** traditional preparations; oh-so-French atmosphere; European wines. *Average main: $29 ✉ 6510 Washington St., Yountville ✣ At Mulberry St. ☎ 707/944–0103 ⊕ www.bistrojeanty.com.*

★ Bouchon Bistro

$$$$ | FRENCH | The team that created The French Laundry is also behind this place, where everything—the lively and crowded zinc-topped bar, the elbow-to-elbow seating, the traditional French onion soup—could have come straight from a Parisian bistro. Pan-seared rib eye with béarnaise and mussels steamed with white wine, saffron, and Dijon mustard—both served with crispy, addictive fries—are among the perfectly executed entrées. **Known for:** bistro classics; raw bar; Bouchon Bakery next door. *Average main: $32 ✉ 6534 Washington St., Yountville ✣ Near Humboldt St. ☎ 707/944–8037 ⊕ www.bouchonbistro.com.*

Ciccio

$$ | MODERN ITALIAN | The ranch of Ciccio's owners, Frank and Karen Altamura, supplies some of the vegetables and herbs for the modern Italian cuisine prepared in the open kitchen of this remodeled former grocery store. Seasonal growing cycles dictate the menu, with fried-seafood appetizers (calamari, perhaps, or softshell crabs), a few pasta dishes, bavette steak with red-wine jus, and pancetta pizzas among the frequent offerings. **Known for:** Negroni bar; prix-fixe chef's dinner; mostly Napa Valley wines, some from owners' winery. *Average main: $19 ✉ 6770 Washington St., Yountville ✣ At Madison St. ☎ 707/945–1000 ⊕ www.ciccionapavalley.com ⏲ Closed Mon. and Tues. No lunch ☞ No reservations, except for prix-fixe chef's dinner (required; for 2–10 guests).*

★ The French Laundry

$$$$ | AMERICAN | An old stone building laced with ivy houses chef Thomas Keller's destination restaurant. Some courses on the two prix-fixe menus, one of which highlights vegetables, rely on luxe ingredients such as *calotte* (cap of the rib eye) while other courses take humble elements like carrots or fava beans and elevate them to art; many courses offer "supplements"—sea urchin, for instance, or black truffles. **Known for:** signature starter "oysters and pearls"; intricate flavors; superior wine list. *Average main: $325 ✉ 6640 Washington St., Yountville ✣ At Creek St. ☎ 707/944–2380 ⊕ www.frenchlaundry.com ⏲ No lunch Mon.–Thurs. Jacket required ☞ Reservations essential wks ahead.*

Mustards Grill

$$$ | **AMERICAN** | Cindy Pawlcyn's Mustards Grill fills day and night with fans of her hearty cuisine, equal parts updated renditions of traditional American dishes—what Pawlcyn dubs "deluxe truck stop classics"—and fanciful contemporary fare. Barbecued baby back pork ribs and a lemon-lime tart piled high with brown-sugar meringue fall squarely in the first category, with sweet corn tamales with tomatillo-avocado salsa and wild mushrooms representing the latter. **Known for:** roadhouse setting; convivial mood; hoppin' bar. *Average main: $28 ✉ 7399 St. Helena Hwy./Hwy. 29, Napa ✣ 1 mile north of Yountville ☎ 707/944–2424 ⊕ www.mustardsgrill.com.*

★ Protéa Restaurant

$$ | **LATIN AMERICAN** | A meal at Yountville's The French Laundry motivated Puerto Rico–born Anita Cartagena to pursue a career as a chef, which she did for several years at nearby Ciccio and elsewhere before opening this perky storefront serving Latin-inspired multiculti fast-food cuisine. What's in season and the chef's whims determine the order-at-the-counter fare, but Puerto Rican rice bowls (often with pork), empanadas, and sweet-and-sour ramen stir-fries make regular appearances. **Known for:** patio and rooftop seating; beer and wine lineup; eager-to-please staff. *Average main: $16 ✉ 6488 Washington St., Yountville ✣ At Oak Circle ☎ 707/415–5035 ⊕ www.proteayv.com ⊗ Closed Wed.*

Redd Wood

$$ | **ITALIAN** | Chef Richard Reddington's casual restaurant specializes in thin-crust wood-fired pizzas and contemporary variations on Italian classics. With potato–and–green garlic soup, pizzas such as the sausage with a blend of goat cheese and mozzarella, and the pork chop entrée enlivened in fall by persimmon, Redd Wood does for Italian comfort food what nearby Mustards Grill does for the American version: it spruces it up but retains its innate pleasures. **Known for:** industrial decor; easygoing service; lunch through late-night menu. *Average main: $22 ✉ North Block Hotel, 6755 Washington St., Yountville ✣ At Madison St. ☎ 707/299–5030 ⊕ www.redd-wood.com.*

Hotels

★ Bardessono

$$$$ | **RESORT** | Tranquillity and luxury with a low carbon footprint are among the goals of this ultragreen wood, steel, and glass resortlike property in downtown Yountville, but there's nothing spartan about its accommodations, arranged around four landscaped courtyards. **Pros:** large rooftop lap pool; in-room spa treatments; smooth service. **Cons:** expensive; limited view from some rooms; a bit of street traffic on hotel's west side. *Rooms from: $700 ✉ 6526 Yount St., Yountville ☎ 707/204–6000 ⊕ www.bardessono.com ⇏ 62 rooms ǁ○ǁ No meals.*

Maison Fleurie

$$ | **B&B/INN** | A stay at this comfortable, reasonably priced inn, said to be the oldest hotel in the Napa Valley, places you within walking distance of Yountville's fine restaurants. **Pros:** smallest rooms a bargain; outdoor hot tub and pool; free bike rental. **Cons:** breakfast room can be crowded at peak times; some rooms pick up noise from nearby Bouchon Bakery; hard to book in high season. *Rooms from: $229 ✉ 6529 Yount St., Yountville ☎ 707/944–2056 ⊕ www.maisonfleurienapa.com ⇏ 13 rooms ǁ○ǁ Breakfast.*

Napa Valley Lodge

$$ | **HOTEL** | Clean rooms in a convenient motel-style setting draw travelers willing to pay more than at comparable lodgings in the city of Napa to be within walking distance of Yountville's tasting rooms, restaurants, and shops. **Pros:** clean rooms; filling continental breakfast; large pool area. **Cons:** no elevator; lacks amenities of other Yountville properties;

pricey on weekends in high season. 💲 *Rooms from: $280* ✉ *2230 Madison St., Yountville* ☎ *707/944–2468, 888/944–3545* 🌐 *www.napavalleylodge.com* *55 rooms* 🍽 *Breakfast.*

★ North Block Hotel

$$$$ | **HOTEL** | A two-story boutique property near downtown Yountville's northern edge, the North Block attracts sophisticated travelers who appreciate its clever but unpretentious style and offhand luxury. **Pros:** extremely comfortable beds; attentive service; room service by Redd Wood restaurant. **Cons:** outdoor areas get some traffic noise; weekend minimum-stay requirement; rates soar on high-season weekends. 💲 *Rooms from: $425* ✉ *6757 Washington St., Yountville* ☎ *707/944–8080* 🌐 *northblockhotel.com* *20 rooms* 🍽 *No meals.*

Vintage House

$$$ | **RESORT** | Part of the 22-acre Estate Yountville complex—other sections include sister lodging Hotel Villagio and the shops and restaurants of V Marketplace—this downtown hotel consists of two-story brick buildings along verdant landscaped paths shaded by mature trees. **Pros:** aesthetically pleasing accommodations; private patios and balconies; secluded feeling yet near shops, tasting rooms, and restaurants. **Cons:** highway noise audible in some exterior rooms; very expensive on summer and fall weekends; weekend minimum-stay requirement. 💲 *Rooms from: $355* ✉ *6541 Washington St., Yountville* ☎ *707/944–1112* 🌐 *www.vintagehouse.com* *80 rooms* 🍽 *Breakfast.*

BALLOONING

Napa Valley Aloft

BALLOONING | Between 8 and 12 passengers soar over the Napa Valley in balloons that launch from downtown Yountville. Rates include preflight refreshments and a huge breakfast. ✉ *V Marketplace, 6525 Washington St., Yountville* ✣ *Near Mulberry St.* ☎ *707/944–4400, 855/944–4408* 🌐 *www.nvaloft.com* *From $200.*

BIKING

Napa Valley Bike Tours

BICYCLING | With dozens of wineries within 5 miles, this shop makes a fine starting point for guided and self-guided vineyard and wine-tasting excursions. The outfit also rents bikes. ✉ *6500 Washington St., Yountville* ✣ *At Mulberry St.* ☎ *707/944–2953* 🌐 *www.napavalleybiketours.com* *From $124 (½-day guided tour).*

Hunter Gatherer

CLOTHING | A Napa Valley play on the classic general store, Colby Hallen's high-end lifestyle shop sells women's clothing and accessories from designers such as Frēda Salvador and Emerson Fry. She carries some men's items, too, along with everything from ceramic flasks and small gifts and cards to artisanal honey and Vintner's Daughter Active Botanical Serum face oil. ✉ *6795 Washington St., Bldg. B, Yountville* ✣ *At Madison St.* 🌐 *www.huntergatherernapavalley.com.*

V Marketplace

SHOPPING CENTERS/MALLS | This two-story redbrick market, which once housed a winery, a livery stable, and a brandy distillery, now contains clothing boutiques, art galleries, a chocolatier, and food, wine, and gift shops. Celebrity chef Michael Chiarello operates a restaurant (Bottega), a tasting room for his wines, and Ottimo, with pizza, fresh mozzarella, and other stands plus retail items. Show some love to the shops upstairs, especially Knickers and Pearls (lingerie and loungewear) and Lemondrops (kids' clothing and toys). ✉ *6525 Washington St., Yountville* ✣ *Near Mulberry St.* ☎ *707/944–2451* 🌐 *www.vmarketplace.com.*

SPAS

B Spa Therapy Center

SPA/BEAUTY | Many of this spa's patrons are Bardessono Hotel guests who take their treatments in their rooms' large, customized bathrooms—all of them equipped with concealed massage tables—but the main facility is open to guests and nonguests. An in-room treatment popular with couples starts with massages in front of the fireplace and ends with a tea bath and a split of sparkling wine. The two-hour Yountville Signature treatment, which can be enjoyed in-room or at the spa, begins with a shea-butter-enriched sugar scrub, followed by a Chardonnay grape-seed oil massage and a hydrating hair-and-scalp treatment. The spa engages massage therapists skilled in Swedish, Thai, and several other techniques. In addition to massages, the services include facials and other skin-care treatments. ✉ *Bardessono Hotel, 6526 Yount St., Yountville* ✣ *At Mulberry St.* ☎ *707/204–6050* 🌐 *www.bardessono.com/spa* 🎫 *Treatments from $165.*

Oakville

2 miles northwest of Yountville.

A large butte that runs east–west just north of Yountville blocks the cooling fogs from the south, facilitating the myriad microclimates of the Oakville AVA, home to several high-profile wineries.

GETTING HERE AND AROUND

Driving along Highway 29, you'll know you've reached Oakville when you see the Oakville Grocery on the east side of the road. You can reach Oakville from the Sonoma County town of Glen Ellen by heading east on Trinity Road from Highway 12. The twisting route, along the mountain range that divides Napa and Sonoma, eventually becomes the Oakville Grade. The views on this drive are breathtaking, though the continual curves make it unsuitable for those who suffer from motion sickness.

Sights

B Cellars

WINERY/DISTILLERY | The chefs take center stage in the open-hearth kitchen of this boutique winery's hospitality house, and with good reason: creating food-friendly wines is B Cellars's raison d'être. Visits to the Oakville facility—all steel beams, corrugated metal, and plate glass yet remarkably cozy—begin with a tour of the winery's culinary garden and in some cases also the caves. Most guests return to the house to sample wines paired with small bites, with some visitors remaining in the caves for exclusive tastings of Cabernet Sauvignons from several historic vineyards of Andy Beckstoffer, a prominent grower. Kirk Venge, whose fruit-forward style well suits the winery's food-oriented approach, crafts these and other wines, among them red and white blends and single-vineyard Cabernets from other noteworthy vineyards. All visits here are strictly by appointment. ✉ *703 Oakville Cross Rd., Oakville* ✣ *West of Silverado Trail* ☎ *707/709–8787* 🌐 *www.bcellars.com* 🎫 *Tastings from $65.*

Far Niente

WINERY/DISTILLERY | Hamden McIntyre, a prominent winery architect of his era also responsible for Inglenook and what's now the Culinary Institute of America at Greystone, designed the centerpiece 1885 stone winery here. Abandoned in the wake of Prohibition and only revived beginning in 1979, Far Niente now ranks as one of the Napa Valley's most beautiful properties. Guests participating in the main tour and tasting learn some of this history while strolling the winery and its aging caves. The trip completed, hosts pour the flagship wines, a Chardonnay and a Cabernet Sauvignon blend. The tasting session concludes with Dolce, a late-harvest Sémillon and Sauvignon

Blanc wine. Two shorter tastings, one highlighting older vintages, the other showcasing the output of affiliated wineries, dispense with the tour. ■ **TIP→ Aged and rare Cabernets from the Far Niente wine library are served at Cave Collection tastings.** ✉ *1350 Acacia Dr., Oakville* ✣ *Off Oakville Grade Rd.* ☎ *707/944–2861* 🌐 *www.farniente.com* 🎫 *Tastings from $80; tour and tasting $80.*

Robert Mondavi Winery

WINERY/DISTILLERY | The graceful arch at the center of the winery's Mission-style building frames the lawn and the vineyard behind, inviting a stroll under the arcades. You can head for one of the walk-in tasting rooms, but if you've not toured a winery before, the 75-minute Signature Tour and Tasting is a good way to learn about enology and the late Robert Mondavi's role in California wine making. Those new to tasting should consider the 45-minute Wine Tasting Basics experience. Serious wine lovers can opt for the Exclusive Cellar tasting, during which a server pours and explains limited-production, reserve, and older vintages. The three-course Harvest of Joy Lunch and wine pairing starts with a tour. All visits except walk-in tastings require reservations. ■ **TIP→ Well-attended concerts take place in summer on the lawn.** ✉ *7801 St. Helena Hwy./Hwy. 29, Oakville* ☎ *888/766–6328* 🌐 *www.robertmondaviwinery.com* 🎫 *Tastings and tours from $25.*

★ Silver Oak

WINERY/DISTILLERY | The first review of this winery's Napa Valley Cabernet Sauvignon declared the debut 1972 vintage not all that good and, at $6 a bottle, overpriced. Oops. The celebrated Bordeaux-style Cabernet blend, still the only Napa Valley wine bearing its winery's label each year, evolved into a cult favorite, and Silver Oak founders Ray Duncan and Justin Meyer received worldwide recognition for their signature use of exclusively American oak to age the wines. At the Oakville tasting room, constructed out of reclaimed stone and other materials from a 19th-century Kansas flour mill, you can sip the current Napa Valley vintage, its counterpart from Silver Oak's Alexander Valley operation, and a library wine without an appointment. One is required for tours, private tastings, and food–wine pairings. ✉ *915 Oakville Cross Rd., Oakville* ✣ *Off Hwy. 29* ☎ *707/942–7022* 🌐 *www.silveroak.com* 🎫 *Tastings from $30, tours from $40 (includes tasting).*

Rutherford

2 miles northwest of Oakville.

With its singular microclimate and soil, Rutherford is an important viticultural center, with more big-name wineries than you can shake a corkscrew at. Cabernet Sauvignon is king here. The well-drained, loamy soil is ideal for those vines, and since this part of the valley gets plenty of sun, the grapes develop exceptionally intense flavors.

GETTING HERE AND AROUND

Wineries around Rutherford are dotted along Highway 29 and the parallel Silverado Trail north and south of Rutherford Road/Conn Creek Road, on which wineries can also be found.

Sights

★ Frog's Leap

WINERY/DISTILLERY | FAMILY | If you're a novice, the tour at Frog's Leap is a fun way to begin your education. You'll taste wines that might include Zinfandel, Merlot, Chardonnay, Sauvignon Blanc, and an estate-grown Cabernet Sauvignon. The winery includes a barn built in 1884, 5 acres of organic gardens, an eco-friendly visitor center, and a frog pond topped with lily pads. Reservations are required for all visits here. ■ **TIP→ The tour is recommended, but you can also just sample wines either inside or on a porch**

overlooking the garden. ✉ *8815 Conn Creek Rd., Rutherford* ☎ *707/963–4704, 800/959–4704* 🌐 *www.frogsleap.com* 🎫 *Tastings from $25, tour $35.*

Honig Vineyard & Winery

WINERY/DISTILLERY | FAMILY | Sustainable farming is the big story at this family-run winery. The Eco Tour, offered seasonally, focuses on the Honig family's environmentally friendly farming and production methods, which include using biodiesel to fuel the tractors, monitoring water use in the vineyard and winery, and generating power for the winery with solar panels. The family produces only Sauvignon Blanc and Cabernet Sauvignon. By appointment, you can taste whites and reds at a standard tasting; the reserve tasting pairs single-vineyard Cabernets with small bites. ✉ *850 Rutherford Rd., Rutherford* ✢ *Near Conn Creek Rd.* ☎ *800/929–2217* 🌐 *www.honigwine.com* 🎫 *Tastings from $30, tour $45.*

★ Inglenook

WINERY/DISTILLERY | Filmmaker Francis Ford Coppola began his wine-making career in 1975, when he bought part of the historic Inglenook estate. Over the decades he reunited the original property acquired by Inglenook founder Gustave Niebaum, remodeled Niebaum's ivy-covered 1880s château, and purchased the rights to the Inglenook name. The Inglenook Experience, an escorted tour of the château, vineyards, and caves, ends with a seated tasting of wines paired with artisanal cheeses. Among the topics discussed are the winery's history and the evolution of Coppola's signature wine, Rubicon, a Cabernet Sauvignon–based blend. The Heritage Tasting, which also includes a Rubicon pour, is held in the opulent Pennino Salon. Reservations are required for some tastings and tours, and are recommended for all. **■ TIP→ Walk-ins can sip wines by the glass or bottle at The Bistro, a wine bar with a picturesque courtyard.** ✉ *1991 St. Helena Hwy./Hwy. 29, Rutherford* ✢ *At Hwy. 128* ☎ *707/968–1100* 🌐 *www.inglenook.com* 🎫 *Tastings from $45, private experiences from $75.*

Mumm Napa

WINERY/DISTILLERY | In Mumm's light-filled tasting room or adjacent outdoor patio you can enjoy bubbly by the flight, but the sophisticated sparkling wines, elegant setting, and vineyard views aren't the only reasons to visit. An excellent gallery displays original Ansel Adams prints and presents temporary exhibitions by premier photographers. Winery tours cover the major steps in making sparklers. For a leisurely tasting of several vintages of the top-of-the-line DVX wines, book an Oak Terrace tasting. Reservations are required for this tasting and the tour; they're recommended for tastings inside or on the patio. ✉ *8445 Silverado Trail, Rutherford* ✢ *1 mile south of Rutherford Cross Rd.* ☎ *707/967–7700, 800/783–5826* 🌐 *www.mummnapa.com* 🎫 *Tastings from $25, tour $40 (includes tasting).*

Restaurants

★ Restaurant at Auberge du Soleil

$$$$ | MODERN AMERICAN | Possibly the most romantic roost for dinner in all the Wine Country is a terrace seat at the Auberge du Soleil resort's illustrious restaurant, and the Mediterranean-inflected cuisine more than matches the dramatic vineyard views. The prix-fixe dinner menu, which relies mainly on local produce, might include crispy veal sweetbreads and chanterelles or prime beef pavé with hearts of palm, arugula pesto, and tomato confit. **Known for:** polished service; comprehensive wine list; over-the-top weekend brunch. $ *Average main: $120* ✉ *Auberge du Soleil, 180 Rutherford Hill Rd., Rutherford* ✢ *Off Silverado Trail* ☎ *707/963–1211, 800/348–5406* 🌐 *www.aubergedusoleil.com.*

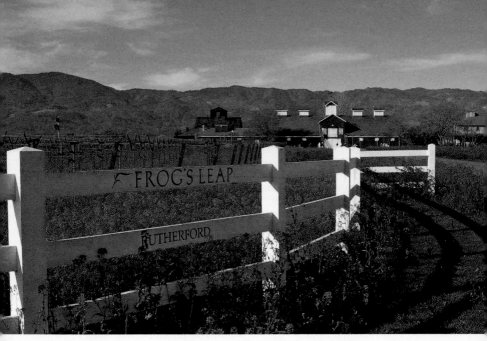

Frog's Leap's picturesque country charm extends all the way to the white picket fence.

★ Rutherford Grill

$$$ | **AMERICAN** | Dark-wood walls, subdued lighting, and red-leather banquettes make for a perpetually clubby mood at this Rutherford hangout whose patio, popular for its bar, fireplace, and rocking chairs, is open for full meal service or drinks and appetizers when the weather's right. Many entrées—steaks, burgers, fish, rotisserie chicken, and barbecued pork ribs—emerge from an oak-fired grill operated by master technicians. **Known for:** signature French dip sandwich and grilled jumbo artichokes; reasonably priced wine list with rarities; patio's bar, fireplace, and rocking chairs. *$ Average main: $30 ✉ 1180 Rutherford Rd., Rutherford ✣ At Hwy. 29 ☎ 707/963–1792 🌐 www.rutherfordgrill.com.*

Hotels

★ Auberge du Soleil

$$$$ | **RESORT** | Taking a cue from the olive-tree-studded landscape, this hotel with a renowned restaurant and spa cultivates a luxurious look that blends French and California style. **Pros:** stunning views over the valley; spectacular pool and spa areas; the most expensive suites are fit for a superstar. **Cons:** stratospheric prices; least expensive rooms get some noise from the bar and restaurant; weekend minimum-stay requirement. *$ Rooms from: $950 ✉ 180 Rutherford Hill Rd., Rutherford ☎ 707/963–1211, 800/348–5406 🌐 www.aubergedusoleil.com 🛏 52 rooms 🍽 Breakfast.*

St. Helena

2 miles northwest of Oakville.

Downtown St. Helena is the very picture of good living in the Wine Country: sycamore trees arch over Main Street (Highway 29), where visitors flit between boutiques, cafés, and storefront tasting rooms housed in sun-faded redbrick buildings. The genteel district pulls in rafts of tourists during the day, though like most Wine Country towns St. Helena more or less rolls up the sidewalks after dark.

The Napa Valley floor narrows between the Mayacamas and Vaca mountains around St. Helena. The slopes reflect heat onto the vineyards below, and since there's less fog and wind, things get pretty toasty. This is one of the valley's hottest AVAs, with midsummer temperatures often reaching the mid-90s. Bordeaux varietals are the most popular grapes grown here—especially Cabernet Sauvignon but also Merlot, Cabernet Franc, and Sauvignon Blanc.

GETTING HERE AND AROUND

Downtown stretches along Highway 29, called Main Street here. Many wineries lie north and south of downtown along Highway 29. More can be found off Silverado Trail, and some of the most scenic spots are on Spring Mountain, which rises southwest of town.

Sights

Beringer Vineyards

WINERY/DISTILLERY | Brothers Frederick and Jacob Beringer opened the winery that still bears their name in 1876. One of California's earliest bonded wineries, it is the oldest one in the Napa Valley never to have missed a vintage—no mean feat, given Prohibition. Frederick's grand Rhine House Mansion, built in 1884, serves as the reserve tasting room. Here, surrounded by Belgian art-nouveau hand-carved oak and walnut furniture and stained-glass windows, you can sample wines that include a limited-release Chardonnay, a few big Cabernets, and a Sauterne-style dessert wine. A less expensive tasting takes place in the original stone winery. Reservations are required for some tastings and recommended for tours. **■ TIP→ The one-hour Taste of Beringer tour of the property and sensory gardens surveys the winery's history and wine making and concludes with a seated wine-and-food pairing.** ✉ *2000 Main St./Hwy. 29, St. Helena* ✣ *Near Pratt Ave.* ☎ *707/963–8989* 🌐 *www.beringer.com* 🎫 *Tastings from $25, tours from $30.*

Charles Krug Winery

WINERY/DISTILLERY | A historically sensitive renovation of its 1874 Redwood Cellar Building transformed the former production facility of the Napa Valley's oldest winery into an epic hospitality center. Charles Krug, a Prussian immigrant, established the winery in 1861 and ran it until his death in 1892. Italian immigrants Cesare Mondavi and his wife, Rosa, purchased Charles Krug in 1943, and operated it with their sons Peter and Robert (who later opened his own winery). The winery, still run by Peter's family, specializes in small-lot Yountville and Howell Mountain Cabernet Sauvignons and makes Chardonnay, Merlot, Pinot Noir, Sauvignon Blanc, Zinfandel, and a Zinfandel port. The tour is by appointment only. ✉ *2800 Main St./Hwy. 29, St. Helena* ✣ *Across from Culinary Institute of America* ☎ *707/967–2229* 🌐 *www.charleskrug.com* 🎫 *Tastings $45, tour $75 (includes tasting).*

Culinary Institute of America at Greystone

COLLEGE | The West Coast headquarters of the country's leading school for chefs is in the 1889 Greystone Cellars, an imposing building once the world's largest stone winery. On the ground floor you can check out the quirky Corkscrew Museum and browse the Spice Islands Marketplace store, stocked with gleaming gadgets and many cookbooks. The Bakery Café by illy serves soups, salads, sandwiches, and baked goods. One-day and multiday cooking and beverage classes often take place. Students run the Gatehouse Restaurant, which serves dinner except during semester breaks. ✉ *2555 Main St./Hwy. 29, St. Helena* ☎ *707/967–1100* 🌐 *www.ciachef.edu/california* 🎫 *Museum free, tour $10; class prices vary.*

Hall St. Helena

WINERY/DISTILLERY | The Cabernet Sauvignons produced here are works of art and the latest in organic-farming science and wine-making technology. A glass-walled tasting room allows guests to see in action some of the high-tech equipment winemaker Steve Leveque employs to craft wines that also include Merlot, Cabernet Franc, and Sauvignon Blanc. Westward from the second-floor tasting area, rows of neatly spaced Cabernet vines capture the eye, and beyond them the tree-studded Mayacamas Mountains. The main guided tour takes in the facility, the grounds, and a restored 19th-century winery, passing artworks by John Baldessari, Jaume Plensa, and other contemporary talents. On Friday and weekends, tastings of limited-production Baca label Zinfandels take place. **■TIP→ Hall Rutherford, an appointment-only sister winery, provides an exclusive, elegant wine-and-food pairing atop a Rutherford hillside.** ✉ *401 St. Helena Hwy./Hwy. 29, St. Helena* ✣ *Near White La.* ☎ *707/967–2626* 🌐 *www.hallwines.com* 🎟 *Tastings from $30, tours from $40.*

★ Joseph Phelps Vineyards

WINERY/DISTILLERY | An appointment is required for tastings at the winery started by the late Joseph Phelps, but it's well worth the effort—all the more so after an inspired renovation of the main redwood structure, a classic of 1970s Northern California architecture. Known for wines crafted with grace and precision, Phelps does produce fine whites, but the blockbusters are red, particularly the Cabernet Sauvignon and the luscious-yet-subtle Bordeaux-style blend called Insignia. In good weather, one-hour seated tastings take place on a terrace overlooking vineyards and oaks. At 90-minute tastings as thoughtfully conceived as the wines, guests explore such topics as wine-and-cheese pairing, wine blending, and the role oak barrels play in wine making. Participants in the blending seminar mix the various varietals that go into the Insignia blend. ✉ *200 Taplin Rd., St. Helena* ✣ *Off Silverado Trail* ☎ *707/963–2745, 800/707–5789* 🌐 *www.josephphelps.com* 🎟 *Tastings and seminars from $75.*

★ Mad Fritz Brewing Co.

WINERY/DISTILLERY | #Beerpassion reigns at this St. Helena tap room where enthusiastic fans and palate-cleansing wine tourists stop to quaff small-lot lagers and ales crafted with a winemaker's sensibility. The goal of founder and master brewer Nile Zacherle, who, when he's not at the brewery, works at a Pritchard Hill winery, isn't merely to make great beers. He and his wife, Whitney Fisher, succeed at that, but they also create what they call "origin specific beers," with each label listing where the couple sourced every ingredient from hops to barley to water. The beers' label art and names, among them The Wind and the Sun and The Donkey and the Thistle, derive from a centuries-old *Aesop's Fables* edition. Along with the label's ingredients list is a summary of the bottling's fable and, in boldface, its moral. ✉ *1282B Vidovich Ave., St. Helena* ✣ *At Hwy. 29* ☎ *707/968–5097* 🌐 *www.madfritz.com* 🎟 *Tastings from $3 per pour.*

Prager Winery & Port Works

WINERY/DISTILLERY | "If door is locked, ring bell," reads a sign outside the weathered-redwood tasting shack at this family-run winery known for red, white, and tawny ports. The sign, the bell, and the thousands of dollar bills tacked to the walls and ceilings inside are your first indications that you're drifting back in time with the old-school Pragers, who have been making regular and fortified wines in St. Helena since the late 1970s. Five members of the second generation, along with two spouses, run this homespun operation founded by Jim and Imogene Prager. In addition to ports the winery makes Petite Sirah and Sweet Claire, a late-harvest Riesling dessert wine. ✉ *1281 Lewelling La., St. Helena* ✣ *Off Hwy. 29* ☎ *707/963–7678* 🌐 *www.pragerport.com* 🎟 *Tastings $30 (includes glass).*

Pride Mountain Vineyards

WINERY/DISTILLERY | This winery 2,200 feet up Spring Mountain straddles Napa and Sonoma counties, confusing enough for visitors but even more complicated for the wine-making staff: government regulations require separate wineries and paperwork for each side of the property. It's one of several amusing Pride Mountain quirks, but winemaker Sally Johnson's "big red wines," including a Cabernet Sauvignon that earned 100-point scores from a major wine critic two years in a row, are serious business. At tastings and on tours you can learn about the farming and cellar strategies behind Pride's acclaimed Cabs (the winery also produces Syrah, a Cab-like Merlot, Viognier, and Chardonnay among others). The tour, which takes in vineyards and caves, also includes tastings of wine still in barrel. ■ **TIP→ The views here are knock-your-socks-off gorgeous.** ✉ *4026 Spring Mountain Rd., St. Helena* ✣ *Off St. Helena Rd. (extension of Spring Mountain Rd. in Sonoma County)* ☎ *707/963–4949* 🌐 *www.pridewines.com* 🎫 *Tastings from $30* 🕒 *Closed Tues.*

The Prisoner Wine Company

WINERY/DISTILLERY | The iconoclastic brand opened an industrial-chic space with interiors by the wildly original Napa-based designer Richard Von Saal to showcase its flagship The Prisoner red blend. "Getting the varietals to play together" is winemaker Chrissy Wittmann's goal with that wine (Zinfandel, Cabernet Sauvignon, Petite Sirah, Syrah, Charbono) and siblings like the Blindfold white (Viognier, Roussanne, Chenin Blanc, Vermentino). Walk-in patrons can sip these and other selections in the Tasting Lounge, more hip hotel bar than traditional tasting room, or outside in the casual open-air The Yard. Southward in The Makery, private appointment-only experiences unfold, some involving boldly flavored plates the winery kitchen turns out. Several alcoves within The Makery contain products for sale inspired by the Wine Country. The Prisoner's tasting space is quite the party, for most of which a reservation is required. ✉ *1178 Galleron Rd., St. Helena* ✣ *At Hwy. 29* ☎ *707/967–3823, 877/283–5934* 🌐 *www.theprisonerwinecompany.com* 🎫 *Tastings from $45.*

Restaurants

Charter Oak

$$$ | **MODERN AMERICAN** | Executive chef Christopher Kostow prepares ornate swoon-worthy haute cuisine at The Restaurant at Meadowood, but he and chef Katianna Hong take a simpler approach (fewer ingredients chosen for maximum effect) at this high-ceilinged, brown-brick downtown restaurant. On a recent menu the strategy translated into dishes like hearth-roasted ham with horseradish, black cod grilled in corn leaves, and cauliflower with raisins and brown butter. **Known for:** exceedingly fresh produce; patio dining in brick courtyard; new chicken-wings appetizer recipe from high-profile restaurant each month. $ *Average main: $29* ✉ *1050 Charter Oak Ave., at Hwy. 29, St. Helena* ☎ *707/302–6996* 🌐 *www.thecharteroak.com* 🕒 *No lunch Mon.–Thurs.*

★ **Cook St. Helena**

$$$ | **ITALIAN** | A curved marble bar spotlit by contemporary art-glass pendants adds a touch of style to this downtown restaurant whose northern Italian cuisine pleases with similarly understated sophistication. Mussels with house-made sausage in a spicy tomato broth, chopped salad with pancetta and pecorino, and the daily changing risotto are among the dishes regulars revere. **Known for:** top-quality ingredients; reasonably priced local and international wines; Cook Tavern two doors down for pizza and small plates. $ *Average main: $23* ✉ *1310 Main St., St. Helena* ✣ *Near Hunt Ave.* ☎ *707/963–7088* 🌐 *www.cooksthelena.com.*

★ Farmstead at Long Meadow Ranch

$$$ | MODERN AMERICAN | Housed in a high-ceilinged former barn, Farmstead revolves around an open kitchen where executive chef Stephen Barber's team prepares meals with grass-fed beef and lamb, fruits and vegetables, and eggs, olive oil, wine, honey, and other ingredients from Long Meadow Ranch. Entrées might include wood-grilled trout with fennel, mushroom, onion and a bacon-mustard vinaigrette; Yukon potato gnocchi with wild mushrooms; or a wood-grilled heritage pork chop with jalapeño grits and chutney. **Known for:** Tuesday fried-chicken night; house-made charcuterie; seasonal cocktails. *Average main: $29* *738 Main St., St. Helena* *At Charter Oak Ave.* *707/963–4555* *www.longmeadowranch.com/eat-drink/restaurant.*

Goose & Gander

$$$ | MODERN AMERICAN | The pairing of food and drink at G&G is as likely to involve cool cocktails as wine. Main courses such as koji-poached sea bass, heritage-pork porterhouse, and dry-aged New York steak with black-lime and pink-peppercorn butter work well with starters that might include blistered shishito peppers and grilled Spanish octopus. **Known for:** intimate main dining room with fireplace; alfresco dining on patio in good weather; basement bar among Napa's best drinking spots. *Average main: $26* *1245 Spring St., St. Helena* *At Oak St.* *707/967–8779* *www.goosegander.com.*

Gott's Roadside

$ | AMERICAN | A 1950s-style outdoor hamburger stand goes upscale at this spot whose customers brave long lines to order breakfast sandwiches, juicy burgers, root-beer floats, and garlic fries. Choices not available a half century ago include the ahi tuna burger and the Vietnamese chicken salad. **Known for:** tasty (if pricey) 21st-century diner cuisine; shaded picnic tables (arrive early or late for lunch to get one); second branch at Napa's Oxbow Public Market. *Average main: $13* *933 Main St./Hwy. 29, St. Helena* *707/963–3486* *www.gotts.com* *Reservations not accepted.*

★ Press

$$$$ | MODERN AMERICAN | Few taste sensations surpass the combination of a sizzling steak and a Napa Valley red, a union the chef and sommeliers at Press celebrate with a reverence bordering on obsession. Grass-fed beef from celebrated California purveyor Bryan Flannery cooked on the cherry-and-almond-wood-fired grill is the star—especially the 38-ounce Porterhouse and the *côte de boeuf* bone-in rib eye, both dry-aged—but the cooks also prepare pork chops, free-range chicken, and fish. **Known for:** extensive wine cellar; impressive cocktails; casual-chic ambience. *Average main: $59* *587 St. Helena Hwy./Hwy. 29, St. Helena* *At White La.* *707/967–0550* *www.pressnapavalley.com* *Closed Tues. No lunch.*

★ The Restaurant at Meadowood

$$$$ | MODERN AMERICAN | Chef Christopher Kostow has garnered rave reviews—and three Michelin stars for several years running—for creating a unique dining experience. Patrons choosing the Tasting Menu option ($285 per person) enjoy their meals in the dining room, its beautiful finishes aglow with warm lighting, but up to four guests can select the Counter Menu ($500 per person) for the chance to sit in the kitchen and watch Kostow's team prepare the food ("the height of our vacation," said four recent guests). **Known for:** complex cuisine; first-class service; romantic setting. *Average main: $275* *900 Meadowood La., St. Helena* *Off Silverado Trail N* *707/967–1205, 800/458–8080* *www.therestaurantatmeadowood.com* *Closed Sun. and Mon. No lunch* *Jacket suggested but not required.*

Hotels

El Bonita Motel

$ | **HOTEL** | A classic 1950s-style neon sign marks the driveway to this well-run roadside motel that—when it isn't sold out—offers great value to budget-minded travelers. **Pros:** cheerful rooms; hot tub; microwaves and mini-refrigerators. **Cons:** road noise a problem in some rooms; noise in ground-floor rooms from second floor; lacks amenities of fancier properties. *Rooms from: $149 195 Main St./Hwy. 29, St. Helena 707/963–3216, 800/541–3284 www.elbonita.com 52 rooms Breakfast.*

Harvest Inn by Charlie Palmer

$$$ | **HOTEL** | Although this inn sits just off Highway 29, its patrons remain mostly above the fray, strolling 8 acres of gardens, enjoying views of the vineyards adjoining the property, partaking in spa services, and drifting to sleep in beds adorned with fancy linens and down pillows. **Pros:** garden setting; spacious rooms; near choice wineries, dining spots, and shops. **Cons:** some lower-price rooms lack elegance; high weekend rates; occasional service lapses. *Rooms from: $354 1 Main St., St. Helena 707/963–9463, 800/950–8466 www.harvestinn.com 78 rooms Breakfast.*

Ink House

$$$$ | **B&B/INN** | The goal of the Castellucci family, which lavishly refurbished an 1885 Italianate along Highway 29, is to provide "a curated luxury experience" in impeccably styled rooms with 11-foot ceilings and vineyard views out tall windows. **Pros:** panoramic views from the cupola; attention to detail; Elvis Presley slept here (but it wasn't this stylish). **Cons:** extremely pricey; lacks on-site pool, fitness center, spa; two bathrooms have showers only (albeit nice ones). *Rooms from: $500 1575 St. Helena Hwy., St. Helena 707/968–9686 www.inkhousenapavalley.com/inn 4 rooms Free Breakfast.*

Inn St. Helena

$$ | **B&B/INN** | A large room at this spiffed-up downtown St. Helena inn is named for author Ambrose Bierce *(The Devil's Dictionary)*, who lived in the main Victorian structure in the early 1900s, but sensitive hospitality and modern amenities are what make a stay worth writing home about. **Pros:** filling breakfast; outdoor porch and swing; convenient to shops, tasting rooms, restaurants. **Cons:** no pool, gym, room service, or other hotel amenities; two-night minimum on weekends (three with Monday holiday); per website "children 16 and older are welcome". *Rooms from: $279 1515 Main St., St. Helena 707/963–3003 www.innsthelena.com 8 rooms Breakfast.*

Las Alcobas Napa Valley

$$$$ | **HOTEL** | Upscale-casual luxury is the goal of this hillside beauty—part of the Starwood chain's Luxury Collection—next to Beringer Vineyards and six blocks north of Main Street shopping and dining. **Pros:** pool, spa, and fitness center; vineyard views from most rooms; chef Chris Cosentino's Acacia House restaurant. **Cons:** pricey; per website no children under age 17 permitted; no self-parking. *Rooms from: $638 1915 Main St., St. Helena 707/963–7000 www.lasalcobasnapavalley.com 68 rooms Breakfast.*

★ Meadowood Napa Valley

$$$$ | **RESORT** | Founded in 1964 as a country club, Meadowood evolved into an elite resort, a gathering place for Napa's wine-making community, and a celebrated dining destination. **Pros:** superb restaurant; all-organic spa; gracious service. **Cons:** very expensive; far from downtown St. Helena; weekend minimum-stay requirement. *Rooms from: $650 900 Meadowood La., St. Helena 707/963–3646, 800/458–8080 www.meadowood.com 85 rooms No meals.*

Wine Country Inn

$$$ | **B&B/INN** | Vineyards flank the three buildings, containing 24 rooms, and five cottages of this pastoral retreat, where blue oaks, maytens, and olive trees provide shade, and gardens feature lantana (small butterflies love it) and lavender. **Pros:** staff excels at anticipating guests' needs; good-size swimming pool; vineyard views from most rooms. **Cons:** some rooms let in noise from neighbors; expensive in high season; weekend minimum-stay requirement. *Rooms from: $349* ✉ *1152 Lodi La., St. Helena* ✥ *East of Hwy. 29* ☎ *707/963–7077, 888/465–4608* 🌐 *www.winecountryinn.com* *29 rooms* *Breakfast.*

Nightlife

The Saint

WINE BARS—NIGHTLIFE | This high-ceilinged downtown wine bar benefits from the grandeur and gravitas of its setting inside a stone-walled late-19th-century former bank. Lit by chandeliers and decked out in contemporary style with plush sofas and chairs and Lucite stools at the bar, it's a classy, loungelike space to expand your enological horizons comparing the many small-lot Napa Valley wines on offer with their counterparts in France and beyond. There's live or DJ music some nights. ✉ *1351 Main St., St. Helena* ✥ *Near Adams St.* ☎ *707/302–5130* 🌐 *www.thesaintnapavalley.com.*

Calistoga

3 miles northwest of St. Helena.

With false-fronted, Old West–style shops and 19th-century inns and hotels lining its main drag, Lincoln Avenue, Calistoga comes across as more down-to-earth than its more polished neighbors. Don't be fooled, though. On its outskirts lie some of the Wine Country's swankest (and priciest) resorts and its most fanciful piece of architecture, the medieval-style Castello di Amorosa winery.

Calistoga was developed as a spa-oriented getaway from the start. Sam Brannan, a gold rush–era entrepreneur, planned to use the area's natural hot springs as the centerpiece of a resort complex. His venture failed, but old-time hotels and bathhouses—along with some glorious new spas—still operate. You can come for an old-school mud bath, or go completely 21st century and experience lavish treatments based on the latest innovations in skin and body care.

GETTING HERE AND AROUND

Highway 29 heads east (turn right) at Calistoga, where in town it is signed as Lincoln Avenue. If arriving via the Silverado Trail, head west at Highway 29/Lincoln Avenue.

Sights

Ca' Toga Galleria d'Arte

MUSEUM | The boundless wit, whimsy, and creativity of the Venetian-born Carlo Marchiori, this gallery's owner-artist, finds expression in paintings, watercolors, ceramics, sculptures, and other artworks. Marchiori often draws on mythology and folktales for his inspiration. A stop at this magical gallery might inspire you to tour Villa Ca' Toga, the artist's fanciful Palladian home, a tromp-l'oeil tour de force open for tours from May through October on Saturday morning only, by appointment. ✉ *1206 Cedar St., Calistoga* ✥ *Near Lincoln Ave.* ☎ *707/942–3900* 🌐 *www.catoga.com* ⏲ *Closed Tues. and Wed.*

Castello di Amorosa

WINERY/DISTILLERY | An astounding medieval structure complete with drawbridge and moat, chapel, stables, and secret passageways, the Castello commands Diamond Mountain's lower eastern slope. Some of the 107 rooms contain artist Fabio Sanzogni's replicas of 13th-century frescoes (cheekily signed with his website address), and the dungeon has an iron maiden from Nuremberg, Germany. You must pay for a tour to see most of Dario Sattui's extensive eight-level property, though with a basic tasting you'll have access to part of the complex. Bottlings of note include several Italian-style wines, including La Castellana, a robust "super Tuscan" blend of Cabernet Sauvignon, Sangiovese, and Merlot; and Il Barone, a deliberately big Cab primarily of Rutherford grapes. **■ TIP→ The 2½-hour Royal Food & Wine Pairing Tour by sommelier Mary Davidek (by appointment only) is among the Wine Country's best.** ✉ *4045 N. St. Helena Hwy./Hwy. 29, Calistoga* ✣ *Near Maple La.* ☎ *707/967–6272* 🌐 *www.castellodiamorosa.com* 🎫 *Tastings from $30, tours from $40 (include tastings).*

Chateau Montelena

WINERY/DISTILLERY | Set amid a bucolic northern Calistoga landscape, this winery helped establish the Napa Valley's reputation for high-quality wine making. At the pivotal Paris tasting of 1976, the Chateau Montelena 1973 Chardonnay took first place, beating out four white Burgundies from France and five other California Chardonnays, an event immortalized in the 2008 movie *Bottle Shock.* A 21st-century Napa Valley Chardonnay is always part of a Current Release Tasting—the winery also makes Sauvignon Blanc, Riesling, a fine estate Zinfandel, and Cabernet Sauvignon—or you can opt for a Limited Release Tasting focusing more on Cabernets. The walking Estate Tour takes in the grounds and covers the history of this stately property whose stone winery building was erected in 1888. Guests board a vehicle for the seasonal Vineyard Tour. Tours and some tastings require a reservation. ✉ *1429 Tubbs La., Calistoga* ✣ *Off Hwy. 29* ☎ *707/942–5105* 🌐 *www.montelena.com* 🎫 *Tastings from $30, tours from $50.*

Frank Family Vineyards

WINERY/DISTILLERY | As a former Disney film and television executive, Rich Frank knows a thing or two about entertainment, and it shows in the chipper atmosphere that prevails in the winery's bright-yellow Craftsman-style tasting room. The site's wine-making history dates from the 19th century, and portions of an original 1884 structure, reclad in stone in 1906, remain standing today. From 1952 until 1990, Hanns Kornell made sparkling wines on this site. Frank Family makes sparklers itself, but the high-profile wines are the Cabernet Sauvignons, particularly the Rutherford Reserve and the Winston Hill red blend. Tastings are mostly sit-down affairs, indoors, on the popular back veranda, or at picnic tables under 100-year-old elms. Reservations are required from Friday through Sunday; they're wise on other days, too. ✉ *1091 Larkmead La., Calistoga* ✣ *Off Hwy. 29* ☎ *707/942–0859* 🌐 *www.frankfamilyvineyards.com* 🎫 *Tastings from $40.*

Tamber Bey Vineyards

WINERY/DISTILLERY | Endurance riders Barry and Jennifer Waitte share their passion for horses and wine at their glam-rustic winery north of Calistoga. Their 22-acre Sundance Ranch remains a working equestrian facility, but the site has been revamped to include a state-of-the-art winery with separate fermenting tanks for grapes from Tamber Bey's vineyards in Yountville, Oakville, and elsewhere. The winemakers produce three Chardonnays and a Sauvignon Blanc, but the stars are several subtly powerful reds, including the flagship Oakville Cabernet Sauvignon and a Yountville Merlot. The top-selling wine, Rabicano, is a Cabernet Sauvignon-heavy blend that in a recent vintage contained the four other main Bordeaux red grapes: Malbec, Merlot, Petit Verdot, and Cabernet Franc. Visits here require an appointment. ✉ *1251 Tubbs La., Calistoga* ✣ *At Myrtledale Rd.*

All it needs is a fair maiden: Castello di Amorosa's re-created castle.

☎ *707/942–2100* 🌐 *www.tamberbey.com* 🎫 *Tastings from $45.*

★ Venge Vineyards

WINERY/DISTILLERY | As the son of Nils Venge, the first winemaker to earn a 100-point score from the wine critic Robert Parker, Kirk Venge had a hard act to follow. Now a consultant to exclusive wineries himself, Kirk is an acknowledged master of balanced, fruit-forward Bordeaux-style blends. At his casual ranch-house tasting room you can sip wines that might include the estate Bone Ash Cabernet Sauvignon, an Oakville Merlot, and the Silencieux Cabernet, a blend of grapes from several appellations. With its views of the well-manicured Bone Ash Vineyard and, west across the valley, Diamond Mountain, the ranch house's porch would make for a magical perch even if Venge's wines weren't works of art in themselves. Tastings are by appointment only. ✉ *4708 Silverado Trail, Calistoga* ✣ *1½ miles south of downtown, near Dunaweal La.* ☎ *707/942–9100* 🌐 *www.vengevineyards.com* 🎫 *Tastings $45* 🕐 *Reservations recommended 3–4 wks in advance for weekend visits.*

Restaurants

★ Evangeline

$$$ | **MODERN AMERICAN** | The gas-lamp-style lighting fixtures, charcoal-black hues, and bistro cuisine at Evangeline evoke old New Orleans with a California twist. Executive chef Gustavo Rios, whose previous stops include Calistoga's Solbar and Yountville's Bouchon Bistro, puts a jaunty spin on dishes that might include shrimp étouffée, duck confit, or steak frites; the elaborate weekend brunch, with everything from avocado toast to buttermilk biscuits and sausage gravy, is an upvalley favorite. **Known for:** outdoor courtyard; palate-cleansing Sazeracs; addictive fried pickles. 💲 *Average main: $27* ✉ *1226 Washington St., Calistoga* ✣ *Near Lincoln Ave.* ☎ *707/341–3131* 🌐 *www.evangelinenapa.com* 🕐 *No lunch weekdays.*

Sam's Social Club

$$$ | **MODERN AMERICAN** | Tourists, locals, and spa guests—some of the latter in bathrobes after treatments—assemble at this resort restaurant for breakfast, lunch, bar snacks, or dinner. Lunch options include pizzas, sandwiches, an aged-cheddar burger, and entrées such as chicken paillard, with the burger reappearing for dinner along with pan-seared Alaskan halibut, rib-eye steak frites, and similar fare, perhaps preceded by oysters and other cocktail-friendly starters. **Known for:** casual atmosphere; active patio scene; thin-crust lunch pizzas. *Average main: $28 Indian Springs Resort and Spa, 1712 Lincoln Ave., Calistoga At Wappo Ave. 707/942–4969 www.samssocialclub.com.*

★ Solbar

$$$$ | **MODERN AMERICAN** | As befits a restaurant at a spa resort, the sophisticated menu at Solbar is divided into "healthy, lighter dishes" and "hearty cuisine," with the stellar wine list's many half-bottle selections encouraging moderation, too. On the lighter side, seared black cod served with bok choy, ginger endive, and carrots, with heartier options recently including hibachi-grilled Wagyu rib eye with new potatoes. **Known for:** stylish dining room; festive outdoor patio; Sunday brunch. *Average main: $35 Solage Calistoga, 755 Silverado Trail, Calistoga At Rosedale Rd. 866/942–7442 solage.aubergeresorts.com/dine.*

Hotels

Calistoga Ranch

$$$$ | **RESORT** | Spacious cedar-shingle lodges throughout this posh wooded Auberge Resorts property have outdoor living areas—even the restaurant, spa, and reception space have outdoor seating and fireplaces. **Pros:** many lodges have private hot tubs on the deck; hiking trails on property; guests have reciprocal facility privileges at Auberge du Soleil and Solage Calistoga. **Cons:** indoor-outdoor concept works better in fine weather than in rain or cold; no self-parking; expensive. *Rooms from: $895 580 Lommel Rd., Calistoga 707/254–2800, 855/942–4220 www.calistogaranch.com 52 lodges No meals.*

★ Embrace Calistoga

$$$ | **B&B/INN** | Extravagant hospitality defines the Napa Valley's luxury properties, but Embrace Calistoga takes the prize in the "small lodging" category. **Pros:** attentive owners; marvelous breakfasts; restaurants, tasting rooms, and shopping within walking distance. **Cons:** light hum of street traffic; no pool or spa; two-night minimum some weekends. *Rooms from: $309 1139 Lincoln Ave., Calistoga 707/942–9797 embracecalistoga.com 5 rooms Breakfast.*

Indian Springs Resort and Spa

$$ | **RESORT** | Palm-studded Indian Springs—operating as a spa since 1862—ably splits the difference between laid-back and chic in accommodations that include lodge rooms, suites, 14 historic cottages, three stand-alone bungalows, and two houses. **Pros:** palm-studded grounds with outdoor seating areas; on-site Sam's Social Club restaurant; enormous mineral pool. **Cons:** lodge rooms are small; many rooms have showers but no tubs; two-night minimum on weekends (three with Monday holiday). *Rooms from: $279 1712 Lincoln Ave., Calistoga 707/942–4913 www.indianspringscalistoga.com 113 rooms No meals.*

★ Solage Calistoga

$$$$ | **RESORT** | The aesthetic at this 22-acre property, where health and wellness are priorities, is Napa Valley barn meets San Francisco loft: guest rooms have high ceilings, polished concrete floors, recycled walnut furniture, and all-natural fabrics in soothingly muted colors. **Pros:** great service; complimentary bikes; separate pools for kids and adults. **Cons:** vibe might not suit

everyone; longish walk from some lodgings to spa and fitness center; expensive in-season. *Rooms from: $481* ✉ *755 Silverado Trail, Calistoga* ☎ *866/942–7442, 707/226–0800* 🌐 *www.solagecalistoga.com* *89 rooms* *No meals.*

Shopping

Calistoga Pottery

CERAMICS/GLASSWARE | You might recognize the dinnerware and other pottery sold by owners Jeff and Sally Manfredi—their biggest customers are the area's inns, restaurants, and wineries. ✉ *1001 Foothill Blvd./Hwy. 29, Calistoga* ✣ *500 feet south of Lincoln Ave.* ☎ *707/942–0216* 🌐 *www.calistogapottery.com* ⏲ *Closed Sun.*

SPAS

Indian Springs Spa

SPA/BEAUTY | Even before Sam Brannan constructed a spa on this site in the 1860s, the Wappo Indians were building sweat lodges over its thermal geysers. Treatments include a Calistoga-classic, pure volcanic-ash mud bath followed by a mineral bath, after which clients are wrapped in a flannel blanket for a 15-minute cool-down session or until called for a massage if they've booked one. Intraceuticals oxygen-infusion facials are another specialty. Spa clients have access to the Olympic-size mineral-water pool, kept at 92°F in summer and a toasty 102°F in winter. ✉ *1712 Lincoln Ave., Calistoga* ✣ *At Wappo Ave.* ☎ *707/942–4913* 🌐 *www.indianspringscalistoga.com/spa* *Treatments from $95.*

★ Spa Solage

This eco-conscious spa reinvented the traditional Calistoga mud-and-mineral-water regimen with the hour-long "Mudslide." The three-part treatment includes a mud body mask self-applied in a heated lounge, a soak in a thermal bath, and a power nap in a sound-vibration chair. The mud here, less gloppy than at other resorts, is a mix of clay, volcanic ash, and essential oils. Traditional spa services—combination Shiatsu-Swedish and other massages, full-body exfoliations, facials, and waxes—are available, as are yoga and wellness sessions. ✉ *755 Silverado Trail, Calistoga* ✣ *At Rosedale Rd.* ☎ *707/226–0825* 🌐 *solage.aubergeresorts.com/spa* *Treatments from $110.*

Activities

Calistoga Bikeshop

BICYCLING | Options here include regular and fancy bikes that rent for $28 and up for two hours, and there's a self-guided Cool Wine Tour ($110) that includes tastings at three or four small wineries. ✉ *1318 Lincoln Ave., Calistoga* ✣ *Near Washington St.* ☎ *707/942–9687* 🌐 *www.calistogabikeshop.net.*

Sonoma

14 miles west of Napa, 45 miles northeast of San Francisco.

One of the few towns in the valley with multiple attractions not related to food and wine, Sonoma has plenty to keep you busy for a couple of hours before you head out to tour the wineries. And you needn't leave town to taste wine. There are about three dozen tasting rooms within steps of the tree-filled Sonoma plaza, some of which pour wines from more than one winery. The valley's cultural center, Sonoma was founded in 1835 when California was still part of Mexico.

GETTING HERE AND AROUND

Highway 12 (signed as Broadway near Sonoma Plaza) heads north into Sonoma from Highway 121 and south from Santa Rosa into downtown Sonoma, where (signed as West Spain Street) it travels east to the plaza. Parking is relatively easy to find on or near the plaza, and you can walk to many restaurants, shops, and tasting rooms. Signs point the way to several wineries a mile or more east of the plaza.

Sights

Bedrock Wine Co.

WINERY/DISTILLERY | Wines, notably Zinfandel, celebrating Sonoma County's heritage vineyards are the focus of Bedrock, whose backstory involves several historical figures. Tastings take place in a home just east of Sonoma Plaza owned in the 1850s by General Joseph Hooker. By coincidence, Hooker planted grapes at what's now the estate Bedrock Vineyard a few miles away. General William Tecumseh Sherman was his partner in the vineyard (a spat over it affected their Civil War interactions), which newspaper magnate William Randolph Hearst's father, George, replanted in the late 1880s. Some Hearst vines still produce grapes. Current owner-winemaker Morgan Twain-Peterson learned about Zinfandel from his dad, Joel Peterson, who started Ravenswood Winery. **TIP→ The shaded patio out back faces the circa-1840 Blue Wing Inn, where Hooker often partied.** ✉ *General Joseph Hooker House, 414 1st St. E, Sonoma* ☎ *707/343–1478* 🌐 *www.bedrockwineco.com* *Tastings $30* ⏲ *Closed Tues.*

Buena Vista Winery

WINERY/DISTILLERY | The birthplace of modern California wine making has been transformed into an entertaining homage to the accomplishments of the 19th-century wine pioneer Count Agoston Haraszthy. Tours pass through the original aging caves dug deep into the hillside by Chinese laborers, and banners, photos, and artifacts inside and out convey the history made on this site. The rehabilitated former press house (used for pressing grapes into wine), which dates to 1862, hosts the standard tastings. Chardonnay, Pinot Noir, several red blends, and a vibrant Petit Verdot are the strong suits here. **TIP→ The high-tech Historic Wine Tool Museum displays implements, some decidedly low-tech, used to make wine over the years.** ✉ *18000 Old Winery Rd., Sonoma* ✢ *Off E. Napa St.* ☎ *800/926–1266* 🌐 *www.buenavistawinery.com* *Tastings from $20; tours from $25.*

★ The Donum Estate

WINERY/DISTILLERY | Anne Moller-Racke, the founder of this prominent Chardonnay and Pinot Noir producer, calls herself a winegrower in the French *vigneron* tradition that emphasizes agriculture—selecting vineyards with the right soils, microclimates, and varietals, then farming with precision—over wine-making wizardry. The Donum Estate, whose white board-and-batten tasting room affords guests hilltop views of Los Carneros, San Pablo Bay, and beyond, farms two vineyards surrounding the structure, along with one in the Russian River Valley and another in Mendocino County's Anderson Valley. All the wines exhibit the "power yet elegance" that sealed the winery's fame in the 2000s. Tastings are by appointment only. **TIP→ Large museum-quality outdoor sculptures by Anselm Kiefer, Lynda Benglis, Ai Weiwei, and three dozen other contemporary talents add a touch of high culture to a visit here.** ✉ *24500 Ramal Rd., Sonoma* ✢ *Off Hwy. 121/12* ☎ *707/732–2200* 🌐 *www.thedonumestate.com* *Tastings $80.*

Gloria Ferrer Caves and Vineyards

WINERY/DISTILLERY | A tasting at Gloria Ferrer is an exercise in elegance: at tables inside the Spanish hacienda–style winery or outside on the terrace (no standing at the bar at Gloria Ferrer), you can take in vistas of gently rolling Carneros hills while sipping sparkling and still wines. The Chardonnay and Pinot Noir grapes from the surrounding vineyards are the product of old-world wine-making knowledge—the same family started the sparkling-wine maker Freixenet in 16th-century Spain—and contemporary soil management techniques and clonal research. The daily tour covers *méthode traditionelle* wine making, the Ferrer family's history, and the winery's vineyard sustainability practices. ✉ *23555 Carneros Hwy./Hwy. 121, Sonoma*

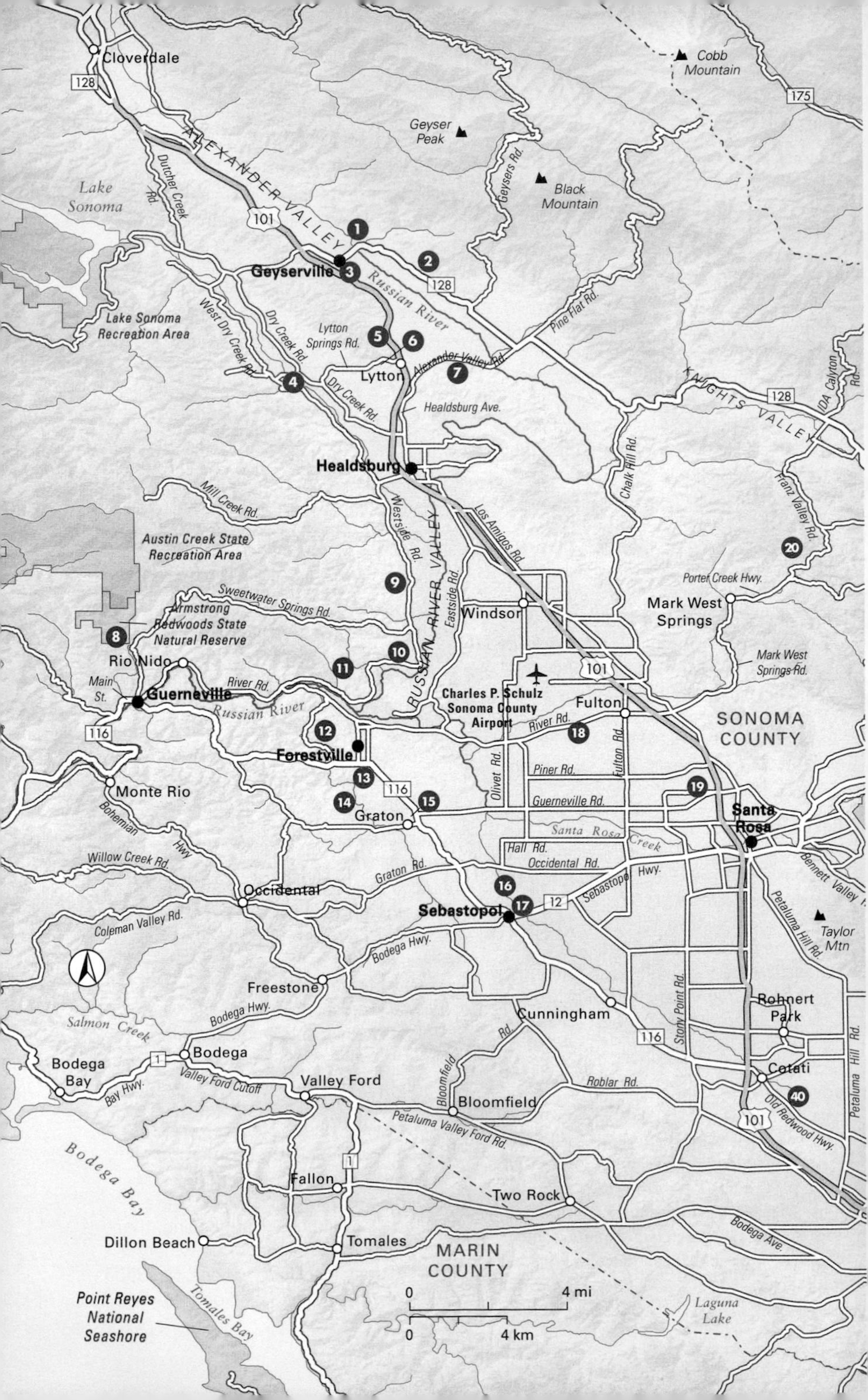

Cloverdale
Cobb Mountain
Geyser Peak
Black Mountain
Lake Sonoma
ALEXANDER VALLEY
Geyserville
Russian River
Lake Sonoma Recreation Area
Lytton
Healdsburg
KNIGHTS VALLEY
Austin Creek State Recreation Area
Armstrong Redwoods State Natural Reserve
RUSSIAN RIVER VALLEY
Windsor
Mark West Springs
Rio Nido
Guerneville
Charles P. Schulz Sonoma County Airport
Fulton
SONOMA COUNTY
Forestville
Monte Rio
Graton
Santa Rosa
Santa Rosa Creek
Occidental
Sebastopol
Taylor Mtn
Freestone
Cunningham
Rohnert Park
Salmon Creek
Bodega
Bodega Bay
Valley Ford
Cotati
Bloomfield
Fallon
Two Rock
Dillon Beach
Tomales
MARIN COUNTY
Point Reyes National Seashore
Tomales Bay
Laguna Lake
0 4 mi
0 4 km

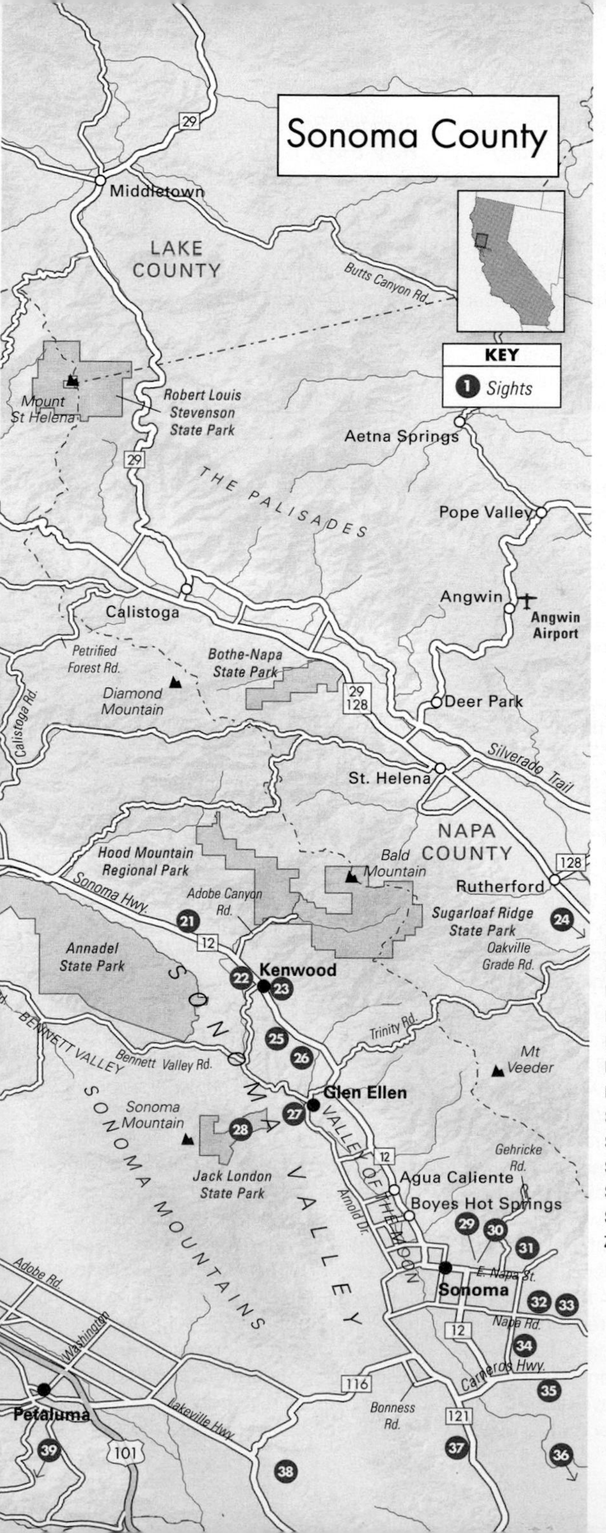

Sights

- Arista Winery 10
- Armstrong Redwoods State Natural Reserve 8
- B Wise Vineyards Tasting Lounge 22
- Balletto Vineyards 16
- The Barlow 17
- Bedrock Wine Co 30
- Benziger Family Winery 27
- Buena Vista Winery 31
- Charles M. Schulz Museum 19
- The Donum Estate 36
- Dry Creek Vineyard 4
- Dutton-Goldfield Winery 15
- Francis Ford Coppola Winery 5
- Gary Farrell Vineyards & Winery 11
- Gloria Ferrer Caves and Vineyard 37
- Gundlach Bundschu 32
- Hanson of Sonoma Organic Vodka 35
- Hartford Family Winery 12
- Iron Horse Vineyards 14
- Jack London State Historic Park 28
- Jordan Vineyard and Winery 7
- Joseph Jewell Wines 13
- Keller Estate 38
- Kunde Estate Winery & Vineyards 23
- Lagunitas Brewing Company 40
- Lasseter Family Winery 26
- Locals Tasting Room 3
- Loxton Cellars 25
- MacRostie Estate House 9
- Martinelli Winery 18
- McEvoy Ranch 39
- Patz & Hall 34
- Ridge Vineyards 6
- Robert Young Estate Winery 2
- Safari West 20
- St. Francis Winery 21
- Scribe 33
- Silver Oak 24
- Sonoma Mission 29
- Zialena 1

☎ 707/933–1917 🌐 *www.gloriaferrer.com* 🎫 *Tastings from $9, tour with tasting $25.*

Gundlach Bundschu

WINERY/DISTILLERY | The Bundschu family, which has owned most of this property since 1858, makes reds that include Cabernet Franc, Cabernet Sauvignon, Merlot, and a Bordeaux-style blend of each vintage's best grapes. Gewürztraminer, Chardonnay, and two rosés are also in the mix. Parts of the 1870 stone winery where standard tastings unfold are still used for wine making. For a more comprehensive experience, book a cave tour, a Pinzgauer vehicle vineyard tour, or a Heritage Reserve pairing of limited-release wines with small gourmet bites. Some tastings and all tours are by appointment only. "Gun lock bun shoe" gets you close to pronouncing this winery's name correctly, though everyone here shortens it to Gun Bun. ✉ *2000 Denmark St., Sonoma* ✣ *At Bundschu Rd., off 8th St. E, 3 miles southeast of Sonoma Plaza* ☎ *707/938–5277* 🌐 *www.gunbun.com* 🎫 *Tastings from $20, tours $45 (includes tastings).*

Hanson of Sonoma Organic Vodka

WINERY/DISTILLERY | The Hanson family makes grape-based organic vodkas, one of them straightforward and four others infused with cucumbers, ginger, mandarin oranges, and habanero and other chili peppers. To produce these vodkas and a few seasonal offerings, white wine is made from three grape types and then distilled. The family pours its vodkas, which have racked up some impressive awards, in an industrial-looking tasting room heavy on the steel, with wood reclaimed from Deep South smokehouses adding a rustic note. Because you're in a tasting room rather than a bar, there's a limit to the amount poured, but it's sufficient to get to know the product. Book distillery tours through Hanson's website. **■ TIP→ A popular tasting involves three vodka sips and a well-mixed cocktail.** ✉ *22985 Burndale Rd., Sonoma* ✣ *Off Carneros Hwy. (Hwy. 121)* ☎ *707/343–1805* 🌐 *hansonofsonoma.com* 🎫 *Tastings from $15, tours from $25 (includes tasting).*

★ Patz & Hall

WINERY/DISTILLERY | Sophisticated single-vineyard Chardonnays and Pinot Noirs are the trademark of this respected winery whose tastings take place in a fashionable single-story residence 3 miles southeast of Sonoma Plaza. It's a Wine Country adage that great wines are made in the vineyard—the all-star fields represented here include Hyde, Durell, and Gap's Crown—but winemaker James Hall routinely surpasses peers with access to the same fruit, proof that discernment and expertise (Hall is a master at oak aging) play a role, too. You can sample wines at the bar and on some days on the vineyard-view terrace beyond it, but to learn how food-friendly these wines are, consider the Salon Tasting, at which they're paired with gourmet bites. Tastings are by appointment only. ✉ *21200 8th St. E, Sonoma* ✣ *Near Peru Rd.* ☎ *707/265–7700* 🌐 *www.patzhall.com* 🎫 *Tastings from $35.*

★ Scribe

WINERY/DISTILLERY | Andrew and Adam Mariani established Scribe in 2007 on land first planted to grapes in 1858 by Emil Dresel, a German immigrant. Dresel's claims to fame include cultivating Sonoma's first Riesling and Sylvaner, an achievement the brothers honor by growing both varietals on land he once farmed. Using natural wine-making techniques, they craft bright, terroir-driven wines from those grapes, along with Chardonnay, Pinot Noir, Syrah, and Cabernet Sauvignon. In restoring their property's 1915 Mission Revival–style hacienda, the brothers preserved various layers of history—original molding and light fixtures, for instance, but also fragments of floral-print wallpaper and 1950s newspapers. Now a tasting space, the hacienda served during

Prohibition as a bootleggers' hideout, and its basement harbored a speakeasy. Tastings, which include meze plates whose ingredients come from Scribe's farm, are by appointment only. ✉ *2100 Denmark St., Sonoma* ✣ *Off Napa Rd.* ☎ *707/939–1858* 🌐 *scribewinery.com* 🎫 *Tastings from $60.*

Sonoma Mission

RELIGIOUS SITE | The northernmost of the 21 missions established by Franciscan friars in California, Sonoma Mission was founded in 1823 as Mission San Francisco Solano. These days it serves as the centerpiece of **Sonoma State Historic Park,** which includes several other sites in Sonoma and nearby Petaluma. Some early mission structures were destroyed, but all or part of several remaining buildings date to the era of Mexican rule over California. Worth a look are the **Sonoma Barracks,** a half block west of the mission at 20 East Spain Street, which housed troops under the command of General Mariano Guadalupe Vallejo, who controlled vast tracts of land in the region. **General Vallejo's Home,** a Victorian-era structure, is a few blocks west. ✉ *114 E. Spain St., Sonoma* ✣ *At 1st St. E* ☎ *707/938–9560* 🌐 *www.parks.ca.gov* 🎫 *$3, includes same-day admission to other historic sites.*

Restaurants

★ Cafe La Haye

$$$ | **AMERICAN** | In a postage-stamp-size open kitchen (the dining room, its white walls adorned with contemporary art, is nearly as compact), chef Jeffrey Lloyd turns out understated, sophisticated fare emphasizing seasonably available local ingredients. Chicken, beef, pasta, and fish get deluxe treatment without fuss or fanfare—the daily risotto special is always good. **Known for:** Napa-Sonoma wine list with French complements; signature butterscotch pudding dessert; owner Saul Gropman on hand to greet diners. 💲 *Average main: $24* ✉ *140 E. Napa St., Sonoma* ✣ *Just off Sonoma Plaza* ☎ *707/935–5994* 🌐 *www.cafelahaye.com* 🕑 *Closed Sun. and Mon. No lunch.*

El Dorado Kitchen

$$$ | **MODERN AMERICAN** | This restaurant owes its visual appeal to its clean lines and handsome decor, but the eye inevitably drifts westward to the open kitchen, where the chefs craft dishes full of subtle surprises. The menu might include ahi tuna tartare with wasabi tobiko caviar as a starter, with paella awash with seafood and dry-cured Spanish chorizo sausage among the entrées. **Known for:** subtle tastes and textures; truffle-oil fries with Parmesan; pot de crème and other desserts. 💲 *Average main: $27* ✉ *El Dorado Hotel, 405 1st St. W, Sonoma* ✣ *At W. Spain St.* ☎ *707/996–3030* 🌐 *eldoradokitchen.com.*

★ Girl & the Fig

$$$ | **FRENCH** | At this hot spot for inventive French cooking inside the historic Sonoma Hotel bar, you can always find a dish with owner Sondra Bernstein's signature figs on the menu, whether it's a fig-and-arugula salad or an aperitif blending sparkling wine with fig liqueur. Also look for duck confit, a burger with matchstick fries, and wild flounder meunière. **Known for:** Rhône-wines emphasis; artisanal cheese platters; croque monsieur and eggs Benedict at Sunday brunch. 💲 *Average main: $28* ✉ *Sonoma Hotel, 110 W. Spain St., Sonoma* ✣ *At 1st St. W* ☎ *707/938–3634* 🌐 *www.thegirlandthefig.com.*

★ Harvest Moon Cafe

$$$ | **AMERICAN** | Everything at this little restaurant with an odd, zigzagging layout is so perfectly executed and the vibe is so genuinely warm that a visit here is deeply satisfying. The ever-changing menu might include homey dishes such as hand-cut tagliatelle with sautéed mushrooms or panfried swordfish with herbed quinoa pilaf. **Known for:** friendly service; patio dining area;

husband-and-wife chefs Nick and Jen Demarest. *Average main: $28* *487 1st St. W, Sonoma* *At W. Napa St.* *707/933–8160* *www.harvestmoon-cafesonoma.com* *Closed Tues. No lunch.*

Oso Sonoma

$$$ | **MODERN AMERICAN** | Chef David Bush, who achieved national recognition for his food pairings at St. Francis Winery, owns this barlike small-plates restaurant whose menu evolves throughout the day. Lunch might see mole-braised pork-shoulder tacos or an achiote chicken sandwich, with dinner fare perhaps of steamed mussels, miso-glazed salmon, or poutine, all of it served in an 1890s structure, erected as a livery stable, that incorporates materials reclaimed from the building's prior incarnations. **Known for:** bar menu between lunch and dinner; smart beer and wine selections; Sonoma Plaza location. *Average main: $29* *9 E. Napa St., Sonoma* *At Broadway* *707/931–6926* *www.ososonoma.com* *No lunch Mon.–Wed.*

Sunflower Caffé

$ | **AMERICAN** | Whimsical art and brightly painted walls set a jolly tone at this casual eatery whose assets include sidewalk seating with Sonoma Plaza views and the verdant patio out back. Omelets and waffles are the hits at breakfast, with the smoked duck *banh mi,* served on a toasted baguette with Sriracha aioli, a favorite for lunch. **Known for:** combination café, gallery, and wine bar; local cheeses and hearty soups; free Wi-Fi. *Average main: $14* *421 1st St. W, Sonoma* *At W. Spain St.* *707/996–6645* *www.sonomasunflower.com* *No dinner.*

Hotels

Inn at Sonoma

$$ | **B&B/INN** | Little luxuries delight at this well-run inn ¼-mile south of Sonoma Plaza: wine and hors d'oeuvres are served every evening in the lobby, where a jar brims with cookies from noon to 8 pm and free beverages are always available. **Pros:** last-minute specials are a great deal; comfortable beds; good soundproofing blocks out Broadway street noise. **Cons:** on a busy street rather than right on the plaza; pet-friendly rooms book up quickly; some rooms on the small side. *Rooms from: $249* *630 Broadway, Sonoma* *707/939–1340* *www.innatsonoma.com* *27 rooms* *Breakfast.*

★ Ledson Hotel

$$$ | **B&B/INN** | With just six rooms the Ledson feels intimate, and the furnishings and amenities—down beds, mood lighting, gas fireplaces, whirlpool tubs, and balconies for enjoying breakfast or a glass of wine—stack up well against Wine Country rooms costing more, especially in high season. **Pros:** convenient Sonoma Plaza location; spacious, individually decorated rooms with whirlpool tubs; complimentary tasting at ground-floor Zina Lounge wine bar. **Cons:** maximum occupancy in all rooms is two people; children must be at least 12 years old; front rooms have plaza views but pick up some street noise. *Rooms from: $350* *480 1st St. E, Sonoma* *707/996–9779* *www.ledsonhotel.com* *6 rooms* *Free Breakfast.*

★ MacArthur Place Hotel & Spa

$$$ | **HOTEL** | Guests at this 7-acre boutique property five blocks south of Sonoma Plaza bask in ritzy seclusion in plush accommodations set amid landscaped gardens. **Pros:** verdant garden setting; tranquil spa; great for a romantic getaway. **Cons:** a bit of a walk from the plaza; some traffic noise audible in street-side rooms; pricey in high season. *Rooms from: $359* *29 E. MacArthur St., Sonoma* *707/938–2929, 800/722–1866* *www.macarthurplace.com* *64 rooms* *No meals.*

Nightlife

Sigh

WINE BARS—NIGHTLIFE | From the oval bar and walls the color of a fine Blanc de Blancs to retro chandeliers that mimic champagne bubbles, everything about this sparkling-wine bar's frothy space screams "have a good time." That owner Jayme Powers and her posse are trained in the fine art of *sabrage* (opening a sparkler with a saber) only adds to the festivity. **■TIP➔ Sigh opens at noon, so it's a good daytime stop, too.** ✉ *120 W. Napa St., Sonoma* ✣ *At 1st St. W* ☎ *707/996–2444* 🌐 *www.sighsonoma.com.*

Shopping

Sonoma Plaza is a shopping magnet, with tempting boutiques and specialty food purveyors facing the square or within a block or two.

★ Sonoma Valley Certified Farmers Market

OUTDOOR/FLEA/GREEN MARKETS | To discover just how bountiful the Sonoma landscape is—and how talented its farmers and food artisans are—head to Depot Park, just north of the Sonoma Plaza, on Friday morning. This market is considered Sonoma County's best. ✉ *Depot Park, 1st St. W, Sonoma* ✣ *At Sonoma Bike Path* ☎ *707/538–7023* 🌐 *www.svcfm.org.*

SPAS

Willow Stream Spa at Fairmont Sonoma Mission Inn & Spa

SPA/BEAUTY | By far the Wine Country's largest spa, the Fairmont resort's 40,000-square-foot facility provides every amenity you could possibly want, including pools and hot tubs fed by local thermal springs. The signature 2½-hour Sonoma Organic Lavender Kur and Facial includes a botanical body wrap, a full-body massage, and a facial. Couples seeking romance often request the treatment room with the two-person copper bathtub. ✉ *100 Boyes Blvd./Hwy. 12, Sonoma* ✣ *2½ miles north of Sonoma Plaza* ☎ *707/938–9000* 🌐 *www.fairmont.com/sonoma/willow-stream* 🎫 *Treatments from $79.*

Glen Ellen

7 miles north of Sonoma.

Unlike its flashier Napa Valley counterparts, Glen Ellen eschews well-groomed sidewalks lined with upscale boutiques and restaurants, preferring instead its crooked streets, some with no sidewalks at all, shaded with stands of old oak trees. Jack London, who represents Glen Ellen's rugged spirit, lived in the area for many years; the town commemorates him with place-names and nostalgic establishments. Hidden among sometimes-ramshackle buildings abutting Sonoma and Calabasas creeks are low-key shops and galleries worth poking through, and several fine dining establishments.

GETTING HERE AND AROUND

Craggy Glen Ellen epitomizes the difference between the Napa and Sonoma valleys. Whereas small Napa towns like St. Helena get their charm from upscale boutiques and restaurants lined up along well-groomed sidewalks, Glen Ellen's crooked streets are shaded with stands of old oak trees and occasionally bisected by the Sonoma and Calabazas creeks. Tucked among the trees of a narrow canyon, where Sonoma Mountain and the Mayacamas pinch in the valley floor, Glen Ellen looks more like a town of the Sierra foothills gold country than a Wine Country village.

Sights

Benziger Family Winery

WINERY/DISTILLERY | One of the best-known Sonoma County wineries sits on a sprawling estate in a bowl with 360-degree sun exposure, the benefits of which are explored on tram tours that depart several times daily. Guides explain Benziger's biodynamic farming practices and provide a glimpse of the extensive cave system. Choose from a regular tram tour or a more in-depth excursion that concludes with a seated tasting. Known for Chardonnay, Cabernet Sauvignon, Merlot, Pinot Noir, and Sauvignon Blanc, the winery is a beautiful spot for a picnic. ■ **TIP➔ Reserve a seat on the tram tour through the winery's website or arrive early in the day on summer weekends and during harvest season.** ✉ *1883 London Ranch Rd., Glen Ellen* ✣ *Off Arnold Dr.* ☎ *888/490–2739* 🌐 *www.benziger.com* 🎫 *Tastings from $20, tours from $30 (includes tastings).*

★ Jack London State Historic Park

NATIONAL/STATE PARK | The pleasures are pastoral and intellectual at author Jack London's beloved Beauty Ranch, where you could easily spend the afternoon hiking some of the 30-plus miles of trails that loop through meadows and stands of oaks, redwoods, and other trees. Manuscripts and personal artifacts depicting London's travels are on view at the House of Happy Walls Museum, which provides an overview of the writer's life, literary passions, humanitarian and conservation efforts, and promotion of organic farming. A short hike away lie the ruins of Wolf House, which burned down just before London was to move in. Also open to visitors are a few outbuildings and the restored wood-framed cottage where London penned many of his later works. He's buried on the property. ■ **TIP➔ Well-known performers headline the park's Broadway Under the Stars series, a hot ticket in summer.** ✉ *2400 London Ranch Rd., Glen Ellen* ✣ *Off Arnold Dr.* ☎ *707/938–5216* 🌐 *www.jacklondonpark.com* 🎫 *Parking $10 ($5 walk-in or bike), includes admission to museum; cottage $4.*

★ Lasseter Family Winery

WINERY/DISTILLERY | Immaculately groomed grapevines dazzle the eye at John and Nancy Lasseter's secluded winery, and it's no accident: Phil Coturri, Sonoma Valley's premier organic vineyard manager, tends them. Even the landscaping, which includes an insectary to attract beneficial bugs, is meticulously maintained. Come harvesttime, the wine-making team oversees gentle processes that transform the fruit into wines of purity and grace: a Sémillon–Sauvignon Blanc blend, two rosés, and Bordeaux and Rhône reds. Evocative labels illustrate the tale behind each wine. These stories are well told on tours that precede some tastings of wines, paired with local artisanal cheeses, in an elegant room whose east-facing window frames vineyard and Mayacamas Mountains views. Tastings, by the glass or flight, also take place on the winery's outdoor patio. All visits are by appointment only. ✉ *1 Vintage La., Glen Ellen* ✣ *Off Dunbar Rd.* ☎ *707/933–2814* 🌐 *www.lasseterfamilywinery.com* 🎫 *Tastings (some including tours) from $30.*

Loxton Cellars

WINERY/DISTILLERY | Back in the day when tasting rooms were low-tech and the winemaker often poured the wines, the winery experience unfolded pretty much the way it does at Loxton Cellars today. The personable Australia-born owner, Chris Loxton, who's on hand many days, crafts Zinfandels, Syrahs, a Pinot Noir, and a Cabernet Sauvignon, all quite good, and some regulars swear by the seductively smooth Syrah Port. You can sample a few current releases without an appointment, but one is needed to taste library- and limited-release wines. ■ **TIP➔ To learn more about Loxton's wine-making philosophy and practices, book a Walkabout tour (weekends only) of the vineyard and winery that's followed by a seated tasting.** ✉ *11466 Dunbar Rd., Glen Ellen* ✣ *At Hwy. 12* ☎ *707/935–7221* 🌐 *www.loxtonwines.com* 🎫 *Tastings from $15, tour $40.*

Hitching a ride on the Benziger Family Winery tram tour

Restaurants

Fig Cafe

$$ | **FRENCH** | The compact menu at this cheerful bistro focuses on California and French comfort food—pot roast and duck confit, for instance, as well as thin-crust pizza. Steamed mussels are served with crispy fries, which also accompany the Chef's Burger (top sirloin with Gruyère), two of the many dependable dishes that have made this restaurant a downtown Glen Ellen fixture. **Known for:** daily three-course prix-fixe specials; no corkage fee; local winemakers pouring wines on Wednesday evening. *Average main: $19 ✉ 13690 Arnold Dr., Glen Ellen ✣ At O'Donnell La. ☎ 707/938–2130 🌐 www.thefigcafe.com ⏲ No lunch.*

★ Glen Ellen Star

$$$ | **ECLECTIC** | Chef Ari Weiswasser honed his craft at The French Laundry, Daniel, and other bastions of culinary finesse, but at his Wine Country outpost he prepares haute-rustic cuisine, much of it emerging from a wood-fired oven that burns a steady 600°F. Crisp-crusted, richly sauced Margherita and other pizzas thrive in the torrid heat, as do tender whole fish entrées and vegetables roasted in small iron skillets. **Known for:** kitchen-view counter for watching chefs cook; prix-fixe Wednesday "neighborhood night" menu with free corkage; Weiswasser's sauces, emulsions, and spices. *Average main: $28 ✉ 13648 Arnold Dr., Glen Ellen ✣ At Warm Springs Rd. ☎ 707/343–1384 🌐 glenellenstar.com ⏲ No lunch.*

Hotels

★ Gaige House + Ryokan

$$$ | **B&B/INN** | There's no other place in Sonoma or Napa quite like the Gaige House + Ryokan, which blends the best elements of a traditional country inn, a boutique hotel, and a longtime expat's classy Asian hideaway. **Pros:** short walk to Glen Ellen restaurants, shops, and tasting rooms; bottomless jar of cookies in the common area; full breakfasts, afternoon wine and appetizers. **Cons:** sound carries

in the main house; the least expensive rooms are on the small side; oriented more toward couples than families with children. *Rooms from: $358 13540 Arnold Dr., Glen Ellen 707/935–0237, 800/935–0237 www.gaige.com 23 rooms Breakfast.*

★ Olea Hotel

$$$ | **B&B/INN** | The husband-and-wife team of Ashish and Sia Patel operate this boutique lodging that's at once sophisticated and down-home country casual, and the attention to detail impresses most visitors almost instantly, from the exterior landscaping, pool, and hot tub to the colors and surfaces in the guest rooms and public spaces. **Pros:** beautiful style; complimentary wine; chef-prepared breakfasts. **Cons:** minor road noise in some rooms; fills up quickly on weekends; weekend minimum-stay requirement. *Rooms from: $308 5131 Warm Springs Rd., Glen Ellen West off Arnold Dr. 707/996–5131 www.oleahotel.com 15 rooms Breakfast.*

Kenwood

4 miles north of Glen Ellen.

Tiny Kenwood consists of little more than a few restaurants, shops, tasting rooms, and a historic train depot, now used for private events. But hidden in this pretty landscape of meadows and woods at the north end of Sonoma Valley are several good wineries, most just off the Sonoma Highway. Varietals grown here at the foot of the Sugarloaf Mountains include Sauvignon Blanc, Chardonnay, Zinfandel, and Cabernet Sauvignon.

GETTING HERE AND AROUND

To get to Kenwood from Glen Ellen, head northeast on Arnold Drive and north on Highway 12. Sonoma Transit Bus 30 and Bus 38 serve Kenwood from Glen Ellen and Sonoma.

Sights

B Wise Vineyards Tasting Lounge

WINERY/DISTILLERY | The stylish roadside tasting room (walk-ins welcome) of this producer of small-lot reds sits on the valley floor, but B Wise's winery and vineyards occupy prime acreage high in the Moon Mountain District AVA. The winery made its name crafting big, bold Cabernets, including one from owner Brion Wise's estate, but in recent years has also focused on Pinot Noirs from Sonoma County and Oregon's Willamette Valley. Among the other stars in the uniformly excellent lineup is the Cabernet-heavy blend Trios, whose grapes, all from Wise's estate, include Merlot, Petit Verdot, Syrah, and Tannat. The winery also makes Chardonnay and a rosé of Pinot Noir that quickly sells out. A tasting here may whet your appetite for a visit to the estate, done by appointment only. *9077 Sonoma Hwy., Kenwood At Shaw Ave. 707/282–9169 www.bwisevineyards.com Tastings $20.*

Kunde Estate Winery & Vineyards

WINERY/DISTILLERY | On your way into Kunde you pass a terrace flanked by fountains, virtually coaxing you to stay for a picnic with views over the vineyard. Family owned for more than a century, Kunde prides itself on producing 100% estate wines from its 1,850-acre property, which rises 1,400 feet from the valley floor. Kunde's whites include several Chardonnays and a Sauvignon Blanc, with Cabernet Sauvignon, Merlot, and a Zinfandel from 1880s vines among the reds. **■TIP→ Make a reservation for the Mountain Top Tasting, a tour by luxury van that ends with a sampling of reserve wines.** *9825 Sonoma Hwy./Hwy. 12, Kenwood 707/833–5501 www.kunde.com Tastings from $15, grounds and cave tour free.*

St. Francis Winery

WINERY/DISTILLERY | Nestled at the foot of Mt. Hood, St. Francis has earned national acclaim for its wine-and-food pairings. With its red-tile roof and bell tower and views of the Mayacamas Mountains just to the east, the winery's California Mission–style visitor center occupies one of Sonoma County's most scenic locations. The charm of the surroundings is matched by the mostly red wines, including rich, earthy Zinfandels from the Dry Creek, Russian River, and Sonoma valleys. Five-course pairings with small bites and wine—chicken medallions with Chardonnay, for instance, or a grilled lamb chop with Cabernet Franc—are offered from Thursday through Monday; pairings with cheeses and charcuterie are available daily. ✉ *100 Pythian Rd., Kenwood* ✣ *Off Hwy. 12* ☎ *707/538–9463, 888/675–9463* 🌐 *www.stfranciswinery.com* 🎫 *Tastings from $15.*

Restaurants

★ Salt & Stone

$$$ | MODERN AMERICAN | The menu at this upscale roadhouse with a sloping wood-beamed ceiling focuses on seafood (salt) and beef, lamb, chicken, duck, and other meats (stone), with many dishes in both categories grilled. Start with the classics, perhaps a martini and oysters Rockefeller, before moving on to well-plated contemporary entrées that might include crispy-skin salmon or duck breast, fish stew, or grilled rib-eye. **Known for:** suave cocktails including signature New York Sour; mountain-view outdoor seating area; Monday–Wednesday "Bistro Nights" three-course dinners. [$] *Average main: $25* ✉ *9900 Sonoma Hwy., Kenwood* ✣ *At Kunde Winery Rd.* ☎ *707/833–6326* 🌐 *www.saltstonekenwood.com* ⏲ *No lunch Tues. and Wed.*

Hotels

Kenwood Inn and Spa

$$$$ | B&B/INN | Fluffy feather beds, custom Italian furnishings, and French doors in most cases opening onto terraces or balconies lend this inn's uncommonly spacious guest rooms a romantic air. **Pros:** large rooms; lavish furnishings; romantic setting. **Cons:** road or lobby noise in some rooms; expensive in high season; geared more to couples than families with children. [$] *Rooms from: $489* ✉ *10400 Sonoma Hwy./Hwy. 12, Kenwood* ☎ *707/833–1293, 800/353–6966* 🌐 *www.kenwoodinn.com* *29 rooms* *Breakfast.*

Healdsburg

17 miles north of Santa Rosa.

Easily Sonoma County's ritziest town and the star of many a magazine spread or online feature, Healdsburg is located at the intersection of the Dry Creek Valley, Russian River Valley, and Alexander Valley AVAs. Several dozen wineries bear a Healdsburg address, and around downtown's plaza you'll find fashionable boutiques, spas, hip tasting rooms, and art galleries, and some of the Wine Country's best restaurants. Star chef Kyle Connaughton, who opened SingleThread Farms Restaurant to much fanfare, has motivated his counterparts all over town to up their game.

Especially on weekends, you'll have plenty of company as you tour the downtown area. You could spend a day just exploring the tasting rooms and shops surrounding Healdsburg Plaza, but be sure to allow time to venture into the surrounding countryside. With orderly rows of vines alternating with beautifully overgrown hills, this is the setting you dream about when planning a Wine Country vacation. Many wineries here are barely visible, often tucked behind groves of eucalyptus or hidden high on fog-shrouded hills. Country stores and roadside farm stands alongside relatively untrafficked roads sell just-plucked fruits and vine-ripened tomatoes.

GETTING HERE AND AROUND

Healdsburg sits just off U.S. 101. Heading north, take the Central Healdsburg exit to reach Healdsburg Plaza; heading south, take the Westside Road exit and pass east under the freeway. Sonoma County Transit Bus 60 serves Healdsburg from Santa Rosa.

Sights

★ Arista Winery

WINERY/DISTILLERY | Brothers Mark and Ben McWilliams own this winery specializing in small-lot Pinot Noirs that was founded in 2002 by their parents. The sons have raised the winery's profile in several ways, most notably by hiring winemaker Matt Courtney, who has earned high praise from the *Wine Spectator* and other publications for his balanced, richly textured Pinot Noirs. Courtney shows the same deft touch with Arista's Zinfandels, Chardonnays, and a Gewürztraminer. One tasting focuses on the regions from which Arista sources its grapes, another on small-lot single-vineyard wines. Visits are by appointment only. **■ TIP→ Guests who purchase a bottle are welcome to enjoy it in the picnic area, near a Japanese garden that predates the winery.** ✉ *7015 Westside Rd.* ☎ *707/473–0606* 🌐 *www.aristawinery.com* 🎫 *Tastings from $35.*

Dry Creek Vineyard

WINERY/DISTILLERY | Sauvignon Blanc marketed as Fumé Blanc brought instant success to the Dry Creek Valley's first new winery since Prohibition, but this area stalwart established in 1972 receives high marks as well for its Zinfandels, Bordeaux-style red blends, and Cabernet Sauvignons. In the nautical-themed tasting room—Dry Creek has featured sailing vessels on its labels since the 1980s—you can choose an all–Sauvignon Blanc flight, an all-Zinfandel one, or a mix of these and other wines. A vineyard walk and an insectary garden enhance a visit to this historic producer, a fine place for a picnic under the shade of a magnolia and several redwood trees. **■ TIP→ You can reserve a boxed lunch two days ahead through the winery, a time-saver on busy weekends.** ✉ *3770 Lambert Bridge Rd.* ✣ *Off Dry Creek Rd.* ☎ *707/433–1000, 800/864–9463* 🌐 *www.drycreekvineyard.com* 🎫 *Tastings from $15, tour $30.*

Gary Farrell Vineyards & Winery

WINERY/DISTILLERY | Pass through an impressive metal gate and wind your way up a steep hill to reach this winery with knockout Russian River Valley views from the elegant two-tiered tasting room and terrace outside. In 2017 *Wine Enthusiast Magazine* named a Gary Farrell Chardonnay wine of the year, one among many accolades for this winery known for sophisticated single-vineyard Chardonnays and Pinot Noirs. The private Exploration Tour & Tasting, which includes a winery tour and artisanal cheeses, provides a solid introduction. The quicker Elevation Tasting (no tour) takes place inside or on the terrace; the Inspiration Tasting, in a private salon, concentrates on gifted winemaker Theresa Heredia's Pinot Noirs. **■ TIP→ All visits are by appointment, but same-day Elevation reservations are usually possible during the week.** ✉ *10701 Westside Rd.* ☎ *707/473–2909* 🌐 *www.garyfarrellwinery.com* 🎫 *Tastings from $35, tour $45.*

★ Jordan Vineyard and Winery

WINERY/DISTILLERY | A visit to this 1,200-acre property revolves around an impressive estate built in the early 1970s to replicate a French château. Founders Tom and Sally Jordan—their son, John, now runs the winery—erected the structure in part to emphasize their goal of producing Sonoma County Chardonnays and Cabernet Sauvignons to rival those in the Napa Valley and France itself. A seated Library Tasting of the current release of each varietal takes place in the château, accompanied by executive chef Todd Knoll's small bites. The tasting concludes with an older vintage Cabernet Sauvignon. The 90-minute Winery Tour &

Tasting includes the above, plus a walk through part of the château. All visits are by appointment only. **■TIP→ For a truly memorable experience, splurge on the three-hour Estate Tour & Tasting, whose pièce de résistance is the Cabernet segment, which unfolds at a 360-degree vista point overlooking vines, olive trees, and countryside.** ✉ *1474 Alexander Valley Rd.* ✧ *1½ miles east of Healdsburg Ave.* ☎ *800/654–1213, 707/431–5250* 🌐 *www.jordanwinery.com* 🎫 *Library tasting $30, winery tour and tasting $40, estate tour and tasting $120* ⊗ *Closed Sun. Dec.–Mar.*

MacRostie Estate House

WINERY/DISTILLERY | A driveway off Westside Road curls through undulating vineyard hills to the steel, wood, and heavy-on-the-glass tasting space of this longtime Chardonnay and Pinot Noir producer. Moments after you've arrived and a host has offered a glass of wine, you'll already feel transported to a genteel, rustic world. Hospitality is clearly a priority here, but so, too, is seeking out top-tier grape sources—30 for the Chardonnays, 15 for the Pinots—among them Dutton Ranch, Bacigalupi, and owner Steve MacRostie's Wildcat. With fruit this renowned, current winemaker Heidi Bridenhagen downplays the oak and other tricks of her trade, letting the vineyard settings, grape clones, and vintage do the talking. Tastings, inside or on balcony terraces with views across the Russian River Valley, are all seated. **■TIP→ Reservations, required on weekends, are a good idea on weekdays, too.** ✉ *4605 Westside Rd.* ✧ *Near Frost Rd.* ☎ *707/473–9303* 🌐 *macrostiewinery.com* 🎫 *Tastings from $25.*

★ Ridge Vineyards

WINERY/DISTILLERY | Ridge stands tall among local wineries, and not merely because its 1971 Monte Bello Cab placed first in a 30th-anniversary rematch of the famous Judgment of Paris blind tasting of California and French reds. The winery built its reputation on Cabernet Sauvignons, Zinfandels, and Chardonnays of unusual depth and complexity, but you'll also find blends of Rhône varietals. Ridge makes wines using grapes from several California locales—including the Dry Creek Valley, Sonoma Valley, Napa Valley, and Paso Robles—but the focus is on single-vineyard estate wines, such as the Lytton Springs Zinfandel from grapes grown near the tasting room. In good weather you can sit outside, taking in views of rolling vineyard hills while you sip. **■TIP→ The $25 tasting includes a pour of the top-of-the-line Monte Bello Cabernet Sauvignon from Santa Cruz Mountains grapes.** ✉ *650 Lytton Springs Rd.* ✧ *Off U.S. 101* ☎ *408/867–3233* 🌐 *www.ridgewine.com/visit/lytton-springs* 🎫 *Tastings from $10, tours from $35.*

★ Silver Oak

WINERY/DISTILLERY | The views and architecture are as impressive as the wines at the Sonoma County outpost of the same-named Napa Valley winery. In 2018, six years after purchasing a 113-acre parcel with 73 acres planted to grapes, Silver Oak debuted its ultramodern, environmentally sensitive winery and glass-walled tasting pavilion. As in Napa, the Healdsburg facility produces just one wine each year: a robust, well-balanced Alexander Valley Cabernet Sauvignon aged in American rather than French oak barrels. The walk-in tasting includes the current Alexander Valley Cabernet and Napa Valley Bordeaux blend plus an older vintage. Tours, worth taking to experience the high-tech winery, are by appointment. The winery's chef prepares several courses (enough to serve as lunch) paired with library and current Cabernets plus two or more wines of sister operation Twomey Cellars, which produces Sauvignon Blanc, Pinot Noir, and Merlot. ✉ *7370 Hwy. 128* ☎ *707/942–7082* 🌐 *www.silveroak.com* 🎫 *Tastings from $20, tours and tastings from $30.*

Restaurants

★ Barndiva

$$$$ | AMERICAN | Music plays quietly in the background while servers ferry the inventive seasonal cocktails of this restaurant that abandons the homey vibe of many Wine Country spots for a more urban feel. Make a light meal out of yellowtail tuna crudo or Dungeness crab salad, or settle in for the evening with pan-seared king salmon with caviar and crème fraîche or sautéed rack of lamb with gnocchi. **Known for:** cool cocktails; stylish cuisine; open-air patio. *Average main: $34* *231 Center St.* *At Matheson St.* *707/431–0100* *www.barndiva.com* *Closed Mon. and Tues.*

Bravas Bar de Tapas

$$$ | SPANISH | Spanish-style tapas and an outdoor patio in perpetual party mode make this restaurant, headquartered in a restored 1920s bungalow, a popular downtown perch. Contemporary Spanish mosaics set a perky tone inside, but unless something's amiss with the weather, nearly everyone heads out back for flavorful croquettes, paella, jamón, *pan tomate* (tomato toast), duck egg with chorizo cracklings, grilled octopus, skirt steak, and crispy fried chicken. **Known for:** casual small plates; specialty cocktails, sangrias, and beer; sherry flights. *Average main: $27* *420 Center St.* *Near North St.* *707/433–7700* *www.barbravas.com.*

Campo Fina

$$ | ITALIAN | Chef Ari Rosen showcases his contemporary-rustic Italian cuisine at this converted storefront that once housed a bar notorious for boozin' and brawlin'. Sandblasted red brick, satin-smooth walnut tables, and old-school lighting fixtures strike a retro note for a menu built around pizzas and gems such as Rosen's variation on his grandmother's tomato-braised chicken with creamy-soft polenta. **Known for:** outdoor patio and boccie court out of an Italian movie set; lunch sandwiches; wines from California and Italy. *Average main: $20* *330 Healdsburg Ave.* *Near North St.* *707/395–4640* *www.campofina.com.*

★ Chalkboard

$$$ | MODERN AMERICAN | Unvarnished oak flooring, wrought-iron accents, and a vaulted white ceiling create a polished yet rustic ambience for executive chef Shane McAnelly's playfully ambitious small-plate cuisine. Starters such as pork-belly biscuits might seem frivolous, but the silky flavor blend—maple glaze, pickled onions, and chipotle mayo playing off feathery biscuit halves—signals a supremely capable tactician at work. **Known for:** festive happy hour; pasta "flights" (choose three or six styles); The Candy Bar dessert. *Average main: $30* *Hotel Les Mars, 29 North St.* *West of Healdsburg Ave.* *707/473–8030* *www.chalkboardhealdsburg.com.*

Costeaux French Bakery

$ | FRENCH | Breakfast, served all day at this bright-yellow French-style bakery and café, includes the signature omelet (sun-dried tomatoes, applewood-smoked bacon, spinach, and Brie) and French toast made from thick slabs of cinnamon-walnut bread. French onion soup, salad Niçoise, and smoked-duck, cranberry-turkey, and French dip sandwiches are among the lunch favorites. **Known for:** breads, croissants, and fancy pastries; quiche and omelets; front patio (arrive early on weekends). *Average main: $14* *417 Healdsburg Ave.* *At North St.* *707/433–1913* *www.costeaux.com* *No dinner.*

★ SingleThread Farms Restaurant

$$$$ | ECLECTIC | The seasonally oriented, multicourse Japanese dinners known as *kaiseki* inspired the prix-fixe vegetarian, meat, and seafood menu at the spare, elegant restaurant—redwood walls, walnut tables, mesquite-tile floors, muted-gray yarn-thread panels—of internationally renowned culinary artists Katina and Kyle Connaughton (she farms, he cooks). As Katina describes the endeavor, the 72 microseasons of their farm—5 acres at a nearby vineyard plus SingleThread's rooftop garden of fruit trees and microgreens—dictate Kyle's rarefied fare, prepared in a theatrically lit open kitchen. **Known for:** culinary precision; new online reservation slots released on first of month; impeccable wine pairings. *$ Average main: $275 ✉ 131 North St. ✣ At Center St. ☎ 707/723–4646 🌐 www.singlethreadfarms.com ⏱ No lunch weekdays.*

★ Valette

$$$$ | **MODERN AMERICAN** | Northern Sonoma native Dustin Valette opened this homage to the area's artisanal agricultural bounty with his brother, who runs the high-ceilinged dining room, its playful contemporary lighting tempering the austerity of the exposed concrete walls and butcher-block-thick wooden tables. Charcuterie is an emphasis, but also consider the signature day-boat scallops *en croûte* (in a pastry crust) or dishes that might include Liberty duck breast with blackberry gastrique or Padrón-pepper-crusted Alaskan halibut. **Known for:** intricate cuisine; "Trust me" (the chef) tasting menu; well-chosen mostly Northern California wines. *$ Average main: $34 ✉ 344 Center St. ✣ At North St. ☎ 707/473–0946 🌐 www.valettehealdsburg.com ⏱ No lunch.*

 Hotels

★ Harmon Guest House

$$ | **HOTEL** | A boutique sibling of the h2hotel two doors away, this downtown delight debuted in late 2018 having already earned LEED Gold status for its eco-friendly construction and operating practices. **Pros:** rooftop bar's cocktails, food menu, and views; connecting rooms and suites; convenient to Healdsburg Plaza action. **Cons:** minor room-to-room noise bleed-through; room gadgetry may flummox some guests; minimum-stay requirements some weekends. *$ Rooms from: $264 ✉ 227 Healdsburg Ave. ☎ 707/922–5262 🌐 harmonguesthouse.com 🛏 39 rooms 🍴 Free Breakfast.*

★ The Honor Mansion

$$$ | **B&B/INN** | There's a lot to like about the photogenic Honor Mansion, starting with the main 1883 Italianate Victorian home, the beautiful grounds, the elaborate breakfasts, and the home-away-from-home atmosphere. **Pros:** homemade sweets available at all hours; pool, putting green, and boccie, croquet, tennis, and basketball courts; secluded vineyard suites with indoor soaking tubs, outdoor hot tubs. **Cons:** almost a mile from Healdsburg Plaza; walls can seem thin; weekend minimum-stay requirement includes Thursday. *$ Rooms from: $380 ✉ 891 Grove St. ☎ 707/433–4277, 800/554–4667 🌐 www.honormansion.com ⏱ Closed 2 wks at Christmas 🛏 13 rooms 🍴 Breakfast.*

Hotel Trio Healdsburg

$$ | **HOTEL** | Named for the three major wine appellations—the Russian River, Dry Creek, and Alexander valleys—whose confluence it's near, this Residence Inn by Marriott a mile and a quarter north of Healdsburg Plaza and its many restaurants and shops caters to families and extended-stay business travelers with spacious rooms equipped with full kitchens. **Pros:** cute robot room service; full kitchens; rooms sleep up to four or six. **Cons:** 30-minute walk to downtown; slightly corporate feel; pricey in high season. *$ Rooms from: $209 ✉ 110 Dry Creek Rd. ☎ 707/433–4000 🌐 www.hoteltrio.com 🛏 122 rooms 🍴 Free Breakfast.*

★ River Belle Inn

$$ | **B&B/INN** | An 1875 Victorian with a storied past and a glorious colonnaded wraparound porch anchors this boutique property along the Russian River. **Pros:** riverfront location near a dozen-plus tasting rooms; cooked-to-order full breakfasts; attention to detail. **Cons:** about a mile from Healdsburg Plaza;

minimum-stay requirement on weekends; lacks on-site pool, fitness center, and other amenities. *Rooms from: $250* *68 Front St.* *707/955–5724* *www.riverbelleinn.com* *12 rooms* *Free Breakfast.*

★ SingleThread Farms Inn

$$$$ | **B&B/INN** | A remarkable Relais & Châteaux property a block north of Healdsburg Plaza, SingleThread is the creation of husband-and-wife team Kyle and Katina Connaughton, who operate the ground-floor destination restaurant and the four guest rooms and a suite above it. **Pros:** multicourse breakfast; in-room amenities from restaurant; rooftop garden. **Cons:** expensive year-round; no pool or fitness center (free passes provided to nearby facility with both); no spa, but in-room massages available. *Rooms from: $1000* *131 North St.* *At Center St.* *707/723–4646* *www.singlethreadfarms.com* *5 rooms* *Breakfast.*

Shopping

ART GALLERIES

★ Gallery Lulo

ART GALLERIES | A collaboration between a local artist and jewelry maker and a Danish-born curator, this gallery presents changing exhibits of jewelry, sculpture, and objets d'art. *303 Center St.* *At Plaza St.* *707/433–7533* *www.gallerylulo.com.*

CRAFTS

★ One World Fair Trade

CRAFTS | Independent artisans in developing countries create the clothing, household items, jewelry, gifts, and toys sold in this bright, well-designed shop whose owners have a shrewd eye for fine craftsmanship. *353 Healdsburg Ave.* *Near North St.* *707/473–0880* *www.oneworldfairtrade.net.*

SPAS

★ Spa Dolce

SPA/BEAUTY | Owner Ines von Majthenyi Scherrer has a good local rep, having run a popular nearby spa before opening this stylish facility just off Healdsburg Plaza. Spa Dolce specializes in skin and body care for men and women, and waxing and facials for women. Curved white walls and fresh-cut floral arrangements set a subdued tone for such treatments as the exfoliating Hauschka body scrub, which combines organic brown sugar with scented oil. There's a romantic room for couples to enjoy massages for two. **■ TIP→ Many guests come just for the European-style facials, which range from a straightforward cleansing to an anti-aging peel.** *250 Center St.* *At Matheson St.* *707/433–0177* *www.spadolce.com* *Treatments from $60.*

Activities

BICYCLING

★ Wine Country Bikes

BICYCLING | This shop several blocks southeast of Healdsburg Plaza is perfectly located for single or multiday treks into the Dry Creek and Russian River valleys. Bikes, including tandems, rent for $39–$145 per day. One-day tours start at $139. **■ TIP→ The owner and staff can help with bicycling itineraries, including a mostly gentle loop, which takes in Westside Road and Eastside Road wineries and a rusting trestle bridge, as well as a more challenging excursion to Lake Sonoma.** *61 Front St.* *At Hudson St.* *707/473–0610, 866/922–4537* *www.winecountrybikes.com.*

Geyserville

8 miles north of Healdsburg.

Several high-profile Alexander Valley AVA wineries, including the splashy Francis Ford Coppola Winery, can be found in the town of Geyserville, a small part of which stretches west of U.S. 101 into northern Dry Creek. Not long ago this was a dusty farm town, and downtown Geyserville retains its rural character, but the restaurants, shops, and tasting rooms along the short main drag hint at Geyserville's growing sophistication.

GETTING HERE AND AROUND

From Healdsburg, the quickest route to downtown Geyserville is north on U.S. 101 to the Highway 128/Geyserville exit. Turn right at the stop sign onto Geyserville Avenue and follow the road north to the small downtown. For a more scenic drive, head north from Healdsburg Plaza along Healdsburg Avenue. About 3 miles north, jog west (left) for a few hundred feet onto Lytton Springs Road, then turn north (right) onto Geyserville Avenue. In town the avenue merges with Highway 128. Sonoma County Transit Bus 60 serves Geyserville from downtown Healdsburg.

Francis Ford Coppola Winery

WINERY/DISTILLERY | **FAMILY** | The fun at what the film director calls his "wine wonderland" is all in the excess. You may find it hard to resist having your photo snapped standing next to Don Corleone's desk from *The Godfather* or beside other memorabilia from Coppola films (including some directed by his daughter, Sofia). A bandstand reminiscent of one in *The Godfather Part II* is the centerpiece of a large pool area where you can rent a changing room, complete with shower, and spend the afternoon lounging poolside, perhaps ordering food from the adjacent café. A more elaborate restaurant, Rustic, overlooks the vineyards. As for the wines, the excess continues in the cellar, where several dozen varietal wines and blends are produced. ✉ *300 Via Archimedes* ✥ *Off U.S. 101* ☎ *707/857–1400* 🌐 *www.franciscoppolawinery.com* 🎫 *Tastings free–$25, tours $50, pool pass from $40.*

★ Locals Tasting Room

WINERY/DISTILLERY | If you're serious about wine, Carolyn Lewis's tasting room alone is worth a trek 8 miles north of Healdsburg Plaza to downtown Geyserville. Connoisseurs who appreciate Lewis's ability to spot up-and-comers head here regularly to sample the output of a dozen or so small wineries, most without tasting rooms of their own. There's no fee for tasting—extraordinary for wines of this quality—and the extremely knowledgeable staff are happy to pour you a flight of several wines so you can compare, say, different Cabernet Sauvignons. ✉ *21023A Geyserville Ave.* ✥ *At Hwy. 128* ☎ *707/857–4900* 🌐 *www.tastelocalwines.com* 🎫 *Tastings free.*

★ Robert Young Estate Winery

WINERY/DISTILLERY | Panoramic Alexander Valley views unfold at Scion House, the stylish yet informal knoll-top tasting space this longtime Geyserville grower opened in 2018. The first Youngs began farming this land in the mid-1800s, raising cattle and growing wheat, prunes, and other crops. In the 1960s the late Robert Young, of the third generation, began cultivating grapes, eventually planting two Chardonnay clones now named for him. Grapes from them go into the Area 27 Chardonnay, noteworthy for the quality of its fruit and craftsmanship. The reds—small-lot Cabernet Sauvignons plus individual bottlings of Cabernet Franc, Malbec, Merlot, and Petit Verdot—shine even brighter. Tastings at Scion House, named for the fourth generation, whose members built on Robert Young's legacy and established the winery, are by appointment, but the winery accommodates walk-ins when possible. ✉ *5120 Red Winery Rd.* ✥ *Off Hwy. 128* ☎ *707/431–4811* 🌐 *www.ryew.com* 🎫 *Tastings from $25* 🕒 *Closed Tues.*

★ Zialena

WINERY/DISTILLERY | Sister-and-brother team Lisa and Mark Mazzoni (she runs the business, he makes the wines) debuted their small winery's first vintage in 2014, but their Italian American family's Alexander Valley wine-making heritage stretches back more than a century. Mark—whose on-the-job teachers included the late Mike Lee of Kenwood Vineyards and Philippe Melka, a premier international consultant—specializes in smooth Zinfandel and nuanced Cabernet Sauvignon. Most of the grapes come from the 120-acre estate vineyard farmed by Lisa and Mark's father, Mike, who sells to Jordan and other big-name wineries. Other Zialena wines include a Sauvignon Blanc and Cappella, a Zin-based blend Lisa describes as "Mark's fun wine." Tastings take place in a contemporary stone, wood, and glass tasting room amid the family's vineyards. Tours, one focusing on production, the other on the vineyards, are by appointment only. ✉ *21112 River Rd.* ✣ *Off Hwy. 128* ☎ *707/955–5992* 🌐 *www.zialena.com* 🎫 *Tastings from $15, tours $50.*

Restaurants

Diavola Pizzeria & Salumeria

$$ | ITALIAN | A dining area with hardwood floors, a pressed-tin ceiling, and exposed-brick walls provides a fitting setting for the rustic cuisine at this Geyserville mainstay. Chef Dino Bugica studied with several artisans in Italy before opening this restaurant that specializes in pizzas pulled from a wood-burning oven and several types of house-cured meats, with a few salads and meaty main courses rounding out the menu. **Known for:** talented chef; smoked pork belly, pancetta, and spicy Calabrese sausage; casual setting. $ *Average main: $20* ✉ *21021 Geyserville Ave.* ✣ *At Hwy. 128* ☎ *707/814–0111* 🌐 *www.diavolapizzeria.com.*

Hotels

Geyserville Inn

$ | HOTEL | Clever travelers give the Healdsburg hubbub and prices the heave-ho but still have easy access to outstanding Dry Creek and Alexander Valley wineries from this modest, motel-like inn. **Pros:** outdoor pool; second-floor rooms in back have vineyard views; picnic area. **Cons:** rooms facing pool or highway can be noisy; not much style; some maintenance issues. $ *Rooms from: $179* ✉ *21714 Geyserville Ave.* ☎ *707/857–4343, 877/857–4343* 🌐 *www.geyservilleinn.com* *41 rooms* *No meals.*

Forestville

13 miles southwest of Healdsburg.

To experience the Russian River AVA's climate and rusticity, follow the river's westward course to the town of Forestville, home to a highly regarded restaurant and inn and a few wineries producing Pinot Noir from the Russian River Valley and well beyond.

GETTING HERE AND AROUND

To reach Forestville from U.S. 101, drive west from the River Road exit north of Santa Rosa. From Healdsburg, follow Westside Road west to River Road and then continue west. Sonoma County Transit Bus 20 serves Forestville.

Sights

★ Hartford Family Winery

WINERY/DISTILLERY | Pinot Noir lovers appreciate the subtle differences in the wines Hartford's Jeff Stewart crafts from grapes grown in four Sonoma County AVAs, along with fruit from nearby Marin and Mendocino counties and Oregon. Stewart also makes highly rated Chardonnays and old-vine Zinfandels. If the weather's good and you've made a

Russian River Valley AVA

As the Russian River winds its way from Mendocino to the Pacific Ocean, it carves out a valley that's a near-perfect environment for growing certain grape varietals. Because of the low elevation, sea fog pushes far inland to cool the soil, yet in summer it burns off, giving the grapes enough sun to ripen properly. Fog-loving Pinot Noir and Chardonnay grapes are king and queen in the Russian River Valley AVA, which extends from Healdsburg west to the town Guerneville. The namesake river does its part by slowly carving its way downward through many layers of rock, depositing a deep layer of gravel that in parts of the valley measures 60 or 70 feet. This gravel forces the roots of grapevines to go deep in search of water and nutrients. In the process, the plants absorb trace minerals that add complexity to the flavor of the grapes.

reservation, you can enjoy a flight of five or six wines on the patio outside the opulent main winery building. Indoors, at seated private library tastings, guests sip current and older vintages. **■TIP→ Hartford also has a tasting room in downtown Healdsburg.** ✉ *8075 Martinelli Rd.* ✣ *Off Hwy. 116 or River Rd.* ☎ *707/887–8030, 800/588–0234* 🌐 *www.hartfordwines.com* 🎫 *Tastings from $25.*

Joseph Jewell Wines

WINERY/DISTILLERY | Micah Joseph Wirth and Adrian Jewell Manspeaker founded this winery whose name combines their middle ones. Pinot Noirs from the Russian River Valley and Humboldt County to the north are the strong suit. Wirth, who worked for seven years for vintner Gary Farrell, credits his interactions with Farrell's Russian River growers, among them the owners of Bucher Vineyard and Hallberg Ranch, with easing the winery's access to prestigious fruit. Manspeaker, a Humboldt native, spearheaded the foray into Pinot Noir grown in the coastal redwood country. Joseph Jewell's playfully rustic storefront tasting room in downtown Forestville provides the opportunity to experience what's unique about the varietal's next Northern California frontier. The bonuses: a Zinfandel from 1970s vines and two Chardonnays. ✉ *6542 Front St.* ☎ *707/820–1621* 🌐 *www.josephjewell.com* 🎫 *Tastings from $10, tours from $105 per couple ($500 tour is in a helicopter).*

Restaurants

Backyard

$$$ | **MODERN AMERICAN** | The folks behind this casually rustic modern American restaurant regard Sonoma County's farms and gardens as their "backyard" and proudly list their purveyors on the menu. Dinner entrées, which change seasonally, might include herb tagliatelle with goat sausage or chicken potpie. **Known for:** buttermilk fried chicken with buttermilk biscuits to stay or go; poplar-shaded outdoor front patio in good weather; Monday locals'-night specials, plus live music. 💲 *Average main: $26* ✉ *6566 Front St./Hwy. 116* ✣ *At 1st St.* ☎ *707/820–8445* 🌐 *backyardforestville.com* 🕒 *Closed Tues.–Thurs.*

Hotels

★ The Farmhouse Inn

$$$$ | **B&B/INN** | With a farmhouse-meets-modern-loft aesthetic, this low-key but upscale getaway with a pale-yellow exterior contains spacious rooms filled with king-size four-poster beds, whirlpool tubs, and hillside-view terraces. **Pros:** fantastic restaurant; luxury bath products; full-service spa. **Cons:** mild road noise audible in rooms closest to the street; two-night minimum on weekends; pricey, especially during high season. *Rooms from: $545 ✉ 7871 River Rd. ☎ 707/887–3300, 800/464–6642 🌐 www.farmhouseinn.com ⇨ 25 rooms 🍽 Breakfast.*

Activities

Burke's Canoe Trips

CANOEING/ROWING/SKULLING | You'll get a real feel for the Russian River's flora and fauna on a leisurely 10-mile paddle downstream from Burke's to Guerneville. A shuttle bus returns you to your car at the end of the journey, which is best taken from late May through mid-October and, in summer, on a weekday—summer weekends can be crowded and raucous. *✉ 8600 River Rd. ✣ At Mirabel Rd. ☎ 707/887–1222 🌐 www.burkescanoetrips.com 🎫 $78 per canoe.*

Guerneville

7 miles northwest of Forestville, 15 miles southwest of Healdsburg.

Guerneville's tourist demographic has evolved over the years—Bay Area families in the 1950s, lesbians and gays starting in the 1970s, and these days a mix of both groups, plus techies and outdoorsy types—with coast redwoods and the Russian River always central to the town's appeal. The area's most famous winery is Korbel Champagne Cellars, established nearly a century and a half ago. Even older are the stands of trees that except on the coldest winter days make Armstrong Redwoods State Natural Reserve such a perfect respite from wine tasting.

GETTING HERE AND AROUND

To get to Guerneville from Healdsburg, follow Westside Road south to River Road and turn west. From Forestville, head west on Highway 116; alternatively, you can head north on Mirabel Road to River Road and then head west. Sonoma County Transit Bus 20 serves Guerneville.

Sights

★ Armstrong Redwoods State Natural Reserve

NATIONAL/STATE PARK | FAMILY | Here's your best opportunity in the western Wine Country to wander amid *Sequoia sempervirens,* also known as coast redwood trees. The oldest example in this 805-acre state park, the Colonel Armstrong Tree, is thought to be more than 1,400 years old. A half mile from the parking lot, the tree is easily accessible, and you can hike a long way into the forest before things get too hilly. **■ TIP→ During hot summer days, Armstrong Redwoods's tall trees help the park keep its cool.** *✉ 17000 Armstrong Woods Rd. ✣ Off River Rd. ☎ 707/869–2958 for visitor center, 707/869–2015 for park headquarters 🌐 www.parks.ca.gov 🎫 $8 per vehicle, free to pedestrians and bicyclists.*

Restaurants

★ boon eat+drink

$$$ | MODERN AMERICAN | A casual storefront restaurant on Guerneville's main drag, boon eat+drink has a menu built around small, "green" (salads and cooked vegetables), and main plates assembled for the most part from locally produced organic ingredients. Like many of chef-owner Crista Luedtke's dishes, the signature polenta lasagna—creamy ricotta salata cheese and polenta served on greens sautéed in garlic, all of it floating upon a spicy marinara sauce—deviates significantly from the lasagna norm but succeeds on its own merits. **Known for:** adventurous culinary sensibility; all wines from Russian River Valley; local organic ingredients. *Average main: $23 ✉ 16248 Main St. ✣ At Church St. ☎ 707/869–0780 🌐 eatatboon.com ⏲ Closed Wed.*

Hotels

boon hotel+spa

$ | HOTEL | Redwoods, Douglas firs, and palms supply shade and seclusion at this lushly landscaped resort ¾ mile north of downtown Guerneville. **Pros:** memorable breakfasts; pool area and on-site spa; complimentary bikes. **Cons:** lacks amenities of larger properties; pool rooms too close to the action for some guests; can be pricey in high season. *Rooms from: $195* *14711 Armstrong Woods Rd.* *707/869–2721* *boonhotels.com* *15 rooms* *Breakfast.*

Sebastopol

6 miles east of Occidental, 7 miles southwest of Santa Rosa.

A stroll through downtown Sebastopol—a town formerly known more for Gravenstein apples than for grapes but these days a burgeoning wine hub—reveals glimpses of the distant and recent past and perhaps the future, too. Many hippies settled here in the 1960s and 70s and, as the old Crosby, Stills, Nash & Young song goes, they taught their children well: the town remains steadfastly, if not entirely, countercultural.

GETTING HERE AND AROUND

Sebastopol can be reached from Occidental by taking Graton Road east to Highway 116 and turning south. From Santa Rosa, head west on Highway 12. Sonoma County Transit Buses 20, 22, 24, and 26 serve Sebastopol.

Sights

The Barlow

MARKET | A multibuilding complex on the site of a former apple cannery, The Barlow celebrates Sonoma County's "maker" culture with tenants who produce or sell wine, beer, spirits, crafts, clothing, art, and artisanal food and herbs. Only club members and guests on the allocation waiting list can visit the anchor wine tenant, Kosta Browne, but MacPhail, Pax, and Friedeman have tasting rooms open to the public. Crooked Goat Brewing and Woodfour Brewing Company make and sell ales, and you can have a nip of vodka, gin, sloe gin, or wheat and rye whiskey at Spirit Works Distillery. A locally renowned mixologist teamed up with the duo behind nearby Lowell's and Handline restaurants to open Fern Bar, whose zero-proof (as in nonalcoholic) cocktails entice as much as the traditional ones. *6770 McKinley St.* *At Morris St., off Hwy. 12* *707/824–5600* *www.thebarlow.net* *Complex free; tasting fees at wineries, breweries, distillery.*

★ Dutton-Goldfield Winery

WINERY/DISTILLERY | An avid cyclist whose previous credits include developing the wine-making program at Hartford Court, Dan Goldfield teamed up with fifth-generation farmer Steve Dutton to establish this small operation devoted to cool-climate wines. Goldfield modestly strives to take Dutton's meticulously farmed fruit and "make the winemaker unnoticeable," but what impresses the most about these wines, which include Pinot Blanc, Chardonnay, Pinot Noir, and Zinfandel, is their sheer artistry. Among the ones to seek out are the Angel Camp Pinot Noir, from Anderson Valley (Mendocino County) grapes, and the Morelli Lane Zinfandel, from grapes grown on the remaining 1.8 acres of an 1880s vineyard Goldfield helped revive. Tastings often begin with Pinot Blanc, a white-wine variant of Pinot Noir, proceed through the reds, and end with a palate-cleansing Chardonnay. *3100 Gravenstein Hwy. N/Hwy. 116* *At Graton Rd.* *707/827–3600* *www.duttongoldfield.com* *Tastings from $20.*

★ Iron Horse Vineyards

WINERY/DISTILLERY | A meandering one-lane road leads to this winery known for its sparkling wines and estate Chardonnays and Pinot Noirs. The sparklers have made history: Ronald Reagan served them at his summit meetings with Mikhail Gorbachev; George H. W. Bush took some along to Moscow for treaty talks; and Barack Obama included them at official state dinners. Despite Iron Horse's brushes with fame, a casual rusticity prevails at its outdoor tasting area (large heaters keep things comfortable on chilly days), which gazes out on acres of rolling, vine-covered hills. Regular tours take place on weekdays at 10 am. Tastings and tours are by appointment only. **■TIP→ When his schedule permits, winemaker David Munksgard leads a private tour by truck at 10 am on Monday.** *✉ 9786 Ross Station Rd. ✣ Off Hwy. 116 ☎ 707/887–1507 ⊕ www.ironhorsevineyards.com 🎫 Tastings $30, tours from $50 (includes tasting).*

Restaurants

Handline Coastal California

$ | **MODERN AMERICAN** | **FAMILY** | Lowell Sheldon and Natalie Goble, who also run a fine-dining establishment (Lowell's) a mile away, converted Sebastopol's former Foster's Freeze location into a 21st-century fast-food palace that won design awards for its rusted-steel frame and translucent panel-like windows. Their menu, a paean to coastal California cuisine, includes oysters raw and grilled, fish tacos, ceviches, tostadas, three burgers (beef, vegetarian, and fish), and, honoring the location's previous incarnation, chocolate and vanilla soft-serve ice cream for dessert. **Known for:** upscale comfort food; outdoor patio; sustainable seafood and other ingredients. *$ Average main: $14 ✉ 935 Gravenstein Hwy. S ✣ Near Hutchins Ave. ☎ 707/827–3744 ⊕ www.handline.com.*

★ Ramen Gaijin

$$ | **JAPANESE** | Inside a tall-ceilinged, brick-walled, vaguely industrial-looking space with reclaimed wood from a coastal building backing the bar, the chefs in Ramen Gaijin's turn out richly flavored ramen bowls brimming with crispy pork belly, woodear mushrooms, seaweed, and other well-proportioned ingredients. *Izakaya* (Japanese pub grub) dishes like *donburi* (meat and vegetables over rice) are another specialty, like the ramen made from mostly local proteins and produce. **Known for:** craft cocktails by renowned mixologist Scott Beattie, Japanese whiskeys; gluten-free, vegetarian dishes; pickle, karage (fried-chicken thigh), and other small plates. *$ Average main: $17 ✉ 6948 Sebastopol Ave. ✣ Near Main St. ☎ 707/827–3609 ⊕ www.ramengaijin.com ⊗ Closed Sun. and Mon.*

Santa Rosa

6 miles east of Sebastopol, 55 miles north of San Francisco.

Urban Santa Rosa isn't as popular with tourists as many Wine Country destinations—which isn't surprising, seeing as there are more office parks than wineries within its limits. Nevertheless, this hardworking town is home to a couple of interesting cultural offerings and a few noteworthy restaurants and vineyards. The city's chain motels and hotels can be handy if you're finding that everything else is booked up, especially since Santa Rosa is roughly equidistant from Sonoma, Healdsburg, and the western Russian River Valley, three of Sonoma County's most popular wine-tasting destinations.

GETTING HERE AND AROUND

To get to Santa Rosa from Sebastopol, drive east on Highway 12. From San Francisco, cross the Golden Gate Bridge and continue north on U.S. 101. Santa Rosa's hotels, restaurants, and wineries are spread over a wide area; factor in extra time when driving around the city, especially during morning and evening rush hour. To get here from downtown San Francisco, take Golden Gate Transit Bus 101. Several Sonoma County Transit buses serve the city and surrounding area.

Sights

Balletto Vineyards

WINERY/DISTILLERY | A few decades ago Balletto was known for quality produce more than for grapes, but the new millennium saw vineyards emerge as the core business. About 90% of the fruit from the family's 650-plus acres goes to other wineries, with the remainder destined for Balletto's estate wines. The house style is light on the oak, high in acidity, and low in alcohol content, a combination that yields exceptionally food-friendly wines. On a hot summer day, sipping a Pinot Gris, rosé of Pinot Noir, or brut rosé sparkler on the outdoor patio can feel transcendent, but the superstars are the Chardonnays and Pinot Noirs. **■TIP→ Look for the Teresa's unoaked and Cider Ridge Chardonnays and the Burnside Road, Sexton Hill, and Winery Block Pinots, but all the wines are exemplary—and, like the tastings, reasonably priced.** ✉ *5700 Occidental Rd.* ✢ *2½ miles west of Hwy. 12* ☎ *707/568–2455* 🌐 *www.ballettovineyards.com* 🎟 *Tastings $10.*

Charles M. Schulz Museum

MUSEUM | FAMILY | Fans of Snoopy and Charlie Brown will love this museum dedicated to the late Charles M. Schulz, who lived his last three decades in Santa Rosa. Permanent installations include a re-creation of the cartoonist's studio, and temporary exhibits often focus on a particular theme in his work. **■TIP→ Children and adults can take a stab at creating cartoons in the Education Room.** ✉ *2301 Hardies La.* ✢ *At W. Steele La.* ☎ *707/579–4452* 🌐 *www.schulzmuseum.org* 🎟 *$12* 🕒 *Closed Tues. early Sept.–late May.*

★ Martinelli Winery

WINERY/DISTILLERY | In a century-old hop barn with the telltale triple towers, Martinelli has the feel of a traditional country store, but the sophisticated wines made here are anything but old-fashioned. The winery's reputation rests on its complex Pinot Noirs, Syrahs, and Zinfandels, including the Jackass Hill Vineyard Zin, made with grapes from 130-year-old vines. Noted winemaker Helen Turley set the Martinelli style—fruit-forward, easy on the oak, reined-in tannins—in the 1990s, and the current team continues this approach. You can sample current releases at a walk-in tasting at the bar or reserve space a couple of days ahead for a seated tasting on the vineyard-view terrace. Rarer and top-rated vintages are poured at appointment-only sessions. ✉ *3360 River Rd., Windsor* ✢ *East of Olivet Rd.* ☎ *707/525–0570, 800/346–1627* 🌐 *www.martinelliwinery.com* 🎟 *Tastings from $25.*

Safari West

NATURE PRESERVE | FAMILY | An unexpected bit of wilderness in the Wine Country, this preserve with African wildlife covers 400 acres. Begin your visit with a stroll around enclosures housing lemurs, cheetahs, giraffes, and rare birds like the brightly colored scarlet ibis. Next, climb with your guide onto open-air vehicles that spend about two hours combing the expansive property, where more than 80 species—including gazelles, cape buffalo, antelope, wildebeests, and zebras—inhabit the hillsides. **■TIP→ If you'd like to extend your stay, lodging in swank Botswana-made tent cabins is available.** ✉ *3115 Porter Creek Rd.* ✢ *Off Mark West Springs Rd.* ☎ *707/579–2551, 800/616–2695* 🌐 *www.safariwest.com* 🎟 *From $83.*

Restaurants

★ Bistro 29

$$$ | **FRENCH** | Chef Brian Anderson prepares steak frites, cassoulet, duck confit, and sautéed fish with precision at his perky downtown restaurant—rich-red walls, white tile floors, and butcher paper atop linen tablecloths set the mood—but the mixed-greens salad with Dijon vinaigrette best illustrates his understated approach: its local produce bursts with freshness, and the dressing delicately balances its savory and acidic components. Start with escargots or bay scallops with béchamel, finishing with beignets or orange crème brûlée for dessert. **Known for:** midweek prix-fixe menu; sweet and savory crepes; beer selection, Sonoma County and French wines. *Average main: $27 620 5th St. Near Mendocino Ave. 707/546–2929 www.bistro29.com Closed Sun. and Mon. No lunch Sat.*

★ The Spinster Sisters

$$$ | **MODERN AMERICAN** | Modern, well-sourced variations on eggs Benedict and other standards are served at this concrete-and-glass hot spot's weekday breakfast and weekend brunch. Lunch might bring carrot soup, wilted kale salad, or a *banh mi* sandwich, with dinner consisting of shareable bites and small and large plates—think kimchi-and-bacon deviled eggs, vegetable *fritto misto,* and grilled hanger steak. **Known for:** local and international wines; happy hour (Tuesday–Friday 4 pm–6 pm) small bites; horseshoe-shaped bar a good perch for dining single, picking up gossip. *Average main: $26 401 S. A St. At Sebastopol Ave. 707/528–7100 thespinstersisters.com No dinner Sun. and Mon.*

Hotels

Vintners Inn

$$ | **HOTEL** | With a countryside location, a sliver of style, and spacious rooms with comfortable beds, the Vintners Inn further seduces with a slew of amenities and a scenic vineyard landscape. **Pros:** John Ash & Co. restaurant; jogging path through the vineyards; online deals pop up year-round. **Cons:** occasional noise from adjacent events center; trips to downtown Santa Rosa or Healdsburg require a car; pricey on summer and fall weekends. *Rooms from: $295 4350 Barnes Rd. 707/575–7350, 800/421–2584 www.vintnersinn.com 78 rooms No meals.*

Petaluma

14 miles west of Sonoma, 39 miles north of San Francisco.

The first thing you should know about Petaluma is that this is a farm town—with more than 60,000 residents, a large one—and the residents are proud of it. Recent years have seen an uptick in the quality of Petaluma cuisine, fueled in part by the proliferation of local organic and artisanal farms and boutique wine production. With the 2018 approval of the Petaluma Gap AVA, the town even has its name on a wine appellation.

Petaluma's agricultural history reaches back to the mid-1800s, when General Mariano Vallejo established Rancho de Petaluma as the headquarters of his vast agrarian empire. From the late 1800s into the 1960s Petaluma marketed itself as the "Egg Capital of the World," and with production totals that peaked at 612 million eggs in 1946, the point was hard to dispute. Although a poultry processor remains Petaluma's second-largest employer, the town has diversified. The adobe, an interesting historical stop, was once the area's *only* employer, but these days its visitation figures are dwarfed by Lagunitas Brewing Company, whose free tour is a hoot. At McEvoy Ranch, which started out producing gourmet olive oil and now also makes wine, you can taste both products and tour parts of the farm.

GETTING HERE AND AROUND

Petaluma lies west of Sonoma and southwest of Glen Ellen and Kenwood. From Highway 12 or Arnold Drive, take Watmaugh Road west to Highway 116 west. Sonoma Transit buses (Nos. 30, 40, and 53) serve Petaluma from the Sonoma Valley. From San Francisco take U.S. 101 (or Golden Gate Transit Bus 101) north.

Sights

Keller Estate

WINERY/DISTILLERY | This boutique winery's guests discover why "wind to wine" is the Petaluma Gap AVA's slogan. The steady Pacific Ocean and San Pablo Bay breezes that mitigate the midday heat give the grapes thick "sailor's skin," heightening their tannins and flavor, says Ana Keller, whose parents planted vineyards three decades ago on former dairy fields. Keller Estate concentrates on Chardonnay, Pinot Noir, and Syrah. In good weather, tastings take place on a stone terrace shaded by umbrellas and flowering pear trees. Book a walking tour to see the property's cave, winery, vineyards, and olive trees, or go farther afield touring in a 1956 Mercedes van. **■TIP→ The winery requires reservations for all tastings and tours, but same-day visits are usually possible if you call ahead.** ✉ *5875 Lakeville Hwy.* ✢ *At Cannon La.* ☎ *707/765–2117* 🌐 *www.kellerestate.com* 🎫 *Tastings $25, tours (with tastings) from $35* 🕑 *Closed Tues. and Wed.*

★ Lagunitas Brewing Company

WINERY/DISTILLERY | These days owned by Heineken International, Lagunitas began as a craft brewery in Marin County in 1993 before moving to Petaluma in 1994. In addition to its large facility, the company operates a taproom, the Schwag Shop, and an outdoor beer garden that in good weather bustles even at midday. Guides leading the free weekday Tasting/Walking Tour, which starts with a flight of four beers, provide an irreverent version of the company's rise to international acclaim. An engaging tale involves the state alcohol board's sting operation commemorated by Undercover Investigation Shut-down Ale, one of several small-batch brews made here. **■TIP→ The taproom closes on Monday and Tuesday, but tours take place and the gift shop stays open.** ✉ *1280 N. McDowell Blvd.* ✢ *½ mile north of Corona Rd.* ☎ *707/769–4495* 🌐 *lagunitas.com/taproom/petaluma* 🎫 *Tour free* 🕑 *Taproom closed Mon. and Tues.*

★ McEvoy Ranch

WINERY/DISTILLERY | The pastoral retirement project of the late Nan McEvoy after departing as board chair of the *San Francisco Chronicle,* the ranch produces organic extra virgin olive oil and Pinot Noir and other wines, the estate ones from the Petaluma Gap AVA. Some guests sip a few selections at the bar inside, but far better is to reserve an At Our Table Tasting of wines, oils, seasonal edibles from the organic gardens, and artisanal cheeses. In good weather these relaxing sessions unfold on a pond's-edge flagstone patio with views of alternating rows of Syrah grapes and mature olive trees. Walkabout Ranch Tours of four guests or more take in vineyards, gardens, a Chinese pavilion, and other sites. All visits require an appointment. ✉ *5935 Red Hill Rd.* ✢ *6½ miles south of downtown* ☎ *866/617–6779* 🌐 *www.mcevoyranch.com* 🎫 *Tastings from $20, tour and tasting $95* 🕑 *Closed Mon. and Tues. No tour Sun.*

Restaurants

★ Central Market

$$$ | MODERN AMERICAN | A participant in the Slow Food movement, Central Market serves creative, upscale Cal-Mediterranean dishes—many of whose ingredients come from the restaurant's organic farm—in a century-old building with exposed brick walls and an open kitchen. The menu, which changes daily depending on chef Tony Najiola's inspiration and what's ripe and ready, might include tortilla soup or a buttermilk-fried halibut-cheeks starter, a slow-roasted-beets salad, pizzas and stews, and wood-grilled fish and meat. **Known for:** chef's tasting menus; superior wine list; historic setting. *Average main: $25* *42 Petaluma Blvd. N* *Near Western Ave.* *707/778–9900* *www.centralmarketpetaluma.com* *Closed Wed. No lunch.*

★ Pearl

$$ | MEDITERRANEAN | Regulars of this southern Petaluma "daytime café" with indoor and outdoor seating rave about its eastern Mediterranean–inflected cuisine—then immediately downplay their enthusiasm lest this 2018 arrival become more popular. The menu, divided into "smaller," "bigger," and "sweeter" options, changes often, but mainstays include buckwheat polenta, a lamb burger dripping with tzatziki (pickled fennel and yogurt sauce), and *shakshuka* (tomato-based stew with chickpeas, fava beans, and baked egg). **Known for:** weekend brunch; zippy beverage lineup; menu prices include gratuity. *Average main: $18* *500 1st St.* *At G St.* *707/559–5187* *pearlpetaluma.com* *Closed Tues. No dinner.*

Chapter 11

THE NORTH COAST

Updated by
Daniel Mangin

Sights ★★★★★ | Restaurants ★★★★☆ | Hotels ★★★★★ | Shopping ★☆☆☆☆ | Nightlife ★☆☆☆☆

WELCOME TO THE NORTH COAST

TOP REASONS TO GO

★ **Scenic coastal drives:** There's hardly a road here that *isn't* scenic.

★ **Wild beaches:** This stretch of California is one of nature's masterpieces. Revel in the unbridled, rugged coastline, without a building in sight.

★ **Dinnertime:** When you're done hiking the beach, refuel with delectable food; you'll find everything from fresh-off-the-boat seafood to haute French cuisine.

★ **Fine wine:** Sip wines at family-owned tasting rooms—cool-climate Pinot Noirs and Chardonnays in the Anderson Valley, then wines from Zinfandel and other heat-loving varietals as you move inland.

★ **Wildlife:** Watch for migrating whales, sunbathing sea lions, and huge Roosevelt elk with majestic antlers.

It's all but impossible to explore the Northern California coast without a car. Indeed, you wouldn't want to—driving here is half the fun. The main road is Highway 1, two lanes that twist and turn (sometimes 180 degrees) up cliffs and down through valleys in Sonoma and Mendocino counties, with U.S. 101 proceeding parallel inland until the two roads join northward in the Redwood Country of Humboldt County. From south to north, below are a few key towns:

1 **Bodega Bay**

2 **Jenner**

3 **Gualala**

4 **Point Arena**

5 **Elk**

6 **Little River**

7 **Mendocino**

8 **Ft. Bragg**

9 **Philo**

10 **Boonville**

11 **Hopland**

12 **Ukiah**

13 **Weott**

14 **Ferndale**

15 **Eureka**

16 **Trinidad**

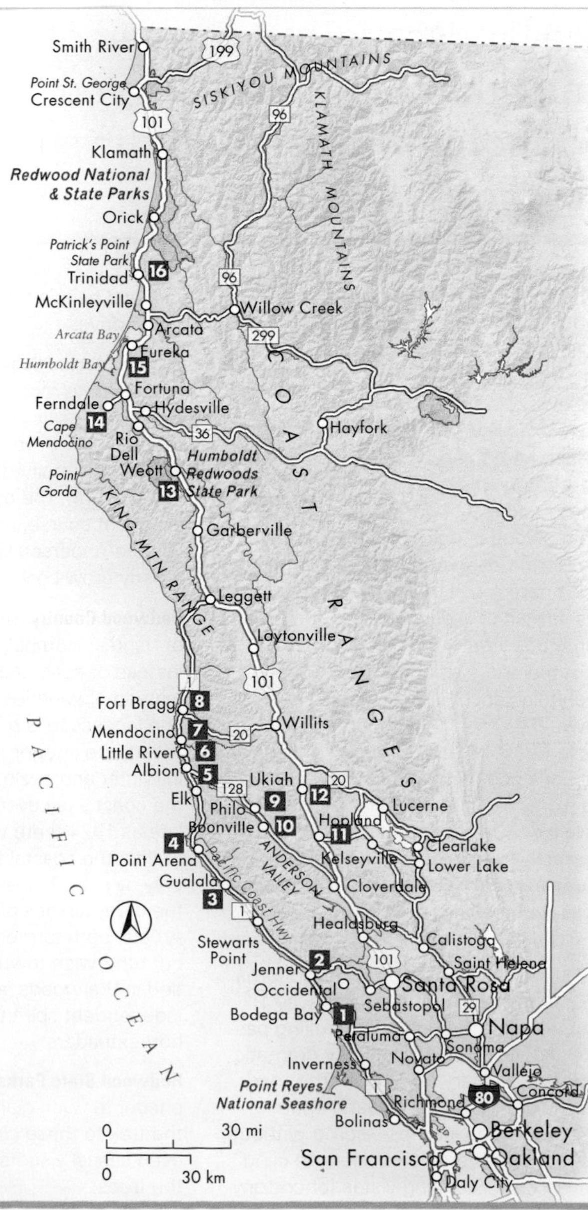
Smith River
199
Point St. George
Crescent City
101
SISKIYOU MOUNTAINS
96
KLAMATH MOUNTAINS
Klamath
Redwood National & State Parks
Orick
Patrick's Point State Park
16
Trinidad
96
McKinleyville
Willow Creek
Arcata
Arcata Bay
299
Eureka
Humboldt Bay
15
Fortuna
Ferndale
Hydesville
14
Cape Mendocino
Rio Dell
36
Hayfork
COAST RANGES
Humboldt Redwoods State Park
Weott
Point Gorda
13
KING MTN RANGE
Garberville
Leggett
Laytonville
1
101
Fort Bragg
8
Mendocino
7
Willits
20
Little River
6
Albion
5
Ukiah
20
128
9
12
Elk
Philo
Lucerne
Boonville
10
Hopland
11
4
Clearlake
Point Arena
ANDERSON VALLEY
Kelseyville
Lower Lake
Gualala
Pacific Coast Hwy
Cloverdale
3
1
PACIFIC OCEAN
Healdsburg
Calistoga
Stewarts Point
2
101
Saint Helena
Jenner
Occidental
Santa Rosa
Sebastopol
29
Bodega Bay
1
Napa
Petaluma
Sonoma
Inverness
Novato
Vallejo
Point Reyes National Seashore
1
Richmond
80
Concord
Bolinas
Berkeley
0
30 mi
0
30 km
San Francisco
Oakland
Daly City

The spectacular coastline between Marin County and the Oregon border defies expectations. The Pacific Ocean defines the landscape, but instead of boardwalks and bikinis there are ragged cliffs and pounding waves—and the sunbathers are mostly sea lions.

Instead of strip malls and freeways, you'll find a two-lane highway that follows a fickle shoreline. Although coastal towns vary from deluxe spa retreat to hippie hideaway, all are reliably sleepy—and that's exactly why many Californians escape here to enjoy nature unspoiled. On a detour inland, you can explore redwoods and taste wines at wineries rarely too crowded or pricey. When you travel the North Coast, turn off your phone; you won't have much of a signal anyway, and this stretch of Highway 1 is made up of numerous little worlds, each different from the last, waiting to be discovered. Everything about life here says slow down. If you don't, you might miss a noble Roosevelt elk grazing in a roadside field or a pod of migrating whales cruising along the shore. ■ **TIP→ Don't plan to drive too far in one day. Some drivers stop frequently to appreciate the views, and you can't safely drive faster than 30 or 40 mph on many portions of the highway.**

MAJOR REGIONS

The Sonoma Coast. As you enter Sonoma County from the south on Highway 1, you pass first through gently rolling pastureland. North of Bodega Bay dramatic shoreline scenery takes over. The road snakes up, down, and around sheer cliffs and steep inclines—some without guardrails—where cows seem to cling precariously. Stunning vistas (or cottony fog) and hairpin turns make for an exhilarating drive.

The Mendocino Coast. The timber industry gave birth to most of the small towns along this stretch of coastline. Although tourism now drives the economy, the region has retained much of its old-fashioned charm. The beauty of the landscape, of course, has not changed. Inland lies the Anderson Valley, whose wineries mostly grow cool-climate grapes.

Redwood Country. There's a different state of mind in Humboldt County. Here, instead of spas, there are old-time hotels. Instead of wineries, there are breweries. The landscape is primarily thick redwood forest; the interior mountains get snow in winter and sizzle in summer while the coast sits covered in fog. Until as late as 1924 there was no road north of Willits; the coastal towns were reachable only by sea. That legacy is apparent in the communities of today: Eureka and Arcata, both former ports, are sizeable, but otherwise towns are tiny and nestled in the woods, and people have an independent spirit that recalls the original homesteaders.

Redwood State Parks. For a pristine encounter with giant redwoods, make the trek to these coastal parks where even casual visitors have easy access to the trees.

Planning

When to Go

The North Coast is a year-round destination, though when you go determines what you will see. The migration of the Pacific gray whales is a wintertime phenomenon, which lasts roughly from mid-December to early April. Wildflowers follow the winter rain, as early as January in southern areas through June and July farther north. Summer is the high season for tourists, but spring, fall, and even winter are arguably better times to visit. The pace is slower, towns are quieter, and lodging is cheaper.

The coastal climate is similar to San Francisco's, although winter nights are colder than in the city. In July and August thick fog can drop temperatures to the high 50s, but fear not: you need only drive inland a few miles to find temperatures that are often 20 degrees higher.

Getting Here and Around

AIR TRAVEL

Arcata/Eureka Airport (ACV), 14 miles north of Eureka in McKinleyville, is served by subsidiaries of United and a few other small airlines. Most arriving passengers rent a car, but you can also taxi ($50–$60), shuttle ($28), or ride share (starting at $22) to Eureka (a little less to Arcata).

AIRPORT CONTACTS Arcata/Eureka Airport ✉ *3561 Boeing Ave., McKinleyville* ☎ *707/445–9651* 🌐 *flyhumboldt.org.*

GROUND TRANSPORTATION CONTACTS City Cab ☎ *707/442–4551* 🌐 *citycab-humboldt.com.* **Door-to-Door Airporter** ☎ *888/338–5497, 707/839–4186* 🌐 *www.doortodoorairporter.com.*

BUS TRAVEL

Greyhound buses travel along U.S. 101 from San Francisco to Garberville, Eureka, and Arcata. Humboldt Transit Authority connects Eureka, Arcata, and Trinidad.

BUS CONTACTS Greyhound ☎ *800/231–2222* 🌐 *www.greyhound.com.* **Humboldt Transit Authority** ☎ *707/443–0826* 🌐 *www.hta.org.*

CAR TRAVEL

U.S. 101 has excellent services, but long stretches separate towns along Highway 1. **■TIP➔ If you're running low on fuel and see a gas station, stop for a refill.** Twisting Highway 1 is the scenic route to Mendocino from San Francisco, but the fastest one is U.S. 101 north to Highway 128 west (from Cloverdale) to Highway 1 north. The quickest route to the far North Coast is straight up U.S. 101 past Cloverdale to Hopland and Ukiah and on to Humboldt County.

ROAD CONDITIONS Caltrans ☎ *800/427–7623* 🌐 *www.dot.ca.gov.*

Restaurants

Restaurants here, a few with regional reputations but most off the culinary world's radar, entice diners with dishes fashioned from the abundant fresh seafood and locally grown vegetables and herbs. Attire is usually informal, though at pricier establishments dressy casual is the norm. Most kitchens close at 8 or 8:30 pm and few places serve past 9:30 pm. Many restaurants close in January or early February.

Hotels

Restored Victorians, rustic lodges, country inns, and vintage motels are among the accommodations available here. Few have air-conditioning (the ocean breezes make it unnecessary), and many have no phones or TVs in the rooms. Except in Fort Bragg and a few other towns, budget accommodations are rare, but in winter you're likely to find reduced rates and nearly empty lodgings. In summer and on the weekends, though, make bed-and-breakfast reservations as far ahead as possible—rooms at the best inns often sell out months in advance. *Hotel reviews have been shortened. For full information, visit Fodors.com.*

WHAT IT COSTS			
$	$$	$$$	$$$$
RESTAURANTS			
under $16	$16–$22	$23–$30	over $30
HOTELS			
under $120	$120–$175	$176–$250	over $250

Visitor Information

CONTACTS Humboldt Visitors Bureau ☎ *707/443–5097, 800/346–3482* 🌐 *www.visitredwoods.com.* **Sonoma County Tourism** ☎ *707/522–5800, 800/576–6662* 🌐 *www.sonomacounty.com.* **Visit Mendocino County** ☎ *707/964–9010, 866/466–3636* 🌐 *www.visitmendocino.com.*

Bodega Bay

23 miles west of Santa Rosa.

From this working town's busy harbor west of Highway 1, commercial boats pursue fish and Dungeness crab. In 1962, Alfred Hitchcock shot *The Birds* here. The Tides Wharf complex, an important location, is no longer recognizable, but a few miles inland, in Bodega, you can find Potter Schoolhouse, now a private residence.

GETTING HERE AND AROUND

To reach Bodega Bay, exit U.S. 101 at Santa Rosa and take Highway 12 west (called Bodega Highway west of Sebastopol) 23 miles to the coast. A scenic alternative is to take U.S. 101's East Washington Street/Central Petaluma exit and follow signs west to Bodega Bay; just after you merge onto Highway 1, you'll pass through down-home Valley Ford. Mendocino Transit Authority (🌐 *mendocinotransit.org*) Route 95 buses serve Bodega Bay.

Sights

Sonoma Coast Vineyards

WINERY/DISTILLERY | This boutique winery with an ocean-view tasting room makes cool-climate Chardonnays and Pinot Noirs from grapes grown close to the Pacific. The Antonio Mountain and Balistreri Family Vineyards Pinot Noirs stand out among wines that also include a mildly oaky Sauvignon Blanc and a well-balanced sparkler. ✉ *555 Hwy. 1* ☎ *707/921–2860* 🌐 *www.sonomacoastvineyards.com* 🎟 *Tastings from $25.*

Beaches

★ Sonoma Coast State Park

BEACH—SIGHT | The park's gorgeous sandy coves stretch for 17 miles from Bodega Head to 4 miles north of Jenner. **Bodega Head** is a popular whale-watching perch in winter and early spring, and **Rock Point, Duncan's Landing,** and **Wright's Beach,** at about the halfway mark, have good picnic areas. Rogue waves have swept people off the rocks at Duncan's Landing Overlook, so don't stray past signs warning you away. Calmer **Shell Beach,** about 2 miles north, is known for beachcombing, tidepooling, and fishing. Walk part of the bluff-top **Kortum Trail** or drive about 2½ miles north of Shell Beach to **Blind Beach.** Near the mouth of the Russian River just north of here at **Goat Rock Beach,** you'll find harbor seals; pupping season is from March through August. Bring binoculars and walk north from the parking lot to view the seals. During summer lifeguards are on duty at some beaches, but strong rip currents and heavy surf keep most visitors onshore. **Amenities:** parking (fee); toilets. **Best for:** solitude; sunset; walking. ✉ *Park Headquarters/Salmon Creek Ranger Station, 3095 Hwy. 1* ⊕ *2 miles north of Bodega Bay* ☎ *707/875–3483* 🌐 *www.parks.ca.gov* 🎟 *$8 per vehicle.*

Restaurants

Spud Point Crab Company

$ | **SEAFOOD** | Crab sandwiches, New England or Manhattan clam chowder, and homemade crab cakes with roasted red pepper sauce star on the brief menu of this food stand. Place your order inside, and enjoy your meal to go or at one of the marina-view picnic tables outside. **Known for:** family-run operation; opens at 9 am; seafood cocktails, superb chowder. $ *Average main: $10* ✉ *1910 Westshore Rd.* ☎ *707/875–9472* ⏲ *No dinner.*

★ Terrapin Creek Cafe & Restaurant

$$$$ | **MODERN AMERICAN** | Intricate but not fussy cuisine based on locally farmed ingredients and *fruits de mer* has made this casual yet sophisticated restaurant with an open kitchen a West County darling. Start with raw Marin Miyagi oysters, rich potato-leek soup, or (in season) Dungeness crabmeat ragout before moving on to halibut or other fish pan-roasted to perfection. **Known for:** intricate cuisine of chefs Liya and Andrew Truong; top Bay Area–foodies' choice; starters and salads. $ *Average main: $32* ✉ *1580 Eastshore Rd.* ☎ *707/875–2700* 🌐 *www.terrapincreekcafe.com* ⏲ *Closed Tues. and Wed. No lunch.*

Hotels

Bodega Bay Lodge

$$$ | **HOTEL** | Looking out to the ocean across a wetland, the lodge's shingle-and-river-rock buildings contain Bodega Bay's finest accommodations. **Pros:** ocean views; spacious rooms; fireplaces and patios or balconies in most rooms. **Cons:** pricey in-season; parking lot in foreground of some rooms' views; fairly long drive to other fine dining. $ *Rooms from: $239* ✉ *103 Coast Hwy. 1* ☎ *707/875–3525* 🌐 *www.bodegabaylodge.com* *83 rooms* *No meals.*

Bodega Harbor Inn

$ | **HOTEL** | As humble as can be, this is one of the few places on this stretch of the coast with rooms for around $100 a night. **Pros:** budget choice; rooms for larger groups; ocean views from public areas and some rooms. **Cons:** older facility; nondescript rooms; behind a shopping center. $ *Rooms from: $99* ✉ *1345 Bodega Ave.* ☎ *707/875–3594* 🌐 *www.bodegaharborinn.com* *16 rooms* *No meals.*

Jenner

10 miles north of Bodega Bay.

The Russian River empties into the Pacific Ocean at Jenner, a wide spot in the road where houses dot a mountainside high above the sea. Facing south, the village looks across the river's mouth to Goat Rock Beach *(see Sonoma Coast State Park, above)*. North of the village, Fort Ross State Historic Park provides a glimpse into Russia's early-19th-century foray into California. South of the fort a winery named for the fort grows Chardonnay and Pinot Noir above the coastal fog line. North of the fort lie more beaches and redwoods to hike and explore.

GETTING HERE AND AROUND

Jenner is north of Bodega Bay on Highway 1; from Guerneville head west on Highway 116 (River Road). Mendocino Transit Authority (🌐 *mendocinotransit.org*) buses serve Jenner from Bodega Bay and other coastal towns.

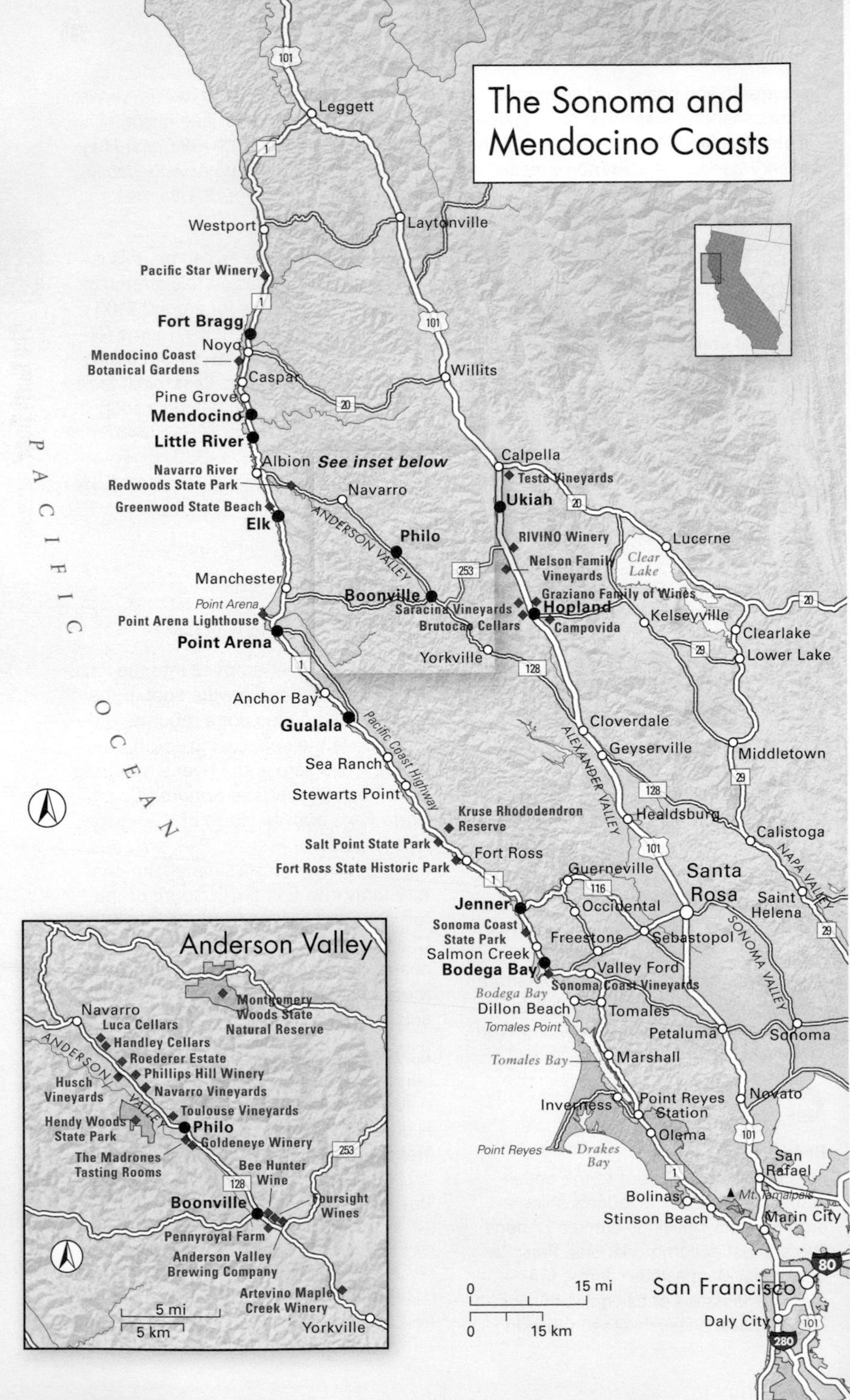

The Sonoma and Mendocino Coasts
Leggett
Westport
Laytonville
Pacific Star Winery
Fort Bragg
Noyo
Mendocino Coast Botanical Gardens
Caspar
Pine Grove
Mendocino
Little River
Willits
Albion
See inset below
Navarro River Redwoods State Park
Greenwood State Beach
Elk
Navarro
Anderson Valley
Philo
Calpella
Testa Vineyards
Ukiah
RIVINO Winery
Nelson Family Vineyards
Graziano Family of Wines
Lucerne
Clear Lake
Manchester
Point Arena
Point Arena Lighthouse
Point Arena
Boonville
Saracina Vineyards
Brutocao Cellars
Hopland
Campovida
Kelseyville
Clearlake
Lower Lake
Yorkville
Anchor Bay
Gualala
Pacific Coast Highway
Sea Ranch
Stewarts Point
Cloverdale
Geyserville
Alexander Valley
Middletown
Healdsburg
Calistoga
Kruse Rhododendron Reserve
Salt Point State Park
Fort Ross
Fort Ross State Historic Park
Guerneville
Santa Rosa
Napa Valley
Jenner
Occidental
Saint Helena
Sonoma Coast State Park
Salmon Creek
Freestone
Sebastopol
Sonoma Valley
Bodega Bay
Valley Ford
Sonoma Coast Vineyards
Bodega Bay
Dillon Beach
Tomales
Tomales Point
Petaluma
Sonoma
Tomales Bay
Marshall
Inverness
Point Reyes Station
Novato
Olema
Point Reyes
Drakes Bay
San Rafael
Bolinas
Mt. Tamalpais
Stinson Beach
Marin City
San Francisco
Daly City
Pacific Ocean
0
15 mi
0
15 km
Anderson Valley
Montgomery Woods State Natural Reserve
Navarro
Luca Cellars
Handley Cellars
Roederer Estate
Phillips Hill Winery
Husch Vineyards
Navarro Vineyards
Toulouse Vineyards
Anderson Valley
Hendy Woods State Park
Philo
Goldeneye Winery
The Madrones Tasting Rooms
Bee Hunter Wine
Boonville
Foursight Wines
Pennyroyal Farm
Anderson Valley Brewing Company
Artevino Maple Creek Winery
Yorkville
5 mi
5 km

Sights

Fort Ross State Historic Park

NATIONAL/STATE PARK | FAMILY | With its reconstructed Russian Orthodox chapel, stockade, and officials' quarters, Fort Ross looks much the way it did after the Russians made it their major California coastal outpost in 1812. Russian settlers established the fort on land they leased from the native Kashia people. The Russians hoped to gain a foothold in the Pacific coast's warmer regions and to produce crops and other supplies for their Alaskan fur-trading operations. In 1841, with the local marine mammal population depleted and farming having proven unproductive, the Russians sold their holdings to John Sutter, later of gold-rush fame. The land, privately ranched for decades, became a state park in 1909. One original Russian-era structure remains, as does a cemetery. The rest of the compound has been reconstructed to look much as it did during Russian times. An excellent small museum documents the history of the fort, the Kashia people, and the ranch and state-park eras. Note that no dogs are allowed past the parking lot and picnic area. ✉ *19005 Hwy. 1* ✥ *11 miles north of Jenner village* ☎ *707/847–3437* 🌐 *www.fortross.org* 🎟 *$8 per vehicle.*

Salt Point State Park

NATIONAL/STATE PARK | For 5 miles, Highway 1 winds through this park, 6,000 acres of forest, meadows, and rocky shoreline. Heading north, the first park entrance (on the right) leads to forest hiking trails and several campgrounds. The next entrance—the park's main road—winds through meadows and along the wave-splashed coastline. This is also the route to the visitor center and **Gerstle Cove,** a favorite spot for scuba divers and sunbathing seals. Next along the highway is **Stump Beach Cove,** with picnic tables, toilets, and a ¼-mile walk to the sandy beach. The park's final entrance is at **Fisk Mill Cove,** where centuries of wind and rain erosion have carved unusual honeycomb patterns in the sandstone called "tafonis." A five-minute walk uphill from the parking lot leads to a dramatic view of **Sentinel Rock,** an excellent spot for sunsets.

Just up the highway, narrow, unpaved Kruse Ranch Road leads to the **Kruse Rhododendron State Reserve**, where each May thousands of rhododendrons bloom within a quiet forest of redwoods and tan oaks. ✉ *25050 Hwy. 1* ✥ *6 miles north of Fort Ross* ☎ *707/847–3221, 707/865–2391* 🌐 *www.parks.ca.gov* 🎟 *$8 per vehicle.*

Restaurants

Coast Kitchen

$$$ | MODERN AMERICAN | On a sunny afternoon or at sunset, glistening ocean views from the Coast Kitchen's outdoor patio and indoor dining space elevate dishes emphasizing seafood and local produce both farmed and foraged. Starters like a baby gem lettuce Caesar and grilled salmon wings precede entrées that may include seared scallops and aged rib eye. **Known for:** ocean-view patio (frequent whale sightings in winter and spring); Sonoma County cheeses, wines, and produce; bar menu 3 pm–5 pm. $ *Average main: $28* ✉ *Timber Cove, 21780 Hwy. 1* ✥ *3 miles north of Fort Ross State Historic Park* ☎ *707/847–3231* 🌐 *www.coastkitchensonoma.com.*

Hotels

★ Timber Cove Resort

$$$$ | RESORT | Restored well beyond its original splendor, this resort anchored to a craggy oceanfront cliff is by far the Sonoma Coast's coolest getaway. **Pros:** dramatic sunsets; grand public spaces; destination restaurant. **Cons:** almost too cool for the laid-back Sonoma Coast; pricey ocean-view rooms; far from nightlife. $ *Rooms from: $314* ✉ *21780 Hwy. 1* ☎ *707/847–3231* 🌐 *www.timbercoveresort.com* *46 rooms* 🍴 *No meals.*

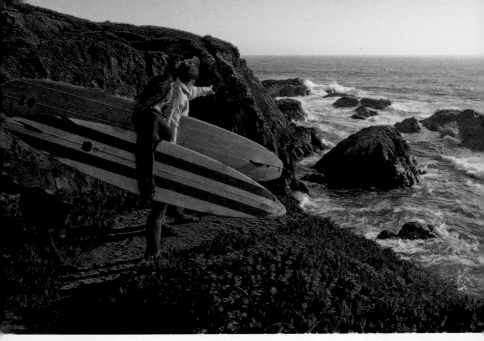

Surfers check out the waves near Bodega Bay on the Sonoma Coast.

Gualala

38 miles north of Jenner, 35 miles south of Mendocino.

This former lumber port on the Gualala River, a good base for exploring the southern Mendocino coast, has all the basic services plus some galleries and gift shops.

GETTING HERE AND AROUND

Gualala is on Highway 1; from U.S. 101 near Santa Rosa, head west on River Road (Exit 494) and turn north at the ocean. Mendocino Transit Authority (*mendocinotransit.org*) buses serve the area.

Restaurants

St. Orres

$$$ | AMERICAN | Underneath one of this lodge's two Russian-style onion-dome towers is a romantic atrium dining room where locally farmed and foraged ingredients appear in dishes such as garlic flan with black chanterelles and rack of wild boar with apple-pear latkes. You can also dine in the bar, where, as with the main room you can choose from the prix-fixe menu (usually about $50) or dine à la carte on wild-mushroom ravioli, baby abalone with seared scallops, and other small plates. **Known for:** elaborate weekend brunch; worthy wine list; lodgings in adjacent hotel and cottages. *Average main: $28 36601 S. Hwy. 1, 3 miles north of Gualala 707/884–3335 www.saintorres.com Closed Mon. and Tues. No lunch weekdays. Occasionally closed some weekdays in winter.*

Hotels

★ Mar Vista Cottages

$$$ | HOTEL | Escape to nature and retro-charm at these refurbished, gadget-free 1930s cottages, four with two bedrooms and eight with one. **Pros:** commune-with-nature solitude; peaceful retreat; walking path to beach. **Cons:** no other businesses within walking distance; no TVs or phones in rooms; two-night minimum on weekends. $ *Rooms from: $190* ✉ *35101 S. Hwy 1* ✣ *5 miles north of Gualala* ☎ *707/884-3522, 877/855-3522* 🌐 *www.marvistamendocino.com* *12 rooms* *No meals.*

Seacliff Motel on the Bluff

$$ | **HOTEL** | Wedged in back of a small shopping center, this motel is not much to look at, but you'll spend your time here staring at the Pacific panorama because all rooms have ocean views. **Pros:** smart budget choice; Trinks restaurant next door for creative breakfasts (lunch served, too); clean rooms with gas fireplaces, free Wi-Fi, and binoculars. **Cons:** nondescript from highway; standard-issue decor; sometimes foggy in summer. $ *Rooms from: $165* ✉ *39140 S. Hwy. 1* ☎ *707/884-1213, 800/400-5053* 🌐 *www.seacliffmotel.com* *16 rooms* *No meals.*

Point Arena

15 miles north of Gualala, 35 miles south of Mendocino.

Occupied by longtime locals and long-haired surfers, this former timber town on Highway 1 is part New Age, part rowdy, and always laid-back. The one road going west out of downtown will lead you to the harbor, where fishing boats unload sea urchins and salmon and someone's nearly always riding the waves.

GETTING HERE AND AROUND

From Gualala follow Highway 1 north; from Mendocino follow it south. Mendocino Transit Authority (🌐 *mendocinotransit.org*) serves the area.

★ Point Arena Lighthouse

LIGHTHOUSE | For an outstanding view of the ocean and, in winter, migrating whales, take the marked road off Highway 1 north of town to the 115-foot lighthouse. Climb the 145 steps, and a 360-degree panorama unfolds. It's possible to stay out here in one of four rental units ($$–$$$$), all with full kitchens (weekend minimum-stay requirement). ✉ *45500 Lighthouse Rd.* ✣ *Off Hwy. 1, 4½ miles northwest of town* ☎ *707/882-2809, 877/725-4448* 🌐 *www.pointarenalighthouse.com* *Tour $8 ($5 if no tour).*

Restaurants

Arena Market and Cafe

$ | **CAFÉ** | The simple café at this all-organic grocery store serves baked goods for breakfast and has hot soups, sandwiches, and an ample salad bar for lunch and early dinner. The market, which specializes in food from local farms, sells cheese, bread, and other picnic items, and you can sip beer and wine in the café. **Known for:** locally owned co-op; espresso drinks; good soups and salad bar. $ *Average main: $9* ✉ *185 Main St.* ☎ *707/882-3663* 🌐 *www.arenamarketandcafe.org* ☞ *No dinner.*

★ Franny's Cup and Saucer

$ | **CAFÉ** | Aided by her mother Barbara, a former pastry chef at famed Chez Panisse in Berkeley, Franny turns out baked goods that are sophisticated and inventive. Morning favorites include scones and sweet and savory pastries; there are fruit tarts and strawberry-apricot crisps, plus a mouthwatering assortment of cookies, candy, jams, and jellies for indulging anytime. **Known for:** dazzling specialty cakes; delightful ambience; croque monsieurs and frittata of the day. $ *Average main: $7* ✉ *213 Main St.* ☎ *707/882-2500* 🌐 *www.frannyscupandsaucer.com* *No credit cards* *Closed Sun.–Tues. No dinner.*

Elk

33 miles north of Gualala.

In this quiet town on the cliff above Greenwood Cove, just about every spot has a view of the rocky coastline and stunning Pacific sunsets. A few restaurants and inns do business here, but the main attraction is highly walkable Greenwood State Beach.

GETTING HERE AND AROUND

Elk is along Highway 1, 6 miles south of its intersection with Highway 128. Mendocino Transit Authority (*mendocinotransit.org*) buses serve the area.

Sights

Greenwood State Beach

BEACH—SIGHT | If you're not staying at one of Elk's cliff-top lodgings, the easiest access to the sandy shore below them is at this state beach whose parking lot sits across Highway 1 from the town's general store. A trail leads from the lot down to the beach, where the waves crashing against the huge offshore rocks are the perfect backdrop. **Amenities:** parking (free). **Good for:** sunset; walking. *6150 Hwy. 1* *707/937–5804* *www.parks.ca.gov* *Free.*

Restaurants

Queenie's Roadhouse Cafe

$ | **AMERICAN** | If the day's sunny, grab one of the picnic tables in front of this beloved hangout for big breakfasts (served until closing, at 3) and lunches that include blue-cheese burgers topped with onions browned in bourbon and butter. The café's wide windows provide Pacific views to enjoy with your meal. **Known for:** omelets, huevos rancheros, waffles, and pancakes; burgers, salads, and sandwiches; local wines and microbrews. *Average main: $14* *6061 S. Hwy. 1* *707/877–3285* *www.queeniesroadhousecafe.com* *Closed Tues. and Wed. Closed late Dec.–mid-Feb. No dinner.*

Hotels

Elk Cove Inn & Spa

$$ | **B&B/INN** | Perched on a bluff above pounding surf and a driftwood-strewn beach, this property has stunning views from most of its accommodations, which include seven rooms, five suites, and four cottages. **Pros:** gorgeous views; filling breakfast; steps to the beach. **Cons:** rooms in main house are smallish; not suitable for young children; spa's massage calendar often full. *Rooms from: $175* *6300 S. Hwy. 1* *707/877–3321, 800/275–2967* *www.elkcoveinn.com* *16 rooms* *Free Breakfast.*

★ Harbor House Inn

$$$$ | **B&B/INN** | Prepare to be bowled over by every aspect of this showcase property that reopened in 2018 after a five-year multimillion-dollar makeover: its rugged Pacific-cliff setting, destination restaurant, sterling hospitality, and luxurious accommodations in a 1916 redwood Craftsman-style house and a few newer cottages. **Pros:** romantic, ocean-view setting; luxurious base for wine tasting and outdoor activities; destination restaurant. **Cons:** not ideal for kids; 16 miles from Mendocino; best accommodations expensive for the area. *Rooms from: $379* *5600 S. Hwy. 1* *707/877–3203, 800/720–7474* *www.theharborhouseinn.com* *10 rooms* *Free Breakfast.*

Little River

13½ miles north of Elk.

The town of Little River is not much more than a post office and a convenience store; Albion, its neighbor to the south, is even smaller. Along this winding portion of Highway 1 you'll find numerous inns and restaurants, all of them quiet and situated to take advantage of the breathtaking ocean views.

GETTING HERE AND AROUND

Little River is along Highway 1, 7 miles north of its junction with Highway 128. Mendocino Transit Authority (*mendocinotransit.org*) buses serve the area.

Sights

Navarro River Redwoods State Park

NATIONAL/STATE PARK | **FAMILY** | Described by locals as the "11-mile-long redwood tunnel to the sea," this park that straddles Highway 128 is great for walks amid second-growth redwoods and for summer swimming in the gentle Navarro River. In late winter and spring, when the river is higher, you also can fish, canoe, and kayak. *Hwy. 128, Albion* *2 miles east of Hwy. 1* *707/937–5804* *www.parks.ca.gov.*

Van Damme State Park

NATIONAL/STATE PARK | Best known for its quiet beach, a prime diving spot, this park is also popular with day hikers. A ¼-mile stroll on a boardwalk leads to the bizarre **Pygmy Forest,** where acidic soil and poor drainage have produced mature cypress and pine trees that are no taller than a person. For more of a challenge, hike the moderate 4¼-mile Pygmy Forest and Fern Canyon Loop past the forest and sword ferns that grow as tall as 4 feet. The visitor center has displays on ocean life and the historical significance of the redwood lumber industry along the coast. *Little River Park Rd., off Hwy. 1* *707/937–5804* *www.parks.ca.gov* *$8 per vehicle, walk-ins free (park at beach).*

Restaurants

Ledford House

$$$ | **FRENCH** | The only thing separating this bluff-top wood-and-glass restaurant from the Pacific Ocean is a great view. Entrées evoke the flavors of southern France and include hearty bistro dishes—stews, cassoulet, and pastas—and large portions of grilled meats and freshly caught fish (though the restaurant also is vegetarian friendly). **Known for:** Mendocino-centric wine list; live jazz nightly; three-course bistro special. *Average main: $27* *3000 N. Hwy. 1, Albion* *707/937–0282* *www.ledfordhouse.com* *Closed Mon. and Tues. and late-Feb.–early Mar. and mid-Oct.–early Nov. No lunch.*

Hotels

Albion River Inn

$$$ | **B&B/INN** | Contemporary New England–style cottages at this inn overlook the dramatic bridge and seascape where the Albion River empties into the Pacific. **Pros:** ocean views; great bathtubs; meat and fresh seafood dishes at romantic glassed-in restaurant. **Cons:** often foggy in summer; no TV in rooms; could use style update. *Rooms from: $195* *3790 N. Hwy. 1, Albion* *707/937–1919, 800/479–7944* *albionriverinn.com* *22 rooms* *Free Breakfast.*

Mendocino

3 miles north of Little River.

A flourishing logging town in the late-19th century, Mendocino seduces 21st-century travelers with windswept cliffs, phenomenal Pacific Ocean views, and boomtown-era New England–style architecture. Following the timber industry's mid-20th-century decline, artists and craftspeople began flocking here, and so did Hollywood: Elia Kazan chose Mendocino as a backdrop for his 1955 film adaptation of John Steinbeck's *East of Eden,* starring James Dean, and the town stood in for fictional Cabot Cove, Maine, in the long-running TV series *Murder, She Wrote.* As the arts community thrived, restaurants, cafés, and inns sprang up. Today, the small downtown area consists almost entirely of places to eat and shop.

GETTING HERE AND AROUND

Main Street is off Highway 1 about 10 miles north of its junction with Highway 128. Mendocino Transit Authority (🌐 *mendocinotransit.org*) buses serve the area.

Sights

Ford House Visitor Center & Museum

HOUSE | The restored Ford House, built in 1854, serves as the visitor center for Mendocino Headlands State Park and the town. The house has a scale model of Mendocino as it looked in 1890, when it had 34 water towers and a 12-seat public outhouse. From the museum, you can head out on a 3-mile trail across the spectacular seaside cliffs that border the town. ✉ *45035 Main St., west of Lansing St.* ☎ *707/937–5397* 🌐 *mendoparks.org/visitor-centers* 🎟 *Museum $2, visitor center free.*

Kelley House Museum

MUSEUM | An 1861 structure holds this museum whose artifacts include Victorian-era furniture and historical photographs of Mendocino coast's logging days. Two-hour walking tours of Mendocino depart from the museum at 11 am on weekends and some weekday holidays. ✉ *45007 Albion St.* ☎ *707/937–5791* 🌐 *www.kelleyhousemuseum.org* 🎟 *Museum $5, walking tours $10* 🕒 *Closed Tues.–Thurs.*

Restaurants

Cafe Beaujolais

$$$$ | **AMERICAN** | A garden of heirloom and exotic plantings surrounds this popular restaurant inside a yellow Victorian cottage. Local ingredients find their way into starters such as a silky-creamy wild-foraged-chanterelle soup or a salad of burrata and Brussels sprouts and entrées like duck breast à l'orange and local black cod with a truffle emulsion. **Known for:** breads from a wood-fired brick oven; Mendocino wines on international list; salads, burgers, sandwiches, pastas, and (some days) pizza for lunch. $ *Average main: $33* ✉ *961 Ukiah St.* ☎ *707/937–5614* 🌐 *www.cafebeaujolais.com* 🕒 *No lunch Mon. and Tues.*

Trillium Cafe & Inn

$$$ | **AMERICAN** | The term "light rustic" applies equally well to this comely cafe's decor—plank flooring, wood-top tables, gas fireplace with brick hearth—and its cuisine, which emphasizes local produce and seafood. The menu changes seasonally, with the homemade rosemary bread, peppered-albacore appetizer, Point Reyes blue cheese salad, and grilled organic pork chop among the year-round crowd-pleasers. **Known for:** outdoor patio area with garden and ocean views; wine list favoring Northern California wines, particularly Mendocino; three upstairs rooms (two sharing a bathroom) a good deal in summer. $ *Average main: $29* ✉ *10390 Kasten St.* ☎ *707/937–3200* 🌐 *www.trilliummendocino.com* 🕒.

Hotels

Blue Door Group Inns of Mendocino

$$$ | **B&B/INN** | Each inn has its own appeal—Blue Door Inn for its garden, Packard House for its serene setting, JD House for its ocean views (and garden, too)—with all three worth consideration for their proximity to restaurants, shops, and the Mendocino Headlands. **Pros:** historic properties with modern decor; service-oriented staff; wide range of prices and room types. **Cons:** some rooms are on the small side; lacks personal touch of on-site owner-innkeeper; best rooms are pricey. $ *Rooms from: $179* ✉ *10481 Howard St.* ☎ *707/937–4892, 888/453–2677* 🌐 *www.bluedoorgroup.com* *19 rooms* 🍽 *Free Breakfast.*

★ Brewery Gulch Inn

$$$$ | **B&B/INN** | The feel is modern yet tasteful at this smallish inn with redwood and leather furnishings and plush beds; two rooms have whirlpool tubs with views. **Pros:** luxury in tune with nature;

peaceful ocean views; complimentary wine hour and light buffet. **Cons:** must drive to town; expensive in-season; two-night minimum on weekends. $ *Rooms from: $385 ✉ 9401 N. Hwy. 1, 1 mile south of Mendocino ☎ 707/937–4752, 800/578–4454 ⊕ www.brewerygulchinn.com ⇨ 11 rooms ⊙ Free Breakfast.*

Glendeven Inn & Lodge

$$ | **B&B/INN** | If Mendocino is the New England village of the West Coast, then Glendeven—an 1867 farmhouse and several other buildings—is the local country manor, with sea views and 8 acres of gardens, complete with llamas and chickens that provide eggs for three-course breakfasts served in-room. **Pros:** romantic setting with acres of gardens; elegant decor; ocean views. **Cons:** not within walking distance of town; some rooms pick up highway noise; weekend minimum-stay requirement. $ *Rooms from: $170 ✉ 8205 N. Hwy. 1 ☎ 707/937–0083, 800/822–4536 ⊕ glendeven.com ⇨ 22 rooms ⊙ Free Breakfast.*

MacCallum House

$$$$ | **B&B/INN** | Set on 2 flower-filled acres in the middle of town, this inn is a perfect mix of Victorian charm and modern luxury. **Pros:** excellent breakfast; central location; outstanding restaurant. **Cons:** luxury suites on a separate property are more modern; some rooms in main house lack charm; some guests find the look dated. $ *Rooms from: $338 ✉ 45020 Albion St. ☎ 707/937–0289, 800/609–0492 ⊕ www.maccallumhouse.com ⇨ 30 rooms ⊙ Free Breakfast.*

Stanford Inn by the Sea

$$$$ | **HOTEL** | This woodsy yet luxurious family-run property a few minutes south of town feels like the Northern California version of an old-time summer resort, with an ecologically friendly twist. **Pros:** lovely grounds; wide variety of activities; on-site vegetarian restaurant. **Cons:** New Age feel won't appeal to everyone; carnivores may find menus challenging; least expensive rooms lack ocean views. $ *Rooms from: $351 ✉ 44850 Comptche Ukiah Rd. ☎ 707/937–5615, 800/331–8884 ⊕ www.stanfordinn.com ⇨ 41 rooms ⊙ Free Breakfast.*

Activities

Catch-A-Canoe and Bicycles Too

KAYAKING | Rent kayaks and regular and outrigger canoes here year-round, as well as mountain and suspension bicycles. The outfit's tours explore Big River and its estuary. ✉ *Stanford Inn by the Sea, 1 S. Big River Rd. ✢ Off Hwy. 1, 1 mile south of town ☎ 707/937–0273 ⊕ www.catchacanoe.com ✉ From $65.*

Fort Bragg

10 miles north of Mendocino.

Fort Bragg is a working-class town that many feel is the most authentic place on the coast. The city maintains a local vibe since most people who work at the area hotels and restaurants also live here, as do many artists and commercial anglers. The pleasures of a visit are mainly outdoors, a stroll through the botanical gardens or along the town's coastal trail, touring by train or boast, tidepooling or fishing at the state park, or tasting wine within steps of the ocean.

GETTING HERE AND AROUND

Highway 20 winds west 33 miles from Willits to Highway 1 just south of Fort Bragg. Mendocino Transit Authority (⊕ *mendocinotransit.org*) buses serve the town.

Sights

Fort Bragg Coastal Trail

TRAIL | A multiuse path, much of it flat and steps from rocky and highly photogenic shoreline, stretches the length of Fort Bragg. A particularly pleasant section, lined with benches created by local artists, follows the coast north

The North Coast is famous for its locally caught Dungeness crab; be sure to try some during your visit.

about 2 miles between Noyo Headlands Park in southern Fort Bragg and Glass Beach. From the beach you can continue well into MacKerricher State Park. **TIP→ There's free parking at both Noyo Headlands Park and Glass Beach.** ✉ *Fort Bragg* ✣ *Noyo Headlands Park, W. Cypress St. off S. Main St. (Hwy. 1); Glass Beach, W. Elm St. off N. Main St.*

★ Mendocino Coast Botanical Gardens

GARDEN | Something beautiful is always abloom in these marvelous gardens. Along 3½ miles of trails, including pathways with ocean views and observation points for whale-watching, lie a profusion of flowers. The rhododendrons are at their peak from April through June; the dahlias begin their spectacular show in July and last through September. In winter the heather and camellias add more than a splash of color. The main trails are wheelchair accessible. ✉ *18220 N. Hwy. 1, 2 miles south of Fort Bragg* ☎ *707/964–4352* 🌐 *www.gardenbythesea.org* 🎫 *$15.*

★ Noyo Harbor Tours with Captain Dan

TOUR—SIGHT | The genial Captain Dan owns two commercial fishing boats that hit the high seas, but for his gentle tours of Noyo Harbor from the river up to (but not into) the ocean he ordered a custom-built 18-foot eco-friendly Duffy electric boat. Having been in Fort Bragg for decades he knows everyone and everyone's story, including those of the harbor seals, sea lions, birds, and other wildlife you'll see on his excursion. ✉ *32399 Basin St.* ✣ *From S. Main St. (Hwy. 1), take Hwy. 20 east ¼ mile, S. Harbor Dr. north ¼ mile, and Basin St. northeast 1 mile* ☎ *707/734–0044* 🌐 *www.noyoharbortours.com* 🎫 *From $35.*

Pacific Star Winery

WINERY/DISTILLERY | When the sun's out and you're sipping wine while viewing whales or other sea creatures swimming offshore, this bluff-top winery's outdoor tasting spaces feel mystical and magical. Equally beguiling on a brooding stormy day, Pacific Star has still more aces up its sleeve: engaging owners, and cheery staffers pouring a lineup of obscure varietals like Charbono and Brunello, a cousin of Sangiovese. The wines, among them a vibrant Mendocino Zin, are good, and they're reasonably priced. ✉ *33000 N. Hwy. 1, 12 miles north of downtown* ☎ *707/964–1155* 🌐 *www.pacificstarwinery.com* 🎫 *Tastings $7* ⏲ *Closed Mon. Dec.–Mar., Tues. and Wed. year-round.*

Skunk Train

TOUR—SIGHT | FAMILY | A reproduction train travels a few miles of the route of its 1920s predecessor, a fume-spewing gas-powered motorcar that shuttled passengers along a rail line dating from the 1880s logging days. Nicknamed the Skunk Train, the original traversed redwood forests inaccessible to automobiles. There are also excursions from the town of Willits as well as seasonal and holiday-themed tours. **■TIP→ For a separate fee you can pedal the same rails as the Skunk Train on two-person side-by-side reclining bikes outfitted for the track, a one-hour ride many patrons find more diverting and a better value than the train trip.** ✉ *100 W. Laurel St., at Main St.* ☎ *707/964–6371* 🌐 *www.skunktrain.com* 🎫 *Train rides $27 Jan.–Mar.; $29, Apr.–May; $42 June–Dec.; rail-bikes $79 for 2 people (no single-rider fee)* ⏲ *No train rides on some weekdays Sept.–May (call or check online calendar); no rail-bike tours Dec.–Feb.*

Triangle Tattoo & Museum

MUSEUM | At the top of a steep staircase, this several-room museum pays homage to Fort Bragg's rough-and-tumble past with memorabilia that includes early-20th-century Burmese tattooing instruments, pictures of astonishing tattoos from around the world, and a small shrine to the late sword-swallowing sideshow king Captain Don Leslie. ✉ *356–B N. Main St.* ☎ *707/964–8814* 🌐 *www.triangletattoo.com* 🎫 *Free.*

Beaches

MacKerricher State Park

NATIONAL/STATE PARK | This park begins at **Glass Beach,** its draw an unfortunately dwindling supply of sea glass (remnants from the city dump once in this area), and stretches north for 9 miles, beginning with rocky headlands that taper into dunes and sandy beaches. The headlands are a good place for whale-watching from December to mid-April. Fishing, canoeing, hiking, tidepooling, jogging, bicycling, beachcombing, camping, and harbor seal watching at Laguna Point are among the popular activities, many of which are accessible to the mobility-impaired. **⚠ Be vigilant for rogue waves—don't turn your back on the sea. Amenities:** parking; toilets. **Best for:** solitude; sunset; walking. ✉ *24100 MacKerricher Park Rd., off Hwy. 1, 3 miles north of town* ☎ *707/937–5804* 🌐 *www.parks.ca.gov* 🎫 *Free.*

Restaurants

Cowlick's Ice Cream

$ | AMERICAN | FAMILY | Candy-cap mushroom (tastes like maple syrup) and black raspberry chocolate chunk are among this fun ice-cream shop's top-selling flavors. Chocolate, mocha almond fudge, and ginger appear year-round, supplemented by blackberry-cheesecake, pumpkin, eggnog, and other seasonal offerings; the sorbets might include lemon, pear, or strawberry. **Known for:** handmade ice cream; chai, yellow-cake batter, and other wiggy flavors; sodas, sundaes, and root-beer floats. 💲 *Average main: $5* ✉ *250 N. Main St.* ☎ *707/962–9271* 🌐 *www.cowlicksicecream.com.*

North Coast Brewing

$$ | AMERICAN | Clam chowder, pork chili, and jumbo chicken wings are among the beer-friendly starters at the brewing company's expansive restaurant—heavy on the oak, especially in the bar—whose headlining entrées include

Neapolitan-style pizzas, burgers, pulled-pork sandwiches, and beer-batter fish or jumbo shrimp and chips. The beers, award-winners worldwide, run the gamut from pilsners and the flagship Red Seal amber ale to the Russian-style Rasputin stout and Old Stock Ale, a 12.5%-alcohol (sometimes more) affair. **Known for:** seasonal beers; sampler flights; beer-wise staffers. *Average main: $18 444 N. Main St. 707/964–3400 northcoast-brewing.com/brewery-taproom.*

Piaci Pub and Pizzeria

$ | **ITALIAN** | The seats are stools and your elbows might bang a neighbor's, but nobody seems to mind at this casual spot for thin-crust pizzas (more than a dozen types), focaccia, and calzones. The food—there are several salads, too—is simple, but everything is carefully prepared and comes out tasty. **Known for:** cash-only; well-chosen beers; dog-friendly outdoor tables. *Average main: $15 120 W. Redwood Ave. 707/961–1133 www.piacipizza.com No credit cards No lunch Sun.*

★ Princess Seafood Market & Deli

$ | **SEAFOOD** | Captain Heather Sears leads her all-woman crew of "girls gone wild for wild-caught seafood" that heads oceanward on the *Princess* troller, returning with some of the seafood served at this shanty astride the vessel's Noyo Harbor dock. Order chowder (might be clam, crab, or salmon), crab rolls and shrimp po'boys, raw or barbecued oysters, or other sturdy fare at the counter, dining under the all-weather tent kept toasty by heaters and a fire pit when the wind's ablowin'. **Known for:** fresh, sustainable seafood; canned wines and beer; crew members who clearly love their jobs. *Average main: $14 32410 N. Harbor Dr., Follow N. Harbor Dr. ½ mile southeast from S. Main St. (Hwy. 1) 707/962–3123 fvprincess.com/p/fish-market Closed Mon.–Wed. No dinner (closes at 6).*

Hotels

★ Inn at Newport Ranch

$$$$ | **B&B/INN** | Attention to detail in both design and hospitality make for an incomparable stay at this 2,000-acre working cattle ranch with 1½ miles of private coastline. **Pros:** over-the-top design; mesmerizing Pacific views; horse riding, ocean-side cocktails by a fire pit, and other diversions. **Cons:** all this design and glamour comes at a price; lengthy drive back from Mendocino and Fort Bragg restaurants at night; coast can be foggy in summer. *Rooms from: $400 31502 N. Hwy. 1 707/962–4818 theinnatnewportranch.com 11 rooms Free Breakfast.*

★ Noyo Harbor Inn

$$$$ | **HOTEL** | Craftsman touches abound in this luxury inn's lavishly restored 1868 main structure, which overlooks Noyo Harbor, and a nearby newer wing with Pacific Ocean views. **Pros:** landscaped grounds; warm service; restaurant with harbor-view outdoor deck. **Cons:** barking of sea lions in harbor at certain times of year; expensive during high season; some rooms lack water views. *Rooms from: $275 500 Casa del Noyo Dr. 707/961–4200 noyoharborinn.com 15 rooms No meals.*

Surf and Sand Lodge

$$ | **HOTEL** | As its name implies, this five-building, two-story property, whose owners run two similar lodgings nearby, sits practically on the beach; pathways lead from the accommodations down to the rock-strewn shore. **Pros:** beach location; gorgeous sunsets from decks and patios of ocean-side rooms; very affordable in the off-season. **Cons:** motel style; no restaurants close by; least expensive rooms lack view. *Rooms from: $159 1131 N. Main St. 707/964–9383 www.surfsandlodge.com 30 rooms No meals.*

Weller House Inn

$$ | B&B/INN | It's hard to believe that this 1886 Victorian was abandoned and slated for demolition when it was purchased in 1994 and carefully restored. **Pros:** handcrafted details; radiant heat in the wood floors; colorful and tasteful rooms. **Cons:** some guests find it too old-fashioned; pet cleaning fee; no TVs in rooms. *Rooms from: $165 ✉ 524 Stewart St. ☎ 707/964–4415 🌐 www.wellerhouse.com 9 rooms Free Breakfast.*

Nightlife

Overtime Brewing

BREWPUBS/BEER GARDENS | Murals depicting logging, fishing, and other local industries adorn the walls of this small-batch brewery two childhood pals opened in 2018. You'll find the expected range of ale types, along with novelties like the Jasmine Green Tea Ale and Overkill Chocolate Raspberry Stout. *✉ 190 E. Elm St ☎ 707/962–3040 🌐 www.overtimebrewing.com.*

Sequoia Room

MUSIC CLUBS | Easily the best jazz venue along the North Coast, this 60-seat room adjoining the North Coast Brewing Company's taproom books name acts like Larry Fuller and Nancy Wright plus talents both established and up-and-coming. Shows take place on Friday and Saturday evenings. *✉ 444 N. Main St. ☎ 707/964–3400 🌐 northcoastbrewing.com/jazz.*

Activities

All Aboard Adventures

FISHING | Captain Tim of All Aboard operates whale-watching trips from late December through April. He also heads out to sea for salmon, crab, rock cod, and other excursions. *✉ Noyo Harbor, 32410 N. Harbor Dr. ☎ 707/964–1881 🌐 www.allaboardadventures.com From $40.*

Ricochet Ridge Ranch

HORSEBACK RIDING | Come here for private and group trail rides through the redwood forest and on the beach. *✉ 24201 N. Hwy. 1 ☎ 707/964–7669, 888/873–5777 🌐 www.horse-vacation.com From $60.*

Philo

34 miles southeast of Mendocino, 5 miles west of Boonville.

Many wineries straddle Highway 128 in Philo and nearby Navarro. Tasting rooms here are more low-key than their counterparts in Napa, but the wineries here produce world-class wines, particularly Pinot Noirs and Gewürztraminers, whose grapes thrive in the moderate coastal climate.

GETTING HERE AND AROUND

Highway 128 travels east from coastal Highway 1 south of Mendocino and west from Boonville to Philo. Mendocino Transit Authority (🌐 *mendocinotransit.org*) buses serve the area.

Sights

Goldeneye Winery

WINERY/DISTILLERY | Established in 1996 by the founders of the Napa Valley's well-respected Duckhorn Wine Company, Goldeneye makes Pinot Noirs from estate and other local grapes, along with a Gewürztraminer, a Pinot Gris, a Chardonnay, and a blush Vin Gris of Pinot Noir. Leisurely tastings, some by appointment only, take place in either a restored farmhouse or on a patio with vineyard views. *✉ 9200 Hwy. 128, Philo ☎ 800/208–0438, 707/895–3202 🌐 www.goldeneyewinery.com Tastings from $15 Closed. Tues. and Wed. in Jan. and Feb.*

Handley Cellars

WINERY/DISTILLERY | International folk art collected by founding winemaker Milla Handley adorns the tasting room at this Anderson Valley pioneer whose lightly oaked Chardonnays and Pinot Noirs earn high praise from wine critics. The winery, which has an arbored outdoor patio picnic area, also makes Gewürztraminer, Pinot Gris, Riesling, Zinfandel, sparklers, and several other wines. ✉ *3151 Hwy. 128, Philo* ☎ *707/895–3876, 800/733–3151* 🌐 *www.handleycellars.com* 🎫 *Tasting free.*

Hendy Woods State Park

NATIONAL/STATE PARK | Two groves of ancient redwoods accessible via short trails from the parking lot are the main attractions at this park that's also perfect for a picnic or a summer swim. ✉ *18599 Philo Greenwood Rd., Philo* ✣ *Entrance ½ mile southwest of Hwy. 128* ☎ *707/937–5804* 🌐 *www.parks.ca.gov* 🎫 *$8 per vehicle.*

Husch Vineyards

WINERY/DISTILLERY | A century-old former pony barn houses the cozy tasting room of the Anderson Valley's oldest winery. Wines of note include Gewürztraminer, Chardonnay, Pinot Noir, and two Zinfandels from old-vine grapes. You can picnic on the deck here or at tables under grape arbors. ✉ *4400 Hwy. 128, Philo* ☎ *800/554–8724* 🌐 *www.huschvineyards.com* 🎫 *Tasting free.*

Lula Cellars

WINERY/DISTILLERY | Seventeen miles inland from Highway 1, the fun, relaxing, and pet-friendly Lula is among the Anderson Valley wineries closest to the coast. Lula produces Sauvignon Blanc, Gewürztraminer, Zinfandel, and a rosé of Zinfandel and Pinot Noir, but the several Pinot Noirs, each flavorful and with its own personality, are the highlights. ✉ *2800 Guntly Rd., at Hwy. 128, Philo* ☎ *707/895–3737* 🌐 *www.lulacellars.com* 🎫 *Tastings from $5.*

★ The Madrones Tasting Rooms

WINERY/DISTILLERY | Expand your palate at this 2-acre complex's trio of tasting rooms pouring wines from a dozen varietals. Chardonnay and Pinot Noir are the focus at **Long Meadow Ranch,** where you can also order well-brewed espresso or tea and pick up olive oil, sauces, and similar items from the ranch's Napa Valley operations. Next door, **Drew Family Wines** specializes in Pinot Noir and Syrah beloved by sommeliers. Nearby **Smith Story,** a crowd-funding success story, makes Anderson Valley Pinots plus wines (among them Cabernet Sauvignon) from Sonoma County grapes. Across from Smith Story, Stone and Embers serves gourmet wood-fired pizzas, and the Madrones also includes a spa, a quirky curiosity shop, and lodgings amid landscaped gardens. **■ TIP→ Days, hours, and fees vary at the tasting rooms; the restaurant (Stone and Embers) opens Thursday–Sunday for lunch and dinner year-round, sometimes other days in summer.** ✉ *9000 Hwy. 128, Philo* ☎ *707/895–2955* 🌐 *www.themadrones.com/tasting-rooms* 🎫 *Tastings from $10.*

Navarro Vineyards

WINERY/DISTILLERY | A visit to this family-run winery is a classic Anderson Valley experience. Make time if you can for a vineyard tour (call ahead)—the guides draw from years of hands-on experience to explain every aspect of production, from sustainable farming techniques to the choices made in aging and blending. Best known for Alsatian varietals such as Gewürztraminer and Riesling, Navarro also makes Chardonnay, Pinot Noir, and other wines. The tasting room sells cheese and charcuterie for picnickers. ✉ *5601 Hwy. 128, Philo* ☎ *707/895–3686, 800/537–9463* 🌐 *www.navarrowine.com* 🎫 *Tasting and tour free.*

★ Phillips Hill Winery

WINERY/DISTILLERY | You're apt to meet owner-winemaker Toby Hill on a visit to this winery whose tasting room occupies the upper floor of a weatherworn former apple dryer barn. The several Pinot Noirs here represent a survey of fruit from the Anderson Valley's floor and hillsides, along with some from the Oppenlander Vineyard in nearby Comptche. Hill also makes Chardonnay that finds its way onto local restaurant lists, plus Gewürztraminer and Tempranillo. **TIP→ Picnic tables on the willow-shaded lawn below the tasting room invite lingering.** *5101 Hwy. 128, Philo 707/895–2209 www.phillipshill.com Tastings $10 Closed Tues. and Wed. except by appt.*

Roederer Estate
WINERY/DISTILLERY | The Anderson Valley is particularly hospitable to Pinot Noir and Chardonnay grapes, the two varietals used to create Roederer's sparkling wines. The view of vineyards and rolling hills from the patio is splendid. *4501 Hwy. 128, Philo 707/895–2288 www.roedererestate.com Tastings $10.*

Toulouse Vineyards & Winery
WINERY/DISTILLERY | Especially at sunset the view west across the Anderson Valley from this winery's tasting room and deck is captivating enough to warrant a visit, but the wines here don't disappoint either. Tastings begin with whites that might include Pinot Gris, Riesling, or Gewürztraminer—there's also a rosé of Pinot Noir that sells out quickly each spring—followed by Pinot Noir from estate and sourced fruit and a silky Petite Sirah from inland fruit. Perhaps because the setting is so inspiring, the hosts here are exceptionally chipper. *8001 Hwy. 128, Philo 707/895–2828 www.toulousevineyards.com Tastings $10.*

Restaurants

★ Bewildered Pig
$$$$ | MODERN AMERICAN | Chef Janelle Weaver cooked for seven years at a prestigious appointment-only Napa Valley winery, perfecting skills that serve her well at the low-key yet polished roadside restaurant. Her Mendo-centric menu might include braised short ribs or extraordinary Peking duck breast from a local provider, with luscious miso deviled eggs and the "Brutus" Caesar salad of petite kale, little gems, garlic crumbs, extra anchovies, and a few daggers of serrano chili. **Known for:** miso deviled eggs starter with sparkling wine; phenomenally fresh salads; Sunday brunch from late May to mid-October. *Average main: $32 1810 Hwy. 128, Philo 707/895–2088 www.bewilderedpig.com Closed Jan. and Mon. and Tues. No lunch.*

Hotels

★ The Madrones Guest Quarters
$$$ | B&B/INN | The centerpiece of a 2-acre spread that includes tasting rooms, a gift shop, a spa, and a restaurant, the nine eclectically decorated accommodations here range from apartment-like studios to duplex cottages, some with patios or balconies facing landscaped gardens. **Pros:** location near wineries and Hendy Woods State Park; on-site Stone and Embers restaurant; nearby sister property The Brambles set among redwoods. **Cons:** weekend minimum-stay requirement; pricey on summer weekends; yogurt, cereal, and coffee/tea provided in-room but no breakfast served. *Rooms from: $210 9000 Hwy. 128, Philo 707/895–2955 www.themadrones.com 9 rooms No meals.*

The Philo Apple Farm
$$$$ | HOTEL | Two founders of the renowned Napa Valley restaurant The French Laundry are among the owners of this farm with three inviting cottages and one guest room set in an organic heirloom apple orchard. **Pros:** rustic-contemporary touches in cottages and room; working farm; relaxing back-to-nature experience. **Cons:** occasionally hot in summer; few "activities"; room service only upon request. *Rooms from: $300 18501 Greenwood Rd., Philo 707/895–2333 www.philoapplefarm.com 4 rooms Breakfast.*

Boonville

6 miles east of Philo, 28 miles northwest of Hopland.

At first glance Boonville, population a little more than 1,000, looks pretty much as it has for decades, with the 19th-century Boonville Hotel anchoring the few-blocks downtown and sheep farms and fruit orchards fanning out on either side of Highway 128, albeit with more grapevines these days. The founding of the Anderson Valley Brewing Company in the late 1980s and the revitalization of the hotel by its current owners, the Schmitt family, jump-started the transformation of Boonville into a haven of artisanal food, wine, and beer. Despite this, the town retains its old-school character—listen carefully and you may hear fragments of the academically recognized Boontling argot, which dates to the time when this stretch of the valley was even more isolated.

GETTING HERE AND AROUND

Boonville lies along Highway 128 at its junction with Highway 253. Mendocino Transit Authority (🌐 *mendocinotransit.org*) buses serve the area.

Sights

Anderson Valley Brewing Company

WINERY/DISTILLERY | Brewery tours, tastings in the Tap Room, and 18 holes of disc golf provide a diversified experience at the home of Boont Amber Ale, double and triple Belgian style ales, and other consistent award-winning brews. Local winemakers clear their palates with the Bourbon Barrel Stout, aged in Wild Turkey barrels. ✉ *17700 Hwy. 253, Boonville* ✣ *At Hwy. 128* ☎ *707/895–2337* 🌐 *www.avbc.com* 🎫 *Tastings from $10.*

Artevino Maple Creek Winery

WINERY/DISTILLERY | Chardonnay, Pinot Noir, and Zinfandel are the specialties of this winery whose artist owner, Tom Rodrigues, also makes Merlot, two dessert wines, and the Cowboy Red blend of Zinfandel, Merlot, and Carignane. If the art that adorns Maple Creek labels looks familiar, there's a reason: Tom's also responsible for ones at the Napa Valley's Far Niente and other top wineries. ■ **TIP→ Picnickers are welcome (wines are sold by the glass).** ✉ *20799 Hwy. 128, Yorkville* ✣ *7½ miles southeast of Boonville* ☎ *707/895–3001* 🌐 *www.maplecreekwine.com* 🎫 *Tastings $10.*

Bee Hunter Wine

WINERY/DISTILLERY | Winemaker Andy DuVigneaud of Bee Hunter Wine prefers vineyards close to the ocean because the cool climate requires that grapes stay longer on the vine, preventing them from ripening before their flavors have fully developed. His restrained yet delicious wines, which he pours in a former car repair shop in Boonville, include Sauvignon Blanc, Chardonnay, and a dry and light rosé of Pinot Noir, along with four Pinot Noirs and a Cabernet Sauvignon–Merlot blend. ✉ *14251 Hwy. 128, Boonville* ☎ *707/895–3995* 🌐 *www.beehunterwine.com* 🎫 *Tasting free.*

★ Foursight Wines

WINERY/DISTILLERY | Four generations of the Charles family have farmed the land that produces this winery's vegan-friendly all-estate lineup of Sauvignon Blanc, Semillon, and Pinot Noirs. From 11.5 acres of Pinot Noir, winemaker Joe Webb employs various techniques to produce four very different wines, from the light Zero, aged solely in used oak barrels, to the "richer, riper" Paraboll, its flavors heightened by new French oak. ■ **TIP→ After a tasting, you can picnic outside the casual wood-frame tasting room, enjoying a glass or bottle.** ✉ *14475 Hwy. 128, Boonville* ☎ *707/895–2889* 🌐 *www.foursightwines.com* 🎫 *Tastings $10* ⏲ *Closed Tues. and 3rd wk of June.*

★ Pennyroyal Farm
WINERY/DISTILLERY | FAMILY | At this Boonville ranch with a contemporary barn tasting room you can sample estate Sauvignon Blanc, one of Mendocino's best rosés, and velvety Pinot Noirs, along with cheeses made on the premises from goat and sheep milk. Tours of the farmstead (reservations required) take place year-round in the morning, with afternoon ones from late spring to early fall. The wines, cheeses, pastoral setting, and adorable goats win most guests' hearts. Chefs prepare a few lunch items you can enjoy on the patio in good weather; cheese boards and other snacks are available throughout the day. ✉ *14930 Hwy. 128, Boonville* ☎ *707/895–2410* 🌐 *www.pennyroyalfarm.com* *Tastings from $5, tour $20.*

Restaurants

Lauren's
$$ | AMERICAN | Boonville locals and frequent visitors love Lauren's for its down-home vibe and healthful comfort food—vegetarian and ground-beef burgers, pizzas, pot roast, chicken tostadas, meat loaf, and curry noodle bowls—many of whose ingredients are grown or produced nearby. Chocolate brownie sundaes and (seasonally) apple tarts and honey-baked pears are among the desserts worth a trip on their own. **Known for:** down-home vibe; diverse Mendocino wine selection; trivia nights second and fourth Thursday of the month. *$ Average main: $16* ✉ *14211 Hwy. 128, Boonville* ☎ *707/895–3869* 🌐 *laurensgoodfood.com* *No dinner Sun. (except for occasional pop-ups) and Mon. No lunch Mon.–Wed.*

Mosswood Market Café and Bakery
$ | AMERICAN | Pastries for breakfast; wraps, salads, hot soup, and sandwiches for lunch; and espresso drinks all day make this sweet café in downtown Boonville a fine stop for a quick bite. Order at the counter and enjoy your meal—the oven-roasted turkey and chicken mango wraps and Reuben and albacore tuna sandwiches are among the lunchtime choices—at tables inside or out front. **Known for:** empanadas; Danishes and scones; vegan options. *$ Average main: $12* ✉ *14111 Hwy. 128, Boonville* ☎ *707/895–3635* *No dinner.*

★ Table 128
$$$$ | AMERICAN | This stylishly funky yet rustic restaurant's chef, Perry Hoffman, got his start (at age five) working in the kitchen of the Napa Valley's The French Laundry, which his grandmother founded and later sold to Thomas Keller. As an adult Hoffman made a name for himself at three Wine Country spots before returning to Boonville in 2019 to prepare prix-fixe California farm-to-table cuisine (including a few original French Laundry dishes) at his family's Table 128. **Known for:** many ingredients grown on-site or nearby; fresh oysters and paella on summer Sundays; alfresco dining on patio April–October. *$ Average main: $65* ✉ *Boonville Hotel, 14050 Hwy. 128, Boonville* ☎ *707/895–2210* 🌐 *www.boonvillehotel.com* *Closed Mon.–Thurs. Nov.–Apr., closed Tues. and Wed. May–Oct. No lunch.*

Hotels

Boonville Hotel
$$$ | HOTEL | From the street this looks like a standard small-town hotel with seven freestanding cottages and a two-room, two-story building out back in the garden, but once you cross the threshold you begin to sense the laid-back sophistication that makes the entire Anderson Valley so appealing. **Pros:** stylish but homey; beautiful gardens and grounds; on-site Table 128 restaurant for prix-fixe meals served family style. **Cons:** minimum-stay requirement most weekends; no TVs or phones, no air-conditioning in some rooms; lacks big-hotel amenities. *$ Rooms from: $215* ✉ *14050 Hwy. 128, Boonville* ☎ *707/895–2210* 🌐 *www.boonvillehotel.com* *17 rooms* *Free Breakfast.*

You'll find excellent wines and great places to taste them in the laid-back Anderson Valley.

Hopland

28 miles east of Boonville, 14 miles south of Ukiah, 32 miles north of Healdsburg.

U.S. 101 briefly narrows to one lane in each direction to become Hopland's main drag. For many years a center for the cultivation and drying of beer hops—the source of its name—the small town of Hopland these days is a center of grape growing and wine making and a pleasant stop for a meal or a tasting.

GETTING HERE AND AROUND

Car travelers from Sonoma and Humboldt counties arrive in Hopland via U.S. 101. Highway 253 will get you here from Boonville. Mendocino Transit Authority (🌐 *mendocinotransit.org*) buses serve the area.

VISITOR INFORMATION

Destination Hopland ☎ *707/564–2582* 🌐 *destinationhopland.com.*

Sights

Brutocao Cellars

WINERY/DISTILLERY | With 1,250 acres of vineyards mostly in the Hopland area but also the cooler Anderson Valley, family-owned Brutocao produces Sauvignon Blanc, Zinfandel, Merlot, and Cabernet Sauvignon along with Chardonnay and Pinot Noir. Some of these wines plus ones from Italian varietals like Sangiovese and Primitivo are poured in Hopland's 1923 former high school building, whose outdoor areas have picnic tables and regulation bocce courts. ■ **TIP→ The winery operates a second tasting room in the Anderson Valley town of Philo.** ✉ *13500 S. U.S. 101, Hopland* ☎ *800/433–3689* 🌐 *www.brutocaocellars.com* 🎫 *Tastings free–$10.*

Campovida

WINERY/DISTILLERY | Wines from Italian and Rhône varietals grown in Mendocino County organic, biodynamic, and sustainable vineyards are the focus of Campovida, on a historic 56-acre property whose previous owners include local railroad magnate A.W. Foster and the Fetzer wine-making clan. The white Tocai Friulano and the red Nero d'Avola are among the wines from grapes rarely seen in California, with Sangiovese among the more familiar offerings. **■ TIP→ After a tasting, you can purchase wine by the glass or bottle to enjoy with a picnic amid the landscaped gardens.** ✉ *13601 Old River Rd., Hopland* ✥ *Head east ¾ mile from U.S. 101 on Hwy. 175* ☎ *707/744–8797* 🌐 *www.campovida.com* 🎫 *Tastings $15* 🕓 *Closed Tues. and Wed.*

Graziano Family of Wines
WINERY/DISTILLERY | A winemaker who never met a grape he didn't want to transform in the cellar, Gregory Graziano creates wines for four separate labels, one devoted to Burgundian grapes like Pinot Noir, two to Italian varietals, and the last to Zinfandel, Rhône, and a few other types. The winery's oldest Mendocino County vineyard was planted just before Prohibition by Gregory's grandfather. The lineup poured in the downtown Hopland tasting space might include Pinot Gris and Arneis whites and Dolcetto and Nebbiolo reds. ✉ *13275 S. U.S. 101, Hopland* ☎ *707/744–8466* 🌐 *grazianofamilyofwines.com* 🎫 *Tasting free.*

Saracina Vineyards
WINERY/DISTILLERY | Guests at the contemporary stone and glass tasting room of this boutique winery enjoy views of a landscaped outdoor picnic area and the vineyards beyond. Tastings sometimes begin with a Sauvignon Blanc that helped establish this winery under its original owners, John Fetzer and his wife, Patty Rock. Some of the wine's organic grapes come from California's oldest Sauvignon Blanc vines (1945). The standout reds include Zinfandel, Cabernet Sauvignon, and Malbec. **■ TIP→ Caves are rare in Mendocino, but there's one here you can tour by appointment.** ✉ *11684 S. U.S. 101, Hopland* ☎ *707/ 670–0199* 🌐 *www.saracina.com* 🎫 *Tastings $10, tour free* 🕓 *Closed Mon. and Tues.*

Restaurants

★ Golden Pig
$$ | **AMERICAN** | Grass-fed burgers, pulled-pork and pork-schnitzel sandwiches, and North Coast cod ceviche with house-made tortilla chips are among the popular items this hip-casual restaurant inside a former grocery store serves all day, with bone-in pork chops, rotisserie chicken, and similar plates appearing for dinner. Well-selected breads and buns, crispy fries with the burgers, perfect pickles with the sandwiches, and slivers of fresh ginger in the ceviche elevate the farm-to-table comfort fare, much of it showcasing ingredients from local purveyors. **Known for:** Northern California beers, Mendocino County wines; everything on menu made gluten-free if desired; specialty cocktails. 💲 *Average main: $22* ✉ *13380 U.S. 101, Hopland* ☎ *707/670–6055* 🌐 *www.thegoldenpig.com.*

Hotels

Stock Farm Hopland Restaurant & Boutique Inn
$$$ | **B&B/INN** | Atop the same-named pizzeria and bar, this inn whose owners also operate Campovida winery less than a mile away sits along Hopland's main drag near shops, tasting rooms, and other restaurants. **Pros:** plush rooms with fireplaces, wet bars, whirlpool tubs, refrigerators, and private balconies; two rooms with pullout couches sleep four; pool privileges at adjoining 18-room sister property the 1890s Thatcher Hotel. **Cons:** single-person whirlpool tubs in two rooms; after check-in (at bar), more self-serve than pampering; weekend minimum-stay requirement. 💲 *Rooms from: $220* ✉ *13441 U.S. 101, Hopland* ☎ *707/744–1977* 🌐 *www.stockfarmhopland.com/inn* 🛏 *7 rooms* 🍽 *No meals.*

Ukiah

14 miles north of Hopland, 21 miles northeast of Boonville.

About 16,000 people live in Ukiah, the Mendocino County seat and largest town. Logging and beer hops were two prominent industries starting in the late-19th century and continuing well into the 20th. Grape plantings date to the late 1800s, though many of the head-trained (no trellising) old vines were planted in the early 1900s, when the Italian Swiss Colony expanded from Sonoma County, and during and just after Prohibition. Warmer than the Anderson Valley, the Ukiah area is known for Zinfandel, Cabernet Sauvignon, and other varietals that thrive in high heat. Should you need to cool off, you can repair to the redwoods of Montgomery Woods State Natural Reserve.

GETTING HERE AND AROUND

Ukiah is off U.S. 101; if coming from Boonville, take Highway 253 northeast to U.S. 101 and head north. Mendocino Transit Authority (🌐 *mendocinotransit.org*) buses serve the area.

VISITOR INFORMATION Ukiah Visitor Center ✉ *200 S. School St.* ☎ *707/467–5766* 🌐 *www.visitukiah.com.*

Sights

Montgomery Woods State Natural Reserve
NATIONAL/STATE PARK | Narrow Orr Springs Road winds 13 miles west from Ukiah to this secluded park whose 3-mile loop trail leads to serene old-growth redwood groves. Only the intermittent breezes, rustling of small wildlife, and calls of resident birds punctuate the prehistoric quiet of the most remote one. The reserve (no dogs allowed) is a place like few others in all of California. **■TIP→ From the town of Mendocino you can access the park by taking the Comptche Ukiah Road to Orr Springs Road.** ✉ *15825 Orr Springs Rd., Ukiah* ✣ *13 miles west of N. State St.* ☎ *707/937–5804* 🌐 *www.parks.ca.gov* 🎟 *Free.*

Nelson Family Vineyards
WINERY/DISTILLERY | The grandparents of the current winemaker and his brother, who manages the estate vineyards, moved to Mendocino County in the early 1950s, establishing a ranch just north of Hopland that now encompasses 2,000 acres. About 10% of the land is devoted to grapes, with olive and pear orchards among the other plantings. Tastings, which take place in the living room of the former family home, usually begin with sparkling wine. **■TIP→ A redwood grove steps from the tasting room has picnic tables.** ✉ *550 Nelson Ranch Rd., Ukiah* ☎ *707/462–3755* 🌐 *www.nelsonfamilyvineyards.com* 🎟 *Tastings $5.*

Rivino Winery
WINERY/DISTILLERY | The open-air tasting room and outdoor spaces at Rivino are oriented to maximize the views of the 215-acre estate's vineyard and pond. As with the architecture, owner-winemaker Jason McConnell takes a minimalist approach with his wines, all from grapes grown on-site. The Sangiovese and Sedulous blend of Merlot, Cabernet Sauvignon, and a touch of Viognier stand out, as does the Amber Eve rosé, a brisk seller. **■TIP→ Talented local musicians perform on Wednesday and Friday in the late afternoon and early evening from April through October.** ✉ *4101 Cox Schrader Rd., Ukiah* ✣ *Exit 545 off U.S. 101* ☎ *707/293–4262* 🌐 *www.rivino.com* 🎟 *Tastings from $7.*

★ Testa Vineyards
WINERY/DISTILLERY | This family-owned winery sells most of its grapes—some from vines planted in the 1930s and 1940s—to notable Napa, Sonoma, and Mendocino brands but withholds some of its output for its small label. Winemaker Maria Testa Martinson, whose great-grandparents established Testa Ranch in 1912, makes Charbono, Carignane, Petite Sirah, Zinfandel, Cabernet

Sauvignon, and other reds from grapes grown on the estate, with a few whites from outside sources. Tastings take place in a spiffed-up former chicken coop with views of a pond and rolling vineyards. On sunny days you can enjoy at tasting on the patio outside. ✉ *6400 N. State St., Calpella* ☎ *707/485–7051* 🌐 *testaranch.com* *Tastings $5* 🕒 *Closed Mon.–Thurs. except by appt.*

Restaurants

Cultivo

$$ | **AMERICAN** | An oasis of low-key sophistication in downtown Ukiah, Cultivo is known for inventive wood-fired pizzas (try the braised-duck or wild-boar-sausage pie or go meatless with one starring trumpet mushrooms) but also plates up oysters on the half shell, fish tacos, a kale Caesar salad (sourdough croutons make it work), quinoa risotto, and a heritage pork chop. Meals are served on thick wooden tables in the downstairs bar area and in the mezzanine; there's also sidewalk dining out front. **Known for:** something for everyone; California beers on tap; gluten-free options. $ *Average main: $19* ✉ *108 W. Standley St., Ukiah* ☎ *707/462–7007* 🌐 *cultivorestaurant.com* 🕒 *Closed Sun.*

Hotels

Vichy Springs Resort

$$$ | **RESORT** | The cottages and multiunit one-story buildings of this historic hot-springs resort—luminaries from Ulysses S. Grant to Nancy Pelosi have unwound here—surround a broad lawn shaded by mature manzanitas and oaks. **Pros:** rural solitude; naturally carbonated hot springs; some accommodations have full kitchens. **Cons:** pool is only heated part of the year; not a pampering-type spa; noise from nearby gun range. $ *Rooms from: $245* ✉ *2605 Vichy Springs Rd., Ukiah* ☎ *707/462–9515* 🌐 *www.vichysprings.com* *26 rooms* *Free Breakfast.*

Weott

86 miles northeast of Fort Bragg, 46 miles south of Eureka.

Conservationists banded together a century ago as the Save the Redwoods League and scored a crucial victory when a memorial grove was dedicated in 1921. That grove is now part of Humboldt Redwoods State Park. Headquartered in the town of Weott, the park these days has grown to nearly 53,000 acres, about a third of which are filled with untouched old-growth coast redwoods.

GETTING HERE AND AROUND

Access the park's visitor center off U.S. 101. Southern Humboldt Intercity (🌐 *hta.org*) buses serve the area.

Sights

★ Avenue of the Giants

NATIONAL/STATE PARK | **FAMILY** | Some of the tallest trees on Earth tower over this magnificent 32-mile stretch of two-lane blacktop, also known as Highway 254, that follows the south fork of the Eel River through Humboldt Redwoods State Park. The highway runs more or less parallel to U.S. 101 from Phillipsville in the south to the town of Pepperwood in the north. A brochure available at either end of the highway or the **visitor center,** 2 miles south of Weott, contains a self-guided tour, with short and long hikes through various redwood groves. A trail at **Founders Grove** passes by several impressive trees, among them the fallen 362-foot-long Dyerville Giant, whose root base points skyward 35 feet. The tree can be reached via a short trail that begins 4 miles north of the visitor center. About 6 miles north of the center lies **Rockefeller Forest.** The largest remaining old-growth coast redwood forest, it contains more than a third of the 100 tallest trees in the world. ✉ *Humboldt Redwoods State Park Visitor Center, 17119 Ave. of the Giants, Weott*

☎ *707/946–2263* 🌐 *www.parks.ca.gov/humboldtredwoods* 🎫 *Free; $8 day-use fee for Williams Grove.*

Briceland Vineyards
WINERY/DISTILLERY | Lean yet flavorful Humboldt County Pinot Noirs are the specialty of this winery set amid the trees. In good weather the delightfully low-key tastings take place in front of the weathered original winery building. Guests sip Gewürztraminer (surprisingly dry), Viognier, or other whites before sampling Pinots and perhaps Syrah or Zinfandel. ■ **TIP→ From late May through August drop-ins are welcome 1–5 on weekends; otherwise tastings are by appointment.** ✉ *5959 Briceland Rd., 10½ miles southwest of Ave. of the Giants southern entrance* ✣ *Take Briceland Rd. 5½ miles west from Redwood Dr. in Redway (from north, U.S. 101 Exit 642; from south, Exit 639B)* ☎ *707/923–2429* 🌐 *bricelandvineyards.com* 🎫 *Tastings $15.*

Ferndale

35 miles northwest of Weott, 19 miles south of Eureka.

Ferndale, best known for its colorful Victorian architecture, much of it Stick-Eastlake style, is worth the 5-mile detour off U.S. 101. Many shops carry a self-guided tour map that highlights the most interesting historic buildings. Gift shops and ice-cream stores comprise a fair share of the businesses here, but Ferndale remains a fully functioning small town, and descendants of the Portuguese and Scandinavian dairy farmers who settled here continue to raise dairy cows in the surrounding pastures.

GETTING HERE AND AROUND

To get to Ferndale from U.S. 101, follow Highway 211 southwest 5 miles. Public transit doesn't serve the town.

Sights

Ferndale Historic Cemetery
CEMETERY | The well-worn gravestones at Ferndale's east-side cemetery provide insight into the hard, often short lives of the European immigrants who cultivated this area in the mid-18th century. At the top of the hill, sweeping (and photogenic) vistas unfold of the town, its farms, and the ocean. ✉ *Craig St. and Berding St.* 🎫 *Free.*

Ferndale Museum
MUSEUM | The main building of this museum exhibits Victoriana and historical photographs and has a display of an old-style barbershop and another of Wiyot Indian baskets. In the annex are a horse-drawn buggy, a re-created blacksmith's shop, and antique farming, fishing, and dairy equipment. Don't miss the Bosch-Omori seismograph, installed in 1933 in Ferndale; it's still checked daily for recordings of earthquake activity. ✉ *515 Shaw Ave.* ☎ *707/786–4466* 🌐 *www.ferndale-museum.org* 🎫 *$2* ⏲ *Closed Mon. and Tues.*

Lost Coast Scenic Drive
SCENIC DRIVE | A loop drive counterclockwise from Ferndale yields amazing ocean views and winds through forests and small towns before heading into Humboldt Redwoods State Park and then back up U.S. 101 toward the starting point. The road has numerous curves and some rugged stretches in need of repair, but driving this 100-or-so-mile stretch is exhilarating. ■ **TIP→ Allot four hours for this excursion.** ✉ *Ferndale* ✣ *Head southwest from Ferndale on Wildcat Ave., which soon becomes Mattole Rd. Follow Mattole west to the coast, south to Petrolia, and east to Honeydew and the park. At U.S. 101 head north back toward Ferndale.* 🌐 *visitredwoods.com/listing/lost-coast-scenic-drive/148.*

Gingerbread Mansion
$$ | **B&B/INN** | A dazzler that rivals San Francisco's "painted ladies," this Victorian mansion has detailed exterior spindle work, turrets, and gables. **Pros:** elegant decor; relaxing atmosphere; friendly staff. **Cons:** some may find the place gaudy; two-night minimum on weekends; lacks standard hotel amenities. *Rooms from: $165* ✉ *400 Berding St.* ☎ *707/786–4000* 🌐 *www.gingerbread-mansion.com* *11 rooms* *Free Breakfast.*

Blacksmith Shop
HOUSEHOLD ITEMS/FURNITURE | With two storefronts in Ferndale, this shop celebrates the survival of traditional blacksmithing arts in the area. The hand-forged works sold here range from flatware to furniture. The rough-handled chef's knives are so sharp there are Band-Aids behind the display, just in case. ✉ *455 and 491 Main St.* ☎ *707/786–4216* 🌐 *www.ferndaleblacksmith.com.*

Eureka

19 miles north of Ferndale.

With a population of 27,200, Eureka is the North Coast's largest city, a good place to fuel up, buy groceries, and learn a little about the region's mining, timber, and fishing pasts. The chamber of commerce visitor center has maps of self-guided driving tours of the town's nearly 100 Victorians, among them the flamboyant 1886 Queen Anne–style **Carson Mansion,** at 143 M Street. The home can only be viewed from outside, but it's worth a look and a photo or two. Art galleries and antiques stores liven up the district from C to I Street between 2nd and 3rd streets, and a walking pier extends into the harbor.

GETTING HERE AND AROUND

U.S. 101 travels through Eureka. Eureka Transit (🌐 *www.eurekatransit.org*) buses serve the town.

VISITOR CENTER

Eureka Chamber of Commerce ✉ *2112 Broadway* ☎ *707/442–3738* 🌐 *www.eurekachamber.com.*

Blue Ox Millworks
FACTORY | This wood-shop is among a handful in the country specializing in Victorian-era architecture, but what makes it truly unique is that its craftspeople use antique tools to do the work. Visitors can watch artisans use printing presses, lathes, and other equipment to create gingerbread trim, fence pickets, and other signature Victorian embellishments. The shop is less interesting on Saturday, when most craftspeople take the day off. ✉ *1 X St.* ☎ *707/444–3437, 800/248–4259* 🌐 *www.blueoxmill.com* *$12* *Closed Sat. Dec.–Mar., Sun. yr-round.*

Clarke Historical Museum
MUSEUM | The Native American Wing of this museum contains a beautiful collection of northwestern California basketry. Artifacts from Eureka's Victorian, logging, and maritime eras fill the rest of the space. ✉ *240 E St.* ☎ *707/443–1947* 🌐 *www.clarkemuseum.org* *$5* *Closed Mon.*

★ Brick & Fire Bistro
$$ | **MODERN AMERICAN** | Just about every seat in the darkly lighted, urbane dining room has a view of this downtown bistro's most important feature, a wood-fired brick oven used to prepare everything from roasted local Kumamoto oysters to a wild-mushroom cobbler topped with a cheesy biscuit—even the "fries," char-roasted potatoes tossed

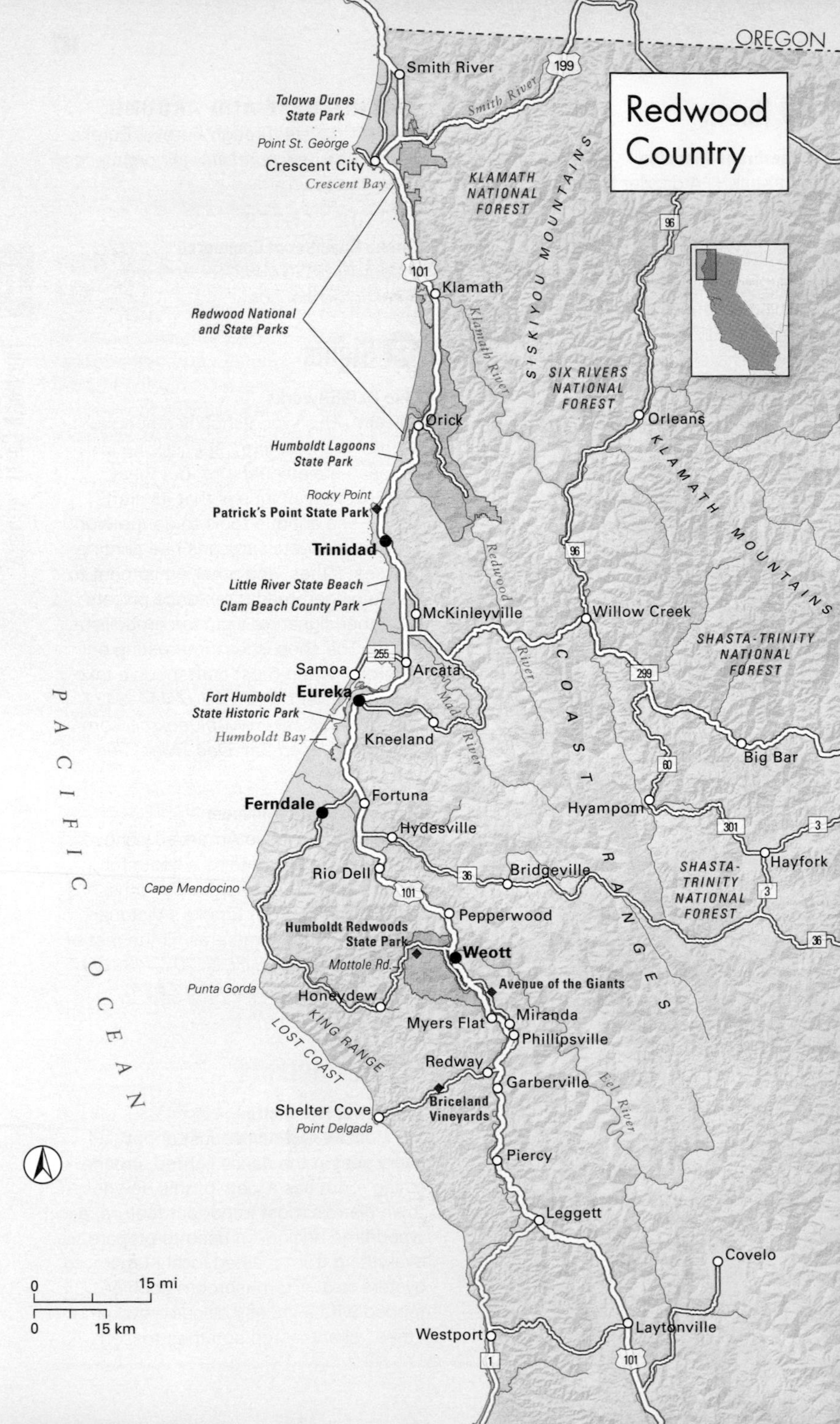

Redwood Country
OREGON
Smith River
199
Smith River
Tolowa Dunes State Park
Point St. George
Crescent City
Crescent Bay
KLAMATH NATIONAL FOREST
SISKIYOU MOUNTAINS
96
101
Klamath
Klamath River
Redwood National and State Parks
SIX RIVERS NATIONAL FOREST
Orleans
Orick
Humboldt Lagoons State Park
KLAMATH MOUNTAINS
Rocky Point
Patrick's Point State Park
Trinidad
Redwood
Little River State Beach
Clam Beach County Park
McKinleyville
Willow Creek
255
Samoa
Arcata
COAST RANGES
SHASTA-TRINITY NATIONAL FOREST
299
Eureka
Fort Humboldt State Historic Park
Mad River
Humboldt Bay
Kneeland
Big Bar
60
PACIFIC OCEAN
Fortuna
Ferndale
Hyampom
301
3
Hydesville
Hayfork
Rio Dell
36
Bridgeville
Cape Mendocino
101
Pepperwood
SHASTA-TRINITY NATIONAL FOREST
Humboldt Redwoods State Park
Weott
Mottole Rd.
Avenue of the Giants
Punta Gorda
Honeydew
Miranda
KING RANGE
LOST COAST
Myers Flat
Phillipsville
Redway
Garberville
Eel River
Briceland Vineyards
Shelter Cove
Point Delgada
Piercy
Leggett
Covelo
0
15 mi
0
15 km
Laytonville
Westport
1
101

in olive oil and spices, come out of the oven. Creatively topped pizzas, sandwiches, and grilled meats and seafood round out the menu. **Known for:** house-made sausage pizzas; eggplant, brisket, and other sandwich fillings char-grilled in a wood-fired oven; house-made ginger ale. *Average main: $19 1630 F St. 707/268–8959 www.brickandfire-bistro.com Closed Tues. No lunch weekends.*

Lost Coast Brewery and Cafe
$ | **AMERICAN** | This bustling microbrewery with surf-tropical decor accents is the best place in town to relax with a pint of ale or porter. Soups and salads, plus burgers, tacos, and light meals are served for lunch and dinner. **Known for:** outstanding beers; happy hour weekdays 4–6; brewery tours. *Average main: $14 617 4th St. 707/445–4480 www.lostcoast.com.*

Samoa Cookhouse
$$ | **AMERICAN** | **FAMILY** | Waiters at this former cafeteria for local mill workers deliver family-style bowls—whatever is being served at the meal you've arrived for—to long, communal tables. For breakfast that means eggs, sausage, biscuits and gravy, and the like; lunch and dinner usually feature soup, potatoes, salad, and pie, plus daily-changing entrées such as pot roast and pork loin. **Known for:** hearty meals for carnivores; blast from the logging past atmosphere; museum in back. *Average main: $18 908 Vance Ave., near Cookhouse Rd., Samoa 707/442–1659 www.samoacookhouse.net.*

Hotels

★ Carter House Inns
$$$ | **HOTEL** | Richly painted and aglow with wood detailing, the rooms, in two main Victorian buildings and several historic cottages, contain a mix of modern and antique furnishings; some have whirlpool tubs and separate sitting areas. **Pros:** elegant ambience; every detail in place; on-site Restaurant 301 ranks among town's best dining spots. **Cons:** not suitable for children; restaurant is a bit pricey; two-night minimum on weekends. *Rooms from: $199 301 L St. 707/444–8062, 800/404–1390 www.carterhouse.com 32 rooms Breakfast.*

Activities

Humboats Kayak Adventures
KAYAKING | You can rent kayaks and book kayaking tours that from December to June include whale-watching trips. Half-day river kayaking trips pass beneath massive redwoods; the whale-watching outings get you close enough for good photos. *Woodley Island Marina, 601 Startare Dr., Dock A 707/443–5157 www.humboats.com From $30 rentals, $55 tours.*

Trinidad

23 miles north of Eureka.

A mellow base for exploring the southern portion of Redwood National Park, coastal Trinidad got its name from the Spanish mariners who entered the bay on Trinity Sunday, June 9, 1775. Formerly the principal trading post for mining camps along the Klamath and Trinity rivers, these days Trinidad is a quiet and genuinely charming community with several beaches and ample sights and activities to entertain low-key visitors.

GETTING HERE AND AROUND

Trinidad sits right off U.S. 101. From Interstate 5, head west from Redding on Highway 299 and north on U.S. 101 north of Arcata. Redwood Transit System (*www.redwoodtransit.org*) provides bus service.

Patrick's Point State Park

NATIONAL/STATE PARK | On a forested plateau almost 200 feet above the surf, the park has stunning views of the Pacific, great whale- and sea lion–watching spots, campgrounds, picnic areas, bike paths, and hiking trails through old-growth spruce forest. There are also tidal pools at Agate Beach, a re-created Yurok Indian village, and a small visitor center with exhibits. It's uncrowded and sublimely quiet here. Dogs are not allowed on trails or the beach. ✉ *4150 Patrick's Point Dr.* ✣ *Off U.S. 101, 5 miles north of town* ☎ *707/677–3570* 🌐 *www.parks.ca.gov* 🎫 *$8 per vehicle.*

 Beaches

Clam Beach County Park and Little River State Beach

BEACH—SIGHT | **FAMILY** | These two adjoining oceanfront areas stretch for several miles south of Trinidad. The sandy beach here is exceptionally wide. Beachcombing and savoring fabulous sunsets are favorite activities. The two parks share day-use facilities. **Amenities:** parking; toilets. **Best for:** solitude; sunset; walking. ✉ *Clam Beach Dr. and U.S. 101, 6 miles south of Trinidad* ☎ *707/445–7651* 🌐 *www.parks.ca.gov* 🎫 *Free (day use).*

 Restaurants

★ Larrupin' Cafe

$$$$ | **AMERICAN** | Set in a two-story house on a quiet country road north of town, this restaurant—one of the best places to eat on the North Coast—is often thronged with people enjoying fresh seafood, Cornish game hen, mesquite-grilled ribs, and vegetarian dishes. The garden setting and candlelight stir thoughts of romance. **Known for:** garden setting; outside patio; smoked beef brisket. Ⓢ *Average main: $31* ✉ *1658 Patrick's Point Dr.* ☎ *707/677–0230* 🌐 *www.larrupin.com* ⏲ *No lunch.*

Trinidad Bay Bed and Breakfast Inn

$$$ | **B&B/INN** | Staying at this small Cape Cod–style inn perched above Trinidad Bay is like spending the weekend at a friend's vacation house. **Pros:** great location above bay; lots of light; tall windows in Tidepool room. **Cons:** main house can feel crowded at full occupancy; expensive in summer; two-night minimum on weekends. Ⓢ *Rooms from: $225* ✉ *560 Edwards St.* ☎ *707/677–0840* 🌐 *www.trinidadbaybnb.com* *4 rooms* *Free Breakfast.*

Turtle Rocks Oceanfront Inn

$$$$ | **B&B/INN** | This comfortable inn has the best view in Trinidad, with the ocean and sunning sea lions seen from private, glassed-in decks in each room. **Pros:** great ocean views; comfortable king beds; surrounding landscape left natural and wild. **Cons:** no businesses within walking distance; interiors may be too spare for some guests; can be foggy here in summer. Ⓢ *Rooms from: $280* ✉ *3392 Patrick's Point Dr., 4½ miles north of town* ☎ *707/677–3707* 🌐 *www.turtlerocksinn.com* *6 rooms* *Free Breakfast.*

Chapter 12

SACRAMENTO AND THE GOLD COUNTRY

Updated by
Daniel Mangin

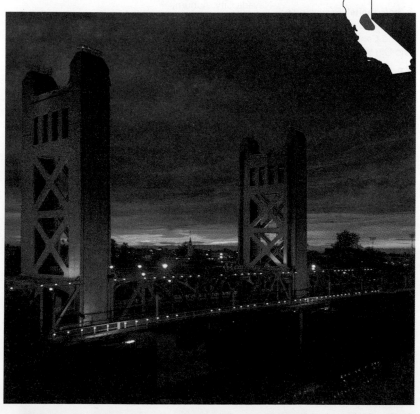

Sights ★★★★☆

Restaurants ★★★★☆

Hotels ★★★★☆

Shopping ★★★☆☆

Nightlife ★★★☆☆

WELCOME TO SACRAMENTO AND THE GOLD COUNTRY

TOP REASONS TO GO

★ **Gold rush:** Marshall Gold Discovery State Park is where it all started—it's a must-see—but there are historic and modern gems all along California Highway 49 from Nevada City to Mariposa.

★ **State capital:** Easygoing Sacramento offers sights like the Capitol and historic Old Sacramento.

★ **Bon appétit:** Sacramento has emerged as a foodie destination in the past decade, but its celebrations of food, drink, and culture date back to the gold-rush parade of immigrants.

★ **Wine tasting:** With bucolic scenery and friendly tasting rooms, the Gold Country's Shenandoah Valley has become an acclaimed wine-making region, specializing in Zinfandel.

★ **Rivers, sequoias, and caverns:** Natural beauty here is rich (stream beds are still lined with gold), high (sequoias in Calaveras Big Trees State Park), and deep (Moaning Cavern's main chamber is big enough to hold the Statue of Liberty).

The Gold Country is a large rural destination popular with those seeking a reasonably priced escape from Southern California and the Bay Area. Sacramento and Davis are in an enormous valley just west of the Sierra Nevada range. Foothill communities Nevada City, Auburn, Placerville, and Sutter Creek were products of the gold rush, and remain popular stopovers with travelers en route to Lake Tahoe.

1 **Sacramento.**

2 **Woodland.**

3 **Davis.**

4 **Lodi.**

5 **Nevada City.**

6 **Grass Valley.**

7 **Auburn.**

8 **Coloma.**

9 **Placerville.**

10 **Plymouth.**

11 **Amador City.**

12 **Sutter Creek.**

13 **Volcano.**

14 **Jackson.**

15 **Angels Camp.**

16 **Murphys.**

17 **Columbia.**

18 **Sonora.**

19 **Jamestown.**

20 **Mariposa.**

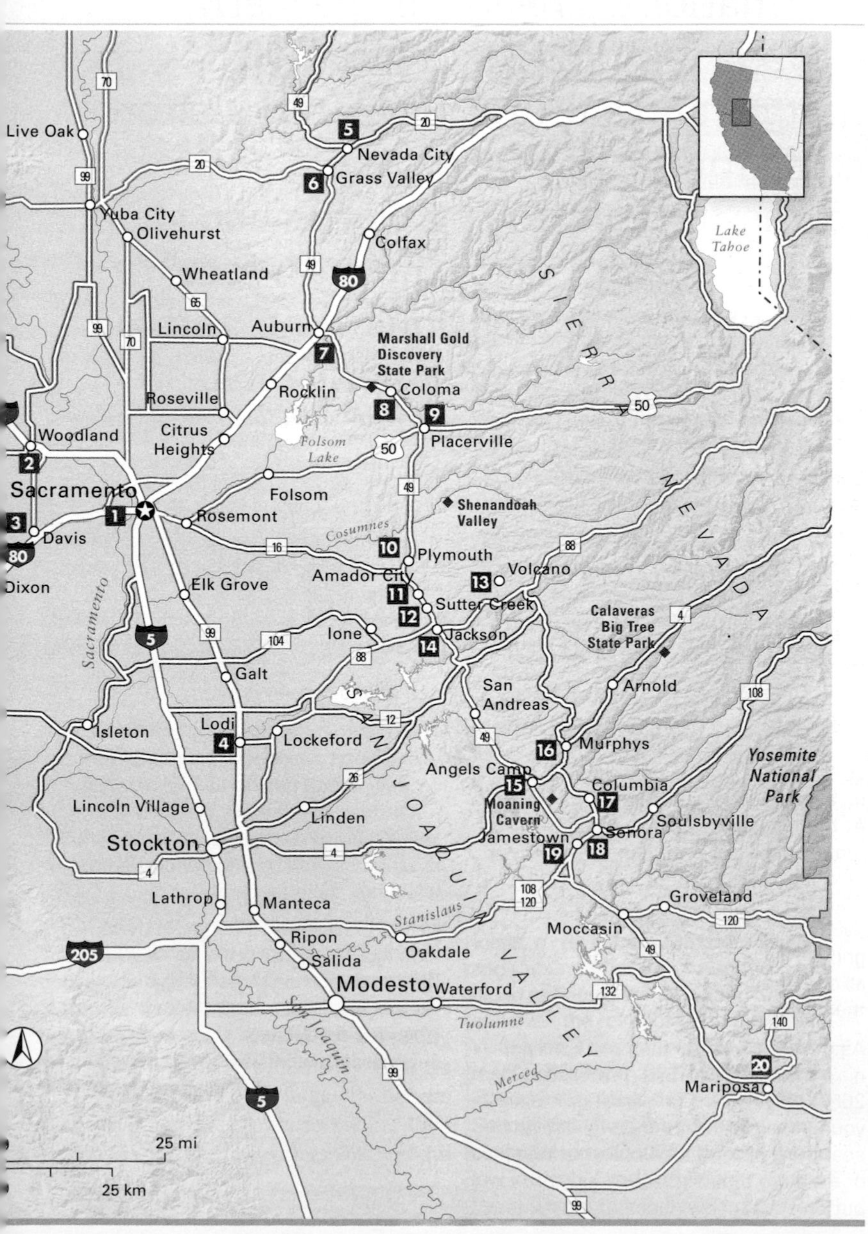
Live Oak
Yuba City
Olivehurst
Wheatland
Lincoln
Auburn
Roseville
Citrus Heights
Rocklin
Woodland
Sacramento
Davis
Dixon
Rosemont
Folsom
Folsom Lake
Elk Grove
Galt
Isleton
Lodi
Lockeford
Lincoln Village
Stockton
Lathrop
Manteca
Ripon
Salida
Modesto
Waterford
Oakdale
Linden
Ione
Jackson
Sutter Creek
Amador City
Plymouth
Volcano
Cosumnes
Shenandoah Valley
Placerville
Coloma
Marshall Gold Discovery State Park
Colfax
Nevada City
Grass Valley
Lake Tahoe
SIERRA NEVADA
SAN JOAQUIN VALLEY
Calaveras Big Tree State Park
Arnold
San Andreas
Murphys
Angels Camp
Moaning Cavern
Columbia
Jamestown
Sonora
Soulsbyville
Yosemite National Park
Groveland
Moccasin
Mariposa
Sacramento
San Joaquin
Stanislaus
Tuolumne
Merced
1
2
3
4
5
6
7
8
9
10
11
12
13
14
15
16
17
18
19
20
25 mi
25 km

The Gold Country is one of California's less expensive and more sublime destinations, a region of the Sierra Nevada foothills that's filled with natural and cultural pleasures. Visitors come for the boomtowns and ghost towns; to explore art galleries and shop for antiques; to savor "farm-to-fork" restaurants and delicious wine; and to rest at friendly, atmospheric inns.

Spring brings wildflowers, and in fall the hills are colored by bright red berries and changing leaves. Because it offers plenty of outdoor diversions, the Gold Country is a great place to take kids. Sacramento is an ethnically diverse city, with sizable Mexican, Hmong, and Ukrainian populations, among many others. Many present-day immigrants are relatively recent arrivals, but the capital city has absorbed several waves of newcomers since 1848, when James Marshall turned up a gold nugget in the American River. At the time, Mexico and the United States were still wrestling for ownership of what would become the Golden State. Marshall's discovery provided the incentive for the United States to tighten its grip on the region, and prospectors from all over the world soon came to seek their fortunes in the Mother Lode.

As gold fever seized the nation, California's population of 15,000 swelled to 265,000 within three years. The mostly young, male adventurers who arrived in search of gold—the '49ers—became part of a culture that discarded many of the button-down conventions of the eastern states. It was also a violent time. Yankee prospectors chased Mexican miners off their claims, and California's leaders initiated a plan to exterminate the local Native American population. Bounties were paid, and private militias were hired to wipe out the Native Americans or sell them into slavery. California was to be dominated by the Anglo.

The gold-rush boom lasted scarcely 20 years, but it changed California forever, producing 546 mining towns, of which fewer than 250 remain. The hills of the Gold Country were alive, not only with prospecting and mining but also with business, the arts, gambling, and a fair share of crime. Opera houses went up alongside brothels, and the California State Capitol, in Sacramento, was built partly with the gold dug out of the hills.

MAJOR REGIONS

Sacramento and Nearby. The gateway to the Gold Country, the seat of state government, and an agricultural hub, Sacramento plays many important contemporary roles. About 2½ million people live in the metropolitan area, which offers up more sunshine and lower prices than coastal California. The Sacramento area's mild climate and fertile soil are responsible for the region's current riches: fresh and bountiful food and high-quality wines. There's a growing local craft-beer scene, too. Visits to Sacramento and nearby towns like Woodland and Davis provide the broad agricultural perspective, Lodi the wine-making one. Wineries here earn national acclaim, yet they're without the high prices of Napa and Sonoma.

The Gold Country—South. South of its junction with U.S. 50, Highway 49 traces in asphalt the famed Mother Lode. The peppy former gold-rush towns strung along the road have for the most part been restored, many with money from a modern-day boom in vineyards and wineries.

The Gold Country—North. Old Sacramento's museums provide an excellent introduction to the Gold Country's illustrious history, but the region's heart lies along Highway 49, which winds the approximately 300-mile north–south length of the historic mining area past or near (from north to south) the following towns: Nevada City, Grass Valley, Auburn, Coloma, Placerville, Plymouth, Amador City, Sutter Creek, Jackson, Angels Camp, Murphys, Columbia, Sonora, Jamestown, and Mariposa. Some can be explored as easy day trips from Sacramento, but to immerse yourself in this storied setting, consider staying overnight at least a day or two, especially if you'll be stopping at the many wineries of the Sierra Foothills appellation. On days when it's not too hot or cold, the highway—a hilly, often twisting two-lane road—begs for a convertible with the top down.

Planning

When to Go

The Gold Country is most pleasant in spring, when the wildflowers are in bloom, and in fall. Summers can be hot in the valley (temperatures of 100°F are fairly common), so head for the hills. Sacramento winters tend to be cool, with occasionally foggy or rainy days. Throughout the year Gold Country towns stage community and cultural celebrations. In December many towns are decked out for Christmas.

Getting Here and Around

AIR TRAVEL

Sacramento International Airport (SMF) is served by Aeromexico, Air Canada, Alaska/Horizon, American, Delta, Frontier, Hawaiian, JetBlue, Southwest, United, and Volaris. A taxi from the airport to Downtown Sacramento costs about $40, but services like Lyft and Uber often cost much less. The Super Shuttle fare starts at $15. Public buses *(see Bus and Light-Rail Travel)* are also an option.

CONTACTS Sacramento International Airport ✉ *6900 Airport Blvd., Sacramento* ✣ *12 miles northwest of Downtown off I–5* ☎ *916/929–5411* 🌐 *www.sacramento.aero/smf.* **Super Shuttle** ☎ *800/258–3826* 🌐 *www.supershuttle.com.*

BUS AND LIGHT-RAIL TRAVEL

Greyhound serves Sacramento from San Francisco and Los Angeles. Sacramento Regional Transit serves the capital area with buses and light-rail vehicles. Yolobus public buses Nos. 42A and 42B connect SMF airport and Downtown Sacramento, West Sacramento, Davis, and Woodland.

CONTACTS Greyhound ✉ *420 Richards Blvd.* ☎ *916/444–6858* 🌐 *www.greyhound.com.* **Sacramento Regional Transit** ☎ *916/321–2877* 🌐 *www.sacrt.com.*

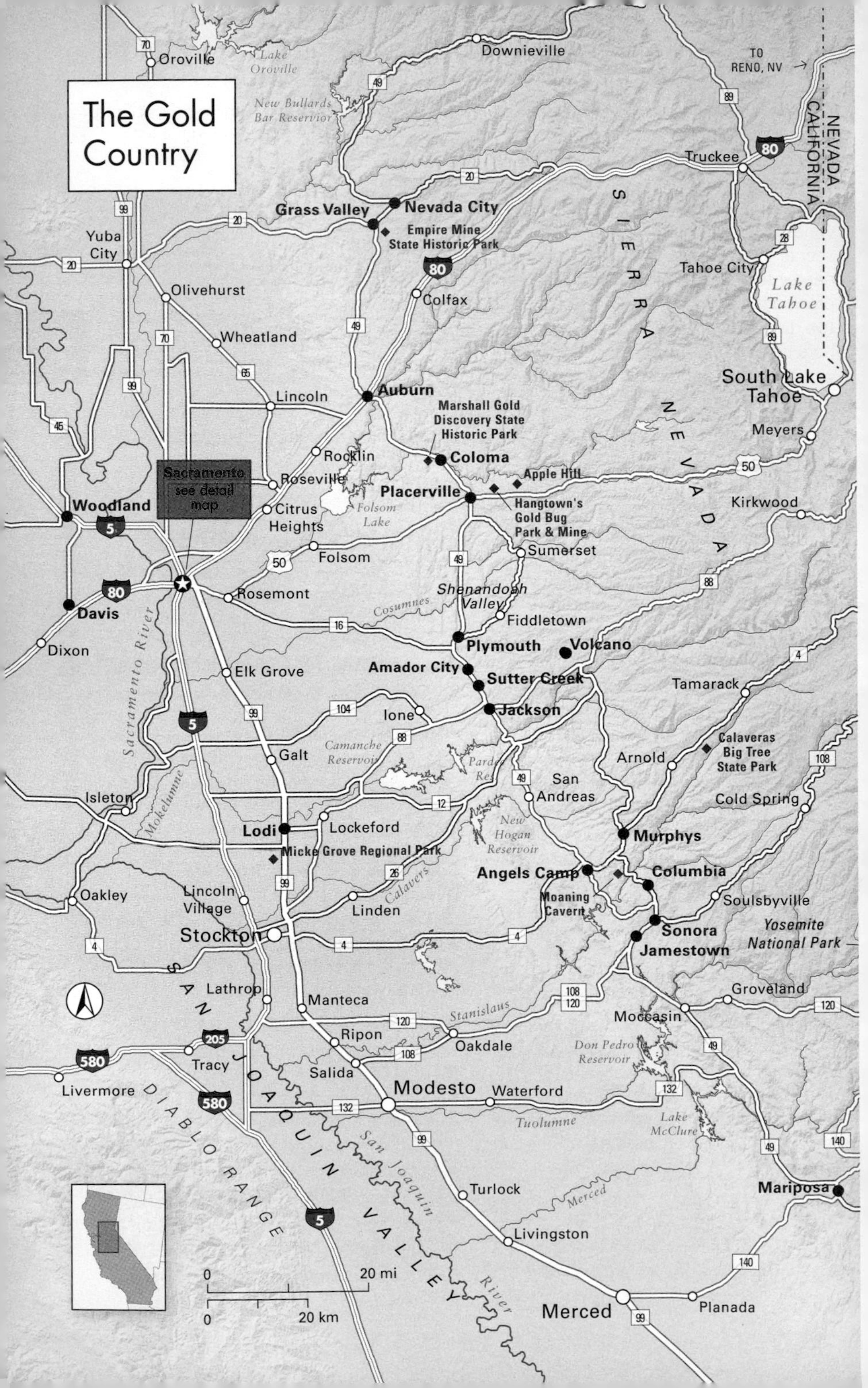

The Gold Country
Sacramento see detail map
Oroville
Lake Oroville
New Bullards Bar Reservior
Downieville
TO RENO, NV
NEVADA
CALIFORNIA
Truckee
Grass Valley
Nevada City
Empire Mine State Historic Park
SIERRA NEVADA
Yuba City
Olivehurst
Wheatland
Colfax
Tahoe City
Lake Tahoe
South Lake Tahoe
Auburn
Lincoln
Marshall Gold Discovery State Historic Park
Meyers
Rocklin
Coloma
Roseville
Apple Hill
Placerville
Woodland
Citrus Heights
Folsom Lake
Hangtown's Gold Bug Park & Mine
Kirkwood
Folsom
Sumerset
Rosemont
Shenandoah Valley
Davis
Cosumnes
Fiddletown
Dixon
Plymouth
Volcano
Sacramento River
Elk Grove
Amador City
Sutter Creek
Tamarack
Jackson
Ione
Calaveras Big Tree State Park
Galt
Camanche Reservoir
Arnold
San Andreas
Isleton
Cold Spring
Mokelumne
New Hogan Reservoir
Lodi
Lockeford
Murphys
Micke Grove Regional Park
Angels Camp
Columbia
Oakley
Lincoln Village
Calavers
Moaning Cavern
Soulsbyville
Linden
Sonora
Yosemite National Park
Stockton
Jamestown
SAN JOAQUIN VALLEY
Lathrop
Manteca
Groveland
Stanislaus
Moccasin
Ripon
Oakdale
Don Pedro Reservoir
Tracy
Salida
Livermore
DIABLO RANGE
Modesto
Waterford
Tuolumne
Lake McClure
San Joaquin
Turlock
Mariposa
Merced
Livingston
River
0
20 mi
0
20 km
Merced
Planada

Yolobus ☎ *530/666–2877, 916/371–2877* 🌐 *www.yolobus.com.*

CAR TRAVEL

Interstate 5 (north–south) and Interstate 80 (east–west) are the two main routes into and out of Sacramento. From Sacramento, three highways fan out toward the east, all intersecting with historic Highway 49: Interstate 80 heads northeast 34 miles to Auburn; U.S. 50 goes east 40 miles to Placerville; and Highway 16 angles southeast 45 miles to Plymouth. Two-lane Highway 49, one of America's great drives, winds and climbs through the foothills and valleys, linking the principal Gold Country towns. Traveling by car is the only practical way to explore the Gold Country.

TRAIN TRAVEL

On the Amtrak *California Zephyr,* you can ride the same route traveled by prospectors in the late 1800s. Amtrak trains also serve Sacramento and Davis from the Bay Area.

CONTACTS Amtrak ✉ *401 I St.* ☎ *800/872–7245* 🌐 *www.amtrak.com.*

Restaurants

American, Italian, Chinese, and Mexican are common Gold Country fare, but chefs also prepare ambitious European, French, and contemporary regional cuisine based on seasonal local ingredients. Although fewer places make them these days, Grass Valley's meat- and vegetable-stuffed *pasties,* introduced by 19th-century gold miners from Cornwall, England, are one of the region's more unusual treats.

Hotels

Sacramento has plenty of full-service hotels, budget motels, and small inns. Larger towns along Highway 49—among them Auburn, Grass Valley, and Jackson—have chain motels and inns. Many Gold Country bed-and-breakfasts occupy former mansions, miners' cabins, and other historic buildings. *Hotel reviews have been shortened. For full information, visit Fodors.com.*

Visitor Information

EVENTS AND ENTERTAINMENT Sacramento 365 🌐 *www.sacramento365.com.*

TOURISM AGENCIES Amador County Chamber of Commerce & Visitors Bureau ✉ *115 Main St., Jackson* ☎ *209/223–0350* 🌐 *amadorchamber.com.* **El Dorado County Visitors Authority** ✉ *542 Main St., Placerville* ☎ *530/621–5885* 🌐 *visit-eldorado.com.* **Grass Valley/Nevada County Chamber of Commerce** ✉ *128 E. Main St., Grass Valley* ☎ *530/273–4667* 🌐 *www.grassvalleychamber.com.* **Tuolumne County Visitors Bureau** ✉ *193 S. Washington St., Sonora* ☎ *209/533–4420, 800/446–1333* 🌐 *www.yosemitegoldcountry.com.* **Yosemite Mariposa County Tourism Bureau** ✉ *5065 Hwy. 140, Suite E, Mariposa* ☎ *209/742–4567* 🌐 *www.yosemite.com.*

What It Costs

	$	$$	$$$	$$$$
RESTAURANTS				
	under $16	$16–$22	$23–$30	over $30
HOTELS				
	under $120	$120–$175	$176–$250	over $250

Sacramento

87 miles northeast of San Francisco, 384 miles north of Los Angeles.

All around the Golden State's seat of government you'll experience echoes of the gold-rush days, most notably in Old Sacramento, whose wooden sidewalks and horse-drawn carriages on cobblestone streets lend the waterfront district a 19th-century feel. The California State Railroad Museum and other venues hold artifacts of state and national significance, and historic buildings house shops and restaurants. River cruises and train rides are fun family diversions.

Due east of Old Sacramento is Downtown, where landmarks include the Capitol building and the surrounding Capitol Park. Golden 1 Center, the new sports and concert venue, is part of DOCO, short for Downtown Commons, which also includes shopping, restaurants, hotels, and a grassy and concrete gathering spaces.

Farther east, starting at about 15th Street, lies Midtown, a mix of genteel Victorian edifices, ultramodern lofts, and innovative restaurants and cozy wine bars. The neighborhood springs to life on the second Saturday evening of the month, when art galleries hold open houses. A few intersections are jumping most evenings when the weather's good; they include the corner of 20th and L streets in what's known as Lavender Heights, the center of the city's gay and lesbian community.

GETTING HERE AND AROUND

Most people drive to Sacramento and get around by car. Yellow Cab, Lyft, and Uber are reliable cab options.

Sacramento Regional Transit buses and light-rail vehicles serve the area. Bus 30 links Old Sacramento, Midtown, and Sutter's Fort.

Assuming that traffic is not a factor (though it often is), Sacramento is a 90-minute drive from San Francisco and a seven-hour drive from Los Angeles. Parking garages serve Old Sacramento and other tourist spots; on-street parking in Downtown can be difficult to find.

TRANSPORTATION CONTACTS Sacramento Regional Transit ☎ *916/321–2877* 🌐 *www.sacrt.com.* **Yellow Cab Co. of Sacramento** ☎ *916/444–2222* 🌐 *www.yellowcabsacramento.com.*

ESSENTIALS

VISITOR INFORMATION Old Sacramento Visitor Information Center ✉ *1002 2nd St.* ☎ *916/442–7644* 🌐 *www.oldsacramento.com.* **Sacramento Convention and Visitors Bureau** ✉ *1608 I St., Downtown* ☎ *916/808–7777* 🌐 *www.visitsacramento.com.*

Sights

California Automobile Museum

MUSEUM | More than 150 automobiles—from Model Ts, Hudsons, and Studebakers to modern-day electric-powered ones—are on display at this museum that pays tribute to automotive history and car culture. Check out a replica of Henry Ford's 1896 Quadracycle and a 1920s roadside café and garage exhibit. The docents are ready to explain everything you see. The museum is south of Downtown and Old Sacramento, with ample free parking. ✉ *2200 Front St., Downtown* ☎ *916/442–6802* 🌐 *www.calautomuseum.org* *$10* *Closed Tues.*

California Museum

MUSEUM | **FAMILY** | Showcasing longtime and temporary residents who helped elevate the Golden State, this museum displays artifacts from the State Constitution to surfing magazines. Permanent exhibits cover topics like statehood, the experiences of California Indians, life for Japanese Americans in World War II internment camps, and the impact of women. The California Hall of Fame honors Walt Disney, Jackie Robinson, Bruce Lee, Amelia Earhart, writer and Sacramento native Joan Didion, and other familiar names. ✉ *1020 O St., at 11th St., Downtown* ☎ *916/653–7524* 🌐 *www.californiamuseum.org* *$9* *Closed Mon.*

★ California State Railroad Museum

MUSEUM | FAMILY | Sprawling over three floors and taking up the equivalent of 2½ acres of space, this museum celebrates the history of trains from their 19th-century English origins and the building of America's transcontinental railroad (Sacramento was its western terminus) to the pre–jet age glory days of rail travel and the high-speed trains in today's Europe and Asia. A permanent exhibit that debuted in 2019 for the 150th anniversary of the transcontinental railroad's completion details the contributions of Chinese laborers, and another section contains a cast gold "Last Spike," one of several spikes issued to commemorate the joining in Utah of the west-to-east Central Pacific and east-to-west Union Pacific lines. Twenty-two of the museum's railroad cars and engines—among them Pullman-style cars and steam locomotives—are on display at any one time, and there are interactive displays and a play area for kids. The exhibits of toy trains delight youngsters and adults. ✉ *125 I St., at 2nd St., Old Sacramento* ☎ *916/323–9280* 🌐 *www.csrmf.org* 🎟 *$12.*

★ Capitol

GOVERNMENT BUILDING | Built in 1869 and topped by a 128-foot gilded dome, the Capitol functions as both a working museum and the active seat of California's government. Wander freely by reproductions of century-old state offices and into legislative chambers (in session from January to September) decorated in the style of the 1890s. Look for the abstract portrait of Edmund G. "Jerry" Brown, alongside those of fellow former governors Ronald Reagan (who succeeded Brown's father, Edmund G. "Pat" Brown) and Arnold Schwarzenegger. Guides conduct tours of the building and the 40-acre Capitol Park, which contains a rose garden, a fragrant display of camellias (Sacramento's city flower), and California Veterans Memorials. ■ **TIP→ The Capitol's diverse trees include more than 1,000 trees from around the world.** ✉ *10th St. and L St., Downtown* ☎ *916/324–0333* 🌐 *capitolmuseum.ca.gov* 🎟 *Free.*

Central Pacific Railroad Passenger Station

TRANSPORTATION SITE (AIRPORT/BUS/FERRY/TRAIN) | FAMILY | At this reconstructed 1876 depot there's rolling stock to admire and a typical waiting room. Part of the year a train departs from the freight depot, south of the passenger station, making a 45-minute out-and-back trip that starts along the banks of the Sacramento River. ■ **TIP→ Cookies and hot chocolate are served aboard sellout Polar Express rides between Thanksgiving and Christmas that include appearances by characters from the famous story.** ✉ *930 Front St., at J St., Old Sacramento* ☎ *916/445–5995* 🌐 *www.csrmf.org/events/train-rides* 🎟 *Train rides from $12* 🕒 *Hrs vary.*

★ Crocker Art Museum

MUSEUM | Established in 1885 with a collection assembled by California Supreme Court judge E.B. Crocker (brother of Charles Crocker, of railroad-baron fame) and his wife, Margaret, Sacramento's premier fine-arts museum specializes in California art, European master drawings, and international ceramics. A highlight is the magnificent *Great Canyon of the Sierra, Yosemite* (1871) by Thomas Hill. Some works are displayed in two architecturally significant 19th-century structures, the original Italianate Crocker residence and the villa-like gallery the judge commissioned. A contemporary 125,000-square-foot space added in 2010 hosts outstanding traveling exhibitions. ■ **TIP→ The museum stays open late on Thursday; pay what you wish on the third Sunday each month.** ✉ *216 O St., at 3rd St., Downtown* ☎ *916/808–7000* 🌐 *www.crockerartmuseum.org* 🎟 *$12* 🕒 *Closed Mon.*

Governor's Mansion

HOUSE | This 15-room Italianate mansion was built in 1877 and used by the state's chief executives from the early 1900s

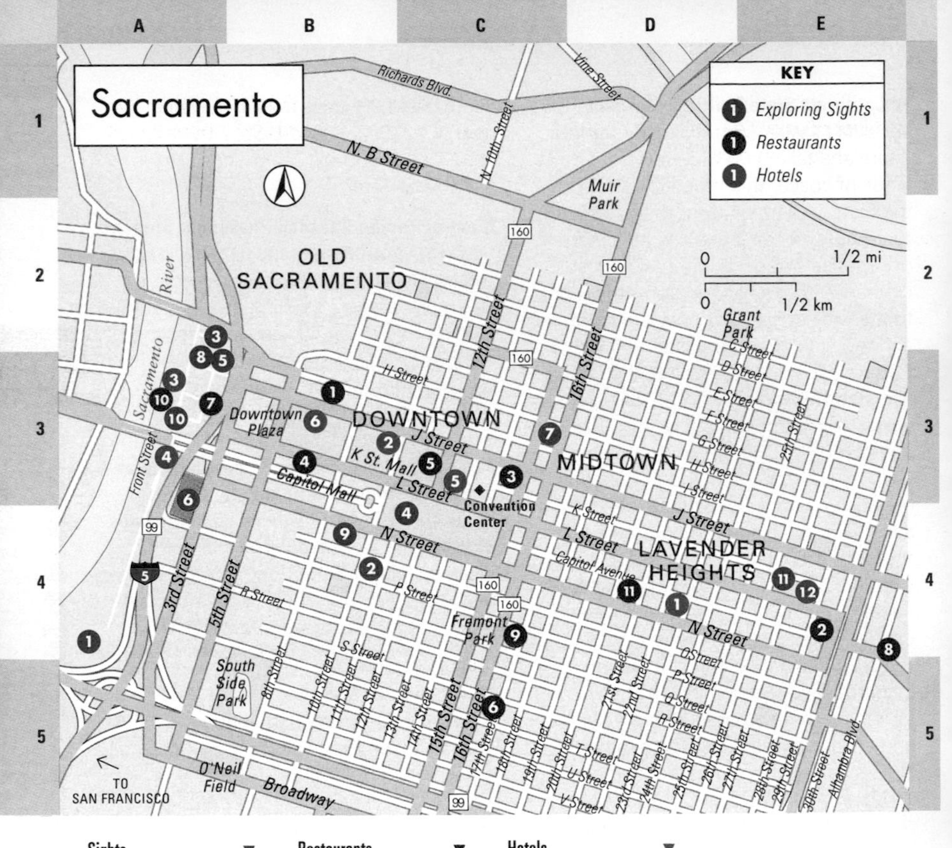

Sights

1 California Automobile Museum **A4**
2 California Museum **B4**
3 California State Railroad Museum **A2**
4 Capitol........ **C4**
5 Central Pacific Railroad Passenger Station...... **A3**
6 Crocker Art Museum... **A4**
7 Governor's Mansion..... **C3**
8 Huntington, Hopkins & Co. Store **A3**
9 Leland Stanford Mansion State Historic Park **B4**
10 Old Sacramento Schoolhouse Museum **A3**
11 State Indian Museum ... **E4**
12 Sutter's Fort **E4**

Restaurants

1 The Bank 629 J........ **B3**
2 Biba **E4**
3 Cafeteria 15L **C3**
4 Camden Spit & Larder **B3**
5 Ella........ **C3**
6 Hook & Ladder Manufacturing Company........ **C5**
7 The Firehouse........ **A3**
8 Kru........ **E4**
9 Magpie Cafe........ **C4**
10 Rio City Cafe........ **A3**
11 The Waterboy........ **D4**

Hotels

1 Amber House Inn of Midtown **D4**
2 Citizen Hotel........ **B3**
3 Delta King........ **A3**
4 Embassy Suites by Hilton Sacramento Riverfront Promenade........ **A3**
5 Hyatt Regency Sacramento **C3**
6 Kimpton Sawyer Hotel........ **B3**

until 1967, when Ronald Reagan vacated it in favor of a modern residence. Many of the interior decorations were ordered from the Huntington, Hopkins & Co. Hardware Store, one of whose partners, Albert Gallatin, was the original occupant. Following renovations completed in 2015, then-governor Jerry Brown began occupying the home, and in early 2019 his successor, Gavin Newsom, moved in—then announced he was decamping with his family to the Sacramento suburbs. You can view the mansion from outside, but it isn't open for tours. ✉ *1526 H St., at 16th St., Midtown.*

Huntington, Hopkins & Co. Store

MUSEUM | Picks, shovels, and other paraphernalia used by gold-rush miners are on display at this re-creation of a 19th-century hardware store that also displays tools and accessories for households, farms, and machine shops. Though it's named for two of the Big Four railroad barons, their store was far more elaborate. ✉ *113 I St., at Front St., Old Sacramento* ☎ *916/323–7234* 🌐 *www.csrmf.org* 🎫 *Free* 🕒 *Closed Mon.–Wed.*

★ Leland Stanford Mansion State Historic Park

HOUSE | In 1856 this structure's original owner built a modest two-story row house purchased a few years later by Leland Stanford, a railroad baron, California governor, and U.S. senator who expanded it in 1862 and the early 1870s into a 19,000-square-foot mansion. The opulent space is open for touring except on days when California's governor hosts official events. Before Stanford's wife and heir, Jane, died, she donated the mansion to Sacramento's Roman Catholic diocese, whose nuns ran it first as an orphanage and later a home for teenage girls. Luckily for the restoration efforts which began in 1986 after the state acquired the property, the nuns had stashed many original furnishings and fixtures in the attic and the renowned photographer Eadweard Muybridge had shot images in the 1870s that made clear what rooms looked like and where things belonged. ■ **TIP→ Guided tours of small groups depart hourly from 10 to 4.** ✉ *800 N St., at 8th St., Downtown* ☎ *916/324–0575 recorded info, 916/324–9266 visitor center* 🌐 *www.parks.ca.gov/stanford-mansion* 🎫 *Free.*

Old Sacramento Schoolhouse Museum

MUSEUM | **FAMILY** | A kid-friendly attraction that shows what one-room schoolhouses were like in central California and the Sierra foothills in the late 1800s, this replica built in 1976 is a fun, quick stop a block from the waterfront. Some of the salient history is written on blackboards in chalk. ✉ *1200 Front St., at L St., Old Sacramento* 🌐 *www.oldsacschoolhouse.org* 🎫 *Free.*

State Indian Museum

MUSEUM | Adjacent to Sutter's Fort, this small but engaging museum explores the lives and history of California's native peoples. Arts-and-crafts exhibits, a demonstration village, and an evocative video offer a fascinating portrait of the state's earliest inhabitants. ✉ *2618 K St., at 26th St., Midtown* ☎ *916/324–0971* 🌐 *www.parks.ca.gov/indianmuseum* 🎫 *$5.*

Sutter's Fort

MUSEUM VILLAGE | **FAMILY** | German-born Swiss immigrant John Augustus Sutter founded Sacramento's earliest Euro-American settlement in 1839. A self-guided tour includes a blacksmith's shop, bakery, prison, living quarters, and livestock areas. Costumed docents sometimes reenact fort life, demonstrating crafts, food preparation, and firearms maintenance. ✉ *2701 L St., at 27th St., Midtown* ☎ *916/445–4422* 🌐 *www.suttersfort.org* 🎫 *From $5.*

Restaurants

The Bank 629 J

$$ | **ECLECTIC** | A sensitive restoration transformed a century-old neoclassical-style bank into a first-floor ensemble of food stations, a classy mezzanine bar, and (down in the former vault, its thick circular door the centerpiece) a self-serve taproom. Under gilded ceilings and ornate chandeliers on the main floor, the various purveyors serve Southern-tinged cuisine, burgers with an Asian-Cajun spin, poké bowls and sushi rolls, sandwiches and salads, vegan gelato, and other delights. **Known for:** sports on 18 TVs, many in the taproom; snacks, quick bites, full meals; near Golden 1 Center arena. *Average main: $18 ✉ 629 J St., at 7th St., Downtown ☎ 916/557–9910 🌐 www.thebank629j.com.*

★ Biba

$$$ | **NORTHERN ITALIAN** | Celebrity chef and owner Biba Caggiano's elegant yet comfortable haven of northern Italian cuisine, opened in 1986 near Sutter's Fort, stands tallest among the restaurants that elevated Sacramento's stature as a food town. The Capitol crowd flocks here for menus that change quarterly, with staples such as a 10-layer lasagna with Bolognese sauce (served only on Thursday and Friday), braised pork shoulder, and house-made gnocchi and pasta dishes. **Known for:** Sacramento institution still going strong; California and Italian wines; signature rum-soaked cake with chocolate ganache for dessert. *Average main: $28 ✉ 2801 Capitol Ave., at 28th St., Midtown ☎ 916/455–2422 🌐 www.biba-restaurant.com ⏲ Closed Sun. No lunch Mon. or Sat.*

Cafeteria 15L

$$ | **AMERICAN** | The exposed brick, reclaimed wood, mismatched chairs, and natural light streaming through large-paned windows of this easygoing hangout for comfort food make a great first impression on newbies and a lasting one on the many repeat local customers. Favorites like tater tots (in truffle oil), sloppy joes (from braised short ribs), and chicken and waffles (with pecan butter and Tabasco-and-black-pepper gravy) prove simultaneously familiar and intriguing. **Known for:** two outdoor patios; nostalgic food with a modern twist; weekend brunch. *Average main: $21 ✉ 1116 15th St., at L St., Downtown ☎ 916/492–1960 🌐 www.cafeteria15l.com.*

★ Camden Spit & Larder

$$$ | **MODERN AMERICAN** | Upscale London haberdasheries reportedly inspired the aesthetic of this impeccably designed, pressed-metal-ceilinged paean to spit-roasted, Brit-influenced meat dishes. Near Golden 1 Center and Downtown Commons, it's a place to share small offerings like sausage rolls, salt-cod fritters, local caviar (Sacramento is a center of caviar production), and Wagyu tartare, perhaps with a craft cocktail incorporating seasonal fruits, herbs, and vegetables, before proceeding to roasted half chicken or the house specialty, roast rib of beef with fermented horseradish. **Known for:** sea-salt fingerling fries with malt vinegar mayo; kitchen bar to watch chefs at work; wine, beer, and cider selections; inventive cocktails. *Average main: $29 ✉ 555 Capitol Mall, at 6th St., Downtown ☎ 916/619–8897 🌐 www.camdenspitandlarder.com ⏲ No lunch.*

Ella

$$$$ | **MODERN AMERICAN** | With fresh white calla lilies on the tables, ivory linen curtains, and distressed-wood shutters installed across the ceiling, this swank restaurant and bar near the Capitol is artfully designed and thoroughly modern. The stellar California–French farm-to-table cuisine served within changes seasonally, but typical dishes include steak tartare with garlic popovers and a farm egg, orange-anise marinated beet salad, a wood-fired pork chop, and bavette steak. **Known for:** fresh, seasonal local ingredients; waitstaff's attention to detail; cocktail and wine selection. *Average main: $39 ✉ 1131 K St., at 12th St., Downtown ☎ 916/443–3772 🌐 www.elladiningroomandbar.com ⏲ Closed Sun. No lunch.*

★ The Firehouse
$$$$ | **AMERICAN** | Sacramento's rich and famous including California governors going back to Ronald Reagan settle into the elegant spaces within the city's restored first brick firehouse to dine on award-winning contemporary cuisine. The creative fare ranges from carpaccio, seasonal oysters, and braised pork belly with sage bread pudding to delicately spiced pan-roasted sea bass and rack of lamb, rib eye, and other specialty meat cuts. **Known for:** steaks and seafood; chef's tasting menu; courtyard patio. *$ Average main: $41 ✉ 1112 2nd St., at L St., Old Sacramento ☎ 916/442–4772 🌐 www.firehouseoldsac.com ⏲ No lunch weekends.*

Hook & Ladder Manufacturing Company
$$$ | **MODERN AMERICAN** | Youthful and compelling, with found-art decorative elements and exposed vents, this historic former fire station is a favorite stop for cocktails, craft beers, and farm-to-fork fare. The area's year-round farmers' markets supply ingredients for the delectable salads and soups, and the carefully sourced beef, poultry, and seafood entrées are always good. **Known for:** carefully sourced ingredients; many local brews and wines; many vegan items. *$ Average main: $26 ✉ 1630 S St., at 17th St., Midtown ☎ 916/442–4885 🌐 www.hookandladder916.com.*

Kru
$$$ | **JAPANESE** | It's worth the drive a little past Sutter's Fort to this blond-wood mod-Japanese restaurant whose owner-chef fashions fresh and wildly creative sushi. Sit at blond-wood tables or the counter and order a sunshine roll, with spicy tuna, escolar, and shrimp tempura enlivened by the tart contribution of green apples and lemon, perhaps pairing it with cooked fare like smoked duck *kushiyaki* with plum-wine katsu sauce or hearty hot or cold ramen, including pork belly, poached shrimp, and mushroom broth. **Known for:** smart decor; nearly two dozen rolls; impressive sake, wine, and whiskeys. *$ Average main: $28 ✉ 3135 Folsom Blvd., at Seville Way ☎ 916/551–1559 🌐 www.krurestaurant.com ⏲ No lunch.*

★ Magpie Cafe
$$$ | **AMERICAN** | This Midtown eatery with a vaguely industrial look and a casual vibe takes its food seriously: nearly all the produce is sourced locally, and the chefs prepare only sustainable seafood. Roasted chicken for two with a chervil-ginger green sauce is a staple, as is the seafood skillet with seasonal vegetables. **Known for:** weekend brunch; happy-hour menu Tuesday–Friday; homemade ice-cream sandwiches. *$ Average main: $25 ✉ 1601 16th St., Midtown ☎ 916/452–7594 🌐 www.magpiecafe.com ⏲ Closed Mon. No dinner Sun.*

Rio City Café
$$$ | **AMERICAN** | Contemporary and seasonal Mediterranean and Californian cuisine, and huge floor-to-ceiling windows and an outdoor deck overlooking the river are the attractions of this restaurant designed to resemble a vintage steamship warehouse. The food—maple bourbon–marinated steaks, filet mignon Wellington, almond-crusted mahimahi, crab and shrimp Louie salads—is generally good, though the big draw is the setting. **Known for:** riverfront location; daytime water views; dinner starts at 4 pm. *$ Average main: $25 ✉ 1110 Front St., at L St., Old Sacramento ☎ 916/442–8226 🌐 www.riocitycafe.com.*

★ The Waterboy
$$$ | **EUROPEAN** | Rural French cooking with locally sourced, seasonal, high-quality often organic ingredients is the hallmark of this upscale white-tablecloth corner storefront restaurant that's as appealing for a casual meal with friends as it is for a drawn-out romantic dinner for two. Among the mains, try the steak du jour, coq au vin, or seasonal seafood, and save room for sweet (profiteroles) or savory (assorted cheeses) desserts.

Known for: exceptional French cooking; quality local ingredients; welcoming chef. *Average main: $30 2000 Capitol Ave., at 20th St., Midtown 916/498–9891 www.waterboyrestaurant.com No lunch weekends.*

Hotels

★ Amber House Inn of Midtown

$$$ | **B&B/INN** | Veer from the beaten path of traditional lodging at Amber House Inn's two historic homes—one a 1905 Craftsman, the other an 1895 Dutch colonial–revival—just 1 mile from the Capitol. **Pros:** Midtown location; attentive service; full breakfast served in-room if desired. **Cons:** freeway access isn't easy; not exactly kid-friendly; lacks spa, fitness center, and other big-hotel amenities. *Rooms from: $179 1315 22nd St., Midtown 916/444–8085 www.amberhouse.com 10 rooms Free Breakfast.*

Citizen Hotel

$$$ | **HOTEL** | This boutique hotel built within the historic 1926 Cal Western Life building is dapper and refined, with marble stairs, striped wallpaper, and plush velvet chairs, lending the place a Roaring '20s charm. **Pros:** hip, sophisticated decor; smooth and solicitous service; terrific restaurant and bar. **Cons:** rooms near elevator can be noisy; rates vary widely depending on conventions, legislature, season; expensive parking. *Rooms from: $208 926 J St., Downtown 916/447–2700 www.thecitizenhotel.com 198 rooms No meals.*

Delta King

$$ | **HOTEL** | Wake up to the sound of geese taking flight along the river when you book a stay in one of Sacramento's most unusual and historic relics, a carefully restored riverboat hotel, permanently moored on Old Sacramento's waterfront. **Pros:** unique lodgings; steps from historic Old Town shopping and dining; period feel. **Cons:** slanted floors can feel a bit jarring; rooms are cramped; some noise issues. *Rooms from: $154 1000 Front St., Old Sacramento At end of K St. 916/444–5464, 800/825–5464 www.deltaking.com 44 rooms Free Breakfast.*

Embassy Suites by Hilton Sacramento Riverfront Promenade

$$$$ | **HOTEL** | Adjacent to Sacramento's iconic Tower Bridge, this property has huge common areas, updated large rooms, public art, and a reputation for customer service. **Pros:** best river view in town; proximity to Old Sacramento and Downtown; made-to-order breakfast included in rate. **Cons:** the atrium feels sterile; ho-hum guest-room style; high prices during events and when legislature is in session. *Rooms from: $298 100 Capitol Mall, Downtown 916/326–5000 embassysuites3.hilton.com 242 suites Free Breakfast.*

Hyatt Regency Sacramento

$$$ | **HOTEL** | With a marble-and-glass lobby and luxurious rooms, this multitiered, glass-dominated hotel across from the Capitol and adjacent to the convention center has a striking Mediterranean design. **Pros:** best rooms have Capitol Park views; some rooms have small balconies; excellent service. **Cons:** nearby streets can feel dodgy at night; somewhat impersonal; many corporate events. *Rooms from: $220 1209 L St., Downtown 916/443–1234, 800/633–7313 sacramento.regency.hyatt.com 505 rooms No meals.*

★ Kimpton Sawyer Hotel

$$$$ | **HOTEL** | Soft shades of brown and gray and furniture milled from California oak lend an haute-rustic feel to the spacious rooms and suites of this full-service hotel amid Sacramento's Downtown Commons (DOCO) shopping and entertainment complex. **Pros:** pool deck; "living room" lobby; convenient to Downtown and Old Sacramento. **Cons:** pricey in-season; no tubs in many rooms; may be too high-style for some guests.

Rooms from: $254 ✉ 500 J St., Downtown ☎ 916/545–7100 front desk, 877/678–6255 reservations 🌐 www.sawyerhotel.com 285 rooms No meals.

Nightlife

Dive Bar

BARS/PUBS | Live "mermaids" and "mermen" swim in a massive tank above the bar at this lively Downtown nightspot known for its extensive list of craft cocktails and local beers. ✉ *1016 K St., Downtown* ☎ *916/737–5999* 🌐 *divebarsacramento.com.*

Drakes: The Barn

BREWPUBS/BEER GARDENS | Drake's Brewing serves up beer, food, and musical and other events at a dramatically curving, cedar-shingled pavilion on 2 acres along the Sacramento River. The anchor food tenant, PizzaSmith, serves thin-crust New Haven–style pies; there are also resident and pop-up food trucks and a brewpub–beer garden (lawn-chair and other seating plus fire pits) pouring 50 Drake's brews on tap, including the potent Denogginizer Double IPA. The Barn is closed on Monday and Tuesday. ✉ *985 Riverfront St., at Garden St., West Sacramento* ↔ *Across Sacramento River from Downtown near Raley Field* ☎ *510/568–2739* 🌐 *drinkdrakes.com/barn.*

Harlow's

MUSIC CLUBS | This sceney restaurant draws a younger crowd to its art-deco bar-nightclub. They have an inviting patio plus live music after 9 pm from a diverse lineup. ✉ *2708 J St., at 27th St., Midtown* ☎ *916/441–4693* 🌐 *www.harlows.com.*

★ Midtown BierGarten

BREWPUBS/BEER GARDENS | The neighborhood feel and the selection of beers, ales, porters, stouts, sours, and ciders make a trip to this boisterous beer garden a fun occasion, with the garlic fries, fresh pretzels with mustard, old-fashioned hot dogs, and other small bites a definite bonus. A 40-foot cargo container holds the bar, and a 20-footer contains the bathrooms, with the rest of the setting alfresco. ✉ *2332 K St., at 24th St.* ☎ *916/346–4572* 🌐 *beergardensacramento.com.*

★ Midtown's Cantina Alley

BARS/PUBS | Flavorful, colorful, fruity cocktails, some served in hollowed-out pineapples or watermelons, are the specialty of this bar and restaurant whose equally rich-hued decor and corrugated-metal ceiling intentionally evoke similar spots throughout Mexico. While sipping sangria, a cerveza, one of several margaritas, or a Tijuana mule (made with tequila and delivered in a 128-ounce copper mug, it serves five), you can nibble on street tacos, posole, *elote* (corn on a stick, rolled in mayonnaise and topped with cheese and spices), and other small plates. ✉ *2320 Jazz Alley, Midtown* ↔ *Off 24th St. between J and K Sts.* ☎ *833/232–0639* 🌐 *www.cantinaalley.com.*

Punch Bowl Social

BARS/PUBS | This restaurant and entertainment complex offers bowling, billiards, table shuffleboard, karaoke, Giant Jenga, virtual reality, pinball, and Skee-Ball. After you've worked up an appetite, dine on updated pub grub and sip well-chosen craft beers, wine, specialty cocktails, or boozeless beverages. ✉ *500 J St., Downtown* ↔ *At 5th St.* ☎ *916/925–5610* 🌐 *www.punchbowlsocial.com/sacramento.*

Revival

BARS/PUBS | The poolside rooftop bar at the Kimpton Sawyer is a chic people-watching perch with views of Downtown Commons and the Golden 1 Center. They offer specialty cocktails and excellent bar bites, and host guest DJs after 9:30 pm Wednesday through Saturday (the bar is closed on other days except for special events). ✉ *Kimpton Sawyer Hotel, 500 J St., Downtown*

☎ *916/545–7111* 🌐 *revivalsacramento.com.*

Streets Pub and Grub

BARS/PUBS | A favorite among Anglophiles, Streets is open until 2 am nightly, with lively karaoke on Wednesday night (with a band on month's second and fourth Thursday). ✉ *1804 J St., at 18th St., Midtown* ☎ *916/498–1388* 🌐 *www.streetspubandgrub.com.*

Tiger

BARS/PUBS | Concrete walls and black-metal beams and railings reinforce the post-industrial mood at this two-level bar with zesty bites like paprika-spiced popcorn, pickled deviled eggs, and chicken-leek meatballs. The signature Tiger's Milk drink riffs off a piña colada with crème de cacao, gin, Frangelico, and coconut milk, and there are several other artisanal offerings and a few classics, including a Manhattan, plus beer and wine. ✉ *722 K St., at 8th St., Downtown* ☎ *916/382–9610* 🌐 *www.tiger700block.com.*

Performing Arts

Broadway Sacramento

THEATER | This group presents Broadway shows at the Community Center Theater and produces summer musicals (think *Oklahoma, Annie*) at the theater-in-the-round Wells Fargo Pavilion. ✉ *1419 H St., at 14th St., Downtown* ☎ *916/557–1999* 🌐 *www.broadwaysacramento.com.*

Crest Theatre

ARTS CENTERS | It's worth peeking inside the Crest even if you don't catch a show, just to see the swirling and flamboyant art-deco design in the foyer, or to dine at the Empress Tavern restaurant within. It's a beloved venue for classic and art-house films, along with concerts and other cultural events. ✉ *1013 K St., at 10th St., Downtown* ☎ *916/476–3356* 🌐 *www.crestsacramento.com.*

Shopping

Downtown Commons (*DOCO*)

SHOPPING CENTERS/MALLS | As its name implies, this multiblock complex adjoining the Golden 1 Center aspires to be a gathering spot for locals and tourists as much as a place to shop, dine, catch a movie, or sip a cocktail. ✉ *660 J St., Downtown* ✣ *Between 5th and 7th Sts., J and L Sts.* ☎ *916/273–8124.*

★ Kulture

GIFTS/SOUVENIRS | Two sons of migrant workers from Jalisco and Michoacán opened this vibrant shop that sells Mexican art, jewelry, and gifts, along with the duo's pithy Keepin It Paisa line of T-shirts, hoodies, and ball caps. Buoyed by the shop's success, the two expanded into the adjacent space where they and other vendors sell furniture, clothing, and other items. ✉ *2331 K St., Midtown* ✣ *At 24th St.* ☎ *916/442–2728* 🌐 *kulturedc.wixsite.com/kulture* ⏱ *Closed Mon.*

Scout Living

HOUSEHOLD ITEMS/FURNITURE | The members of this collective are specialists in home accessories and antique, vintage, and modern furniture. Even if you're not looking to redecorate, the shop's a wonder to walk through. ✉ *1215 18th St., at L St., Midtown* ☎ *916/594–7971* 🌐 *www.scoutliving.com* ⏱ *Closed Mon.*

Activities

American River Bicycle Trail

BICYCLING | The Jedediah Smith Memorial Trail, as it's formally called, runs for 32 miles from Old Sacramento to Beals Point in Folsom. Walk or ride a bit of it and you'll see why local cyclists and pedestrians adore its scenic lanes. Enjoy great views of the American River and the bluffs overlooking it. **■ TIP→ Bring lunch or a snack. Pretty parks and picnic areas dot the trail.** ✉ *Old Sacramento* 🌐 *www.americanriverbiketrail.com.*

Sacramento Kings

BASKETBALL | The Sacramento Kings of the NBA play at the LEED-certified Golden 1 Center, which opened in 2016 as the centerpiece of the DOCO (Downtown Commons) complex of restaurants, hotels, and shops. ✉ *500 David J. Stern Walk, Downtown* ⊕ *At 5th and L Sts.* 🌐 *www.sacramentokings.com.*

Sacramento River Cats

BASEBALL/SOFTBALL | **FAMILY** | The top minor-league affiliate of the San Francisco Giants plays before big crowds just across the Sacramento River from Downtown. ✉ *Raley Field, 400 Ballpark Dr., West Sacramento* ⊕ *Across Sacramento River from Downtown* ☎ *916/376–4700* 🌐 *www.rivercats.com.*

Woodland

20 miles northwest of Sacramento.

In its heyday, Woodland was among California's wealthiest cities. Established by gold seekers and entrepreneurs, it later became an agricultural gold mine. The legacy of the old land barons lives on in the restored Victorian and Craftsman architecture downtown; the best examples are south of Main Street on College, Elm, 1st, and 2nd streets. The town's top attractions pay tribute to car culture and motorized agriculture vehicles.

GETTING HERE AND AROUND

Yolobus (🌐 *www.yolobus.com*) serves Woodland from Sacramento, but it's far more practical to drive here via Interstate 5.

ESSENTIALS

VISITOR INFORMATION Woodland Chamber of Commerce ✉ *307 1st St., at Dead Cat Alley* ☎ *530/662–7327* 🌐 *www.woodlandchamber.org.*

Sights

California Agriculture Museum

MUSEUM | **FAMILY** | This gigantic space provides a marvelous overview of the entire history of motorized agricultural vehicles through dozens and dozens of threshers, harvesters, combines, tractors, and more. A separate wing surveys the evolution of the truck, with an emphasis on ones used for farm work. ✉ *1962 Hays La., off County Rd. 102* ☎ *530/666–9700* 🌐 *www.CaliforniaAgMuseum.org* 🎫 *$10* ⏲ *Closed Sun. and Mon.*

★ Reiff's Gas Station Museum

MUSEUM | Mark Reiff, an inveterate collector of gas-station pumps and signs, converted his home in a residential neighborhood into a joyful homage to 20th-century car culture. A yellow-and-orange "Roar with Gilmore" pump got Reiff going in 1999, and he's never stopped, adding more pumps and signs (Sinclair, Flying A, Sunray), along with a flood of nostalgia-inducing memorabilia. Reiff describes his creation as "labor of love and a butt load of fun"—and it is. Contact him to arrange a tour. ✉ *52 Jefferson St., at McKinley Ave.* ☎ *530/666–1758* 🌐 *reiffsgasstation.com* 🎫 *$7.*

Woodland Opera House

ARTS VENUE | On the U.S. National Register of Historic Places, this 1896 structure hosted minstrel shows, John Philip Sousa's marching band, and early vaudeville acts before closing for six decades. Now restored, it hosts plays, musicals, and concerts year-round. If the box office is open, ask for a backstage tour or a peek at the auditorium. ✉ *340 2nd St.* ☎ *530/666–9617* 🌐 *www.woodlandoperahouse.org.*

Restaurants

Kitchen428 and Mojo's Lounge

$$ | **AMERICAN** | Erected in 1891 to house luxury apartments, the Jackson building roared back to life as a showcase for locally sourced California cuisine from filet mignon to miso-marinated salmon. The menu at this stylish exposed-brick restaurant also includes vegetarian and vegan items. **Known for:** local and sustainable menu; cocktail bar with craft beers on tap; weekend brunch. *Average main: $21 428 1st St., off Main St. 530/661–0428 www.mojoskitchen428.com.*

Davis

10 miles west of Sacramento.

Davis began as a rich agricultural area and remains one, but it doesn't feel like a cow town. It's home to the University of California at Davis, whose 38,000-plus students hang at downtown cafés, galleries, and bookstores (most of the action takes place between 1st and 4th and C and G streets), lending the city a decidedly college-town feel.

GETTING HERE AND AROUND

Most people arrive here by car via Interstate 80. In a pinch, you can get here via Yolobus (*www.yolobus.com*) from Sacramento. Downtown is walkable. Touring by bicycle is also a popular option—Davis is very flat.

ESSENTIALS

VISITOR INFORMATION Davis Chamber of Commerce *640 3rd St. 530/756–5160 www.davischamber.com.*

Sights

University of California, Davis

COLLEGE | A top research university, UC Davis educates many of the Wine Country's vintners and grape growers, in addition to farmers, veterinarians, and brewmasters, too. Campus tours depart from Buehler Alumni and Visitors Center. On a tour or not, worthy stops include the **Arboretum,** the **Manetti Shrem Museum of Art,** and the **Mondavi Center,** a striking modern glass structure that presents top-tier performing artists. *Visitor Center, 550 Alumni La. 530/752–8111 for tour information visit.ucdavis.edu.*

Restaurants

Mustard Seed

$$$$ | **AMERICAN** | Many patrons at this restaurant serving eclectic seasonal California cuisine are attending performing-arts events at the Mondavi Center a short walk away or visiting their kids at UC Davis. With hardwood floors and tables topped with white linen, the dining room is cozy and romantic, but when the weather's fine, the tree-shaded patio out back is the best place to enjoy dishes like tomato bisque topped with a puff pastry and herb-crusted rack of lamb. **Known for:** lunchtime soups, salads, and sandwiches; smooth service; reasonably priced California wines. *Average main: $32 222 D St., Suite 11 530/758–5750 www.mustardseeddavis.com Closed Mon. No lunch weekends.*

Hotels

Aggie Inn

$$ | **HOTEL** | A 2016 renovation added a touch of style to this basic hotel less than a block from the UC Davis campus whose spacious cottages work well for families. **Pros:** great location; full breakfast with hot entrée; suites with kitchens. **Cons:** can get a little noisy; motel feel; lacks amenities. *Rooms from: $155 245 1st St. 530/756–0352 www.aggieinn.com 33 rooms Breakfast.*

Best Western Plus Palm Court Hotel

$$ | **HOTEL** | Rich accents of gold and cobalt blue add boutique flair to the spacious rooms of this dependable choice for business and leisure travelers. **Pros:** convenient location; good on-site restaurant; congenial staff. **Cons:** pricey during major UC Davis events; no pool; chain's usual free breakfast not offered. *Rooms from: $163 234 D St.*

☎ 530/753–7100 🌐 www.palmcourtdavis.com 🛏 27 rooms 🍽 No meals.

Lodi

34 miles south of Sacramento.

With with more than 110,000 acres of mostly alluvial soils planted to more than six dozen grape varietals—more types than in any other California viticultural area—Lodi is a major grape-growing hub. Eighty-five or so wineries do business in Lodi, the self-proclaimed Zinfandel Capital of the World, and neighboring towns. (Although plenty of Zin grows here, these days farmers devote even more land to Cabernet Sauvignon.) Founded on agriculture, Lodi was once the country's watermelon capital. Today it's surrounded by fields of asparagus, pumpkins, beans, safflowers, sunflowers, melons, squashes, peaches, and cherries. Lodi retains an old rural charm. You can stroll downtown or visit a wildlife refuge, all the while benefiting from a Sacramento River delta breeze that keeps this microclimate cooler in summer than anyplace else in the area.

GETTING HERE AND AROUND

Most of Lodi lies west of Highway 99 and east of Interstate 5. Amtrak trains stop here frequently. GrapeLine (☎ *209/333–6806*) buses pass by many wineries, but touring by car is more efficient.

ESSENTIALS

VISITOR INFORMATION Lodi Conference & Visitors Bureau ✉ *25 N. School St.* ☎ *209/365–1195, 800/798–1810* 🌐 *www.visitlodi.com.*

Sights

Berghold Estate Winery

WINERY/DISTILLERY | The tasting room at Berghold recalls an earlier wine era with its vintage Victorian interior, including restored, salvaged mantlepieces, leaded glass, and a 26-foot-long bar. The wines—among them Viognier, Cabernet Sauvignon, Syrah, and Zinfandel—pay homage to French wine-making styles. ✉ *17343 N. Cherry Rd., off E. Victor Rd./Hwy. 12* ☎ *209/333–9291* 🌐 *berghold-vineyards.com* 🎟 *Tastings $10* ⏲ *Closed Mon.–Wed.*

Bokisch Vineyards

WINERY/DISTILLERY | This operation 11 miles outside of downtown comes highly recommended for its excellent Spanish varietals and warm hospitality. The Albariño white and Tempranillo and Graciano reds often receive favorable critical notice, but everything is well made, including the non-Spanish old-vine Zinfandel. **■TIP→ Bokisch welcomes picnickers; pick up fixings in town and enjoy vineyard views while you dine.** ✉ *18921 Atkins Rd.* ✣ *From Hwy. 99 head east on Hwy. 12, north on Hwy. 88, and east on Brandt Rd.* ☎ *209/642–8880* 🌐 *www.bokischvineyards.com* 🎟 *Tastings $10* ⏲ *Closed Tues.–Thurs.*

Harney Lane Winery

WINERY/DISTILLERY | The Harney family has grown grapes in Lodi since the 1900s dawned but only started a winery in 2006. Three Zinfandels star in a lineup that includes Albariño, Chardonnay, a multigrape rosé, Petite Sirah, Tempranillo, and an old-vine Zinfandel port-style dessert wine. Extend your tasting with a glass in the "forest" garden, where three-century-old cedars supply the shade. **■TIP→ Learn about the family and Lodi on the Grape to Glass tour.** ✉ *9010 E. Harney La.* ✣ *About 6½ miles south of downtown, Hwy. 99 to E. Harney La. exit* ☎ *209/365–1900* 🌐 *www.harneylane.com* 🎟 *Tastings $10, tour $25.*

Jeremy Wine Co.

WINERY/DISTILLERY | Originally a downtown bank, its original floors unfinished and as timeworn as the centerpiece bar Trettevik bought on eBay, the place has the feel of a chic old-time saloon. Sangiovese, Tempranillo, and a few other reds, most from well-sourced Lodi appellation grapes, are the specialty here, with Chardonnay among the few whites, and a chocolate port-style dessert wine for anyone with a sweet tooth. ✉ *6 W. Pine St. , at S. Sacramento St.* ☎ *209/367–3773* 🌐 *jeremywineco.com* 🎫 *Tastings $10.*

Lodi Wine & Visitor Center

WINERY/DISTILLERY | A fine place to sample Lodi wines, the center has a tasting bar and viticultural exhibits. You can also buy wine and pick up a free winery map. The knowledgeable staff can suggest wineries to explore. ✉ *2545 W. Turner Rd., at Woodhaven La.* ☎ *209/365–0621* 🌐 *www.lodiwine.com* 🎫 *Tastings $8.*

Lucas Winery

WINERY/DISTILLERY | David Lucas was one of the first local producers to start making serious wine, and today his Zinfandels are among Lodi's most sought-after vintages. In addition to Zin, Lucas makes a light Chardonnay with subtle oaky flavors. The 90-minute tour, for which reservations are required, will get you up to speed on the Lodi wine appellation. ✉ *18196 N. Davis Rd., at W. Turner Rd.* ☎ *209/368–2006* 🌐 *www.lucaswinery.com* 🎫 *Tastings from $10, tour (includes tasting) $75* ⏲ *Closed Mon. and Tues.*

★ M2 Wines

WINERY/DISTILLERY | With its translucent polycarbonate panels, concrete floor, and metal framing, this winery's high-ceilinged tasting room strikes an iconoclastic, industrial-sleek pose along an otherwise relentlessly rural lane north of Lodi. The Soucie Vineyard old-vine Zinfandel and the Trio Red Wine blend are the flagships. ✉ *2900 E. Peltier Rd., Acampo* ✣ *Take Hwy. 99 north from downtown to Peltier Rd. exit and head west* ☎ *209/339–1071* 🌐 *www.m2wines.com* 🎫 *Tastings $10.*

★ McCay Cellars

WINERY/DISTILLERY | Wine critics applaud owner-winemaker Michael McCay's pursuit of balance and restraint with his flagship TruLux Zinfandel and Faith Lot 13 Zin from century-old vines. A longtime grower who started his namesake label in 2007, McCay also makes several rosés and whites, plus reds from Spanish (Tempranillo), Rhône (Grenache, Syrah), and lesser-seen varietals like Cinsaut and Carignane. He's often on-site at his lively downtown tasting room. ✉ *100 S. Sacramento St.* ✣ *At W. Oak St.* ☎ *209/368–9463* 🌐 *www.mccaycellars.com* 🎫 *Tastings $10.*

★ Michael David Winery

WINERY/DISTILLERY | *Wine Enthusiast* magazine anointed Adam Mettler of Michael David its winemaker of the year in 2018 in recognition of his skill at creating smooth but characterful red blends like Petite Petit (Petite Sirah and Petit Verdot) and Freakshow Zinfandel. Taste these and other wines at the sprawling roadside **Phillips Farms Fruit Stand,** where fifth-generation farmers turned winery owners Michael and David Philips also sell their family's gorgeous produce. ■ **TIP→ Breakfast or lunch at the stand's café is a treat.** ✉ *4580 W. Hwy. 12, at N. Ray Rd.* ☎ *209/368–7384* 🌐 *www.michaeldavidwinery.com* 🎫 *Tastings from $10.*

Micke Grove Regional Park

AMUSEMENT PARK/WATER PARK | **FAMILY** | This 258-acre, oak-shaded park has a Japanese tea garden, picnic tables, children's play areas, an agricultural museum, a zoo, a golf course, and a water-play feature. **Fun Town at Micke Grove,** a family-oriented amusement park, is geared toward younger children. ✉ *11793 N. Micke Grove Rd.* ✣ *Off Hwy. 99 Armstrong Rd. exit* ☎ *209/953–8800 park info* 🎫 *From $5.*

St. Amant Winery

WINERY/DISTILLERY | Although its estate vineyards are east of town in Amador County, St. Amant is among the wineries that helped raise the profile of Lodi as a wine-growing region. Known for Tempranillo, Zinfandel, and port-style wines, the winery hosts guests in an industrial-park facility. Turn right immediately after passing through the gate. ✉ *1 Winemaster Way, Suite I* ✥ *Take E. Turner Rd. east to N. Guild Ave. north; turn right after 100 feet* ☎ *209/367–0646* 🌐 *www.stamantwinery.com* 🎟 *Tastings $5* ⏲ *Closed Mon.–Wed.*

Van Ruiten Family Winery

WINERY/DISTILLERY | To experience what Lodi's hardworking old Zinfandel vines can produce, sample the Van Ruiten Old Vine Zin and the Reserve Sideways Lot 69 Old Vine Zin. Other wines of note include the Chardonnays and the Cabernet-Shiraz blend. ✉ *340 W. Hwy. 12* ✥ *¾ mile west of Lower Sacramento Rd.* ☎ *209/334–5722* 🌐 *www.vrwinery.com* 🎟 *Tastings $10.*

The Dancing Fox Winery and Bakery

$ | **AMERICAN** | A good downtown stop especially for lunch, the Dancing Fox also has a tasting room for its eponymous wines. The restaurant, with decor that shimmers with fairy-tale whimsy, sandwiches, salads, pizzas, burgers, and wraps and has more than a dozen beers on tap. **Known for:** Sunday brunch; many dishes baked in Spanish wood-fired oven; historic downtown setting. $ *Average main: $14* ✉ *203 S. School St.* ☎ *203/366–2634* 🌐 *www.dancingfoxwinery.com* ⏲ *Closed Mon. No dinner Sun.*

Pietro's Trattoria

$$$ | **ITALIAN** | Lodi's go-to spot for Italian American classics wins fans for its quality ingredients, Tuscan-courtyard ambience, and plant-filled outdoor patio (reservations essential on weekends). Expect straightforward, well-executed renditions of chicken piccata and veal cacciatore, filling lasagna and fettuccine Alfredo (with chicken or prawns), pizzas, and the like, all delivered with informal good cheer by the cadre of servers. **Known for:** wine list focused on local vintages; Italian American classics; meatball and chicken pesto with cheese sandwiches for lunch. $ *Average main: $23* ✉ *317 E. Kettleman La.* ☎ *209/368–0613* 🌐 *www.pietroslodi.com* ⏲ *Closed Sun.*

★ Towne House Restaurant

$$$$ | **MODERN AMERICAN** | Lodi power breakfasts and lunches and special-occasion dinners often take place in the distinguished rooms of this former residence behind, and part of, the Wine and Roses hotel. Painted in rich, textured hues offset by wide white molding, the rooms exude a subtle sophistication matched by seasonal dishes that might include a Niman Ranch pork chop with miso-molasses glaze or Hawaiian opah with nori risotto. **Known for:** dozens of local wines by the glass; nightly live music; fresh seasonal local ingredients. $ *Average main: $38* ✉ *2505 W. Turner Rd., at Woodhaven La.* ☎ *209/371–6160* 🌐 *winerose.com/the-restaurant.*

The Inn at Locke House

$$ | **B&B/INN** | Built between 1862 and 1882, the inn occupies a pioneer doctor's family home that rates a listing on the National Register of Historic Places. **Pros:** eager-to-please hosts; peace and quiet; local farm products in full breakfast. **Cons:** remote location; can be hard to find; lacks amenities of a full-service hotel. $ *Rooms from: $149* ✉ *19960 Elliott Rd., Lockeford* ☎ *209/727–5715* 🌐 *www.theinnatlockehouse.com* *5 rooms* 🍽 *Free Breakfast.*

Wine & Roses Hotel

$$$ | **HOTEL** | Set on 7 acres amid a tapestry of informal gardens, this hotel has cultivated a sense of refinement typically associated with Napa or Carmel. **Pros:** luxurious setting; popular restaurant; spa treatments. **Cons:** expensive for the area; some guests mention that walls are thin; many events. $ *Rooms from: $249* ✉ *2505 W. Turner Rd.* ☎ *209/334–6988*

www.winerose.com 66 rooms
No meals.

Nevada City

4 miles north of Grass Valley.

Nevada City, once known as the Queen City of the Northern Mines, is the most appealing of the northern Mother Lode towns. The iron-shutter brick buildings that line downtown streets contain antiques shops, galleries, boutiques, B&Bs, restaurants, a winery, and some tasting rooms. Gas street lamps add to the romance. At one point in the 1850s, Nevada City had a population of nearly 10,000—enough to support much cultural activity. Today, about 3,000 people live here, but the performing-arts scene remains vibrant.

GETTING HERE AND AROUND

You'll need a car to get here. Take Highway 20 east from Interstate 5 or west from Interstate 80. Highway 49 is the north–south route into town. Gold Country Stage vehicles (*530/477–0103*) serve some attractions on weekdays.

ESSENTIALS

VISITOR INFORMATION Nevada City Chamber of Commerce *132 Main St. 530/265–2692 www.nevadacitychamber.com.*

Sights

Firehouse No. 1
BUILDING | With its gingerbread-trim bell tower, Firehouse No. 1 has been one of the Gold Country's most distinctive buildings since 1861. The museum inside, worth a peek if it's open, houses artifacts from the gold rush, the Nisenan people, the ill-fated Donner Party, and the altar from a Chinese joss house (temple). *214 Main St. 530/265–3937 www.nevadacountyhistory.org Donation suggested Closed Mon. and Tues. and Nov.–Apr.*

Nevada City Winery
WINERY/DISTILLERY | The area's oldest winery, established in 1980 in the Miners Foundry garage, pours its wines, many from Sierra Foothills grapes, in a newer nearby tasting room whose patio perches over the operation's current wine-making facility. Chardonnay is the best-seller, with Cabernet Franc and Rhône and Italian reds among the other specialties. *321 Spring St., at Bridge St. 530/265–9463, 800/203–9463 www.ncwinery.com Tastings from $8.*

Szabo Vineyards
WINERY/DISTILLERY | Taste for yourself what makes Sierra Foothills wines unique at the brick-walled sipping salon of owner-winemaker Alex Szabo. In addition to growing the grapes 7 miles west of his downtown tasting room and making the wines, Alex is often the one pouring them. His Zinfandel, Petite Sirah, Grenache, Syrah, and other wines impress with their soft tannins, ample acidity, and long finish. *316 Broad St., at York St. 530/265–8792 www.szabovineyards.com Tastings $9 Closed Mon.–Wed.*

Restaurants

Friar Tuck's
$$$ | **EUROPEAN** | Popular Friar Tuck's specializes in creative, interactive fondues and has an extensive menu of seafood, steaks, and pasta dishes. The sparkling interior has a late-19th-century ambience—it's one of Nevada City's best indoor spaces. **Known for:** cheese fondue; varied selection of mostly California wines; live music nightly. *Average main: $28 111 N. Pine St. 530/265–9093 friartucks.com No lunch.*

New Moon Cafe
$$$$ | **AMERICAN** | Although not eye-catching from outside, New Moon Cafe hugs you in an exquisite dining experience once you enter. Organic salads, homemade ravioli, fresh line-caught fish, and locally sourced beef, chicken, and pork

dishes appear on the seasonally changing menu. **Known for:** a cosmopolitan meal in rural Gold Country; crème brûlée and other desserts; well-selected California and international wines. *Average main: $32* *203 York St.* *530/265–6399* *www.thenewmooncafe.com* *Closed Mon. No lunch weekends.*

South Pine Cafe

$ | **AMERICAN** | Locals flock here at breakfast time for lobster Benedict, chorizo tacos, and other dishes that are anything but your ordinary eggs and pancakes. Imaginative burritos and burgers and more lobster in the form of a melt sandwich appear for lunch. **Known for:** homemade muffins; vegan and gluten-free options; additional Grass Valley location. *Average main: $13* *110 S. Pine St.* *530/265–0260* *www.southpinecafe.com* *No dinner.*

Three Forks Bakery & Brewing Co.

$ | **AMERICAN** | Baked goods, wood-fired pizzas, excellent coffee (teas and kombucha, too), and microbrews made on-site draw locals and tourists to this redbrick spot with a high, heavy-beamed open ceiling. The food's ingredients come from nearby organic sources; the beers on tap range from a blonde and a pale ale to a double IPA and a porter. **Known for:** lunch and dinner menu changes with the seasons; breads, muffins, scones, cookies, and cakes; soups and salads. *Average main: $14* *211 Commercial St.* *530/470–8333* *www.threeforksnc.com* *Closed Tues.*

Hotels

Deer Creek Inn

$$$ | **B&B/INN** | The main veranda of this cozy 1860 Queen Anne Victorian overlooks lush gardens that roll past a rose-covered arbor to the creek below (where you can pan for gold). **Pros:** relaxing creek sounds; afternoon wine gathering; gourmet breakfast. **Cons:** expensive for the area; minimum weekend-stay requirement; lacks full-service hotel amenities. *Rooms from: $195* *116 Nevada St.* *530/264–7038* *www.deercreekinn.net* *4 rooms* *Free Breakfast.*

Madison House Bed & Breakfast

$$$ | **B&B/INN** | A convenient downtown location, filling breakfasts showcasing local organic products, and welcoming hosts who exceed expectations make for a winning combination at this northern Gold Country bed-and-breakfast inside a romantic Victorian house. **Pros:** landscaped garden and sun porch; homemade baked goods; historic, romantic atmosphere. **Cons:** no elevator to upper-floor rooms; some noise and sun in front rooms; weekend minimum-stay requirement. *Rooms from: $185* *427 Broad St.* *530/470–6127* *www.themadisonhouse.net* *5 rooms* *Free Breakfast.*

Outside Inn

$ | **HOTEL** | **FAMILY** | It looks like a typical one-story motel, but the Outside Inn offers a variety of unique accommodations inspired by nature or activities in nature (there's a climbing wall in the rock-climbing suite), in an ideal location to enjoy Northern California's four seasons. **Pros:** fun reinvention of a motel; convenient to trails and hikes; affiliated Inn Town Campground for camping and glamping. **Cons:** rooms are on the small side; a half mile from town; weekend minimum-stay requirement. *Rooms from: $99* *575 E. Broad St.* *530/265–2233* *www.outsideinn.com* *15 rooms* *No meals.*

Performing Arts

Miners Foundry

ARTS CENTERS | The foundry, erected in 1856, produced machines for gold mining and logging. The Pelton Water Wheel, a power source for the mines (the wheel also jump-started the hydroelectric power industry), was invented here. The building is now used to stage art, dance, music, and film events. ✉ *325 Spring St.* ☎ *530/265–5040* 🌐 *www.minersfoundry.org.*

Nevada Theatre

ARTS VENUE | Mark Twain, Emma Nevada, and Jack London have all appeared on stage at this 1865 redbrick edifice. The West Coast's longest continuously operating theater building, today it presents art and independent films, spoken-word artists, comedians, local theater groups, and live music. ✉ *401 Broad St., at Commercial St.* ☎ *530/265–6161* 🌐 *www.nevadatheatre.com.*

Grass Valley

24 miles north of Auburn.

More than half of California's total gold production was extracted from mines around Grass Valley, including the Empire Mine, which, along with the North Star Mining Museum, is among the Gold Country's most fascinating attractions. Nearby Nevada City has better dining and lodging options, though.

GETTING HERE AND AROUND

You'll need a car to get here. Take Highway 20 east from Interstate 5 or west from Interstate 80. Highway 49 is the north–south route into town. Gold Country Stage (☎ *530/477–0103*) provides public transit. Expect a moderate wait.

Sights

★ Empire Mine State Historic Park

NATIONAL/STATE PARK | **FAMILY** | Starting with the "secret map" that mine management hid from miners, you can relive the days of gold, grit, and glory, when this mine was one of the biggest and most prosperous hard-rock gold mines in North America. Empire Mine yielded an estimated 5.8 million ounces of gold from 367 miles of underground passages. You can walk into a mine shaft and peer into dark, deep recesses, and almost imagine what it felt like to work this vast operation. Dressed-up docents portraying colorful characters who shaped Northern California's history share stories about the period. The grounds have the exquisite Bourn Cottage (call for tour times), picnic tables, and gentle trails—perfect for a family outing. ✉ *10791 E. Empire St.* ☎ *530/273–8522* 🌐 *www.empiremine.org* 🎟 *$7.*

Holbrooke Hotel

HOTEL—SIGHT | A Main Street icon built in 1851, the hotel hosted entertainer Lola Montez and writer Mark Twain as well as Ulysses S. Grant and other U.S. presidents. New owners who took over in 2018 are renovating the property a section at a time. If it's open when you visit, the saloon is worth a peek as one of the oldest operating west of the Mississippi. ✉ *212 W. Main St.* ☎ *530/273–1353* 🌐 *www.holbrooke.com.*

North Star Mining Museum

MUSEUM | **FAMILY** | Housed in a former power house, the museum displays the 32-foot-high Pelton Water Wheel, said to be the largest ever built. It was used to power mining operations and was a forerunner of the modern turbines that generate hydroelectricity. Other exhibits, some geared to children, document life in the mines and the environmental effects mining had on the area. You can picnic nearby. ✉ *10933 Allison Ranch Rd.* ☎ *530/264–7569* 🌐 *www.nevadacounty-history.org* 🎟 *Donation requested.*

Restaurants

Cirino's at Main Street

$$ | **ITALIAN** | **FAMILY** | A family-owned spot with exposed brick walls, a tall ceiling, and a well-worn bar and floor, Cirino's serves up a vast menu of hefty Italian American favorites like Corsican rosemary chicken, steak à la Gorgonzola, and pork chop Milanese. The bar crew, which slings the signature Bloody Mary and other specialty cocktails, is as friendly as the rest of the team. **Known for:** house-made soups and sauces; family-friendly attitude; full-dinner "butcher shop" menu items with soup or salad, starch, and vegetable. *Average main: $22* ✉ *213 W. Main St.* ☎ *530/477–6000* 🌐 *www.cirinosatmainstreet.com.*

Valentina's Organic Bistro & Bakery

$ | **AMERICAN** | The emphasis is on wellness and organic non–genetically modified ingredients at this wide-windowed, simply decorated roadside restaurant, whose owners' inspiration for providing healthful cuisine to their community grew out of the lengthy illness of one of their daughters. Locals love the pastries, burritos, quesadillas, waffles, and "wamlets" (omelets cooked in a waffle iron) for breakfast and the burgers, sandwiches, burritos, burrito bowls, and salads for lunch. **Known for:** coffee, chai and other teas, smoothies, and blended juices; muffins, scones, brownies, and cinnamon rolls; outdoor patio. *Average main: $12* ✉ *841 Sutton Way* ☎ *530/272–4470* 🌐 *www.valentinasbistro.com* ⏲ *Closed Sun. No dinner.*

Nightlife

The Pour House

BARS/PUBS | The owners of this downtown bar across from the Holbrooke Hotel aim to please lovers of beer and wine with a dozen-plus pours of each, many from local and regional craft breweries and boutique wineries. The storefront space (closed Monday), with a long redbrick wall on the bar side, serves soups, dips, soft pretzels, and other comfort bites; there's live music some nights. ✉ *217 W. Main St., at Church St.* ☎ *530/802–5414* 🌐 *www.thepourhousegv.com.*

Auburn

18 miles northwest of Coloma, 34 miles northeast of Sacramento.

Halfway between San Francisco and Reno, Auburn convenient to gold-rush sites, outdoor recreation opportunities, and wineries. The self-proclaimed "endurance capital of the world" is abuzz almost every summer weekend with running, cycling, rafting or kayaking, and equestrian events. Old Town Auburn has its own gold-rush charm, with narrow climbing streets, cobblestone lanes, wooden sidewalks, and many original buildings. **■ TIP→ Fresh produce, flowers, and baked goods are for sale at the farmers' market, held on Saturday morning year-round.**

GETTING HERE AND AROUND

Amtrak serves Auburn, though most visitors arrive by car on Highway 49 or Interstate 80. Once downtown, you can tour on foot.

Sights

Bernhard Museum Complex

MUSEUM | Party like it's 1889 at this space whose main structure opened in 1851 as the Traveler's Rest Hotel and for 100 years was the residence of the Bernhard family. The congenial docents, dressed in Victorian garb, describe the family's history and 19th-century life in Auburn. ✉ *291 Auburn–Folsom Rd.* ☎ *530/889–6500* 🌐 *www.placer.ca.gov* *Free.*

Placer County Courthouse

MUSEUM | Visible from the highway, Auburn's standout structure is the Placer County Courthouse. The classic bronze-domed building houses the Placer County Museum, which documents the area's history—Native American, railroad, agricultural, and mining—from the early 1700s to 1900. Look for the wall safe housing gold nuggets valued at more than $300,000 today. ✉ *101 Maple St.* ☎ *530/889–6500* 🌐 *www.placer.ca.gov/departments/facility/placermuseums* 🎫 *Free.*

Restaurants

Auburn Alehouse

$ | **AMERICAN** | **FAMILY** | Inside the historic American Block building, which dates to 1856, you can see this craft operation's beers being made through glass walls behind the dining room, which serves burgers, nachos, salads, wraps, and other decent gastropub fare. Gold Country Pilsner, Old Town Brown, Gold Digger IPA, and Hop Donkey Red Ale are all Great American Beer Festival award winners. **Known for:** chicken, pork, and fish tacos; herb-brined buttermilk fried chicken; kids menu. *$ Average main: $13* ✉ *289 Washington St.* ☎ *530/885–2537* 🌐 *www.auburnalehouse.com.*

Awful Annie's

$ | **AMERICAN** | **FAMILY** | One of Auburn's favorite old-time breakfast and lunch spots entices patrons with waffles, pancakes, Monte Cristo French toast, and a slew of egg dishes you can wash down with an award-winning Bloody Mary or two. Expect burgers, sandwiches, and more Bloody Marys for lunch. **Known for:** heartiest breakfast in the foothills; Grandma's bread pudding with brandy sauce; second location in nearby Lincoln. *$ Average main: $12* ✉ *13460 Lincoln Way* ☎ *530/888–9857* 🌐 *www.awfulannies.com* ⏲ *No dinner.*

★ Carpe Vino

$$$ | **MODERN AMERICAN** | What started as a boutique wine retailer has become a must-visit experience for foodies who appreciate the hearty and imaginative French-inspired dishes served in this gem's charming setting, a restored 19th-century saloon. Sophisticated seasonal fare that always includes a vegan option is presented in a nonchalant, almost effortless way, as if ingredients rolled right from the farm basket onto your plate. **Known for:** extensive and varied wine list; impeccable service; 21-plus only. *$ Average main: $27* ✉ *1568 Lincoln Way* ☎ *530/823–0320* 🌐 *www.carpevinoauburn.com* ⏲ *Closed Sun. and Mon. No lunch.*

The Pour Choice

$ | **AMERICAN** | Black subway tiles, contemporary bistro furniture, and a gray-marble counter lit by orb-shape Edison bulbs lend urban flair to this fine spot for a craft coffee or one of more than two dozen local, national, and international brews on tap. In a sliver of a space once occupied by a drugstore, the Pour Choice, which bills itself as Auburn's living room, serves light fare that might include a chèvre and Gouda grilled-cheese sandwich on ciabatta with bacon. **Known for:** upbeat vibe; talented baristas; outdoor terrace in good weather. *$ Average main: $12* ✉ *177 Sacramento St.* ☎ *530/820–3451* 🌐 *thepourchoice.com.*

Hotels

Holiday Inn Auburn Hotel

$$ | **HOTEL** | **FAMILY** | Above the freeway across from Old Town, this hotel renovated in 2016 has a welcoming lobby and chain-standard but well-organized rooms. **Pros:** work areas in all rooms; suitable base for Gold Country exploring; on-site restaurant. **Cons:** lacks style; some traffic noise; can't walk to Old Town restaurants and shops. *$ Rooms from: $165* ✉ *120 Grass Valley Hwy.* ☎ *530/887–8787, 800/814–8787* 🌐 *www.auburnhi.com* *96 rooms* *No meals.*

★ Park Victorian

$$$$ | **B&B/INN** | A walking path leads down to Old Town Auburn from this boutique hotel inside a lavishly restored 1867 mansion set on 6½ secluded acres atop Snowden Hill. **Pros:** stunning views; within walking distance of Old Town restaurants; some original architectural details retained. **Cons:** pricey for the Gold

Almost 6 million ounces of gold were extracted from the Empire Mine.

Country but the gracious hosts deliver; minimum weekend-stay requirement; one room suitable for one adult only. $ *Rooms from: $295* ✉ *195 Park St.* ☎ *530/330–4411* 🌐 *www.parkvictorian.com* 🛏 *6 rooms* 🍽 *Free Breakfast.*

Coloma

On Hwy. 49 between Placerville (8 miles) and Auburn (18 miles).

The California gold rush started in Coloma. "My eye was caught with the glimpse of something shining in the bottom of the ditch," James Marshall recalled.

GETTING HERE AND AROUND

A car is the only practical way to get to Coloma, via Highway 49. Once parked, you can walk to all the worthwhile sights.

Sights

★ Marshall Gold Discovery State Historic Park

NATIONAL/STATE PARK | FAMILY | Most of Coloma lies within the historic park along the banks of the south fork of the American River. Though crowded with tourists in summer, Coloma hardly resembles the mob scene it was in 1849, when 2,000 prospectors staked out claims along the streambed. The town's population grew to 4,000, supporting seven hotels, three banks, and many stores and businesses. But when reserves of the precious metal dwindled, prospectors left as quickly as they had come. A working reproduction of an 1840s mill lies near the spot where James Marshall first saw gold. Trails lead to the mill, remnants of buildings and mining equipment, and a statue of Marshall with sublime views. **■ TIP→ For $7 per person, rangers give gold-panning lessons on the hour, year-round.** ✉ *310 Back St., off Hwy. 49* ☎ *530/622–3470* 🌐 *www.parks.ca.gov/marshallgold* 🎟 *$8 per vehicle.*

Placerville

44 miles east of Sacramento.

It's hard to imagine now, but in 1849 about 4,000 miners staked out every gully and hillside in Placerville, turning the town into a rip-roaring camp of log cabins, tents, and clapboard houses. The area was then known as Hangtown, a graphic allusion to the nature of frontier justice. It took on the name Placerville in 1854 and became an important supply center for the miners. (*Placer* is defined roughly as valuable minerals found in riverbeds or lakes.) Mark Hopkins, Philip Armour, and John Studebaker were among the industrialists who got their starts here. Today Placerville ranks among the hippest towns in the region, its Main Street abuzz with indie shops, coffeehouses, and wine bars, many of them inside rehabbed historic buildings.

GETTING HERE AND AROUND

You'll need a car to get to and around Placerville; it's a 45-minute drive from Sacramento via U.S. 50.

Sights

Apple Hill

FARM/RANCH | **FAMILY** | From July to late December, Apple Hill Growers Association members open their orchards and vineyards for apple and berry picking, picnicking, and wine, cider, pressed-juice, and other tastings. With treasure hunts, pond fishing, pie making, and other activities, the area is a magnet for families, but there's plenty to entice adults as well. Stop at Wofford Acres Vineyard if only see the dramatic view of the American River canyon below. The Apple Hill website has a printable map and an up-to-date events calendar, or download the Official Apple Hill Growers app. **■ TIP→ Traffic often backs up on weekends, so take U.S. 50's Camino exit or visit during the week (although kids-oriented events are on weekends).** ✉ *Placerville* ✣ *Starting 2 miles east of Hwy. 49, Exits 48–57 off U.S. 50* ☎ *530/644–7692* 🌐 *www.applehill.com.*

Boeger Winery

WINERY/DISTILLERY | Founder Greg Boeger's ancestors established a Napa Valley winery in the late 19th century. In 1972, he revived a gold rush–era farm that once supported fruit and nut orchards, a winery, and a distillery. These days Boeger produces estate wines from 30 varietals grown on two parcels totaling 100 acres, with Sauvignon Blanc and Barbera the best sellers and Zinfandel and Primitivo also worth seeking out. **■ TIP→ The creek-side picnic area fronting the tasting room hosts bands and food vendors on Friday evenings in summer (reserve space well ahead).** ✉ *1709 Carson Rd.* ✣ *Head north from U.S. 50, Exit 48, then northeast (right) on Carson Rd.* ☎ *530/622–8094* 🌐 *www.boegerwinery.com* 🎫 *Tastings from $5.*

Hangtown's Gold Bug Park & Mine

MINE | **FAMILY** | Take a self-guided tour of this fully lighted mine shaft within a park owned by the City of Placerville. The worthwhile audio tour (included) makes clear what you're seeing. **■ TIP→ A shaded stream runs through the park, and there are picnic facilities.** ✉ *2635 Goldbug La., Exit U.S. 50 at Bedford Ave. and follow signs* ☎ *530/642–5207* 🌐 *www.goldbugpark.org* 🎫 *Park free; mine tour $7* ⏲ *Closed weekdays Nov.–Mar. except for a few holidays.*

★ Holly's Hill Vineyards

WINERY/DISTILLERY | The founders of this woodsy hilltop winery 7 miles south of Apple Hill tasted Châteauneuf-du-Pape on their honeymoon, sparking a lifetime passion for Rhône wines made in classic French style. Mourvèdre is a specialty, by itself and in blends with Grenache, Syrah, or both. Carignane, Counoise, and other lower-profile Rhône reds are also made, along with whites that include the Roussanne-dominant Patriarche Blanc blend. Taste these beautifully crafted estate wines in a space with views that extend 75 miles on a clear day, and picnic outside when you're done. ✉ *3680 Leisure La., off Pleasant Valley Rd.* ✣ *From U.S. 50, Exit 49, follow Broadway east to Newtown Rd. and Pleasant Valley Rd. southeast* ☎ *530/344–0227* 🌐 *www.hollyshill.com* 🎫 *Tastings $5.*

★ Lava Cap Winery

WINERY/DISTILLERY | Nineteenth-century miners knew if they found the type of volcanic rocks visible everywhere on this winery's property that gold was nearby. These days the rocky soils and vineyard elevations as high as 2,800 feet play pivotal roles in the creation of fruit forward yet elegant wines with a hint of minerals. Zinfandel, Grenache, Cabernet Franc, and Petite Sirah star among the reds, Chardonnay and Viognier among the whites. **■ TIP→ After a tasting you can picnic on the patio and enjoy Sierra foothills vistas.** ✉ *2221 Fruitridge Rd.* ☎ *530/621–0175* 🌐 *www.lavacap.com* 🎫 *Tastings from $5.*

Lewis Grace Winery

WINERY/DISTILLERY | A bright red 1890 barn greets visitors to this winery on land whose vineyards were replaced with apples during Prohibition. Wine critics praise the estate Tempranillo and Cabernet Sauvignon for their structure and elegance, with Grenache, Syrah, and Cabernet Franc the other noteworthy reds and Viognier and Pinot Gris the standout whites. Grapevines surround the high-ceilinged tasting room and adjacent patio on two sides, with views of the Crystal Range, its peaks snowcapped more than half the year, in the distance. ✉ *2701 Carson Rd.* ☎ *530/642–8424* 🌐 *gracepatriotwines.com* 🎫 *Tastings $5* ⏲ *Closed Tues.*

Restaurants

Allez

$$ | **FRENCH** | The tale of how the couple running this spot for to-go or dine-in French food came to be husband and wife says all one needs to know about their passion for beautifully crafted cuisine: he won her heart with his escargot sauce. In a casual space with ocher walls, six utilitarian stools at the wine bar, and a few tables inside and out, the two serve baguette sandwiches, salads, crepes, stews, and entrées like steak au poivre and wild-mushroom pasta. **Known for:** all-day prix-fixe menu (a deal), plus à la carte; sandwich, salad, and dessert lunch boxes; French pastries. $ *Average main: $21* ✉ *4242 Fowler La., Diamond Springs* ✣ *Off Hwy. 49, 3 miles south of downtown Placerville* ☎ *530/621–1160* 🌐 *www.allezeldorado.com* ⏲ *Closed Sun. and Mon.*

Heyday Cafe

$$ | **AMERICAN** | Inside an exposed-brick 1857 former assay office where miners exchanged gold nuggets for the coin of the realm, the Heyday is a happy haven for salads, panini, and thin-crust pizzas at lunch and dinner entrées that might include seared salmon with coffee-smoked carrot puree and duck-fat confit half-roasted chicken. The mood here is casual, but the food is prepared with style. **Known for:** sherry-infused lobster bisque; local to international wine list; molasses gingerbread cake. $ *Average main: $22* ✉ *325 Main St.* ☎ *530/626–9700* 🌐 *www.heydaycafe.com.*

★ Smith Flat House

$$$ | **MODERN AMERICAN** | Carefully sourced ingredients from local purveyors, meticulous execution, and a historic setting at a former mine site have made this restaurant 3 miles east of downtown a hit among locals, Gold Country tourists, and travelers heading to or from Tahoe. The seasonally changing menu might include crab ravioli, bouillabaisse, and the Black and White entrée of filet mignon and perfectly grilled prawns. **Known for:** waffle Benedict at Sunday brunch; salads, pizzas, burgers for weekend lunch; "hyper local, domestic, and international" wine list. [$] *Average main: $29* ✉ *2021 Smith Flat Rd.* ✥ *From U.S. 50, Exit 49, head north on Point View Dr. and Jacquier Rd. and east on Smith Flat Rd.* ☎ *530/621–1003* 🌐 *www.smithflathouse.com* ⏲ *Closed Mon. and Tues. No lunch Wed.–Fri.*

Solid Ground Brewing

$ | **ECLECTIC** | The chef at this brewpub with a no-nonsense industrial decor (high ceilings, concrete floor, huge garage doors) tailors the cuisine to the namesake beers produced by two Sierra foothills natives, one with an enology degree, the other with extensive experience in European beer making. Along with gastropub stalwarts like spicy wings, smoked bratwurst, and sliders (both with grass-fed beef, one with IPA bacon jam and Brie), chicken korma or salmon tartine might also appear on the menu. **Known for:** cheesy fried polenta tots; wine blended into some beers; live music at Sunday brunch and other times. [$] *Average main: $12* ✉ *553 Pleasant Valley Rd., Diamond Springs* ✥ *Off Hwy. 49, 3 miles south of downtown Placerville* ☎ *530/344–7442* 🌐 *solidgroundbrewing.com.*

Hotels

★ Eden Vale Inn

$$$$ | **B&B/INN** | **FAMILY** | Handcrafted by the owners, this lavish but rustic B&B occupies a converted turn-of-the-20th-century hay barn, the centerpiece of which is a 27-foot slate fireplace that rises to a sloping ceiling of timber beams. **Pros:** rooms are exceptionally plush; the patio and grounds are stunning; plenty of places outside for kids to run. **Cons:** expensive for the area; summer weekends book up far ahead; weekend minimum-stay requirement. [$] *Rooms from: $365* ✉ *1780 Springvale Rd.* ☎ *530/621–0901* 🌐 *www.edenvaleinn.com* *7 rooms* *Free Breakfast.*

★ Lucinda's Country Inn

$$$ | **B&B/INN** | Effusive but not intrusive hospitality is the trademark of this contemporary inn between Placerville and Plymouth whose spacious light-filled suites have views of the oaks, firs, and other trees surrounding the property. **Pros:** romantic setting; convenient for wine touring; filling breakfast and catered dinner option. **Cons:** some rooms sleep only two; long drive to Placerville or Plymouth restaurants; weekend minimum-stay requirement. [$] *Rooms from: $180* ✉ *6701 Perry Creek Rd., Fair Play* ☎ *530/409–4169* 🌐 *www.lucindascountryinn.com* *5 rooms* *Free Breakfast.*

Plymouth

20 miles south of Placerville.

The most concentrated Gold Country wine-touring area lies in the hills of the Shenandoah Valley, east of Plymouth—you could easily spend two or three days just hitting the highlights. Zinfandel is the primary grape grown here, but area vineyards produce many other varietals, from Rhônes like Syrah and Mourvèdre to Italian Barberas and Sangioveses. Most wineries are open for tastings at least on Friday and weekends, and some of the top ones are open daily; many welcome picnickers.

GETTING HERE AND AROUND

Highway 49 runs north–south through Plymouth's small downtown. Reach the Shenandoah Valley by heading east from the highway on Fiddletown Road and then north on Plymouth-Shenandoah Road. You will need a car to explore the valley and its vineyards.

Sights

Amador Cellars

WINERY/DISTILLERY | Larry and Linda Long made wine out of their home in Truckee for 15 years before opening their down-home Amador County winery. Their son Michael is head winemaker, daughter Ashley his assistant. Estate-grown Zinfandel is the biggest seller, but this small operation also does well with Syrah, Barbera, Tempranillo, and the Portuguese varietal Touriga (one of the Port grapes), and there's a GSM (Grenache, Syrah, and Mourvèdre) Rhône-style blend. Just outside the modest tasting space, two oak trees shade a patio where guests are welcome to picnic. ✉ *11093 Shenandoah Rd., Plymouth* ☎ *209/245–6150* 🌐 *amadorcellars.com.*

Bella Grace Vineyards

WINERY/DISTILLERY | For all the Gold Country's caverns and underground mines, few opportunities exist to taste wine in a cave, but at Bella Grace you can do so in one with vineyard views from the entrance while you sip. Barbera and old-vine Zinfandel earn the most critical acclaim; the Vermentino, Viognier, and Primitivo are worth checking out, too. ■ **TIP→ Cave tastings take place only three days a week (picnickers welcome), but the winery's downtown Sutter Creek space is open daily.** ✉ *22715 Upton Rd., off Steiner Rd., Plymouth* ☎ *209/418–5040* 🌐 *www.bellagracevineyards.com* ⏲ *Closed Mon.–Thurs.*

Charles Spinetta Winery and Wildlife Gallery

WINERY/DISTILLERY | A casual, family-owned winery that appeals to non–wine drinkers with wildlife watercolors, sculptures, and other artworks and to lovers of sweet wines with orange and black muscats and the Zinfandel-based Zinetta, Charles Spinetta, in business since 1984, also makes dry reds. Petite Sirah, Barbara, Zinfandel, and its cousin Primitivo are among the latter ones that stand out. ✉ *12557 Steiner Rd., off Shenandoah Rd., Plymouth* ☎ *209/245–3384* 🌐 *www.charlesspinettawinery.com* ⏲ *Closed Tues. and Wed.*

★ Jeff Runquist Wines

WINERY/DISTILLERY | Judges at the 2018 San Francisco International Wine Competition bestowed Winery of the Year honors on this operation whose tasting room ranks among the Shenandoah Valley's jolliest. Known for elegant, fruit-forward wines with velvety tannins, Jeff Runquist specializes in Barbera, Zinfandel, and Petite Sirah but makes red wines from nearly two dozen varietals from Amador County, Lodi, Clarksburg, and several other appellations. ✉ *10776 Shenandoah Rd., Plymouth* ☎ *916/245–6282* 🌐 *www.jeffrunquistwines.com* 🎫 *Free* ⏲ *Closed Tues. and Wed.*

★ Scott Harvey Wines

WINERY/DISTILLERY | Owner-winemaker Scott Harvey helped elevate the profile of Amador County wines in the 1970s, later developing two wine programs in the Napa Valley before returning full time to the Sierra foothills. Harvey describes the foothills as similar to Italy's Piemonte region, where Barbera originated, but with one additional benefit: it's sunnier here, which this grape loves. Barbera, Zinfandel (one from vines planted in 1869), and Syrah are the focus, but you'll also find Cabernet Sauvignon and other reds along with Sauvignon Blanc, Riesling, and sparkling wine. ✉ *10861 Shenandoah Rd., Plymouth* ☎ *209/245–3670* 🌐 *www.scottharveywines.com* 🎫 *Tastings $7.*

Sobon Estate

WINERY/DISTILLERY | You can sip fruity, robust Zinfandels—old vine and new—and learn about wine making and Shenandoah Valley pioneer life at the museum here. This winery was established in 1856 and has been run since 1989 by the owners of Shenandoah Vineyards (whose wines you can also taste). To sample the best of the Zins, pay the modest fee for the reserve tasting. ✉ *14430 Shenandoah Rd., Plymouth* ☎ *209/245–4455* 🌐 *www.sobonwine.com* 🎫 *Tastings from $5.*

Terre Rouge and Easton Wines

WINERY/DISTILLERY | The winery of Bill Easton and Jane O'Riordan achieves success with two separate labels: terre Rouge, which focuses on Rhône-style wines, makes some of the area's best Syrahs. The Easton label specializes in Zinfandel from old and new vines, including an Amador County bottling. **■ TIP→ You can picnic on the shaded patio here, and there's a pétanque court nearby.** ✉ *10801 Dickson Rd., Plymouth* ☎ *209/245–4277* 🌐 *www.terrerougewines.com* 🎫 *Tastings $5* ⏲ *Closed Tues. and Wed.*

★ Turley Wine Cellars

WINERY/DISTILLERY | Zinfandel fans won't want to miss Turley, which makes a dozen and a half single-vineyard wines (collectors love them) from old-vine grapes grown all over California. Some of the wines, including a few from Amador County, are available only in the tasting room. Petite Sirah and Cabernet Sauvignon are two other emphases. Guests are welcome to purchase wine by the glass or bottle and picnic amid old olive trees when the weather's good, under an awning if not. **■ TIP→ Customized "focused tastings," offered twice daily by reservation, showcase wines from key vineyard sites.** ✉ *10851 Shenandoah Rd., Plymouth* ☎ *209/245–3938* 🌐 *www.turleywinecellars.com/amador* 🎫 *Tastings from $10.*

Vino Noceto

WINERY/DISTILLERY | Owners Suzy and Jim Gullett draw raves for their Sangioveses, which range from light and fruity to rich and heavy. They also produce small lots of Pinot Grigio, Barbera, Zinfandel, and other varietals. Tastings take place in the red barn where the couple began operations in the 1980s. ✉ *11011 Shenandoah Rd., at Dickson Rd., Plymouth* ☎ *209/245–6556* 🌐 *www.noceto.com* 🎫 *Tastings free, tour $18.*

Restaurants

Amador Vintage Market

$ | AMERICAN | Area caterer Beth Sogaard spiffed up Plymouth's original general store, transforming its handsome red- and sand-color brick building into a dandy stop for quiche and other breakfast fare and gourmet sandwiches and deli specialties like Muscovy duck confit, Dijon potato salad, and house-smoked salmon. A recent turkey meat loaf pepped up with blue cheese and porcini mushrooms is typical of Sogaard's reimagining of comfort-food staples you can enjoy on-site, at nearby wineries, or on picnic tables at the park next door. **Known for:** homemade truffle potato chips; selection of local wines (good way to tell where to go tasting); order for pickup or nearby delivery. $ *Average main: $9* ✉ *9393 Main St., Plymouth* ☎ *209/245–3663* 🌐 *bethsogaard.com/vintage-market* ⏲ *No dinner.*

★ Taste

$$$$ | MODERN AMERICAN | A serendipitous find in downtown Plymouth, Taste serves eclectic modern dishes made from fresh local fare. Phyllo-wrapped mushroom "cigars" are a small-plate staple, and seared day boat scallops, rack of lamb, and duck confit are examples of owner-chef Mark Berkner's sustainably sourced, creative entrées. **Known for:** superb beer and wine list; knowledgeable sommeliers; Monday prix-fixe menu. $ *Average main: $37* ✉ *9402 Main St., Plymouth* ☎ *209/245–3463* 🌐 *www.restauranttaste.com* ⏲ *Closed Wed. No lunch Mon.–Thurs.*

Hotels

Amador Harvest Inn

$$ | B&B/INN | This B&B adjacent to the Deaver Vineyards tasting room occupies a bucolic lakeside spot in the Shenandoah Valley. **Pros:** rustic charm; hospitable innkeeper; hearty breakfasts. **Cons:** no children allowed; somewhat spare

Reliving the Gold Rush

When James W. Marshall burst into John Sutter's Mill on January 24, 1848, carrying flecks of gold in his hat, the millwright unleashed the glittering California gold rush with these immortal words: "Boys, I believe I've found a gold mine!" In short order, California's coastal communities began to empty as prospectors flocked to the hills, getting a jump on East Coasters, who didn't hear about the gold boom until the *New York Herald* reported it in mid-August. The gold rush began in earnest in 1849. Before it was over, Columbia's mines alone had yielded $87,000,000, and California's Mother Lode—a vein of gold-bearing quartz that stretched 150 miles across the Sierra Nevada foothills—had been nearly tapped dry.

Pure Vacation Treasure

The gold rush soon became the gold bust—by 1855 digging for the precious mineral had become increasingly difficult, and large corporations had monopolized mining operations—but today you can relive the era. Journey down the serpentine, nearly 300-mile-long Gold Country Highway, a two-lane route appropriately numbered 49, to find pure vacation treasure: fascinating Mother Lode towns, rip-roaring mining camps, and significant strike sites.

Pan the Streams

In Placerville and other towns you can still pan the streams. Grab a non-Teflon-coated pan with sloping sides and head to the hills. Find a stream—preferably one containing black sand—you can stoop beside, and then scoop out sediment to fill your pan. Add water, then gently shake the pan sideways, back and forth. Doing this allows any gold to settle at the bottom. Pick out and toss away any larger rocks. Keep adding water, keep shaking the pan, and slowly pour the loosened waste gravel over the rim of the pan. If you're left with gold, yell "Eureka!" (California's state motto) then put it in a glass container. Your findings may not make you rich, but will entitle you to bragging rights. If you'd rather go with a guide, plenty of attractions and museums in the Gold Country will let you try your hand at prospecting.

decor; minimum weekend-stay requirement. *$ Rooms from: $150 ✉ 12455 Steiner Rd., Plymouth ☎ 209/245–5512, 800/217–2304 🌐 amadorharvestinn.com ⇆ 4 rooms 🍽 Free Breakfast.*

★ Rest Hotel Plymouth

$$ | **B&B/INN** | The team behind Plymouth's Taste restaurant converted two adjacent run-down buildings into this boutique hotel whose individually decorated rooms rank among the area's finest. **Pros:** attention to detail; continental breakfast's baked goods; evening wine hour. **Cons:** minimum stay requirement some weekends; lacks big-city hotel amenities; some noise in street-side rooms. *$ Rooms from: $142 ✉ 9372 Main St., Plymouth ☎ 209/245–6315 🌐 www.hotel-rest.net ⇆ 16 rooms 🍽 Free Breakfast.*

Amador City

6 miles south of Plymouth.

The history of tiny Amador City (population 200) mirrors the boom-bust-boom cycle of many Gold Country towns. With an output of $42 million in gold, its Keystone Mine was one of the most productive in the Mother Lode. After all the gold

Did You Know?

You can still pan for gold, but any shiny stuff will usually be worthless iron pyrite. Here a young prospector tries his hand at Marshall Gold Discovery State Park.

was extracted, the miners cleared out, and the area suffered. Amador City now derives its wealth from tourists, who come to browse through its antiques and specialty shops.

GETTING HERE AND AROUND

Park where you can along Old Highway 49 (a bypass diverts Highway 49 traffic around Sutter Creek and Amador City), and walk around.

Hotels

Imperial Hotel

$$ | **B&B/INN** | An 1879 hotel on the bend in this one-block town, the Imperial charms its guests with six second-floor rooms whose antique furnishings include iron-and-brass beds, gingerbread flourishes, and, in one instance, art-deco appointments. **Pros:** history-evoking stay; good restaurant and bar; two rooms with balconies. **Cons:** hotel and bar are the town nightlife; rooms and hotel could use a refresh; noise issues in street-side rooms. *Rooms from: $130* *14202 Old Hwy. 49* *209/267–9172* *www.imperialamador.com* *9 rooms* *Free Breakfast.*

Sutter Creek

2 miles south of Amador City.

Sutter Creek is a charming conglomeration of balconied buildings, Victorian homes, and neo–New England structures. At any time of year Main Street (formerly part of Highway 49) is worth a stroll for its shops selling antiques and works by local artists and craftspeople. Tasting rooms of note include Bella Grace and Scott Harvey. Sites like the 19th-century water-powered Knight Foundry and Monteverde Store Museum are worth a peek if you're in town on the rare days they're open, but always accessible is the open-air Miners' Bend Historic Gold Mining Park.

GETTING HERE AND AROUND

Arrive here by car on Highway 49. There's no public transit, but downtown is walkable. The visitor center organizes walking tours.

ESSENTIALS

INFORMATION Sutter Creek Visitor Center *71A Main St.* *209/267–1344* *www.suttercreek.org.*

Sights

Miners' Bend Historic Gold Mining Park

CITY PARK | A dedicated band of volunteers converted a parking lot into a compact open-air tribute to the area's mining legacy. Signs along the path describe 19th-century mining operations and the 16 pieces of equipment used to extract or process ore on display. *29 Old Hwy. 49* *209/560–6880* *suttercreekfoundation.org* *Free.*

Monteverde Store Museum

MUSEUM | This store, opened 1896, is a relic from the past: its final owner walked out more than four decades ago and never returned. These days you can peruse what he left behind, including typical wares from a century ago, an elaborate antique scale, and a chair-encircled potbellied stove. *3 Randolph St.* *209/267–0493.*

Restaurants

Gold Dust Pizza

$$ | **PIZZA** | Zesty well-made pies like the Miner Moe's BBQ Chicken, with red onions, pineapple, bacon, and cheese make this casual spot a few steps off Main Street an excellent choice, particularly for lunch or a mid-afternoon snack. You can also build your own pizza or order a sandwich; there's some indoor seating, but when the weather's good most folks eat outside on the front patio or the creek-side one out back. **Known for:** ultracrispy crust; chicken wings and calzone; combo meals. *Average main:*

$16 ✉ 20 Eureka St., off Main St., Davis ☎ 209/267–1900.

Hotels

Eureka Street Inn

$$ | **B&B/INN** | The lead- and stained-glass windows and the original redwood paneling, wainscoting, and beams lend a cozy feel to this 1914 Craftsman-style bungalow whose rooms, furnished with antiques, all have a gas stove or fireplace. **Pros:** quiet location; large bathrooms; engaging innkeeper. **Cons:** weekend minimum-stay requirement; lacks pool, room service, and other hotel amenities; old-time feel may not work for all travelers. *Rooms from: $165 ✉ 55 Eureka St. ☎ 209/267–5500 🌐 www.eurekastreet-inn.com 4 rooms Free Breakfast.*

The Foxes Inn of Sutter Creek

$$$ | **B&B/INN** | The rooms in this 1857 yellow-clapboard house are handsome, with high ceilings, antique beds, and armoires; five have gas fireplaces. **Pros:** lovely inside and out; friendly owners; discounts at Helwig Winery for guests (same ownership). **Cons:** minimum weekend-stay requirement; pricey in season; per website inn is "most suitable" for children 12 and over. *Rooms from: $199 ✉ 77 Main St. ☎ 209/267–5882, 800/987–3344 🌐 www.foxesinn.com 7 rooms Free Breakfast.*

Grey Gables Inn

$$$ | **B&B/INN** | Charming if you like lace and frills, this inn—with rooms named after British poets—brings the English countryside to Gold Country. **Pros:** English-manor feel; tasteful interiors and grounds; complimentary bottle of wine. **Cons:** adjacent town's busy main drag; minimum weekend-stay requirement; dated design. *Rooms from: $220 ✉ 161 Hanford St. ☎ 209/267–1039, 800/473–9422 🌐 www.greygables.com 10 rooms Free Breakfast.*

Volcano

12½ miles northeast of Jackson, 13 miles east of Sutter Creek, 17 miles southeast of Plymouth.

Many roads, all of them winding, all of them scenic, lead to Volcano, an off-the-beaten-path former mining town of about 120 people, the entirety of which is a California Historical Landmark. Pick up a pastry at the Kneading Dough Bakery and head out any time of year to the main attraction, Black Chasm Cavern. In early spring, weather and other factors permitting, combine the cave visit with one to see Daffodil Hill's namesake flowers in bloom.

GETTING HERE AND AROUND

A car is the practical way to get to Volcano, via Highway 88 east from Jackson; Ridge Road and Highway 88 east from Sutter Creek (alternate route: Sutter Creek–Volcano Road, also east); or Fiddletown Road east from Plymouth to Shake Ridge Road southwest to Charleston Road southeast. GPS can be sketchy here, so plot and save your route when you have good coverage.

Sights

Black Chasm Cavern National Natural Landmark

CAVE | **FAMILY** | Guided 50-minute tours take you past stalactites, stalagmites, and rare formations of delicate helictites in three underground chambers, one of which also contains a lake. Black Chasm isn't the largest cave in the Gold Country, but its crystals dazzle both eye and camera—the Landmark Chamber, the tour's third stop, inspired a scene in the 2003 film *The Matrix Reloaded*. Outside is an area where kids can "pan" for crystals. *✉ 15701 Pioneer Volcano Rd., Volcano ↔ ¾ mile south of Volcano off Pine Grove–Volcano Rd. ☎ 209/296–5007 🌐 blackchasmcavern.com $19 Closed Mon.–Thurs. in Jan.*

Daffodil Hill

GARDEN | Each spring a 7-acre hillside east of Sutter Creek erupts in a riot of yellow and gold as (in a good year) hundreds of thousands of daffodils burst into bloom. The garden is the work of the McLaughlin family, which has owned this site since 1887. Daffodil plantings began in the 1930s. The display usually takes place between mid-March and mid-April. **■ TIP→ Call for daily weather updates.** ✉ *18310 Rams Horn Grade Rd., Volcano* ✣ *From Main St., Hwy. 49, in Sutter Creek, take Shake Ridge Rd. east 13 miles* ☎ *209/296–7048* 🌐 *suttercreek.org/sutter-creek-events-daffodil-hill-amador-county* 🎫 *Free* ⏲ *Closed late Apr.–early Mar.*

Restaurants

Kneading Dough Bakery

$ | **AMERICAN** | Breakfast entrées, soups, soufflés, and sandwiches are on the menu at this beloved spot for pastries, tarts, coffee cakes, scones, cookies, muffins, cupcakes, and other baked goods, all so well composed you'll wonder why your larger town doesn't have bakers this accomplished. Inside a 19th-century stone-and-wood building, the bakery has indoor and outdoor seating. **Known for:** enthusiastic owner and staff; Nana's Famous Cinnamon Rolls; order ahead (see website) for pickup or delivery to Sutter Creek or Jackson. $ *Average main: $9* ✉ *16154 Main St., Volcano* ☎ *209/296–4663* 🌐 *www.kneadingdoughbakery.com.*

Hotels

Volcano Pub + Inn

$ | **B&B/INN** | The folks behind Plymouth's Taste restaurant and Rest hotel operate this four-room second-floor inn whose first incarnation, from the 1880s into the 1920s, was as a saloon and boardinghouse for miners and other mostly long-term guests. **Pros:** daily specials at pub; simple but pleasing decor; homemade full breakfast with egg dish, fresh fruit, and baked goods. **Cons:** per website "not suited for small children"; two rooms have a shower but no tub; minimum weekend-stay requirement. $ *Rooms from: $97* ✉ *21375 Consolation St., Volcano* ☎ *209/296–7711* 🌐 *www.volcanounion.com* *4 rooms* *Free Breakfast.*

Jackson

8 miles south of Sutter Creek.

Jackson wasn't the Gold Country's rowdiest town, but the party lasted longer here than most anywhere else: "girls' dormitories" (aka brothels) and nickel slot machines flourished until the mid-1950s. Jackson also had the world's deepest and richest gold mines, the Kennedy and the Argonaut, which together produced $70 million in gold. Most of the miners who worked the lode were of Serbian or Italian origin, and they gave the town a European character that persists to this day. Jackson has pioneer cemeteries whose headstones tell the stories of local Serbian and Italian families. The city's official website (🌐 *ci.jackson.ca.us; click on "Visitor Center"*) has cemetery and walking-tour maps.

GETTING HERE AND AROUND

Arrive by car on Highway 49. You can walk to downtown sights but otherwise will need a car.

Sights

Kennedy Gold Mine

HISTORIC SITE | On weekends, docents offer guided 90-minute surface tours of one of the most prolific mines of the gold-rush era and one of the deepest gold mines in the world. Exhibits inside the remaining buildings illustrate how gold flakes were melted for shipment to San Francisco and how "skips" were used to lower miners and materials into the mile-long shaft and carry ore to the surface. *Kennedy Mine Rd., at Argonaut La. ½ mile east of Hwy. 49 209/223–9542 www.kennedy-goldmine.com Free; guided tour $12 Closed weekdays year-round, weekends Nov.–Feb.*

Preston Castle

HISTORIC SITE | History buffs and ghost hunters regularly make the trip to this fantastically creepy 156-room Romanesque Revival structure erected in 1894 to house troubled youth. Having fallen into disrepair, the building is slowly undergoing a full restoration. On tours, which take place on many Saturdays between April and August, you'll hear all sorts of spine-tingling tales. *909 Palm Dr., Ione 12 miles west of Jackson via Hwys. 88 and 104 209/256–3623 www.prestoncastle.com $20 Closed Sept.–Mar.*

Restaurants

Mel and Faye's Diner

$ | AMERICAN | FAMILY | Since 1956, the Gillman family has been serving up its famous "Moo Burger" with two patties and special sauce—so big it still makes cow sounds, presumably. Breakfast is available all day at this homey diner. **Known for:** loads of atmosphere; milk shakes and floats; freshly baked pies. *Average main: $14 31 Hwy. 88 209/223–0853 melandfayes.homestead.com.*

Teresa's Place

$$ | ITALIAN | Ease back in time at this rustic roadside favorite of Gold Country residents and regulars that dates back to 1921, when its namesake, an Italian immigrant, opened a boardinghouse for local miners. Run by her descendants, the restaurant serves unfussy renditions of Italian American classics—pastas, wood-fired pizzas, veal and chicken dishes, and steak and seafood. **Known for:** full bar; local wines and microbrews; minestrone soup from family recipe. *Average main: $21 1235 Jackson Gate Rd. From downtown head north 1¼ miles on N. Main St.; from Hwy. 49 north of town take Jackson Gate Rd. east 1½ miles 209/223–1786 www.teresas-place.com Closed Wed. and Thurs. No lunch Sat.–Tues.*

Hotels

Hotel Léger

$ | HOTEL | A rowdy miners' haunt during the gold rush, this convivial saloon and hotel about 8 miles south of Jackson contains 13 rooms decorated with a mishmash of Victorian antiques and more utilitarian pieces. **Pros:** rich in history, including a 2013 "Hotel Impossible" makeover; individually decorated rooms with antiques and utilitarian pieces; on-site restaurant and saloon. **Cons:** creaky wooden floors; rooms above the saloon can be noisy; some rooms feel cramped. *Rooms from: $110 8304 Main St., Mokelumme Hill 209/286–1401 www.hotelleger.com 13 rooms No meals.*

Angels Camp

20 miles south of Jackson.

Angels Camp is famous chiefly for its May jumping-frog contest, based on Mark Twain's short story "The Celebrated Jumping Frog of Calaveras County." The writer reputedly heard the story of the jumping frog from Ross Coon, proprietor of Angels Hotel, which opened in 1856. Sidewalk plaques downtown à la the Hollywood Walk of Fame celebrate the winning frogs in the continuing competition. Either training's gotten way better, or something else is in play—the 1929 victor jumped only 4 feet, but for the last three decades most of the leaps have been from 18- to 20-plus feet. In addition to the contests, Angels Camp's draws include its explorable subterranean caverns and river and lake fishing spots for salmon, trout, and bass.

GETTING HERE AND AROUND

Angels Camp is at the intersection of Highway 49 and Highway 4. You'll need a car to get here and around.

★ Angels Camp Museum

HISTORIC SITE | FAMILY | Learn a little bit about Mark Twain's "The Celebrated Jumping Frog of Calaveras County"—and Angels Camp's celebrated frog-jumping contests—at this museum's street-side facility, then head to the 3-acre spread behind it for a fascinating survey of gold rush–era mining history. The grounds include a carriage house with pre-automotive farming and passenger coaches and wagons, a large building with mining equipment, and, outside in its original mountings, the 27-foot-diameter water wheel that powered machinery at the area's Angels Quartz Mine. ✉ *753 S. Main St.* ☎ *209/736–2963* 🌐 *angelscamp.gov/museum* 🎫 *$7.*

★ Moaning Cavern

CAVE | FAMILY | For a different sort of underground jewel, wander into an ancient limestone cave, where stalactites and stalagmites, not gold and silver, await. Take the 235-step Spiral Tour down a staircase built in 1922 into this vast cavern, or descend farther on the Expedition Tour caving adventure. Outside are zip lines and a climbing tower. ✉ *5350 Moaning Cave Rd., Vallecito* ✥ *About 2 miles south of Vallecito off Parrotts Ferry Rd.* ☎ *209/736–2708* 🎫 *Tours from $20, zip line $50.*

Murphys

10 miles northeast of Angels Camp.

Murphys is the Gold Country's most compact, orderly town, with enough shops and restaurants to keep families busy for at least a half day, and more than 20 tasting rooms within walking distance. To learn about the full lineup, drop by the Calaveras Wine Alliance's visitor center, whose staffers are good at pairing visitors with the right space, in some case providing discount passes. A well-preserved hamlet of white-picket fences and Victorian houses, Murphys exhibits an upscale vibe. Horatio Alger, Ulysses S. Grant, and other celebs passed through here, staying at what's now called the Murphys Historic Hotel & Lodge when they, along with many other 19th-century tourists, came to investigate the giant sequoia groves in nearby Calaveras Big Trees State Park.

GETTING HERE AND AROUND

Murphys is 10 miles northeast of Highway 49 on Highway 4. You'll need to drive here. Parking can be difficult on summer weekends.

CONTACT Calaveras Wine Alliance ✉ *202 Main St.* ☎ *209/728–9467* 🌐 *calaveraswines.org.*

★ Calaveras Big Tree State Park

NATIONAL/STATE PARK | FAMILY | The park protects hundreds of the largest and rarest living things on the planet—magnificent giant sequoia redwood trees. Some are 3,000 years old, 90 feet around at the base, and 250 feet tall. There are campgrounds, cabin rentals, and picnic areas; swimming, wading, fishing, and sunbathing on the Stanislaus River are popular in summer. Enjoy the "three senses" trail, designated for the blind, with interpretive signs in braille that guide visitors to touch the bark and encourage children to slow down and enjoy the forest in a more sensory way. ✉ *1170 E. Hwy. 4, Arnold* ✥ *15 miles northeast of Murphys, 4 miles northeast of Arnold* ☎ *209/795–2334* 🌐 *www.parks.ca.gov/calaverasbigtrees* 🎫 *$10 per vehicle.*

DEA Bathroom Machineries

STORE/MALL | History resides inside this two-story plumbing shop, and not just because it occupies the 1901 former I.O.O.F. (International Order of Odd Fellows) Hall, constructed of lumber milled nearby. Though it exists primarily as a specialist in antique plumbing fixtures and vintage parts, the museumlike shop displays (all for sale) old tobacco tins, stereoscope cards, lamps, sewing machines, glassware, and similar items, plus souvenirs. **■TIP→ Be sure to slip upstairs to check out the deluxe porcelain toilets, some as ornate as fine china and selling in the thousands.** ✉ *495 Main St.* ☎ *209/728–2031* 🌐 *deabath.com.*

Ironstone Vineyards

WINERY/DISTILLERY | Tours here take in spectacular gardens and underground tunnels cooled by a waterfall and include the automated performance of a restored silent-movie-era pipe organ. On display near the tasting room is a 44-pound specimen of crystalline gold. The winery, known for Merlot, Cabernet Sauvignon, Cabernet Franc, and old-vine Zinfandel, hosts concerts and other events. Its deli has picnic items. **■TIP→ Ironstone is worth a visit even if you don't drink wine.** ✉ *1894 6 Mile Rd.* ✣ *From Main St. in town, head south on Scott St.* ☎ *209/728–1251* 🌐 *www.ironstonevineyards.com* 🎫 *Tastings $5.*

Lavender Ridge

WINERY/DISTILLERY | A stone building dating to 1859 houses this boutique winery's tasting room, which also sells artisanal cheeses and lavender products. Lavender Ridge's longtime owner-winemaker uses traditional French methods to craft wines from organically farmed Rhône grapes. The lineup includes single-varietal Viognier, Roussane, and Grenache Blanc whites (also Rolle, aka Vermentino) and Grenache, Syrah, and Mourvèdre reds, single varietal and in a blend. Cheeses accompany all tastings, a nice touch. ✉ *425 Main St.* ☎ *209/728–2441* 🌐 *lavenderridgevineyard.com* 🎫 *Tastings from $10.*

Mercer Caverns

CAVE | Light-hearted, well-informed guides lead 45-minute tours (208 steps down, 232 steps up) into caverns a prospector named Walter J. Mercer discovered in 1885. Millions of years in the making, the sheer, draperylike formations and aragonite crystals that resemble snowflakes enthrall visitors. **■TIP→ Dress in layers (even in summer) and wear nonskid closed-toe shoes for this mildly strenuous adventure.** ✉ *1665 Sheep Ranch Rd.* ☎ *209/728–2101* 🌐 *mercercaverns.net* 🎫 *$18.*

Murphys Old Timers Museum

MUSEUM | A quirky blast from the past in a stone building that survived three 19th-century fires that destroyed downtown, the museum documents Murphys history with artifacts of the gold-rush period, the area's native people, and pioneer families, among them the town's namesake clan. **■TIP→ Historic walking tours take place on Saturday at 10 am.** ✉ *470 Main St.* ☎ *209/728–1160* 🎫 *Free (donation encouraged)* ⏲ *Closed Tues.–Thurs. and Mon. except holidays.*

Newsome Harlow Wines

WINERY/DISTILLERY | Single-vineyard Sierra Foothills Zinfandels are the passion of Newsome Harlow's part owner and winemaker Scott Klann. The ebullient Klann also makes Petite Sirah, Syrah, Carignane, and the Meritage blend of Cabernet Sauvignon and other Bordeaux varietals—whites include a Sauvignon Blanc on several local restaurants' wine lists. The lively in-town tasting room benefits from its upbeat staff, playful atmosphere, and indoor and outdoor tasting spaces, the latter with a fire pit and large sofa affectionately dubbed the Big A$$ Couch. ✉ *403 Main St.* ☎ *209/728–9817* 🌐 *nhvino.com.*

Restaurants

★ Alchemy Cafe

$$ | **AMERICAN** | A casual spot on the eastern edge of town with yellow walls and artsy French posters, Alchemy serves sturdy comfort food like braised lamb shank over fried polenta, drunken noodles with shrimp and Asian vegetables, and grilled Atlantic salmon. Pork belly, fried calamari with roasted jalapeños, and mussels with fries are among the starters that pair well with a bourbon rosemary sour specialty cocktail or perhaps the Alchemy Bloody Mary, hopped up with a splash of Firestone Pivo Pilsner. **Known for:** Calaveras County wines well represented; open continuously from lunch through dinner; mildly pricey but reliable. *Average main: $22* *191 Main St.* *209/728–0700* *alchemymurphys.com.*

Aria Bakery & Espresso Cafe

$ | **BAKERY** | For a place as small as it is, this bakery café often smelled before seen turns out a staggering array of sweet and savory pastries, sandwiches, salads, and desserts you can enjoy with a well-brewed (if not always swiftly made) coffee, espresso drink, or tea. The croissants are golden and flaky, the quiches moist and filling, and the scones large and flavorful; the breads for lunchtime sandwiches include sourdough, focaccia, and polenta wheat. **Known for:** limited seating inside and out; blueberry muffins, savory croissants, and other baked goods; vegetarian, vegan, gluten-free options. *Average main: $12* *458 Main St., Suite B* *209/728–9250* *Closed Tues. and Wed. in winter. No dinner.*

Dogwood

$$$ | **AMERICAN** | One of Calaveras County's shining stars serves fresh seasonal cuisine in a cabinlike white-walled space with an open kitchen and hardwood floors and tables. The meat-heavy menu might include grilled flat-iron steak, grilled pork porterhouse with bourbon-maple jus, and short ribs with caramelized shallot whipped potatoes, with grilled salmon and rice pilaf, three-cheese flamed-roasted pasilla pepper, and roasted cauliflower for those seeking lighter fare. **Known for:** woodsy setting; warm hospitality; alfresco dining in good weather. *Average main: $29* *1224 Oak Circle, Arnold* *12 miles north of Murphys off Hwy. 4* *209/813–7101* *No lunch.*

Grounds

$$ | **AMERICAN** | From potato pancakes for breakfast to grilled rib eye for dinner, this bustling bistro with a series of wainscoted rooms and an outdoor patio has something for all palates. Lighter grilled vegetables, chicken, sandwiches, salads, and homemade soups always shine here, as do heartier fare that might include elk medallions and prawns, manicotti with goat cheese and ricotta, and a robust cioppino. **Known for:** full bar; wines by local producers; attentive service. *Average main: $22* *402 Main St.* *209/728–8663* *www.groundsrestaurant.com* *No dinner Mon. and Tues.*

Hotels

Dunbar House 1880

$$$ | **B&B/INN** | The oversize rooms in this elaborate Italianate-style home have brass beds, down comforters, gas-burning stoves, and claw-foot tubs. **Pros:** great breakfasts; colorful gardens; accommodating staff. **Cons:** expensive in-season; not kid-friendly; minimum-stay requirement on weekends. *Rooms from: $186* *271 Jones St.* *209/728–2897* *www.dunbarhouse.com* *6 rooms* *Free Breakfast.*

Murphys Historic Hotel & Lodge

$$ | **HOTEL** | Mark Twain, John Wayne, Susan B. Anthony, Ulysses S. Grant, and the guy who invented Lipton tea are among the past guests of this 19th-century throwback in the heart of Murphys that's intriguing more for its place in

history than the pedestrian experience it delivers in the present. **Pros:** historic ambience; old-time saloon; proximity to shops, restaurants, and tasting rooms. **Cons:** original building lacks modern amenities; newer building has motel feel; restaurant can be noisy. *Rooms from: $139 457 Main St. 209/728–3444, 800/532–7684 www.murphyshotel.com 29 rooms No meals.*

Murphys Inn Motel
$ | **HOTEL** | Reasonably well run if steadfastly nondescript, this two-story motel built in the late 1990s has two things going for it: a convenient location on the edge of downtown and bargain rates most of the year. **Pros:** clean rooms; bargain rates; convenient location. **Cons:** thin walls; some road noise; lacks style and big-hotel amenities. *Rooms from: $93 76 Main St. 209/728–1818, 888/796–1800 reservations www.murphysinnmotel.com 37 rooms No meals.*

Victoria Inn
$$ | **B&B/INN** | Decorated with contemporary furnishings with 19th-century accents, this inn benefits from a prime Main Street location within walking distance of restaurants, shops, and wine-tasting rooms. **Pros:** convenient location; romantic feel; filling continental breakfast. **Cons:** no TVs in rooms; minimum weekend-stay requirement; noise issues in some rooms. *Rooms from: $161 420 Main St. 209/728–8933 www.victoriainn-murphys.com 23 rooms Free Breakfast.*

Columbia

14 miles south of Angels Camp.

Columbia is the gateway for Columbia State Historic Park, one of the Gold Country's most visited sites. It's a great place for families to participate in living-history activities, like candle dipping and soap making on weekends. There are several inviting spots for a picnic in the area.

GETTING HERE AND AROUND

The only way to get here is by car, via either Highway 4 (the northern route) or Highway 49 (the southern) from Angels Camp.

Sights

★ Columbia State Historic Park
NATIONAL/STATE PARK | **FAMILY** | Columbia is both a functioning community and a historically preserved gold-rush town. Usually you can ride a stagecoach, pan for gold, and watch a blacksmith working at an anvil. Street musicians perform in summer. Restored or reconstructed buildings include a Wells Fargo Express office, a Masonic temple, an old-fashioned candy store, saloons, a firehouse, churches, a school, and a newspaper office. At times, all are staffed to simulate a working 1850s town. The park also includes the **Historic Fallon House Theater,** a gorgeous Victorian structure where Broadway-quality shows are performed. The town's two 19th-century historic lodgings, the Fallon Hotel ($) and City Hotel ($–$$) perch you in the past; reserve a room or cottage at *www.reservecalifornia.com. 11255 Jackson St. 209/588–9128 www.parks.ca.gov/columbia Free.*

Performing Arts

Sierra Repertory Theater Company
THEATER | The company, established in 1979, presents a full season of dramas, comedies, and musicals at the Historic Fallon House Theater and another venue in east Sonora. *11175 Washington St. 209/532–3120 www.sierrarep.org From $37.*

Sonora

4 miles south of Columbia.

Miners from Mexico founded Sonora and made it the biggest town in the Mother Lode. Following a period of racial and ethnic strife, the Mexican settlers moved on, and Yankees built the commercial city visible today. Sonora's historic downtown section sits atop the Big Bonanza Mine, one of the richest in the state. Another mine, on the site of nearby Sonora High School, yielded 990 pounds of gold in a single week in 1879. Reminders of the gold rush are everywhere in Sonora, in prim Victorian houses, typical Sierra-stone storefronts, and awning-shaded sidewalks. Reality intrudes beyond the town's historic heart, with strip malls, shopping centers, and modern motels.

If the countryside surrounding Sonora seems familiar, that's because it has been the backdrop for many movies over the years. Scenes from *High Noon, For Whom the Bell Tolls, The Virginian, Back to the Future III, Unforgiven,* and many other films were shot here.

GETTING HERE AND AROUND

Arrive in Sonora by car via Highway 49 (if coming from Columbia, drive south on Parrots Ferry Road). Parking can be difficult on the busy main drag, Washington Street (Highway 49).

Sights

Tuolumne County Museum and History Centers

MUSEUM | The small museum occupies a historic gold-rush-era building that served as a jail until 1960. Vintage firearms and paraphernalia, gold specimens, and Me-Wuk baskets are among the many artifacts on display. *158 Bradford St. 209/532–1317 www.tchistory.org Free Closed Sun.*

Restaurants

Diamondback Grill and Wine Bar

$ | AMERICAN | The bright decor and refined atmosphere suggest more ambitious fare, but massive half-pound burgers and sandwiches like the Ultimate Grilled Cheese with smoked bacon and tomato between three thick slices of sourdough bread are what this place inside a late-19th-century stone-walled building is about. Locals crowd the tables, especially after 6 pm, for the ground-meat patties, beer-battered onion rings, veggie burgers, and fine wines. **Known for:** garlic fries; wine bar and wine club; homemade desserts. *Average main: $13 93 S. Washington St. 209/532–6661 diamondbackgrillsonora.com.*

Hotels

Barretta Gardens Bed and Breakfast Inn

$$ | B&B/INN | Perfect for a romantic getaway or peaceful escape, this elegant 1904 inn evokes days gone by with three antiques-filled parlors but doesn't skimp on creature comforts in the well-tended guest rooms, also decorated in period style. **Pros:** mature gardens; delicious breakfasts; great location. **Cons:** only eight rooms; minimum-stay requirement; period look may not appeal to all travelers. *Rooms from: $159 700 S. Barretta St. 209/532–6039 www.barrettagardens.com 8 rooms Free Breakfast.*

Best Western Sonora Oaks Hotel & Conference Center

$$ | HOTEL | The standard-motel-issue rooms, some upgraded in 2019, are clean and spacious at this east Sonora establishment; the larger ones have outdoor sitting areas. **Pros:** clean rooms and public areas; great location for Gold Country and Stanislaus forest; suites have hillside views. **Cons:** front rooms can be noisy (ask for room away from highway); chain feel; minor housekeeping lapses in public areas. $ *Rooms from: $159* ✉ *19551 Hess Ave.* ☎ *209/533–4400, 800/780–7234* 🌐 *www.bwsonoraoaks.com* *100 rooms* 🍴 *Breakfast.*

Jamestown

4 miles south of Sonora.

Compact Jamestown supplies a touristy view of gold-rush-era life. Shops in brightly colored buildings along Main Street sell antiques and gift items, and there are a couple of wine-tasting rooms, Inner Sanctum for Spanish varietals and Gianelli's for Italian ones. You can try your hand at panning for gold here or explore a bit of railroad history.

GETTING HERE AND AROUND

Jamestown lies at the intersection of north–south Highway 49 and east–west Highway 108. You'll need a car to tour here.

Sights

Gold Prospecting Adventures

TOUR—SIGHT | FAMILY | You'll get a real feel (sort of) for the life of a prospector on the three-hour gold-panning excursions (reservations recommended) led by this outfit's congenial tour guides. You might even strike gold at the Jimtown Mine. Even if you're not panning, it's fun to look at the gold-rush artifacts on display here. ✉ *18170 Main St.* ☎ *209/984–4653* 🌐 *www.goldprospecting.com* *Call for prices.*

★ Railtown 1897 State Historic Park

NATIONAL/STATE PARK | FAMILY | A must for rail enthusiasts and families with kids, this is one of the most intact early roundhouses (maintenance facilities) in North America. You can hop aboard a steam train for a 40-minute journey—bring along the family dog if you'd like. The docents entertain guests with tales about the history of locomotion. Listen to the original rotor and pulleys in the engine house and take in the smell of axle grease. Walk through a genteel passenger car with dusty-green velvet seats and ornate metalwork, where Grace Kelly and Gary Cooper filmed a scene in the epic Western *High Noon.* **■TIP→ Polar Express excursions at Christmastime sell out quickly.** ✉ *18115 5th Ave.* ☎ *209/984–3953* 🌐 *www.railtown1897.org* *Roundhouse tour $5; rides from $15.*

Restaurants

Service Station

$$ | AMERICAN | Exposed brick walls and a pressed-metal ceiling lend an air of nostalgia that's heightened by this restaurant's theme, the golden age of road trips and automobile service stations. Half-pounder burgers and pulled-pork, tri-tip, and other sandwiches and wraps count among the menu's highlights, along with small plates like nacho fries and fried calamari and entrées that might include chicken, grilled salmon, or filet mignon. **Known for:** upbeat vibe; local wines, craft beers on tap; salads and vegetarian wraps and burgers for noncarnivores. $ *Average main: $20* ✉ *18242 Main St.* ☎ *209/782–5122* 🌐 *jamestownservicestation.com.*

Hotels

Black Oak Casino Resort

$ | RESORT | About 12 miles east of Jamestown off Highway 108, this flashy, contemporary property appeals heavily to casino gamers, but it's also a nice place to stay, with well-outfitted rooms and a Gold Country location. **Pros:** clean and spacious rooms; diversions for kids and adults; lounge hosts talented acts on weekends. **Cons:** smoking permitted in some casino areas; nothing quaint or historic about the place; far from town. $ *Rooms from: $109* ✉ *19400 Tuolumne Rd. N, Tuolumne* ☎ *209/928–9300, 877/747–8777* 🌐 *www.blackoakcasino.com/lodging* *148 rooms* 🍴 *No meals.*

Jamestown Hotel

$$ | **HOTEL** | The spacious light-filled rooms of this hotel that celebrated its 100th anniversary in 2019 are decorated simply but with flair, and all have updated bathrooms with a period feel. **Pros:** convenient to shops, restaurants, and tasting rooms; balcony overlooking Main Street; on-site dining. **Cons:** rooms lack refrigerators, microwaves, TVs, and other amenities; rooms are above saloon and restaurant (some noise bleeds though); no elevator. *Rooms from: $138 ✉ 18153 Main St. ☎ 209/984–3902 🌐 www.thejamestownhotel.com 8 rooms No meals.*

McCaffrey House Bed and Breakfast Inn

$$$ | **B&B/INN** | Surrounded by trees on the edge of the Stanislaus National Forest, McCaffrey's appeals to travelers seeking a remote retreat, in this case run by innkeepers with an eye for detail and a zeal for green practices. **Pros:** rooms outfitted with stoves and Amish quilts; nearby hiking; romantically remote. **Cons:** too remote for some; lacks amenities of larger properties; weekend minimum-stay requirement. *Rooms from: $189 ✉ 23251 Hwy. 108, Twain Harte ✣ 20 miles east of Jamestown ☎ 209/586–0757, 888/586–0757 🌐 www.mccaffreyhouse.com 8 rooms Free Breakfast.*

National Hotel and Restaurant

$$ | **B&B/INN** | In business since 1859, the National has survived the gold rush, gambling, prostitution, at least two fires, a ghost named Flo, and Prohibition, and stands today a well-maintained property with all the authentic character and charm its storied past suggests. **Pros:** authentic character—feels straight out of a Western movie; views from odd-numbered rooms (plus Room 2); popular restaurant (good brunches). **Cons:** some rooms are small; most even-numbered rooms have no view; some noise issues. *Rooms from: $150 ✉ 18183 Main St. ☎ 209/984–3446 🌐 www.national-hotel.com 9 rooms Free Breakfast.*

Mariposa

50 miles south of Jamestown.

Mariposa marks the southern end of the Mother Lode. Much of the land in this area was part of a 44,000-acre land grant Colonel John C. Fremont acquired from Mexico before gold was discovered and California became a state. Many people stop here on the way to Yosemite National Park, about an hour's drive east on Highway 140.

GETTING HERE AND AROUND

If driving, take Highway 49 or Highway 140. YARTS (🌐 *www.yarts.com*), the regional transit system, can get you to Mariposa from the Central Valley town of Merced (where you can also transfer from Amtrak) or from Yosemite Valley. Otherwise, you'll need a car to get here and around.

Restaurants

Charles Street Dinner House

$$$ | **AMERICAN** | Centrally located Charles Street, its rustic decor heavy on the wood and Old West adornments, at once evokes gold-rush days and the 1980s, when it opened. The extensive straightforward menu includes hand-cut steaks, honey-barbecue baby back ribs, several pasta dishes, chicken, pork loin, lamb, a few well-adorned burgers, and some vegetarian options. **Known for:** excellent steaks; cheesecake, sundae, crème brûlée for dessert; local feel. *Average main: $27 ✉ Hwy. 140 and 7th St. ☎ 209/966–2366 🌐 www.charlesstreetdinnerhouse.net ⏲ No lunch weekends.*

Savoury's

$$ | **AMERICAN** | Seafood, pasta, and portobello mushrooms are some of the savory treats that draw high praise from locals at the kind of refined space you'd expect

in an urban environment, not in mellow Mariposa. Contemporary paintings and photography set aglow by track lighting create a gallerylike atmosphere. **Known for:** well-prepared steak and seafood; full bar; vegetarian and vegan options. *Average main: $20* *5034 Hwy. 140* *209/966–7677* *Closed Wed. No lunch.*

Hotels

Mariposa Lodge

$$ | **HOTEL** | Modern and tastefully landscaped, the lodge is a solid option for those who want to stay within 30 miles of Yosemite National Park without spending a fortune. **Pros:** convenient location; relatively inexpensive; clean rooms. **Cons:** no frills; lacks amenities of big-city properties; rooms near front pick up road noise. *Rooms from: $159* *5052 Hwy. 140* *209/966–3607, 800/966–8819* *www.mariposalodge.com* *45 rooms* *No meals.*

Chapter 13

LAKE TAHOE

Updated by
Daniel Mangin

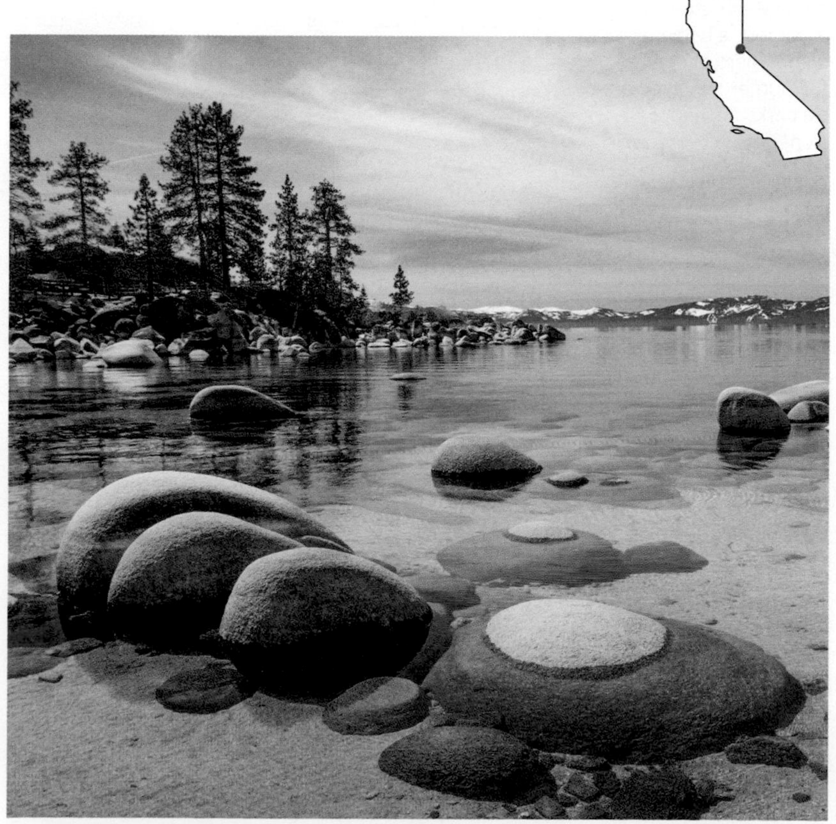

Sights ★★★★★ | Restaurants ★★★★☆ | Hotels ★★★★★ | Shopping ★☆☆☆☆ | Nightlife ★☆☆☆☆

WELCOME TO LAKE TAHOE

TOP REASONS TO GO

★ **The lake:** Blue, deep, and alpine pure, Lake Tahoe is far and away the main reason to visit this High Sierra paradise.

★ **Skiing:** Daring black-diamond runs or baby-bunny bumps—whether you're an expert, a beginner, or somewhere in between, the numerous Tahoe-area ski parks abound with slopes to suit your skills.

★ **The great outdoors:** A ring of national forests and recreation areas linked by miles of trails makes Tahoe excellent for nature lovers.

★ **Dinner with a view:** You can picnic lakeside at state parks or dine in restaurants perched along the shore.

★ **A date with lady luck:** Whether you want to roll dice, play the slots, or hope the blackjack dealer goes bust before you do, you'll find round-the-clock gambling at the casinos on the Nevada side of the lake and in Reno.

In the Sierra Nevada range's northern section, the Lake Tahoe area covers portions of four national forests, several state parks, and rugged wilderness areas. Lake Tahoe, the star attraction, straddles California and Nevada and is one of the world's largest, clearest, and deepest alpine lakes.

1 **South Lake Tahoe.**

2 **Pope-Baldwin Recreation Area.**

3 **Emerald Bay.**

4 **D.L. Bliss State Park.**

5 **Ed Z'berg Sugar Pine Point State Park.**

6 **Tahoma.**

7 **Tahoe City.**

8 **Olympic Valley.**

9 **Truckee.**

10 **Carnelian Bay to Kings Beach.**

11 **Incline Village.**

12 **Zephyr Cove.**

13 **Stateline.**

14 **Reno.**

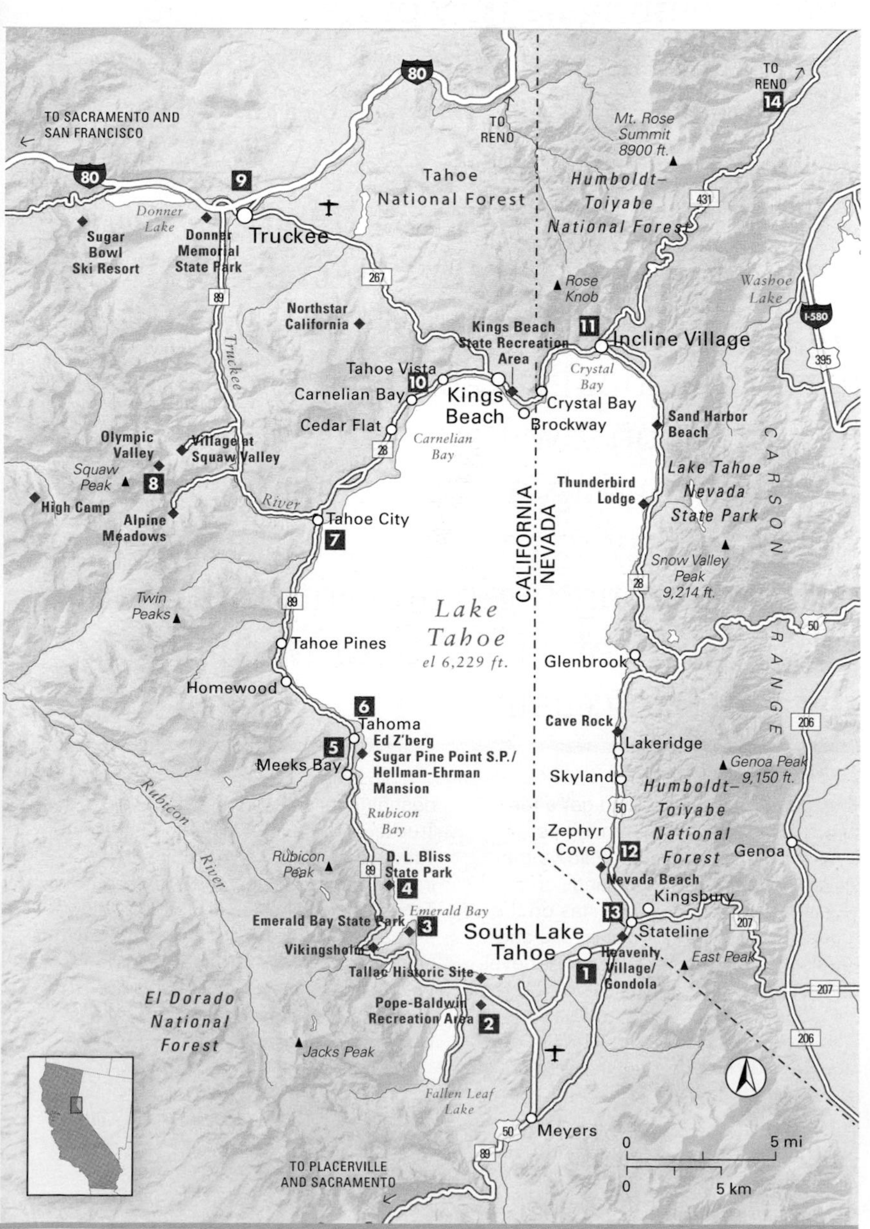
TO SACRAMENTO AND SAN FRANCISCO
80
TO RENO
Tahoe National Forest
Mt. Rose Summit 8900 ft.
Humboldt–Toiyabe National Forest
TO RENO
14
431
9
Donner Lake
Sugar Bowl Ski Resort
Donner Memorial State Park
Truckee
267
89
Rose Knob
Washoe Lake
I-580
395
Northstar California
Kings Beach State Recreation Area
11
Incline Village
Crystal Bay
Tahoe Vista
10
Carnelian Bay
Kings Beach
Crystal Bay
Brockway
Cedar Flat
Sand Harbor Beach
Carnelian Bay
28
Olympic Valley
Village at Squaw Valley
Squaw Peak
8
High Camp
Alpine Meadows
Truckee River
Tahoe City
7
Thunderbird Lodge
Lake Tahoe Nevada State Park
CARSON RANGE
CALIFORNIA
NEVADA
Snow Valley Peak 9,214 ft.
Twin Peaks
Lake Tahoe el 6,229 ft.
50
Tahoe Pines
Glenbrook
Homewood
6
Tahoma
Ed Z'berg Sugar Pine Point S.P./ Hellman-Ehrman Mansion
5
Meeks Bay
Cave Rock
Lakeridge
206
Skyland
Genoa Peak 9,150 ft.
Humboldt–Toiyabe National Forest
Rubicon River
Rubicon Bay
Zephyr Cove
12
Genoa
Rubicon Peak
D. L. Bliss State Park
4
Nevada Beach
Kingsbury
Emerald Bay
13
Emerald Bay State Park
3
South Lake Tahoe
Stateline
207
Vikingsholm
Heavenly Village/ Gondola
1
East Peak
Tallac Historic Site
Pope-Baldwin Recreation Area
2
El Dorado National Forest
Jacks Peak
Fallen Leaf Lake
Meyers
0
5 mi
5 km
TO PLACERVILLE AND SACRAMENTO

Whether you swim, fish, sail, or simply rest on its shores, you'll be wowed by the overwhelming beauty of Lake Tahoe, the largest alpine lake in North America. Famous for its cobalt-blue water and surrounding snowcapped peaks, Lake Tahoe straddles the state line between California and Nevada. The border gives this popular Sierra Nevada resort region a split personality: about half its visitors are intent on low-key sightseeing, hiking, camping, and boating; the rest head directly to the Nevada side, where bargain dining, big-name entertainment, and the lure of a jackpot draw them into the glittering casinos.

To explore the lake area and get a feel for its many differing communities, drive the 72-mile road that follows the shore through wooded flatlands and past beaches, climbing to vistas on the rugged southwest side of the lake and passing through busy commercial developments and casinos on its northeastern and southeastern edges. Another option is to actually go out *on* the 22-mile-long, 12-mile-wide lake on a sightseeing cruise or kayaking trip.

The lake, the communities around it, the state parks, national forests, and protected tracts of wilderness are the region's main draws, but other nearby destinations are gaining in popularity. Truckee, with an Old West feel and innovative restaurants, entices visitors looking for a relaxed pace and easy access to Tahoe's north shore and Olympic Valley ski parks. And today Reno, once known only for its casinos, attracts tourists with its buzzing arts scene, downtown riverfront, and campus events at the University of Nevada.

Planning

When to Go

A sapphire-blue lake shimmering deep in the center of an ice-white wonderland—that's Tahoe in winter. But those blankets of snow mean lots of storms that often close roads and force chain requirements on the interstate. In summer the roads are open, but the lake and lodgings are clogged with visitors seeking respite from valley heat. If you don't ski, the best times to visit are early fall—September and October—and late spring. The crowds thin, prices dip, and you can count on Tahoe being beautiful.

Most Lake Tahoe accommodations, restaurants, and even a handful of parks are open year-round, but many visitor centers, mansions, state parks, and beaches are closed from October through May. During those months, winter-sports enthusiasts swamp Tahoe's downhill resorts and cross-country centers, North America's largest concentration of skiing facilities. In summer it's cooler here than in the scorched Sierra Nevada foothills, the clean mountain air is bracingly crisp, and the surface temperature of Lake Tahoe is an invigorating 65°F to 70°F (compared with 40°F to 50°F in winter). This is also the time, however, when it may seem as if every tourist at the lake—100,000 on peak weekends—is in a car on the main road circling the shoreline (especially on Highway 89, just south of Tahoe City; on Highway 28, east of Tahoe City; and on U.S. 50 in South Lake Tahoe). Christmas week and July 4th are the busiest times, and prices go through the roof; plan accordingly.

Getting Here and Around

AIR TRAVEL

The nearest airport to Lake Tahoe is Reno–Tahoe International Airport (RNO), in Reno, 50 miles northeast of the closest point on the lake. Airlines serving RNO include Alaska, Allegiant, American, Delta, JetBlue, Southwest, United, and Volaris. Except for Allegiant, these airlines plus Aeromexico and Hawaiian serve Sacramento International Airport (SMF), 112 miles from South Lake Tahoe. North Lake Tahoe Express runs buses ($49 each way) between RNO and towns on the lake's western and northern shores, plus Incline Village, Truckee, Squaw Valley, and Northstar. South Tahoe Airporter runs buses ($29.75 one-way, $53 round-trip) between Reno–Tahoe Airport and resort hotels in the South Lake Tahoe area.

AIRPORT CONTACTS Reno Tahoe International Airport ✉ *2001 E. Plumb La., off U.S. 395/I–580, Reno* ☎ *775/328–6400* 🌐 *www.renoairport.com.* **Sacramento International Airport** ✉ *6900 Airport Blvd., Sacramento* ✣ *Off I–5, 12 miles northwest of downtown* ☎ *916/929–5411* 🌐 *www.sacramento.aero/smf.*

TRANSFER CONTACTS North Lake Tahoe Express ☎ *866/216–5222* 🌐 *www.northlaketahoeexpress.com.* **South Tahoe Airporter** ☎ *775/325–8944* 🌐 *southtahoeairporter.com.*

BUS TRAVEL

Greyhound stops in San Francisco, Sacramento, Truckee, and Reno. BlueGO ($2 per ride) provides year-round local service in South Lake Tahoe. On the north shore, Tahoe Area Regional Transit (TART; $1.75) operates buses between Tahoma and Incline Village and runs shuttles to Truckee. RTC RIDE buses ($2) serve the Reno area. All local rides require exact change.

In winter, BlueGO provides free ski shuttle service from South Lake Tahoe hotels and resorts to various Heavenly

Mountain ski lodge locations. Most of the major ski resorts offer shuttle service to nearby lodging.

BUS CONTACTS Greyhound ☎ *800/231–2222* 🌐 *www.greyhound.com.* **BlueGO** ☎ *530/541–7149* 🌐 *www.tahoetransportation.org/transit/south-shore-services.* **RTC RIDE** ☎ *775/348–7433* 🌐 *www.rtcwashoe.com.* **Tahoe Area Regional Transit (TART)** ☎ *530/550–1212, 800/736–6365* 🌐 *www.placer.ca.gov/departments/works/transit/tart.*

CAR TRAVEL

Lake Tahoe is 198 miles northeast of San Francisco, a drive of less than four hours in good weather and light traffic—if possible avoid heavy weekend traffic, particularly leaving the San Francisco area for Tahoe on Friday afternoon and returning on Sunday afternoon. The major route is Interstate 80, which cuts through the Sierra Nevada about 14 miles north of the lake. From there Highway 89 and Highway 267 reach the west and north shores, respectively.

U.S. 50 is the more direct route to the south shore, a two-hour drive from Sacramento. From Reno you can get to the north shore by heading south on U.S. 395/Interstate 580 for 10 miles, then west on Highway 431 for 25 miles. For the south shore, head south on U.S. 395/Interstate 580 through Carson City, and then turn west on U.S. 50 (56 miles total).

The scenic 72-mile highway around the lake is marked Highway 89 on the southwest and west shores, Highway 28 on the north and northeast shores, and U.S. 50 on the east and southeast. Sections of Highway 89 sometimes close during snowy periods, usually at Emerald Bay because of avalanche danger, which makes it impossible to complete the circular drive around the lake. Interstate 80, U.S. 50, and U.S. 395/Interstate 580 are all-weather highways, but there may be delays while snow is cleared during major storms.

Interstate 80 is a four-lane freeway; much of U.S. 50 is only two lanes with no center divider. Carry tire chains from October through May, or rent a four-wheel-drive vehicle. Most rental agencies do not allow tire chains to be used on their vehicles; ask when you book.

CONTACTS California Highway Patrol ☎ *530/577–1001 South Lake Tahoe* 🌐 *www.chp.ca.gov.* **Caltrans Current Highway Conditions** ☎ *800/427–7623* 🌐 *www.dot.ca.gov.* **Nevada Department of Transportation Road Information** ☎ *877/687–6237* 🌐 *nvroads.com.* **Nevada Highway Patrol** ☎ *775/687–5300* 🌐 *nhp.nv.gov.*

TRAIN TRAVEL

Amtrak's cross-country rail service makes stops in Truckee and Reno. Amtrak also operates several buses daily between Reno and Sacramento to connect with coastal train routes.

TRAIN CONTACT Amtrak ☎ *800/872–7245* 🌐 *www.amtrak.com.*

Restaurants

On weekends and in high season, expect a long wait at the more popular restaurants. And expect to pay resort prices almost everywhere. During the "shoulder seasons" (from April to May and September to November), some places may close temporarily or limit their hours, so call ahead. Also, check local papers for deals and discounts during this time, especially two-for-one coupons. Many casinos use their restaurants to attract gamblers. Marquees often tout "$8.99 prime rib dinners" or "$4.99 breakfast specials." Some of these meals are downright lousy and they are usually available only in the coffee shops and buffets, but at those prices, it's hard to complain. The finer restaurants in casinos deliver pricier food, as well as reasonable service and a bit of atmosphere.

Unless otherwise noted, even the most expensive area restaurants welcome customers in casual clothes. *Restaurant reviews have been shortened. For full information, visit Fodors.com.*

Hotels

Quiet inns on the water, suburban-style strip motels, casino hotels, slope-side ski lodges, and house and condo rentals throughout the area constitute the lodging choices at Tahoe. The crowds come in summer and during ski season; reserve as far in advance as possible, especially for holiday periods when prices skyrocket. Spring and fall give you a little more leeway and lower—sometimes significantly lower, especially at casino hotels—rates. Check hotel websites for the best deals.

Head to South Lake Tahoe for the most activities and the widest range of lodging options. Heavenly Village in the heart of town has an ice rink, cinema, shops, fine-dining restaurants, and simple cafés, plus a gondola that will whisk you up to the ski park. Walk two blocks south from downtown, and you can hit the casinos.

Tahoe City, on the west shore, has a small-town atmosphere and is accessible to several nearby ski resorts. A few miles northwest of the lake, Squaw Valley USA has its own self-contained upscale village, an aerial tram to the slopes, and numerous outdoor activities once the snow melts.

Looking for a taste of Old Tahoe? The north shore with its woodsy backdrop is your best bet, with Carnelian Bay and Tahoe Vista on the California side. And across the Nevada border are casino resorts where Hollywood's glamour-stars once romped. *Hotel reviews have been shortened. For full information, visit Fodors.com.*

What It Costs

	$	$$	$$$	$$$$
RESTAURANTS				
	under $16	$16–$22	$23–$30	over $30
HOTELS				
	under $120	$120–$175	$176–$250	over $250

Outdoors and Backcountry Tips

If you're planning to spend any time outdoors around Lake Tahoe, whether hiking, climbing, skiing, or camping, be aware that weather conditions can change quickly in the Sierra. To avoid hypothermia, always bring a pocket-size, fold-up rain poncho (available in all sporting-goods stores) to keep you dry. Wear long pants and a hat. Carry plenty of water. Because you'll likely be walking on granite, wear sturdy, closed-toe hiking boots, with soles that grip rock. If you're going into the backcountry, bring a signaling device (such as a mirror), emergency whistle, compass, map, energy bars, and water purifier. When heading out alone, tell someone where you're going and when you expect to return.

If you plan to ski, be aware of resort elevations. In the event of a winter storm, determine the snow level before you choose the resort you'll ski. Often the level can be as high as 7,000 feet, which means rain at some resorts' base areas but snow at others.

BackCountry, in Truckee, operates an excellent website with current information about how and where to (and where not to) ski, mountain bike, and hike in the backcountry around Tahoe. The store also stocks everything from crampons to transceivers. For storm information, check the National Weather Service's website; for ski conditions, visit

🌐 *onthesnow.com*. For reservations at campgrounds in California state parks, contact Reserve California. If you plan to camp in the backcountry of the national forests, you'll need to purchase a wilderness permit, which you can pick up at the forest service office or at a ranger station at any forest entrance. If you plan to ski the backcountry, check the U.S. Forest Service's recorded information for conditions.

CONTACTS AND INFORMATION Back-Country ✉ *11400 Donner Pass Rd., at Meadow Way, Truckee* ☎ *530/582–0909 Truckee* 🌐 *www.thebackcountry.net.* **National Weather Service** 🌐 *www.wrh.noaa.gov/rev.* **OntheSnow.com** 🌐 *www.onthesnow.com/california/skireport.html.* **Reserve California** 🌐 *www.reservecalifornia.com.* **U.S. Forest Service** ✉ *Office, 35 College Dr., South Lake Tahoe* ☎ *530/543–2600 general backcountry information, 530/587–3558 backcountry information recording after office hrs* 🌐 *www.fs.usda.gov/ltbmu.*

Skiing and Snowboarding

The mountains around Lake Tahoe are bombarded by blizzards throughout most winters and sometimes in fall and spring; 10- to 12-foot bases are common. Indeed, the Sierras often have the deepest snowpack on the continent, but because of the relatively mild temperatures over the Pacific, falling snow can be very heavy and wet—it's nicknamed "Sierra Cement" for a reason. The upside is that you can sometimes ski and board as late as May (snowboarding is permitted at all Tahoe ski areas). The major resorts get extremely crowded on weekends. If you're going to ski on a Saturday, arrive early and quit early. Avoid moving with the masses: eat at 11 am or 1:30 pm, not noon. Also consider visiting the ski areas with few high-speed lifts or limited lodging and real estate at their bases: Alpine Meadows, Sugar Bowl, Homewood, Mt. Rose, Sierra-at-Tahoe, Diamond Peak, and Kirkwood. And to find out the true ski conditions, talk to waiters and bartenders—most of them are ski bums.

The Lake Tahoe area is also a great destination for Nordic skiers. Cross-country skiing at the resorts can be costly, but you get the benefits of machine grooming and trail preparation. If it's bargain Nordic you're after, take advantage of thousands of acres of public forest and parkland trails.

Tours

Lake Tahoe Balloons

BALLOONING | Take a hot-air balloon flight over the lake from mid-May through mid-October with this company that launches and lands its balloons on a boat. The four-hour excursion (the flight is 45–60 minutes) begins shortly after sunrise and ends with a traditional champagne toast. ✉ *Tahoe Keys Marina, 2435 Venice Dr. E, South Lake Tahoe* ✣ *Tahoe Keys Blvd. off Lake Tahoe Blvd.* ☎ *530/544–1221, 800/872–9294* 🌐 *www.laketahoeballoons.com* 🎫 *From $299.*

MS *Dixie II*

BOAT TOURS | The 520-passenger MS *Dixie II*, a stern-wheeler, sails year-round from Zephyr Cove to Emerald Bay on sightseeing and dinner cruises. ✉ *Zephyr Cove Marina, 760 U.S. Hwy. 50, near Church St., Zephyr Cove* ☎ *800/238–2463* 🌐 *www.zephyrcove.com/cruises* 🎫 *From $65.*

North Lake Tahoe Ale Trail

SELF-GUIDED | Bike or walk one of North Lake Tahoe's dozens of trails, then reward yourself with a craft brew at an alehouse near the end of your chosen route. The largest concentration of beer stops is around Incline Village, but you'll find drinking spots in from Tahoma to Zephyr Cove. A dedicated website has an interactive map, descriptions, and short videos pairing trails and drinking spots. There are also suggestions for paddleboarders and kayakers. 🌐 *www.gotahoenorth.com/things/north-lake-tahoe-ale-trail.*

Sierra Cloud

BOAT TOURS | The *Sierra Cloud*, a 41-passenger catamaran, departs from the Hyatt Regency beach at Incline Village and cruises the north and east shore areas for two hours. ✉ *Hyatt Regency Lake Tahoe, 111 Country Club Dr., Incline Village* ☎ *775/831–4386* 🌐 *www.awsincline.com* 🎫 *From $90* ⏲ *Closed Oct.–Apr.*

Tahoe Gal

BOAT TOURS | Docked in Tahoe City this old-style 120-passenger paddle wheeler departs daily from June through September and on some days in May on brunch, lunch, happy hour, and sunset tours of Emerald Bay and Lake Tahoe's north and west shores. Specialty excursions include ones with live music or other entertainment. ⚠ **Closed October–April and some days in May.** ✉ *Departures from Lighthouse Center, 952 N. Lake Blvd., Tahoe City* ☎ *800/218–2464* 🌐 *www.tahoegal.com* 🎫 *From $35.*

Tahoe Cruises

BOAT TOURS | This outfit operates cruises year-round on two boats, the *Safari Rose*, an 80-foot-long wooden motor yacht, and the *Spirit of Tahoe*, added in 2019. From mid-May to mid-October, Tahoe Cruises offers barbecue lunch, happy-hour, sunset, and champagne cruises. Shuttle-bus pickup service is available. ✉ *Ski Run Marina, 900 Ski Run Blvd., South Lake Tahoe* ☎ *888/867–6394* 🌐 *www.tahoecruises.com* 🎫 *Call for prices.*

★ Thunderbird Lodge Cruise & Tour

BOAT TOURS | The captain of the *Tahoe*, a classic wooden boat, takes passengers on an east shore cruise whose highlights are a walking tour and picnic lunch at the Thunderbird Lodge, a historic mansion. ✉ *Departures from Zephyr Cove Pier, 760 U.S. 50, Zephyr Cove* ☎ *775/230–8907* 🌐 *www.cruisetahoe.com/public-cruises* 🎫 *$149.*

Visitor Information

CONTACTS Go Tahoe North ☎ *530/581–6900* 🌐 *www.gotahoenorth.com.* **Tahoe South** ☎ *775/542–4637 California, 800/588–4591 Nevada* 🌐 *tahoesouth.com.*

South Lake Tahoe

60 miles south of Reno, 198 miles northeast of San Francisco.

The city of South Lake Tahoe's raison d'être is tourism: the casinos of adjacent Stateline, Nevada; the ski slopes at Heavenly Mountain; the beaches, docks, bike trails, and campgrounds all around the south shore; and the backcountry of Eldorado National Forest and Desolation Wilderness. Less appealing are the strip malls, old-school motels, and low-rise prefab buildings lining U.S. 50, the city's main drag. Although in recent years a few jazzed-up motels and new boutique hotels have joined a few longtime high-quality inns, many places provide little more than basic accommodation. The small city's saving grace is its convenient location, bevy of services, and gorgeous lake views.

GETTING HERE AND AROUND

The main route into and through South Lake Tahoe is U.S. 50; signs say "Lake Tahoe Boulevard" in town. Arrive by car or, if coming from Reno airport, take the South Tahoe Express bus. BlueGO operates daily bus service in the south shore area year-round, plus a ski shuttle from the large hotels to Heavenly Mountain Resort in the winter.

ESSENTIALS

VISITOR INFORMATION Visit Lake Tahoe South ✉ *Visitor Center, 169 U.S. Hwy. 50, at Kingsbury Grade, Stateline* ☎ *775/588–5900* 🌐 *tahoesouth.com* ✉ *Visitor Center, 3066 Lake Tahoe Blvd., at San Francisco Ave.* ☎ *530/541–5255* 🌐 *tahoesouth.com.*

Sights

★ Heavenly Gondola

VIEWPOINT | FAMILY | Whether you ski or not, you'll appreciate the impressive view of Lake Tahoe from the Heavenly Gondola. Its eight-passenger cars travel from Heavenly Village 2.4 miles up the mountain in 15 minutes. When the weather's fine, you can take one of three hikes around the mountaintop and then have lunch at Tamarack Lodge. ✉ *4080 Lake Tahoe Blvd.* ☎ *775/586–7000, 800/432–8365* 🌐 *www.skiheavenly.com* 🎫 *$61.*

Heavenly Village

STORE/MALL | This lively complex at the base of the Heavenly Gondola has good shopping, an arcade for kids, a cinema, a brewpub, a skating rink in winter, miniature golf in summer, and the Loft for magic shows and other live entertainment. Base Camp Pizza Co., Azul Latin Kitchen, and Kalani's for seafood stand out among the several restaurants. ✉ *1001 Heavenly Village Way, at U.S. 50* 🌐 *www.theshopsatheavenly.com.*

Restaurants

Artemis Lakefront Cafe

$$ | MEDITERRANEAN | A festive marina restaurant with a heated outdoor patio, Artemis reveals its Greek influences in breakfast dishes like baklava French toast and gyros and egg pita wraps. All day, though, the menus encompass more familiar options (eggs Benedict in the morning, burgers and grilled mahimahi later on). **Known for:** heated outdoor patio; outgoing staff; marina location. [$] *Average main: $19* ✉ *900 Ski Run Blvd.* ☎ *530/542–3332* 🌐 *www.artemislakefrontcafe.com.*

Blue Angel Café

$$ | ECLECTIC | A favorite of locals, who fill the dozen or so wooden tables, this cozy spot with Wi-Fi serves basic sandwiches and salads along with internationally inspired dishes like chipotle shrimp tacos and Thai curry. On cold days warm up with wine or an espresso in front of the stone fireplace. **Known for:** varied menu; daily 3–6 happy hour; easygoing staff. [$] *Average main: $17* ✉ *1132 Ski Run Blvd., at Larch Ave.* ☎ *530/544–6544* 🌐 *www.blueangelcafe.com.*

★ Evan's American Gourmet Cafe

$$$$ | ECLECTIC | Its excellent service, world-class cuisine, and superb wine list make this intimate restaurant the top choice for high-end dining in South Lake. Inside a converted cabin, Evan's serves creative American cuisine that might include pan-seared day boat scallops and meat dishes such as rack of lamb marinated with rosemary and garlic and served with raspberry demi-glace. **Known for:** intimate atmosphere; world-class cuisine; superb wine list. [$] *Average main: $38* ✉ *536 Emerald Bay Rd., Hwy. 89, at 15th St.* ☎ *530/542–1990* 🌐 *evanstahoe.com* ⊙ *No lunch.*

Kalani's at Lake Tahoe

$$$$ | ASIAN | The white-tablecloth dining room at Heavenly's sleekest (and priciest) restaurant is decked out with carved bamboo, a burnt-orange color palette, and a modern-glass sculpture, all of which complement Pacific Rim–influenced dishes like fillet of beef with miso-garlic butter and the signature Chilean sea bass with Thai-basil mash, wilted balsamic greens, and ponzu butter sauce. Sushi selections with inventive rolls and sashimi combos, plus less expensive vegetarian dishes, add depth to the menu. **Known for:** fresh-off-the-plane Hawaiian seafood; thoughtful wine selections; upscale setting. [$] *Average main: $37* ✉ *1001 Heavenly Village Way, #26, at U.S. 50* ☎ *530/544–6100* 🌐 *www.kalanis.com.*

My Thai Cuisine

$ | THAI | Fantastic flavors and gracious owners have earned this humble roadside restaurant with river-stone columns, pine-paneled walls and ceilings, Thai statues and ornamentation the loyalty of Tahoe residents and regular visitors. The aromatic dishes include crab pad Thai, basil lamb, sizzling shrimp, and numerous curries. **Known for:** many vegetarian options; lunch specials a steal; lively atmosphere. *$ Average main: $14 ✉ 2108 Lake Tahoe Blvd., ¼ mile northeast of "Y" intersection of U.S. 50 and Hwy. 89 ☎ 530/544–3232 🌐 www.thairestaurantsouthlaketahoe.com.*

Red Hut Café

$ | **AMERICAN** | A vintage-1959 Tahoe diner, all chrome and red plastic, the Red Hut is a tiny place with a wildly popular breakfast menu: huge omelets; banana, pecan, and coconut waffles; and other tasty vittles. A second South Lake branch has a soda fountain and is the only one that serves dinner, and there's a third location in Stateline. **Known for:** huge omelets; variety of waffles; old-school feel. *$ Average main: $10 ✉ 2723 Lake Tahoe Blvd., near Blue Lake Ave. ☎ 530/541–9024 🌐 www.redhutcafe.com ⏲ No dinner.*

Scusa! Italian Ristorante

$$$ | **ITALIAN** | This longtime favorite turns out big plates of veal scaloppine, chicken piccata, and garlicky linguine with clams—straightforward Italian American food (and lots of it), served in an intimate dining room warmed by a crackling fire on many nights. There's an outdoor patio that's open in warm weather. **Known for:** classic Italian American recipes; fritto misto, grilled radicchio, and fresh-baked mozzarella appetizers; sticky-bun bread pudding for dessert. *$ Average main: $23 ✉ 2543 Lake Tahoe Blvd., at Sierra Blvd. ☎ 530/542–0100 🌐 www.scusalaketahoe.com ⏲ No lunch.*

★ Sprouts Natural Foods Cafe

$ | **AMERICAN** | If it's in between normal mealtimes and you're hungry for something healthful, head to this order-at-the-counter café for salads, overstuffed wraps, hot sandwiches, homemade vegan soups, all-day breakfasts, and the best smoothies in town. Dine at wooden tables in the cheery contemporary indoor space or out front on the patio, or just order food to go. **Known for:** fresh, healthy cuisine; vegan and vegetarian friendly; congenial staff. *$ Average main: $10 ✉ 3123 Harrison Ave., U.S. 50 at Alameda Ave. ☎ 530/541–6969 🌐 www.sprouts-cafetahoe.com.*

Hotels

Base Camp South Lake Tahoe

$$ | **HOTEL** | This three-floor boutique hotel near the Heavenly Gondola, Stateline casinos, and several good restaurants provides solid value in a hip yet family-friendly setting. **Pros:** convenient location; great for groups; cool public spaces include rooftop hot tub with mountain views. **Cons:** communal dinners won't appeal to all travelers; near a busy area; not on the lake. *$ Rooms from: $129 ✉ 4143 Cedar Ave., off U.S. 50 ☎ 530/208–0180 🌐 www.basecamptahoesouth.com ⇆ 74 rooms 🍴 Free Breakfast.*

★ Black Bear Lodge

$$$ | **B&B/INN** | The rooms and cabins at this well-appointed inn feature 19th-century American antiques, fine art, and fireplaces; cabins also have kitchenettes—built in the 1990s with meticulous attention to detail, the entire complex feels like one of the grand old lodges of the Adirondacks. **Pros:** near Heavenly skiing; within walking distance of good restaurants; good for groups. **Cons:** no room service; lacks big-hotel amenities; social types may find setting too sedate. *$ Rooms from: $199 ✉ 1202 Ski Run Blvd. ☎ 530/544–4451 🌐 www.tahoeblackbear.com ⇆ 9 rooms 🍴 Free Breakfast.*

Camp Richardson

$ | **RESORT** | **FAMILY** | The pluses of this old-fashioned family resort on 80 acres fronting Lake Tahoe are also its minuses: Camp Richardson earns retro cred for its 1920s rustic log cabin–style lodge, few dozen cabins, and small inn—all tucked beneath giant pine trees—but wins no style points for its straightforward accommodations and lack of amenities many travelers take for granted. **Pros:** lakeside location with wide choice of lodgings; great for families; inexpensive daily and weekly rates. **Cons:** dated style; lacks upscale amenities (and even phones and TVs in some rooms); some cabins available in summer only. *$ Rooms from: $105 ✉ 1900 Jameson Beach Rd. ☎ 530/541–1801, 800/544–1801 🌐 www.camprichardson.com ⇒ 74 rooms 🍴 No meals.*

Hotel Azure

$$$$ | HOTEL | High-end motel meets boutique hotel at this totally revamped (to the tune of $3.5 million) property across the road from a beach. **Pros:** clean, spacious rooms; good work spaces and tech amenities; short drive to Heavenly Mountain. **Cons:** on busy Lake Tahoe Boulevard; no bell or room service; some sound bleed-through from room to room. *$ Rooms from: $262 ✉ 3300 Lake Tahoe Blvd. ☎ 530/542–0330, 800/877–1466 🌐 www.hotelazuretahoe.com ⇒ 99 rooms 🍴 No meals.*

Marriott's Grand Residence and Timber Lodge

$$$ | RESORT | You can't beat the location of these two gigantic, modern condominium complexes right at the base of Heavenly Gondola, smack in the center of town. **Pros:** central location; great for families; near excellent restaurants. **Cons:** can be jam-packed on weekends; no room service; lacks serenity. *$ Rooms from: $195 ✉ 1001 Heavenly Village Way ☎ 530/542–8400 Marriott's Grand Residence, 800/845–5279, 530/542–6600 Marriott's Timber Lodge 🌐 www.marriott.com ⇒ 431 rooms 🍴 No meals.*

Sorensen's Resort

$$ | RESORT | Escape civilization at this woodsy 165-acre resort within the Eldorado National Forest, 20 minutes south of town. **Pros:** gorgeous rustic setting; good on-site café serves three meals a day (nonguests welcome); outdoor activities. **Cons:** nearest nightlife is 20 miles away; lacks amenities of larger properties; basic furnishings. *$ Rooms from: $145 ✉ 14255 Hwy. 88, Hope Valley ☎ 530/694–2203, 800/423–9949 🌐 www.sorensensresort.com ⇒ 36 rooms 🍴 No meals.*

Nightlife

Most of the area's nightlife is concentrated in the casinos over the border in Stateline. To avoid slot machines and blinking lights, try the California-side nightspots in and near Heavenly Village.

BARS

The Loft

THEMED ENTERTAINMENT | Crowd-pleasing magic shows and other entertainment and a casual-industrial setting keep patrons happy at this Heavenly Village bar and lounge where kids aren't out of place. The mood is upbeat, the specialty cocktails are potent, and if you're in the mood for dinner the kitchen turns out Italian fare more tasty than one might expect at such a venue. *✉ 1001 Heavenly Village Way ☎ 530/523–8024 🌐 www.thelofttahoe.com.*

Mc P's Taphouse & Grill

BARS/PUBS | You can hear live bands—rock, jazz, blues, alternative—on most nights at Mc P's while you sample a few of the 40 beers on draft. Lunch and dinner (pub grub) are served daily. *✉ 4125 Lake Tahoe Blvd., Ste A, near Friday Ave. ☎ 530/542–4435.*

Activities

FISHING

Tahoe Sport Fishing

FISHING | One of the area's largest and oldest fishing-charter services offers morning and afternoon trips. Outings include all necessary gear and bait, and the crew cleans and packages your catch. *✉ 900 Ski Run Blvd., off Lake*

Tahoe Blvd. ☎ *530/541–5448* 🌐 *www.tahoesportfishing.com* 🎫 *From $125.*

HIKING

Desolation Wilderness

HIKING/WALKING | Trails within the 63,960-acre wilderness lead to gorgeous backcountry lakes and mountain peaks. It's called Desolation Wilderness for a reason, so bring a topographic map and compass, and carry water and food. You need a permit for overnight camping (☎ *877/444–6777*). In summer you can access this area by boarding a boat taxi ($14 one-way) at **Echo Chalet** (*9900 Echo Lakes Rd., off U.S. 50,* ☎ *530/659–7207,* 🌐 *www.echochalet.com*) and crossing Echo Lake. The Pacific Crest Trail also traverses Desolation Wilderness. ✉ *El Dorado National Forest Information Center* ☎ *530/644–2349* 🌐 *www.fs.usda.gov/eldorado.*

Pacific Crest Trail

HIKING/WALKING | Hike a couple of miles on this famous mountain trail that stretches from Mexico to Canada. ✉ *Echo Summit, about 12 miles southwest of South Lake Tahoe off U.S. 50* ☎ *916/285–1846* 🌐 *www.pcta.org.*

ICE-SKATING

Heavenly Village Outdoor Ice Rink

ICE SKATING | **FAMILY** | If you're here in winter, practice your jumps and turns at this rink between the gondola and the cinema. ✉ *1001 Heavenly Village Way* ☎ *530/542–4230* 🌐 *www.theshopsatheavenly.com* 🎫 *$22, includes skate rental.*

South Lake Tahoe Ice Arena

ICE SKATING | For year-round fun, head to this NHL regulation–size indoor rink where you can rent equipment and sign up for lessons. ■ **TIP→ Hours vary; call or check website for public skate times.** ✉ *1176 Rufus Allen Blvd.* ☎ *530/544–7465* 🌐 *tahoearena.com* 🎫 *$15; includes skate rental.*

KAYAKING

Kayak Tahoe

KAYAKING | Sign up for lessons and excursions (to the south shore, Emerald Bay, and Sand Harbor), offered from May through September. You can also rent a kayak and paddle solo on the lake. ✉ *Timber Cove Marina, 3411 Lake Tahoe Blvd., at Balbijou Rd.* ☎ *530/544–2011* 🌐 *www.kayaktahoe.com* 🎫 *Rentals from $28, tours from $55.*

MOUNTAIN BIKING

Tahoe Sports Ltd.

BICYCLING | You can rent road and mountain bikes and get tips on where to ride from the friendly staff at this full-service sports store. ✉ *Tahoe Crescent V Shopping Center, 4000 Lake Tahoe Blvd., Suite 7* ☎ *530/542–4000* 🌐 *www.tahoesportsltd.com.*

SKIING

If you don't want to pay the high cost of rental equipment at the resorts, you'll find reasonable prices and expert advice at Tahoe Sports Ltd. *(see Mountain Biking, above).*

★ Heavenly Mountain Resort

SKIING/SNOWBOARDING | Straddling two states, vast Heavenly Mountain Resort—composed of nine peaks, two valleys, and four base-lodge areas, along with the largest snowmaking system in the western United States—pairs terrain for every skier with exhilarating Tahoe Basin views. Beginners can choose wide, well-groomed trails, accessed from the California Lodge or the gondola from downtown South Lake Tahoe; kids have short and gentle runs in the Enchanted Forest area all to themselves. The Sky Express high-speed quad chair whisks intermediate and advanced skiers to the summit for wide cruisers or steep tree-skiing. Mott and Killebrew canyons draw experts to the Nevada side for steep chutes and thick-timber slopes.

The ski school is big and offers everything from learn-to-ski packages to canyon-adventure tours. Call about ski and boarding camps. Skiing lessons are available for children ages four and up; there's day care for infants older than six weeks. Summertime thrill seekers participate in Epic Discovery—fun for the whole family that includes a mountain coaster, zip lines, a climbing wall, ropes courses, hiking opportunities, and a learning center. **Facilities:** 97 trails; 4,800 acres; 3,500-foot vertical drop; 28 lifts. ✉ *Ski Run Blvd., off U.S. 50* ☎ *775/586–7000, 800/432–8365* 🌐 *www.skiheavenly.com* 🎫 *Lift ticket $154.*

Hope Valley Outdoors

SKIING/SNOWBOARDING | Operating from a yurt at Pickett's Junction, Hope Valley provides lessons and equipment rentals to prepare you for cross-country skiing and snowshoeing. The outfit has more than 60 miles of trails through Humboldt–Toiyabe National Forest, several miles of which are groomed. ✉ *Hwy. 88, at Hwy. 89, Hope Valley* ☎ *530/721–2015* 🌐 *www.hopevalleycrosscountry.com.*

Kirkwood Ski Resort

SKIING/SNOWBOARDING | Thirty-six miles south of Lake Tahoe, Kirkwood is the hard-core skiers' and boarders' favorite south-shore mountain, known for its craggy gulp-and-go chutes, sweeping cornices, steep-aspect glade skiing, and high base elevation. But there's also fantastic terrain for newbies and intermediates down wide-open bowls, through wooded gullies, and along rolling tree-lined trails. Families often head to the Timber Creek area, a good spot to learn to ski or snowboard. Tricksters can show off in two terrain parks on jumps, wall rides, rails, and a half-pipe. The mountain gets hammered with an average of 354 inches of snow annually. If you're into out-of-bounds skiing, check out Expedition Kirkwood, a backcountry-skills program that teaches basic safety awareness. If you're into cross-country, the resort has 80 km (50 miles) of superb groomed-track skiing, with skating lanes, instruction, and rentals. Nonskiers can snowshoe, snow-skate, and go dog-sledding or snow-tubing. The children's ski school has programs for ages 3 to 12. **Facilities:** 86 trails; 2,300 acres; 2,000-foot vertical drop; 15 lifts. ✉ *1501 Kirkwood Meadows Dr., Kirkwood* ✣ *Off Hwy. 88, 14 miles west of Hwy. 89* ☎ *209/258–6000* 🌐 *www.kirkwood.com* 🎫 *Lift ticket $117.*

Sierra-at-Tahoe

SKIING/SNOWBOARDING | Wind-protected and meticulously groomed slopes, excellent tree-skiing, and gated back-country skiing are among the draws at this low-key but worthy resort. Extremely popular with snowboarders, Sierra has several terrain parks, including Halfpipe, with 18-foot walls and a dedicated chairlift. For beginners, Sierra-at-Tahoe has more than 100 acres of learning terrain, and there are two snow-tubing lanes. **Facilities:** 46 trails; 2,000-plus acres; 2,250-foot vertical drop; 14 lifts. ✉ *1111 Sierra-at-Tahoe Rd., Twin Bridges* ✣ *12 miles from South Lake Tahoe off U.S. 50, past Echo Summit* ☎ *530/659–7453 information, 530/659–7475 snow phone* 🌐 *www.sierraattahoe.com* 🎫 *Lift ticket $110.*

Pope-Baldwin Recreation Area

5 miles west of South Lake Tahoe.

To the west of downtown South Lake Tahoe, U.S. 50 and Highway 89 come together, forming an intersection nicknamed "the Y." If you head northwest on Highway 89, also called Emerald Bay Road, and follow the lakefront, commercial development gives way to national forests and state parks. One of these is Pope-Baldwin Recreation Area.

GETTING HERE AND AROUND

The entrance to the Pope-Baldwin Recreation Area is on the east side of Emerald Bay Road. The area is closed to vehicles in winter, but you can cross-country ski here.

Sights

★ Tallac Historic Site

HISTORIC SITE | At this site you can stroll or picnic lakeside year-round, and then in late spring and summer you can also explore three historic estates. The **Pope House** is the magnificently restored 1894 mansion of George S. Pope, who made his money in shipping and lumber and played host to the business and cultural elite of 1920s America. The **Baldwin Museum** is in the estate that once belonged to entrepreneur "Lucky" Baldwin; today it houses a collection of family memorabilia and Washoe Indian artifacts. The **Valhalla** (🌐 *valhallatahoe.com*), with a spectacular floor-to-ceiling stone fireplace, was occupied for years by Walter and Claire Heller (tidbit: after their divorce, each visited the property on alternate weekends, though she held the title). Its Grand Hall, Grand Lawn, and a lakeside boathouse refurbished as a theater, host the summertime Valhalla Art, Music and Theatre Festival of concerts, plays, and cultural activities. Docents conduct tours of the Pope House in summer; call for tour times. ✉ *Pope Baldwin Recreation Area Hwy. 89* ☎ *530/541–5227 late May–mid-Sept., 530/543–2600 year-round* 🌐 *tahoeheritage.org* 🎫 *Free, summer guided site walk $5, Pope House tour $10* ⏲ *House and museum closed late Sept.–late May.*

Taylor Creek Visitor Center

INFO CENTER | **FAMILY** | At this center operated by the U.S. Forest Service you can visit the site of a Washoe Indian settlement; walk self-guided trails through meadow, marsh, and forest; and inspect the Stream Profile Chamber, an underground display with windows right into Taylor Creek. In fall you may see spawning kokanee salmon digging their nests. In summer Forest Service naturalists organize discovery walks and evening programs. ✉ *Hwy. 89, 3 miles north of junction with U.S. 50* ☎ *530/543–2674 late May–Oct., 530/543–2600 year-round* 🌐 *www.fs.usda.gov* 🎫 *Free.*

Emerald Bay State Park

4 miles west of Pope-Baldwin Recreation Area.

You can hike, bike, swim, camp, scuba dive, kayak, or tour a lookalike Viking castle at this state park. Or you can simply enjoy the most popular tourist stop on Lake Tahoe's circular drive: the high cliff overlooking Emerald Bay, famed for its jewel-like shape and color.

GETTING HERE AND AROUND

The entrance to Emerald Bay State Park is on the east side of a narrow, twisting section of Highway 89. Caution is the key word for both drivers and pedestrians. The park is closed to vehicles in winter.

Sights

★ Emerald Bay State Park

NATIONAL/STATE PARK | A massive glacier millions of years ago carved this 3-mile-long and 1-mile-wide fjordlike inlet. Famed for its jewel-like shape and colors, the bay surrounds Fannette, Tahoe's only island. Highway 89 curves high above the lake through Emerald Bay State Park; from the Emerald Bay lookout, the centerpiece of the park, you can survey the whole scene. This is one of the don't-miss views of Lake Tahoe. The light is best in mid- to late morning, when the bay's colors really pop. ✉ *Hwy. 89* ☎ *530/525–7232* 🌐 *www.parks.ca.gov* 🎫 *$10 parking fee.*

Vikingsholm

HOUSE | This 38-room estate was completed in 1929 and built as a precise copy of a 1,200-year-old Viking castle, using

Fjord-like Emerald Bay is possibly the most scenic part of Lake Tahoe.

materials native to the area. Its original owner, Lora Knight, furnished it with Scandinavian antiques and hired artisans to build period reproductions. The sod roof sprouts wildflowers each spring. There are picnic tables nearby and a gray-sand beach for strolling. A steep 1-mile-long trail from the Emerald Bay lookout leads down to Vikingsholm, and the hike back up is hard (especially if you're not yet acclimated to the elevation), although there are benches and stone culverts to rest on. At the 150-foot peak of Fannette Island are the ruins of a stone structure known as the Tea House, built so that Knight's guests could have a place to enjoy afternoon refreshments after a motorboat ride. The island is off-limits from February through mid-June to protect nesting Canada geese. The rest of the year it's open for day use—kayak and paddleboard rentals are available at Emerald Bay State Park's beach. ✉ *Hwy. 89* ☎ *530/525–7232* 🌐 *www.vikingsholm.com* 🎟 *Day-use parking fee $10; mansion tour $10* ⏲ *Closed late Sept.–late May.*

Activities

HIKING

Eagle Falls

HIKING/WALKING | To reach these falls, leave your car in the parking lot of the Eagle Falls picnic area (near Vikingsholm; arrive early for a good spot), and walk up the short but fairly steep canyon nearby. You'll have a brilliant panorama of Emerald Bay from this spot near the boundary of Desolation Wilderness. For a strenuous full-day hike, continue 5 miles, past Eagle Lake (a good spot for an alpine swim), to Upper and Middle Velma lakes. Pick up trail maps at Taylor Creek Visitor Center in summer, or year-round at the main U.S. Forest Service Office in South Lake Tahoe, at 35 College Drive. ✉ *Hwy. 89 at Emerald Bay State Park.*

D.L. Bliss State Park

3 miles north of Emerald Bay State Park, 17 miles south of Tahoe City.

This park shares 6 miles of shoreline with adjacent Emerald Bay State Park, and has two white-sand beaches. Hike the Rubicon Trail for stunning views of the lake.

GETTING HERE AND AROUND

The entrance to D.L. Bliss State Park is on the east side of Highway 89 just north of Emerald Bay. No vehicles are allowed in when the park is closed for the season.

Sights

D.L. Bliss State Park

NATIONAL/STATE PARK | This park takes its name from Duane LeRoy Bliss, a 19th-century lumber magnate. At one time Bliss owned nearly 75% of Tahoe's lakefront, along with local steamboats, railroads, and banks. The park shares 6 miles of shoreline with Emerald Bay State Park; combined the two parks cover 1,830 acres, 744 of which the Bliss family donated to the state. At the north end of Bliss is Rubicon Point, which overlooks one of the lake's deepest spots. Short trails lead to an old lighthouse and Balancing Rock, which weighs 250,000 pounds and balances on a fist of granite. The 4.5-mile Rubicon Trail—one of Tahoe's premier hikes—leads to Vikingsholm and provides stunning lake views. Two white-sand beaches front some of Tahoe's warmest water. ✉ *Hwy. 89* ✣ *Entrance east side of Hwy. 89, 3 miles north of Emerald Bay State Park* ☎ *530/525–3345* 🌐 *www.parks.ca.gov* 🎫 *$10 per vehicle, day-use.*

Ed Z'berg Sugar Pine Point State Park

8 miles north of D. L. Bliss State Park, 10 miles south of Tahoe City.

Visitors love to hike, swim, and fish here in the summer, but this park is also popular in winter, when a small campground remains open. Eleven miles of cross-country ski and snowshoe trails allow beginners and experienced enthusiasts alike to whoosh through pine forests and glide past the lake.

GETTING HERE AND AROUND

The entrance to Sugar Pine Point is on the east side of Highway 89, about a mile south of Tahoma. A bike trail links Tahoe City to the park.

Sights

Ed Z'Berg Sugar Pine Point State Park

NATIONAL/STATE PARK | Visitors love to hike, swim, and fish in the summer at this park named for a state lawmaker who sponsored key conservation legislation, but it's also popular in winter, when a small campground remains open. Eleven miles of cross-country ski and snowshoe trails allow beginners and experienced enthusiasts alike to whoosh through pine forests and glide past the lake. Rangers lead full-moon snowshoe tours from January to March. With 2,000 densely forested acres and nearly 2 miles of shore frontage, this is Lake Tahoe's largest state park. ✉ *Hwy. 89, 1 mile south of Tahoma* ☎ *530/525–7982 summer, 530/525–7232 year-round* 🌐 *www.parks.ca.gov* 🎫 *$10 per vehicle, day-use.*

Hellman-Ehrman Mansion

HOUSE | The main attraction at Sugar Pine Point State Park is the Hellman-Ehrman Mansion, a 1903 stone-and-shingle summer home furnished in period style. In its day the height of modernity, the mansion had electric lights and full indoor plumbing. Also in the park are a trapper's log cabin from the mid-19th century, a nature preserve with wildlife exhibits, a lighthouse, the start of the 10-mile biking trail to Tahoe City, and an extensive system of hiking and cross-country skiing trails. If you're feeling less ambitious, you can relax on the sun-dappled lawn behind the mansion and gaze out at the lake. **TIP→ Purchase tour tickets at the Sugar Pine nature center.** ✉ *Hwy. 89* ☎ *530/525–7982 summer, 530/525–7232 year-round* 🌐 *www.parks.ca.gov* 🎫 *$10 per vehicle, day-use; mansion tour $10.*

Tahoma

1 mile north of Ed Z'berg Sugar Pine Point State Park, 23 miles south of Truckee.

With its rustic waterfront vacation cottages, Tahoma exemplifies life on the lake in its quiet early days before bright-lights casinos and huge crowds proliferated. In 1960 Tahoma was host of the Olympic Nordic-skiing competitions. Today there's little to do here except stroll by the lake and listen to the wind in the trees, making it a favorite home base for mellow families and nature buffs.

GETTING HERE AND AROUND

Approach Tahoma by car on Highway 89, called West Lake Boulevard in this section. From the northern and western communities, take a TART bus to Tahoma. A bike trail links Tahoe City to Tahoma.

Tahoma Meadows B&B Cottages

$$ | **B&B/INN** | **FAMILY** | With 16 individually decorated little red cottages sitting beneath towering pine trees, it's hard to beat this serene property for atmosphere and woodsy charm. **Pros:** lovely setting; good choice for families; close to Homewood ski resort. **Cons:** far from the casinos; may be too serene for some guests; old-style decor. $ *Rooms from: $149* ✉ *6821 W. Lake Blvd.* ☎ *530/525–1553, 866/525–1553* 🌐 *www.tahomameadows.com* *16 rooms* *No meals.*

SKIING

Homewood Mountain Resort

SKIING/SNOWBOARDING | Schuss down these slopes for fantastic views—the mountain rises across the road from the Tahoe shoreline. This small, usually uncrowded resort is the favorite area of locals on a snowy day, because you can find lots of untracked powder. It's also the most protected and least windy Tahoe ski area during a storm; when every other resort's lifts are on wind hold, you can almost always count on Homewood's to be open. There's only one high-speed chairlift, but there are rarely any lines. The resort may look small as you drive by, but most of it isn't visible from the road. **Facilities:** 67 trails; 1,260 acres; 1,650-foot vertical drop; 8 lifts. ✉ *5145 W. Lake Blvd., Homewood* ✣ *Hwy. 89, 5 miles south of Tahoe City* ☎ *530/525–2992 information, 530/525–2900 snow phone* 🌐 *www.skihomewood.com* 🎫 *Lift ticket $129.*

Tahoe City

9 miles north of Tahoma, 14 miles south of Truckee.

Tahoe City is the only lakeside town with a charming downtown area good for strolling and window-shopping. Stores and restaurants are all within walking distance of the Outlet Gates, where water is spilled into the Truckee River to control the surface level of the lake.

GETTING HERE AND AROUND

Tahoe City is at the junction of Highway 28, also called North Lake Boulevard, and Highway 89 where it turns northwest

Sugar Pine Point State Park.

toward Squaw Valley and Truckee. TART buses serve the area.

ESSENTIALS

VISITOR INFORMATION Go Tahoe North ☎ *530/581–6900* 🌐 *www.gotahoenorth.com.*

Sights

Gatekeeper's Museum

MUSEUM | This museum preserves a little-known part of the region's history. Between 1910 and 1968 the gatekeeper who lived on this site was responsible for monitoring the level of the lake, using a winch system (still used today and visible just outside the museum) to keep the water at the correct level. Also here, the fantastic Marion Steinbach Indian Basket Museum displays intricate baskets from 85 tribes. ✉ *130 W. Lake Blvd.* ☎ *530/583–1762* 🌐 *www.northtahoemuseums.org* 🎟 *$5* 🕒 *Closed Mon.–Wed. early-Sept.–late May.*

Watson Cabin Living Museum

MUSEUM | In the middle of Tahoe City sits a 1909 hand-hewn log cabin, the town's oldest structure still on its original site. Now a museum open during the summer, it's filled with century-old furnishings and many reproductions. ✉ *560 N. Lake Blvd.* ☎ *530/583–1762* 🌐 *www.northtahoemuseums.org* 🎟 *Free* 🕒 *Closed Tues.–Wed. and early Sept.–May.*

Restaurants

Cafe Zenon

$ | **ECLECTIC** | Straightforward Vietnamese pho noodle soup is served all day at this restaurant at Tahoe City's public golf course, but the chef also prepares everything from poutine and kimchi hot dogs to green beans with pork or prawns. The Vietnamese French Dip, a local favorite, substitutes pho broth for the traditional beef. **Known for:** roasted-chicken, Polish sausage, and other sides; Hawaiian buns and gravy with fried egg at weekend brunch; golf course setting (skating rink in winter). $ *Average main: $11* ✉ *251 N. Lake Blvd.* ✥ *Behind Bank of America building* ☎ *530/583–1517* 🌐 *www.cafezenon.com* ⏲ *Closed Tues.*

★ Christy Hill

$$$$ | **MODERN AMERICAN** | Huge windows reveal stellar lake views at this Euro–Cal restaurant serving seafood, beef, and vegetarian entrées, along with small-plate offerings. The extensive wine list and exceptional desserts earn accolades; the atmosphere is casual. **Known for:** tasting menu a good deal; romantic choice; dinner on the deck in fine weather. $ *Average main: $37* ✉ *115 Grove St., at N. Lake Blvd.* ☎ *530/583–8551* 🌐 *www.christyhill.com* ⏲ *No lunch.*

Fire Sign Cafe

$ | **AMERICAN** | There's often a wait for breakfast and lunch at this great little diner with pine paneling, hardwood floors, and an exposed-beam ceiling, but it's worth it. The pastries are made from scratch, the salmon is smoked in-house, the salsa is hand cut, and there's real maple syrup for the many types of pancakes and waffles. **Known for:** pastries from scratch; many pancakes and waffles; fruit cobbler for dessert. $ *Average main: $12* ✉ *1785 W. Lake Blvd.* ✥ *Hwy. 89, 2 miles south of downtown Tahoe City at Fountain Ave.* ☎ *530/583–0871* 🌐 *www.firesigncafe.com* ⏲ *No dinner.*

Wolfdale's

$$$$ | **ECLECTIC** | Consistent, inspired cuisine served in an elegantly simple dining room makes Wolfdale's one of the top restaurants on the lake, albeit among the most expensive. The imaginative entrées, many involving seafood, merge Asian and European cooking, and everything from teriyaki glaze to smoked fish is made in-house. **Known for:** multiple martinis and other cocktails; lake-view setting; happy hour wines and small plates (5–6:30 except Saturday and holidays). $ *Average main: $39* ✉ *640 N. Lake Blvd., near Grove St.* ☎ *530/583–5700* 🌐 *www.wolfdales.com* ⏲ *Closed Tues. No lunch.*

Hotels

Basecamp Tahoe City

$$ | **B&B/INN** | **FAMILY** | A downtown motel for the 21st century, Basecamp charms its guests with a combination of industrial, retro, and rustic styles. **Pros:** lively public spaces; stylish rooms; convenient to commercial strip with restaurants and grocery stores. **Cons:** some road noise; lacks amenities of large properties; eight-minute walk to local beach. $ *Rooms from: $149* ✉ *955 N. Lake Blvd.* ☎ *530/580–8430* 🌐 *www.basecamptahoecity.com* *24 rooms* 🍽 *Free Breakfast.*

Cottage Inn

$$ | **B&B/INN** | Avoid the crowds by staying in one of these charming circa-1938 log cottages under the towering pines on the lake's west shore. **Pros:** romantic, woodsy setting; all rooms have gas fireplaces, some two-person tubs; private beach access. **Cons:** guests must be older than 12; most cottages accommodate two people maximum; minimum weekend-stay requirement. $ *Rooms from: $150* ✉ *1690 W. Lake Blvd.* ☎ *530/581–4073, 800/581–4073* 🌐 *www.thecottageinn.com* *22 rooms* 🍽 *Free Breakfast.*

Granlibakken Tahoe

$$ | **RESORT** | A condo community with its own snow-play area in winter, this secluded 74-acre resort's name means "a hillside sheltered by fir trees" in Norwegian—adventure fitness, and wellness activities are a key focus. **Pros:** range of lodging options, from studio condos to town houses; secluded location; pool and spa treatments. **Cons:** some guests find the location too secluded; more for families than romantic interludes; conference activities and weddings. $ *Rooms from: $171* ✉ *725 Granlibakken Rd.* ☎ *530/583–4242 front desk, 800/543–3221 reservations* 🌐 *granlibakken.com* *165 rooms* 🍽 *Free Breakfast.*

Mother Nature's Inn
$ | **HOTEL** | This Tahoe City bargain is a two-story, motel-style array of rooms behind a home-furnishings store. **Pros:** good value; comfortable rooms; in the middle of town near the beach. **Cons:** pet-friendly rooms may bother those with allergies; no views; rooms get little light. *Rooms from: $80* *551 N. Lake Blvd.* *530/581-4278* *www.mothernaturesinn.com* *8 rooms* *No meals.*

★ **Sunnyside Steakhouse and Lodge**
$$$ | **HOTEL** | The views are superb and the hospitality gracious at this lakeside lodge 3 miles south of Tahoe City. **Pros:** complementary continental breakfast and afternoon tea; most rooms have balconies overlooking the lake; lively bar and restaurants. **Cons:** can be pricey for families; noisy in summer; pricey entrées at steak house. *Rooms from: $199* *1850 W. Lake Blvd.* *530/583-7200, 800/822-2754* *www.sunnysideresort.com* *23 rooms* *Free Breakfast.*

Activities

RAFTING

Truckee River Rafting
WHITE-WATER RAFTING | **FAMILY** | In summer you can take a self-guided raft trip down a gentle 5-mile stretch of the Truckee River. This outfitter will shuttle you back to Tahoe City at the end of your two- to three-hour trip. ■ **TIP→ On a warm day this makes a great family outing.** *175 River Rd., near W. Lake Blvd.* *530/583-1111* *www.truckeeriverrafting.com* *From $48.*

SKIING

Alpine Meadows Ski Area
SKIING/SNOWBOARDING | With an average 450 inches of snow annually, Alpine has some of Tahoe's most reliable conditions. It's usually one of the first areas to open in November and one of the last to close in May or June. Alpine isn't the place for show-offs; instead, you'll find down-to-earth alpine fetishists. The two peaks here are well suited to intermediate skiers, with a number of runs for experts only. Snowboarders and hot-dog skiers will find a terrain park with a super-pipe, rails, and tabletops, as well as a boarder-cross course. Alpine is a great place to learn to ski and has a ski school for kids and adults. On Saturday, because of the limited parking, there's more acreage per person than at other resorts. Lift tickets are good at neighboring Squaw Valley; a free shuttle runs all day between the two ski parks. **Facilities:** 100-plus trails; 2,400 acres; 1,802-foot vertical drop; 13 lifts. *2600 Alpine Meadows Rd.* *Off Hwy. 89, 6 miles northwest of Tahoe City, 13 miles south of Truckee* *530/583-4232, 800/403-0206* *www.squawalpine.com* *Lift ticket $169.*

Tahoe Dave's Skis and Boards
SKIING/SNOWBOARDING | You can rent skis, boards, and snowshoes at this shop, which has the area's best selection of downhill rental equipment. *590 N. Lake Blvd.* *530/583-6415* *www.tahoedaves.com.*

Olympic Valley

7 miles north of Tahoe City to Squaw Valley Road; 8½ miles south of Truckee.

Olympic Valley got its name in 1960, when Squaw Valley USA, the ski resort here, hosted the Winter Olympics. Snow sports remain the primary activity, but once summer comes, you can hike into the adjacent Granite Chief Wilderness, explore wildflower-studded alpine meadows, or lie by a swimming pool in one of the Sierra's prettiest valleys.

GETTING HERE AND AROUND

Squaw Valley Road, the only way into Olympic Valley, branches west off Highway 89 about 8 miles south of Truckee. TART connects the Squaw Valley ski area with the communities along the north and west shores, and Truckee, with year-round public transportation. Squaw Valley

Squaw Valley USA has runs for skiers of all ability levels, from beginner to expert trails.

Ski Resort provides a free shuttle to many stops in those same areas.

Sights

High Camp

VIEWPOINT | Ride the Squaw Valley Aerial Tram to this activity hub, which at 8,200 feet commands superb views of Lake Tahoe and the surrounding mountains. In summer, go for a hike, sit by the pool, or have a cocktail and watch the sunset. In winter you can ski or snow-tube. There's also a restaurant, a lounge, and a small Olympic museum. Pick up trail maps at the tram building. *Aerial Tram Bldg., Squaw Valley 800/403–0206 www.squawalpine.com/events-things-do/aerial-tram-rides Aerial Tram, $46.*

Village at Squaw Valley

COMMERCIAL CENTER | **FAMILY** | The centerpiece of Olympic Valley is a pedestrian mall at the base of several four-story ersatz Bavarian stone-and-timber buildings, where you'll find restaurants, high-end condo rentals, boutiques, and cafés. *1750 Village East Rd. 530/584–1000, 800/403–0206 information www.squawalpine.com/explore/about/squaw-valley-village-map.*

Restaurants

Fireside Pizza Company

$ | **PIZZA** | **FAMILY** | Adults might opt for the signature pear-and-Gorgonzola pizza at this modern Italian restaurant, but most kids clamor for the house favorite: an Italian-sausage-and-pepperoni combo with a bubbly blend of four cheeses. Salads and pasta dishes round out the menu at this family-friendly spot. **Known for:** inventive pizzas; good, inexpensive dining option in a pricey area; family friendly. *Average main: $15 The Village at Squaw Valley, 1985 Squaw Valley Rd., #25 530/584–6150 www.firesidepizza.com.*

Graham's at Squaw Valley

$$$ | **ECLECTIC** | Sit by a floor-to-ceiling river-rock hearth under a knotty-pine peaked ceiling in this well-run restaurant's intimate dining room. The southern

European–inspired menu changes often, but expect hearty entrées such as grilled beef tenderloin with wild mushroom sauce, along with lighter-fare small plates like quail with fig demi-glace or cassoulet. **Known for:** forest feel inside and out; highly regarded wine list; fireside bar for appetizers. *Average main: $30* *Christy Inn Lodge, 1650 Squaw Valley Rd.* *530/581–0454* *www.dinewine.com* *Closed Mon. and Tues. No lunch.*

★ PlumpJack Cafe

$$$$ | **AMERICAN** | The menu at this silver-tone white-tablecloth restaurant whose wide windows reveal Squaw in all its glory changes seasonally, but look for rib-eye steak, seared diver scallops with risotto, and a filling, inventive vegetarian dish. Rather than complicated, heavy sauces, the chef uses simple reductions to complement a dish, resulting in clean, dynamic flavors. **Known for:** specialty cocktails; less expensive but equally adventurous bar menu; varied, reasonably priced wines. *Average main: $42* *1920 Squaw Valley Rd.* *530/583–1578* *www.plumpjackcafe.com* *No lunch (except at bar).*

Hotels

★ PlumpJack Squaw Valley Inn

$$$ | **HOTEL** | Stylish and luxurious, this two-story, cedar-sided inn has a snappy, sophisticated look and laid-back sensibility, perfect for the Bay Area cognoscenti who flock here on weekends. **Pros:** small and intimate; loaded with amenities; personable and attentive service. **Cons:** not the best choice for families with small children; not all rooms have tubs; laid-back sensibility may not work for some guests. *Rooms from: $225* *1920 Squaw Valley Rd.* *530/583–1576, 800/323–7666* *www.plumpjacksquawvalleyinn.com* *56 rooms* *Free Breakfast.*

Resort at Squaw Creek

$$$ | **RESORT** | This Squaw Valley multifacility offers restaurants, a golf course, spa, heated swimming pool, ice skating rink, chairlift to the mountain, and groomed cross-country ski tracks on the property, plus all the amenities and services you could possibly want in the Tahoe area. **Pros:** every conceivable amenity; private chairlift to Squaw Valley USA for ski-in, ski-out; attractive furnishings. **Cons:** so large it can feel impersonal; high in-season rates; a lot of hubbub during ski season. *Rooms from: $219* *400 Squaw Creek Rd.* *530/583–6300, 800/327–3353* *www.squawcreek.com* *405 rooms* *No meals.*

The Village at Squaw Valley USA

$$$ | **HOTEL** | **FAMILY** | Right at the base of the slopes, at the center point of Olympic Valley, the Village's condominiums (from studio to three bedrooms) come complete with gas fireplaces, daily maid service, and heated slate-tile bathroom and kitchen floors. **Pros:** each condo sleeps at least four people; near Village restaurants and shops; at base of slopes. **Cons:** village often gets crowded on weekends; nicely appointed but not high style; lacks room service and other hotel amenities. *Rooms from: $199* *1750 Village East Rd.* *530/584–1000, 888/259–1428* *www.squawalpine.com/lodging* *198 rooms* *No meals.*

Activities

GOLF

Resort at Squaw Creek Golf Course

GOLF | For beautiful views of Squaw Valley's surrounding peaks, play this narrow, challenging championship course designed by Robert Trent Jones Jr. The design emphasizes accuracy over distance, especially on the front nine. All fees include a golf cart plus valet parking; rates drop after noon and again after 3 pm. *400 Squaw Creek Rd.* *530/583–6300, 530/581–6637 pro shop* *www.destinationhotels.com/squawcreek/*

recreation *From $89* *18 holes, 6931 yards, par 71.*

SKIING

★ Squaw Valley USA

SKIING/SNOWBOARDING | Known for some of the toughest skiing in the Tahoe area, this park was the centerpiece of the 1960 Winter Olympics. Today it's the definitive North Tahoe ski resort and among the top-three megaresorts in California (the other two are Heavenly and Mammoth). Although Squaw has changed significantly since the Olympics, the skiing is still world-class and extends across vast bowls stretched between six peaks. Experts often head directly to the untamed terrain of the infamous KT-22 face, which has bumps, cliffs, and gulp-and-go chutes, or to the nearly vertical Palisades, where many famous extreme-skiing films have been shot. Fret not, beginners and intermediates: you have plenty of wide-open, groomed trails at High Camp (which sits at the *top* of the mountain) and around the more challenging Snow King Peak. Snowboarders and show-off skiers can tear up the five fantastic terrain parks, which include a giant super-pipe. Ski passes are good at neighboring Alpine Meadows; free shuttles run all day between the two ski parks. (By the early 2020s a gondola will connect them.) **Facilities:** 178 trails; 3,600 acres; 2,840-foot vertical drop; 30 lifts. ✉ *1960 Squaw Valley Rd.* ✣ *Off Hwy. 89, 7 miles northwest of Tahoe City* ☎ *800/403–0206* 🌐 *www.squawalpine.com* *Lift ticket $179.*

Tahoe Dave's Skis and Boards

SKIING/SNOWBOARDING | If you don't want to pay resort prices, you can rent and tune downhill skis and snowboards at this shop. ✉ *3039 Hwy. 89, at Squaw Valley Rd.* ☎ *530/583–5665* 🌐 *www.tahoedaves.com.*

Truckee

13 miles northwest of Kings Beach, 14 miles north of Tahoe City.

Formerly a decrepit railroad town in the mountains, Truckee is now the trendy first stop for many Tahoe visitors. The town was officially established around 1863, and by 1868 it had gone from a stagecoach station to a major stopover for trains bound for the Pacific via the new transcontinental railroad. Every day, freight trains and Amtrak's *California Zephyr* still idle briefly at the depot in the middle of town. The visitor center inside the depot has a walking-tour map of historic Truckee.

Across from the station, where Old West facades line the main drag, you'll find galleries, gift shops, boutiques, a wine-tasting room, old-fashioned diners, and several good restaurants.

GETTING HERE AND AROUND

Truckee is off Interstate 80 between Highways 89 and 267. Greyhound and Amtrak stop here, and TART buses serve the area.

ESSENTIALS

VISITOR INFORMATION Truckee Donner Chamber of Commerce and the California Welcome Center ✉ *Amtrak depot, 10065 Donner Pass Rd., near Spring St.* ☎ *530/587–2757* 🌐 *www.truckee.com.*

Sights

Donner Memorial State Park and Emigrant Trail Museum

NATIONAL/STATE PARK | The park and museum commemorate the 89 members of the Donner Party, westward-bound pioneers who became trapped in the Sierra in the winter of 1846–47 in snow 22 feet deep. Barely more than half survived, some by resorting to cannibalism. The absorbing Emigrant Trail Museum in the visitor center contains exhibits about the Donner Party, regional Native Americans, and railroad and transportation development in the area. In the park, you can picnic, hike, camp, and go boating, fishing, and waterskiing in summer; winter brings cross-country skiing and snowshoeing on groomed trails. ✉ *12593 Donner Pass Rd.* ✥ *Off I–80, Exit 184, 2 miles west of Truckee* ☎ *530/582–7892* 🌐 *www.parks.ca.gov/donnermemorial* 🎫 *$10 parking, day-use ($5 in winter).*

Restaurants

★ Cottonwood Restaurant & Bar
$$$ | ECLECTIC | Perched above town on the site of North America's first chairlift, this local institution has a bar decked out with old wooden skis, sleds, skates, and photos of Truckee's early days. The ambitious menu includes grilled steak, baby-back short ribs with chipotle barbecue jus, and house-special pasta dishes like chicken linguine. **Known for:** early-bird three-course dinner except in high season; wine selection; hilltop views from atmospheric bar. 💲 *Average main: $28* ✉ *10142 Rue Hilltop Rd., off Brockway Rd., ¼ mile south of downtown* ☎ *530/587–5711* 🌐 *www.cottonwoodrestaurant.com* ⏲ *No lunch.*

FiftyFifty Brewing Company
$$ | AMERICAN | In this Truckee brewpub the warm red tones and comfy booths, plus a pint of the Donner Party porter (or a shot of bourbon), will take the nip out of a cold day on the slopes. The menu includes salads, burgers, inventive pizzas, barbecued ribs, pan-seared salmon, and the house specialty, a pulled-pork sandwich. **Known for:** high-quality burger beef; 2018 Brewery Group of the Year honors at top beer fest; après-ski action. 💲 *Average main: $21* ✉ *11197 Brockway Rd., near Martis Valley Rd.* ☎ *530/587–2337* 🌐 *www.fiftyfiftybrewing.com.*

★ Marty's Cafe
$ | AMERICAN | You'd never know from this downtown café's laid-back decor that the namesake owner-chef's resume includes stints at fancy restaurants from Beverly Hills to Kennebunkport. Marty's hearty breakfasts (like the house-made granola or the fried egg sandwich with bacon and Gruyère on toasted French bread) and lunches—burgers, hoagies, "char dogs," sloppy joes, and a winning chicken-and-avocado BLT—are served from opening until closing. **Known for:** well-executed cuisine; daily specials and seasonal salads; ebullient hospitality. 💲 *Average main: $15* ✉ *10115 Donner Pass Rd.* ☎ *530/550–8208* 🌐 *martyscafetruckee.com* ⏲ *No dinner.*

Moody's Bistro, Bar & Beats
$$$ | ECLECTIC | Head here for contemporary-Cal cuisine in a sexy dining room with pumpkin-color walls, burgundy velvet banquettes, and art-deco fixtures. The earthy, sure-handed cooking features organically grown ingredients: look for ahi poke, snazzy pizzas bubbling-hot from a brick oven, braised lamb shanks, pan-roasted wild game, fresh seafood, and organic beef. **Known for:** lighter fare for lunch; summer alfresco dining; live music in bar some nights. 💲 *Average main: $27* ✉ *10007 Bridge St., at Donner Pass Rd.* ☎ *530/587–8688* 🌐 *www.moodysbistro.com.*

Pianeta Ristorante
$$$ | ITALIAN | A longtime town favorite, Pianeta serves high-style Italian cuisine in a warmly lit bi-level redbrick space on Truckee's historic main drag. Start with a beef carpaccio antipasto plate or perhaps house-made spicy-fennel and mild sausages, following up with a pasta course of ravioli Bolognese (both pasta and sauce made in-house), an entrée of ragout with spicy sausage and Mexican prawns—or both. **Known for:** welcoming atmosphere; tiramisu and panna cotta for dessert; West Coast and Italian wine selections. 💲 *Average main: $29* ✉ *10096 Donner Pass Rd.* ☎ *530/587–4694* 🌐 *www.pianetarestauranttruckee.com* ⏲ *No lunch.*

Squeeze In

$ | **AMERICAN** | Meet the locals at Truckee's top choice for breakfast, thanks to the dozens of omelets and several variations on eggs Benedict along with banana-walnut pancakes and French toast oozing with cream cheese. At lunch savor homemade soups and sandwiches. **Known for:** cheeseburger omelet; homemade soups; gluten-free variations. *Average main: $14* *10060 Donner Pass Rd., near Bridge St.* *530/587–9814* *www.squeezein.com* *No dinner.*

Truckee Tavern and Grill

$$$ | **AMERICAN** | The wood-fired grill in this second-floor downtown restaurant turns out steaks, chicken, and chops along with fish dishes that might include Mt. Lassen trout with white beans and mushrooms. As with the food, the decor is New West contemporary—bricks line the wall behind the bar, where mixologists craft wiggy drinks like the Salvador (as in Dalí, with rye, mescal, blood orange, and egg white), and, in tribute to Truckee's bootlegging past, pour artisanal small-batch gin and whiskey. **Known for:** buffalo tri-tip; pasta and fish entrées; deck overlooking downtown action. *Average main: $26* *10118 Donner Pass Rd., near Spring St.* *530/587–3766* *www.truckeetavern.com* *No lunch Mon.–Wed.*

Hotels

Cedar House Sport Hotel

$$ | **HOTEL** | The clean, spare lines of the Cedar House's wooden exterior evoke a modern European feel, while energy-saving heating, cooling, and lighting systems emphasize the owners' commitment to sustainability. **Pros:** environmentally friendly; hip yet comfortable; heated-tile bathroom floors. **Cons:** some bathrooms on the small side; not all bathrooms have tubs; about a mile from historic downtown Truckee. *Rooms from: $170* *10918 Brockway Rd.* *530/582–5655, 866/582–5655* *www.cedarhousesporthotel.com* *40 rooms* *Free Breakfast.*

Northstar California Resort

$$$ | **RESORT** | The area's most complete destination resort entices families with its sports activities and concentration of restaurants, shops, and accommodations. **Pros:** array of lodging types; on-site shuttle; several dining options in Northstar Village. **Cons:** family accommodations can be pricey; lacks intimacy; some units not as attractive as others. *Rooms from: $185* *5001 Northstar Dr.* *Off Hwy. 267, 6 miles southeast of Truckee* *530/562–1010, 800/466–6784* *www.northstarcalifornia.com* *250 rooms* *No meals.*

★ Ritz-Carlton Highlands Court, Lake Tahoe

$$$$ | **RESORT** | Nestled mid-mountain on the Northstar ski resort, the plush accommodations of the four-story Ritz-Carlton have floor-to-ceiling windows for maximum views, along with fireplaces, cozy robes, and down comforters. **Pros:** superb service; gorgeous setting; ski-in, ski out convenience. **Cons:** in-season prices as breathtaking as the views; resort fee and mandatory valet parking add to cost of stay; must go off-site for golf and tennis. *Rooms from: $342* *13031 Ritz-Carlton Highlands Court* *530/562–3000, 800/241–3333* *www.ritzcarlton.com/laketahoe* *170 rooms* *No meals.*

River Street Inn

$$ | **B&B/INN** | On the banks of the Truckee River, this 1882 wood-and-stone inn has uncluttered, comfortable rooms that are simply decorated, with attractive, country-style wooden furniture and extras like flat-screen TVs. **Pros:** tidy rooms; good value; in historic downtown Truckee. **Cons:** parking is a half block from inn; decor is simple; noise from on-site restaurant and bar and nearby trains. *Rooms from: $145* *10009 E. River St.* *530/550–9290 inn, 530/550–9222 restaurant* *www.riverstreetinntruckee.com* *7 rooms* *Free Breakfast.*

Truckee Hotel

$$$ | **HOTEL** | A four-story hotel in business in various forms since 1873, the Truckee Hotel attracts history buffs and skiers, the latter for the reasonable rates when in-season prices skyrocket at Northstar, Sugar Bowl, and other nearby resorts. **Pros:** historic atmosphere; convenient to shops and restaurants; same owners operate a modern Hampton Inn nearby. **Cons:** no pool, fitness center, elevator; train and other noise issues (when booking ask for a quiet room); most rooms lack a private bathroom (though all have a sink). *Rooms from: $189 ✉ 10007 Bridge St. ☎ 530/587–4444, 800/659–6921 ⊕ www.truckeehotel.com 32 rooms, 24 with shared baths Free Breakfast.*

Activities

GOLF

Coyote Moon Golf Course

GOLF | With pine trees lining the fairways and no houses to spoil the view, this course is as beautiful as it is challenging. Fees include a shared cart; the greens fee drops at 1 pm and dips again at 3. *✉ 10685 Northwoods Blvd., off Donner Pass Rd. ☎ 530/587–0886 ⊕ www.coyotemoongolf.com $175 18 holes, 7177 yards, par 72 Closed late fall–late spring.*

Northstar Golf

GOLF | Robert Muir Graves designed this course that combines hilly terrain and open meadows. The front nine holes here are open-links style, while the challenging back nine move through tight, tree-lined fairways. Rates, which include a cart, drop successively after 11, 1, and 4. *✉ 168 Basque Dr. ↔ Off Northstar Dr., west off Hwy. 267 ☎ 530/562–3290 pro shop ⊕ www.northstarcalifornia.com $95 for 18 holes 18 holes, 6781 yards, par 72.*

MOUNTAIN BIKING

Cyclepaths Mountain Bike Adventures

BICYCLING | This combination full-service bike shop and bike-adventure outfitter offers instruction in mountain biking, guided tours, tips for self-guided bike touring, bike repairs, and books and maps on the area. *✉ Pioneer Center, 10825 Pioneer Trail, Suite 105 ☎ 530/582–1890 ⊕ www.cyclepaths.net.*

Northstar California Bike Park

BICYCLING | From late May through September Northstar's ski slopes transform into a magnificent lift-served bike park with 100 miles of challenging terrain, including the aptly named Livewire trail. Guided tours, multiday retreats, and downhill, cross-country, and endurance races are available for riders of all abilities. *✉ Northstar Dr., off Hwy. 267 ☎ 530/562–1010 ⊕ www.northstarcalifornia.com Lift $60.*

SKIING

★ Northstar California

SKIING/SNOWBOARDING | Meticulous grooming and long cruisers make this resort a paradise for intermediate skiers and a fine choice for families. Although the majority of the trails are intermediate in difficulty, advanced skiers and riders have access to Lookout Mountain's more than two dozen expert trails and 347 acres of gated terrain and steeps. The diversity of terrain in proximity makes it easier for families and groups with varying skills to hang out with each other. As for terrain parks, the ones here are considered among North America's best, with features that include a 420-foot-long super-pipe, a half-pipe, rails and boxes, and lots of kickers. The Cross Country, Telemark and Snowshoe Center, located mid-mountain, is the starting point for a network of 35 km (22 miles) of groomed trails, including double-set tracks and skating lanes. The trails are also fat-bike friendly, so nonskiers can enjoy the park, too. The school has programs for skiers ages three and up, and on-site care is available for tots two and older. **Facilities:** 100 trails; 3,170 acres; 2,280-foot vertical drop; 20 lifts. ✉ *5001 Northstar Dr.* ☎ *530/562–2267* 🌐 *www.northstarcalifornia.com* 🎫 *Lift ticket $160.*

★ Royal Gorge

SKIING/SNOWBOARDING | If you love to cross-country, don't miss Royal Gorge, which serves up 140 km (124 miles) of track for all abilities, six trail systems on a whopping 6,000 acres, a ski school, and nine warming huts. Because the complex, affiliated with Sugar Bowl, sits right on the Sierra Crest, the views are drop-dead gorgeous. ✉ *9411 Pahatsi Dr., Soda Springs* ✣ *Off I–80, Soda Springs/Norden exit* ☎ *530/426–3871, 530/426–3871* 🌐 *www.royalgorge.com* ☞ *All-day pass $35.*

Sugar Bowl Ski Resort

SKIING/SNOWBOARDING | Opened in 1939 by Walt Disney, this is the oldest—and one of the best—resorts at Tahoe. Atop Donner Summit, it receives an incredible 500 inches of snowfall annually. Four peaks are connected by 1,650 acres of skiable terrain, with everything from gentle groomed corduroy to wide-open bowls to vertical rocky chutes and outstanding tree skiing. Snowboarders can hit two terrain parks with numerous boxes, rails, and jumps. Because it's more compact than some of the area's megaresorts, there's a gentility here that distinguishes Sugar Bowl from its competitors, making this a great place for families and a low-pressure, low-key place to learn to ski. It's not huge, but there's some very challenging terrain (experts: head to the Palisades). There is limited lodging at the base area. Facilities: 100 trails; 1,650 acres; 1,500-foot vertical drop; 12 lifts. ✉ *629 Sugar Bowl Rd., Norden* ✣ *Off Donner Pass Rd., 3 miles east of I–80 Soda Springs/Norden exit, 10 miles west of Truckee* ☎ *530/426–9000, 530/426–1111 snow phone* 🌐 *www.sugarbowl.com* 🎫 *Lift ticket from $118.*

Tahoe Dave's

SKIING/SNOWBOARDING | You can save money by renting skis and boards at this shop, which has the area's best selection and also repairs and tunes equipment. ✉ *10200 Donner Pass Rd., near Spring St.* ☎ *530/582–0900* 🌐 *www.tahoedaves.com.*

Tahoe Donner Cross Country Ski Center

SKIING/SNOWBOARDING | Just north of Truckee, the center, which ranks among the nation's best cross-country venues for the skiing and the magnificent Sierra Crest views, includes 65 trails on 100 km (62 miles) of groomed tracks on more than 2,800 acres. In addition to cross-country skiing, there are fat-biking, dog, and snowshoeing trails. ✉ *15275 Alder Creek Rd.* ☎ *530/587–9484* 🌐 *www.tahoedonner.com/xc.*

Carnelian Bay to Kings Beach

5–10 miles northeast of Tahoe City.

The small lakeside commercial districts of Carnelian Bay and Tahoe Vista service the thousand or so locals who live in the area year-round and the thousands more who have summer residences or launch their boats here. Kings Beach, the last town heading east on Highway 28 before the Nevada border, is full of basic motels and rental condos, restaurants, and shops.

GETTING HERE AND AROUND

To reach Kings Beach and Carnelian Bay from the California side, take Highway 89 north to Highway 28 north and then east. From the Nevada side, follow Highway 28 north and then west. TART provides public transportation in this area.

Beaches

Kings Beach State Recreation Area

BEACH—SIGHT | FAMILY | The north shore's 28-acre Kings Beach State Recreation Area, one of the largest such areas on the lake, is open year-round. The 700-foot-long sandy beach gets crowded in summer with people swimming, sunbathing, Jet Skiing, riding in paddleboats, spiking volleyballs, and tossing Frisbees. If you're going to spend the day, come early to snag a table in the picnic area; there's also a good playground. **Amenities:** food and drink; parking (fee); toilets; water sports. **Best for:** sunrise; sunset; swimming; windsurfing. *8318 N. Lake Blvd., Kings Beach 530/546–7248 www.parks.ca.gov $10 parking fee.*

Restaurants

Gar Woods Grill and Pier

$$$$ | ECLECTIC | The view's the thing at this lakeside stalwart, where you can watch the sun shimmer on the water through the dining room's plateglass windows or from the heated outdoor deck. Price wise, this is a better bet for lunch or weekend breakfast than for dinner, at which grilled steak and fish are menu mainstays, but specialties like crab chiles rellenos and pomegranate braised pork ribs also merit consideration. **Known for:** lake views; grilled steak and fish; specialty cocktails. *Average main: $36 5000 N. Lake Blvd., Carnelian Bay Hwy. 28, 2 miles west of Tahoe Vista 530/546–3366 www.garwoods.com.*

Jason's Beachside Grille

$$ | AMERICAN | If the kids want burgers but you want bourbon, area mainstay Jason's has a full bar as well as steaks, 10 kinds of burgers, teriyaki chicken, and a big salad bar. The whole place is wood, from floor to ceiling, lending it an ultrarustic feel. **Known for:** salad bar; summer dining on deck overlooking the lake; tables by fireplace in winter. *Average main: $19 8338 N. Lake Blvd., Kings Beach 530/546–3315 jasonsbeachsidegrille.com.*

Soule Domain

$$$ | ECLECTIC | Rough-hewn wood beams, a vaulted wood ceiling, and in winter, a roaring fireplace, lend high romance to this cozy 1927 pine-log cabin next to the Tahoe Biltmore casino. Chef-owner Charlie Soule's specialties include curried almond chicken, fresh sea scallops poached in champagne with a kiwi-and-mango cream sauce, and a vegan sauté judiciously flavored with ginger, jalapeños, sesame seeds, and teriyaki sauce. **Known for:** romance by candlelight; skillfully prepared cuisine; suave service. *Average main: $30 9983 Cove St., ½ block up Stateline Rd. off Hwy. 28, Kings Beach Restaurant is just west of Tahoe Biltmore casino at California-Nevada border. 530/546–7529 www.souledomain.com No lunch.*

Spindleshanks American Bistro and Wine Bar

$$$ | AMERICAN | A local favorite on the Old Brockway Golf Course, Spindleshanks serves mostly classic American cooking—ribs, steaks, and seafood updated with adventurous sauces—as well as house-made ravioli. Savor a drink from the full bar or choose a wine from the extensive list while you enjoy views of Lake Tahoe or the historic greens where Bing Crosby hosted his first golf tournament in 1934. **Known for:** classic American cooking; Lake Tahoe views; patio dining. *Average main: $28 400 Brassie Ave., Kings Beach At Hwy. 267 and N. Lake Tahoe Blvd. 530/546–2191 www.spindleshankstahoe.com.*

Hotels

Ferrari's Crown Resort

$ | HOTEL | FAMILY | Great for families with kids and all travelers on a budget willing to trade style and amenities for below-average rates and (from some rooms) impressive water views, the family-owned Ferrari's has straightforward rooms in two formerly separate vintage-1950s motels, sitting side-by-side on the lake. **Pros:** family-friendly; lakeside location; a few rooms value-priced. **Cons:** older facility with unappealing exterior; thin walls; uninspired breakfast. *Rooms from: $99 8200 N. Lake Blvd., Kings Beach 530/546–3388, 800/645–2260 www.tahoecrown.com 72 rooms Free Breakfast.*

Mourelatos Lakeshore Resort

$$ | **B&B/INN** | At first glance this family-run waterfront property looks like a slightly above-average two-story motel, but with a private beach, two hot tubs, ceaselessly alluring lake and mountain vistas, and summertime barbecuing, kayaking, and other extras it legitimately lays claim to the title of resort. **Pros:** private beach; some rooms have full kitchens; summertime barbecuing and kayaking. **Cons:** decor a tad dated; books up quickly for summer; some rooms lack sufficient heat in winter. *Rooms from: $160 6834 N. Lake Blvd., Tahoe Vista 530/546–9500 www.mlrtahoe.com 32 rooms Free Breakfast.*

Rustic Cottages

$ | **HOTEL** | **FAMILY** | These charming clapboard cottages sit clustered beneath tall pine trees across the road from Lake Tahoe and a little beach. **Pros:** woodsy Old Tahoe feel; expanded continental breakfast; good value. **Cons:** older facility; some rooms are very small; lacks big-hotel amenities. *Rooms from: $119 7449 N. Lake Blvd., Tahoe Vista 530/546–3523, 888/778–7842 www.rusticcottages.com 20 rooms Free Breakfast.*

Incline Village

3 miles east of Crystal Bay.

Incline Village dates to the early 1960s, when an Oklahoma developer bought 10,000 acres north of Lake Tahoe. His idea was to sketch out a plan for a town without a central commercial district, hoping to prevent congestion and to preserve the area's natural beauty. One-acre lakeshore lots originally fetched $12,000 to $15,000; today you couldn't buy the same land for less than several million.

GETTING HERE AND AROUND

From the California side, reach Incline Village via Highway 89 or 267 to Highway 28. From South Lake Tahoe, take U.S. 50 north to Highway 28 north. TART serves the communities along Lake Tahoe's north and west shores from Incline Village to Tahoma.

ESSENTIALS

VISITOR INFORMATION Lake Tahoe Incline Village/Crystal Bay Visitors Bureau *969 Tahoe Blvd. 775/832–1606, 800/468–2463 www.gotahoenorth.com.*

Lakeshore Drive

SCENIC DRIVE | Take this beautiful drive to see some of the most expensive real estate in Nevada. The route is discreetly marked: to find it, start at the Hyatt hotel and drive westward along the lake. *Incline Village.*

★ Thunderbird Lodge

HOUSE | George Whittell, a San Francisco socialite who once owned 40,000 acres of property along the lake, began building this lodge in 1936, completing it in 1941. You can tour the mansion and the grounds by reservation only, and though it's pricey to do so, you'll be rewarded with a rare glimpse of a time when only the very wealthy had homes at Tahoe. The lodge is accessible via a bus from the Incline Village–Crystal Bay Visitors Bureau, several boats from the Hyatt in Incline Village, and a 1950 wooden cruiser from Zephyr Cove. *5000 Hwy. 28 775/832–8750 www.thunderbirdtahoe.org/tours From $50 for bus tour, $140 for boat tours.*

Beaches

Lake Tahoe–Nevada State Park and Sand Harbor Beach

BEACH—SIGHT | Protecting much of the lake's eastern shore from development, this park comprises several sections that stretch from Incline Village to Zephyr Cove. Beaches and trails provide access to a wilder side of the lake, whether you're into cross-country skiing, hiking, or just relaxing at a picnic. With a gently sloping beach for lounging, crystal-clear water for swimming and snorkeling, and a picnic area shaded by cedars and pines, **Sand Harbor Beach** sometimes reaches capacity by 11 am on summer weekends. A handicap-accessible nature trail has interpretive signs and beautiful lake views. Pets are not allowed on the beach from mid-April through mid-October. **Amenities**: food and drink; parking ($12 mid-April–mid-October, $7 rest of the year); toilets; water sports. **Best for**: boating; snorkeling; sunset; swimming; walking. ✉ *Sand Harbor Beach, Hwy. 28, 3 miles south of Incline Village* ☎ *775/831–0494* 🌐 *parks.nv.gov/parks/sand-harbor.*

Restaurants

Azzara's

$$ | **ITALIAN** | This dependable if not fabulous Italian family restaurant serves a dozen pasta dishes and many pizzas, as well as chicken, veal, shrimp, and beef. Prices initially might seem high, but once you factor in soup or salad and garlic bread, it's a pretty good value. **Known for:** family run; daily specials; excellent tiramisu. $ *Average main: $22* ✉ *Raley's Shopping Center, 930 Tahoe Blvd., near Village Blvd.* ☎ *775/831–0346* 🌐 *www.azzaras.com* ⏲ *Closed Mon. No lunch.*

Fredrick's Fusion Bistro

$$$ | **ECLECTIC** | Copper-top tables lend a chic look to the dining room at this intimate bistro. The menu consists of a mélange of European and Asian dishes—braised short ribs, roasted duck with caramel-pecan glaze, fresh sushi rolls—most of them prepared with organic produce and free-range meats. **Known for:** chic and intimate; organic, free-range meat in most dishes; fireside tables. $ *Average main: $24* ✉ *907 Tahoe Blvd., at Village Blvd.* ☎ *775/832–3007* 🌐 *fredricksbistro.com* ⏲ *Closed Sun. and Mon. No lunch.*

Le Bistro

$$$$ | **FRENCH** | Incline Village's hidden gem (this restaurant is hard to find, so ask for directions when you book) serves French-country cuisine in a romantic dining room with single-stem roses adorning linen-dressed tables. The five-course prix-fixe menu may include starters like flame-broiled eggplant with ratatouille or escargots, followed by one of several salads (try the gem lettuce Caesar) and lamb loin with lentils and tomato chutney or *coquille St.-Jacques* (scallops in cream sauce), paired with award-winning wines if you choose. **Known for:** romantic setting; five-course prix-fixe meal with wine pairings; gracious, attentive service. $ *Average main: $65* ✉ *120 Country Club Dr., #29* ✥ *Off Lakeshore Blvd.* ☎ *775/831–0800* 🌐 *www.lebistrotahoe.com* ⏲ *Closed Sun. and Mon. No lunch.*

★ Mountain High Sandwich Company

$ | **AMERICAN** | A casual plank-floored all-natural deli serving breakfast and lunch, Mountain High may well be the only place in Tahoe to find coconut chia seed pudding and similar delicacies. More familiar fare—biscuits and sausage gravy for breakfast, house-smoked tri-tip sandwiches for lunch—is also on the menu, with many selections gluten-free and vegan or vegetarian friendly. **Known for:** grab-and-go items; inventive soups; sustainable practices. $ *Average main: $10* ✉ *120 Country Club Dr., Suite 28* ☎ *775/298–2636* 🌐 *www.mountainhigh-sandwichco.com* ⏲ *Closed Mon. No dinner.*

Get to Sand Harbor Beach in Lake Tahoe–Nevada State Park early; the park sometimes fills to capacity before lunchtime in summer.

Hotels

Hyatt Regency Lake Tahoe

$$$ | RESORT | A full-service destination resort on 26 acres of prime lakefront property, the Hyatt has a range of luxurious accommodations, from tower-hotel rooms to lakeside cottages. **Pros:** incredible views; low-key casino; luxurious accommodations. **Cons:** pricey (especially for families); feels corporate; smallish beach. *Rooms from: $227* ✉ *111 Country Club Dr.* ☎ *775/832–1234, 888/899–5019* 🌐 *www.laketahoe.hyatt.com* *422 rooms* *No meals.*

Activities

GOLF

Incline Championship

GOLF | Robert Trent Jones Sr. designed this challenging course of tightly cut, tree-lined fairways laced with water hazards that demand accuracy as well as distance skills. Greens fee includes a cart, except for the 4:30 pm Super Twilight rate of $3 per hole (cart $25). ✉ *955 Fairway Blvd., at Northwood Blvd., north off Hwy. 28* ☎ *866/925–4653 reservations, 775/832–1146 pro shop* 🌐 *www.yourtahoeplace.com/golf-incline* *$190 weekdays, $200 weekends* *18 holes, 7106 yards, par 72.*

Incline Mountain

GOLF | Robert Trent Jones Jr. designed this executive (shorter) course that requires accuracy more than distance skills. The greens fee includes a cart. ✉ *690 Wilson Way, at Golfer's Pass, south off Hwy. 431* ☎ *866/925–4653 reservations, 775/832–1150 pro shop* 🌐 *www.yourtahoeplace.com/golf-incline* *From $65* *18 holes, 3527 yards, par 58.*

MOUNTAIN BIKING

Flume Trail Bikes

BICYCLING | You can rent bikes and get helpful tips from this company, which also operates a bike shuttle to popular trailheads. ✉ *1115 Tunnel Creek Rd., at Ponderosa Ranch Rd., off Hwy. 28* ☎ *775/298–2501* 🌐 *www.flumetrailtahoe.com* *From $45.*

SKIING

Diamond Peak

SKIING/SNOWBOARDING | Diamond Peak has affordable rates and many special programs. Snowmaking covers 75% of the mountain, and runs are groomed nightly. The ride up the 1-mile Crystal Express rewards you with fantastic views. Diamond Peak is less crowded than Tahoe's larger ski parks and provides free shuttles to nearby lodgings. A great place for beginners and intermediates, it's appropriately priced for families. Though there are some steep-aspect black-diamond runs, advanced skiers may find the acreage too limited. For snowboarders there's a small terrain park. **Facilities:** 30 trails; 655 acres; 1,840-foot vertical drop; 7 lifts. ✉ *1210 Ski Way, off Country Club Dr.* ☎ *775/832–1177* 🌐 *www.diamondpeak.com* 🎫 *Lift ticket from $89.*

Mt. Rose Ski Tahoe

SKIING/SNOWBOARDING | At this park, ski some of Tahoe's highest slopes and take in bird's-eye views of Reno, the lake, and Carson Valley. Though more compact than the bigger Tahoe resorts, Mt. Rose has the area's highest base elevation and consequently the driest snow. The mountain has a wide variety of terrain. The most challenging is the Chutes, 200 acres of gulp-and-go advanced-to-expert vertical. Intermediates can choose steep groomers or mellow, wide-open boulevards. Beginners have their own corner of the mountain, with gentle, wide slopes. Boarders and tricksters have several terrain parks to choose from, on opposite sides of the mountain, allowing them to follow the sun as it tracks across the resort. The mountain gets hit hard in storms; check conditions before heading up during inclement weather or on a windy day. **Facilities:** 61 trails; 1,200 acres; 1,800-foot vertical drop; 8 lifts. ✉ *22222 Mt. Rose Hwy., Reno* ✣ *Hwy. 431, 11 miles north of Incline Village* ☎ *775/849–0704* 🌐 *www.skirose.com* 🎫 *Lift ticket $135.*

Tahoe Meadows Snowplay Area

SKIING/SNOWBOARDING | This is the most popular area near the north shore for noncommercial cross-country skiing, sledding, tubing, snowshoeing, and snowmobiling. ✉ *Off Hwy. 431* ✣ *From Hwy. 28 at Incline Village, head north about 6½ miles on Hwy. 431 toward Mt. Rose Ski Area.*

Zephyr Cove

22 miles south of Incline Village.

The largest settlement between Incline Village and the Stateline area is Zephyr Cove, a tiny resort. It has a beach, marina, campground, picnic area, coffee shop in a log lodge, rustic cabins, and nearby riding stables.

GETTING HERE AND AROUND

From the north shore communities, reach Zephyr Cove by following Highway 28 along the eastern side of the lake. From South Lake Tahoe, take U.S. 50 north and then west. Public transportation isn't available in Zephyr Cove.

Sights

Cave Rock

NATURE SITE | Near Zephyr Cove, this 75 feet of solid stone at the southern end of Lake Tahoe–Nevada State Park is the throat of an extinct volcano. The impressive outcropping towers over a parking lot, a lakefront picnic ground, and a boat launch. The views are some of the best on the lake; this is a good spot to stop and take a picture. ⚠ **Cave Rock is a sacred burial site for the Washoe Indians. Climbing to it or through it is prohibited.** ✉ *U.S. 50, 4 miles north of Zephyr Cove* ☎ *775/831–0494* 🌐 *www.parks.nv.gov/parks/lake-tahoe-nevada-state-park-2* 🎫 *$10.*

Restaurants

Capisce?
$$$ | **ITALIAN** | The signature mushroom-and-tomato sauce is so thick it's called "gravy" at this roadside restaurant whose menu emphasizes old favorites from the Italian American side of the family that runs it. The mildly spicy concoction adds zest to cioppino (seafood stew), lasagna, and pasta dishes that include house-made ravioli that some diners prefer slathered instead with a velvety butter-and-Parmesan-cheese sauce. **Known for:** old family recipes; full bar patronized by many locals; desserts including gooey-wonderful cinnamon bun. *$ Average main: $27 ✉ 178 U.S. 50 ☎ 775/580–7500 ⊕ www.capiscelaketahoe.com ⊙ Closed Mon. No lunch.*

Hotels

Zephyr Cove Resort
$$$ | **RENTAL** | **FAMILY** | Beneath towering pines at the lake's edge stand 28 cozy, modern vacation cabins with peaked knotty-pine ceilings. **Pros:** family-friendly; cozy cabins; old-school ambience. **Cons:** lodge rooms are basic; can be noisy in summer; not all cabins have fireplaces. *$ Rooms from: $209 ✉ 760 U.S. 50, 4 miles north of Stateline ☎ 775/589–4906, 800/238–2463 ⊕ www.zephyrcove.com 32 rooms No meals.*

Stateline

5 miles south of Zephyr Cove.

Stateline is the archetypal Nevada border town. Its four high-rise casinos are as vertical and contained as the commercial district of South Lake Tahoe, on the California side, is horizontal and sprawling. And Stateline is as relentlessly indoors-oriented as the rest of the lake is focused on the outdoors. This small strip is where you'll find the most concentrated action at Lake Tahoe: restaurants (including typical casino buffets), showrooms with semi-famous headliners and razzle-dazzle revues, tower-hotel rooms and suites, and 24-hour casinos.

GETTING HERE AND AROUND

From South Lake Tahoe take U.S. 50 north across the Nevada border to reach Stateline and its casinos. If coming from Reno's airport, take U.S. 395/Interstate 580 south to Carson City, and then head west on U.S. 50 to the lake and head south. Or take the South Tahoe Express bus. BlueGO operates daily bus service.

Beaches

Nevada Beach
BEACH—SIGHT | Although less than a mile long, this is the widest beach on the lake and especially good for swimming (many Tahoe beaches are rocky). You can boat and fish here, and there are picnic tables, barbecue grills, and a campground beneath the pines. This is the best place to watch the July 4th or Labor Day fireworks, but most of the summer the subdued atmosphere attracts families and those seeking a less-touristy spot. **Amenities:** parking; water sports; toilets. **Best for:** sunrise; swimming; walking. *✉ Elk Point Rd., off U.S. 50, 3 miles north of Stateline ☎ 530/543–2600 ⊕ www.fs.usda.gov/recarea/ltbmu/recarea/?recid=11757 $8 day-use fee ☞ Dogs permitted on leash in picnic areas but not on beach.*

Restaurants

★ Edgewood Tahoe
$$$ | **AMERICAN** | The three restaurants at Stateline's classy resort, all in impeccably designed spaces that make the most of the lakeside setting, offer some of the area's best dining, if on the pricey side. Head to the Bistro for casual-fancy breakfast, lunch, and dinner; Brooks Bar & Grill for inventive comfort food during lunch and dinner; and the Edgewood Restaurant for evening fine dining with views

across the lake to Mt. Tallac. **Known for:** a venue for all moods; vegan and gluten-free options; golf-course views from outdoor deck at Brooks. *Average main: $27* *Edgewood Tahoe, 100 Lake Pkwy.* *775/588–2787* *www.edgewoodtahoe.com/dine-imbibe.*

Hotels

Harrah's Tahoe Hotel/Casino

$ | **HOTEL** | The 18-story hotel's major selling point is that every room has two full bathrooms, a boon if you're traveling with family. **Pros:** lake and mountain views from upper-floor rooms; good midweek values; top-floor steak house with good views from all tables. **Cons:** can get noisy; uneven housekeeping; lacks intimacy. *Rooms from: $109* *15 U.S. 50, at Stateline Ave.* *775/588–6611, 800/427–7247* *www.caesars.com/harrahs-tahoe* *512 rooms* *No meals.*

Harveys Lake Tahoe Resort Hotel and Casino

$ | **HOTEL** | This resort began as a cabin in 1944, and now it's Tahoe's largest casino-hotel; premium rooms have custom furnishings, oversize marble baths, minibars, and excellent lake views. **Pros:** live entertainment; 19 Kitchen and Sage Room Steakhouse restaurants; lake views from upper-floor rooms. **Cons:** can get loud at night; high summer rates; large property. *Rooms from: $119* *18 U.S. 50, at Stateline Ave.* *775/588–2411, 800/648–3361* *www.caesars.com/harveys-tahoe* *742 rooms* *No meals.*

Lakeside Inn and Casino

$ | **HOTEL** | The smallest of the Stateline casinos, the property has good promotional room rates and simple, attractive accommodations in two-story motel-style buildings separate from the casino. **Pros:** daily dining specials; casino separate from accommodations; free Wi-Fi and no resort or parking fee. **Cons:** some rooms are dark and on the small side; motel-style buildings; despite name lake is a short walk away. *Rooms from: $109* *168 U.S. 50, at Kingsbury Grade* *775/588–7777, 800/624–7980* *lakesideinn.com* *124 rooms* *No meals.*

★ The Lodge at Edgewood Tahoe

$$$$ | **RESORT** | The lodge, which debuted in mid-2017 on a prime lakefront parcel, makes a bold impression with its stone-and-walnut Great Hall, whose four-story wall of windows frames views across Lake Tahoe to grand Mt. Tallac. **Pros:** prime lakefront location; haute-rustic design; all rooms have balconies and fireplaces. **Cons:** high rates in-season; some rooms have no lake views; long walk to pool and hot tub from some rooms. *Rooms from: $400* *100 Lake Pkwy.* *775/588–2787, 888/769–1924* *www.edgewoodtahoe.com/lodge* *154 rooms* *No meals.*

Nightlife

Each of the major casinos has its own showroom, featuring everything from comedy to magic acts to sexy floor shows to Broadway musicals.

LIVE MUSIC

Harveys Outdoor Summer Concert Series

CONCERTS | Headliners such as Robert Plant, Amy Schumer, Janet Jackson, and Keith Urban perform at this weekend concert series. *Harveys Lake Tahoe, 18 U.S. 50* *775/588–2411* *www.caesars.com/harveys-tahoe/shows.*

South Shore Room

CABARET | Classic acts like Chris Botti and Todd Rundgren play Harrah's big showroom, along with the psychedelic Pink Floyd Laser Spectacular show and comedians like Sinbad. *Harrah's Lake Tahoe, 15 U.S. 50* *775/586–6244 tickets, 775/588–6611* *www.caesars.com/harrahs-tahoe/shows.*

Activities

GOLF

Edgewood Tahoe

GOLF | Golfers of all skill levels enjoy this scenic lakeside course that has four sets of tees, offering a variety of course lengths. The greens fee includes an optional cart. ✉ *100 Lake Pkwy., at U.S. 50* ☎ *775/588–3566* 🌐 *www.edgewood-tahoe.com/golf* 🎫 *From $150 (varies throughout season)* ⛳ *18 holes, 7529 yards, par 72.*

Reno

32 miles east of Truckee, 38 miles northeast of Incline Village.

Established in 1859 as a trading station at a bridge over the Truckee River, Reno grew along with the silver mines of nearby Virginia City and the transcontinental railroad that chugged through town. Train officials named it in 1868, but gambling—legalized in 1931—put Reno on the map. This is still a gambling town, with most of the casinos crowded into five square blocks downtown, but a thriving university scene and outdoor activities also attract tourists.

Parts of downtown are sketchy, but things are changing. Reno now touts family-friendly activities like kayaking on the Truckee, museums, and a downtown climbing wall. With over 300 days of sunshine annually, temperatures year-round in this high-mountain-desert climate are warmer than at Tahoe, though rarely as hot as in Sacramento and the Central Valley, making strolling around town a pleasure.

GETTING HERE AND AROUND

Interstate 80 bisects Reno east–west, U.S. 395 north–south (south of town the road is signed U.S. 395/Interstate 580). Greyhound and Amtrak stop here, and several airlines fly into Reno-Tahoe International Airport. RTC Ride provides bus service.

ESSENTIALS

BUS CONTACT RTC Ride ✉ *Transit Center, E. 4th and Lake Sts.* ☎ *775/348–7433* 🌐 *www.rtcwashoe.com.*

VISITOR INFORMATION Reno Tahoe Visitor Center ✉ *135 N. Sierra St.* ☎ *800/367–7366* 🌐 *www.visitrenotahoe.com.*

Sights

★ National Automobile Museum

MUSEUM | FAMILY | An absolute delight filled with antique and classic cars with obscure and familiar names like Packard, Studebaker, Maxwell, Oldsmobile, and Lincoln, the museum, one of the best of its kind in the country, surveys automotive history. Celebrity vehicles include the Lana Turner Chrysler (one of only six made), an Elvis Presley Cadillac, and a Mercury coupe driven by James Dean in the movie *Rebel Without a Cause.* Hard to miss are the experimental and still futuristic-looking 1938 Phantom Corsair and a gold-plated 1980 DeLorean. ✉ *10 S. Lake St., at Mill St.* ☎ *775/333–9300* 🌐 *www.automuseum.org* 🎫 *$12.*

Nevada Museum of Art

MUSEUM | A dramatic four-level structure designed by Will Bruder houses this splendid museum's collection, which focuses on themes such as the Sierra Nevada/Great Basin and altered-landscape photography. The building's exterior torqued walls are sided with a black zinc-based material that has been fabricated to resemble textures found in the Black Rock Desert. Inside the building, a staircase installed within the central atrium is lit by skylights and suspended by a single beam attached to the atrium ceiling. ✉ *160 W. Liberty St., and Hill St.* ☎ *775/329–3333* 🌐 *www.nevadaart.org* 🎫 *$10* 🕒 *Closed Mon. and Tues.*

Riverwalk District

PROMENADE | A formerly dilapidated section of Reno's waterfront is now the toast of the town. The Riverwalk itself is a half-mile promenade on the north side of the Truckee River, which flows around Wingfield Park, where outdoor festivals and other events take place. On the third Saturday of each month, local merchants host a **Wine Walk** between 2 and 5. For $20 you receive a glass and can sample fine wines at participating shops, bars, restaurants, and galleries. In July, look for outdoor art, opera, dance, and kids' performances as part of the monthlong **Artown festival** (🌐 *artown.org*), presented mostly in Wingfield Park. Also at Wingfield is the **Truckee River Whitewater Park.** With activities for all skill levels, it's become a major attraction for water-sports enthusiasts. ✉ *North side of Truckee River between Lake and Ralston Sts.* 🌐 *www.renoriver.org.*

Restaurants

Beaujolais Bistro

$$$$ | **FRENCH** | Across from the Truckee River, this Reno favorite serves earthy, country-style French food—escargots, steak frites with red wine sauce, cassoulet, and crisp sweetbreads with Madeira, along with fish and vegetarian selections—with zero pretension. Wood floors, large windows, and brick walls with a fireplace create a welcoming and intimate atmosphere. **Known for:** inventive cocktails; intimate atmosphere; more casual experience at the bar. [$] *Average main: $35* ✉ *753 Riverside Dr., near Winter St.* ☎ *775/323–2227* 🌐 *www.beaujolaisbistro.com* ⏲ *Closed Mon. No lunch.*

★ **4th St. Bistro**

$$$ | **AMERICAN** | Tablecloths from Provence and a roaring fireplace in winter warm the dining room of this pert, petite bistro on the edge of town. The deliciously simple, smartly prepared cuisine might include oven-roasted fish with citrus beurre blanc or roasted duck breast with yams, tender kale, and port-poached tart cherries. **Known for:** desserts incorporating local fruit; global wine list; fireplace in winter, deck dining in summer. [$] *Average main: $30* ✉ *3065 W. 4th St.* ☎ *775/323–3200* 🌐 *www.4thstbistro.com* ⏲ *Closed Sun. and Mon. No lunch.*

Hotels

Eldorado Resort Casino

$ | **HOTEL** | In the middle of glittering downtown, this resort's huge tower has rooms overlooking either the mountains or the lights of the city. **Pros:** spacious rooms; skywalk connects hotel to Circus Circus and Silver Legacy casinos; amusingly kitschy decor. **Cons:** noisy atmosphere; some housekeeping lapses; faux-everything decor can overwhelm. [$] *Rooms from: $60* ✉ *345 N. Virginia St.* ☎ *775/786–5700, 800/879–8879* 🌐 *www.eldoradoreno.com* *816 rooms* *No meals.*

Peppermill Reno

$ | **HOTEL** | A few miles removed from downtown's flashy main drag, this property set a high standard for luxury in Reno, especially in the Tuscan Tower, whose 600 baroque suites have plush king-size beds, marble bathrooms, and European soaking tubs. **Pros:** luxurious rooms; casino decor; good coffee shop. **Cons:** deluge of neon may be off-putting to some; enormous size; mostly expensive dining. [$] *Rooms from: $109* ✉ *2707 S. Virginia St.* ☎ *775/826–2121, 866/821–9996* 🌐 *www.peppermillreno.com* *1,623 rooms* *No meals.*

Nightlife

CASINOS

Eldorado Resort Casino

CASINOS | Action packed, with lots of slots and popular bar-top video poker, this casino also has good coffee-shop and food-court fare. Don't miss the Fountain of Fortune with its massive

Florentine-inspired sculptures. ✉ *345 N. Virginia St., at W. 4th St.* ☎ *775/786–5700, 800/879–8879* 🌐 *www.eldoradoreno.com.*

Harrah's Reno

CASINOS | Occupying two city blocks, this landmark property has a sprawling casino and an outdoor promenade. ✉ *219 N. Center St., at E. 2nd St.* ☎ *775/786–3232, 800/427–7247* 🌐 *www.harrahsreno.com.*

Peppermill

CASINOS | A few miles from downtown, this casino is known for its excellent restaurants and neon-bright gambling areas. The Fireside cocktail lounge is a blast. ✉ *2707 S. Virginia St., at Peppermill La.* ☎ *775/826–2121, 866/821–9996* 🌐 *www.peppermillreno.com.*

Silver Legacy

CASINOS | A 120-foot-tall mining rig and video poker games draw gamblers to this razzle-dazzle casino. ✉ *407 N. Virginia St., at W. 4th St.* ☎ *775/325–7411, 800/215–7721* 🌐 *www.silverlegacyreno.com/gaming.*

Chapter 14

REDWOOD NATIONAL AND STATE PARKS

Updated by
Andrew Collins

Sights ★★★★★ | Restaurants ★★★★☆ | Hotels ★★★★★ | Shopping ★☆☆☆☆ | Nightlife ★☆☆☆☆

WELCOME TO REDWOOD NATIONAL AND STATE PARKS

TOP REASONS TO GO

★ **Giant trees:** These mature coastal redwoods are the tallest trees in the world.

★ **Hiking to the sea:** The park's trails wind through majestic redwood groves, and many connect to the Coastal Trail, which runs along the western edge of the park.

★ **Rare wildlife:** Mighty Roosevelt elk favor the park's flat prairie and open lands; seldom-seen black bears roam the backcountry; trout and salmon leap through streams; and Pacific gray whales swim along the coast during their spring and fall migrations.

★ **Stepping back in time:** Hike mossy and mysterious Fern Canyon Trail and explore a prehistoric scene of lush vegetation and giant ferns—a memorable scene in *Jurassic Park 2* was shot here.

★ **Getting off-the-grid:** Amid the majestic redwoods you're usually out of cell phone range and often free from crowds, offering a rare opportunity to disconnect.

U.S. 101 weaves through the southern portion of Redwood National and State parks, skirts around the center, and then slips back through redwoods in the north and on to Crescent City. The entire park spans about 50 miles north to south. The Kuchel Visitor Center, Humboldt Lagoons State Park, Prairie Creek Redwoods State Park, Tall Trees Grove, Fern Canyon, and Lady Bird Johnson Grove are in the southern section. In the central section, where the Klamath River Overlook is the dominant feature, the narrow, mostly graveled Coastal Drive loop yields ocean vistas. To the north are Mill Creek Trail, Enderts Beach, and Crescent Beach Overlook in Del Norte Coast Redwoods State Park, as well as Jedediah Smith Redwoods State Park, Stout Grove, Little Bald Hills, and Simpson-Reed Grove.

1 Del Norte Coast Redwoods State Park. The rugged terrain of this far northwestern corner of California combines stretches of treacherous surf, steep cliffs, and forested ridges. On a clear day it's postcard-perfect; with fog, it's mysterious and mesmerizing.

2 Jedediah Smith Redwoods State Park. Gargantuan old-growth redwoods dominate the scenery here. The Smith River cuts through canyons and splits across boulders, carrying salmon to the inland creeks where they spawn.

3 Prairie Creek Redwoods State Park. The forests here give way to spacious, grassy plains where abundant wildlife thrives. Roosevelt elk are a common sight in the meadows and down to Gold Bluffs Beach, where a short trail leads to Fern Canyon.

4 Orick Area. The highlight of the southern portion of Redwood National and State parks is the Tall Trees Grove. It's difficult to reach and requires a special pass, but it's worth the hassle—this section has some of the tallest coast redwood trees. The current world-record holder, a 379-footer named Hyperion, was discovered outside the grove in 2006.

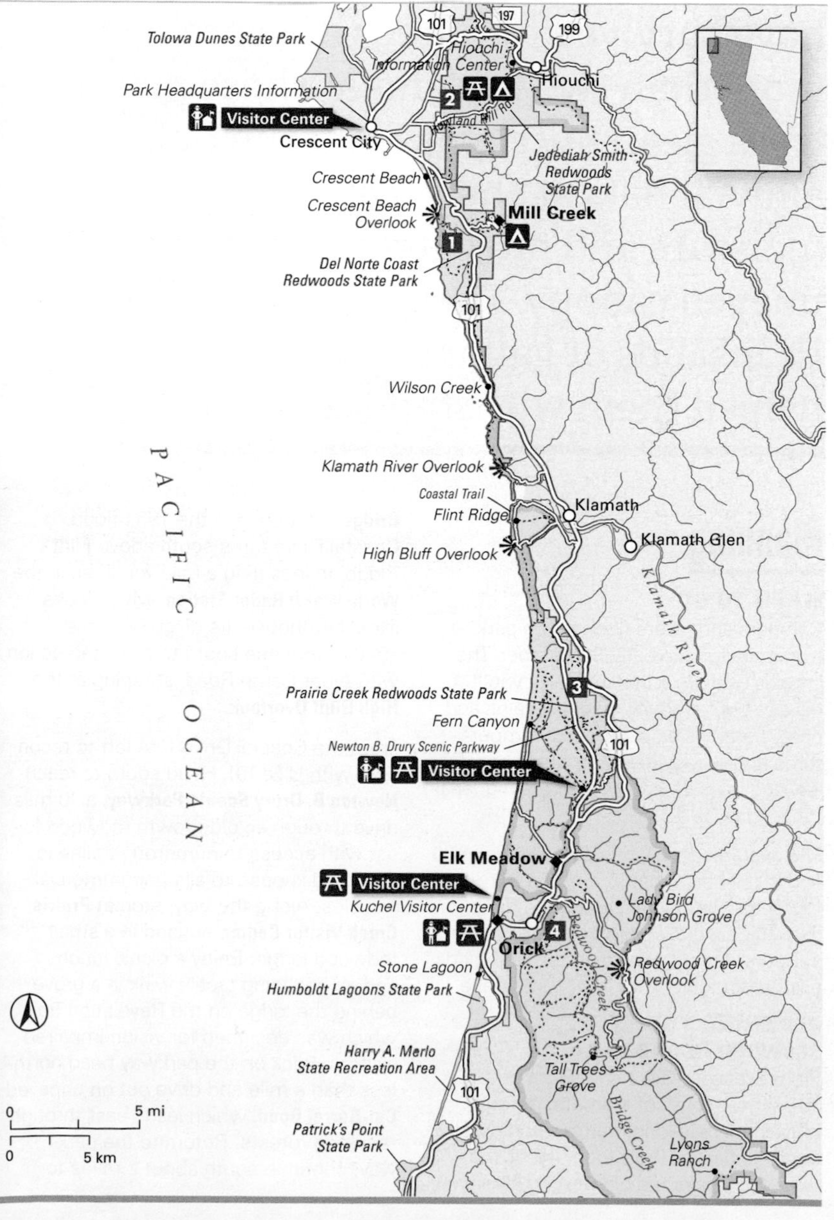
101
197
199
Tolowa Dunes State Park
Hiouchi Information Center
Hiouchi
Park Headquarters Information
Visitor Center
Crescent City
Howland Hill Rd.
Jedediah Smith Redwoods State Park
Crescent Beach
Crescent Beach Overlook
Mill Creek
Del Norte Coast Redwoods State Park
Wilson Creek
PACIFIC OCEAN
Klamath River Overlook
Coastal Trail
Flint Ridge
Klamath
Klamath Glen
High Bluff Overlook
Klamath River
Prairie Creek Redwoods State Park
Fern Canyon
Newton B. Drury Scenic Parkway
Visitor Center
Elk Meadow
Visitor Center
Kuchel Visitor Center
Lady Bird Johnson Grove
Orick
Redwood Creek
Stone Lagoon
Redwood Creek Overlook
Humboldt Lagoons State Park
Harry A. Merlo State Recreation Area
Tall Trees Grove
Bridge Creek
Patrick's Point State Park
Lyons Ranch
0 5 mi
0 5 km
1
2
3
4

Soaring more than 350 feet high, the coastal redwoods that give this park its name are miracles of efficiency—some have survived hundreds of years, a few more than two millennia. These massive trees glean nutrients from the rich alluvial flats at their feet and from the moisture and nitrogen trapped in their uneven canopy. Their thick bark can hold thousands of gallons of water, which has helped them withstand centuries of fires.

Planning

WHEN TO GO

Campers and hikers flock to the park from mid-June to early September. The crowds disappear in winter, but you'll have to contend with frequent rains and nasty potholes on side roads. Temperatures fluctuate widely: the foggy coastal lowland is much cooler than the higher-altitude interior.

The average annual rainfall is between 60 and 80 inches, most of it falling between November and April. During the dry summer, thick fog rolling in from the Pacific veils the forests, providing the redwoods a large portion of their moisture intake.

PLANNING YOUR TIME

REDWOOD IN ONE DAY

From Crescent City head south on U.S. 101. A mile south of Klamath, detour onto the 8-mile-long, narrow, and mostly unpaved **Coastal Drive** loop. Along the way, you'll pass the old **Douglas Memorial Bridge,** destroyed in the 1964 flood. Coastal Drive turns south above Flint Ridge. In less than a mile you'll reach the **World War II Radar Station,** which looks like a farmhouse, its disguise in the 1940s. Continue south to the intersection with Alder Camp Road, stopping at the **High Bluff Overlook.**

From the Coastal Drive turn left to reconnect with U.S. 101. Head south to reach **Newton B. Drury Scenic Parkway,** a 10-mile drive through an old-growth redwood forest with access to numerous trailheads. This road is open to all noncommercial vehicles. Along the way, stop at **Prairie Creek Visitor Center,** housed in a small redwood lodge. Enjoy a picnic lunch and an engaging tactile walk in a grove behind the lodge on the Revelation Trail, which was designed for vision-impaired visitors. Back on the parkway head north less than a mile and drive out on unpaved **Cal-Barrel Road,** which leads east through redwood forests. Return to the parkway, continue south about 2 miles to

AVERAGE HIGH/LOW TEMPERATURES					
JAN.	**FEB.**	**MAR.**	**APR.**	**MAY**	**JUNE**
54/39	56/41	57/41	59/42	62/45	65/48
JULY	**AUG.**	**SEPT.**	**OCT.**	**NOV.**	**DEC.**
67/51	67/51	68/49	64/46	58/43	55/40

reconnect with U.S. 101, and turn west on mostly unpaved **Davison Road** (motor homes/RVs and trailers are prohibited). In about 30 minutes you'll curve right to **Gold Bluffs Beach.** Continue north to the **Fern Canyon** trailhead. Return to U.S. 101, and drive south to the turnoff for the **Thomas H. Kuchel Visitor Center.** Pick up a free permit—a limited number are granted daily—to visit the **Tall Trees Grove** and head north on U.S. 101 to the turnoff for **Bald Hills Road,** a steep route (motor homes/RVs and trailers are not advised). If you visit the grove, allow at least four hours round-trip from the Kuchel Visitor Center. You could also bypass the turnoff to the grove and continue south on Bald Hills Road to 3,097-foot **Schoolhouse Peak.** For a simpler jaunt, turn onto Bald Hills Road and follow it for 2 miles to the **Lady Bird Johnson Grove Nature Loop Trail.** Take the footbridge to the easy 1-mile loop, which follows an old logging road through a mature redwood forest. **■ TIP→ Motor homes/RVs and trailers are not allowed on Coastal Drive, Cal-Barrel Road, and Davison Road, and are not advised on Bald Hills Road. Conditions on these roads can sometimes lead to closures or the requirement of high-clearance vehicles—check with the visitor centers before you set out.**

GETTING HERE AND AROUND

AIR TRAVEL

United Airlines flies a few times daily between San Francisco and the most practical gateway, Arcata/Eureka Airport, between Trinidad and Arcata, about 16 miles north of Eureka. The regional carrier Contour offers daily service from Oakland to Del Norte County Regional Airport in Crescent City. Another option is Oregon's Rogue Valley International Medford Airport, which is served by Alaska, Allegiant, American, Delta, and United, and is about a two-hour drive from the northern end of the park in Crescent City.

CAR TRAVEL

U.S. 101 runs north–south the entire length of the park. You can access all the main park roads via U.S. 101 and U.S. 199, which runs east–west through the park's northern portion. Many roads within the park aren't paved, and winter rains can turn them into obstacle courses; sometimes they're closed completely. Motor homes/RVs and trailers aren't permitted on some routes. The drive from San Francisco to the park's southern end takes about six hours via U.S. 101. From Portland it takes roughly the same amount of time to reach the park's northern section via Interstate 5 to U.S. 199. **■ TIP→ Don't rely solely on GPS, which is inaccurate in parts of the park; closely consult official park maps.**

PARK ESSENTIALS

PARK FEES AND PERMITS

Admission to Redwood National Park is free; several of the state parks collect day-use fees of $8, including the Gold Bluffs Beach and Fern Canyon sections of Prairie Creek Redwoods State Park, and the day-use areas accessed via the campground entrances in Jedediah Smith and Del Norte Coast state parks (the fee for camping overnight is $35). To visit the popular Tall Trees Grove, you must get a free permit at the Kuchel Visitor Center in Orick. Free permits, available at the Kuchel, Crescent City, and (summer only) Hiouchi visitor centers, are needed to stay at all designated backcountry camps.

PARK HOURS
The park is open year-round, 24 hours a day.

CELL PHONE RECEPTION
It's difficult to pick up a signal in much of the park, especially in the camping and hiking areas. If you need a public telephone, go to the Prairie Creek or Jedediah Smith visitor centers.

EDUCATIONAL OFFERINGS
RANGER PROGRAMS
All summer long, ranger-led programs explore the mysteries of both the redwoods and the sea. Topics include how the trees grow from fleck-size seeds to towering giants, what causes those weird fungi on old stumps, why the ocean fog is so important to redwoods, and exactly what those green-tentacled creatures are that float in tide pools. Campfire programs can include slide shows, storytelling, music, and games. Check with visitor centers for offerings and times.

Junior Ranger Program
TOUR—SIGHT | **FAMILY** | From June to early September, rangers lead one-hour programs for children between ages 7 and 12. Activities include nature walks and lessons in bird identification and outdoor survival. ☎ *707/465–7306* 🌐 *www.nps.gov/redw.*

Ranger Talks
TOUR—SIGHT | From mid-May through mid-September, state park rangers regularly lead discussions on the redwoods, tide pools, geology, and Native American culture. Check schedules at the visitor centers. ☎ *707/465–7335* 🌐 *www.nps.gov/redw.*

Redwood EdVentures
TOUR—SIGHT | **FAMILY** | Fun and engaging nature Redwood EdVentures scavenger hunts for kids, called Quests, include ones in the park. Visit the website for "treasure map" PDFs detailing the Quests, which typically take no more than an hour. Participants receive a patch upon completion. 🌐 *www.redwood-edventures.org.*

RESTAURANTS
The park has no restaurants, but Eureka and Arcata have diverse dining establishments—everything from hip oyster bars to some surprisingly good ethnic restaurants. The dining options are more limited, though decent, in Crescent City, and there are a few good choices in Klamath, Orick, and Trinidad. Most small-town restaurants close early, around 7:30 or 8 pm.

HOTELS
The only lodgings within park boundaries are the Elk Meadow Cabins, near Prairie Creek Redwoods Visitor Center. Orick, to the south of Elk Meadow, and Klamath, to the north, have basic motels, and in Klamath there's the Requa Inn bed-and-breakfast. Elegant Victorian inns, seaside motels, and fully equipped vacation rentals are among the options in towns north and south of the park. In summer, try to book at least a week ahead at lodgings near the park entrance. *Hotel reviews have been shortened. For full information, visit Fodors.com.*

What It Costs

$	$$	$$$	$$$$
RESTAURANTS			
under $12	$12–$20	$21–$30	over $30
HOTELS			
under $100	$100–$150	$151–$200	over $200

VISITOR INFORMATION
PARK CONTACT INFORMATION Redwood National and State Parks ✉ *1111 2nd St., Crescent City* ☎ *707/465–7335* 🌐 *www.nps.gov/redw.*

VISITOR CENTERS
Crescent City Information Center
INFO CENTER | At the park's headquarters, this downtown visitor center with

a gift shop and picnic area is the main information stop if you're approaching the Redwoods from the north. In winter, hours are limited and dependent on funding; call ahead to confirm. ✉ *1111 2nd St., Crescent City* ☎ *707/465–7335* 🌐 *www.nps.gov/redw.*

Hiouchi Information Center

INFO CENTER | This small center at Jedediah Smith Redwoods State Park has exhibits about the area flora and fauna and screens a 12-minute park film. A starting point for ranger programs, the center has restrooms and a picnic area. ✉ *U.S. 199* ✣ *Opposite entrance to Jedediah Smith Campground, 9 miles east of Crescent City* ☎ *707/458–3294* 🌐 *www.nps.gov/redw.*

Jedediah Smith Visitor Center

INFO CENTER | Adjacent to the Jedediah Smith Redwoods State Park main campground, this seasonal center has information about ranger-led walks and evening campfire programs. Also here are nature and history exhibits, a gift shop, and a picnic area. ✉ *U.S. 199, Hiouchi* ✣ *At Jedediah Smith Campground* ☎ *707/458–3496* 🌐 *www.nps.gov/redw* 🕑 *Closed Oct.–May.*

★ Prairie Creek Visitor Center

INFO CENTER | FAMILY | In a small redwood lodge, this center has a massive stone fireplace. The wildlife displays include a section of a tree a young elk died beside. Because of the peculiar way the redwood grew around the elk's skull, the tree appears to have antlers. The center has information about summer programs in Prairie Creek Redwoods State Park, and you'll find a gift shop, a picnic area, restrooms, and exhibits on flora and fauna. Roosevelt elk often roam the vast field adjacent to the center, and several trailheads begin nearby. Stretch your legs with an easy stroll along **Revelation Trail,** a short loop that starts behind the lodge. ✉ *Prairie Creek Rd., Orick* ✣ *Off southern end of Newton B. Drury Scenic Pkwy.* ☎ *707/488–2039* 🌐 *www.nps.gov/redw.*

★ Thomas H. Kuchel Visitor Center

INFO CENTER | FAMILY | The park's southern section contains the largest and best of the Redwoods visitor centers. Rangers here dispense brochures, advice, and free permits to drive up the access road to Tall Trees Grove. Whale-watchers find the center's deck an excellent observation point, and bird-watchers enjoy the nearby Freshwater Lagoon, a popular layover for migrating waterfowl. Many of the center's exhibits are hands-on and kid-friendly. ✉ *U.S. 101, Orick* ✣ *Redwood Creek Beach County Park* ☎ *707/465–7765* 🌐 *www.nps.gov/redw.*

Sights

SCENIC DRIVES

★ Coastal Drive Loop

SCENIC DRIVE | The 9-mile, narrow, and partially unpaved Coastal Drive Loop takes about one hour to traverse. Weaving through stands of redwoods, the road yields close-up views of the Klamath River and expansive panoramas of the Pacific. Recurring landslides have closed sections of the original road; this loop, closed to trailers and RVs, is all that remains. Hikers access the Flint Ridge section of the Coastal Trail off the drive. ✉ *Klamath* ✣ *Off Klamath Beach Rd. exit from U.S. 101.*

Howland Hill Road/Stout Grove

SCENIC DRIVE | Take your time as you drive this 10-mile route along Mill Creek, which winds through old-growth redwoods and past the Smith River. Trailers and RVs are prohibited on this route. ✣ *Access from Elk Valley Rd., off U.S. 101.*

★ Newton B. Drury Scenic Parkway/Big Tree Wayside

SCENIC DRIVE | This paved 10-mile route threads through Prairie Creek Redwoods State Park and old-growth redwoods. It's open to all noncommercial vehicles. North of the Prairie Creek Visitor Center you can make the 0.8-mile walk to Big Tree Wayside and observe Roosevelt elk

Plants and Wildlife in Redwood

Coast redwoods, the world's tallest trees, grow in the moist, temperate climate of California's North Coast. The current record holder, topping out at 379 feet (or 386, depending on who's measuring), was found in the Redwood Creek watershed in 2006. These ancient giants thrive in an environment that exists in only a few hundred coastal miles along the Pacific Ocean. They commonly live 600 years—though some have been around for more than 2,000 years.

Diverse, Complex

A healthy redwood forest is diverse and includes Douglas firs, western hemlocks, tan oaks, and madrone trees. The complex soils of the forest floor support a profusion of ferns, mosses, and fungi, along with numerous shrubs and berry bushes. In spring, California rhododendron bloom all over, providing a dazzling purple and pink contrast to the dense greenery.

Old-Growth Forests

Redwood National and State parks hold nearly 50% of California's old-growth redwood forests, but only about a third of the forests in the park are old-growth. Of the original 3,125 square miles (2 million acres) in the Redwoods Historic Range, only 4% survived logging that began in 1850. A quarter of these trees are privately owned and on managed land. The rest are on public tracts.

Wildlife Species

In the park's backcountry, you might spot mountain lions, black bears, black-tailed deer, river otters, beavers, and minks. Roosevelt elk roam the flatlands, and the rivers and streams teem with salmon and trout. Gray whales, seals, and sea lions cavort near the coastline. More than 280 species of birds have been recorded in the parks, which are located along the Pacific Flyway.

in the prairie. ✉ *Orick* ✧ *Entrances off U.S. 101 about 5 miles south of Klamath and 5 miles north of Orick.*

SCENIC STOPS

Crescent Beach Overlook

VIEWPOINT | The scenery here includes views of the ocean and, in the distance, Crescent City and its working harbor. In balmy weather this is a great place for a picnic. You may spot migrating gray whales between November and April. ✉ *Enderts Beach Rd.* ✧ *4½ miles south of Crescent City.*

Del Norte Coast Redwoods State Park

BEACH—SIGHT | This park southeast of Crescent City contains 15 memorial redwood groves and 8 miles of pristine coastline, which you can most easily access at Wilson Beach or False Klamath Cove. The old-growth forest extends down steep slopes almost to the shore. ✉ *U.S. 101, Crescent City* ✧ *9 miles southeast of Crescent City* ☎ *707/465–7335* 🌐 *www.parks.ca.gov.*

★ Fern Canyon

CANYON | Enter another world and be surrounded by 50-foot canyon walls covered with sword, deer, and five-finger ferns. Allow an hour to explore the ¼-mile-long vertical garden along a 0.7-mile loop. From the northern end of Gold Bluffs Beach it's an easy walk, although you'll have to wade across or scamper along planks that traverse a small stream several times (in addition to driving across a couple of streams on the way to the parking area). But the lush, otherworldly surroundings, which appeared in *Jurassic Park 2,* are a must-see when creeks aren't running too high. Motor homes/RVs and all trailers are prohibited. You can also hike to the canyon from Prairie Creek Visitor Center along the moderately challenging West Ridge–Friendship Ridge–James Irvine Loop, 12½ miles round-trip. ✉ *Orick* ✣ *2¾ miles north of Orick, take Davison Rd. northwest off U.S. 101 and follow signs to Gold Bluffs Beach.*

★ Jedediah Smith Redwoods State Park

NATIONAL/STATE PARK | Home to the Stout Memorial Grove, this park with 20 miles of hiking and nature trails is named after a trapper who in 1826 became the first white man to explore Northern California's interior. If coming from interior Oregon, this is your first chance to drive and hike among stands of soaring redwoods. ✉ *U.S. 199, Hiouchi* ✣ *9 miles east of Crescent City* ☎ *707/458–4396* 🌐 *www.parks.ca.gov.*

Klamath River Overlook

VIEWPOINT | This grassy, windswept bluff rises 650 feet above the confluence of the Klamath River and the Pacific. It's one of the best spots in the park for spying migratory whales in early winter and late spring, and it accesses a section of the Coastal Trail. Warm days are ideal for picnicking at one of the tables. ✉ *End of Requa Rd., Klamath* ✣ *2¼ miles west of U.S. 101.*

Lady Bird Johnson Grove

FOREST | One of the park's most accessible spots to view big trees, the grove was dedicated by, and named for, the former first lady. An easy 1-mile nature loop follows an old logging road through a redwood forest. ✉ *Bald Hills Rd., Orick* ✣ *2 miles east of U.S. 101.*

★ Prairie Creek Redwoods State Park

NATIONAL/STATE PARK | **FAMILY** | Spectacular redwoods and lush ferns make up this park traversed by the stunning Newton B. Drury Scenic Parkway. Extra space has been paved alongside the parklands, providing fine places to observe herds of Roosevelt elk, which at one time neared extinction, in adjoining meadows. The park also includes famously spectacular Gold Bluffs Beach and Fern Canyon. If your time is limited, Prairie Creek is one of the best spots for a full day hiking and exploring. ✉ *Prairie Creek Rd., Orick* ✣ *Off southern end of Newton B. Drury Scenic Pkwy.* ☎ *707/488–2039* 🌐 *www.parks.ca.gov.*

Tall Trees Grove

FOREST | At the Kuchel Visitor Center you can obtain a free permit to make the steep 14-mile drive to this redwood grove that once contained the world-record holder for tallest tree. Rangers dispense a limited number per day, first come, first served. The hike from the trailhead parking lot is 4 miles round-trip. No trailers or RVs. ✉ *Tall Trees Access Rd., off Bald Hills Rd., Orick* ✣ *Off Bald Hills Rd., 7 miles from U.S. 101, then 6½ miles to trailhead.*

Activities

BICYCLING

Besides the roadways, you can bike on several trails, many of them along former logging roads. Best bets include the 11-mile Lost Man Creek Trail, which begins 3 miles north of Orick; the 12-mile round-trip Coastal Trail (Last Chance Section), which starts at the southern end of Enderts Beach Road and becomes steep and narrow as it travels through dense slopes of foggy redwood forests; and the 19-mile, single-track Ossagon Trail Loop, on which you're likely to see elk as you cruise through redwoods before coasting ocean side toward the end.

BIRD-WATCHING

Many rare and striking winged specimens inhabit the area, including chestnut-backed chickadees, brown pelicans, great blue herons, pileated woodpeckers, northern spotted owls, and marbled murrelets.

FISHING

Deep-sea and freshwater fishing are popular here. Anglers often stake out sections of the Klamath and Smith rivers seeking salmon and trout. A single state license (🌐 *www.wildlife.ca.gov/licensing/fishing*) covers both ocean and river fishing. A two-day license costs about $24. You can go crabbing and clamming on the coast, but check the tides carefully: rip currents and sneaker waves can be deadly. No license is needed to fish from the long B Street Pier in Crescent City.

HIKING

★ Coastal Trail

HIKING/WALKING | This easy-to-difficult trail, depending on how much of it you tackle, runs most of the park's length; smaller sections that vary in difficulty are accessible at frequent, well-marked trailheads. The moderate-to-difficult **DeMartin section** leads past 6 miles of old-growth redwoods and through prairie. If you're up for a real workout, hike the brutally difficult but stunning **Flint Ridge section,** 4½ miles of steep grades and numerous switchbacks past redwoods and Marshall Pond (check ahead to be sure this section has reopened, following a closure as a result of bridge damage in 2018). The moderate 5½-mile-long **Klamath section,** which connects the Wilson Creek Picnic Area and the Klamath River Overlook, with a short detour to Hidden Beach and its tide pools, provides coastal views and whale-watching opportunities. *Moderate.* ✉ *Klamath* ⊕ *Trailheads: DeMartin, U.S. 101 mile markers 12.8 (south) and 15.6 (north); Flint Ridge, Alder Camp Rd. at Douglas Bridge parking area, north end of Coastal Dr. (east), and off Klamath Beach Rd. (west); Klamath, Requa Rd. at Klamath River Overlook (south), Wilson Creek Picnic Area, off U.S. 101 (north)* 🌐 *www.nps.gov/redw.*

West Ridge–Friendship Ridge–James Irvine Loop

HIKING/WALKING | For a long, moderately strenuous trek, try this 12½-mile loop. The difficult West Ridge segment passes redwoods looming above a carpet of ferns. The difficult Friendship Ridge portion slopes down toward the coast through forests of spruce and hemlock and accesses iconic Fern Canyon. The moderate James Irvine Trail portion winds along a small creek and amid dense stands of redwoods. *Difficult.* ✉ *Orick* ⊕ *Trailhead: Prairie Creek Visitor Center* 🌐 *www.nps.gov/redw.*

KAYAKING

With many miles of often shallow rivers, streams, and estuarial lagoons, kayaking is a popular pastime in the park.

Humboats Kayak Adventures

KAYAKING | You can rent kayaks and book kayaking tours that from December to June include whale-watching trips. Half-day river kayaking trips pass beneath massive redwoods; the whale-watching outings get you close enough for good photos. ✉ *Woodley Island Marina, 601 Startare Dr., Dock A, Eureka* ☎ *707/443–5157* 🌐 *www.humboats.com* 🎫 *From $30 rentals, $55 tours.*

★ Kayak Zak's

KAYAKING | This outfit rents kayaks and stand-up paddleboards, good for touring the beautiful estuarial and freshwater lagoons of Humboldt Lagoons State Park. You can also book a guided nature paddle. Rentals at the Stone Lagoon Visitor Center take place year-round, and on most summer weekends Kayak Zak's sets up a trailer at nearby Big Lagoon. The lagoons are stunning. Herds of Roosevelt elk sometimes traipse along the shoreline of Big Lagoon; raptors, herons, and waterfowl abound in both lagoons; and you can paddle across Stone Lagoon to a spectacular secluded Pacific-view beach. ✉ *Humboldt Lagoons State Park Visitor Center, 115336 U.S. 101, about 5½ miles south of Orick, Trinidad*

707/498–1130 *www.kayakzak.com* *From $30.*

WHALE-WATCHING
Good vantage points for whale-watching include Crescent Beach Overlook, the Kuchel Visitor Center in Orick, points along the Coastal Trail, and the Klamath River Overlook. From late November through January is the best time to see their southward migrations; from February through April the whales return, usually passing closer to shore.

Nearby Towns

Crescent City, north of the park, is Del Norte County's largest town (population about 6,700) and home to the Redwood National and State parks headquarters. Though it curves around a beautiful stretch of ocean, rain and bone-chilling fog often prevail. Very small **Klamath** is outside park boundaries though near to the middle section. The town has a few lodgings but not much dining. Roughly 50 miles south of Crescent City (20 miles north of Eureka), little **Trinidad** has a cove harbor that attracts fishermen and photographers. The picturesque town has a few notable dining and lodging options and is a good base for exploring Prairie Creek Redwoods State Park and other southerly attractions. Farther south, **Arcata** began life in 1850 as a base camp for miners and lumberjacks and had fewer than 1,000 residents until the early 1900s. Today this artsy, progressive town has about 17,200 citizens, plus another 8,500 students enrolled in Humboldt State University. Activity centers on the grassy Arcata Plaza, which is surrounded by restored buildings containing funky bars, cafés, and indie shops. Nearby **Eureka,** population 27,200 and the Humboldt County seat, was named after a gold miner's hearty exclamation. Its Old Town has an alluring waterfront boardwalk, several excellent restaurants and shops, and the region's largest selection of lodgings. The visitor center here is the area's best overall resource for tourism information. Strip malls dominate the city's outskirts, but the city center has much to recommend it.

VISITOR INFORMATION Arcata Humboldt Visitor Center *1635 Heindon Rd., Arcata* *707/822–3619* *www.arcatachamber.com.* **Crescent City/Del Norte County Chamber of Commerce** *1001 Front St., Crescent City* *707/464–3174, 800/343–8300* *www.delnorte.org.* **Eureka-Humboldt Visitors Bureau** *322 1st St., Eureka* *707/443–5097, 800/346–3482* *www.visitredwoods.com.*

Sights

Battery Point Lighthouse
LIGHTHOUSE | Only during low tide, you can walk from the pier across the ocean floor to this working lighthouse, which was built in 1856. It houses a museum with nautical artifacts and photographs of shipwrecks. There's even a resident ghost. *Lighthouse parking, 235 Lighthouse Way, Crescent City* *707/464–3089, 707/464–3922* *www.delnortehistory.org/lighthouse* *$5* *Closed weekdays Oct.–Mar.*

Northcoast Marine Mammal Center
ZOO | The nonprofit center rescues and rehabilitates stranded, sick, and injured seals, sea lions, dolphins, and porpoises. Its facility isn't a museum or an aquarium, but placards and kiosks provide information about marine mammals and coastal ecosystems, and even when the place is closed you can observe the rescued animals through a fence enclosing individual pools. The gallery and gift shop is open on most weekends and some weekdays, especially in summer, and volunteers are often on hand to answer questions. It's worth calling the day of your visit to find out when feedings will take place. *424 Howe Dr., Crescent City* *707/465–6265* *www.northcoastmmc.org* *Free.*

Sequoia Park Zoo

ZOO | FAMILY | Animal lovers of all ages appreciate visiting California's oldest zoo (it opened in 1907). A highlight here is strolling high above the forest on the nation's only redwood canopy walk. Although it's a relatively small zoo, it is conservation-focused and fully accredited, and it's developed a number of excellent new exhibits in recent years, Favorite areas for wildlife viewing include the red panda exhibit, a barnyard petting zoo, and a walk-in aviary with both local and exotic birds. ✉ *3414 W St., Eureka* ☎ *707/441–4263* 🌐 *www.sequoiapark-zoo.net* 🎫 *$10.*

Trees of Mystery

FOREST | FAMILY | Since opening in 1946, this unabashedly goofy but endearing roadside attraction has been doling out family fun. From the moment you pull your car up to the 49-foot-tall talking statue of Paul Bunyan (alongside Babe the Blue Ox), the kitschy thrills begin. You can then explore a genuinely informative museum of Native American artifacts, admire intricately carved redwood figures, and browse tacky souvenirs. For a fee you can ride a six-passenger gondola over the redwood treetops for a majestic view of the forest canopy, and stroll along several mostly easy trails through the adjacent forest of redwoods, Sitka spruce, and Douglas firs. ✉ *15500 U.S. 101 N, between Klamath and Del Norte Coast Redwoods State Park, Klamath* ☎ *707/482–2251* 🌐 *www.treesofmystery.net* 🎫 *Museum free, trails and gondola $18.*

Restaurants

IN THE PARK

PICNIC AREAS

Crescent Beach

RESTAURANT—SIGHT | This beach has a grassy picnic area with tables, fire pits, and restrooms. There's an overlook south of the beach. ✉ *Enderts Beach Rd., Crescent City* ✣ *4 miles south of Crescent City.*

Elk Prairie

RESTAURANT—SIGHT | In addition to many elk, this spot has a campground, a nature trail, and a ranger station. ✉ *Prairie Creek Redwoods State Park, 127011 Newton B. Drury Scenic Pkwy., Orick.*

★ High Bluff Overlook

RESTAURANT—SIGHT | This picnic area's sunsets and whale-watching are unequaled. A ½-mile trail leads from here to the beach. ✉ *Coastal Dr. loop, Klamath* ✣ *Off U.S. 1010, via Alder Camp Rd.*

OUTSIDE THE PARK

ARCATA

★ Cafe Brio

$$ | AMERICAN | With an inviting indoor dining room and outside seating overlooking bustling Arcata Plaza, this artisan bakery and restaurant is known for its savory and sweet breads. Notable noshes include ham-and-cheese breakfast croissants, focaccia sandwiches with avocado and Humboldt Fog goat cheese from Arcata's Cypress Grove creamery, and farm-to-table dinner fare. **Known for:** lemon cream tarts and other pastries available all day; small but terrific wine selection; Blue Bottle coffees. 💲 *Average main: $14* ✉ *791 G St., Arcata* ☎ *707/822–5922* 🌐 *www.cafebrioarcata.com* 🕓 *No dinner Sun. and Mon.*

Wildberries Marketplace

$ | DELI | This market with juice and salad bars and a small café carries a great selection of deli items, cheeses, and picnic provisions, many of them produced regionally. **Known for:** burgers and jerk chicken sandwiches; organic produce; excellent pizzas, tarts, pies, and other baked goods. 💲 *Average main: $8* ✉ *747 13th St., Arcata* ☎ *707/822–0095* 🌐 *www.wildberries.com* 💳 *No credit cards.*

Redwood trees, and the moss that often coats them, grow best in damp, shady environments.

CRESCENT CITY

Good Harvest Cafe

$$ | **AMERICAN** | The café, which serves great breakfasts and espresso drinks, lives up to its name with ample use of locally grown and organic ingredients. For lunch and dinner there are salads, burgers, sandwiches, vegetarian specialties, and several fish entrées, plus a nice range of local beers and West Coast wines. **Known for:** fish-and-chips and other local seafood; hearty, delicious breakfasts; plenty of vegetarian items. *Average main: $16 ✉ 575 U.S. 101 S, Crescent City ☎ 707/465–6028.*

★ SeaQuake Brewing

$$ | **PIZZA** | Water from the cool and clean Smith River goes into the dozen or so beers poured at this microbrewery with a modern-industrial look. They pair well with wood-fired thin-crust pizzas that include one with grilled chicken, bacon, artichoke hearts, garlic cream sauce, and cheeses from the local Rumiano Cheese Company. **Known for:** tacos, wings, salads, and other starters; well-crafted beers on tap; the caramel stout sundae. *Average main: $15 ✉ 400 Front St., Crescent City ☎ 707/465–4444 🌐 seaquakebrewing.com ⏲ Closed Sun. and Mon.*

Vita Cucina

$ | **AMERICAN** | Although set in a nondescript downtown shopping center, this casual café, bakery, and takeout market serves fresh, creative food that's anything but ordinary. Come by in the morning for pastries, eggs, or quiche, or later on for fare that includes Vietnamese *banh mi* and sushi-grade-ahi sandwiches, whole smoked chicken with garlic-mashed potatoes, and barbecue-pork pizzas. **Known for:** great stop for picnic supplies before venturing into the park; daily-changing quiche (always with a vegetarian option); nice selection of fresh salads. *Average main: $8 ✉ 1270 Front St., Crescent City ☎ 707/464–1076 ⏲ Closed Sun. No dinner.*

Hotels

IN THE PARK

★ Elk Meadow Cabins

$$$$ | **B&B/INN** | **FAMILY** | From the porches of these beautifully restored 1,200-square-foot former mill workers' cottages, guests often see Roosevelt elk meandering in the meadows. **Pros:** in a stunning part of Prairie Creek State Park yet conveniently located on U.S. 101; spacious enough for four to six guests; kitchens. **Cons:** a bit of a drive from most area restaurants; expensive for just two occupants, though reasonable for families or groups; furnishings are comfortable but plain. *Rooms from: $299 ✉ 7 Valley Green Camp Rd., off U.S. 101 north of Davison Rd., Orick ☎ 707/488–2222, 866/733–9637 www.elkmeadowcabins.com 7 cabins No meals.*

OUTSIDE THE PARK

CRESCENT CITY

Curly Redwood Lodge

$ | **HOTEL** | A single redwood tree produced the 57,000 board feet of lumber used to build this budget 1957 motor lodge. **Pros:** large rooms; several restaurants within walking distance; cool retro furnishings. **Cons:** road noise can be bothersome; very basic amenities; no breakfast. *Rooms from: $79 ✉ 701 U.S. 101 S, Crescent City ☎ 707/464–2137 www.curlyredwoodlodge.com 36 rooms No meals.*

Ocean View Inn & Suites

$$ | **HOTEL** | This clean, comfortable, and reasonably priced hotel doesn't have a lot of bells and whistles, but it does enjoy a great location on the edge of downtown Crescent City very close to the water. **Pros:** views of the water; many restaurants nearby; good value. **Cons:** on a busy road; cookie-cutter furnishings; nearby foghorn can be a little noisy. *Rooms from: $125 ✉ 270 U.S. 101, Crescent City ☎ 707/465–1111, 855/623–2611 www.oceanviewinncrescentcity.com 65 rooms Free Breakfast.*

KLAMATH

★ Historic Requa Inn

$$ | **B&B/INN** | This serene 1914 inn overlooks the Klamath River a mile east of where it meets the ocean. **Pros:** serene; relaxing yet central location with river views; excellent restaurant. **Cons:** walls are thin; not a good choice for families with kids; not many dining options in the area. *Rooms from: $119 ✉ 451 Requa Rd., Klamath ☎ 707/482–1425 www.requainn.com 12 rooms Breakfast.*

Ravenwood Motel

$ | **HOTEL** | Attentive on-site owners converted a dowdy roadside motel into this class act consisting of 10 rooms and five suites—four with full kitchens—beautifully decorated with different themes. **Pros:** handy to park's central section; exceptionally clean rooms; a bargain. **Cons:** nonsuite rooms small; along a business strip with no view to speak of; no pets. *Rooms from: $75 ✉ 151 Klamath Blvd., Klamath ☎ 707/482–5911, 866/520–9875 www.ravenwoodmotel.com 15 rooms Breakfast.*

NEAR PARK'S SOUTHERN SECTION

Redwood Coast Vacation Rentals

$$ | **RENTAL** | Given the relatively limited number of hotels and inns close to the park, renting a vacation home in the area can be a good strategy, especially for groups of friends or families who appreciate kitchen facilities. **Pros:** properties for all budgets; all rentals have kitchens; many rentals have multiple bedrooms and baths. **Cons:** 10 am checkout; one-time cleaning fee adds a lot to the cost for travelers only staying a night or two; quality and furnishings vary from unit to unit. *Rooms from: $150 ✉ McKinleyville ☎ 707/834–6555 www.redwoodcoastvacationrentals.com 75 units No meals.*

Chapter 15

THE FAR NORTH

Updated by
Daniel Mangin

Sights
★★★★☆

Restaurants
★★★☆☆

Hotels
★★★☆☆

Shopping
★★★☆☆

Nightlife
★★★☆☆

WELCOME TO THE FAR NORTH

TOP REASONS TO GO

★ **Mother Nature's wonders:** California's Far North has more rivers, streams, lakes, forests, and mountains than you'll ever have time to explore.

★ **Volcanoes:** With two volcanoes to view—Lassen and Shasta—you can learn firsthand what happens when a mountain blows its top.

★ **Fantastic fishing:** Whether you like casting from a riverbank or letting your line bob beside a boat, you'll find fabulous fishing in all the northern counties.

★ **Cool hops:** On a hot day there's nothing quite as inviting as a visit to Chico's world-famous Sierra Nevada Brewery. Take the tour, and then savor a chilled glass on tap at the adjacent brewpub.

★ **Shasta:** Wonderful in all its forms: lake, dam, river, mountain, forest, and town.

1 Chico. A state university and a famous brewery help set the mood in this city also known for its artisans and farmers.

2 Corning. Olive-oil tasting rooms have made this small town a fun stop for many travelers along Interstate 5.

3 Red Bluff. One of several gateway towns to Lassen Volcanic National Park, Red Bluff makes a good base for outdoor adventures.

4 Redding. A northern gateway to Lassen Volcanic National Park, Redding has several points of interest within city limits, and day trips to Weaverville, Shasta Dam, and Lake Shasta Caverns National Natural Landmark are easily undertaken from here.

5 Weaverville. A 19th-century temple erected by Chinese miners is the centerpiece of this laid-back town's historic district.

6 Shasta Lake. Caverns, Shasta Dam, and vacation houseboats count among this quiet town's draws.

7 Dunsmuir. The upper Sacramento River near Dunsmuir consistently ranks among the country's best fishing spots. Most of the accommodations at a popular resort here were formerly cabooses.

8 Mt. Shasta. The town named for the peak that towers above it lures outdoorsy types year-round—hikers and golfers in summer, skiers in winter.

9 Chester. The southern gateway to Lassen Volcanic National Park sits on the forested edge of Lake Almanor.

10 Mineral. Lassen's official address is this town within the 165-square-mile national treasure.

11 Burney. President Theodore Roosevelt was among the fans of two magnificent waterfalls here.

12 Tulelake. Hundreds of underground lava tube caves make this town's Lava Beds National Monument well worth the remote drive.

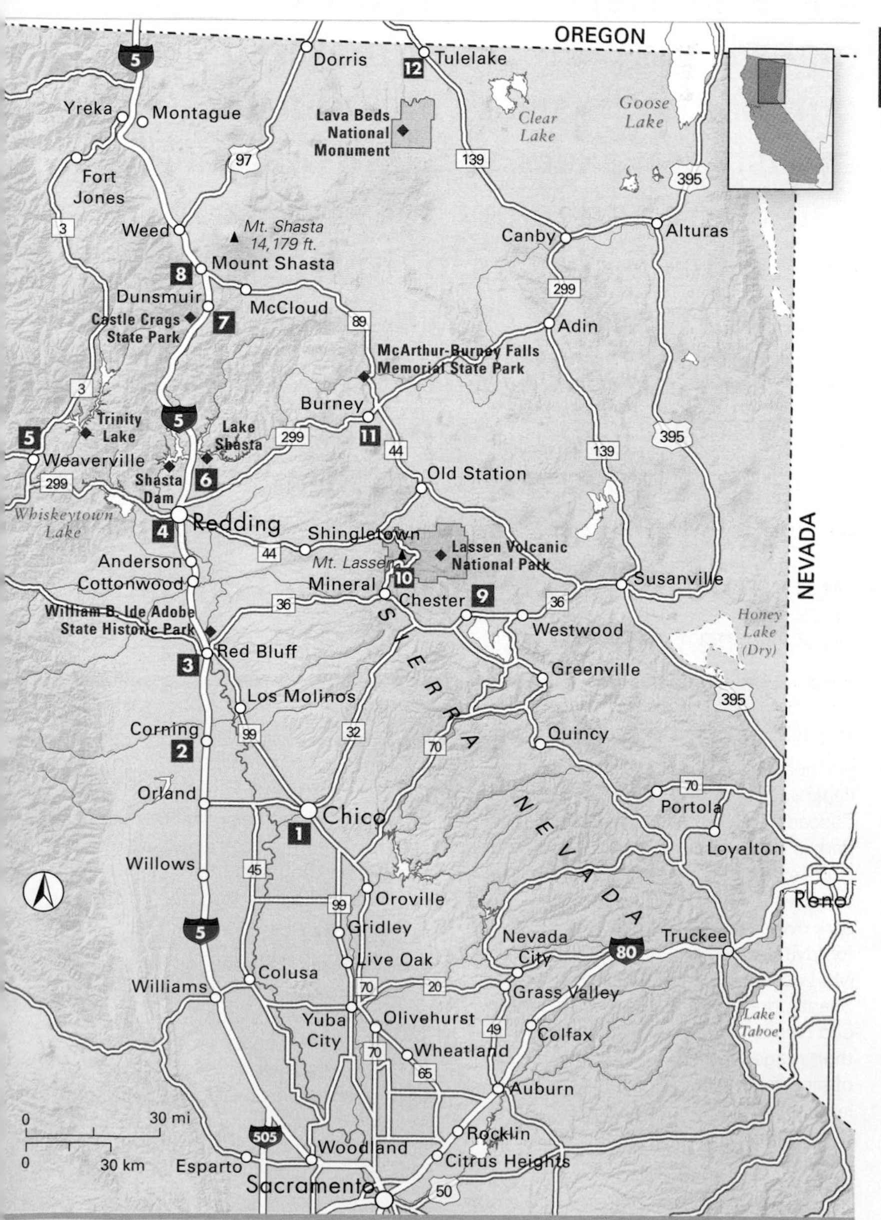
OREGON
Dorris
12
Tulelake
Lava Beds National Monument
Clear Lake
Goose Lake
5
Yreka
Montague
97
139
395
Fort Jones
3
Weed
Mt. Shasta
14,179 ft.
Canby
Alturas
8
Mount Shasta
Dunsmuir
McCloud
299
Castle Crags State Park
7
89
Adin
McArthur-Burney Falls Memorial State Park
Burney
3
Trinity Lake
5
Lake Shasta
299
11
395
5
Weaverville
44
139
Shasta Dam
6
Old Station
299
Whiskeytown Lake
Redding
4
Shingletown
Lassen Volcanic National Park
44
Mt. Lassen
Anderson
Cottonwood
Mineral
10
Chester
9
Susanville
NEVADA
William B. Ide Adobe State Historic Park
36
36
Westwood
Honey Lake (Dry)
Red Bluff
3
Greenville
Los Molinos
SIERRA NEVADA
395
Corning
99
32
70
Quincy
2
Orland
Chico
1
70
Portola
Loyalton
Willows
45
Reno
99
Oroville
Gridley
5
Nevada City
80
Truckee
Live Oak
Colusa
Williams
70
20
Grass Valley
Lake Tahoe
Yuba City
Olivehurst
49
Colfax
70
Wheatland
65
Auburn
0
30 mi
0
30 km
505
Rocklin
Woodland
Esparto
Citrus Heights
Sacramento
50

The Far North's soaring mountain peaks, trail-filled national forests, alpine lakes, and wild rivers teeming with trout make it the perfect destination for outdoor enthusiasts, including hikers, cyclists, kayakers, and bird-watchers. You won't find many hot nightspots or cultural enclaves in this region, but you will discover crowd-free national and state parks, crystal-clear mountain streams, superlative hiking and fishing, plus small towns worth exploring. And the spectacular landscapes of Lassen Volcanic National Park and Mt. Shasta are sure to impress.

The wondrous landscape of California's northeastern corner is the product of volcanic activity. At the southern end of the Cascade Range, Lassen Volcanic National Park is the best place to witness the Far North's fascinating geology. Beyond the sulfur vents and bubbling mud pots, the park owes much of its beauty to 10,457-foot Mt. Lassen and 50 wilderness lakes. Mt. Lassen and another volcano, Mt. Shasta, draw amateur geologists, weekend hikers, and avid mountain climbers to their rugged terrain. An intricate network of high-mountain watersheds feeds lakes large and small, plus streams and rivers that course through several forests.

The most enduring image of the region, though, is Mt. Shasta, whose 14,179-foot snowcapped peak beckons outdoor adventurers of all kinds. There are many versions of Shasta to enjoy—the mountain, the lake, the river, the town, the dam, and the forest—all named after the Native Americans known as the Shatasla, or Sastise, who once inhabited the region.

MAJOR REGIONS

From Chico to Mt Shasta. The Far North is bisected, south to north, by Interstate 5, which passes through several historic towns and state parks, as well as miles of mountainous terrain. Halfway to the Oregon border is Lake Shasta, a favorite recreation destination, and farther north stands the spectacular snowy peak of Mt. Shasta.

The Backcountry. East of Interstate 5, the Far North's main corridor, dozens of scenic two-lane roads crisscross the wilderness, leading to dramatic mountain peaks and fascinating natural wonders. Small towns settled in the second half of the 19th century seem frozen in time, except that they are well equipped with tourist amenities.

Note: Two of the most destructive fires in California history swept through the southern portions of this region in 2018, one centered just east of Chico, the other west of Redding. Collectively the two fires burned nearly 400,000 acres, destroying more than 20,000 structures, and killing 94 people. Although rebuilding efforts have begun and major tourist areas survived, you may see evidence of the blazes as you travel.

Planning

When to Go

Heat scorches the valley in summer. Temperatures above 110°F are common, but the mountains provide cool respite. Fall throughout the Far North is beautiful, rivaled only by spring, when wildflowers bloom and mountain creeks fed by the snowmelt splash through the forests. Winter is usually temperate in the valley, but cold and snowy in the high country. Some tourist attractions are closed in winter or have sharply curtailed hours.

Getting Here and Around

AIR TRAVEL

For the cheapest fares, fly into Sacramento and then rent a car—you'll need one anyway—and drive north. Redding, which is served by United Express, has a small airport. There's no shuttle service, but you can take a taxi for about $30 to downtown Redding, or rideshare starting at about $15.

AIR CONTACTS Redding Municipal Airport ✉ *6751 Woodrum Circle, off Airport Rd., Redding* ☎ *530/224–4320* 🌐 *www.cityofredding.org/departments/airports.*

GROUND TRANSPORTATION Anytime Taxi ☎ *530/828–7962 for Chico transfers.* **Road Runner Taxi** ☎ *530/241–7433 for Redding transfers* 🌐 *www.roadrunnertaxicab.com.*

BUS TRAVEL

Greyhound buses stop in Chico, Red Bluff, Redding, and Weed. TRAX buses serve Corning and Red Bluff. STAGE buses serve Dunsmuir and Mt. Shasta. Various other transit authorities provide local public transit *(see individual town listings for details).*

BUS CONTACTS Greyhound ☎ *800/231–2222* 🌐 *www.greyhound.com.* **STAGE** ☎ *530/842–8295* 🌐 *www.co.siskiyou.ca.us/generalservices/page/stage-schedule.* **TRAX** ☎ *530/385–2877* 🌐 *www.taketrax.com.*

CAR TRAVEL

Interstate 5 runs up the center of California through Red Bluff and Redding. Chico is east of Interstate 5 where Highways 32 and 99 intersect. Lassen Volcanic National Park can be reached by Highway 36 from Red Bluff or (except in winter) Highway 44 from Redding. Highway 299 connects Weaverville and Redding. Check weather reports and carry detailed maps, warm clothing, and tire chains whenever you head into mountainous terrain in winter.

ROAD CONDITIONS Caltrans ☎ *800/427–7623* 🌐 *www.dot.ca.gov.*

TRAIN TRAVEL

Amtrak serves Chico, Redding, and Dunsmuir.

TRAIN CONTACT Amtrak ☎ *800/872–7245* 🌐 *www.amtrak.com.*

Restaurants

Redding, the urban center of the Far North, and college-town Chico have the greatest selection of restaurants. Cafés and simple eateries are the rule in the smaller towns. Dress is always informal.

Hotels

Chain hotels and motels predominate in this region, with the occasional small rustic or Victorian inn. Wilderness resorts close in fall and reopen in mid-spring after the snow season ends. In summer in towns such as Mt. Shasta, Dunsmuir, and Chester, and at camping sites within state or national parks, make lodging reservations well in advance. *Hotel reviews have been shortened. For full information, visit Fodors.com.*

What It Costs

$	$$	$$$	$$$$
RESTAURANTS			
under $16	$16–$22	$23–$30	over $30
HOTELS			
under $120	$120–$175	$176–$250	over $250

Visitor Information

CONTACTS Shasta Cascade Wonderland Association ✉ *Shasta Outlets, 1699 Hwy. 273, off I-5, Exit 667, Anderson* ☎ *530/365–7500* 🌐 *www.shastacascade.com.* **Trinity County Chamber of Commerce** ✉ *509 Main St., Weaverville* ☎ *530/623–6101* 🌐 *www.trinitycounty.com.* **Visit Siskiyou** ☎ *530/926–3696 Mt. Shasta Chamber of Commerce* 🌐 *visitsiskiyou.org.*

Chico

86 miles north of Sacramento.

The Sacramento Valley town of Chico (Spanish for "small") offers a welcome break from the monotony of Interstate 5. The Chico campus of California State University, the scores of local artisans, and the area's agriculture (primarily almond orchards) all influence the culture here. Chico's claim to fame, however, is the Sierra Nevada Brewery, which keeps beer drinkers across the country happy with its distinctive brews.

GETTING HERE AND AROUND

Highway 99, off Interstate 5 from the north or south, and Highway 32 east off the interstate, intersect Chico. Amtrak and Greyhound stop here, and Butte Regional Transit's B-Line buses serve the area. Chico's downtown neighborhoods are great for walking.

ESSENTIALS

BUS CONTACT B-Line ☎ *530/342–0221* 🌐 *www.blinetransit.com.*

VISITOR INFORMATION Chico Chamber of Commerce ✉ *180 E. 4th St., Suite 120* ☎ *530/891–5556, 800/852–8570* 🌐 *www.chicochamber.com.*

Bidwell Mansion State Historic Park
HOUSE | Built between 1865 and 1868 by General John Bidwell, the founder of Chico, this mansion was designed by Henry W. Cleaveland, a San Francisco architect. Bidwell and his wife, Annie, welcomed many distinguished guests to their pink Italianate home, including President Rutherford B. Hayes, naturalist John Muir, suffragist Susan B. Anthony, and General William T. Sherman. A one-hour tour takes you through most of the three-story mansion's 26 rooms. ✉ *525 Esplanade, at Memorial Way* ☎ *530/895–6144* 🌐 *bidwellmansionpark.com* 🎟 *$6* ⏲ *Closed Tues.–Fri.*

Bidwell Park

CITY PARK | The sprawling 3,670-acre Bidwell Park is a community green space straddling Big Chico Creek, where scenes from *Gone With the Wind* and the 1938 version of *Robin Hood* (starring Errol Flynn) were filmed. The region's recreational hub, it includes a golf course, swimming areas, and biking, hiking, horseback riding, and skating trails. Chico Creek Nature Center serves as the official information site for Bidwell Park. ✉ *1968 E. 8th St., off Hwy. 99* ☎ *530/891–4671* 🌐 *ccnaturecenter.org* 🎫 *Park free, nature center $4* ⏲ *Nature center closed Sun.–Tues.*

Chico Museum

MUSEUM | Immerse yourself in all things Chico at this small but engaging museum near Chico State University. Past exhibits have surveyed the city's Native American legacy, its former Chinatowns and agricultural past, and area movers and shakers. ✉ *141 Salem St., at 2nd St.* ☎ *530/891–4336* 🌐 *www.chicohistorymuseum.org* 🎫 *$5* ⏲ *Closed Mon.–Wed.*

Museum of Northern California Art

MUSEUM | After several years of successful pop-up exhibitions around town, this engaging museum found a permanent home in the Veterans Memorial Building, a handsome 1927 Classical Revival structure designed by the local architecture firm of Cole & Brouchaud. The focus is contemporary art produced from San Jose north to Oregon, some of it by area artists. ✉ *900 Esplanade, at E. Washington Ave.* ☎ *530/487–7272* 🌐 *www.monca.org* 🎫 *$5* ⏲ *Closed Mon.–Wed.*

National Yo-Yo Museum

MUSEUM | Cast aside images of a grand edifice and curators of renown: this yo-yo collection spanning multiple decades occupies the back of a downtown toy and novelty shop, itself a throwback to some era or another. If you've ever aspired to Walk the Dog or venture Around the World, you'll find this a diverting 15-minute stop. Highlights include the 256-pound No-Jive 3-in-1 yo-yo and comedian Tom Smothers's collection. ■ **TIP→ In the shop, don't miss the posters for years of Chico events.** ✉ *Bird in Hand, 320 Broadway, near W. 3rd St.* ☎ *530/893–0545* 🌐 *nationalyoyo.org* 🎫 *Free.*

★ Sierra Nevada Brewing Company

WINERY/DISTILLERY | This pioneer of the microbrewery movement still has a hands-on approach to beer making. Take the free Brewery Tour and see how the beer is produced—from the sorting of hops through fermentation and bottling, and concluding with a tasting. Other tours, for which there is a fee, focus on topics like hops, the brewery's history, and its sustainability initiatives. For the ultimate deep dive sign up for the 3½-hour Beer Geek Tour. ■ **TIP→ Tours fill up fast; reserve by phone or online before you visit.** ✉ *1075 E. 20th St., at Sierra Nevada St.* ☎ *530/345–2739 taproom, 530/899–4776 tours* 🌐 *www.sierranevada.com* 🎫 *Tours free–$50 (includes tasting).*

Restaurants

★ Bidwell Perk

$ | **AMERICAN** | It's name a play on nearby Bidwell Park, this clean and tidy many-windowed chain alternative for coffee (six different roasts daily) and pastries also serves full breakfasts and light lunches. Bagels, French toast, quiche, and croissant sandwiches in the morning give way to small plates, salads, bruschetta, and sliders as the day moves along. **Known for:** mostly small-batch beers and wines; outdoor patio; well-crafted espresso drinks. 💲 *Average main: $9* ✉ *664 E. 1st Ave., at Mangrove Ave.* ☎ *530/899–1500* 🌐 *bidwellperk.com.*

★ 5th Street Steakhouse

$$$$ | **STEAKHOUSE** | Hand-cut steak is the star in this refurbished early 1900s building, the place to come when you're craving red meat, a huge baked potato, or some fresh seafood. Exposed redbrick walls warm the dining rooms, and a long mahogany bar catches the overflow crowds that jam the place on weekends. **Known for:** alfresco dining on outdoor patio; weekend crowds; prime cuts of beef with white-tablecloth service. *$ Average main: $35 ✉ 345 W. 5th St., at Normal Ave. ☎ 530/891–6328 🌐 www.5thstreetsteakhouse.com ⏲ No lunch Sat.–Thurs.*

Leon Bistro

$$$ | **MODERN AMERICAN** | The chef's experience at this local fave for romantic fine dining and special occasions includes a stint at the illustrious Chez Panisse restaurant in Berkeley, and her menu, based on locally sourced high-quality ingredients subtly spiced and presented with flair, reflects that influence. The main dining areas, with high-backed wooden booths in one section and tables and chairs elsewhere, is decorated with art by Dennis Leon, the chef's father, and a few other local artists of renown. **Known for:** mushroom fonduta and other starters; seasonal vegetable sampler a menu staple; Wagyu and elk burgers served with house-made potato chips. *$ Average main: $28 ✉ 817 Main St., at E. 8th St. ☎ 530/899–1105 🌐 www.leonbistro.com ⏲ Closed Sun.–Tues. No lunch.*

Red Tavern

$$$ | **MEDITERRANEAN** | With its burgundy carpet, white linen tablecloths, and mellow lighting, this is one of Chico's coziest restaurants. The Mediterranean-influenced menu, inspired by fresh local produce, with vegetarian and pescatarian fare in addition to meat and poultry dishes, changes seasonally—fettuccine with beef short-rib ragout and seared salmon with citrus beurre blanc are among recent offerings. **Known for:** California wine list; nightly specials; popular Sunday brunch. *$ Average main: $29 ✉ 1250 Esplanade, at E. 3rd Ave. ☎ 530/894–3463 🌐 www.redtavern.com ⏲ Closed Mon. No lunch Tues.–Thurs.*

Sierra Nevada Brewery Taproom

$$ | **AMERICAN** | An easy choice, especially if you've just done a tour and are steeped in company lore, the famous brewery's high-ceilinged, heavy-on-the-wood taproom bustles day and night with patrons washing down well-conceived gastropub grub with the best-selling Pale Ale and smaller-batch offerings, some of which are only available here. The open kitchen turns out burgers, wood-oven pizzas, and fish-and-chips (the fish's batter made with Pale Ale) with remarkable speed. **Known for:** beer-cheese and pretzels starters with mustard; soups and salads; no reservations except for large parties (come early to avoid the crowds). *$ Average main: $16 ✉ 1075 E. 20th St. ✈ ½ mile west of Hwy. 99, Exit 384 ☎ 530/345–2739 🌐 www.sierranevada.com/brewery/california/taproom.*

Hotels

Hotel Diamond

$$ | **HOTEL** | Crystal chandeliers and gleaming century-old wood floors and banisters welcome guests into the foyer of this restored 1904 gem near Chico State University. **Pros:** downtown location; refined rooms, some with bay windows and fireplaces; Diamond Steakhouse. **Cons:** street scene can be noisy on weekends; some rooms are small; some rooms lack tubs. *$ Rooms from: $160 ✉ 220 W. 4th St., near Broadway ☎ 530/893–3100, 866/993–3100 🌐 www.hoteldiamondchico.com 43 rooms 🍴 Free Breakfast.*

Activities

Sacramento River Eco Tours

TOUR—SPORTS | Wildlife biologist Henry Lomeli guides boat tours on the Sacramento River to explore its diverse fish, fowl, and plant life. *✉ Chico ☎ 530/864–8594 🌐 www.sacramentorivereco tours.com 🎟 From $85.*

Corning

29 miles northwest of Chico, 50 miles south of Redding.

Signs along Highway 99 and Interstate 5 beckon travelers to Corning, whose favorable soil and plentiful sunshine have made the town a center of olive cultivation and olive-oil manufacturing. At several tasting rooms you can sample olives, olive oil, and other products.

GETTING HERE AND AROUND

Corning lies just off Interstate 5 at Exit 631. From Chico take Highway 99 for 17½ miles and follow signs west to Corning. TRAX provides weekday bus service from Red Bluff.

 Sights

★ Lucero Olive Oil

LOCAL INTEREST | As a brand Lucero dates back to the mid-2000s, but the family that started the company began farming olives in the Corning area in 1947. Lucero's extra-virgin olive oils have won countless awards in California and abroad. In the tasting room adjacent to the mill you can taste oils like Ascalona and Koroneiki and ones infused with lemon, chili, and other flavors, sometimes paired with excellent balsamic vinegars. ✉ *2120 Loleta Ave., Corning* ✣ *Off Hwy. 99W, 1 mile south of Solano St.* ☎ *530/824–2190* 🌐 *www.lucerooliveoil.com* 🎫 *Tastings from $5.*

New Clairvaux Vineyard

WINERY/DISTILLERY | History converges in fascinating ways at this winery and vineyard whose tale involves pioneer-rancher Peter Lassen (Mt. Lassen is named for him), railroad baron Leland Stanford, newspaper magnate William Randolph Hearst, the Napa Valley's five-generation Nichelini wine-making family, and current owners the Trappist-Cistercian monks. In the 1890s the rambling redbrick tasting room, erected by Stanford, stored 2 million gallons of wine. These days hosts here pour Viognier, Tempranillo, Barbera, and other small-lot bottlings from grapes mostly grown nearby. The Syrah and Cabernet stand out, but everything's well made. The on-site chapel (the Hearst connection) has a convoluted story all its own. ✉ *26240 7th St., Vina, Vina* ✣ *10 miles from Corning, Hoag Rd. east to Hill Rd. south to Rhode Island and South Aves. east* ☎ *530/839–2434* 🌐 *www.newclairvauxvineyard.com* 🎫 *Tastings $5.*

Olive Pit

FARM/RANCH | **FAMILY** | Three generations of the Craig family run this combination café, store, and tasting room where you can learn all about California olive production and sample olive products, craft beers and small-lot wines, and artisanal foods. Sandwich selections at the café include muffulettas and olive burgers. Wash your choice down with a balsamic shake in flavors that include peach, coconut, strawberry, and French prune. ■ **TIP→ The Olive Pit opens at 7 am and closes at 8 pm.** ✉ *2156 Solano St., Corning, Corning* ✣ *Off I–5, Exit 631 (Corning Rd.)* ☎ *530/824–4667* 🌐 *www.olivepit.com* 🎫 *Tastings free for olive oil, $5 for beer and wine.*

Red Bluff

41 miles north of Chico.

Red Bluff is a gateway to Lassen Volcanic National Park. Established in the mid-19th century as a shipping center on the Sacramento River, and named for the color of its soil, the town, filled with dozens of restored Victorians, makes a good base for outdoor adventures in the area. The Tehama Country Visitor Center has information about wine tasting and other activities.

GETTING HERE AND AROUND

Access Red Bluff via exits off Interstate 5, or by driving north on Highway 99. Highway 36 travels east–west through town; east of the freeway it's called Antelope Boulevard, west of it Oak Street. Greyhound buses stop in Red Bluff and provide connecting service to Amtrak. TRAX (Tehama Rural Area Express) provides weekday bus service.

ESSENTIALS

VISITOR INFORMATION Tehama Country Visitor Center ✉ *250 Antelope Blvd., ¼-mile east of I–5* ☎ *530/529–0133.*

Sights

★ Gaumer's Jewelry

STORE/MALL | The Gaumer family has been making and selling jewelry in Red Bluff since the 1960s, and has been collecting rocks, gems, and minerals for even longer. When the jewelry shop is open, you can tour its fascinating museum, whose displays include crystals, gemstone carvings, fossils, and fluorescent minerals. ✉ *78 Belle Mill Rd.* ✥ *From I–5, Exit 649, head west on Hwy. 36 (Antelope Blvd.); make a right on Center Ave. and immediately make another right onto Belle Mill* ☎ *530/527–6166* 🌐 *www.gaumers.com* 🎫 *Free* ⏲ *Closed weekends.*

Tuscan Ridge Estate Winery

WINERY/DISTILLERY | Depending on the day, this crowd-pleasing winery with a vineyard-view tasting room serves pizzas or antipasti to accompany some of the nearly two dozen reds and whites made here. Most of the grapes for them come from the Sierra foothills; the Zinfandel and Syrah in particular are worth seeking out. **■ TIP→ The winery opens in the late afternoon on Thursday and Friday.** ✉ *19260 Ridge Rd.* ☎ *530/527–7393* 🌐 *www.tuscanridgeestate.com* 🎫 *Tastings $10* ⏲ *Closed Mon.–Wed.*

William B. Ide Adobe State Historic Park

NATIONAL/STATE PARK | Named for the first and only president of the short-lived California Republic of 1846, this peaceful park is on an oak-lined bank of the Sacramento River. The park's main attraction, an adobe home built in the 1850s and outfitted with period furnishings, reopened in 2019, completely renovated following damage that occurred when a giant oak tree fell on it during a 2015 storm. ✉ *21659 Adobe Rd.* ✥ *At Park Pl., ½ mile east of I–5* ☎ *530/529–8599* 🌐 *www.parks.ca.gov/ideadobe* 🎫 *$6 per vehicle* ⏲ *Visitor center and museum closed Mon.–Thurs.*

Red Bluff Round-up

Check out old-time rodeo at its best during the Red Bluff Round-Up. Held the third weekend of April, this annual event attracts some of the best cowboys in the country. For more information, visit 🌐 *redbluffroundup.com.*

Restaurants

Green Barn Whiskey Kitchen

$$$ | **STEAKHOUSE** | In late 2018, new owners and a new chef renovated the dining room, revamped the menu, and added a layer of Kentucky charm to Red Bluff's premier steak house, which opened in 1959. As before, you're likely to find cowboys sporting Stetsons and spurs feasting on Angus beef steaks, tenderloin medallions, baby back ribs, and prime rib; for lighter fare, try the seafood dishes or entrée-size salads, and leave room for the bourbon-infused desserts. **Known for:** full bar; top-quality beef; convivial atmosphere. 💲 *Average main: $25* ✉ *5 Chestnut Ave., at Antelope Blvd.* ☎ *530/527–3161* ⏲ *Closed Sun.*

Hotels

Hampton Inn & Suites Red Bluff

$$ | **HOTEL** | In a town filled with budget chain properties, this three-story hotel with clean, spacious rooms and a high-ceilinged lobby qualifies as the grande

dame. **Pros:** clean, spacious rooms; Wi-Fi works well; pool and business and fitness centers. **Cons:** pricey for the area; on the north end of town away from most attractions; lacks personality. *Rooms from: $133 ✉ 520 Adobe Rd. ☎ 530/529–4178 ⊕ www.hamptoninn3.hilton.com 97 rooms Free Breakfast.*

Redding

32 miles north of Red Bluff on I–5.

A gateway to Lassen Volcanic National Park's northern entrance, Redding is an ideal headquarters for exploring the surrounding countryside.

GETTING HERE AND AROUND

Interstate 5 is the major north–south route into Redding. Highway 299 bisects the city east–west, and Highway 44 connects Redding and Lassen Park's north entrance. Amtrak and Greyhound stop here.

ESSENTIALS

BUS INFORMATION Redding Area Bus Authority *☎ 530/241–2877 ⊕ www.rabaride.com.*

VISITOR INFORMATION Redding Convention and Visitors Bureau *✉ Visitor center, 844 Sundial Bridge Dr. ☎ 530/225–4100, 800/874–7562 ⊕ www.visitredding.com.*

Sights

Moseley Family Cellars

WINERY/DISTILLERY | Although its street name conjures up pastoral images, this winery whose grapes come from Napa, Sonoma, Lodi, and some local vineyards is actually in an industrial park. It's still worth a visit for its two Chardonnays and Syrah, Mourvèdre, old-vine Zinfandel, and other reds. *✉ 4712 Mountain Lakes Blvd., Suite 300 ☎ 530/229–9463 ⊕ www.moseleyfamilycellars.com Tastings $10 Closed Mon.–Wed. (except by appointment).*

Shasta State Historic Park

HISTORIC SITE | Six miles west of downtown lies the former town of Shasta City, which thrived in the mid- to late 1800s. The park's 19 acres of half-ruined brick buildings, accessed via trails, are a reminder of the glory days of the California gold rush. The former county courthouse building (whose exhibits include rare California landscape paintings), jail, and gallows have been restored to their 1860s appearance. The Litsch General Store, in operation from 1850 to 1950, is now a museum, with displays of items once sold here. Some trails and trees were damaged and a 1928 schoolhouse was destroyed when a 2018 fire burned through the park, though by early 2019 the main remaining structures, which include Shorty's Eatery (good sandwiches) had reopened. *✉ 15312 Hwy. 299 ☎ 530/243–8194 ⊕ www.parks.ca.gov/shastashp Free to park, $3 Courthouse Museum Courthouse Museum closed Mon.–Wed.*

★ Turtle Bay Exploration Park

CITY PARK | FAMILY | This park has walking trails, an aquarium, an arboretum and botanical gardens, and many interactive exhibits for kids. The main draw is the stunning Santiago Calatrava–designed **Sundial Bridge,** a metal and translucent glass pedestrian walkway, suspended by cables from a single tower, spanning a broad bend in the Sacramento River. On sunny days the 217-foot tower lives up to the bridge's name, casting a shadow on the ground below to mark time. Access to the bridge and arboretum is free, but there's a fee for the museum and gardens. *✉ 844 Sundial Bridge Dr. ☎ 530/243–8850 ⊕ www.turtlebay.org Museum $16 Museum closed Mon. and Tues. early Sept.–mid-Mar.*

Restaurants

Armando's Gallery House

$$ | **ECLECTIC** | Dining is an enchanting adventure at Armando Mejorado's combination restaurant, art gallery, and occasional performance space in downtown Redding. The four-course menu, which changes weekly, has included everything from a modern take on shepherd's pie to Indonesian satay. **Known for:** fun, artsy, out of the ordinary; congenial host; à la carte and prix-fixe options. *Average main: $20* *1350 Butte St.* *530/768–1241* *Closed Sun.–Tues. No lunch.*

Clearie's Restaurant and Lounge

$$$$ | **AMERICAN** | The granddaughter of "Doc" Clearie, who ran a popular Redding restaurant long ago, returned the family name to fine-dining prominence with this white-tablecloth lounge and restaurant. Many guests begin with the signature blackberry lavender lemon drop "martini," bubbling like a cauldron courtesy of dry ice, and perhaps a baked Brie appetizer before, depending on the season, a main course like short-rib beef Stroganoff or pan-seared ahi tuna. **Known for:** white-tablecloth ambience; well-executed if not cutting-edge cuisine; great wine list. *Average main: $32* *1325 Eureka Way* *530/241–4535* *www.cleariesrestaurant.com* *Closed Sun.*

From the Hearth Artisan Bakery & Café

$ | **AMERICAN** | A homegrown variation on the Panera theme, this extremely popular operation (as in expect a wait at peak dining hours) serves pastries, eggs and other hot dishes, and good coffee drinks, juices, and smoothies for breakfast, adding a diverse selection of wraps, panini, sandwiches, burgers, rice bowls, and soups the rest of the day. Some sandwiches are made with a bread that FTH bills as "Redding's original sourdough." **Known for:** baked goods; diverse selection; two other Redding locations (one downtown) plus another in Red Bluff. *Average main: $11* *2650 Churn Creek Rd.* *530/424–2233* *www.fthcafe.com.*

Jack's Grill

$$$ | **STEAKHOUSE** | The original Jack opened his grill (and an upstairs brothel) in 1938. Tamer these days but often jam-packed and noisy, this place is famous for its 16-ounce steaks and deep-fried shrimp and chicken dishes. **Known for:** 1930s atmosphere; great martinis; thick slabs of beef. *Average main: $28* *1743 California St., near Sacramento St.* *530/241–9705* *www.jacksgrillredding.com* *Closed Sun. No lunch.*

Moonstone Bistro

$$ | **AMERICAN** | About 1½ miles southwest of downtown this light-filled restaurant in a strip mall prides itself on its use of seasonal organic produce, free-range meats, sustainable line-caught fish, and cage-free eggs. All day you can dine on fish tacos, a large mixed-greens salad, or burgers (standard, veggie, or teriyaki mushroom Swiss), with fish, chicken, and pasta dishes available at lunch, and heavier pork and beef dishes added for dinner. **Known for:** organic produce; all-day bistro menu; Sunday brunch. *Average main: $22* *3425 Placer St., near Buenaventura Blvd.* *530/241–3663* *www.moonstonebistro.com* *Closed Mon. No dinner Sun.*

Nello's Place

$$$ | **ITALIAN** | Fine Italian dining and romantic old-style ambience go hand-in-hand at Nello's Place, where you'll find a varied selection of veal, chicken, beef, and pasta dishes along with lighter fish and vegetarian fare. For special presentations, order a Caesar salad prepared table-side for two, and bananas flambé for dessert. **Known for:** Caesar salad prepared table-side; cherries jubilee and bananas flambé for dessert; step-back-in-time feel. *Average main: $28* *3055 Bechelli La., near Hartnell Ave.* *530/223–1636* *www.nellosrestaurant.net* *Closed Mon. No lunch.*

View 202

$$$ | **MODERN AMERICAN** | The view at this glass-walled hilltop restaurant is of the Sacramento River below the wide outdoor patio and well beyond the waterway to snowcapped mountains. It's best to stick with the least complicated preparations on the New American menu, which emphasizes grilled meats and fish from noted California purveyors but also includes bouillabaisse and house-made ravioli. **Known for:** gluten-free options; specialty cocktails; wine list among the North State's best. *Average main: $26 202 Hemsted Dr., off E. Cypress Ave. 530/226–8439 www.view202redding.com.*

Vintage Public House

$$ | **AMERICAN** | A late-2018 decor refresh initiated by new owners added a touch of class to this comfort-food haven across from downtown's 1935 Cascade movie palace. The fare includes hearty soups, candied-bacon sliders, fish tacos, creative wraps, ahi wonton nachos, a locally revered mac and cheese, and plenty of burgers. **Known for:** patio dining; vegan selections; live music some days. *Average main: $21 1790 Market St., at Sacramento St. 530/229–9449 vintageredding.com No lunch Sat., no dinner Sun.*

Hotels

Best Western Plus Hilltop Inn

$$ | **HOTEL** | **FAMILY** | Comfortable Serta mattresses and strong free Wi-Fi are among the selling points of this hotel just off the freeway 3 miles southeast of downtown Redding. **Pros:** dependable chain property; comfortable beds; hot tub and pool area. **Cons:** rooms facing freeway can be noisy; microwave ovens only by request; minor housekeeping lapses. *Rooms from: $140 2300 Hilltop Dr. 530/221–6100 www.thehilltopinn.com 114 rooms Free Breakfast.*

★ Bridgehouse Bed & Breakfast

$ | **B&B/INN** | In a residential area a block from the Sacramento River and a ½-mile from downtown Redding, this inn contains six rooms in two side-by-side homes. **Pros:** easy hospitality; proximity to downtown and Turtle Bay; freshly baked scones at full breakfast. **Cons:** lacks pool, fitness center, and other standard hotel amenities; the two least expensive rooms are small; books up well ahead in summer. *Rooms from: $119 1455 Riverside Dr. 530/247–7177 www.bridgehousebb.com 6 rooms Free Breakfast.*

Fairfield Inn & Suites Redding

$$ | **HOTEL** | **FAMILY** | The three-story Fairfield's clean rooms, amiable service, 24-hour business center, mountain views from some rooms, and bright, chipper public areas make it the best choice among Redding's many chain properties. **Pros:** clean rooms; amiable service; many amenities. **Cons:** prices often higher than competitors; corporate feel; some rooms are small. *Rooms from: $136 164 Caterpillar Rd. 530/243–3200 www.marriott.com/hotels/travel/rddre 72 rooms Free Breakfast.*

Nightlife

Final Draft Brewing Company

BREWPUBS/BEER GARDENS | This spacious brick-walled brewpub opened in 2017 to high acclaim for its accessible ales and above-average pub grub. Try the beer-battered fish-and-chips with swirly fries instead of regular ones. While they're cooking, order a sampler flight to decide which of the brews to wash them down with. Monday night's trivia contests are wildly fun. *1600 California St., at Placer St. 530/338–1198 www.finaldraftbrewingcompany.com.*

Wildcard Brewing Tied House

BREWPUBS/BEER GARDENS | At the mellow outpost of this brewery founded in 2012 you can sample an adventurous lineup that includes a pilsner, a red ale, several IPAs, and an almost chewy oatmeal porter. The flagship North State IPA's citrus notes are amped up to good effect in the Ruby Red Grapefruit, worth checking out if on tap when you visit. ✉ *1321 Butte St., at Pine St.* ☎ *530/255–8582* 🌐 *www.wildcardbrewingco.com.*

Woody's Brewing Company
BREWPUBS/BEER GARDENS | A fun downtown hangout with a party vibe, Woody's has built a loyal following for its Polish nachos (kettle chips, beer cheese, smoked sausage, and sauerkraut), special-recipe tater tots, and range of beers from fruited wheat ales to an unfiltered dry-hopped IPA and the Pray for Powder porter. The reasonably priced sampler flights provide a good introduction. ✉ *1257 Oregon St., at Shasta St.* ☎ *530/768–1034* 🌐 *www.woodysbrewing.com.*

Weaverville

46 miles west of Redding on Hwy. 299.

Chinese miners erected the 1874 Joss House that anchors Weaverville's impressive downtown historic district. The town, population about 3,600, is also a popular headquarters for family vacations and hiking, fishing, and gold-panning excursions.

GETTING HERE AND AROUND

Highway 299, east from the Pacific Coast or west from Redding, becomes Main Street in central Weaverville. Highway 36 from Red Bluff to Highway 3 heading north leads to Weaverville. Trinity Transit provides bus service.

ESSENTIALS

VISITOR INFORMATION Trinity County Visitors Bureau ✉ *509 Main St.* ☎ *530/623–6101* 🌐 *www.visittrinity.com.*

Sights

Trinity County Hal Goodyear Historical Park
HISTORIC SITE | For a vivid sense of Weaverville's past, visit this park, especially its **Jake Jackson Memorial Museum.** A blacksmith shop and a stamp mill (where ore is crushed) from the 1890s are still in use during certain community events. ✉ *780 Main St., at Bartlett La.* ☎ *530/623–5211* 🌐 *www.trinitymuseum.org* ⏲ *Museum closed various days Jan.–Apr. and Oct.–Dec.*

★ Weaverville Joss House State Historic Park
HISTORIC SITE | Weaverville's main attraction is the Joss House, a Taoist temple built in 1874 and called Won Lim Miao ("the temple of the forest beneath the clouds") by Chinese miners. The oldest continuously used Chinese temple in California, it attracts worshippers from around the world. With its golden altar, antique weaponry, and carved wooden canopies, the Joss House is a piece of California history that can best be appreciated on a guided 30-minute tour. ✉ *630 Main St., at Oregon St.* ☎ *530/623–5284* 🌐 *www.parks.ca.gov/?page_id=457* 🎫 *Museum free; guided tour $4* ⏲ *Closed Mon.–Wed.*

Restaurants

Mamma Llama Eatery & Café
$ | AMERICAN | Tap into the spirit of 21st-century Weaverville at this mellow café that serves breakfast (all day) and lunch and in winter specializes in hot soups to warm body and soul. Expect all the usual suspects at breakfast along with Country Cheesy Potatoes (topped with green chili) and sausage between two biscuits topped with homemade sausage gravy; a spicy club wrap and several vegetarian sandwiches are among the lunch offerings. **Known for:** mellow vibe; good soups; espresso drinks. 💲 *Average main: $8* ✉ *490 Main*

St. ☎ 530/623–6363 🌐 www.mammallama.com ⏲ Closed Sun. No dinner.

Hotels

Weaverville Hotel
$$ | HOTEL | Originally built during the gold rush, this beautifully restored hotel is filled with antiques and period furniture. **Pros:** gracious on-site owners; in heart of town's historic district; beautifully restored. **Cons:** no breakfast on-site; children under 12 not permitted; only one room has a TV. *$ Rooms from: $140 ✉ 481 Main St., near Court St. ☎ 530/623–2222, 800/750–8853 🌐 www.weavervillehotel.com 7 rooms No meals.*

★ Whitmore Inn
$$ | B&B/INN | Amid Weaverville's historic district and shaded by black locust trees, this Victorian inn near shops and restaurants has five rooms, some with a shared bathroom. **Pros:** Victorian style with modern touches; convenient historic district location; innkeeper generous with sightseeing tips. **Cons:** some rooms share a bathroom; Victorian style in most rooms not for everyone; young children (age 5 and under) not permitted. *$ Rooms from: $125 ✉ 761 Main St. ☎ 530/623–2509 🌐 www.whitmoreinn.com 5 rooms Free Breakfast.*

Shopping

Highland Art Center Gallery
ART GALLERIES | Inside a historic Main Street home, this gallery showcases and sells painting, photography, fiber arts, ceramics, sculpture, and other handcrafted works produced by local artists and those from surrounding mountain communities. *✉ 691 Main St. ☎ 530/623–5111 🌐 www.highlandartcenter.org ⏲ Closed Sun. and Mon.*

Activities

Weaverville Ranger Station
HIKING/WALKING | Check here for maps, free wilderness and campfire permits, and information about local fishing and the 600 miles of hiking trails in the 500,000-acre Trinity Alps Wilderness. *✉ 360 Main St. ☎ 530/623–2121.*

Shasta Lake

10 miles north of Redding.

The city of Shasta Lake, population about 10,000, is a portal to water, wilderness, dazzling stalagmites, and a fabulous human-made project, Shasta Dam, in the midst of it all.

GETTING HERE AND AROUND

Shasta Lake lies at the intersection of Interstate 5 and Highway 151. There is no local bus service.

Sights

Lake Shasta
BODY OF WATER | Numerous types of fish inhabit the lake, including rainbow trout, salmon, bass, brown trout, and catfish. The lake region also has California's largest nesting population of bald eagles. You can rent fishing boats, ski boats, sailboats, canoes, paddleboats, Jet Skis, and windsurfing boards at marinas and resorts along the 370-mile shoreline. *✉ Shasta Lake 🌐 www.shastacascade.com.*

★ Lake Shasta Caverns National Natural Landmark
NATURE SITE | FAMILY | Stalagmites, stalactites, flowstone deposits, and crystals entice visitors to the Lake Shasta Caverns. To see this impressive spectacle, you must take the two-hour tour, which includes a catamaran ride across the McCloud arm of Lake Shasta and a bus ride up North Grey Rocks Mountain to the cavern entrance. The temperature

in the caverns is 58°F year-round, making them a cool retreat on a hot summer day. The most awe-inspiring of the limestone rock formations is the glistening Cathedral Room, which appears to be gilded. ■ **TIP→ In summer it's wise to purchase tickets online a day or more ahead of your visit.** ✉ *20359 Shasta Caverns Rd., Lakehead* ✣ *Exit 695 off I–5, 13 miles north of Shasta Lake* ☎ *530/238–2341, 800/795–2283* 🌐 *www.lakeshastacaverns.com* 🎫 *$30.*

Shasta Dam

DAM | This is the second-largest concrete dam in the United States (only Grand Coulee in Washington is bigger). The visitor center has computerized photographic tours of the dam construction, video presentations, fact sheets, and historical displays. ■ **TIP→ Hour-long guided tours inside the dam and its powerhouse leave from the center every other hour from 9 to 3; arrive 30 minutes early.** ✉ *16349 Shasta Dam Blvd., Shasta Lake* ✣ *From downtown Shasta Lake, take Hwy. 151 (Shasta Dam Rd.) west to Lake Blvd. north* ☎ *530/275–4463* 🌐 *www.usbr.gov/mp/ncao/dam-tours.html* 🎫 *Free.*

Activities

Bridge Bay Resort

BOATING | This resort 7½ miles north of Shasta Lake offers modest lakeside lodging, a restaurant, boat and Jet Ski rentals, and a full-service marina. The company's houseboats, available for rent, sleep from 8 to 13 people—before setting out you'll receive a short course in how to maneuver your launch. The resort outfits the boats with cooking utensils, dishes, and most of the equipment you'll need (you supply the food and linens). ✉ *10300 Bridge Bay Rd., Redding* ✣ *Take I–5 Exit 690* ☎ *800/752–9669, 530/275–3021* 🌐 *www.bridgebayhouseboats.com* 🎫 *From $600 per night in summer, 2-night minimum.*

★ **Shasta Marina at Packers Bay**

BOATING | FAMILY | Packed with amenities, well maintained, and clean, this highly regarded operator's deluxe houseboats sleep from 14 to 16 people. Some even have a hot tub on board. ✉ *16814 Packers Bay Rd., Lakehead* ✣ *West from I–5, Exit 693* ☎ *800/959–3359* 🌐 *shastalake.net* 🎫 *From $1250 per night in summer, 3-night minimum.*

Dunsmuir

10 miles south of Mt. Shasta.

Surrounded by towering forests and boasting world-class fly-fishing in the Upper Sacramento River, tiny Dunsmuir was named for a 19th-century Scottish coal baron who offered to build a fountain if the town was renamed in his honor. You can spend the night in restored cabooses at the fun Railroad Park Resort.

GETTING HERE AND AROUND

Reach Dunsmuir via exits off Interstate 5 at the north and south ends of town. Amtrak stops here; Greyhound stops in Weed, 20 miles north. On weekdays, STAGE buses serve Dunsmuir.

ESSENTIALS

VISITOR INFORMATION Dunsmuir Chamber of Commerce ✉ *5915 Dunsmuir Ave., Suite 100* ☎ *530/235–2177* 🌐 *dunsmuir.com.*

Sights

★ **Castle Crags State Park**

NATIONAL/STATE PARK | Named for its 6,000-foot glacier-polished crags, which were formed by volcanic activity centuries ago, this park offers fishing on the upper Sacramento River, hiking in the backcountry, and a view of Mt. Shasta. The crags draw climbers and hikers from around the world. The 4,350-acre park has 28 miles of hiking trails, including a 2¾-mile access trail to **Castle Crags Wilderness,** part of the **Shasta-Trinity National**

Forest. There are excellent trails at lower altitudes, too, including the ¼-mile Vista Point Trail (near the entrance), which leads to views of Castle Crags and Mt. Shasta. ✉ *6 miles south of Dunsmuir, Castella/Castle Crags exit off I–5, 20022 Castle Creek Rd., Castella* ☎ *530/235–2684* 🌐 *www.castlecragspark.org* *$10 per vehicle, day-use.*

Restaurants

Café Maddalena

$$$ | **MEDITERRANEAN** | The chef here gained experience working in top San Francisco restaurants before moving north to prepare adventurous Mediterranean fare with a French influence. Selections change seasonally but always feature a vegetarian dish, along with fish, beef, and chicken entrées. **Known for:** Euro-centric wine list; daily prix-fixe menu; outdoor dining under grape arbor. $ *Average main: $27* ✉ *5801 Sacramento Ave.* ☎ *530/235–2725* 🌐 *www.cafemaddalena.com* ⏲ *Closed Mon.–Wed. and Jan.–mid-Feb. No lunch.*

Yaks on the 5

$$ | **AMERICAN** | Renowned for bacon-jalapeño and many other grass-fed burgers (which get a lot of love on social media), this festive joint, painted in bright colors and with a few interior murals and other artworks, wins most diners' hearts with its house-made ingredients (even buns), dozens of beers, and upbeat staff. You'll pay more than expected but will likely leave feeling you got your money's worth. **Known for:** garlic, duck-chili, barbecue, and other burgers; many beers on tap; upbeat decor and staffer. $ *Average main: $18* ✉ *4917 Dunsmuir Ave.* ☎ *530/678–3517* 🌐 *www.yaks.com.*

Hotels

Railroad Park Resort

$$ | **HOTEL** | **FAMILY** | The antique cabooses here were collected over more than three decades and have been converted into 23 cozy motel rooms in honor of Dunsmuir's railroad legacy; there are also four cabins. **Pros:** gorgeous setting; unique accommodations; kitschy fun. **Cons:** cabooses can feel cramped; must drive to Dunsmuir restaurants; some guests find location too remote. $ *Rooms from: $135* ✉ *100 Railroad Park Rd.* ☎ *530/235–4440* 🌐 *www.rrpark.com* *27 rooms* 🍽 *No meals.*

Fine Fishing

The upper Sacramento River near Dunsmuir is consistently rated one of the best fishing spots in the country. Check with the chamber of commerce for local fishing guides.

Mt. Shasta

34 miles north of Lake Shasta.

While a snow-covered dormant volcano is the area's dazzling draw, the town of Mt. Shasta charms visitors with its small shops, friendly residents, and beautiful scenery in all seasons.

GETTING HERE AND AROUND

Three exits off Interstate 5 lead to the town of Mt. Shasta. When snow hasn't closed the route, you can take Highway 89 from the Lassen Park area toward Burney then northwest to Mt. Shasta. The ski park is off Highway 89. Greyhound stops at Weed, 10 miles north; Amtrak stops at Dunsmuir, 10 miles south. STAGE provides bus service.

ESSENTIALS

VISITOR INFORMATION Visit Mt. Shasta
✉ *Visitor Center, 300 Pine St., at W. Lake St.* ☎ *530/926–4865, 800/926–4865* 🌐 *visitmtshasta.com.*

Sights

★ Mt. Shasta

VOLCANO | The crown jewel of the 2.5-million-acre Shasta-Trinity National Forest, Mt. Shasta, a 14,179-foot-high dormant volcano, is a mecca for day hikers. It's especially enticing in spring, when fragrant Shasta lilies and other flowers adorn the rocky slopes. A paved road, the Everitt Memorial Highway, reaches only as far as the timberline; the final 6,000 feet are a tough climb of rubble, ice, and snow (the summit is perpetually ice-packed). Hiking enthusiasts include this trek with those to the peaks of Kilimanjaro and Mt. Fuji in lists of iconic must-do mountain hikes. **■TIP→ Always check weather predictions; sudden storms have trapped climbers with snow and freezing temperatures.** ✉ *Mt. Shasta* 🌐 *visitmtshasta.com/activities/mountaineering.*

Restaurants

Lilys

$$$ | **ECLECTIC** | This restaurant in a white-clapboard home, framed by a picket fence and arched trellis, offers an eclectic menu, starting with bourbon-glazed French toast for breakfast. Lunch and dinner selections vary seasonally but often include roasted beet salad, herb-stuffed fresh trout, a walnut garbanzo veggie burger, and marinated pork chops with cannellini beans. **Known for:** Wednesday sushi night; flavorful vegetarian options; weekend brunch. [$] *Average main: $24* ✉ *1013 S. Mt. Shasta Blvd., at Holly St.* ☎ *530/926–3372* 🌐 *www.lilysrestaurant.com.*

Poncho & Lefkowitz

$ | **MEXICAN** | The cuisine is Mexican and American at this small stand popular with locals and visitors for its burritos, quesadillas, fish tacos, tamales, sausages, and hot dogs. Order at the window and enjoy your meal at outdoor picnic tables with Mt. Shasta views (there's some indoor seating, too). **Known for:** fish tacos; strawberry lemonade; Mt. Shasta views. [$] *Average main: $8* ✉ *401 S. Mt. Shasta Blvd.* ☎ *530/926–1505* ⊗ *Closed Sun.*

Seven Suns Coffee and Cafe

$ | **CAFÉ** | A favorite gathering spot for locals, this small coffee shop in a stone building serves specialty wraps and burritos for breakfast and lunch (both served all day), plus soups and salad. Pastries, made daily, include muffins, cinnamon rolls, cookies, and scones (great blackberry ones in season). **Known for:** coffee, tea, chai, and spiced cider; outside patio; vegetarian offerings. [$] *Average main: $10* ✉ *1011 S. Mt. Shasta Blvd., at Holly St.* ☎ *530/926–9701* ⊗ *No dinner.*

Hotels

Best Western Tree House Motor Inn

$$ | **HOTEL** | The clean, standard rooms at this motel less than a mile from downtown Mt. Shasta are decorated with natural-wood furnishings. **Pros:** close to ski park; heated indoor pool; lobby's roaring fireplace is a big plus on winter days. **Cons:** not all lodging buildings have elevators; pricier than other chain properties (though it delivers more); some wear and tear. [$] *Rooms from: $165* ✉ *111 Morgan Way* ☎ *530/926–3101, 800/545–7164* 🌐 *www.bestwesterncalifornia.com/hotels/best-western-plus-tree-house* *98 rooms* *No meals.*

Inn at Mount Shasta

$$ | **HOTEL** | This two-story motel-style property conveniently located on Mt. Shasta's main drag wins points for its cleanliness, comfortable beds, and spacious rooms with Wi-Fi, microwaves, refrigerators, hair dryers, and flat-screen TVs with satellite HDTV. **Pros:** clean, spacious rooms; 500-square-foot family suite with three beds; convenient location. **Cons:** minimal style; few amenities; no elevator to second-floor rooms. [$] *Rooms from: $158* ✉ *710 S. Mt. Shasta Blvd.* ☎ *530/918–9292* 🌐 *innatmountshasta.com* *30 rooms* *No meals.*

Pacific Flyway

You don't need wings to catch the Pacific Flyway. All it takes is a car, a good map, and high-powered binoculars to follow the flight path of more than 250 bird species that migrate through far Northern California and stop at wildlife refuges on their way.

Eagles and hawks make their visits in winter; more than a million waterfowl pass through in fall. Returning migrants such as pelicans, cranes, and songbirds such as the marsh wren and ruby-crowned kinglet arrive in March, just in time to herald the spring; goslings, ducklings, and other newly hatched waterfowl paddle through the wetlands in summer.

February and March are especially good viewing times, when people are scarce but wildlife thrives in the cold climate. Many birds enter their breeding season during these months, and you can hear their unusual mating calls and witness aerial ballets as vividly plumed males pursue females.

One of the most impressive Pacific Flyway stopovers is on the California–Oregon border: the 50,092-acre Lower Klamath National Wildlife Refuge, established by President Theodore Roosevelt in 1908 as the country's first waterfowl refuge. The Klamath Basin area has the largest winter concentration of bald eagles in the lower 48 states. You can take a 10-mile auto tour through parts of the refuge, where the eagles feed from December through mid-March. (From Interstate 5 north of Mt. Shasta, take the U.S. 97 turnoff to Highway 161 and follow the signs.) Even if you're not already an avid birdwatcher, you likely will be after a visit to this special place.

—Christine Vovakes

Mount Shasta Resort

$$$ | RENTAL | Private chalets are nestled among tall pine trees along the shore of Lake Siskiyou, all with gas-log fireplaces. **Pros:** romantic woodsy setting with incredible views; full kitchens in many lodgings; largest chalets sleep up to six people. **Cons:** kids may get bored; must drive to Mt. Shasta restaurants; some hospitality lapses. *Rooms from: $179* *1000 Siskiyou Lake Blvd.* *530/926–3030, 800/958–3363* *www.mountshastaresort.com* *65 rooms* *No meals.*

Activities

Fifth Season Mountaineering Shop

CLIMBING/MOUNTAINEERING | This shop rents bicycles and skiing and climbing equipment, and operates a recorded 24-hour climber-skier report. *300 N. Mt. Shasta Blvd.* *530/926–3606, 530/926–5555 ski phone* *www.thefifthseason.com.*

Jack Trout Fly Fishing

FISHING | The Upper Sacramento River is a world-class fly-fishing destination, and few anglers have as much experience fishing it as Jack Trout. He and his guides also book trips to several other Northern California rivers. *1004 S. Mt. Shasta Blvd.* *530/926–4540* *www.jacktrout.com* *Rates vary depending on trip, number of guests.*

Mount Shasta Resort Golf Course

GOLF | At a bit under 6,100 yards, the Mount Shasta Resort golf course isn't long, but it's beautiful and challenging, with narrow, tree-lined fairways and natural alpine terrain. Carts rent for $15; fabulous views are free. *1000 Siskiyou Lake Blvd.* *530/926–3052* *www.mountshastaresort.com/course/* *$45* *weekdays, $60 weekends* ⛳ *18 holes, 6035 yards, par 70.*

Mt. Shasta Board & Ski Park
SKIING/SNOWBOARDING | FAMILY | Three-quarters of the trails at this ski park on Mt. Shasta's southeast flank are for beginning or intermediate skiers. A package for beginners, available through the ski school, includes a lift ticket, ski rental, and a lesson. There's twilight skiing on some nights for those who want to see the moon rise as they schuss. The base lodge has a bar, a few dining options, a ski shop, and a ski-snowboard rental shop. **Facilities:** 32 trails; 425 skiable acres; 1,435-foot vertical drop; 5 lifts. ✉ *4500 Ski Park Hwy.* ✥ *Hwy. 89 exit east from I–5, south of Mt. Shasta City* ☎ *530/926–8610 winter only, 530/926–8686 snow phone* 🌐 *www.skipark.com* 🎫 *Lift ticket $65.*

Mt. Shasta Forest Service Ranger Station
HIKING/WALKING | Check in here for current trail conditions and avalanche reports. ✉ *204 W. Alma St., at Pine St.* ☎ *530/926–4511, 530/926–9613 avalanche conditions* 🌐 *www.fs.usda.gov/main/stnf.*

Mt. Shasta Nordic Center
SKIING/SNOWBOARDING | This center, run by a nonprofit, maintains 15 miles of groomed cross-country ski trails. ✉ *Ski Park Hwy.* ✥ *North off Hwy. 89, 7 miles southeast of Mt. Shasta City* ☎ *530/926–2142* 🌐 *mtshastanordic.org.*

★ Shasta Mountain Guides
CLIMBING/MOUNTAINEERING | These guides lead hiking, climbing, and skiing tours to Mt. Shasta's summit. ✉ *Mt. Shasta* ☎ *530/926–3117* 🌐 *shastaguides.com.*

Chester

71 miles east of Red Bluff.

The population of this small town on Lake Almanor swells from 2,500 to nearly 5,000 in summer as tourists come to visit. Chester serves as a gateway to Lassen Volcanic National Park.

GETTING HERE AND AROUND

Chester is on Highway 36E, the main route from Red Bluff. When snow doesn't close Highway 89 in Lassen Park, visitors can take Highway 44 from Redding to Highway 89 through the park and to Highway 36E and onto Chester and Lake Almanor. Plumas County Transit provides local bus service.

ESSENTIALS

BUS INFORMATION Plumas County Transit ☎ *530/283–2538* 🌐 *www.plumastransit.com.*

VISITOR INFORMATION Lake Almanor Area Chamber of Commerce ✉ *278 Main St.* ☎ *530/258–2426* 🌐 *www.lakealmanorarea.com.*

Sights

Lake Almanor
BODY OF WATER | This lake's 52 miles of forested shoreline are popular with hikers, campers, swimmers, waterskiers, and anglers. At an elevation of 4,500 feet, the lake warms to above 70°F for about eight weeks in summer. ✉ *Off Hwys. 89 and 36* ☎ *530/258–2426* 🌐 *www.lakealmanorarea.com.*

★ Volcanic Legacy Scenic Byway
SCENIC DRIVE | A 500-mile scenic drive that connects Lassen with Oregon's Crater Lake National Park, the byway's southern loop begins in Chester and winds for about 185 miles through the forests, volcanic peaks, hydrothermal springs, and lava fields of Lassen National Forest and Lassen Volcanic National Park, providing an all-day excursion into dramatic wilderness. From Chester, take Highway 36 west to Highway 89 north, which within the park is called Lassen National Park Highway. Upon exiting the park, follow Highway 44 southeast to Highway 36, which leads you back to Chester and around Lake Almanor. Parts of this route

are inaccessible in from mid-fall to mid-to-late spring. ✉ *Lassen Volcanic National Park* ☎ *800/474–2782* 🌐 *www.volcaniclegacybyway.org.*

Restaurants

★ Cravings Cafe Espresso Bar & Bakery
$ | **AMERICAN** | This casual breakfast and lunch place inside a white clapboard house satisfies diners' cravings with dishes like homemade slow-cooked corned-beef hash topped with two eggs and accompanied by a slice of sourdough bread. You can get breakfast and excellent pastries all day, with soups, salads, sandwiches, and burgers on the menu for lunch. **Known for:** waffles with applewood-smoked bacon in the batter; vegetarian options; outdoor patio. *$ Average main: $10* ✉ *278 Main St.* ☎ *530/258–2229* ⏲ *Closed Tues. and Wed. No dinner.*

Hotels

Best Western Rose Quartz Inn
$$ | **HOTEL** | Down the road from Lake Almanor and close to Lassen Volcanic National Park, this mid-range chain property is basically a motel, but the helpful staff (especially with touring plans) and amenities like good Wi-Fi, comfortable bedding, and spacious breakfast area make it a good choice for a short stay. **Pros:** within easy walking distance of town's restaurants; convenient to Lassen Volcanic National Park's southwest entrance; good Wi-Fi and other amenities. **Cons:** a little pricey for what you get; cookie-cutter decor; noise audible between rooms. *$ Rooms from: $160* ✉ *306 Main St.* ☎ *530/258–2002* 🌐 *www.bestwestern.com* *50 rooms* *Free Breakfast.*

★ Drakesbad Guest Ranch
$$$$ | **B&B/INN** | With propane furnaces and kerosene lamps, everything about this century-old property in the Lassen Volcanic National Park's remote but beautiful southeastern corner harks back to a simpler time. **Pros:** back-to-nature experience; great for family adventures; only full-service lodging inside the park. **Cons:** on a remote partially paved road 45 minutes' drive from nearest town (Chester); rustic, with few in-room frills; not open year-round. *$ Rooms from: $384* ✉ *14423 Warner Valley Rd.* ☎ *866/999–0914* 🌐 *www.drakesbad.com* ⏲ *Closed mid-Oct.–early June* *19 rooms* *All meals.*

Mineral

58 miles east of Redding, 42 miles east of Red Bluff.

Fewer than 200 people live in Mineral, the town that serves as Lassen Volcanic National Park's official address.

GETTING HERE AND AROUND

Whether coming from the west or the east, reach the park's southern entrance via Highway 36E, and turn onto Highway 89 for a short drive to the park. The northwest entrance is reached via Highway 44 from Redding. No buses serve the area.

Sights

★ Lassen Volcanic National Park
NATIONAL/STATE PARK | A dormant plug dome, Lassen Peak is the main focus of Lassen Volcanic National Park, but this 165-square-mile tract of dense forests and alpine meadows also abounds with memorable opportunities for hiking, camping, and wildlife photography.
The famed peak began erupting in May 1914, sending pumice, rock, and snow thundering down the mountain and gas and hot ash billowing into the atmosphere. Lassen's most spectacular outburst occurred in 1915, when it blew a cloud of ash almost 6 miles high. The resulting mudflow destroyed vegetation for miles; the evidence is still visible today, especially in the Devastated Area.

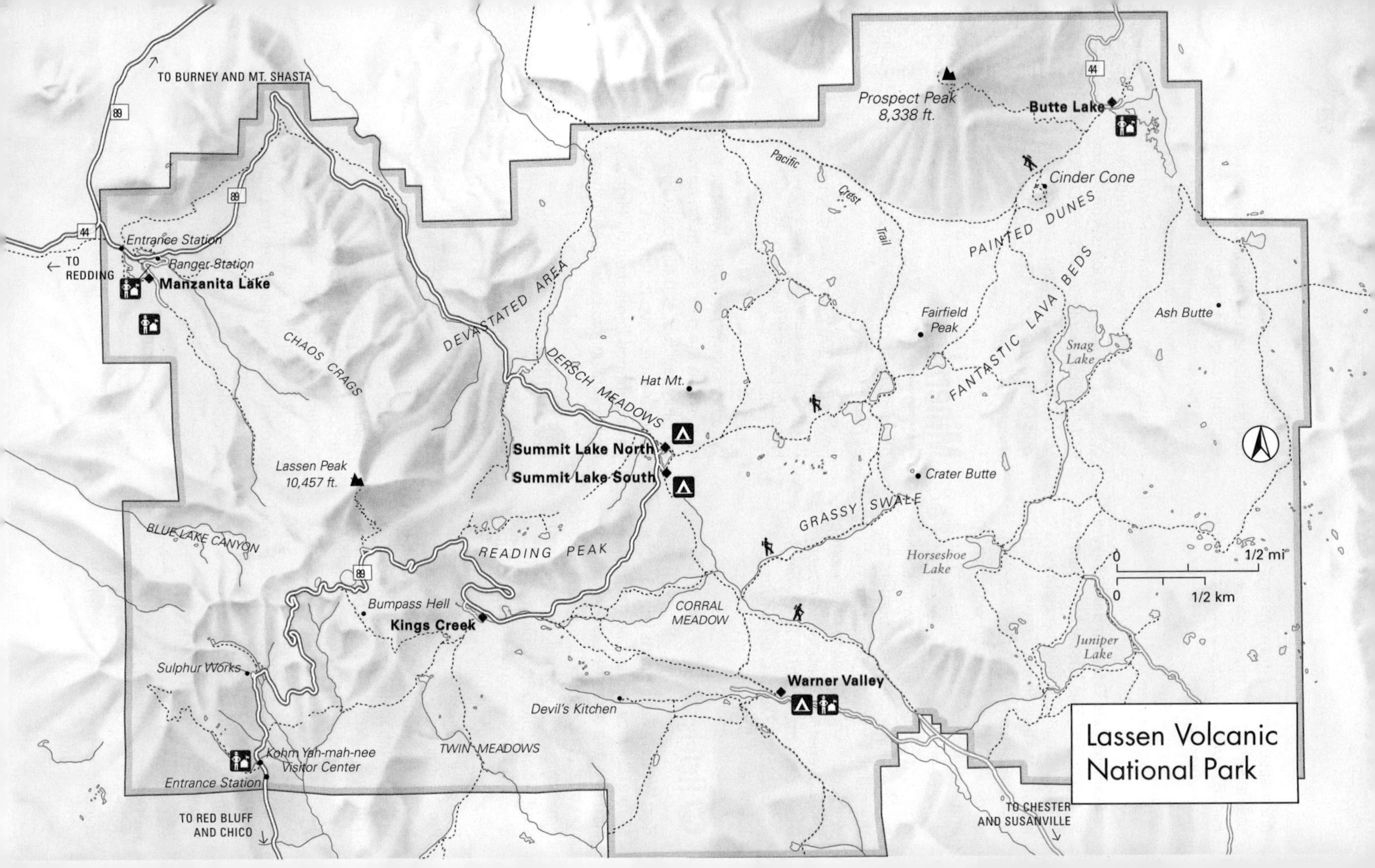

Lassen Volcanic National Park
TO BURNEY AND MT. SHASTA
89
44
Entrance Station
Ranger Station
TO REDDING
Manzanita Lake
CHAOS CRAGS
DEVASTATED AREA
DERSCH MEADOWS
Hat Mt.
Summit Lake North
Summit Lake South
Lassen Peak
10,457 ft.
BLUE LAKE CANYON
READING PEAK
Bumpass Hell
Kings Creek
Sulphur Works
Kohm Yah-mah-nee
Visitor Center
Entrance Station
TO RED BLUFF
AND CHICO
TWIN MEADOWS
Devil's Kitchen
Warner Valley
CORRAL
MEADOW
GRASSY SWALE
Horseshoe
Lake
Juniper
Lake
TO CHESTER
AND SUSANVILLE
Crater Butte
Fairfield
Peak
FANTASTIC LAVA BEDS
PAINTED DUNES
Snag
Lake
Ash Butte
Prospect Peak
8,338 ft.
Butte Lake
Cinder Cone
Pacific
Crest
Trail
0
1/2 mi
0
1/2 km

The volcano finally came to rest in 1921 but is not considered dormant: fumaroles, mud pots, lakes, and bubbling hot springs create a fascinating if dangerous landscape that can be viewed throughout the park, especially via a hiked descent into Bumpass Hell. Because of its significance as a volcanic landscape, Lassen became a national park in 1916. Several volcanoes—the largest of which is now Lassen Peak—have been active in the area for roughly 600,000 years. Lassen Park Road (the continuation of Highway 89 within the park) and 150 miles of hiking trails provide access to many of these wonders. The café at the main Kohm Yah-mah-nee Visitor Center, in the park's southern section, serves pizza, salads, sandwiches, burgers, and the like, along with coffee and hot cocoa, and beer (some of it from local producer Lassen Ale Works) and wine. ⚠ **Heed signs warning visitors to stay on the trails and railed boardwalks to avoid falling into boiling water or through thin-crusted areas.** *Mineral www.nps.gov/lavo $25 per car, $20 per motorcycle, $12 per person if not in motor vehicle Visitor center closed Mon. and Tues. Nov.–Apr.*

Sulphur Works Thermal Area
NATURE SITE | FAMILY | Proof of Lassen Peak's volatility becomes evident shortly after you enter the park at the southwest entrance. Sidewalks skirt boiling springs and sulfur-emitting steam vents. This area is usually the last site to close in winter, but even when the road is closed, you can access the area via a 2-mile round-trip hike through the snow. *Lassen Park Hwy., Lassen Volcanic National Park 1 mile from southwest entrance.*

Restaurants

★ Highlands Ranch Restaurant and Bar
$$$ | AMERICAN | Dining at the Highlands Ranch Resort's contemporary roadhouse restaurant is in a stained-wood, high-ceilinged room indoors, or out on the deck, which has views of a broad serene meadow and the hillside beyond. Among the few sophisticated eating options within Lassen Volcanic National Park's orbit, the restaurant serves updated classics like rib-eye steak (up to 22 ounces), balsamic-marinated Muscovy duck, and blackened ahi with carrot-cucumber slaw. **Known for:** striking views inside and out; small plates and burgers in the bar; inventive sauces and preparations. *Average main: $25 41515 Hwy. 36 E, Mill Creek 530/595–3388 www.highlandsranchresort.com/restaurant Closed Mon.–Wed. Nov.–late May.*

Hotels

★ Highlands Ranch Resort
$$$ | B&B/INN | On a gorgeous 175-acre alpine meadow 10 miles from Lassen's southwest entrance, this cluster of smartly designed upscale bungalows is peaceful and luxurious. **Pros:** stunning views; most luxurious accommodations near the park; friendly and helpful staff. **Cons:** pricey for the area (but you get a lot for what you pay); remote location 20 miles from Chester, the nearest big town; books up months ahead for summer stays. *Rooms from: $249 41515 Hwy. 36 E, Mill Creek 530/595–3388 www.highlandsranchresort.com Closed Mon.–Wed. Nov.–late May 7 cottages Free Breakfast.*

Activities

★ Bumpass Hell Trail
HIKING/WALKING | Boiling springs, steam vents, and mud pots are the highlights of this 3-mile round-trip hike. Expect the loop to take about two hours. During the first mile there's a slight, gradual climb before a steep 300-foot descent to the basin. You'll encounter rocky patches, so wear hiking boots. Stay on trails and boardwalks near the thermal areas, as what appears to be firm ground may be only a thin crust over scalding mud. Due to ongoing trail rehabilitation, this hike

may be fully or partially closed through 2020. *Moderate.* ✉ *Lassen Park Hwy., Lassen Volcanic National Park* ✣ *Trailhead: 6 miles from southwest entrance.*

★ Lassen Peak Hike
HIKING/WALKING | This trail winds 2½ miles to the mountaintop. It's a tough climb—2,000 feet uphill on a steady, steep grade—but the reward is a spectacular view. At the peak you can see into the rim and view the entire park (and much of California's Far North). Bring sunscreen, water, snacks, a first-aid kit, and, because it can be windy and cold at the summit, a jacket. *Difficult.* ✉ *Lassen Park Hwy., Lassen Volcanic National Park* ✣ *Trailhead: 7 miles north of southwest entrance.*

Burney

62 miles southeast of Mt. Shasta, 41 miles north of Lassen Volcanic National Park.

One of the most spectacular sights in the Far North is Burney Falls, where countless ribbon-like streams pour from moss-covered crevices. You have to travel forested back roads to reach this gem in a state park 10 miles north of the town of Burney, but the park's beauty is well worth the trek.

GETTING HERE AND AROUND

To get to the falls, head east off Interstate 5 on Highway 89 at Mt. Shasta. From Redding, head east on Highway 299 to Highway 89; follow signs 6 miles to the park.

Sights

★ McArthur–Burney Falls Memorial State Park
NATIONAL/STATE PARK | **FAMILY** | Just inside this park's southern boundary, Burney Creek wells up from the ground and divides into two falls that cascade over a 129-foot cliff into a pool below. Countless ribbon-like streams pour from hidden moss-covered crevices; resident bald eagles are frequently seen soaring overhead. You can walk a self-guided nature trail that descends to the foot of the falls, which Theodore Roosevelt—according to legend—called "the eighth wonder of the world." On warm days, swim at Lake Britton; lounge on the beach; rent motorboats, paddleboats, and canoes; or relax at one of the campsites or picnic areas. ✉ *24898 Hwy. 89, 6 miles north of Hwy. 299, Burney* ☎ *530/335–2777* 🌐 *www.burneyfallspark.org* 🎟 *$10 per vehicle, day-use.*

Tulelake

89 miles from Burney, 85 miles from Mt. Shasta City.

Lava Beds National Monument, the chief attraction of Tulelake, is so far north that one of the two main routes to it briefly passes into Oregon before looping back south into California. Stunning underground lava tube caves make the trip to this off-the-beaten-path geological site well worth the detour.

GETTING HERE AND AROUND

From McArthur-Burney state park, take Highway 89 south to Highway 299 east to Bieber-Lookout Road and Highway 139 north. At Forest Service Rte. 97 turn left (west) and follow signs. From Mt. Shasta City, take Highway 89 to Forest Service Routes 97 and 10. There's no public transportation.

Sights

★ Lava Beds National Monument
NATURE SITE | **FAMILY** | Thousands of years of volcanic activity created this rugged landscape, which is distinguished by cinder cones, lava flows, spatter cones, pit craters, and more than 400 underground lava tube caves. During the Modoc War

Did You Know?

President Theodore Roosevelt supposedly called McArthur–Burney Falls "the eighth wonder of the world."

(1872–73), Modoc Indians under the leadership of their chief "Captain Jack" Kintpuash took refuge in a natural lava fortress now known as Captain Jack's Stronghold. They managed to hold off U.S. Army forces, which outnumbered them 20 to 1, for five months. When exploring this area, be sure to wear hard-soled boots and a bump hat. Bring a flashlight with you, although some are available for borrowing at the Indian Well Visitor Center, at the park's southern end. This is where summer activities such as guided walks, cave tours, and campfire programs depart from. ■ **TIP→ Lava Beds is extremely remote; see website for detailed driving instructions.** ✉ *1 Indian Well, Tulelake* ✣ *Take Forest Rte. 97 to Forest Rte. 10* ☎ *530/667–8113* 🌐 *www.nps.gov/labe* 🎫 *$20 per vehicle.*

Index

R

S

Photo Credits

Front Cover: Eric Gross [Description: Upper Yosemite Falls in Yosemite National Park.] **Back cover, from left to right:** Celso Diniz/Shutterstock, Dan Harmeson/iStockphoto, (c) Mblach/Dreamstime. **Spine:** S. Greg Panosian/iStockphoto. **Interior, from left to right:** Ethan Daniels/shutterstock (1). Geartooth Productions/shutterstock (2). Robert Holmes (5). **Chapter 1: Experience Northern California:** ewoerlen (6-7). Max Whittaker/Visit California (8-9). Lynn Yeh/shutterstock (9). Oscity/Shutterstock (9). Jill Krueger (10). Eric Broder Van Dyke/shutterstock (10). California Travel and Tourism Commission/Visit California(10). Mike Peters/shutterstock (10). Jill Krueger (11). Joseph Phelps Vineyard (11). Courtesy of Musée Mécanique (12). Visit California/Carol Highsmith (12). Toms Auzins/shutterstock (12). BottleRock Media (12). Michael Lauffenburger/shutterstock (13). Visit California/Andreas Hub (13). Remy Hale (16). nito/shutterstock (17). **Chapter 3: Northern California's Best Road Trips:** PauloZimmermann/istockphoto (37). **Chapter 4: Sequoia and Kings Canyon National Parks:** Robert Holmes (49). urosr/Shutterstock (63). **Chapter 5: Monterey Bay Area:** haveseen/shutterstock (77). Nadezhdasarkisian/Dreamstime (86). Sergio TB/shutterstock (94). Wolterk/Dreamstime (104). Mike Brake/Dreamstime (116). **Chapter 6: Yosemite National Park:** Ershov_Maks/istockphoto (127). Sky_Sajjaphot/istockphoto (137). Jane Rix / Shutterstock (143). Simon Dannhauer (146). Katrina Leigh/Shutterstock (152-153). **Chapter 7: Eastern Sierra:** Glenn Pettersen/shutterstock (161). Mark Sayer/shutterstock (171). Zack Frank/shutterstock (181). Marc Venema (182). **Chapter 8: San Francisco:** San Francisco Travel Association/Scott Chernis (185). San Francisco Travel Association/Scott Chernis (188). Walleyelj/Dreamstime (189). T photography/Shutterstock (189). San Francisco Travel Association/Scott Chernis (197). CURAphotography (201). Arnold Genthe (Public Domain) (202). Library of Congress Prints and Photographs Division (202). Sandor Balatoni/SFCVB (203). Library of Congress (203). Brett Shoaf/Artistic Visual Photography (204). Canadastock (221). Pius Lee (223). San Francisco Municipal Railway Historical Archives (224). Andresr/Dreamstime (231). Robert Holmes (243). Aprillilacs (253). Rafael Ramirez Lee/iStockphoto (257). **Chapter 9: The Bay Area:** Gary Crabbe/Alamy Stock Photo (269). California Travel and Tourism Commission/Bongo (278). Nancy Hoyt Belcher/Alamy (281). Robert Holmes (302). **Chapter 10: Napa and Sonoma:** Infinity Visuals (311). Robert Holmes (318). Far Niente+Dolce+Nickel & Nickel (319). kevin miller/iStockphoto (319). Robert Holmes (320). Robert Holmes (320). Domaine Carneros (321). star5112/Flickr, [CC BY 2.0] (321). Robert Holmes (322). Robert Holmes (322). Gundolf Pftoenhauer (322). Robert Holmes (323). Robert Holmes (323). Agence Images/Alamy (324). Cephas Picture Library/Alamy (324). PHILIPPE ROY/Alamy (324). Napa Valley Conference Bureau (325). Wild Horse Winery/ Forrest L. Doud (Second and Third from Top). (325). Napa Valley Conference Bureau (325). Panther Creek Cellars/Ron Kaplan (325). Clos du Val (Marvin Coffin) (325). Panther Creek Cellars/ Ron Kaplan (325). Warren H. White (325). Courtesy of the di Rosa Collection (328). Terry Joanis/Frog's Leap (342). Courtesy of Castello di Amorosa (350). Robert Holmes (361). **Chapter 11: The North Coast:** MWP/istockphoto (379). Robert Holmes (388). naturediver/istockphoto (394). Robert Holmes (402). **Chapter 12: Sacramento and the Gold Country:** heyengel/istockphoto (411). RickC/Flickr, [CC BY 2.0] (437). Ambient Images Inc./Alamy (444). **Chapter 13: Lake Tahoe:** MariuszBlach/istockphoto (457). Mblach/Dreamstime (472). thetahoeguy/shutterstock (475). Tom Zikas/North Lake Tahoe (478). Christopher Russell/iStockphoto (488). Chapter 14: Redwood National and State Parks: Ericliu08/istockphoto (495). istockphoto (507). **Chapter 15: The Far North:** NPS (509). Stephen Moehle/shutterstock (533). **All author photos are courtesy of the writers.**

*Every effort has been made to trace the copyright holders, and we apologize in advance for any accidental errors. We would be happy to apply the corrections in the subsequent printing of this publication.

Fodor's NORTHERN CALIFORNIA

Publisher: Stephen Horowitz, *General Manager*

Editorial: Douglas Stallings, *Editorial Director*, Jacinta O'Halloran, Amanda Sadlowski, *Senior Editors*; Kayla Becker, Alexis Kelly, Teddy Minford, Rachael Roth, *Editors*

Design: Tina Malaney, *Director of Design and Production*; Jessica Gonzalez, *Graphic Designer;* Mariana Tabares, *Design & Production Intern*

Production: Jennifer DePrima, *Editorial Production Manager*, Carrie Parker, *Senior Production Editor*, Elyse Rozelle, *Production Editor;* Jackson Pranica, *Editorial Production Assistant*

Maps: Rebecca Baer, *Senior Map Editor*, David Lindroth, Mark Stroud (Moon Street Cartography), *Cartographers*

Photography: Viviane Teles, *Senior Photo Editor;* Namrata Aggarwal, Ashok Kumar, Carl Yu, *Photo Editors;* Rebecca Rimmer, *Photo Intern*

Business & Operations: Chuck Hoover, *Chief Marketing Officer*, Robert Ames, *Group General Manager*, Tara McCrillis, *Director of Publishing Operations;* Victor Bernal, *Business Analyst*

Public Relations and Marketing: Joe Ewaskiw, *Senior Director Communications & Public Relations*; Esther Su, *Senior Marketing Manager*

Fodors.com: Jeremy Tarr, *Editorial Director;* Rachael Levitt, *Managing Editor*

Technology: Jon Atkinson, *Director of Technology;* Rudresh Teotia, *Lead Developer*, Jacob Ashpis, *Content Operations Manager*

Writers: Cheryl Crabtree, Andrew Collins, Denise M. Leto, Daniel Mangin, Andrea Powell, Rebecca Flint Marx, and Monique Peterson

Editor: Rachael Roth

Production Editor: Jennifer DePrima

15th Edition

ISBN 978-1-64097-188-2

ISSN 1543–1045

Library of Congress Control Number 2019903949

All details in this book are based on information supplied to us at press time. Always confirm information when it matters, especially if you're making a detour to visit a specific place. Fodor's expressly disclaims any liability, loss, or risk, personal or otherwise, that is incurred as a consequence of the use of any of the contents of this book.

SPECIAL SALES

This book is available at special discounts for bulk purchases for sales promotions or premiums. For more information, e-mail SpecialMarkets@fodors.com.

PRINTED IN THE UNITED STATES OF AMERICA

10 9 8 7 6 5 4 3 2 1

About Our Writers

Former Fodor's staff editor **Andrew Collins** updated the Redwood National Park chapter. He's based in Mexico City but travels regularly throughout the United States, especially in Oregon and New Mexico. A long-time contributor to dozens of Fodor's guidebooks, including Pacific Northwest, Santa Fe, and New England, he's also written for dozens of mainstream and LGBTQ publications— *Travel + Leisure, New Mexico Magazine, AAA Living, The Advocate,* and *Canadian Traveller* among them. Additionally, Collins produces the website *LoveWinsUSA.com* and teaches travel writing and food writing for New York City's Gotham Writers Workshop.

Native Californian **Cheryl Crabtree** has worked as a freelance writer since 1987 and regularly travels up, down, and around California for work and fun. She has contributed to *Fodor's California* since 2003 and also contributes to the *Fodor's National Parks of the West* guide. Cheryl is editor of *Montecito Magazine* and co-authors *The California Directory of Fine Wineries* book series, Central Coast and Napa, Sonoma, Mendocino editions. Her articles have appeared in many regional and national magazines. Cheryl updated the Monterey Bay Area, Eastern Sierra, Yosemite National Park, and Sequoia & Kings Canyon National Park chapters this edition.

Daniel Mangin returned to California, where he's maintained a home for three decades, after two stints at the Fodor's editorial offices in New York City, the second one as the editorial director of Fodors.com and the Compass American Guides. With several dozen wineries less than a half-hour's drive from home, he often finds himself transported as if by magic to a tasting room bar, communing with a sophisticated Cabernet or savoring the finish of a smooth Pinot Noir. For this edition, Daniel, the writer of *Fodor's Napa & Sonoma,* updated the Napa and Sonoma, North Coast, Far North, Lake Tahoe, and Travel Smart chapters.

Monique Peterson A Northern California native, writer and editor Monique Peterson navigates Bay Area cities and landscapes with ease to share her insights on favorite places and new experiences, from Lake Merritt to Point Reyes Station. For many years, Monique's wanderlust landed her in New York City writing and editing books about art, science, history, and nature for The Walt Disney Company, Discovery Channel School, and Random House. She is also co-founder of a regional writing guild (*tell-tailors.com*), where she leads fiction and nonfiction workshops when she's not hiking, biking, or pursuing new adventures.

Updating our San Francisco chapter was a team of writers from *Fodor's San Francisco*: **Denise M. Leto, Daniel Mangin, Andrea Powell,** and **Rebecca Flint Marx.**